Lecture Notes in Computer Science   11275

Commenced Publication in 1973
Founding and Former Series Editors:
Gerhard Goos, Juris Hartmanis, and Jan van Leeuwen

More information about this series at http://www.springer.com/series/7408

Sukyoung Ryu (Ed.)

Programming Languages and Systems

16th Asian Symposium, APLAS 2018
Wellington, New Zealand, December 2–6, 2018
Proceedings

 Springer

Editor
Sukyoung Ryu (ID)
Korea Advanced Institute of Science
and Technology
Daejeon, South Korea

ISSN 0302-9743   ISSN 1611-3349   (electronic)
Lecture Notes in Computer Science
ISBN 978-3-030-02767-4   ISBN 978-3-030-02768-1   (eBook)
https://doi.org/10.1007/978-3-030-02768-1

Library of Congress Control Number: 2018958466

LNCS Sublibrary: SL2 – Programming and Software Engineering

This Springer imprint is published by the registered company Springer Nature Switzerland AG
The registered company address is: Gewerbestrasse 11, 6330 Cham, Switzerland

Preface

This volume contains the proceedings of the 16th Asian Symposium on Programming Languages and Systems (APLAS 2018), held in Wellington, New Zealand during December 2–6, 2018. APLAS aims to stimulate programming language research by providing a forum for the presentation of the latest results and the exchange of ideas in programming languages and systems. APLAS is based in Asia but is an international forum that serves the worldwide programming languages community.

APLAS 2018 solicited submissions in two categories: regular research papers and system and tool demonstrations. The conference solicits contributions in, but is not limited to, the following topics: semantics, logics, and foundational theory; design of languages, type systems, and foundational calculi; domain-specific languages; compilers, interpreters, and abstract machines; program derivation, synthesis, and transformation; program analysis, verification, and model-checking; logic, constraint, probabilistic, and quantum programming; software security; concurrency and parallelism; and tools and environments for programming and implementation.

APLAS 2018 employed a lightweight double-blind reviewing process with an author-response period. Within the review period, APLAS 2018 used an internal two-round review process where each submission received three first-round reviews on average to drive the possible selection of additional expert reviews as needed before the author response. The author-response period was followed by a two-week Program Committee discussion period to finalize the selection of papers.

This year APLAS reviewed 51 submissions. After thoroughly evaluating the relevance and quality of each paper, the Program Committee decided to accept 22 contributions including four tool papers. We were also honored to include three invited talks by distinguished researchers:

- Amal Ahmed (Northeastern University, USA) on "Compositional Compiler Verification for a Multi-Language World"
- Azalea Raad (MPI-SWS, Germany) on "Correctness in a Weakly Consistent Setting"
- Bernhard Scholz (University of Sydney, Australia) on "Soufflé: A Datalog Engine for Static Analysis"

This program would not have been possible without the substantial efforts of many people, whom I sincerely thank. The Program Committee, sub-reviewers, and external expert reviewers worked hard in selecting strong papers while providing constructive and supportive comments in their reviews. Alex Potanin (Victoria University of Wellington, New Zealand) serving as the general chair of APLAS 2018 checked every detail of the conference well in advance. David Pearce (Victoria University of Wellington, New Zealand) serving as the Web and venues chair and Jens Dietrich (Massey University, Palmerston North, New Zealand) serving as the sponsorship and accessibility chair were always responsive. I also greatly appreciate the APLAS

Steering Committee for their leadership, as well as APLAS 2017 PC chair Bor-Yuh Evan Chang (University of Colorado Boulder, USA) for his advice.

Lastly, I would like to acknowledge the organizers of the associated events that make APLAS a successful event: the Poster Session and Student Research Competition (David Pearce, Victoria University of Wellington, New Zealand) and the APLAS Workshop on New Ideas and Emerging Results (Wei-Ngan Chin, National University of Singapore and Atsushi Igarashi, Kyoto University, Japan).

September 2018   Sukyoung Ryu

Organization

General Chair

Alex Potanin — Victoria University of Wellington, New Zealand

Web and Venues Chair

David Pearce — Victoria University of Wellington, New Zealand

Sponsorship and Accessibility Chair

Jens Dietrich — Massey University, Palmerston North, New Zealand

Program Chair

Sukyoung Ryu — KAIST, South Korea

Program Committee

Sam Blackshear	Facebook, UK
Bernd Burgstaller	Yonsei University, South Korea
Cristina David	University of Cambridge, UK
Huimin Cui	Institute of Computing Technology, CAS, China
Benjamin Delaware	Purdue University, USA
Julian Dolby	IBM Thomas J. Watson Research Center, USA
Yuxi Fu	Shanghai Jiao Tong University, China
Aquinas Hobor	National University of Singapore, Singapore
Tony Hosking	Australian National University/Data61, Australia
Chung-Kil Hur	Seoul National University, South Korea
Atsushi Igarashi	Kyoto University, Japan
Joxan Jaffar	National University of Singapore, Singapore
Alexander Jordan	Oracle Labs., Australia
Hakjoo Oh	Korea University, South Korea
Bruno C. d. S. Oliveira	The University of Hong Kong, SAR China
Xiaokang Qiu	Purdue University, USA
Tamara Rezk	Inria, France
Xavier Rival	CNRS/ENS/Inria, France
Ilya Sergey	University College London, UK
Manuel Serrano	Inria, France
Xipeng Shen	North Carolina State University, USA
Guy L. Steele Jr.	Oracle Labs., USA

Alex Summers   ETH, Switzerland
Tachio Terauchi   Waseda University, Japan
Peter Thiemann   Universität Freiburg, Germany
Ashutosh Trivedi   University of Colorado Boulder, USA
Jingling Xue   UNSW Sydney, Australia
Nobuko Yoshida   Imperial College London, UK
Danfeng Zhang   Pennsylvania State University, USA
Xin Zhang   MIT, USA

Workshop on New Ideas and Emerging Results Organizers

Wei-Ngan Chin   National University of Singapore, Singapore
Atsushi Igarashi   Kyoto University, Japan

Additional Reviewers

Astrauskas, Vytautas   Neykova, Rumyana
Avanzini, Martin   Ng, Nicholas
Castro, David   Ngo, Minh
Ferreira, Francisco   Paolini, Luca
Hague, Matthew   Petit, Bertrand
Hoshino, Naohiko   Poli, Federico
Krishnan, Paddy   Radanne, Gabriel
Lewis, Matt   Scalas, Alceste
Muroya, Koko   Schwerhoff, Malte

Contents

Types

Non-linear Pattern Matching with Backtracking for Non-free Data Types

Satoshi Egi[1]($\boxtimes$) and Yuichi Nishiwaki[2]

[1] Rakuten Institute of Technology, Tokyo, Japan
satoshi.egi@rakuten.com
[2] University of Tokyo, Tokyo, Japan
nyuichi@is.s.u-tokyo.ac.jp

Abstract. *Non-free data types* are data types whose data have no canonical forms. For example, multisets are non-free data types because the multiset $\{a, b, b\}$ has two other equivalent but literally different forms $\{b, a, b\}$ and $\{b, b, a\}$. *Pattern matching* is known to provide a handy tool set to treat such data types. Although many studies on pattern matching and implementations for practical programming languages have been proposed so far, we observe that none of these studies satisfy all the *criteria of practical pattern matching*, which are as follows: (i) efficiency of the backtracking algorithm for non-linear patterns, (ii) extensibility of matching process, and (iii) polymorphism in patterns.

This paper aims to design a new *pattern-matching-oriented* programming language that satisfies all the above three criteria. The proposed language features clean Scheme-like syntax and efficient and extensible pattern matching semantics. This programming language is especially useful for the processing of complex non-free data types that not only include multisets and sets but also graphs and symbolic mathematical expressions. We discuss the importance of our criteria of practical pattern matching and how our language design naturally arises from the criteria. The proposed language has been already implemented and open-sourced as the Egison programming language.

1 Introduction

Pattern matching is an important feature of programming languages featuring data abstraction mechanisms. Data abstraction serves users with a simple method for handling data structures that contain plenty of complex information. Using pattern matching, programs using data abstraction become concise, human-readable, and maintainable. Most of the recent practical programming languages allow users to extend data abstraction e.g. by defining new types or classes, or by introducing new abstract interfaces. Therefore, a good programming language with pattern matching should allow users to extend its pattern-matching facility akin to the extensibility of data abstraction.

Earlier, pattern-matching systems used to assume one-to-one correspondence between patterns and data constructors. However, this assumption became problematic when one handles data types whose data have multiple representations.

© Springer Nature Switzerland AG 2018
S. Ryu (Ed.): APLAS 2018, LNCS 11275, pp. 3–23, 2018.
https://doi.org/10.1007/978-3-030-02768-1_1

To overcome this problem, Wadler proposed the pattern-matching system views [28] that broke the symmetry between patterns and data constructors. Views enabled users to pattern-match against data represented in many ways. For example, a complex number may be represented either in polar or Cartesian form, and they are convertible to each other. Using views, one can pattern-match a complex number internally represented in polar form with a pattern written in Cartesian form, and vice versa, provided that mutual transformation functions are properly defined. Similarly, one can use the Cons pattern to perform pattern matching on lists with joins, where a list [1,2] can be either (Cons 1 (Cons 2 Nil)) or (Join (Cons 1 Nil) (Cons 2 Nil)), if one defines a normalization function of lists with join into a sequence of Cons.

However, views require data types to have a distinguished canonical form among many possible forms. In the case of lists with join, one can pattern-match with Cons because any list with join is canonically reducible to a list with join with the Cons constructor at the head. On the other hand, for any list with join, there is no such canonical form that has Join at the head. For example, the list [1,2] may be decomposed with Join into three pairs: [] and [1,2], [1] and [2], and [1,2] and []. For that reason, views do not support pattern matching of lists with join using the Join pattern.

Generally, data types without canonical forms are called *non-free data types*. Mathematically speaking, a non-free data type can be regarded as a quotient on a free data type over an equivalence. An example of non-free data types is, of course, list with join: it may be viewed as a non-free data type composed of a (free) binary tree equipped with an equivalence between trees with the same leaf nodes enumerated from left to right, such as (Join Nil (Cons 1 (Cons 2 Nil))) = (Join (Cons 1 Nil) (Cons 2 Nil)). Other typical examples include sets and multisets, as they are (free) lists with obvious identifications. Generally, as shown for lists with join, pattern matching on non-free data types yields multiple results.[1] For example, multiset {1,2,3} has three decompositions by the insert pattern: insert(1,{2,3}), insert(2,{1,3}), and insert(3,{1,2}). Therefore, how to handle multiple pattern-matching results is an extremely important issue when we design a programming language that supports pattern matching for non-free data types.

On the other hand, *pattern guard* is a commonly used technique for filtering such multiple results from pattern matching. Basically, pattern guards are applied after enumerating all pattern-matching results. Therefore, substantial unnecessary enumerations often occur before the application of pattern guards. One simple solution is to break a large pattern into nested patterns to apply pattern guards as early as possible. However, this solution complicates the program and makes it hard to maintain. It is also possible to statically transform the program in the similar manner at the compile time. However, it makes the compiler implementation very complex. *Non-linear pattern* is an alternative method for

---

[1] In fact, this phenomenon that "pattern matching against a single value yields multiple results" does not occur for free data types. This is the unique characteristic of non-free data types.

pattern guard. Non-linear patterns are patterns that allow multiple occurrences of same variables in a pattern. Compared to pattern guards, they are not only syntactically beautiful but also compiler-friendly. Non-linear patterns are easier to analyze and hence can be implemented efficiently (Sects. 3.1 and 4.2). However, it is not obvious how to extend a non-linear pattern-matching system to allow users to define an algorithm to decompose non-free data types. In this paper, we introduce *extensible pattern matching* to remedy this issue (Sects. 3.2, 4.4, and 6). Extensibility of pattern matching also enables us to define *predicate patterns*, which are typically implemented as a built-in feature (e.g. pattern guards) in most pattern-matching systems. Additionally, we improve the usability of pattern matching for non-free data types by introducing a syntactic generalization for the match expression, called *polymorphic patterns* (Sects. 3.3 and 4.3). We also present a non-linear pattern-matching algorithm specialized for backtracking on infinite search trees and supports pattern matching with infinitely many results in addition to keeping efficiency (Sect. 5).

This paper aims to design a programming language that is oriented toward pattern matching for non-free data types. We summarize the above argument in the form of three criteria that must be fulfilled by a language in order to be used in practice:

1. Efficiency of the backtracking algorithm for non-linear patterns,
2. Extensibility of pattern matching, and
3. Polymorphism in patterns.

We believe that the above requirements, called together *criteria of practical pattern matching*, are fundamental for languages with pattern matching. However, none of the existing languages and studies [5,10,15,26] fulfill all of them. In the rest of the paper, we present a language which satisfies the criteria, together with comparisons with other languages, several working examples, and formal semantics. We emphasize that our proposal has been already implemented in Haskell as the *Egison* programming language, and is open-sourced [6]. Since we set our focus in this paper on the design of the programming language, detailed discussion on the implementation of Egison is left for future work.

2   Related Work

In this section, we compare our study with the prior work.

First, we review previous studies on pattern matching in functional programming languages. Our proposal can be considered as an extension of these studies.

The first non-linear pattern-matching system was the symbol manipulation system proposed by MacBride [21]. This system was developed for Lisp. Their paper demonstrates some examples that process symbolic mathematical expressions to show the expressive power of non-linear patterns. However, this approach does not support pattern matching with multiple results, and only supports pattern matching against a list as a collection.

Miranda laws [24,25,27] and Wadler's views [22,28] are seminal work. These proposals provide methods to decompose data with multiple representations by explicitly declaring transformations between each representation. These are the earliest studies that allow users to customize the execution process of pattern matching. However, the pattern-matching systems in these proposals treat neither multiple pattern matching results nor non-linear patterns. Also, these studies demand a canonical form for each representation.

Active patterns [15,23] provides a method to decompose non-free data. In active patterns, users define a *match function* for each pattern to specify how to decompose non-free data. For example, `insert` for multisets is defined as a match function in [15]. An example of pattern matching against graphs using matching function is also shown in [16]. One limitation of active patterns is that it does not support backtracking in the pattern matching process. In active patterns, the values bound to pattern variables are fixed in order from the left to right of a pattern. Therefore, we cannot write non-linear patterns that require backtracking such as a pattern that matches with collections (like sets or multisets) that contain two identical elements. (The pattern matching fails if we unfortunately pick an element that appears more than twice at the first choice.)

First-class patterns [26] is a sophisticated system that treats patterns as first-class objects. The essence of this study is a *pattern function* that defines how to decompose data with each data constructor. First-class patterns can deal with pattern matching that generates multiple results. To generate multiple results, a pattern function returns a list. A critical limitation of this proposal is that first-class patterns do not support non-linear pattern matching.

Next, we explain the relation with logic programming.

We have mentioned that non-linear patterns and backtracking are important features to extend the efficiency and expressive power of pattern matching especially on non-free data types. Unification of logic programming has both features. However, how to integrate non-determinism of logic programming and pattern matching is not obvious [18]. For example, the pattern-matching facility of Prolog is specialized only for algebraic data types.

Functional logic programming [10] is an approach towards this integration. It allows both of non-linear patterns and multiple pattern-matching results. The key difference between the functional logic programming and our approach is in the method for defining pattern-matching algorithms. In functional logic programming, we describe the pattern-matching algorithm for each pattern in the logic-programming style. A function that describes such an algorithm is called a *pattern constructor*. A pattern constructor takes decomposed values as its arguments and returns the target data. On the other hand, in our proposal, pattern constructors are defined in the functional-programming style: pattern constructors take a target datum as an argument and returns the decomposed values. This enables direct description of algorithms.

3   Motivation

In this section, we discuss the requirements for programming languages to establish practical pattern matching for non-free data types.

3.1   Pattern Guards vs. Non-linear Patterns

Compared to pattern guards, non-linear patterns are a compiler-friendly method for filtering multiple matching results efficiently. However, non-linear pattern matching is typically implemented by converting them to pattern guards. For example, some implementations of functional logic programming languages convert non-linear patterns to pattern guards [8,9,18]. This method is inefficient because it leads to enumerating unnecessary candidates. In the following program in Curry, seqN returns "Matched" if the argument list has a sequential N-tuple. Otherwise it returns "Not matched". insert is used as a pattern constructor for decomposing data into an element and the rest ignoring the order of elements.

```
insert x [] = [x]
insert x (y:ys) = x:y:ys ? y:(insert x ys)

seq2 (insert x (insert (x+1) _)) = "Matched"
seq2 _ = "Not matched"

seq3 (insert x (insert (x+1) (insert (x+2) _))) = "Matched"
seq3 _ = "Not matched"

seq4 (insert x (insert (x+1) (insert (x+2) (insert (x+3) _)))) = "Matched"
seq4 _ = "Not matched"

seq2 (take 10 (repeat 0)) -- returns "Not matched" in O(n^2) time
seq3 (take 10 (repeat 0)) -- returns "Not matched" in O(n^3) time
seq4 (take 10 (repeat 0)) -- returns "Not matched" in O(n^4) time
```

When we use a Curry compiler such as PAKCS [4] and KiCS2 [11], we see that "seq4 (take n (repeat 0))" takes more time than "seq3 (take n (repeat 0))" because seq3 is compiled to seq3' as follows. Therefore, seq4 enumerates $\binom{n}{4}$ candidates, whereas seq3 enumerates $\binom{n}{3}$ candidates before filtering the results. If the program uses non-linear patterns as in seq3, we easily find that we can check no sequential triples or quadruples exist simply by checking $\binom{n}{2}$ pairs. However, such information is discarded during the program transformation into pattern guards.

```
seq3' (insert x (insert y (insert z _))) | y == x+1 && z == x+2 = "Matched"
seq3' _ = "Not matched"
```

One way to make this program efficient in Curry is to stop using non-linear patterns and instead use a predicate explicitly in pattern guards. The following illustrates such a program.

```
isSeq2 (x:y:rs) = y == x+1
isSeq3 (x:rs) = isSeq2 (x:rs) && isSeq2 rs

perm [] = []
perm (x:xs) = insert x (perm xs)
```

```
seq3 xs | isSeq3 ys = "Matched" where ys = perm xs
seq3 _ = "Not matched"

seq3 (take 10 (repeat 0))   -- returns "Not matched" in O(n^2) time
```

In the program, because of the laziness, only the head part of the list is evaluated. In addition, because of *sharing* [17], the common head part of the list is pattern-matched only once. Using this call-by-need-like strategy enables efficient pattern matching on sequential n-tuples. However, this strategy sacrifices readability of programs and makes the program obviously redundant. In this paper, instead, we base our work on non-linear patterns and attempt to improve its usability keeping it compiler-friendly and syntactically clean.

3.2   Extensible Pattern Matching

As a program gets more complicated, data structures involved in the program get complicated as well. A pattern-matching facility for such data structures (e.g. graphs and mathematical expressions) should be extensible and customizable by users because it is impractical to provide the data structures for these data types as built-in data types in general-purpose languages.

In the studies of computer algebra systems, efficient non-linear pattern-matching algorithms for mathematical expressions that avoid such unnecessary search have already been proposed [2,20]. Generally, users of such computer algebra systems control the pattern-matching method for mathematical expressions by specifying attributes for each operator. For example, the `Orderless` attribute of the Wolfram language indicates that the order of the arguments of the operator is ignored [3]. However, the set of attributes available is fixed and cannot be changed [1]. This means that the pattern-matching algorithms in such computer algebra systems are specialized only for some specific data types such as multisets. However, there are a number of data types we want to pattern-match other than mathematical expressions, like unordered pairs, trees, and graphs.

Thus, extensible pattern matching for non-free data types is necessary for handling complicated data types such as mathematical expressions. This paper designs a language that allows users to implement efficient backtracking algorithms for general non-free data types by themselves. It provides users with the equivalent power to adding new attributes freely by themselves. We discuss this topic again in Sect. 4.4.

3.3   Monomorphic Patterns vs. Polymorphic Patterns

Polymorphism of patterns is useful for reducing the number of names used as pattern constructors. If patterns are monomorphic, we need to use different names for pattern constructors with similar meanings. As such, monomorphic patterns are error-prone.

For example, the pattern constructor that decomposes a collection into an element and the rest ignoring the order of the elements is bound to the name insert in the sample code of Curry [8] as in Sect. 3.1. The same pattern constructor's name is Add' in the sample program of Active Patterns [15]. However, these can be considered as a generalized cons pattern constructor for lists to multisets, because they are same at the point that both of them are a pattern constructor that decomposes a collection into an element and the rest.

Polymorphism is important, especially for value patterns. A value pattern is a pattern that matches when the value in the pattern is equal to the target. It is an important pattern construct for expressing non-linear patterns. If patterns are monomorphic, we need to prepare different notations for value patterns of different data types. For example, we need to have different notations for value patterns for lists and multisets. This is because equivalence of objects as lists and multisets are not equal although both lists and multisets are represented as a list.

```
pairsAsLists (insert x (insert x _)) = "Matched"
pairsAsLists _ = "Not matched"

pairsAsMultisets (insert x (insert y _)) | (multisetEq x y) = "Matched"
pairsAsMultisets _ = "Not matched"

pairsAsLists [[1,2],[2,1]]      -- returns "Not matched"
pairsAsMultisets [[1,2],[2,1]] -- returns "Matched"
```

4 Proposal

In this section, we introduce our pattern-matching system, which satisfies all requirements shown in Sect. 3. Our language has Scheme-like syntax. It is dynamically typed, and as well as Curry, based on lazy evaluation.

4.1 The match-all and match expressions

We explain the match-all expression. It is a primitive syntax of our language. It supports pattern matching with multiple results.

We show a sample program using match-all in the following. In this paper, we show the evaluation result of a program in the comment that follows the program. ";" is the inline comment delimiter of the proposed language.

```
(match-all {1 2 3} (list integer) [<join $xs $ys> [xs ys]])
; {[{} {1 2 3}] [{1} {2 3}] [{1 2} {3}] [{1 2 3} {}]}
```

Our language uses three kinds of parenthesis in addition to "(" and ")", which denote function applications. "<" and ">" are used to apply pattern and data constructors. In our language, the name of a data constructor starts with uppercase, whereas the name of a pattern constructor starts with lowercase. "[" and "]" are used to build a tuple. "{" and "}" are used to denote a collection.

In our implementation, the collection type is a built-in data type implemented as a lazy 2–3 finger tree [19]. This reason is that we thought data structures that support a wider range of operations for decomposition are more suitable for our pattern-matching system. (2–3 finger trees support efficient extraction of the last element.)

match-all is composed of an expression called *target*, *matcher*, and *match clause*, which consists of a *pattern* and *body expression*. The match-all expression evaluates the body of the match clause for each pattern-matching result and returns a (lazy) collection that contains all results. In the above code, we pattern-match the target {1 2 3} as a list of integers using the pattern <join $xs $ys>. (list integer) is a matcher to pattern-match the pattern and target as a list of integer. The pattern is constructed using the join pattern constructor. $xs and $ys are called *pattern variables*. We can use the result of pattern matching referring to them. A match-all expression first consults the matcher on how to pattern-match the given target and the given pattern. Matchers know how to decompose the target following the given pattern and enumerate the results, and match-all then collects the results returned by the matcher. In the sample program, given a join pattern, (list integer) tries to divide a collection into two collections. The collection {1 2 3} is thus divided into two collections by four ways.

match-all can handle pattern matching that may yield infinitely many results. For example, the following program extracts all twin primes from the infinite list of prime numbers[2]. We will discuss this mechanism in Sect. 5.2.

```
(define $twin-primes
  (match-all primes (list integer)
    [<join _ <cons $p <cons ,(+ p 2) _>>> [p (+ p 2)]]))

(take 6 twin-primes) ; {[3 5] [5 7] [11 13] [17 19] [29 31] [41 43]}
```

There is another primitive syntax called match expression. While match-all returns a collection of all matched results, match short-circuits the pattern matching process and immediately returns if any result is found. Another difference from match-all is that it can take multiple match clauses. It tries pattern matching starting from the head of the match clauses, and tries the next clause if it fails. Therefore, match is useful when we write conditional branching.

However, match is inessential for our language. It is implementable in terms of the match-all expression and macros. The reason is because the match-all expression is evaluated lazily, and, therefore, we can extract the first pattern-matching result from match-all without calculating other pattern-matching results simply by using car. We can implement match by combining the match-all and if expressions using macros. Furthermore, if is also implementable in terms of the match-all and matcher expression as follows. We will explain the matcher expression in Sect. 6. For that reason, we only discuss the match-all expression in the rest of the paper.

---

[2] We will explain the meaning of the value pattern ,(+ p 2) and the cons pattern constructor in Sects. 4.2 and 4.3, respectively.

```
(define $if
  (macro [$b $e1 $e2]
    (car (match-all b (matcher {[$ something {[<True> {e1}] [<False> {e2}]}]})
         [$x x])))))
```

4.2 Efficient Non-linear Pattern Matching with Backtracking

Our language can handle non-linear patterns efficiently. For example, the calculation time of the following code does not depend on the pattern length. Both of the following examples take $O(n^2)$ time to return the result.

```
(match-all (take n (repeat 0)) (multiset integer)
  [<insert $x <insert ,(+ x 1) _>> x])
; returns {} in O(n^2) time

(match-all (take n (repeat 0)) (multiset integer)
  [<insert $x <insert ,(+ x 1) <insert ,(+ x 2) _>>> x])
; returns {} in O(n^2) time
```

In our proposal, a pattern is examined from left to right in order, and the binding to a pattern variable can be referred to in its right side of the pattern. In the above examples, the pattern variable $x is bound to any element of the collection since the pattern constructor is insert. After that, the patterns ", (+ x 1)" and ", (+ x 2)" are examined. A pattern that begins with "," is called a *value pattern*. The expression following "," can be any kind of expressions. The value patterns match with the target data if the target is equal to the content of the pattern. Therefore, after successful pattern matching, $x is bound to an element that appears multiple times.

We can more elaborately discuss the difference of efficiency of non-linear patterns and pattern guards in general cases. The time complexity involved in pattern guards is $O(n^{p+v})$ when the pattern matching fails, whereas the time complexity involved in non-linear patterns is $O(n^{p+min(1,v)})$, where n is the size of the target object[3], p is the number of pattern variables, and v is the number of value patterns. The difference between v and $min(1,v)$ comes from the mechanism of non-linear pattern matching that backtracks at the first mismatch of the value pattern.

Table 1 shows micro benchmark results of non-linear pattern matching for Curry and Egison. The table shows execution times of the Curry program presented in Sect. 3.1 and the corresponding Egison program as shown above. The environment we used was Ubuntu on VirtualBox with 2 processors and 8 GB memory hosted on MacBook Pro (2017) with 2.3 GHz Intel Core i5 processor. We can see that the execution times in two implementations follow the theoretical computational complexities discussed above. We emphasize that this benchmark results do not mean Curry is slower than Egison. We can write the

---

[3] Here, we suppose that the number of decompositions by each pattern constructor can be approximated by the size of the target object.

Table 1. Benchmarks of Curry (PAKCS version 2.0.1 and Curry2Prolog(swi 7.6) compiler environment) and Egison (version 3.7.12)

Curry	n=15	n=25	n=30	n=50	n=100
seq2	1.18s	1.20s	1.29s	1.53s	2.54s
seq3	1.42s	2.10s	2.54s	7.40s	50.66s
seq4	3.37s	16.42s	34.19s	229.51s	3667.49s

Egison	n=15	n=25	n=30	n=50	n=100
seq2	0.26s	0.34s	0.43s	0.84s	2.72s
seq3	0.25s	0.34s	0.46s	0.82s	2.66s
seq4	0.25s	0.34s	0.42s	0.78s	2.47s

efficient programs for the same purpose in Curry if we do not persist in using non-linear patterns. Let us also note that the current implementation of Egison is not tuned up and comparing constant times in two implementations is nonsense.

Value patterns are not only efficient but also easy to read once we are used to them because it enables us to read patterns in the same order the execution process of pattern matching goes. It also reduces the number of new variables introduced in a pattern. We explain the mechanism how the proposed system executes the above pattern matching efficiently in Sect. 5.

4.3   Polymorphic Patterns

The characteristic of the proposed pattern-matching expression is that they take a matcher. This ingredient allows us to use the same pattern constructors for different data types.

For example, one may want to pattern-match a collection {1 2 3} sometimes as a list and other times as a multiset or a set. For these three types, we can naturally define similar pattern-matching operations. One example is the `cons` pattern, which is also called `insert` in Sects. 3.1 and 4.2. Given a collection, pattern `<cons $x $rs>` divides it into the "head" element and the rest. When we use the `cons` pattern for lists, it either yields the result which is uniquely determined by the constructor, or just fails when the list is empty. On the other hand, for multisets, it non-deterministically chooses an element from the given collection and yields many results. By explicitly specifying which matcher is used in match expressions, we can uniformly write such programs in our language:

```
(match-all {1 2 3} (list integer) [<cons $x $rs> [x rs]])
; {[1 {2 3}]}
(match-all {1 2 3} (multiset integer) [<cons $x $rs> [x rs]])
; {[1 {2 3}] [2 {1 3}] [3 {1 2}]}
(match-all {1 2 3} (set integer) [<cons $x $rs> [x rs]])
; {[1 {1 2 3}] [2 {1 2 3}] [3 {1 2 3}]}
```

In the case of lists, the head element $x is simply bound to the first element of the collection. On the other hand, in the case of multisets or sets, the head element can be any element of the collection because we ignore the order of elements. In the case of lists or multisets, the rest elements $rs are the collection that is made by removing the "head" element from the original collection.

However, in the case of sets, the rest elements are the same as the original collection because we ignore the redundant elements. If we interpret a set as a collection that contains infinitely many copies of an each element, this specification of cons for sets is natural. This specification is useful, for example, when we pattern-match a graph as a set of edges and enumerate all paths with some fixed length including cycles without redundancy.

Polymorphic patterns are useful especially when we use value patterns. As well as other patterns, the behavior of value patterns is dependent on matchers. For example, an equality {1 2 3} = {2 1 3} between collections is false if we regard them as mere lists but true if we regard them as multisets. Still, thanks to polymorphism of patterns, we can use the same syntax for both of them. This greatly improves the readability of the program and makes programming with non-free data types easy.

```
(match-all {1 2 3} (list integer) [,{2 1 3} "Matched"]) ; {}
(match-all {1 2 3} (multiset integer) [,{2 1 3} "Matched"]) ; {"Matched"}
```

We can pass matchers to a function because matchers are first-class objects. It enables us to utilize polymorphic patterns for defining function. The following is an example utilizing polymorphism of value patterns.

```
(define $member?/m
  (lambda [$m $x $xs]
    (match xs (list m) {[<join _ <cons ,x _>> #t] [_ #f]})))
```

4.4 Extensible Pattern Matching

In the proposed language, users can describe methods for interpreting patterns in the definition of matchers. Matchers appeared up to here are defined in our language. We show an example of a matcher definition. We will explain the details of this definition in Sect. 6.1.

```
(define $unordered-pair
  (lambda [$a]
    (matcher {[<pair $ $> [a a] {[<Pair $x $y> {[x y] [y x]}]}]
              [$ [something] {[$tgt {tgt}]}]})))
```

An *unordered pair* is a pair ignoring the order of the elements. For example, <Pair 2 5> is equivalent to <Pair 5 2>, if we regard them as unordered pairs. Therefore, datum <Pair 2 5> is successfully pattern-matched with pattern <pair ,5 $x>.

```
(match-all <Pair 2 5> (unordered-pair integer) [<pair ,5 $x> x]) ; {2}
```

We can define matchers for more complicated data types. For example, Egi constructed a matcher for mathematical expressions for building a computer algebra system on our language [7, 13, 14]. His computer algebra system is implemented as an application of the proposed pattern-matching system. The matcher for mathematical expressions is used for implementing simplification algorithms of mathematical expressions. A program that converts a mathematical expression object $n\cos^2(\theta) + n\sin^2(\theta)$ to n can be implemented as follows. (Here, we introduced the `math-expr` matcher and some syntactic sugar for patterns.)

```
(define $rewrite-rule-for-cos-and-sin-poly
  (lambda [$poly]
    (match poly math-expr
      {[<+ <* $n <,cos $x>^,2 $y> <* ,n <,sin ,x>^,2 ,y> $r>
        (rewrite-rule-for-cos-and-sin-poly <+' r <*' n y>>)]
      [_ poly]})))
```

1	MState {[<cons $m <cons ,m _>> (multiset integer) {2 8 2}]} env {}
	MState {[$m integer 2] [<cons ,m _> (multiset integer) {8 2}]} env {}
2	MState {[$m integer 8] [<cons ,m _> (multiset integer) {2 2}]} env {}
	MState {[$m integer 2] [<cons ,m _> (multiset integer) {2 8}]} env {}
3	MState {[$m something 2] [<cons ,m _> (multiset integer) {8 2}]} env {}
4	MState {[<cons ,m _> (multiset integer) {8 2}]} env {[m 2]}
5	MState {[,m integer 8] [_ (multiset integer) {2}]} env {[m 2]}
	MState {[,m integer 2] [_ (multiset integer) {8}]} env {[m 2]}
6	MState {[_ (multiset integer) {8}]} env {[m 2]}
7	MState {[_ something {8}]} env {[m 2]}
8	MState {} env {[m 2]}

Fig. 1. Reduction path of matching states

5 Algorithm

This section explains the pattern-matching algorithm of the proposed system. The formal definition of the algorithm is given in Sect. 7. The method for defining matchers explained in Sect. 6 is deeply related to the algorithm.

5.1 Execution Process of Non-linear Pattern Matching

Let us show what happens when the system evaluates the following pattern-matching expression.

```
(match-all {2 8 2} (multiset integer) [<cons $m <cons ,m _>> m]) ; {2 2}
```

Figure 1 shows one of the execution paths that reaches a matching result. First, the initial *matching state* is generated (step 1). A matching state is a datum that represents an intermediate state of pattern matching. A matching state is a compound type consisting of a stack of *matching atoms*, an environment, and intermediate results of the pattern matching. A matching atom is a tuple of a pattern, a matcher, and an expression called *target*. `MState` denotes the data constructor for matching states. `env` is the environment when the evaluation enters the `match-all` expression. A stack of matching atoms contains a single matching atom whose pattern, target and matcher are the arguments of the `match-all` expression.

In our proposal, pattern matching is implemented as reductions of matching states. In a reduction step, the top matching atom in the stack of matching atoms is popped out. This matching atom is passed to the procedure called *matching function*. The matching function is a function that takes a matching atom and returns a list of lists of matching atoms. The behavior of the matching function is controlled by the matcher of the argument matching atom. We can control the behavior of the matching function by defining matchers properly. For example, we obtain the following results by passing the matching atom of the initial matching state to the matching function.

```
matchFunction [<cons $m <cons ,m _>> (multiset integer) {2 8 2}] =
  { {[$m integer 2] [<cons ,m _> (multiset integer) {8 2}]}
    {[$m integer 8] [<cons ,m _> (multiset integer) {2 2}]}
    {[$m integer 2] [<cons ,m _> (multiset integer) {2 8}]} }
```

Each list of matching atoms is prepended to the stack of the matching atoms. As a result, the number of matching states increases to three (step 2). Our pattern-matching system repeats this step until all the matching states vanish.

For simplicity, in the following, we only examine the reduction of the first matching state in step 2. This matching state is reduced to the matching state shown in step 3. The matcher in the top matching atom in the stack is changed to `something` from `integer`, by definition of `integer` matcher. `something` is the only built-in matcher of our pattern-matching system. `something` can handle only wildcards or pattern variables, and is used to bind a value to a pattern variable. This matching state is then reduced to the matching state shown in step 4. The top matching atom in the stack is popped out, and a new binding `[m 2]` is added to the collection of intermediate results. Only `something` can append a new binding to the result of pattern matching.

Similarly to the preceding steps, the matching state is then reduced as shown in step 5, and the number of matching states increases to 2. ",m" is pattern-matched with 8 and 2 by `integer` matcher in the next step. When we pattern-match with a value pattern, the intermediate results of the pattern matching is used as an environment to evaluate it. In this way, "m" is evaluated to 2. Therefore, the first matching state fails to pattern-match and vanishes. The second matching state succeeds in pattern matching and is reduced to the matching state shown in step 6. In step 7, the matcher is simply converted from (`multiset integer`) to `something`, by definition of (`multiset integer`). Finally, the matching state is reduced to the empty collection (step 8). No new binding is added because the pattern is a wildcard. When the stack of matching atoms is empty, reduction finishes and the matching patching succeeds for this reduction path. The matching result { [m 2] } is added to the entire result of pattern matching.

We can check the pattern matching for sequential triples and quadruples are also efficiently executed in this algorithm.

5.2   Pattern Matching with Infinitely Many Results

The proposed pattern-matching system can eventually enumerate all successful matching results when matching results are infinitely many. It is performed by reducing the matching states in a proper order. Suppose the following program:

```
(take 8 (match-all nats (set integer) [<cons $m <cons $n _>> [m n]]))
; {[1 1] [1 2] [2 1] [1 3] [2 2] [3 1] [1 4] [2 3]}
```

Figure 2 shows the search tree of matching states when the system executes the above pattern matching expression. Rectangles represent matching states, and circles represent final matching states of successful pattern matching. The rectangle at the upper left is the initial matching state. The rectangles in the second row are the matching states generated from the initial matching state one step. Circles o8, r9, and s9 correspond to pattern-matching results { [m 1] [n 1] }, { [m 1] [n 2] }, and { [m 2] [n 1] }, respectively.

One issue on naively searching this search tree is that we cannot enumerate all matching states either in depth-first or breadth-first manners. The reason is that widths and depths of the search tree can be infinite. Widths can be infinite because a matching state may generate infinitely many matching states (e.g., the width of the second row is infinite), and depths can be infinite when we extend the language with a notion such as recursively defined patterns [12].

To resolve this issue, we reshape the search tree into a *reduction tree* as presented in Fig. 3. A node of a reduction tree is a list of matching states, and a node has at most two child nodes, left of which is the matching states generated from the head matching state of the parent, and right of which is a copy of the tail part of the parent matching states. At each reduction step, the system has a list of nodes. Each row in Fig. 3 denotes such a list. One reduction step in our system proceeds in the following two steps. First, for each node, it generates a node from the head matching state. Then, it constructs the nodes for the next step by collecting the generated nodes and the copies of the tail parts of the nodes. The index of each node denotes the depth in the tree the node is checked at. Since widths of the tree are at most 2^n for some n at any depth, all nodes can be assigned some finite number, which means all nodes in the tree are eventually checked after a finite number of reduction steps.

We adopt breadth-first search strategy as the default traverse method because there are cases that breadth-first traverse can successfully enumerate all pattern-matching results while depth-first traverse fails to do so when we handle pattern matching with infinitely many results. However, of course, when the size of the reduction tree is finite, the space complexity for depth-first traverse is less expensive. Furthermore, there are cases that the time complexity

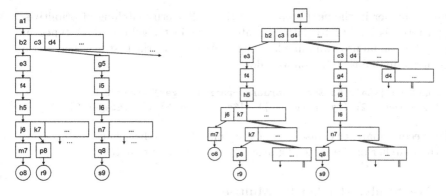

Fig. 2. Search tree   **Fig. 3.** Binary reduction tree

for depth-first traverse is also less expensive when we extract only the first several successful matches. Therefore, to extend the range of algorithms we can express concisely with pattern matching keeping efficiency, providing users with a method for switching search strategy of reduction trees is important. We leave further investigation of this direction as interesting future work.

6   User Defined Matchers

This section explains how to define matchers.

6.1   Matcher for Unordered Pairs

We explain how the `unordered-pair` matcher shown in Sect. 4.4 works. `unordered-pair` is defined as a function that takes and returns a matcher to specify how to pattern-match against the elements of a pair. `matcher` takes matcher clauses. A matcher clause is a triple of a primitive-pattern pattern, next-matcher expressions, and primitive-data-match clauses. The formal syntax of the `matcher` expression is found in Fig. 4 in Sect. 7.

   `unordered-pair` has two matcher clauses. The primitive-pattern pattern of the first matcher clause is `<pair $ $>`. This matcher clause defines the interpretation of `pair` pattern. `pair` takes two pattern holes `$`. It means that it interprets the first and second arguments of `pair` pattern by the matchers specified by the next-matcher expression. In this example, since the next-matcher expression is `[a a]`, both of the arguments of `pair` are pattern-matched using the matcher given by `a`. The primitive-data-match clause of the first matcher clause is `{[<Pair $x $y> {[x y] [y x]}]}`. `<Pair $x $y>` is pattern-matched with the target datum such as `<Pair 2 5>`, and `$x` and `$y` is matched with 2 and 5, respectively. The primitive-data-match clause returns `{[2 5] [5 2]}`. A primitive-data-match clause returns a collection of *next-targets*. This means the patterns ",5" and `$x` are matched with the targets 2 and 5, or 5 and 2 using the

integer matcher in the next step, respectively. Pattern matching of primitive-data-patterns is similar to pattern matching against algebraic data types in ordinary functional programming languages. As a result, the first matcher clause works in the matching function as follows.

```
matchFunction [<pair $x $y> (unordered-pair integer) <Pair 2 5>] =
  { {[$x integer 2] [$y integer 5]} {[$x integer 5] [$y integer 2]} }
```

The second matcher clause is rather simple; this matcher clause simply converts the matcher of the matching atom to the **something** matcher.

6.2 Case Study: Matcher for Multisets

As an example of how we can implement matchers for user-defined non-free data types, we show the definition of **multiset** matcher. We can define it simply by using the **list** matcher. **multiset** is defined as a function that takes and returns a matcher.

```
(define $multiset
  (lambda [$a]
    (matcher
      {[<nil> [] {[{} {[]}] [_ {}]}]
       [<cons $ $> [a (multiset a)]
        {[$tgt (match-all tgt (list a)
                  [<join $hs <cons $x $ts>>
                   [x (append hs ts)]])])]}]
       [,$val []
        {[$tgt (match [val tgt] [(list a) (multiset a)]
                  {[[<nil> <nil>] {[]}]
                   [[<cons $x $xs> <cons ,x ,xs>] {[]}]
                   [[_ _] {}]})]}]
       [$ [something] {[$tgt {tgt}]}]})))
```

The **multiset** matcher has four matcher clauses. The first matcher clause handles the **nil** pattern, and it checks if the target is an empty collection. The second matcher clause handles the **cons** pattern. The **match-all** expression is effectively used to destruct a collection in the primitive-data-match clause. Because the **join** pattern in the **list** matcher enumerates all possible splitting pairs of the given list, **match-all** lists up all possible consing pairs of the target expression. The third matcher clause handles value patterns. ",$val" is a value-pattern pattern that matches with a value pattern. This matcher clause checks if the content of a value pattern (bound to **val**) is equal to the target (bound to **tgt**) as multisets. Note that the definition involves recursions on the **multiset** matcher itself. The fourth matcher clause is completely identical to **unordered-pair** and **integer**.

6.3 Value-Pattern Patterns and Predicate Patterns

We explain the generality of our extensible pattern-matching framework taking examples from the `integer` matcher. How to implement value patterns and predicate patterns in our language is shown.

```
(define $integer
  (matcher {[,$n [] {[$tgt (if (eq? tgt n) {[]} {})]}]
           [<lt ,$n> [] {[$tgt (if (lt? tgt n) {[]} {})]}]
           [$ [something] {[$tgt {tgt}]}]}))
```

Value patterns are patterns that successfully match if the target expression is equal to some fixed value. For example, ,5 only matches with 5 if we use `integer` matcher. The first matcher clause in the above definition exists to implement this. The primitive-pattern pattern of this clause is ,$n, which is a value-pattern pattern that matches with value patterns. The next-matcher expression is an empty tuple because no pattern hole $ is contained. If the target expression `tgt` and the content of the value pattern n are equal, the primitive-data-match clause returns a collection consisting of an empty tuple, which denotes success. Otherwise, it returns an empty collection, which denotes failure.

Predicate patterns are patterns that succeed if the target expression satisfies some fixed predicate. Predicate patterns are usually implemented as a built-in feature, such as pattern guards, in ordinary programming languages. Interestingly, we can implement this on top of our pattern-matching framework. The second matcher clause defines a predicate pattern which succeeds if the target integer is less than the content of the value pattern n. A technique similar to the first clause is used.

$$M ::= x \mid c \mid (\text{lambda } [\$x \cdots] \ M) \mid (M \ M \cdots)$$
$$\mid [M \cdots] \mid \{M \cdots\} \mid <C \ M \cdots>$$
$$\mid (\text{match-all } M \ M \ [p \ M])$$
$$\mid (\text{match } M \ M \ \{[p \ M] \cdots\})$$
$$\mid \text{something} \mid (\text{matcher } \{\phi \cdots\})$$

$$p ::= \_ \mid \$x \mid ,M \mid <C \ p \cdots>$$
$$\phi ::= [pp \ M \ \{[dp \ M] \cdots\}]$$
$$pp ::= \$ \mid ,\$x \mid <C \ pp \cdots>$$
$$dp ::= \$x \mid <C \ dp \cdots>$$

Fig. 4. Syntax of our language

7   Formal Semantics

In this section, we present the syntax and big-step semantics of our language (Fig. 4 and 5). We use metavariables $x, y, z, \ldots$, $M, N, L, \ldots$, $v, \ldots$, and $p, \ldots$ for variables, expressions, values, and patterns respectively. In Fig. 4, c denotes a constant expression and C denotes a data constructor name. $X \cdots$ in Fig. 4 means a finite list of X. The syntax of our language is similar to that of the Lisp language. As explained in Sect. 4.1, $[M \ \cdots]$, $\{M \ \cdots\}$, and $<C \ M \ \cdots>$ denote tuples, collections, and data constructions. All formal arguments are decorated

Evaluation of `matcher` and `match-all`:

$$\overline{\Gamma, (\text{matcher } [pp_i \ M_i \ [dp_j \ N_j]_j]_i\,) \Downarrow ([pp_i, M_i, [dp_j, N_j]_j]_i, \Gamma)}$$

$$\frac{\Gamma, M \Downarrow v \qquad \Gamma, N \Downarrow m \qquad [[[p \sim_m v], \Gamma, \varnothing]] \Rrightarrow [\Delta_i]_i \qquad \Gamma \cup \Delta_i, L \Downarrow v_i \quad (\forall i)}{\Gamma, (\text{match-all } M \ N \ [p \ L]) \Downarrow [v_i]_i}$$

Matching states:

$$\overline{\epsilon \to \textbf{none}, \textbf{none}, \textbf{none}} \qquad \overline{(\epsilon, \Gamma, \Delta) : \vec{s} \to (\text{some } \Delta), \textbf{none}, (\text{some } \vec{s})}$$

$$\frac{p \sim_m^{\Gamma \cup \Delta} v \Downarrow [\vec{a}_i]_i, \Delta'}{((p \sim_m v) : \vec{a}, \Gamma, \Delta) : \vec{s} \to \textbf{none}, (\text{some}[\vec{a}_i + \vec{a}, \Gamma, \Delta \cup \Delta']_i), (\text{some } \vec{s})}$$

$$\frac{\vec{s}_i \to \text{opt } \Gamma_i, \text{opt } \vec{s'}_i, \text{opt } \vec{s''}_i \quad (\forall i)}{[\vec{s}_i]_i \Rrightarrow \sum_i (\text{opt } \Gamma_i), \sum_i (\text{opt } \vec{s'}_i) + \sum_i (\text{opt } \vec{s''}_i)} \qquad \overline{\epsilon \Rrightarrow \epsilon} \qquad \frac{\vec{s} \Rrightarrow \vec{\Gamma}, \vec{s'} \qquad \vec{s'} \Rrightarrow \vec{\Delta}}{\vec{s} \Rrightarrow \vec{\Gamma} + \vec{\Delta}}$$

Matching atoms:

$$\overline{\$x \sim_{\text{something}}^{\Gamma} v \Downarrow [\epsilon], \{x \mapsto v\}} \qquad \frac{pp \approx^{\Gamma} p \Downarrow \textbf{fail} \qquad p \sim_{(\vec{\phi}, \Delta)}^{\Gamma} v \Downarrow \vec{a}, \Gamma'}{p \sim_{((pp, M, \vec{\sigma}):\vec{\phi}, \Delta)}^{\Gamma} v \Downarrow \vec{a}, \Gamma'}$$

$$\frac{pp \approx^{\Gamma} p \Downarrow [p'_i]_i, \Delta' \qquad dp \approx v \Downarrow \textbf{fail} \qquad p \sim_{((pp, M, \vec{\sigma}):\vec{\phi}, \Delta)}^{\Gamma} v \Downarrow \vec{a}, \Gamma'}{p \sim_{((pp, M, (dp, N):\vec{\sigma}):\vec{\phi}, \Delta)}^{\Gamma} v \Downarrow \vec{a}, \Gamma'}$$

$$\frac{pp \approx^{\Gamma} p \Downarrow [p'_j]_j, \Delta' \qquad dp \approx v \Downarrow \Delta'' \qquad \Delta \cup \Delta' \cup \Delta'', N \Downarrow [[v'_{ij}]_j]_i \qquad \Delta, M \Downarrow [m'_j]_j}{p \sim_{((pp, M, (dp, N):\vec{\sigma}):\vec{\phi}, \Delta)}^{\Gamma} v \Downarrow [[p'_j \sim_{m'_j} v'_{ij}]_j]_i, \varnothing}$$

Pattern matching on patterns:

$$\overline{\$ \approx^{\Gamma} p \Downarrow [p], \varnothing} \qquad \frac{\Gamma, M \Downarrow v}{, \$y \approx^{\Gamma}, M \Downarrow \epsilon, \{y \mapsto v\}} \qquad \frac{pp_i \approx^{\Gamma} p_i \Downarrow \vec{p}_i, \Gamma_i \quad (\forall i)}{<\text{C } pp_1 \ldots pp_n> \approx^{\Gamma} <\text{C } p_1 \ldots p_n> \Downarrow \sum_i \vec{p}_i, \bigcup_i \Gamma_i}$$

Pattern matching on data:

$$\overline{\$z \approx v \Downarrow \{z \mapsto v\}} \qquad \frac{dp_i \approx v_i \Downarrow \Gamma_i \quad (\forall i)}{<\text{C } dp_1 \ldots dp_n> \approx <\text{C } v_1 \ldots v_n> \Downarrow \bigcup_i \Gamma_i}$$

Fig. 5. Formal semantics of our language

with the dollar mark. ϕ, pp and dp are called matcher clauses, primitive-pattern patterns and primitive-data patterns respectively.

In Fig. 5, the following notations are used. We write $[a_i]_i$ to mean a list $[a_1, a_2, \ldots]$. Similarly, $[[a_{ij}]_j]_i$ denotes $[[a_{11}, a_{12}, \ldots], [a_{21}, a_{22}, \ldots], \ldots]$, but each list in the list may have different length. List of tuples $[(a_1, b_1), (a_2, b_2), \ldots]$ may be often written as $[a_i, b_i]_i$ instead of $[(a_i, b_i)]_i$ for short. Concatenation of lists l_1, l_2 are denoted by $l_1 + l_2$, and $a : l$ denotes $[a] + l$ (adding at the front). ϵ denotes the empty list. In general, $\vec{x}$ for some metavariable x is a metavariable denoting a list of what x denotes. However, we do *not* mean by $\vec{x}_i$ the i-th element of $\vec{x}$; if we write $[\vec{x}_i]_i$, we mean a list of a list of x. $\Gamma, \Delta, \ldots$ denote variable assignments, i.e., partial functions from variables to values.

Our language has some special primitive types: matching atoms $a, \ldots$, matching states $s, \ldots$, primitive-data-match clauses $\sigma, \ldots$, and matchers $m, \ldots$. A matching atom consists of a pattern p, a matcher m, and a value v, and written as $p \sim_m v$. A matching state is a tuple of a list of matching atoms and two variable assignments. A primitive-data-match clause is a tuple of a primitive-data pattern and an expression, and a matcher clause is a tuple of a primitive-pattern pattern, an expression, and a list of data-pattern clauses. A matcher is a pair containing a list of matcher clauses and a variable assignment. Note that matchers, matching states, etc. are all values.

Evaluation results of expressions are specified by the judgment $\Gamma, e \Downarrow \vec{v}$, which denotes given a variable assignment Γ and an expression e one gets a list of values $\vec{v}$. In the figure, we only show the definition of evaluation of `matcher` and `match-all` expressions (other cases are inductively defined as usual). The definition of `match-all` relies on another type of judgment $\vec{s} \Rightarrow \Gamma$, which defines how the search space is examined. $\Rightarrow$ is inductively defined using $\vec{s} \Rightarrow \Gamma, \vec{s'}$, which is again defined using $\vec{s} \rightarrow \text{opt}\, \Gamma, \text{opt}\, \vec{s'}, \text{opt}\, \vec{s''}$. In their definitions, we introduced notations for (meta-level) option types. `none` and `some` x are the constructors of the option type, and $\text{opt}\, x$ is a metavariable for an optional value (possibly) containing what the metavariable x denotes. $\sum_i (\text{opt}\, x_i)$ creates a list by collecting all the valid (non-`none`) x_i preserving the order.

$p \sim_m^\Gamma v \Downarrow \vec{a}, \Delta$ is a 6-ary relation. One reads it "performing pattern matching on v against p using the matcher m under the variable assignment Γ yields the result Δ and continuation $\vec{a}$." The result is a variable assignment because it is a result of unifications. $\vec{a}$ being empty means the pattern matching failed. If $[\epsilon]$ is returned as $\vec{a}$, it means the pattern matching succeeded and no further search is necessary. As explained in Sect. 6, one needs to pattern-match patterns and data to define user-defined matchers. Their formal definitions are given by judgments $pp \approx^\Gamma p \Downarrow \vec{p'}, \Delta$ and $dp \approx v \Downarrow \Gamma$.

8   Conclusion

We designed a user-customizable efficient non-linear pattern-matching system by regarding pattern matching as reduction of matching states that have a stack of matching atoms and intermediate results of pattern matching. This system enables us to concisely describe a wide range of programs, especially when non-free data types are involved. For example, our pattern matching architecture is useful to implement a computer algebra system because it enables us to directly pattern-match mathematical expressions and rewrite them.

The major significance of our pattern matching system is that it greatly improves the expressivity of the programming language by allowing programmers to freely extend the process of pattern matching by themselves. Furthermore, in the general cases, use of the `match` expression will be as readable as that in other general-purpose programming languages. Although we consider that the current syntax of matcher definition is already clean enough, we leave further refinement of the syntax of our surface language as future work.

We believe the direct and concise representation of algorithms enables us to implement really new things that go beyond what was considered practical before. We hope our work will lead to breakthroughs in various fields.

Acknowledgments. We thank Ryo Tanaka, Takahisa Watanabe, Kentaro Honda, Takuya Kuwahara, Mayuko Kori, and Akira Kawata for their important contributions to implement the interpreter. We thank Michal J. Gajda, Yi Dai, Hiromi Hirano, Kimio Kuramitsu, and Pierre Imai for their helpful feedback on the earlier versions of the paper. We thank Masami Hagiya, Yoshihiko Kakutani, Yoichi Hirai, Ibuki Kawamata, Takahiro Kubota, Takasuke Nakamura, Yasunori Harada, Ikuo Takeuchi, Yukihiro Matsumoto, Hidehiko Masuhara, and Yasuhiro Yamada for constructive discussion and their continuing encouragement.

References

1. Attributes::attnf - Wolfram Language Documentation. http://reference.wolfram.com/language/ref/message/Attributes/attnf.html. Accessed 14 June 2018
2. Introduction to Patterns - Wolfram Language Documentation. http://reference.wolfram.com/language/tutorial/Introduction-Patterns.html. Accessed 14 June 2018
3. Orderless - Wolfram Language Documentation. http://reference.wolfram.com/language/ref/Orderless.html. Accessed 14 June 2018
4. PAKCS. https://www.informatik.uni-kiel.de/~pakcs/. Accessed 14 June 2018
5. ViewPatterns - GHC. https://ghc.haskell.org/trac/ghc/wiki/ViewPatterns. Accessed 14 June 2018
6. The Egison programming language (2011). https://www.egison.org. Accessed 14 June 2018
7. Egison Mathematics Notebook (2016). https://www.egison.org/math. Accessed 14 June 2018
8. Antoy, S.: Programming with narrowing: a tutorial. J. Symb. Comput. **45**(5), 501–522 (2010)
9. Antoy, S.: Constructor-based conditional narrowing. In: Proceedings of the 3rd ACM SIGPLAN International Conference on Principles and Practice of Declarative Programming (2001)
10. Antoy, S., Hanus, M.: Functional logic programming. Commun. ACM **53**(4), 74–85 (2010)
11. Braßel, B., Hanus, M., Peemöller, B., Reck, F.: KiCS2: a new compiler from Curry to Haskell. In: Kuchen, H. (ed.) WFLP 2011. LNCS, vol. 6816, pp. 1–18. Springer, Heidelberg (2011). https://doi.org/10.1007/978-3-642-22531-4_1
12. Egi, S.: Non-linear pattern matching against non-free data types with lexical scoping. arXiv preprint arXiv:1407.0729 (2014)
13. Egi, S.: Scalar and tensor parameters for importing tensor index notation including Einstein summation notation. In: The Scheme and Functional Programming Workshop (2017)
14. Egi, S.: Scalar and tensor parameters for importing the notation in differential geometry into programming. arXiv preprint arXiv:1804.03140 (2018)
15. Erwig, M.: Active patterns. In: Kluge, W. (ed.) IFL 1996. LNCS, vol. 1268, pp. 21–40. Springer, Heidelberg (1997). https://doi.org/10.1007/3-540-63237-9_17

16. Erwig, M.: Functional programming with graphs. In: ACM SIGPLAN Notices, vol. 32 (1997)
17. Fischer, S., Kiselyov, O., Shan, C.: Purely functional lazy non-deterministic programming. In: ACM Sigplan Notices, vol. 44 (2009)
18. Hanus, M.: Multi-paradigm declarative languages. In: Dahl, V., Niemelä, I. (eds.) ICLP 2007. LNCS, vol. 4670, pp. 45–75. Springer, Heidelberg (2007). https://doi.org/10.1007/978-3-540-74610-2_5
19. Hinze, R., Paterson, R.: Finger trees: a simple general-purpose data structure. J. Funct. Program. **16**(2), 197–217 (2006)
20. Krebber, M.: Non-linear associative-commutative many-to-one pattern matching with sequence variables. arXiv preprint arXiv:1705.00907 (2017)
21. McBride, F., Morrison, D., Pengelly, R.: A symbol manipulation system. Mach. Intell. **5**, 337–347 (1969)
22. Okasaki, C.: Views for standard ML. In: SIGPLAN Workshop on ML (1998)
23. Syme, D., Neverov, G., Margetson, J.: Extensible pattern matching via a lightweight language extension. In: ACM SIGPLAN Notices, vol. 42 (2007)
24. Thompson, S.: Lawful functions and program verification in Miranda. Sci. Comput. Program. **13**(2–3), 181–218 (1990)
25. Thompson, S.: Laws in Miranda. In: Proceedings of the 1986 ACM Conference on LISP and Functional Programming (1986)
26. Tullsen, M.: First class patterns? In: Pontelli, E., Santos Costa, V. (eds.) PADL 2000. LNCS, vol. 1753, pp. 1–15. Springer, Heidelberg (1999). https://doi.org/10.1007/3-540-46584-7_1
27. Turner, D.A.: Miranda: a non-strict functional language with polymorphic types. In: Jouannaud, J.-P. (ed.) FPCA 1985. LNCS, vol. 201, pp. 1–16. Springer, Heidelberg (1985). https://doi.org/10.1007/3-540-15975-4_26
28. Wadler, P.: Views: a way for pattern matching to cohabit with data abstraction. In: Proceedings of the 14th ACM SIGACT-SIGPLAN Symposium on Principles of Programming Languages (1987)

Factoring Derivation Spaces
via Intersection Types

Pablo Barenbaum[1,2]([✉]) and Gonzalo Ciruelos[1]

[1] Departamento de Computación, FCEyN, UBA, Buenos Aires, Argentina
pbarenbaum@dc.uba.ar, gonzalo.ciruelos@gmail.com
[2] IRIF, Université Paris 7, Paris, France

Abstract. In typical non-idempotent intersection type systems, proof
normalization is not confluent. In this paper we introduce a confluent non-idempotent intersection type system for the λ-calculus. Typing
derivations are presented using proof term syntax. The system enjoys
good properties: subject reduction, strong normalization, and a very regular theory of residuals. A correspondence with the λ-calculus is established by simulation theorems. The machinery of non-idempotent intersection types allows us to track the usage of resources required to obtain
an answer. In particular, it induces a notion of *garbage*: a computation
is garbage if it does not contribute to obtaining an answer. Using these
notions, we show that the derivation space of a λ-term may be factorized using a variant of the Grothendieck construction for semilattices.
This means, in particular, that any derivation in the λ-calculus can be
uniquely written as a garbage-free prefix followed by garbage.

Keywords: Lambda calculus · Intersection types · Derivation space

1 Introduction

Our goal in this paper is attempting to understand the spaces of computations
of programs. Consider a hypothetical functional programming language with
arithmetic expressions and tuples. All the possible computations starting from
the tuple $(1+1,\ 2*3+1)$ can be arranged to form its "space of computations":

$$
\begin{array}{ccccc}
(1+1,\ 2*3+1) & \longrightarrow & (1+1,\ 6+1) & \longrightarrow & (1+1,\ 7) \\
\downarrow & & \downarrow & & \downarrow \\
(2,\ 2*3+1) & \longrightarrow & (2,\ 6+1) & \longrightarrow & (2,\ 7)
\end{array}
$$

In this case, the space of computations is quite easy to understand, because the
subexpressions $(1+1)$ and $(2*3+1)$ cannot interact with each other. Indeed, the
space of computations of a tuple (A, B) can always be understood as the *product*
of the spaces of A and B. In the general case, however, the space of computations

Work partially supported by CONICET.

S. Ryu (Ed.): APLAS 2018, LNCS 11275, pp. 24–44, 2018.
https://doi.org/10.1007/978-3-030-02768-1_2

of a program may have a much more complex structure. For example, it is not easy to characterize the space of computations of a function application $f(A)$. The difficulty is that f may use the value of A zero, one, or possibly many times.

The quintessential functional programming language is the pure λ-calculus. Computations in the λ-calculus have been thoroughly studied since its conception in the 1930s. The well-known theorem by Church and Rosser [10] states that β-reduction in the λ-calculus is *confluent*, which means, in particular, that terminating programs have unique normal forms. Another result by Curry and Feys [13] states that computations in the λ-calculus may be *standardized*, meaning that they may be converted into a computation in canonical form. A refinement of this theorem by Lévy [26] asserts that the canonical computation thus obtained is equivalent to the original one in a strong sense, namely that they are *permutation equivalent*. In a series of papers [30–32], Melliès generalized many of these results to the abstract setting of *axiomatic rewrite systems*.

Let us discuss "spaces of computations" more precisely. The *derivation space* of an object x in some rewriting system is the set of all *derivations*, *i.e.* sequences of rewrite steps, starting from x. In this paper, we will be interested in the pure λ-calculus, and we will study *finite* derivations only. In the λ-calculus, a transitive relation between derivations may be defined, the *prefix order*. A derivation ρ is a prefix of a derivation σ, written $\rho \sqsubseteq \sigma$, whenever ρ performs less computational work than σ. Formally, $\rho \sqsubseteq \sigma$ is defined to hold whenever the *projection* ρ/σ is empty[1]. For example, if $K = \lambda x.\lambda y.x$, the derivation space of the term $(\lambda x.xx)(Kz)$ can be depicted with the *reduction graph* below. Derivations are directed paths in the reduction graph, and ρ is a prefix of σ if there is a directed path from the target of ρ to the target of σ. For instance, SR_2 is a prefix of $RS'T'$:

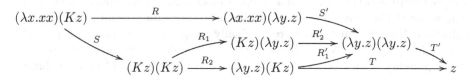

Remark that $\sqsubseteq$ is reflexive and transitive but not antisymmetric, *i.e.* it is a quasi-order but not an order. For example $RS' \sqsubseteq SR_1R_2' \sqsubseteq RS'$ but $RS' \neq SR_1R_2'$. Antisymmetry may be recovered as usual when in presence of a quasi-order, by working modulo *permutation equivalence*: two derivations ρ and σ are said to be permutation equivalent, written $\rho \equiv \sigma$, if $\rho \sqsubseteq \sigma$ and $\sigma \sqsubseteq \rho$. Working modulo permutation equivalence is reasonable because Lévy's formulation of the standardization theorem ensures that permutation equivalence is decidable.

Derivation spaces are known to exhibit various regularities [2, 25–27, 29, 35]. In his PhD thesis, Lévy [26] showed that the derivation space of a term is an upper semilattice: any two derivations ρ, σ from a term t have a *least upper bound* $\rho \sqcup \sigma$, defined as $\rho(\sigma/\rho)$, unique up to permutation equivalence. On the other

---

[1] The notion of projection defined by means of residuals is the standard one, see *e.g.* [4, Chap. 12] or [33, Sect. 8.7].

hand, the derivation space of a term t is not an easy structure to understand in general[2]. For example, relating the derivation space of an application ts with the derivation spaces of t and s appears to be a hard problem. Lévy also noted that the *greatest lower bound* of two derivations does not necessarily exist, meaning that the derivation space of a term does not form a lattice in general. Even when it forms a lattice, it may not necessarily be a *distributive* lattice, as observed for example by Laneve [25]. In [30], Melliès showed that derivation spaces in any rewriting system satisfying certain axioms may be factorized using two spaces, one of *external* and one of *internal* derivations.

The difficulty to understand derivation spaces is due to three pervasive phenomena of *interaction* between computations. The first phenomenon is *duplication*: in the reduction graph of above, the step S duplicates the step R, resulting in two copies of R: the steps R_1 and R_2. In such situation, one says that R_1 and R_2 are *residuals* of R, and, conversely, R is an *ancestor* of R_1 and R_2. The second phenomenon is *erasure*: in the diagram above, the step T erases the step R'_1, resulting in no copies of R'_1. The third phenomenon is *creation*: in the diagram above, the step R_2 creates the step T, meaning that T is not a residual of a step that existed prior to executing R_2; that is, T has no ancestor.

These three interaction phenomena, especially duplication and erasure, are intimately related with the management of *resources*. In this work, we aim to explore the hypothesis that **having an explicit representation of resource management may provide insight on the structure of derivation spaces**.

There are many existing λ-calculi that deal with resource management explicitly [6, 16, 21, 22], most of which draw inspiration from Girard's Linear Logic [19]. Recently, calculi endowed with *non-idempotent intersection type systems*, have received some attention [5, 7, 8, 15, 20, 23, 34]. These type systems are able to statically capture non-trivial dynamic properties of terms, particularly *normalization*, while at the same time being amenable to elementary proof techniques by induction. Intersection types were originally proposed by Coppo and Dezani-Ciancaglini [12] to study termination in the λ-calculus. They are characterized by the presence of an *intersection* type constructor $\mathcal{A} \cap \mathcal{B}$. *Non-idempotent* intersection type systems are distinguished from their usual idempotent counterparts by the fact that intersection is not declared to be idempotent, *i.e.* $\mathcal{A}$ and $\mathcal{A} \cap \mathcal{A}$ are not equivalent types. Rather, intersection behaves like a multiplicative connective in linear logic. Arguments to functions are typed many times, typically once per each time that the argument will be used. Non-idempotent intersection types were originally formulated by Gardner [18], and later reintroduced by de Carvalho [9].

In this paper, we will use a non-idempotent intersection type system based on system $\mathcal{W}$ of [8] (called system $\mathcal{H}$ in [7]). Let us recall its definition. Terms are as usual in the λ-calculus ($t ::= x \mid \lambda x.t \mid t\,t$). Types $\mathcal{A}, \mathcal{B}, \mathcal{C}, \dots$ are defined by the grammar:

$$\mathcal{A} ::= \alpha \mid \mathcal{M} \to \mathcal{A} \qquad\qquad \mathcal{M} ::= [\mathcal{A}_i]_{i=1}^n \quad \text{ with } n \geq 0$$

---

[2] Problem 2 in the RTA List of Open Problems [14] poses the open-ended question of investigating the properties of "spectra", *i.e.* derivation spaces.

where α ranges over one of denumerably many *base types*, and $\mathcal{M}$ represents a *multiset of types*. Here $[\mathcal{A}_i]_{i=1}^n$ denotes the multiset $\mathcal{A}_1, \ldots, \mathcal{A}_n$ with their respective multiplicities. A multiset $[\mathcal{A}_i]_{i=1}^n$ intuitively stands for the (non-idempotent) intersection $\mathcal{A}_1 \cap \ldots \cap \mathcal{A}_n$. The *sum of multisets* $\mathcal{M} + \mathcal{N}$ is defined as their union (adding multiplicities). A *typing context* Γ is a partial function mapping variables to multisets of types. The domain of Γ is the set of variables x such that $\Gamma(x)$ is defined. We assume that typing contexts always have *finite domain* and hence they may be written as $x_1 : \mathcal{M}_1, \ldots, x_n : \mathcal{M}_n$. The *sum of contexts* $\Gamma + \Delta$ is their pointwise sum, *i.e.* $(\Gamma + \Delta)(x) := \Gamma(x) + \Delta(x)$ if $\Gamma(x)$ and $\Delta(x)$ are both defined, $(\Gamma + \Delta)(x) := \Gamma(x)$ if $\Delta(x)$ is undefined, and $(\Gamma + \Delta)(x) := \Delta(x)$ if $\Gamma(x)$ is undefined. We write $\Gamma +_{i=1}^n \Delta_i$ to abbreviate $\Gamma + \Delta_1 + \ldots + \Delta_n$. The *disjoint sum of contexts* $\Gamma \oplus \Delta$ stands for $\Gamma + \Delta$, provided that the domains of Γ and Δ are disjoint. A *typing judgment* is a triple $\Gamma \vdash t : \mathcal{A}$, representing the knowledge that the term t has type $\mathcal{A}$ in the context Γ. Type assignment rules for system $\mathcal{W}$ are as follows.

Definition 1.1 (System $\mathcal{W}$)

$$\frac{}{x : [\mathcal{A}] \vdash \mathcal{A}} \; \text{var} \qquad \frac{\Gamma \oplus (x : \mathcal{M}) \vdash t : \mathcal{A}}{\Gamma \vdash \lambda x.t : \mathcal{M} \to \mathcal{A}} \; \text{lam} \qquad \frac{\Gamma \vdash t : [\mathcal{B}_i]_{i=1}^n \to \mathcal{A} \quad (\Delta_i \vdash s : \mathcal{B}_i)_{i=1}^n}{\Gamma +_{i=1}^n \Delta_i \vdash ts : \mathcal{A}} \; \text{app}$$

Observe that the **app** rule has $n + 1$ premises, where $n \geq 0$. System $\mathcal{W}$ enjoys various properties, nicely summarized in [8].

There are two obstacles to adopting system $\mathcal{W}$ for studying derivation spaces. The first obstacle is mostly a matter of presentation—typing derivations use a tree-like notation, which is cumbersome. One would like to have an alternative notation based on proof terms. For example, one may define proof terms for the typing rules above using the syntax $\pi ::= x^{\mathcal{A}} \mid \lambda x.\pi \mid \pi[\pi, \ldots, \pi]$, in such a way that $x^{\mathcal{A}}$ encodes an application of the **var** axiom, $\lambda x.\pi$ encodes an application of the **lam** rule to the typing derivation encoded by π, and $\pi_1[\pi_2, \ldots, \pi_n]$ encodes an application of the **app** rule to the typing derivations encoded by $\pi_1, \pi_2, \ldots, \pi_n$. For example, using this notation $\lambda x.x^{[\alpha, \alpha] \to \beta}[x^\alpha, x^\alpha]$ would represent the following typing derivation:

$$\frac{\dfrac{}{x : [\alpha, \alpha] \to \beta \vdash x : [\alpha, \alpha] \to \beta} \; \text{var} \quad \dfrac{}{x : [\alpha] \vdash x : \alpha} \; \text{var} \quad \dfrac{}{x : [\alpha] \vdash x : \alpha} \; \text{var}}{\dfrac{x : [[\alpha, \alpha] \to \beta, \alpha, \alpha] \vdash xx : \beta}{\vdash \lambda x.xx : [[\alpha, \alpha] \to \beta, \alpha, \alpha] \to \beta} \; \text{lam}} \; \text{app}$$

The second obstacle is a major one for our purposes: *proof normalization* in this system is not confluent. The reason is that applications take multiple arguments, and a β-reduction step must choose a way to distribute these arguments among the occurrences of the formal parameters. For instance, the following critical pair cannot be closed:

$$(\lambda x.y^{[\alpha]\to[\alpha]\to\beta}[x^\alpha][x^\alpha])[z^{[\gamma]\to\alpha}[z^\gamma], z^{[]\to\alpha}[]]$$

$$y^{[\alpha]\to[\alpha]\to\beta}[z^{[\gamma]\to\alpha}[z^\gamma]][z^{[]\to\alpha}[]] \qquad\qquad y^{[\alpha]\to[\alpha]\to\beta}[z^{[]\to\alpha}[]][z^{[\gamma]\to\alpha}[z^\gamma]]$$

The remainder of this paper is organized as follows:

- In Sect. 2, we review some standard notions of order and rewriting theory.
- In Sect. 3, we introduce a confluent calculus $\lambda^\#$ based on system $\mathcal{W}$. The desirable properties of system $\mathcal{W}$ of [8] still hold in $\lambda^\#$. Moreover, $\lambda^\#$ is confluent. We impose confluence forcibly, by decorating subtrees with distinct labels, so that a β-reduction step may distribute the arguments in a unique way. Derivation spaces in $\lambda^\#$ have very regular structure, namely they are distributive lattices.
- In Sect. 4, we establish a correspondence between derivation spaces in the λ-calculus and the $\lambda^\#$-calculus via simulation theorems, which defines a morphism of upper semilattices.
- In Sect. 5, we introduce the notion of a garbage derivation. Roughly, a derivation in the λ-calculus is *garbage* if it maps to an empty derivation in the $\lambda^\#$-calculus. This gives rise to an orthogonal notion of *garbage-free* derivation. The notion of garbage-free derivation is closely related with the notions of *needed step* [33, Sect. 8.6], *typed occurrence of a redex* [8], and *external derivation* [30]. Using this notion of garbage we prove a *factorization theorem* reminiscent of Melliès' [30]. The upper semilattice of derivations of a term in the λ-calculus is factorized using a variant of the Grothendieck construction. Every derivation is uniquely decomposed as a garbage-free prefix followed by a garbage suffix.
- In Sect. 6, we conclude.

Note. Detailed proofs have been omitted from this paper due to lack of space. Refer to the second author's master's thesis [11] for the full details.

2   Preliminaries

We recall some standard definitions. An *upper semilattice* is a poset $(A, \leq)$ with a least element or *bottom* $\bot \in A$, and such that for every two elements $a, b \in A$ there is a least upper bound or *join* $(a \vee b) \in A$. A *lattice* is an upper semilattice with a greatest element or *top* $\top \in A$, and such that for every two elements $a, b \in A$ there is a greatest lower bound or *meet* $(a \wedge b) \in A$. A lattice is *distributive* if $\wedge$ distributes over $\vee$ and vice versa. A *morphism* of upper semilattices is given by a monotonic function $f : A \to B$, i.e. $a \leq b$ implies $f(a) \leq f(b)$, preserving the bottom element, *i.e.* $f(\bot) = \bot$, and joins, *i.e.* $f(a \vee b) = f(a) \vee f(b)$ for all $a, b \in A$. Similarly for morphisms of lattices. Any poset $(A, \leq)$ forms a category whose objects are the elements of A and morphisms are of the form $a \hookrightarrow b$ for all $a \leq b$. The category of posets with monotonic functions is denoted by Poset. In fact, we regard it as a 2-category: given morphisms $f, g : A \to B$ of posets, we have that $f \leq g$ whenever $f(a) \leq g(a)$ for all $a \in A$.

An *axiomatic rewrite system* (*cf.* [29, Definition 2.1]) is given by a set of objects Obj, a set of steps Stp, two functions src, tgt : Stp $\twoheadrightarrow$ Obj indicating the source and target of each step, and a *residual function* (/) such that given any two steps $R, S \in$ Stp with the same source, yields a set of steps R/S such that $\mathsf{src}(R') = \mathsf{tgt}(S)$ for all $R' \in R/S$. Steps are ranged over by $R, S, T, \ldots$. A step $R' \in R/S$ is called a *residual* of R after S, and R is called an *ancestor* of R'. Steps are *coinitial* (resp. *cofinal*) if they have the same source (resp. target). A *derivation* is a possibly empty sequence of composable steps $R_1 \ldots R_n$. Derivations are ranged over by $\rho, \sigma, \tau, \ldots$. The functions src and tgt are extended to derivations. Composition of derivations is defined when $\mathsf{tgt}(\rho) = \mathsf{src}(\sigma)$ and written $\rho\sigma$. Residuals after a derivation can be defined by $R_n \in R_0/S_1 \ldots S_n$ if and only if there exist $R_1, \ldots, R_{n-1}$ such that $R_{i+1} \in R_i/S_{i+1}$ for all $0 \leq i \leq n - 1$. Let $\mathcal{M}$ be a set of coinitial steps. A *development* of $\mathcal{M}$ is a (possibly infinite) derivation $R_1 \ldots R_n \ldots$ such that for every index i there exists a step $S \in \mathcal{M}$ such that $R_i \in S/R_1 \ldots R_{i-1}$. A development is *complete* if it is maximal.

An *orthogonal* axiomatic rewrite system (*cf.* [29, Sect. 2.3]) has four additional axioms[3]:

1. *Autoerasure.* $R/R = \varnothing$ for all $R \in$ Stp.
2. *Finite Residuals.* The set R/S is finite for all coinitial $R, S \in$ Stp.
3. *Finite Developments.* If $\mathcal{M}$ is a set of coinitial steps, all developments of $\mathcal{M}$ are finite.
4. *Semantic Orthogonality.* Let $R, S \in$ Stp be coinitial steps. Then there exist a complete development ρ of R/S and a complete development σ of S/R such that ρ and σ are cofinal. Moreover, for every step $T \in$ Stp such that T is coinitial to R, the following equality between sets holds: $T/(R\sigma) = T/(S\rho)$.

In [29], Melliès develops the theory of orthogonal axiomatic rewrite systems. A notion of *projection* ρ/σ may be defined between coinitial derivations, essentially by setting $\epsilon/\sigma \overset{\text{def}}{=} \epsilon$ and $R\rho'/\sigma \overset{\text{def}}{=} (R/\sigma)(\rho'/(\sigma/R))$ where, by abuse of notation, R/σ stands for a (canonical) complete development of the set R/σ. Using this notion, one may define a transitive relation of *prefix* ($\rho \sqsubseteq \sigma$), a *permutation equivalence* relation ($\rho \equiv \sigma$), and the *join* of derivations ($\rho \sqcup \sigma$). Some of their properties are summed up in the figure below:

---

[3] In [29], Autoerasure is called Axiom A, Finite Residuals is called Axiom B, and Semantic Orthogonality is called PERM. We follow the nomenclature of [1].

Summary of properties of orthogonal axiomatic rewrite systems

$\epsilon\rho = \rho$	$\rho \sqsubseteq \sigma \overset{\text{def}}{\iff} \rho/\sigma = \epsilon$	$\rho \sqsubseteq \sigma \implies \rho/\tau \sqsubseteq \sigma/\tau$
$\rho\epsilon = \rho$		
$\epsilon/\rho = \epsilon$	$\rho \equiv \sigma \overset{\text{def}}{\iff} \rho \sqsubseteq \sigma \wedge \sigma \sqsubseteq \rho$	$\rho \sqsubseteq \sigma \iff \tau\rho \sqsubseteq \tau\sigma$
$\rho/\epsilon = \rho$	$\rho \sqcup \sigma \overset{\text{def}}{=} \rho(\sigma/\rho)$	$\rho \sqcup \sigma \equiv \sigma \sqcup \rho$
$\rho/\sigma\tau = (\rho/\sigma)/\tau$	$\rho \equiv \sigma \implies \tau/\rho = \tau/\sigma$	$(\rho \sqcup \sigma) \sqcup \tau = \rho \sqcup (\sigma \sqcup \tau)$
$\rho\sigma/\tau = (\rho/\tau)(\sigma/(\tau/\rho))$	$\rho \sqsubseteq \sigma \iff \exists \tau.\ \rho\tau \equiv \sigma$	$\rho \ \sqsubseteq \ \rho \sqcup \sigma$
$\rho/\rho = \epsilon$	$\rho \sqsubseteq \sigma \iff \rho \sqcup \sigma \equiv \sigma$	$(\rho \sqcup \sigma)/\tau = (\rho/\tau) \sqcup (\sigma/\tau)$

Let $[\rho] = \{\sigma \mid \rho \equiv \sigma\}$ denote the permutation equivalence class of ρ. In an orthogonal axiomatic rewrite system, the set $\mathbb{D}(x) = \{[\rho] \mid \mathsf{src}(\rho) = x\}$ forms an upper semilattice [29, Theorems 2.2 and 2.3]. The order $[\rho] \sqsubseteq [\sigma]$ is declared to hold if $\rho \sqsubseteq \sigma$, the join is $[\rho] \sqcup [\sigma] = [\rho \sqcup \sigma]$, and the bottom is $\bot = [\epsilon]$. The λ-calculus is an example of an orthogonal axiomatic rewrite system. Our structures of interest are the semilattices of derivations of the λ-calculus, written $\mathbb{D}^\lambda(t)$ for any given λ-term t. As usual, β-reduction in the λ-calculus is written $t \to_\beta s$ and defined by the contextual closure of the axiom $(\lambda x.t)s \to_\beta t\{x := s\}$.

3   The Distributive λ-Calculus

In this section we introduce the *distributive λ-calculus* ($\lambda^\#$), and we prove some basic results. Terms of the $\lambda^\#$-calculus are typing derivations of a non-idempotent intersection type system, written using proof term syntax. The underlying type system is a variant of system $\mathcal{W}$ of [7,8], the main difference being that $\lambda^\#$ uses *labels* and a suitable invariant on terms, to ensure that the formal parameters of all functions are in 1–1 correspondence with the actual arguments that they receive.

Definition 3.1 (Syntax of the $\lambda^\#$-calculus). *Let* $\mathscr{L} = \{\ell, \ell', \ell'', \ldots\}$ *be a denumerable set of labels. The set of* **types** *is ranged over by* $\mathcal{A}, \mathcal{B}, \mathcal{C}, \ldots$, *and defined inductively as follows:*

$$\mathcal{A} ::= \alpha^\ell \mid \mathcal{M} \overset{\ell}{\to} \mathcal{A} \qquad\qquad \mathcal{M} ::= [\mathcal{A}_i]_{i=1}^n \quad \text{with } n \geq 0$$

where α *ranges over one of denumerably many* **base types**, *and* $\mathcal{M}$ *represents a* **multiset of types**. *In a type like* α^ℓ *and* $\mathcal{M} \overset{\ell}{\to} \mathcal{A}$, *the label* ℓ *is called the* **external label**. *The* **typing contexts** *are defined as in Sect. 1 for system* $\mathcal{W}$. *We write* dom Γ *for the domain of* Γ. *A type* $\mathcal{A}$ *is said to* **occur** *inside another type* $\mathcal{B}$, *written* $\mathcal{A} \preceq \mathcal{B}$, *if* $\mathcal{A}$ *is a subformula of* $\mathcal{B}$. *This is extended to say that a type* $\mathcal{A}$ *occurs in a multiset* $[\mathcal{B}_1, \ldots, \mathcal{B}_n]$, *declaring that* $\mathcal{A} \preceq [\mathcal{B}_1, \ldots, \mathcal{B}_n]$ *if* $\mathcal{A} \preceq \mathcal{B}_i$ *for some* $i = 1..n$, *and that a type* $\mathcal{A}$ *occurs in a typing context* Γ, *declaring that* $\mathcal{A} \preceq \Gamma$ *if* $\mathcal{A} \preceq \Gamma(x)$ *for some* $x \in$ dom Γ.

The set of **terms**, *ranged over by* $t, s, u, \ldots$, *is given by the grammar* $t ::= x^{\mathcal{A}} \mid \lambda^\ell x.t \mid t\,\bar{t}$, *where* $\bar{t}$ *represents a (possibly empty)* **finite list** *of terms. The notations* $[x_i]_{i=1}^n$, $[x_1, \ldots, x_n]$, *and* $\bar{x}$ *all stand simultaneously for multisets and* for lists of elements. Note that there is no confusion since we only work with **multisets of types**, and with **lists of terms**. The concatenation of the lists $\bar{x}, \bar{y}$ is denoted by $\bar{x} + \bar{y}$. A sequence of n lists $(\bar{x}_1, \ldots, \bar{x}_n)$ is a **partition** of $\bar{x}$ if $\bar{x}_1 + \ldots + \bar{x}_n$ is a permutation of $\bar{x}$. The set of **free variables** of a term t is written $\mathsf{fv}(t)$ and defined as expected. We also write $\mathsf{fv}([t_i]_{i=1}^n)$ for $\cup_{i=1}^n \mathsf{fv}(t_i)$. A **context** is a term C with an occurrence of a distinguished **hole** $\square$. We write $\mathsf{C}\langle t \rangle$ for the capturing substitution of $\square$ by t. **Typing judgments** are triples $\Gamma \vdash t : \mathcal{A}$ representing the knowledge that the term t has type $\mathcal{A}$ in the context Γ. Type assignment rules are:

$$\frac{}{x : [\mathcal{A}] \vdash x^{\mathcal{A}} : \mathcal{A}} \ \text{var} \qquad \frac{\Gamma \oplus (x : \mathcal{M}) \vdash t : \mathcal{B}}{\Gamma \vdash \lambda^{\ell} x.t : \mathcal{M} \xrightarrow{\ell} \mathcal{B}} \ \text{lam}$$

$$\frac{\Gamma \vdash t : [\mathcal{B}_1, \ldots, \mathcal{B}_n] \xrightarrow{\ell} \mathcal{A} \qquad (\Delta_i \vdash s_i : \mathcal{B}_i)_{i=1}^n}{\Gamma +_{i=1}^n \Delta_i \vdash t[s_1, \ldots, s_n] : \mathcal{A}} \ \text{app}$$

For example $\vdash \lambda^1 x.x^{[\alpha^2, \alpha^3] \xrightarrow{4} \beta^5}[x^{\alpha^3}, x^{\alpha^2}] : [[\alpha^2, \alpha^3] \xrightarrow{4} \beta^5, \alpha^2, \alpha^3] \xrightarrow{1} \beta^5$ is a derivable judgment (using integer labels).

Remark 3.2 (Unique typing). Let $\Gamma \vdash t : \mathcal{A}$ and $\Delta \vdash t : \mathcal{B}$ be derivable judgments. Then $\Gamma = \Delta$ and $\mathcal{A} = \mathcal{B}$. Moreover, the derivation trees coincide.

This can be checked by induction on t. It means that $\lambda^{\#}$ is an *à la Church* type system, that is, types are an *intrinsic* property of the syntax of terms, as opposed to an *à la Curry* type system like $\mathcal{W}$, in which types are *extrinsic* properties that a given term might or might not have.

   To define a confluent rewriting rule, we impose a further constraint on the syntax of terms, called *correctness*. The $\lambda^{\#}$-calculus will be defined over the set of correct terms.

Definition 3.3 (Correct terms). *A multiset of types $[\mathcal{A}_1, \ldots, \mathcal{A}_n]$ is **sequential** if the external labels of $\mathcal{A}_i$ and $\mathcal{A}_j$ are different for all $i \neq j$. A typing context Γ is sequential if $\Gamma(x)$ is sequential for every $x \in \mathrm{dom}\,\Gamma$. A term t is correct if it is typable and it verifies the following three conditions:*

1. **Uniquely labeled lambdas.** *If $\lambda^{\ell} x.s$ and $\lambda^{\ell'} y.u$ are subterms of t at different positions, then ℓ and ℓ' must be different labels.*
2. **Sequential contexts.** *If s is a subterm of t and $\Gamma \vdash s : \mathcal{A}$ is derivable, then Γ must be sequential.*
3. **Sequential types.** *If s is a subterm of t, the judgment $\Gamma \vdash s : \mathcal{A}$ is derivable, and there exists a type such that $(\mathcal{M} \xrightarrow{\ell} \mathcal{B} \preceq \Gamma) \vee (\mathcal{M} \xrightarrow{\ell} \mathcal{B} \preceq \mathcal{A})$, then $\mathcal{M}$ must be sequential.*

*The set of **correct** terms is denoted by $\mathcal{T}^{\#}$.*

For example, $x^{[\alpha^1]\overset{2}{\to}\beta^3}[x^{\alpha^1}]$ is a correct term, $\lambda^1 x.\lambda^1 y.y^{\alpha^2}$ is not a correct term since labels for lambdas are not unique, and $\lambda^1 x.x^{\alpha^2 \overset{3}{\to}[\beta^4,\beta^4]\overset{5}{\to}\gamma^6}$ is not a correct term since $[\beta^4,\beta^4]$ is not sequential.

Substitution is defined explicitly below. If t is typable, $\mathtt{T}_x(t)$ stands for the multiset of types of the free occurrences of x in t. If $t_1,\ldots,t_n$ are typable, $\mathtt{T}([t_1,\ldots,t_n])$ stands for the multiset of types of $t_1,\ldots,t_n$. For example, $\mathtt{T}_x(x^{[\alpha^1]\overset{2}{\to}\beta^3}[x^{\alpha^1}]) = \mathtt{T}([y^{\alpha^1}, z^{[\alpha^1]\overset{2}{\to}\beta^3}]) = [[\alpha^1]\overset{2}{\to}\beta^3, \alpha^1]$. To perform a substitution $t\{x := [s_1,\ldots,s_n]\}$ we will require that $\mathtt{T}_x(t) = \mathtt{T}([s_1,\ldots,s_n])$.

Definition 3.4 (Substitution). *Let t and $s_1,\ldots,s_n$ be correct terms such that $\mathtt{T}_x(t) = \mathtt{T}([s_1,\ldots,s_n])$. The capture-avoiding substitution of x in t by $\bar{s} = [s_1,\ldots,s_n]$ is denoted by $t\{x := \bar{s}\}$ and defined as follows:*

$$
\begin{aligned}
x^{\mathcal{A}}\{x := [s]\} &\overset{\text{def}}{=} s \\
y^{\mathcal{A}}\{x := []\} &\overset{\text{def}}{=} y^{\mathcal{A}} && \text{if } x \neq y \\
(\lambda^\ell y.u)\{x := \bar{s}\} &\overset{\text{def}}{=} \lambda^\ell y.u\{x := \bar{s}\} && \text{if } x \neq y \text{ and } y \notin \mathsf{fv}(\bar{s}) \\
u_0[u_j]_{j=1}^m\{x := \bar{s}\} &\overset{\text{def}}{=} u_0\{x := \bar{s}_0\}[u_j\{x := \bar{s}_j\}]_{j=1}^m
\end{aligned}
$$

In the last case, $(\bar{s}_0,\ldots,\bar{s}_m)$ is a partition of $\bar{s}$ such that $\mathtt{T}_x(u_j) = \mathtt{T}(\bar{s}_j)$ for all $j = 0..m$.

Remark 3.5. Substitution is *type-directed*: the arguments $[s_1,\ldots,s_n]$ are propagated throughout the term so that s_i reaches the free occurrence of x that has the same type as s_i. Note that the definition of substitution requires that $\mathtt{T}_x(t) = \mathtt{T}([s_1,\ldots,s_n])$, which means that the types of the terms $s_1,\ldots,s_n$ are in 1–1 correspondence with the types of the free occurrences of x. Moreover, since t is a correct term, the multiset $\mathtt{T}_x(t)$ is sequential, which implies in particular that each free occurrence of x has a different type. Hence there is a *unique* correspondence matching the free occurrences of x with the arguments $s_1,\ldots,s_n$ that respects their types. As a consequence, in the definition of substitution for an application $u_0[u_j]_{j=1}^m\{x := \bar{s}\}$ there is essentially a unique way to split $\bar{s}$ into $n+1$ lists $(\bar{s}_0,\bar{s}_1,\ldots,\bar{s}_n)$ in such a way that $\mathtt{T}_x(u_i) = \mathtt{T}(\bar{s}_i)$. More precisely, if $(\bar{s}_0,\bar{s}_1,\ldots,\bar{s}_n)$ and $(\bar{u}_0,\bar{u}_1,\ldots,\bar{u}_n)$ are two partitions of $\bar{s}$ with the stated property, then $\bar{s}_i$ is a permutation of $\bar{u}_i$ for all $i = 0..n$. Using this argument, it is easy to check by induction on t that the value of $t\{x := \bar{s}\}$ is uniquely determined and does not depend on this choice.

For example, $(x^{[\alpha^1]\overset{2}{\to}\beta^3}[x^{\alpha^1}])\{x := [y^{[\alpha^1]\overset{2}{\to}\beta^3}, z^{\alpha^1}]\} = y^{[\alpha^1]\overset{2}{\to}\beta^3} z^{\alpha^1}$ while, on the other hand, $(x^{[\alpha^1]\overset{2}{\to}\beta^3}[x^{\alpha^1}])\{x := [y^{\alpha^1}, z^{[\alpha^1]\overset{2}{\to}\beta^3}]\} = z^{[\alpha^1]\overset{2}{\to}\beta^3} y^{\alpha^1}$.

The operation of substitution preserves term correctness and typability:

Lemma 3.6 (Subject Reduction). *If $\mathtt{C}\langle(\lambda^\ell x.t)\bar{s}\rangle$ is a correct term such that the judgment $\Gamma \vdash \mathtt{C}\langle(\lambda^\ell x.t)\bar{s}\rangle : \mathcal{A}$ is derivable, then $\mathtt{C}\langle t\{x := \bar{s}\}\rangle$ is correct and $\Gamma \vdash \mathtt{C}\langle t\{x := \bar{s}\}\rangle : \mathcal{A}$ is derivable.*

Proof. By induction on C.

Definition 3.7 (The $\lambda^{\#}$-calculus). *The* $\lambda^{\#}$*-calculus is the rewriting system whose objects are the set of correct terms* $\mathcal{T}^{\#}$*. The rewrite relation* $\to_{\#}$ *is the closure under arbitrary contexts of the rule* $(\lambda^{\ell}x.t)\bar{s} \to_{\#} t\{x := \bar{s}\}$*. Lemma 3.6 justifies that* $\to_{\#}$ *is well-defined, i.e. that the right-hand side is a correct term. The label of a step is the label* ℓ *decorating the contracted lambda. We write* $t \xrightarrow{\ell}_{\#} s$ *whenever* $t \to_{\#} s$ *and the label of the step is* ℓ.

Example 3.8. Let $I^3 \overset{\mathrm{def}}{=} \lambda^3 x.x^{\alpha^2}$ and $I^4 \overset{\mathrm{def}}{=} \lambda^4 x.x^{\alpha^2}$. The reduction graph of the term $(\lambda^1 x.x^{[\alpha^2]\overset{3}{\to}\alpha^2}[x^{\alpha^2}])[I^3, I^4[z^{\alpha^2}]]$ is:

$$
\begin{array}{ccccc}
(\lambda^1 x.x^{[\alpha^2]\overset{3}{\to}\alpha^2}[x^{\alpha^2}])[I^3, I^4[z^{\alpha^2}]] & \xrightarrow[S]{1} & I^3[I^4[z^{\alpha^2}]] & \xrightarrow[T]{3} & I^4[z^{\alpha^2}] \\[2mm]
4\downarrow R & & 4\downarrow R' & & 4\downarrow R'' \\[2mm]
(\lambda^1 x.x^{[\alpha^2]\overset{3}{\to}\alpha^2}[x^{\alpha^2}])[I^3, z^{\alpha^2}] & \xrightarrow[S']{1} & I^3[z^{\alpha^2}] & \xrightarrow[T']{3} & z^{\alpha^2}
\end{array}
$$

Note that numbers over arrows are the labels of the steps, while $R, R', S, \ldots$ are metalanguage names to refer to the steps. Next, we state and prove some basic properties of $\lambda^{\#}$.

Proposition 3.9 (Strong Normalization). *There is no infinite reduction* $t_0 \to_{\#} t_1 \to_{\#} \cdots$.

Proof. Observe that a reduction step $\mathsf{C}\langle(\lambda^{\ell}x.t)\bar{s}\rangle \to_{\#} \mathsf{C}\langle t\{x := \bar{s}\}\rangle$ decreases the number of lambdas in a term by exactly 1, because substitution is *linear*, i.e. the term $t\{x := [s_1, \ldots, s_n]\}$ uses s_i exactly once for all $i = 1..n$. Note: this is an adaptation of [8, Theorem 4.1].

The substitution operator may be extended to work on lists, by defining $[t_i]_{i=1}^n\{x := \bar{s}\} \overset{\mathrm{def}}{=} [t_i\{x := \bar{s}_i\}]_{i=1}^n$ where $(\bar{s}_1, \ldots, \bar{s}_n)$ is a partition of $\bar{s}$ such that $\mathsf{T}_x(t_i) = \mathsf{T}(\bar{s}_i)$ for all $i = 1..n$.

Lemma 3.10 (Substitution Lemma). *Let* $x \neq y$ *and* $x \notin \mathsf{fv}(\bar{u})$*. If* $(\bar{u}_1, \bar{u}_2)$ *is a partition of* $\bar{u}$ *then* $t\{x := \bar{s}\}\{y := \bar{u}\} = t\{y := \bar{u}_1\}\{x := \bar{s}\{y := \bar{u}_2\}\}$*, provided that both sides of the equation are defined.* **Note:** *there exists a list* $\bar{u}$ *that makes the left-hand side defined if and only if there exist lists* $\bar{u}_1, \bar{u}_2$ *that make the right-hand side defined.*

Proof. By induction on t.

Proposition 3.11 (Permutation). *If* $t_0 \xrightarrow{\ell_1}_{\#} t_1$ *and* $t_0 \xrightarrow{\ell_2}_{\#} t_2$ *are different steps, then there exists a term* $t_3 \in \mathcal{T}^{\#}$ *such that* $t_1 \xrightarrow{\ell_2}_{\#} t_3$ *and* $t_2 \xrightarrow{\ell_1}_{\#} t_3$.

Proof. By exhaustive case analysis of permutation diagrams. Two representative cases are depicted below. The proof uses the **Substitution Lemma** (Lemma 3.10).

$$(\lambda^\ell x.(\lambda^{\ell'} y.u)\bar{r})\bar{s} \xrightarrow{\ell} ((\lambda^{\ell'} y.u)\bar{r})\{x := \bar{s}\}$$

$$\ell' \downarrow \qquad\qquad\qquad \ell' \downarrow$$

$$(\lambda^\ell x.u\{y := \bar{r}\})\bar{s} \xrightarrow{\ell} u\{y := \bar{r}\}\{x := \bar{s}\}$$

$$(\lambda^\ell x.t)[\bar{s}_1, (\lambda^{\ell'} y.u)\bar{r}, \bar{s}_2] \xrightarrow{\ell} t\{x := [\bar{s}_1, (\lambda^{\ell'} y.u)\bar{r}, \bar{s}_2]\}$$

$$\ell' \downarrow \qquad\qquad\qquad \ell' \downarrow$$

$$(\lambda^\ell x.t)[\bar{s}_1, u\{y := \bar{r}\}, \bar{s}_2] \xrightarrow{\ell} t\{x := [\bar{s}_1, u\{y := \bar{r}\}, \bar{s}_2]\}$$

As a consequence of Proposition 3.11, reduction is subcommutative, *i.e.* ($\leftarrow_\#$ $\circ \rightarrow_\#$) $\subseteq$ ($\rightarrow_\#^= \circ \leftarrow_\#^=$) where $\leftarrow_\#$ denotes $(\rightarrow_\#)^{-1}$ and $R^=$ denotes the reflexive closure of R. Moreover, it is well-known that subcommutativity implies **confluence**, *i.e.* ($\leftarrow_\#^* \circ \rightarrow_\#^*$) $\subseteq$ ($\rightarrow_\#^* \circ \leftarrow_\#^*$); see [33, Proposition 1.1.10] for a proof of this fact.

Proposition 3.12 (Orthogonality). $\lambda^\#$ *is an orthogonal axiomatic rewrite system.*

Proof. Let $R : t \rightarrow_\# s$ and $S : t \rightarrow_\# u$. Define the set of residuals R/S as the set of steps starting on u that have the same label as R. Note that R/S is empty if $R = S$, and it is a singleton if $R \neq S$, since terms are correct so their lambdas are uniquely labeled. Then it is immediate to observe that axioms *Autoerasure* and *Finite Residuals* hold. The *Finite Developments* axiom is a consequence of **Strong Normalization** (Proposition 3.9). The *Semantic Orthogonality* axiom is a consequence of **Permutation** (Proposition 3.11).

For instance, in the reduction graph of Example 3.8, $ST/RS' = T'$, $S \sqcup R = SR'$, and $SR'T' \equiv RS'T'$. Observe that in Example 3.8 there is no duplication or erasure of steps. This is a general phenomenon. Indeed, **Permutation** (Proposition 3.11) ensures that all non-trivial permutation diagrams are closed with exactly one step on each side.

Let us write $\mathbb{D}^\#(t)$ for the set of derivations of t in the $\lambda^\#$-calculus, modulo permutation equivalence. As a consequence of **Orthogonality** (Proposition 3.12) and axiomatic results [29], the set $\mathbb{D}^\#(t)$ is an upper semilattice. Actually, we show that moreover the space $\mathbb{D}^\#(t)$ is a *distributive lattice*. To prove this, let us start by mentioning the property that we call **Full Stability**. This is a strong version of stability in the sense of Lévy [27]. It means that steps are created in an essentially unique way. In what follows, we write $\mathsf{lab}(R)$ for the label of a step, and $\mathsf{labs}(R_1 \ldots R_n) = \{\mathsf{lab}(R_i) \mid 1 \leq i \leq n\}$ for the set of labels of a derivation.

Lemma 3.13 (Full Stability). *Let ρ, σ be coinitial derivations with disjoint labels, i.e. $\mathsf{labs}(\rho) \cap \mathsf{labs}(\sigma) = \varnothing$. Let T_1, T_2, T_3 be steps such that $T_3 = T_1/(\sigma/\rho) = T_2/(\rho/\sigma)$. Then there is a step T_0 such that $T_1 = T_0/\rho$ and $T_2 = T_0/\sigma$.*

Proof The proof is easily reduced to a **Basic Stability** result: a particular case of **Full Stability** when ρ and σ consist of single steps. **Basic Stability** is proved by exhaustive case analysis.

Proposition 3.14. $\mathbb{D}^{\#}(t)$ *is a lattice.*

Proof. The missing components are the *top* and the *meet*. The top element is given by $\top := [\rho]$ where $\rho : t \to_{\#}^{*} s$ is a derivation to normal form, which exists by **Strong Normalization** (Proposition 3.9). The meet of $\{[\rho], [\sigma]\}$ is constructed using **Full Stability** (Lemma 3.13). If $\mathsf{labs}(\rho) \cap \mathsf{labs}(\sigma) = \varnothing$, define $(\rho \sqcap \sigma) := \epsilon$. Otherwise, the stability result ensures that there is a step R coinitial to ρ and σ such that $\mathsf{lab}(R) \in \mathsf{labs}(\rho) \cap \mathsf{labs}(\sigma)$. Let R be one such step, and, recursively, define $(\rho \sqcap \sigma) := R((\rho/R) \sqcap (\sigma/R))$. It can be checked that recursion terminates, because $\mathsf{labs}(\rho/R) \subset \mathsf{labs}(\rho)$ is a strict inclusion. Moreover, $\rho \sqcap \sigma$ is the greatest lower bound of $\{\rho, \sigma\}$, up to permutation equivalence.

For instance, in Example 3.8 we have that $ST \sqcap R = \epsilon$, $ST \sqcap RS' = S$, and $ST \sqcap RS'T' = ST$.

Proposition 3.15. *There is a monomorphism of lattices* $\mathbb{D}^{\#}(t) \to \mathcal{P}(X)$ *for some set* X. *The lattice* $(\mathcal{P}(X), \subseteq, \varnothing, \cup, X, \cap)$ *consists of the subsets of* X, *ordered by inclusion.*

Proof. The morphism is the function labs, mapping each derivation to its set of labels.

This means that a derivation in $\lambda^{\#}$ is characterized, up to permutation equivalence, by the set of labels of its steps. Since $\mathcal{P}(X)$ is a distributive lattice, in particular we have:

Corollary 3.16. $\mathbb{D}^{\#}(t)$ *is a distributive lattice.*

4 Simulation of the λ-Calculus in the $\lambda^{\#}$-Calculus

In this section we establish a precise relationship between derivations in the λ-calculus and derivations in $\lambda^{\#}$. To begin, we need a way to relate λ-terms and correct terms ($T^{\#}$):

Definition 4.1 (Refinement). *A correct term* $t' \in T^{\#}$ **refines** *a* λ-term t, *written* $t' \ltimes t$, *according to the following inductive definition:*

$$\frac{}{x^{\mathcal{A}} \ltimes x} \text{ r-var} \qquad \frac{t' \ltimes t}{\lambda^{\ell} x.t' \ltimes \lambda x.t} \text{ r-lam} \qquad \frac{t' \ltimes t \quad s_i' \ltimes s \text{ for all } i = 1..n}{t'[s_i']_{i=1}^{n} \ltimes ts} \text{ r-app}$$

A λ-term may have many refinements. For example, the following terms refine $(\lambda x.xx)y$:

$$(\lambda^1 x.x^{[]\xrightarrow{2}\alpha^3}[])[y^{[]\xrightarrow{2}\alpha^3}] \qquad (\lambda^1 x.x^{[\alpha^2]\xrightarrow{3}\beta^4}[x^{\alpha^2}])[y^{[\alpha^2]\xrightarrow{3}\beta^4}, y^{\alpha^2}]$$

$$(\lambda^1 x.x^{[\alpha^2,\beta^3]\overset{4}{\to}\gamma^5}[x^{\alpha^2},x^{\beta^3}])[y^{[\alpha^2,\beta^3]\overset{4}{\to}\gamma^5},y^{\alpha^2},y^{\beta^3}]$$

The refinement relation establishes a relation of *simulation* between the λ-calculus and $\lambda^{\#}$.

Proposition 4.2 (Simulation). *Let $t' \ltimes t$. Then:*

1. *If $t \to_\beta s$, there exists s' such that $t' \to_{\#}^* s'$ and $s' \ltimes s$.*
2. *If $t' \to_{\#} s'$, there exist s and s'' such that $t \to_\beta s$, $s' \to_{\#}^* s''$, and $s'' \ltimes s$.*

Proof. By case analysis. The proof is constructive. Moreover, in item @newin-linkPar76reversespssimulationspsitemspsfwd1, the derivation $t' \to_{\#}^* s'$ is shown to be a *multistep*, i.e. the complete development of a set $\{R_1, \ldots, R_n\}$.

The following example illustrates that a β-step in the λ-calculus may be simulated by zero, one, or possibly many steps in $\lambda^{\#}$, depending on the refinement chosen.

Example 4.3. The following are simulations of the step $x\,((\lambda x.x)y) \to_\beta x\,y$ using $\to_{\#}$-steps:

The next result relates typability and normalization. This is an adaptation of existing results from non-idempotent intersection types, e.g. [8, Lemma 5.1]. Recall that a *head normal form* is a term of the form $\lambda x_1 \ldots \lambda x_n.y\,t_1 \ldots t_m$.

Proposition 4.4 (Typability characterizes head normalization). *The following are equivalent:*

1. *There exists $t' \in \mathcal{T}^{\#}$ such that $t' \ltimes t$.*
2. *There exists a head normal form s such that $t \to_\beta^* s$.*

Proof. The implication $(1 \implies 2)$ relies on **Simulation** (Proposition 4.2). The implication $(2 \implies 1)$ relies on the fact that head normal forms are typable, plus an auxiliary result of *Subject Expansion*.

The first item of **Simulation** (Proposition 4.2) ensures that every step $t \to_\beta s$ can be simulated in $\lambda^{\#}$ starting from a term $t' \ltimes t$. Actually, a finer relationship can be established between the derivation spaces $\mathbb{D}^\lambda(t)$ and $\mathbb{D}^{\#}(t')$. For this, we introduce the notion of *simulation residual*.

Definition 4.5 (Simulation residuals). *Let $t' \ltimes t$ and let $R : t \to_\beta s$ be a step. The constructive proof of **Simulation** (Proposition 4.2) associates the $\to_\beta$-step R to a possibly empty set of $\to_\#$-steps $\{R_1, \ldots, R_n\}$ all of which start from t'. We write $R/t' \stackrel{\text{def}}{=} \{R_1, \ldots, R_n\}$, and we call $R_1, \ldots, R_n$ the **simulation residuals of R after t'**. All the complete developments of R/t' have a common target, which we denote by t'/R, called the **simulation residual of t' after R**.*

Recall that, by abuse of notation, R/t' stands for some complete development of the set R/t'. By **Simulation** (Proposition 4.2), the following diagram always holds given $t' \ltimes t \to_\beta s$:

$$
\begin{array}{ccc}
t & \xrightarrow[\;\;R\;\;]{\beta} & s \\
\ltimes & & \ltimes \\
t' & \xrightarrow[\;\;R/t'\;\;]{\#} & t'/R
\end{array}
$$

Example 4.6 (Simulation residuals). Let $R : x\,((\lambda x.x)y) \to_\beta x\,y$ and consider the terms:

$$
\begin{aligned}
t'_0 &= (x^{[\alpha^1,\beta^2]}\xrightarrow{3}\gamma^4\,[(\lambda^5 x.x^{\alpha^1})[y^{\alpha^1}], (\lambda^6 x.x^{\beta^2})[y^{\beta^2}]]) \\
t'_1 &= x^{[\alpha^1,\beta^2]}\xrightarrow{3}\gamma^4\,[y^{\alpha^1}, (\lambda^6 x.x^{\beta^2})[y^{\beta^2}]] \\
t'_2 &= x^{[\alpha^1,\beta^2]}\xrightarrow{3}\gamma^4\,[(\lambda^5 x.x^{\alpha^1})[y^{\alpha^1}], y^{\beta^2}] \\
t'_3 &= x^{[\alpha^1,\beta^2]}\xrightarrow{3}\gamma^4\,[y^{\alpha^1}, y^{\beta^2}]
\end{aligned}
$$

Then $t'_0/R = t'_3$ and $R/t'_0 = \{R_1, R_2\}$, where $R_1 : t'_0 \to_\# t'_1$ and $R_2 : t'_0 \to_\# t'_2$.

The notion of simulation residual can be extended for many-step derivations.

Definition 4.7 (Simulation residuals of/after derivations). *If $t' \ltimes t$ and $\rho : t \to_\beta^* s$ is a derivation, then ρ/t' and t'/ρ are defined as follows by induction on ρ:*

$$
\epsilon/t' \stackrel{\text{def}}{=} \epsilon \qquad R\sigma/t' \stackrel{\text{def}}{=} (R/t')(\sigma/(t'/R)) \qquad t'/\epsilon \stackrel{\text{def}}{=} t' \qquad t'/R\sigma \stackrel{\text{def}}{=} (t'/R)/\sigma
$$

It is then easy to check that $\rho/t' : t' \to_\#^* t'/\rho$ and $t'/\rho \ltimes s$, by induction on ρ. Moreover, simulation residuals are well-defined modulo permutation equivalence:

Proposition 4.8 (Compatibility). *If $\rho \equiv \sigma$ and $t \ltimes \mathsf{src}(\rho)$ then $\rho/t \equiv \sigma/t$ and $t/\rho = t/\sigma$.*

Proof. By case analysis, studying how permutation diagrams in the λ-calculus are transported to permutation diagrams in $\lambda^\#$ via simulation.

The following result resembles the usual Cube Lemma [4, Lemma 12.2.6]:

Lemma 4.9 (Cube). *If $t \ltimes \mathsf{src}(\rho) = \mathsf{src}(\sigma)$, then $(\rho/\sigma)/(t/\sigma) \equiv (\rho/t)/(\sigma/t)$.*

Proof. By induction on ρ and σ, relying on an auxiliary result, the *Basic Cube Lemma*, when ρ and σ are single steps, proved by exhaustive case analysis.

As a result, $(\rho \sqcup \sigma)/t = \rho(\sigma/\rho)/t = (\rho/t)((\sigma/\rho)/(t/\rho)) \equiv (\rho/t)((\sigma/t)/(\sigma/\rho)) = (\rho/t) \sqcup (\sigma/t)$. Moreover, if $\rho \sqsubseteq \sigma$ then $\rho\tau \equiv \sigma$ for some τ. So we have that $\rho/t \sqsubseteq (\rho/t)(\tau/(t/\rho)) = \rho\tau/t \equiv \sigma/t$ by **Compatibility** (Proposition 4.8). Hence we may formulate a stronger simulation result:

Corollary 4.10 (Algebraic Simulation). *Let $t' \ltimes t$. Then the mapping $\mathbb{D}^\lambda(t) \to \mathbb{D}^\#(t')$ given by $[\rho] \mapsto [\rho/t']$ is a morphism of upper semilattices.*

Example 4.11. Let $I = \lambda x.x$ and $\Delta = (\lambda^5 x.x^{\alpha^2})[z^{\alpha^2}]$ and let $\hat{y} = y^{[\alpha^2] \overset{3}{\to} [] \overset{4}{\to} \beta^5}$. The refinement $t' := (\lambda^1 x.\hat{y}[x^{\alpha^2}][])[\Delta] \ltimes (\lambda x.yxx)(Iz)$ induces a morphism between the upper semilattices represented by the following reduction graphs:

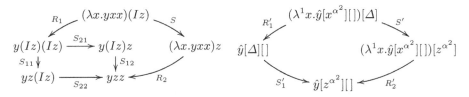

For example $(R_1 \sqcup S)/t' = (R_1 S_{11} S_{22})/t' = R_1' S_1' = R_1' \sqcup S' = R_1/t' \sqcup S/t'$. Note that the step S_{22} is erased by the simulation: $S_{22}/(\hat{y}[z^{\alpha^2}][]) = \varnothing$. Intuitively, S_{22} is "garbage" with respect to the refinement $\hat{y}[z^{\alpha^2}][]$, because it lies inside an *untyped* argument.

5   Factoring Derivation Spaces

In this section we prove that the upper semilattice $\mathbb{D}^\lambda(t)$ may be factorized using a variant of the Grothendieck construction. We start by formally defining the notion of *garbage*.

Definition 5.1 (Garbage). *Let $t' \ltimes t$. A derivation $\rho : t \to_\beta^* s$ is t'-garbage if $\rho/t' = \epsilon$.*

The informal idea is that each refinement $t' \ltimes t$ specifies that some subterms of t are "useless". A subterm u is useless if it lies inside the argument of an application $s(...u...)$ in such a way that the argument is not typed, *i.e.* the refinement is of the form $s'[] \ltimes s(...u...)$. A single step R is t'-garbage if the pattern of the contracted redex lies inside a useless subterm. A sequence of steps $R_1 R_2 \ldots R_n$ is t'-garbage if R_1 is t'-garbage, R_2 is (t'/R_1)-garbage, ..., R_i is $(t'/R_1 \ldots R_{i-1})$-garbage, ..., and so on.

Usually we say that ρ is just *garbage*, when t' is clear from the context. For instance, in Example 4.11, S_{21} is garbage, since $S_{21}/(\hat{y}[\Delta][]) = \epsilon$. Similarly, S_{22} is garbage, since $S_{22}/(\hat{y}[z^{\alpha^2}][]) = \epsilon$. On the other hand, $R_1 S_{21}$ is not garbage, since $R_1 S_{21}/((\lambda^1 x.\hat{y}[x^{\alpha^2}][])[\Delta]) = R_1' \neq \epsilon$. For each $t' \ltimes t$, the set of t'-garbage derivations forms an *ideal* of the upper semilattice $\mathbb{D}^\lambda(t)$. More precisely:

Proposition 5.2 (Properties of garbage). *Let $t' \ltimes t$. Then:*

1. *If ρ is t'-garbage and $\sigma \sqsubseteq \rho$, then σ is t'-garbage.*
2. *The composition $\rho\sigma$ is t'-garbage if and only if ρ is t'-garbage and σ is (t'/ρ)-garbage.*
3. *If ρ is t'-garbage then ρ/σ is (t'/σ)-garbage.*
4. *The join $\rho \sqcup \sigma$ is t'-garbage if and only if ρ and σ are t'-garbage.*

Proof. The proof is easy using Proposition 4.8 and Lemma 4.9.

Our aim is to show that given $\rho : t \to_\beta^* s$ and $t' \ltimes t$, there is a unique way of decomposing ρ as $\sigma\tau$, where τ is t'-garbage and σ "has no t'-garbage". Garbage is well-defined modulo permutation equivalence, *i.e.* given $\rho \equiv \sigma$, we have that ρ is garbage if and only if σ is garbage. In contrast, it is not immediate to give a well-defined notion of "having no garbage". For example, in Example 4.11, SR_2 has no garbage steps, so it appears to have no garbage; however, it is permutation equivalent to $R_1 S_{11} S_{22}$, which does contain a garbage step (S_{22}). The following definition seems to capture the right notion of having no garbage:

Definition 5.3 (Garbage-free derivation). *Let $t' \ltimes t$. A derivation $\rho :$ $t \to_\beta^* s$ is t'-garbage-free if for any derivation σ such that $\sigma \sqsubseteq \rho$ and ρ/σ is (t'/σ)-garbage, then $\rho/\sigma = \epsilon$.*

Again, we omit the t' if clear from the context. Going back to Example 4.11, the derivation SR_2 is not garbage-free, because $R_1 S_{11} \sqsubseteq SR_2$ and $SR_2/R_1 S_{11} = S_{22}$ is garbage but non-empty. Note that Definition 5.3 is defined in terms of the prefix order $(\sqsubseteq)$, so:

Remark 5.4. If $\rho \equiv \sigma$, then ρ is t'-garbage-free if and only if σ is t'-garbage-free.

Next, we define an effective procedure (*sieving*) to erase all the garbage from a derivation. The idea is that if $\rho : t \to_\beta^* s$ is a derivation in the λ-calculus and $t' \ltimes t$ is any refinement, we may constructively build a t'-garbage-free derivation $(\rho \Downarrow t') : t \to_\beta^* u$ by erasing all the t'-garbage from ρ. Our goal will then be to show that $\rho \equiv (\rho \Downarrow t')\sigma$ where σ is garbage.

Definition 5.5 (Sieving). *Let $t' \ltimes t$ and $\rho : t \to_\beta^* s$. A step R is **coarse for** (ρ, t') if $R \sqsubseteq \rho$ and $R/t' \neq \varnothing$. The **sieve of ρ with respect to t'**, written $\rho \Downarrow t'$, is defined as follows.*

- *If there are no coarse steps for (ρ, t'), then $(\rho \Downarrow t') \stackrel{\text{def}}{=} \epsilon$.*
- *If there is a coarse step for (ρ, t'), then $(\rho \Downarrow t') \stackrel{\text{def}}{=} R_0((\rho/R_0) \Downarrow (t'/R_0))$ where R_0 is the leftmost such step.*

Lemma 5.6. *The sieving operation $\rho \Downarrow t'$ is well-defined.*

Proof. To see that recursion terminates, consider the measure M given by $M(\rho, t') := \#\mathsf{labs}(\rho/t')$, and note that $M(\rho, t') > M(\rho/R_0, t'/R_0)$.

For example, in Example 4.11, we have that $S \Downarrow t' = S$ and $SR_2 \Downarrow t' = R_1 S_{11}$.

Proposition 5.7 (Properties of sieving). *Let $t' \ltimes t$ and $\rho : t \to_\beta^* s$. Then:*

1. $\rho \Downarrow t'$ *is t'-garbage-free and $\rho \Downarrow t' \sqsubseteq \rho$.*
2. $\rho/(\rho \Downarrow t')$ *is $(t'/(\rho \Downarrow t'))$-garbage.*
3. ρ *is t'-garbage if and only if $\rho \Downarrow t' = \epsilon$.*
4. ρ *is t'-garbage-free if and only if $\rho \Downarrow t' \equiv \rho$.*

Proof. By induction on the length of $\rho \Downarrow t'$, using various technical lemmas.

As a consequence of the definition of the sieving construction and its properties, given any derivation $\rho : t \to_\beta^* s$ and any refinement $t' \ltimes t$, we can always write ρ, modulo permutation equivalence, as of the form $\rho \equiv \sigma\tau$ in such a way that σ is garbage-free and τ is garbage. To prove this take $\sigma := \rho \Downarrow t'$ and $\tau := \rho/(\rho \Downarrow t')$, and note that σ is garbage-free by item 1. of Proposition 5.7, τ is garbage by item 2. of Proposition 5.7, and $\rho \equiv \sigma(\rho/\sigma) = \sigma\tau$ because $\sigma \sqsubseteq \rho$ by item 1. of Proposition 5.7.

In the following we give a stronger version of this result. The **Factorization** theorem below (Theorem 5.10) states that this decomposition is actually an isomorphism of upper semilattices. This means, on one hand, that given any derivation $\rho : t \to_\beta^* s$ and any refinement $t' \ltimes t$ there is a *unique* way to factor ρ as of the form $\rho \equiv \sigma\tau$ where σ is garbage-free and τ is garbage. On the other hand, it means that the decomposition $\rho \mapsto (\rho \Downarrow t', \rho/(\rho \Downarrow t'))$ mapping each derivation to a of a garbage-free plus a garbage derivation is *functorial*. This means, essentially, that the set of pairs (σ, τ) such that σ is garbage-free and τ is garbage can be given the structure of an upper semilattice in such a way that:

- If $\rho \mapsto (\sigma, \tau)$ and $\rho' \mapsto (\sigma', \tau')$ then $\rho \sqsubseteq \rho' \iff (\sigma, \tau) \leq (\sigma', \tau')$.
- If $\rho \mapsto (\sigma, \tau)$ and $\rho' \mapsto (\sigma', \tau')$ then $(\rho \sqcup \rho') \mapsto (\sigma, \tau) \vee (\sigma', \tau')$.

The upper semilattice structure of the set of pairs (σ, τ) is given using a variant of the Grothendieck construction:

Definition 5.8 (Grothendieck construction for partially ordered sets). *Let A be a poset, and let $B : A \to \mathsf{Poset}$ be a mapping associating each object $a \in A$ to a poset $B(a)$. Suppose moreover that B is a **lax 2-functor**. More precisely, for each $a \leq b$ in A, the function $B(a \hookrightarrow b) : B(a) \to B(b)$ is monotonic and such that:*

1. $B(a \hookrightarrow a) = \mathrm{id}_{B(a)}$ *for all $a \in A$,*
2. $B((b \hookrightarrow c) \circ (a \hookrightarrow b)) \leq B(b \hookrightarrow c) \circ B(a \hookrightarrow b)$ *for all $a \leq b \leq c$ in A.*

*The **Grothendieck construction** $\int_A B$ is defined as the poset given by the set of objects $\{(a, b) \mid a \in A,\ b \in B(a)\}$ and such that $(a, b) \leq (a', b')$ is declared to hold if and only if $A \leq a'$ and $B(a \hookrightarrow a')(b) \leq b'$.*

The following proposition states that garbage-free derivations form a finite lattice, while garbage derivations form an upper semilattice.

Proposition 5.9 (Garbage-free and garbage semilattices). *Let $t' \ltimes t$.*

1. *The set* $F = \{[\rho] \mid \mathsf{src}(\rho) = t \text{ and } \rho \text{ is } t'\text{-garbage-free}\}$ *of* t'-*garbage-free derivations forms a finite lattice* $\mathbb{F}(t', t) = (F, \trianglelefteq, \bot, \triangledown, \top, \triangle)$, *with:*
   - **Partial order:** $[\rho] \trianglelefteq [\sigma] \overset{\text{def}}{\Longleftrightarrow} \rho/\sigma \text{ is } (t'/\sigma)$-*garbage.*
   - **Bottom:** $\bot := [\epsilon]$.
   - **Join:** $[\rho]\triangledown[\sigma] \overset{\text{def}}{=} [(\rho \sqcup \sigma) \Downarrow t']$.
   - **Top:** $\top$, *defined as the join of all the* $[\tau]$ *such that* τ *is* t'-*garbage-free.*
   - **Meet:** $[\rho] \triangle [\sigma]$, *defined as the join of all the* $[\tau]$ *such that* $[\tau] \trianglelefteq [\rho]$ *and* $[\tau] \trianglelefteq [\sigma]$.
2. *The set* $G = \{[\rho] \mid \mathsf{src}(\rho) = t \text{ and } \rho \text{ is } t'\text{-garbage}\}$ *of* t'-*garbage derivations forms an upper semilattice* $\mathbb{G}(t', t) = (G, \sqsubseteq, \bot, \sqcup)$, *with the structure inherited from* $\mathbb{D}^\lambda(t)$.

Proof. The proof relies on the properties of garbage and sieving (Propositions 5.2 and 5.7).

Suppose that $t' \ltimes t$, and let $\mathcal{F} \overset{\text{def}}{=} \mathbb{F}(t', t)$ denote the lattice of t'-garbage-free derivations. Let $\mathcal{G} : \mathcal{F} \to \mathsf{Poset}$ be the lax 2-functor $\mathcal{G}([\rho]) \overset{\text{def}}{=} \mathbb{G}(t'/\rho, \mathsf{tgt}(\rho))$ with the following action on morphisms:

$$\mathcal{G}([\rho] \hookrightarrow [\sigma]) : \mathcal{G}([\rho]) \to \mathcal{G}([\sigma])$$
$$[\alpha] \quad \mapsto \quad [\rho\alpha/\sigma]$$

Using the previous proposition (Proposition 5.9) it can be checked that $\mathcal{G}$ is indeed a lax 2-functor, and that the Grothendieck construction $\int_{\mathcal{F}} \mathcal{G}$ forms an upper semilattice. The join is given by $(a, b) \vee (a', b') = (a \triangledown a', \mathcal{G}(a \hookrightarrow a \triangledown a')(b) \sqcup \mathcal{G}(a' \hookrightarrow a \triangledown a')(b'))$. Finally we can state the main theorem:

Theorem 5.10 (Factorization). *The following maps form an isomorphism of upper semilattices:*

$$\mathbb{D}^\lambda(t) \to \int_{\mathcal{F}} \mathcal{G} \qquad\qquad \int_{\mathcal{F}} \mathcal{G} \to \mathbb{D}^\lambda(t)$$
$$[\rho] \mapsto ([\rho \Downarrow t'], [\rho/(\rho \Downarrow t')]) \qquad ([\rho], [\sigma]) \mapsto [\rho\sigma]$$

Proof. The proof consists in checking that both maps are morphisms of upper semilattices and that they are mutual inverses, resorting to Propositions 5.2 and 5.7.

Example 5.11. Let $t = (\lambda x.yxx)(Iz)$ and t' be as in Example 4.11. The upper semilattice $\mathbb{D}^\lambda(t)$ can be factorized as $\int_{\mathcal{F}} \mathcal{G}$ as follows. Here posets are represented by their Hasse diagrams:

For example $([S], [\epsilon]) \le ([R_1 S_{11}], [S_{22}])$ because $[S] \trianglelefteq [R_1 S_{11}]$, that is, $S/R_1 S_{11} = S_{22}$ is garbage, and $\mathcal{G}([S] \hookrightarrow [R_1 S_{11}])([\epsilon]) = [S/R_1 S_{11}] = [S_{22}] \sqsubseteq [S_{22}]$.

6 Conclusions

We have defined a calculus ($\lambda^{\#}$) based on non-idempotent intersection types. Its syntax and semantics are complex due to the presence of an admittedly *ad hoc* correctness invariant for terms, enforced so that reduction is confluent. In contrast, derivation spaces in this calculus turn out to be very simple structures: they are representable as *rings of sets* (Proposition 3.15) and as a consequence they are distributive lattices (Corollary 3.16). Derivation spaces in the λ-calculus can be mapped to these much simpler spaces using a strong notion of simulation (Corollary 4.10) inspired by residual theory. Building on this, we showed how the derivation space of any typable λ-term may be factorized as a "twisted product" of garbage-free and garbage derivations (Theorem 5.10).

We believe that this validates the (soft) hypothesis that explicitly representing resource management can provide insight on the structure of derivation spaces.

Related Work. The **Factorization** theorem (Theorem 5.10) is reminiscent of Melliès' abstract factorization result [30]. Given an axiomatic rewriting system fulfilling a number of axioms, Melliès proves that every derivation can be uniquely factorized as an *external* prefix followed by an *internal* suffix. We conjecture that each refinement $t' \ltimes t$ should provide an instantiation of Melliès' axioms, in such a way that our t'-garbage-free/t'-garbage factorization coincides with his external/internal factorization. Melliès notes that any evaluation strategy that always selects external steps is hypernormalizing. A similar result should hold for evaluation strategies that always select *non-garbage* steps.

The notion of *garbage-free* derivation is closely related with the notion of X-*neededness* [3]. A step R is X-needed if every reduction to a term $t \in X$ contracts a residual of R. Recently, Kesner et al. [23] have related typability in a non-idempotent intersection type system $\mathcal{V}$ and weak-head neededness. Using similar techniques, it should be possible to prove that t'-garbage-free steps are X-needed, where $X = \{s \mid s' \ltimes s\}$ and s' is the $\rightarrow_{\#}$-normal form of t'.

There are several resource calculi in the literature which perhaps could play a similar role as $\lambda^{\#}$ to recover factorization results akin to Theorem 5.10. Kfoury [24] embeds the λ-calculus in a *linear* λ-calculus that has no duplication nor erasure. Ehrard and Regnier prove that the Taylor expansion of λ-terms [17] commutes with normalization, similarly as in **Algebraic Simulation** (Corollary 4.10). Mazza et al. [28] study a general framework for *polyadic approximations*, corresponding roughly to the notion of *refinement* in this paper.

Acknowledgements. To Eduardo Bonelli and Delia Kesner for introducing the first author to these topics. To Luis Scoccola and the anonymous reviewers for helpful suggestions.

References

1. Accattoli, B., Bonelli, E., Kesner, D., Lombardi, C.: A nonstandard standardization theorem. In: POPL 2014, 20–21 January 2014, San Diego, CA, USA, pp. 659–670 (2014)
2. Asperti, A., Lévy, J.: The cost of usage in the lambda-calculus. In: 28th Annual ACM/IEEE Symposium on Logic in Computer Science, LICS 2013, 25–28 June 2013, New Orleans, LA, USA, pp. 293–300 (2013)
3. Barendregt, H.P., Kennaway, J.R., Klop, J.W., Sleep, M.R.: Needed reduction and spine strategies for the lambda calculus. Inf. Comput. **75**(3), 191–231 (1987)
4. Barendregt, H.: The Lambda Calculus: Its Syntax and Semantics, vol. 103. Elsevier, Amsterdam (1984)
5. Bernadet, A., Lengrand, S.J.: Non-idempotent intersection types and strong normalisation. arXiv preprint arXiv:1310.1622 (2013)
6. Boudol, G.: The lambda-calculus with multiplicities. In: Best, E. (ed.) CONCUR 1993. LNCS, vol. 715, pp. 1–6. Springer, Heidelberg (1993). https://doi.org/10.1007/3-540-57208-2_1
7. Bucciarelli, A., Kesner, D., Ronchi Della Rocca, S.: The inhabitation problem for non-idempotent intersection types. In: Diaz, J., Lanese, I., Sangiorgi, D. (eds.) TCS 2014. LNCS, vol. 8705, pp. 341–354. Springer, Heidelberg (2014). https://doi.org/10.1007/978-3-662-44602-7_26
8. Bucciarelli, A., Kesner, D., Ventura, D.: Non-idempotent intersection types for the lambda-calculus. Log. J. IGPL **25**(4), 431–464 (2017)
9. Carvalho, D.D.: Sémantiques de la logique linéaire et temps de calcul. Ph.D. thesis, Ecole Doctorale Physique et Sciences de la Matière (Marseille) (2007)
10. Church, A., Rosser, J.B.: Some properties of conversion. Trans. Am. Math. Soc. **39**(3), 472–482 (1936)
11. Rodríguez, G.C.: Factorización de derivaciones a través de tipos intersección. Master's thesis, Facultad de Ciencias Exactas y Naturales, Universidad de Buenos Aires, June 2018. http://www.dc.uba.ar/academica/tesis-de-licenciatura/2018/ciruelos.pdf
12. Coppo, M., Dezani-Ciancaglini, M.: A new type assignment for lambda-terms. Arch. Math. Log. **19**(1), 139–156 (1978)
13. Curry, H., Feys, R.: Combinatory Logic, vol. 1. North-Holland Publishing Company, Amsterdam (1958)
14. Dershowitz, N., Jouannaud, J.-P., Klop, J.W.: Open problems in rewriting. In: Book, R.V. (ed.) RTA 1991. LNCS, vol. 488, pp. 445–456. Springer, Heidelberg (1991). https://doi.org/10.1007/3-540-53904-2_120
15. Ehrhard, T.: Collapsing non-idempotent intersection types. In: LIPIcs-Leibniz International Proceedings in Informatics, vol. 16. Schloss Dagstuhl-Leibniz-Zentrum fuer Informatik (2012)
16. Ehrhard, T., Regnier, L.: The differential lambda-calculus. Theor. Comput. Sci. **309**(1), 1–41 (2003)
17. Ehrhard, T., Regnier, L.: Uniformity and the taylor expansion of ordinary lambda-terms. Theor. Comput. Sci. **403**(2–3), 347–372 (2008)
18. Gardner, P.: Discovering needed reductions using type theory. In: Hagiya, M., Mitchell, J.C. (eds.) TACS 1994. LNCS, vol. 789, pp. 555–574. Springer, Heidelberg (1994). https://doi.org/10.1007/3-540-57887-0_115
19. Girard, J.Y.: Linear logic. Theor. Comput. Sci. **50**(1), 1–101 (1987)

20. Kesner, D.: Reasoning about call-by-need by means of types. In: Jacobs, B., Löding, C. (eds.) FoSSaCS 2016. LNCS, vol. 9634, pp. 424–441. Springer, Heidelberg (2016). https://doi.org/10.1007/978-3-662-49630-5_25
21. Kesner, D., Lengrand, S.: Resource operators for λ-calculus. Inf. Comput. **205**(4), 419–473 (2007)
22. Kesner, D., Renaud, F.: The prismoid of resources. In: Královič, R., Niwiński, D. (eds.) MFCS 2009. LNCS, vol. 5734, pp. 464–476. Springer, Heidelberg (2009). https://doi.org/10.1007/978-3-642-03816-7_40
23. Kesner, D., Ríos, A., Viso, A.: Call-by-need, neededness and all that. In: Baier, C., Dal Lago, U. (eds.) FoSSaCS 2018. LNCS, vol. 10803, pp. 241–257. Springer, Cham (2018). https://doi.org/10.1007/978-3-319-89366-2_13
24. Kfoury, A.J.: A linearization of the lambda-calculus and consequences. Technical report, Boston University, Computer Science Department (1996)
25. Laneve, C.: Distributive evaluations of λ-calculus. Fundam. Inform. **20**(4), 333–352 (1994)
26. Lévy, J.J.: Réductions correctes et optimales dans le lambda-calcul. Ph.D. thesis, Université de Paris 7 (1978)
27. Lévy, J.J.: Redexes are stable in the λ-calculus. Math. Struct. Comput. Sci. **27**(5), 738–750 (2017)
28. Mazza, D., Pellissier, L., Vial, P.: Polyadic approximations, fibrations and intersection types. Proc. ACM Program. Lang. **2**(POPL), 6 (2018)
29. Melliès, P.A.: Description abstraite des systèmes de réécriture. Ph.D. thesis, Université Paris 7, December 1996
30. Melliès, P.-A.: A factorisation theorem in rewriting theory. In: Moggi, E., Rosolini, G. (eds.) CTCS 1997. LNCS, vol. 1290, pp. 49–68. Springer, Heidelberg (1997). https://doi.org/10.1007/BFb0026981
31. Melliès, P.-A.: Axiomatic rewriting theory VI: residual theory revisited. In: Tison, S. (ed.) RTA 2002. LNCS, vol. 2378, pp. 24–50. Springer, Heidelberg (2002). https://doi.org/10.1007/3-540-45610-4_4
32. Melliès, P.-A.: Axiomatic rewriting theory I: a diagrammatic standardization theorem. In: Middeldorp, A., van Oostrom, V., van Raamsdonk, F., de Vrijer, R. (eds.) Processes, Terms and Cycles: Steps on the Road to Infinity. LNCS, vol. 3838, pp. 554–638. Springer, Heidelberg (2005). https://doi.org/10.1007/11601548_23
33. Terese: Term Rewriting Systems, Cambridge Tracts in Theoretical Computer Science, vol. 55. Cambridge University Press (2003)
34. Vial, P.: Non-idempotent typing operators, beyond the lambda-calculus. Ph.D. thesis, Université Paris 7, December 2017
35. Zilli, M.V.: Reduction graphs in the lambda calculus. Theor. Comput. Sci. **29**, 251–275 (1984). https://doi.org/10.1016/0304-3975(84)90002-1

Types of Fireballs

Beniamino Accattoli[1] and Giulio Guerrieri[2]([✉])

[1] Inria & LIX, École Polytechnique, UMR 7161, Palaiseau, France
`beniamino.accattoli@inria.fr`
[2] Dipartimento di Informatica—Scienza e Ingegneria (DISI), Università di Bologna, Bologna, Italy
`giulio.guerrieri@unibo.it`

Abstract. The good properties of Plotkin's call-by-value lambda-calculus crucially rely on the restriction to weak evaluation and closed terms. Open call-by-value is the more general setting where evaluation is weak but terms may be open. Such an extension is delicate and the literature contains a number of proposals. Recently, we provided operational and implementative studies of these proposals, showing that they are equivalent with respect to termination, and also at the level of time cost models.

This paper explores the denotational semantics of open call-by-value, adapting de Carvalho's analysis of call-by-name via multi types (aka non-idempotent intersection types). Our type system characterises normalisation and thus provides an adequate relational semantics. Moreover, type derivations carry quantitative information about the cost of evaluation: their size bounds the number of evaluation steps and the size of the normal form, and we also characterise derivations giving exact bounds.

The study crucially relies on a new, refined presentation of the fireball calculus, the simplest proposal for open call-by-value, that is more apt to denotational investigations.

1 Introduction

The core of functional programming languages and proof assistants is usually modelled as a variation over the λ-calculus. Even when one forgets about type systems, there are in fact many λ-calculi rather than a single λ-calculus, depending on whether evaluation is weak or strong (that is, only outside or also inside abstractions), call-by-name (CbN for short), call-by-value (CbV),[1] or call-by-need, whether terms are closed or may be open, not to speak of extensions with continuations, pattern matching, fix-points, linearity constraints, and so on.

Benchmark for λ-calculi. A natural question is *what is a good λ-calculus?* It is of course impossible to give an absolute answer, because different settings value different properties. It is nonetheless possible to collect requirements that seem

---

[1] In CbV, function's arguments are evaluated before being passed to the function, so β-redexes can fire only when their arguments are values, i.e. abstractions or variables.

© Springer Nature Switzerland AG 2018
S. Ryu (Ed.): APLAS 2018, LNCS 11275, pp. 45–66, 2018.
https://doi.org/10.1007/978-3-030-02768-1_3

desirable in order to have an abstract framework that is also useful in practice. We can isolate at least six principles to be satisfied by a good λ-calculus:

1. *Rewriting*: there should be a small-step operational semantics having nice rewriting properties. Typically, the calculus should be non-deterministic but confluent, and a deterministic evaluation strategy should emerge naturally from some good rewriting property (factorisation/standardisation theorem, or the diamond property). The *strategy emerging from the calculus* principle guarantees that the chosen evaluation is not ad-hoc.
2. *Logic*: typed versions of the calculus should be in Curry-Howard correspondences with some proof systems, providing logical intuitions and guiding principles for the features of the calculus and the study of its properties.
3. *Implementation*: there should be a good understanding of how to decompose evaluation in micro-steps, that is, at the level of abstract machines, in order to guide the design of languages or proof assistants based on the calculus.
4. *Cost model*: the number of steps of the deterministic evaluation strategy should be a reasonable time cost model,[2] so that cost analyses of λ-terms are possible, and independent of implementative choices.
5. *Denotations*: there should be denotational semantics, that is, syntax-free mathematical interpretations of the calculus that are invariant by evaluation and that reflect some of its properties. Well-behaved denotations guarantee that the calculus is somewhat independent from its own syntax, which is a further guarantee that it is not ad-hoc.
6. *Equality*: contextual equivalence can be characterised by some form of bisimilarity, showing that there is a robust notion of program equivalence. Program equivalence is indeed essential for studying program transformations and optimisations at work in compilers.

Finally, there is a sort of meta-principle: the more principles are connected, the better. For instance, it is desirable that evaluation in the calculus corresponds to cut-elimination in some logical interpretation of the calculus. Denotations are usually at least required to be *adequate* with respect to the rewriting: the denotation of a term is non-degenerated if and only if its evaluation terminates. Additionally, denotations are *fully abstract* if they reflect contextual equivalence. And implementations have to work within an overhead that respects the intended cost semantics. Ideally, all principles are satisfied and perfectly interconnected.

Of course, some specific cases may drop some requirements—for instance, a probabilistic λ-calculus would not be confluent—some properties may also be strengthened—for instance, equality may be characterised via a separation theorem akin to Bohm's—and other principles may be added—categorical semantics, graphical representations, etc.

What is usually considered *the* λ-calculus, is, in our terminology, the strong CbN λ-calculus with (possibly) open terms, and all points of the benchmark have been studied for it. Plotkin's original formulation of CbV [45], conceived

---

[2] Here *reasonable* is a technical word meaning that the cost model is polynomially equivalent to the one of Turing machines.

for weak evaluation and closed terms and here referred to as *Closed CbV*, also boldly passes the benchmark. Unfortunately Plotkin's setting fails the benchmark as soon as it is extended to open terms, which is required when using CbV for implementing proof assistants, see Grégoire and Leroy's [29]. Typically, denotations are no longer adequate, as first noticed by Paolini and Ronchi Della Rocca [48], and there is a mismatch between evaluation in the calculus and cut-elimination in its linear logic interpretation, as shown by Accattoli [1]. The failure can be observed also at other levels not covered by our benchmark, *e.g.* the incompleteness of CPS translations, already noticed by Plotkin himself [45].

Benchmarking Open Call-by-Value. The problematic interaction of CbV and open terms is well known, and the fault is usually given to the rewriting—the operational semantics has to be changed somehow. The literature contains a number of proposals for extensions of CbV out of the closed world, some of which were introduced to solve the incompleteness of CPS translations. In [3], we provided a comparative study of four extensions of Closed CbV (with weak evaluation on possibly open terms), showing that they have equivalent rewriting theories (namely, they are equivalent from the point of view of termination), they are all adequate with respect to denotations, and they share the same time cost models—these proposals have then to be considered as different incarnations of a more abstract framework, which we call *open call-by-value* (Open CbV). Together with Sacerdoti Coen, we provided also a theory of implementations respecting the cost semantics [4, 7], and a precise linear logic interpretation [1]. Thus, Open CbV passes the first five points of the benchmark.

This paper deepens the analysis of the fifth point, by refining the denotational understanding of Open CbV with a quantitative relationship with the rewriting and the cost model. We connect the size of type derivations for a term with its evaluation via rewriting, and the size of elements in its denotation with the size of its normal form, in a model coming from the linear logic interpretation of CbV and presented as a type system: Ehrhard's relational semantics for CbV [23].

The last point of the benchmark—contextual equivalence for Open CbV— was shown by Lassen to be a difficult question [39], and it is left to future work.

Multi Types. Intersection types are one of the standard tools to study λ-calculi, mainly used to characterise termination properties—classical references are Coppo and Dezani [19,20], Pottinger [46], and Krivine [38]. In contrast to other type systems, they do not provide a logical interpretation, at least not as smoothly as for simple or polymorphic types—see Ronchi Della Rocca and Roversi's [49] or Bono, Venneri, and Bettini's [9] for details. They are better understood, in fact, as syntactic presentations of denotational semantics: they are invariant under evaluation and type all and only the terminating terms, thus naturally providing an adequate denotational model.

Intersection types are a flexible tool that can be formulated in various ways. A flavour that emerged in the last 10 years is that of *non-idempotent* intersection types, where the intersection $A \cap A$ is not equivalent to A. They were first considered by Gardner [26], and then Kfoury [37], Neergaard and Mairson [41], and de Carvalho [14, 16] provided a first wave of works abut them—a survey can be found in Bucciarelli, Kesner, and Ventura's [12]. Non-idempotent intersections can be seen as multisets, which is why, to ease the language, we prefer to call them *multi types* rather than *non-idempotent intersection types*.

Multi types retain the denotational character of intersection types, and they actually refine it along two correlated lines. First, taking types with multiplicities gives rise to a *quantitative* approach, that reflects resource consumption in the evaluation of terms. Second, such a quantitative feature turns out to coincide exactly with the one at work in linear logic. Some care is needed here: multi types do not correspond to linear logic formulas, rather to the relational denotational semantics of linear logic (two seminal references for such a semantic are Girard's [28] and Bucciarelli and Ehrhard's [10]; see also [15, 34])—similarly to intersection types, they provide a denotational rather than a logical interpretation.

An insightful use of multi types is de Carvalho's connection between the size of types and the size of normal forms, and between the size of type derivations and evaluation lengths for the CbN λ-calculus [16].

Types of Fireballs. This paper develops a denotational analysis of Open CbV akin to de Carvalho's. There are two main translations of the λ-calculus into linear logic, due to Girard [27], the CbN one, that underlies de Carvalho's study [14, 16], and the CbV one, that is explored here. The literature contains denotational semantics of CbV and also studies of multi types for CbV. The distinguishing feature of our study is the use of multi types to provide bounds on the number of evaluation steps and on the size of normal forms, which has never been done before for CbV, and moreover we do it for the open case—the result for the closed case, refining Ehrhard's study [23], follows as a special case. Besides, we provide a characterisation of types and type derivations that provide *exact* bounds, similarly to de Carvalho [14, 16], Bernadet and Lengrand [8], and de Carvalho, Pagani, and Tortora de Falco [17], and along the lines of a very recent work by Accattoli, Graham-Lengrand, and Kesner [2], but using a slightly different approach.

Extracting exact bounds from the multi types system is however only half of the story. The other, subtler half is about tuning up the presentation of Open CbV as to accommodate as many points of the benchmark as possible. Our quantitative denotational inquire via multi types requires the following properties:

0. *Compositionality*: if two terms have the same type assignments, then the terms obtained by plugging them in the same context do so.
1. *Invariance under evaluation*: type assignments have to be stable by evaluation.
2. *Adequacy*: a term is typable if and only if it terminates.
3. *Elegant normal forms*: normal forms have a simple structure, so that the technical development is simple and intuitive.
4. *Number of steps*: type derivations have to provide the number of steps to evaluate to normal forms, and this number must be a reasonable cost model.

5. *Matching of sizes*: the size of normal forms has to be bounded by the size of their types.

While property 0 is not problematic (type systems/denotational models are conceived to satisfy it), it turns out that none of the incarnations of Open CbV we studied in [3] (namely, Paolini and Ronchi Della Rocca's *fireball calculus* λ_{fire} [7,29,44,48], Accattoli and Paolini's *value substitution calculus* λ_{vsub} [1,6], and Carraro and Guerrieri's *shuffling calculus* λ_{sh} [13,30–33])[3] satisfies all the properties 1–5 at the same time: λ_{fire} lacks property 1 (as shown here in Sect. 2); λ_{vsub} lacks property 3 (the inelegant characterisation of normal forms is in [6]); and λ_{sh}, which in [13] is shown to satisfy 1, 2, and partially 3, lacks properties 4 (the number of steps does not seem to be a reasonable cost model, see [3]) and 5 (see the end of Sect. 6 in this paper).

We then introduce the *split fireball calculus*, that is a minor variant of the fireball calculus λ_{fire}, isomorphic to it but integrating some features of the value substitution calculus λ_{vsub}, and satisfying all the requirements for our study. Thus, the denotational study follows smooth and natural, fully validating the design and the benchmark.

To sum up, our study adds new ingredients to the understanding of Open CbV, by providing a simple and quantitative denotational analysis via an adaptation of de Carvalho's approach [14,16].

The main features of our study are:

1. *Split fireball calculus*: a new incarnation of Open CbV more apt to denotational studies, and conservative with respect to the other properties of the setting.
2. *Quantitative characterisation of termination*: proofs that typable terms are exactly the normalising ones, and that types and type derivations provide bounds on the size of normal forms and on evaluation lengths.
3. *Tight derivations and exact bounds*: a class of type derivations that provide the exact length of evaluations, and such that the types in the final judgements provide the exact size of normal forms.

Related Work. Classical studies of the denotational semantics of Closed CbV are due to Sieber [50], Fiore and Plotkin [25], Honda and Yoshida [35], and Pravato, Ronchi Della Rocca and Roversi [47]. A number of works rely on multi types or relational semantics to study property of programs and proofs. Among them, Ehrhard's [23], Diaz-Caro, Manzonetto, and Pagani's [22], Carraro and Guerrieri's [13], Ehrhard and Guerrieri's [24], and Guerrieri's [31] deal with CbV, while de Carvalho's [14,16], Bernadet and Lengrand's [8], de Carvalho, Pagani, and Tortora de Falco's [17], Accattoli, Graham-Lengrand, and Kesner's [2] provide exact bounds. Further related work about multi types is by Bucciarelli, Ehrhard, and Manzonetto [11], de Carvalho and Tortora de Falco [18], Kesner and Vial [36], and Mazza, Pellissier, and Vial [40]—this list is not exhaustive.

---

[3] In [3] a fourth incarnation, the *value sequent calculus* (a fragment of Curien and Herbelin's $\bar{\lambda}\tilde{\mu}$ [21]), is proved isomorphic to a fragment of λ_{vsub}, which then subsumes it.

(No) Proofs. All proofs are in the Appendix of [5], the long version of this paper.

TERMS	$t, u, s, r ::= x \mid \lambda x.t \mid tu$
VALUES	$v, v', v'' ::= x \mid \lambda x.t$
FIREBALLS	$f, f', f'' ::= v \mid i$
INERT TERMS	$i, i', i'' ::= x f_1 \dots f_n \quad n > 0$
RIGHT EVALUATION CONTEXTS	$C ::= \langle \cdot \rangle \mid tC \mid Cf$

RULE AT TOP LEVEL	CONTEXTUAL CLOSURE
$(\lambda x.t)v \ \mapsto_{\beta_v} \ t\{x\leftarrow v\}$	$C\langle t \rangle \to_{\beta_v} C\langle u \rangle \quad \text{if } t \mapsto_{\beta_v} u$
$(\lambda x.t)i \ \mapsto_{\beta_i} \ t\{x\leftarrow i\}$	$C\langle t \rangle \to_{\beta_i} C\langle u \rangle \quad \text{if } t \mapsto_{\beta_i} u$

$$\text{REDUCTION} \qquad \to_{\beta_f} \ := \ \to_{\beta_v} \cup \to_{\beta_i}$$

Fig. 1. The fireball calculus λ_{fire}.

2   The Rise of Fireballs

In this section we recall the fireball calculus λ_{fire}, the simplest presentation of Open CbV. For the issues of Plotkin's setting with respect to open terms and for alternative presentations of Open CbV, we refer the reader to our work [3].

The fireball calculus was introduced without a name and studied first by Paolini and Ronchi Della Rocca in [44,48]. It has then been rediscovered by Grégoire and Leroy in [29] to improve the implementation of Coq, and later by Accattoli and Sacerdoti Coen in [7] to study cost models, where it was also named. We present it following [7], changing only inessential, cosmetic details.

The Fireball Calculus. The fireball calculus λ_{fire} is defined in Fig. 1. The idea is that the values of the CbV λ-calculus—i.e. abstractions and variables—are generalised to *fireballs*, by extending variables to more general *inert terms*. Actually fireballs (noted $f, f', \dots$) and inert terms (noted $i, i', \dots$) are defined by mutual induction (in Fig. 1). For instance, x and $\lambda x.y$ are fireballs as values, while $y(\lambda x.x)$, xy, and $(z(\lambda x.x))(zz)(\lambda y.(zy))$ are fireballs as inert terms.

The main feature of inert terms is that they are open, normal, and that when plugged in a context they cannot create a redex, hence the name. Essentially, they are the *neutral terms* of Open CbV. In Grégoire and Leroy's presentation [29], inert terms are called *accumulators* and fireballs are simply called *values*.

Terms are always identified up to α-equivalence and the set of free variables of a term t is denoted by $\text{fv}(t)$. We use $t\{x\leftarrow u\}$ for the term obtained by the capture-avoiding substitution of u for each free occurrence of x in t.

Variables are, morally, both values and inert terms. In [7] they were considered as inert terms, while here, for minor technical reasons we prefer to consider them as values and not as inert terms—the change is inessential.

Evaluation Rules. Evaluation is given by *call-by-fireball* β-reduction $\to_{\beta_f}$: the β-rule can fire, *lighting* the argument, only if the argument is a fireball (*fireball* is a catchier version of *fire-able term*). We actually distinguish two sub-rules: one that *lights* values, noted $\to_{\beta_v}$, and one that *lights* inert terms, noted $\to_{\beta_i}$ (see Fig. 1). Note that evaluation is *weak*: it does not reduce under abstractions.

We endow the calculus with the (deterministic) right-to-left evaluation strategy, defined via right evaluation contexts C—note the production Cf, forcing the right-to-left order. A more general calculus is defined in [3], for which the right-to-left strategy is shown to be complete. The left-to-right strategy, often adopted in the literature on Closed CbV, is also complete, but in the open case the right-to-left one has stronger invariants that lead to simpler abstract machines (see [4]), which is why we adopt it here. We omit details about the rewriting theory of the fireball calculus because our focus here is on denotational semantics.

Properties. A famous key property of Closed CbV (whose evaluation is exactly $\to_{\beta_v}$) is *harmony*: given a closed term t, either it diverges or it evaluates to an abstraction, i.e. t is β_v-normal if and only if t is an abstraction. The fireball calculus λ_{fire} satisfies an analogous property in the (more general) *open* setting by replacing abstractions with fireballs (Proposition 1.1). Moreover, the fireball calculus is a *conservative extension* of Closed CbV: on closed terms it collapses on Closed CbV (Proposition 1.2). No other presentation of Open CbV has these good properties.

Proposition 1 (Distinctive properties of λ_{fire}). *Let t be a term.*

1. Open harmony: *t is β_f-normal if and only if t is a fireball.*
2. Conservative open extension: *$t \to_{\beta_f} u$ if and only if $t \to_{\beta_v} u$, when t is closed.*

Example 2. Let $t := (\lambda z.z(yz))\lambda x.x$. Then, $t \to_{\beta_f} (\lambda x.x)(y\,\lambda x.x) \to_{\beta_f} y\,\lambda x.x$, where the final term $y\,\lambda x.x$ is a fireball (and β_f-normal).

The key property of inert terms is summarised by the following proposition: substitution of inert terms does not create or erase β_f-redexes, and hence can always be avoided. It plays a role in Sect. 4.

Proposition 3 (Inert substitutions and evaluation commute). *Let t, u be terms, i be an inert term. Then, $t \to_{\beta_f} u$ if and only if $t\{x\leftarrow i\} \to_{\beta_f} u\{x\leftarrow i\}$.*

With general terms (or even fireballs) instead of inert ones, evaluation and substitution do not commute, in the sense that both directions of Proposition 3 do not hold. Direction $\Leftarrow$ is false because substitution can create β_f-redexes, as in $(xy)\{x\leftarrow\lambda z.z\} = (\lambda z.z)y$; direction $\Rightarrow$ is false because substitution can erase β_f-redexes, as in $((\lambda x.z)(xx))\{x\leftarrow\delta\} = (\lambda x.z)(\delta\delta)$ where $\delta := \lambda y.yy$.[4]

---

[4] As well-known, Proposition 3 with ordinary (i.e. CbN) β-reduction $\to_\beta$ instead of $\to_{\beta_f}$ and general terms instead of inert ones holds only in direction $\Rightarrow$.

3   The Fall of Fireballs

Here we introduce Ehrhard's multi type system for CbV [23] and show that—with respect to it—the fireball calculus λ_{fire} fails the denotational test of the benchmark sketched in Sect. 1. This is an issue of λ_{fire}: to our knowledge, all denotational models that are adequate for (some variant of) CbV are not invariant under the evaluation rules of λ_{fire}, because of the rule $\to_{\beta_i}$ substituting inert terms[5].

In the next sections we shall use this type system, while the failure is not required for the main results of the paper, and may be skipped on a first reading.

Relational Semantics. We analyse the failure considering a concrete and well-known denotational model for CbV: *relational semantics*. For Plotkin's original CbV λ-calculus, it has been introduced by Ehrhard [23]. More generally, relational semantics provides a sort of canonical model of linear logic [10,15,27,34], and Ehrhard's model is the one obtained by representing the CbV λ-calculus into linear logic, and then interpreting it according to the relational semantics. It is also strongly related to other denotational models for CbV based on linear logic such as Scott domains and coherent semantics [23,47], and it has a well-studied CbN counterpart [2,11,14,16,40,42,43].

Relational semantics for CbV admits a nice syntactic presentation as a *multi type system* (aka non-idempotent intersection types), introduced right next. This type system, first studied by Ehrhard in [23], is nothing but the CbV version of de Carvalho's System R for CbN λ-calculus [14,16].

Multi Types. Multi types and linear types are defined by mutual induction:

$$\begin{array}{lll} \text{Linear types} & L, L' ::= M \multimap N \\ \text{Multi types} & M, N ::= [L_1, \ldots, L_n] & (\text{with } n \in \mathbb{N}) \end{array}$$

where $[L_1, \ldots, L_n]$ is our notation for multisets. Note the absence of base types: their role is played by the *empty multiset* $[\,]$ (obtained for $n = 0$), that we rather note $\mathbf{0}$ and refer to as *the empty (multi) type*. A multi type $[L_1, \ldots, L_n]$ has to be intended as a conjunction $L_1 \wedge \cdots \wedge L_n$ of linear types $L_1, \ldots, L_n$, for a commutative and associative conjunction connective $\wedge$ that is not idempotent (morally a tensor $\otimes$) and whose neutral element is $\mathbf{0}$.

The intuition is that a linear type corresponds to a single use of a term t, and that t is typed with a multiset M of n linear types if it is going to be used (at most) n times. The meaning of *using a term* is not easy to define precisely. Roughly, it means that if t is part of a larger term u, then (at most) n copies of

---

[5] Clearly, any denotational model for the CbN λ-calculus is invariant under β_f-reduction (since $\to_{\beta_f} \subseteq \to_\beta$), but there is no hope that it could be adequate for the fireball calculus. Indeed, such a model would identify the interpretations of $(\lambda x.y)\Omega$ (where Ω is a diverging term and $x \neq y$) and y, but in a CbV setting these two terms have a completely different behaviour: y is normal, whereas $(\lambda x.y)\Omega$ cannot normalise.

t shall end up in evaluation position during the evaluation of u. More precisely, the n copies shall end up in evaluation positions where they are applied to some terms.

The derivation rules for the multi types system are in Fig. 2—they are exactly the same as in [23]. In this system, *judgements* have the shape $\Gamma \vdash t : M$ where t is a term, M is a multi type and Γ is a *type context*, that is, a total function from variables to multi types such that the set $\mathsf{dom}(\Gamma) := \{x \mid \Gamma(x) \neq \mathbf{0}\}$ is finite. Note that terms are always assigned a multi type, and never a linear type—this is dual to what happens in de Carvalho's System R for CbN [14,16].

The application rule has a multiplicative formulation (in linear logic terminology), as it collects the type contexts of the two premises. The involved operation is the *sum of type contexts* $\Gamma \uplus \Delta$, that is defined as $(\Gamma \uplus \Delta)(x) := \Gamma(x) \uplus \Delta(x)$, where the $\uplus$ in the RHS stands for the multiset sum. A type context Γ such that $\mathsf{dom}(\Gamma) \subseteq \{x_1, \ldots, x_n\}$ with $x_i \neq x_j$ and $\Gamma(x_i) = M_i$ for all $1 \leq i \neq j \leq n$ is often written as $\Gamma = x_1 : M_1, \ldots, x_n : M_n$. Note that the sum of type contexts $\uplus$ is commutative and associative, and its neutral element is the type context Γ such that $\mathsf{dom}(\Gamma) = \emptyset$, which is called the *empty type context* (all types in Γ are $\mathbf{0}$). The notation $\pi \triangleright \Gamma \vdash t : M$ means that π is a *type derivation* π (i.e. a tree constructed using the rules in Fig. 2) with conclusion the judgement $\Gamma \vdash t : M$.

$$\frac{}{x : M \vdash x : M} \text{ ax} \qquad \frac{\Gamma \vdash t : [M \multimap N] \qquad \Delta \vdash u : M}{\Gamma \uplus \Delta \vdash tu : N} @$$

$$\frac{\Gamma_1, x : M_1 \vdash t : N_1 \qquad {}^{n \in \mathbb{N}} \qquad \Gamma_n, x : M_n \vdash t : N_n}{\Gamma_1 \uplus \cdots \uplus \Gamma_n \vdash \lambda x.t : [M_1 \multimap N_1, \ldots, M_n \multimap N_n]} \lambda$$

Fig. 2. Multi types system for Plotkin's CbV λ-calculus [23].

Intuitions: the empty type $\mathbf{0}$. Before digging into technical details let us provide some intuitions. A key type specific to the CbV setting is the empty multiset $\mathbf{0}$, also known as the empty (multi) type. The idea is that $\mathbf{0}$ is the type of terms that can be erased. To understand its role in CbV, we first recall its role in CbN.

In the CbN multi type system [2,14,16] every term, even a diverging one, is typable with $\mathbf{0}$. On the one hand, this is correct, because in CbN every term can be erased, and erased terms can also be divergent, because they are never evaluated. On the other hand, adequacy is formulated with respect to non-empty types: a term terminates if and only if it is typable with a non-empty type.

In CbV, instead, terms have to be evaluated before being erased. And, of course, their evaluation has to terminate. Therefore, terminating terms and erasable terms coincide. Since the multi type system is meant to characterise terminating terms, in CbV a term is typable if and only if it is typable with $\mathbf{0}$, as we shall prove in Sect. 8. Then the empty type is not a degenerate type, as in CbN, it rather is *the* type, characterising (adequate) typability altogether.

Note that, in particular, in a typing judgement $\Gamma \vdash e : M$ the type context Γ may give the empty type to a variable x occurring in e, as for instance in the axiom $x : \mathbf{0} \vdash x : \mathbf{0}$—this may seem very strange to people familiar with CbN multi types. We hope that instead, according to the provided intuition that $\mathbf{0}$ is the type of termination, it would rather seem natural.

The Model. The idea to build the denotational model from the type system is that the interpretation (or semantics) of a term is simply the set of its type assignments, i.e. the set of its derivable types together with their type contexts. More precisely, let t be a term and $x_1, \ldots, x_n$ (with $n \geq 0$) be pairwise distinct variables. If $\mathsf{fv}(t) \subseteq \{x_1, \ldots, x_n\}$, we say that the list $\vec{x} = (x_1, \ldots, x_n)$ is *suitable for t*. If $\vec{x} = (x_1, \ldots, x_n)$ is suitable for t, the *(relational) semantics of t for $\vec{x}$* is

$$\llbracket t \rrbracket_{\vec{x}} := \{((M_1, \ldots, M_n), N) \mid \exists\, \pi \,\triangleright\, x_1 : M_1, \ldots, x_n : M_n \vdash t : N\}.$$

Ehrhard proved that this is a denotational model for Plotkin's CbV λ-calculus [23, p. 267], in the sense that the semantics of a term is invariant under β_v -reduction.

Theorem 4 (Invariance for $\to_{\beta_v}$, [23]). *Let t and u be two terms and $\vec{x} = (x_1, \ldots, x_n)$ be a suitable list of variables for t and u. If $t \to_{\beta_v} u$ then $\llbracket t \rrbracket_{\vec{x}} = \llbracket u \rrbracket_{\vec{x}}$.*

Note that terms are not assumed to be closed. Unfortunately, relational semantics is not a denotational model of the fireball calculus λ_{fire}: Theorem 4 does not hold if we replace $\to_{\beta_v}$ with $\to_{\beta_i}$ (and hence with $\to_{\beta_f}$), as we show in the following example—the reader can skip it on a first reading.

Example 5 (On a second reading: non-invariance of multi types in the fireball calculus). Consider the fireball step $(\lambda z.y)(xx) \to_{\beta_f} y$, where the inert sub-term xx is erased. Let us construct the interpretations of the terms $(\lambda z.y)(xx)$ and y. All type derivations for xx are as follows (M and N are arbitrary multi types):

$$\pi_{M,N} = \cfrac{\cfrac{}{x : [M \multimap N] \vdash x : [M \multimap N]}\ \mathsf{ax} \qquad \cfrac{}{x : M \vdash x : M}\ \mathsf{ax}}{x : [M \multimap N] \uplus M \vdash xx : N}\ @$$

Hence, all type derivations for $(\lambda z.y)(xx)$ and y have the following forms:

$$\cfrac{\cfrac{\cfrac{}{y : N \vdash y : N}\ \mathsf{ax}}{y : N \vdash \lambda z.y : [\mathbf{0} \multimap N]}\ \lambda \qquad \cfrac{\vdots\, \pi_{M,\mathbf{0}}}{x : [M \multimap \mathbf{0}] \uplus M \vdash xx : \mathbf{0}}}{x : [M \multimap \mathbf{0}] \uplus M, y : N \vdash (\lambda z.y)(xx) : N}\ @ \qquad \cfrac{}{x : \mathbf{0}, y : N \vdash y : N}\ \mathsf{ax}$$

Therefore,

$$\llbracket (\lambda z.y)(xx) \rrbracket_{x,y} = \{(([M \multimap \mathbf{0}] \uplus M, N), N) \mid M, N \text{ multi types}\}$$
$$\llbracket y \rrbracket_{x,y} = \{((\mathbf{0}, N), N) \mid N \text{ multi type}\}$$

To sum up, in the fireball calculus $(\lambda z.y)(xx) \to_{\beta_f} y$, but $\llbracket (\lambda z.y)(xx) \rrbracket_{x,y} \not\subseteq \llbracket y \rrbracket_{x,y}$ as $(([\mathbf{0} \multimap \mathbf{0}], \mathbf{0}), \mathbf{0}) \in \llbracket (\lambda z.y)(xx) \rrbracket_{x,y} \smallsetminus \llbracket y \rrbracket_{x,y}$, and $\llbracket y \rrbracket_{x,y} \not\subseteq \llbracket (\lambda z.y)(xx) \rrbracket_{x,y}$ because $((\mathbf{0}, \mathbf{0}), \mathbf{0}) \in \llbracket y \rrbracket_{x,y} \smallsetminus \llbracket (\lambda z.y)(xx) \rrbracket_{x,y}$.

TERMS, VALUES, FIREBALLS, INERT TERMS, RIGHT EV. CONTEXTS	as for the fireball calculus λ_{fire}

$$\text{ENVIRONMENTS} \qquad E ::= \epsilon \mid [x{\leftarrow}i] : E$$
$$\text{PROGRAMS} \qquad p ::= (t, E)$$

$$\text{RULES} \qquad (C\langle(\lambda x.t)\ v\rangle, E) \to_{\beta_v} (C\langle t\{x{\leftarrow}v\}\rangle, E)$$
$$(C\langle(\lambda x.t)\ i\rangle, E) \to_{\beta_i} (C\langle t\rangle), [x{\leftarrow}i] : E)$$

$$\text{REDUCTION} \qquad \to_{\beta_f} := \to_{\beta_v} \cup \to_{\beta_i}$$

Fig. 3. The split fireball calculus Splitλ_{fire}.

An analogous problem affects the reduction step $(\lambda z.zz)(xx) \to_{\beta_f} (xx)(xx)$, where the inert term xx is instead duplicated. In general, all counterexamples to the invariance of the relational semantics under β_f-reduction are due to β_i-reduction, when the argument of the fired β_f-redex is an inert term that is erased or duplicated. Intuitively, to fix this issue, we should modify the syntax and operational semantics of λ_{fire} in such a way that the β_i-step destroys the β-redex without erasing nor duplicating its inert argument: Proposition 3 guarantees that this modification is harmless. This new presentation of λ_{fire} is in the next section.

Remark 6 (On a second reading: additional remarks about relational semantics).

1. Relational semantics is invariant for Plotkin's CbV even in presence of *open* terms, but *it no longer is an adequate model*: the term $(\lambda y.\delta)(xx)\delta$ (where $\delta := \lambda z.zz$) has an empty semantics (i.e. is not typable in the multi type system of Fig. 2) but it is β_v-normal. Note that, instead, it diverges in λ_{fire} because a β_i-step "unblocks" it: $(\lambda y.\delta)(xx)\delta \to_{\beta_i} \delta\delta \to_{\beta_v} \delta\delta \to_{\beta_v} \cdots$

2. Even though it is not a denotational model for the fireball calculus, relational semantics is *adequate* for it, in the sense that a term is typable in the multi types system of Fig. 2 if and only if it β_f-normalises. This follows from two results involving the shuffling calculus, an extension of Plotkin's CbV that is another presentation of Open CbV:
   - the adequacy of the relational semantics for the shuffling calculus [13,31];
   - the equivalence of the fireball calculus λ_{fire} and shuffling calculus λ_{sh} from the termination point of view, i.e. a term normalises in one calculus if and only if it normalises in the other one [3].

Unfortunately, the shuffling calculus λ_{sh} has issues with respect to the quantitative aspects of the semantics (it is unknown whether its number of steps is a reasonable cost model [3]; the size of λ_{sh}-normal forms is not bounded by the size of their types, as we show in Example 16), which instead better fit the fireball calculus λ_{fire}. This is why in the next section we slightly modify λ_{fire}, rather than switching to λ_{sh}.

4   Fireballs Reloaded: The Split Fireball Calculus Splitλ_{fire}

This section presents the *split fireball calculus* Splitλ_{fire}, that is the refinement of the fireball calculus λ_{fire} correcting the issue explained in the previous section (Example 5), namely the non-invariance of type assignments by evaluation.

The calculus Splitλ_{fire} is defined in Fig. 3. The underlying idea is simple: the problem with the fireball calculus is the substitution of inert terms, as discussed in Example 5; but some form of β_i-step is needed to get the adequacy of relational semantics in presence of open terms, as shown in Remark 6. Inspired by Proposition 3, the solution is to keep trace of the inert terms involved in β_i-steps in an auxiliary environment, without substituting them in the body of the abstraction. Therefore, we introduce the syntactic category of *programs* p, that are terms with an *environment* E, which in turn is a list of explicit (i.e. delayed) substitutions paring variables and inert terms. We use *expressions* $e, e', \ldots$ to refer to the union of terms and programs. Note the new form of the rewriting rule $\rightarrow_{\beta_i}$, that does not substitute the inert term and rather adds an entry to the environment. Apart from storing inert terms, the environment does not play any active role in β_f-reduction for Splitλ_{fire}. Even though $\rightarrow_{\beta_f}$ is a binary relation on programs, we use '*normal expression*' to refer to either a normal (with respect to $\rightarrow_{\beta_f}$) program or a term t such that the program (t, E) is normal (for any environment E).

The good properties of the fireball calculus are retained. Harmony in Splitλ_{fire} takes the following form (for arbitrary fireball f and environment E):

Proposition 7 (Harmony). *A program p is normal if and only if $p = (f, E)$.*

So, an expression is normal iff it is a fireball f or a program of the form (f, E).

Conservativity with respect to the closed case is also immediate, because in the closed case the rule $\rightarrow_{\beta_i}$ never fires and so the environment is always empty.

On a Second Reading: No Open Size Explosion. Let us mention that avoiding the substitution of inert terms is also natural at the implementation/cost model level, as substituting them causes *open size explosion*, an issue studied at length in previous work on the fireball calculus [4,7]. Avoiding the substitution of inert terms altogether is in fact what is done by the other incarnations of Open CbV, as well as by abstract machines. The split fireball calculus Splitλ_{fire} can in fact be seen as adding the environment of abstract machines but without having to deal with the intricacies of decomposed evaluation rules. It can also be seen as the (open fragment of) Accattoli and Paolini's *value substitution calculus* [6], where indeed inert terms are never substituted. In particular, it is possible to prove that the normal forms of the split fireball calculus are isomorphic to those of the value substitution up to its structural equivalence (see [3] for the definitions).

On a Second Reading: Relationship with the Fireball Calculus. The split and the (plain) fireball calculus are isomorphic at the rewriting level. To state the relationship we need the concept of *program unfolding* $(t, E)\!\downarrow$, that is, the term obtained

$$\dfrac{}{x:M \vdash x:M} \; \text{ax} \qquad \dfrac{\Gamma \vdash t:[M \multimap N] \qquad \Delta \vdash u:M}{\Gamma \uplus \Delta \vdash tu:N} \; @$$

$$\dfrac{\Gamma_1, x:M_1 \vdash t:N_1 \qquad \overset{n \in \mathbb{N}}{\cdots} \qquad \Gamma_n, x:M_n \vdash t:N_n}{\Gamma_1 \uplus \cdots \uplus \Gamma_n \vdash \lambda x.t:[M_1 \multimap N_1, \ldots, M_n \multimap N_n]} \; \lambda$$

$$\dfrac{\Gamma \vdash t:M}{\Gamma \vdash (t,\epsilon):M} \; \text{es}_\epsilon \qquad \dfrac{\Gamma, x:M \vdash (t,E):N \qquad \Delta \vdash i:M}{\Gamma \uplus \Delta \vdash (t,E@[x \leftarrow i]):N} \; \text{es}_@$$

Fig. 4. Multi types system for the split fireball calculus.

by substituting the inert terms in the environment E into the main term t:

$$(t,\epsilon){\downarrow} := t \qquad\qquad (t,[y \leftarrow i]:E){\downarrow} := (t\{x \leftarrow i\}, E){\downarrow}$$

From the commutation of evaluation and substitution of inert terms in the fireball calculus (Proposition 3), it follows that normal programs (in $\mathsf{Split}\lambda_{\mathsf{fire}}$) unfold to normal terms (in λ_{fire}), that is, fireballs. Conversely, every fireball can be seen as a normal program with respect to the empty environment.

For evaluation, the same commutation property easily gives the following strong bisimulation between the split $\mathsf{Split}\lambda_{\mathsf{fire}}$ and the plain λ_{fire} fireball calculi.

Proposition 8 (Strong bisimulation). *Let p be a program (in $\mathsf{Split}\lambda_{\mathsf{fire}}$).*

1. Split to plain: *if $p \to_{\beta_f} q$ then $p{\downarrow} \to_{\beta_f} q{\downarrow}$.*
2. Plain to split: *if $p{\downarrow} \to_{\beta_f} u$ then there exists q such that $p \to_{\beta_f} q$ and $q{\downarrow} = u$.*

It is then immediate that termination in the two calculi coincide, as well as the number of steps to reach a normal form. Said differently, the split fireball calculus can be seen as an *isomorphic* refinement of the fireball calculus.

5 Multi Types for $\mathsf{Split}\lambda_{\mathsf{fire}}$

The multi type system for the split fireball calculus $\mathsf{Split}\lambda_{\mathsf{fire}}$ is the natural extension to terms with environments of the multi type system for Plotkin's CbV λ-calculus seen in Sect. 2. Multi and linear types are the same. The only novelty is that now judgements type expressions, not only terms, hence we add two new rules for the two cases of environment, es_ϵ and $\text{es}_@$, see Fig. 4. Rule es_ϵ is trivial, it is simply the coercion of a term to a program with an empty environment. Rule $\text{es}_@$ uses the *append* operation $E@[x \leftarrow i]$ that appends an entry $[x \leftarrow i]$ to the end of an environment E, formally defined as follows:

$$\epsilon@[x \leftarrow i] := [x \leftarrow i] \qquad ([y \leftarrow i']:E)@[x \leftarrow i] := [y \leftarrow i']:(E@[x \leftarrow i])$$

We keep all the notations already used for multi types in Sect. 3.

Sizes, and Basic Properties of Typing. For our quantitative analyses, we need the notions of size for terms, programs and type derivations.

The *size $|t|$ of a term t* is the number of its applications not under the scope of an abstraction. The *size $|(t, E)|$ of a program (t, E)* is the size of t plus the size of the (inert) terms in the environment E. Formally, they are defined as follows:

$$|v| := 0 \quad |tu| := |t| + |u| + 1 \qquad |(t, \epsilon)| := |t| \quad |(t, E@[x \leftarrow i])| := |(t, E)| + |i|$$

The *size $|\pi|$ of a type derivation π* is the number of its @ rules.

The proofs of the next basic properties of type derivations are straightforward.

Lemma 9 (Free variables in typing). *If $\pi \triangleright \Gamma \vdash e : M$ then $\mathsf{dom}(\Gamma) \subseteq \mathsf{fv}(e)$.*

The next lemma collects some basic properties of type derivations for values.

Lemma 10 (Typing of values). *Let $\pi \triangleright \Gamma \vdash v : M$ be a type derivation for a value v. Then,*

1. *Empty multiset implies null size: if $M = \mathbf{0}$ then $\mathsf{dom}(\Gamma) = \emptyset$ and $|\pi| = 0 = |v|$.*
2. *Multiset splitting: if $M = N \uplus O$, then there are two type contexts Δ and Π and two type derivations $\sigma \triangleright \Delta \vdash v : N$ and $\rho \triangleright \Pi \vdash v : O$ such that $\Gamma = \Delta \uplus \Pi$ and $|\pi| = |\sigma| + |\rho|$.*
3. *Empty judgement: there is a type derivation $\sigma \triangleright \vdash v : \mathbf{0}$.*
4. *Multiset merging: for any two type derivations $\pi \triangleright \Gamma \vdash v : M$ and $\sigma \triangleright \Delta \vdash v : N$ there is a type derivation $\rho \triangleright \Gamma \uplus \Delta \vdash v : M \uplus N$ such that $|\rho| = |\pi| + |\sigma|$.*

The next two sections prove that the multi type system is correct (Sect. 6) and complete (Sect. 7) for termination in the split fireball calculus $\mathsf{Split}\lambda_{\mathsf{fire}}$, also providing bounds for the length $|d|$ of a normalising evaluation d and for the size of normal forms. At the end of Sect. 7 we discuss the adequacy of the relational model induced by this multi type system, with respect to $\mathsf{Split}\lambda_{\mathsf{fire}}$. Section 8 characterises types and type derivations that provide exact bounds.

6   Correctness

Here we prove correctness (Theorem 14) of multi types for $\mathsf{Split}\lambda_{\mathsf{fire}}$, refined with quantitative information: if a term is typable then it terminates, and the type derivation provides bounds for both the number of steps to normal form and the size of the normal form. After the correctness theorem we show that even types by themselves—without the derivation—bound the size of normal forms.

Correctness. The proof technique is standard. Correctness is obtained from subject reduction (Proposition 13) plus a property of typings of normal forms (Proposition 11).

Proposition 11 (Type derivations bound the size of normal forms).
Let $\pi \rhd \Gamma \vdash e : M$ be a type derivation for a normal expression e. Then $|e| \leq |\pi|$.

As it is standard in the study of type systems, subject reduction requires a substitution lemma for typed terms, here refined with quantitative information.

Lemma 12 (Substitution). *Let $\pi \rhd \Gamma, x : N \vdash t : M$ and $\sigma \rhd \Delta \vdash v : N$ (where v is a value). Then there exists $\rho \rhd \Gamma \uplus \Delta \vdash t\{x{\leftarrow}v\} : M$ such that $|\rho| = |\pi| + |\sigma|$.*

The key point of the next *quantitative* subject reduction property is the fact that the size of the derivation decreases by *exactly* 1 at each evaluation step.

Proposition 13 (Quantitative subject reduction). *Let p and p' be programs and $\pi \rhd \Gamma \vdash p : M$ be a type derivation for p. If $p \to_{\beta_f} p'$ then $|\pi| > 0$ and there exists a type derivation $\pi' \rhd \Gamma \vdash p' : M$ such that $|\pi'| = |\pi| - 1$.*

Correctness now follows as an easy induction on the size of the type derivation, which bounds both the length $|d|$ of the—normalising—evaluation d (i.e. the number of β_f-steps in d) by Proposition 13, and the size of the normal form by Proposition 11.

Theorem 14 (Correctness). *Let $\pi \rhd \Gamma \vdash p : M$ be a type derivation. Then there exist a normal program q and an evaluation $d : p \to_{\beta_f}^* q$ with $|d| + |q| \leq |\pi|$.*

Types Bound the Size of Normal Forms. In our multi type system, not only type derivations but also multi types provide quantitative information, in this case on the size of normal forms.

First, we need to define the size for multi types and type contexts, which is simply given by the number of occurrences of $\multimap$. Formally, the size of linear and multi types are defined by mutual induction by $|M \multimap N| := 1 + |M| + |N|$ and $|[L_1, \ldots, L_n]| := \sum_{i=1}^{n} |L_i|$. Clearly, $|M| \geq 0$ and $|M| = 0$ if and only if $M = \mathbf{0}$.

Given a type context $\Gamma = x_1 : M_1, \ldots, x_n : M_n$ we often consider the list of its types, noted $\underline{\Gamma} := (M_1, \ldots, M_n)$. Since any list of multi types $(M_1, \ldots, M_n)$ can be seen as extracted from a type context Γ, we use the notation $\underline{\Gamma}$ for lists of multi types. The size of a list of multi types is given by $|(M_1, \ldots, M_n)| := \sum_{i=1}^{n} |M_i|$. Clearly, $\mathrm{dom}(\Gamma) = \emptyset$ if and only if $|\underline{\Gamma}| = 0$.

The quantitative information is that the size of types bounds the size of normal forms. In the case of inert terms a stronger bound actually holds.

Proposition 15 (Types bound the size of normal forms). *Let e be a normal expression. For any type derivation $\pi \rhd \Gamma \vdash e : M$, one has $|e| \leq |(\underline{\Gamma}, M)|$. If moreover e is an inert term, then $|e| + |M| \leq |\underline{\Gamma}|$.*

Example 16 (On a second reading: types, normal forms, and λ_{sh}). The fact that multi types bound the size of normal forms is a quite delicate result that holds in the split fireball calculus $\mathsf{Split}\lambda_{fire}$ but does not hold in other presentations of Open CbV, like the shuffling calculus λ_{sh} [13,31], as we now show—this is one of the reasons motivating the introduction of $\mathsf{Split}\lambda_{fire}$. Without going into the details of λ_{sh}, consider $t := (\lambda z.z)(xx)$: it is normal for λ_{sh} but it—or, more precisely, the program $p := (t, \epsilon)$—is not normal for $\mathsf{Split}\lambda_{fire}$, indeed $p \to^*_{\beta_f}$ $(z, [y{\leftarrow}xx]) =: q$ and q is normal in $\mathsf{Split}\lambda_{fire}$. Concerning sizes, $|t| = |p| = 2$ and $|q| = 1$. Consider the following type derivation for t (the type derivation $\pi_{0,0}$ is defined in Example 5):

$$\cfrac{\cfrac{\cfrac{}{z:\mathbf{0} \vdash z:\mathbf{0}} \text{ ax}}{\vdash \lambda z.z : [\mathbf{0} \multimap \mathbf{0}]} \lambda \qquad \cfrac{\vdots \pi_{0,0}}{x:[\mathbf{0} \multimap \mathbf{0}] \vdash xx:\mathbf{0}}}{x:[\mathbf{0} \multimap \mathbf{0}] \vdash (\lambda z.z)(xx):\mathbf{0}} \text{ @}$$

So, $|t| = 2 > 1 = |([\mathbf{0} \multimap \mathbf{0}], \mathbf{0})|$, which gives a counterexample to Proposition 15 in λ_{sh}.

7   Completeness

Here we prove completeness (Theorem 20) of multi types for $\mathsf{Split}\lambda_{fire}$, refined with quantitative information: if a term terminates then it is typable, and the quantitative information is the same as in the correctness theorem (Theorem 14 above). After that, we discuss the adequacy of the relational semantics induced by the multi type system, with respect to termination in $\mathsf{Split}\lambda_{fire}$.

Completeness. The proof technique, again, is standard. Completeness is obtained by a subject expansion property plus the fact that all normal forms are typable.

Proposition 17 (Normal forms are typable)

1. Normal expression: *for any normal expression e, there exists a type derivation $\pi \rhd \Gamma \vdash e:M$ for some type context Γ and some multi type M.*
2. Inert term: *for any multi type N and any inert term i, there exists a type derivation $\sigma \rhd \Delta \vdash i:N$ for some type context Δ.*

In the proof of Proposition 17, the stronger statement for inert terms is required, to type a normal expression that is a program with non-empty environment.

For quantitative subject expansion (Proposition 19), which is dual to subject reduction (Proposition 13 above), we need an anti-substitution lemma that is the dual of the substitution one (Lemma 12 above).

Lemma 18 (Anti-substitution). *Let t be a term, v be a value, and $\pi \rhd$ $\Gamma \vdash t\{x{\leftarrow}v\} : M$ be a type derivation. Then there exist two type derivations $\sigma \rhd \Delta, x:N \vdash t:M$ and $\rho \rhd \Pi \vdash v:N$ such that $\Gamma = \Delta \uplus \Pi$ and $|\pi| = |\sigma| + |\rho|$.*

Subject expansion follows. Dually to subject reduction, the size of the type derivation grows by *exactly* 1 along every expansion (i.e. along every anti-β_f-step).

Proposition 19 (Quantitative subject expansion). *Let p and p' be programs and $\pi' \rhd \Gamma \vdash p' : M$ be a type derivation for p'. If $p \to_{\beta_f} p'$ then there exists a type derivation $\pi \rhd \Gamma \vdash p : M$ for p such that $|\pi'| = |\pi| - 1$.*

Theorem 20 (Completeness). *Let $d : p \to^*_{\beta_f} q$ be a normalising evaluation. Then there is a type derivation $\pi \rhd \Gamma \vdash p : M$, and it satisfies $|d| + |q| \leq |\pi|$.*

Relational Semantics. Subject reduction (Proposition 13) and expansion (Proposition 19) imply that the set of typing judgements of a term is invariant by evaluation, and so they provide a denotational model of the split fireball calculus (Corollary 21 below).

The definitions seen in Sect. 2 of the interpretation $[\![t]\!]_{\vec{x}}$ of a term with respect to a list $\vec{x}$ of suitable variables for t extends to the split fireball calculus by simply replacing terms with programs, with no surprises.

Corollary 21 (Invariance). *Let p and q be two programs and $\vec{x} = (x_1, \ldots, x_n)$ be a suitable list of variables for p and q. If $p \to_{\beta_f} q$ then $[\![p]\!]_{\vec{x}} = [\![q]\!]_{\vec{x}}$.*

From correctness (Theorem 14) and completeness (Theorem 20) it follows that the relational semantics is adequate for the split fireball calculus $\mathsf{Split}\lambda_{\mathsf{fire}}$.

Corollary 22 (Adequacy). *Let p be a program and $\vec{x} = (x_1, \ldots, x_n)$ be a suitable list of variables for p. The following are equivalent:*

1. Termination*: the evaluation of p terminates;*
2. Typability*: there is a type derivation $\pi \rhd \Gamma \vdash p : M$ for some Γ and M;*
3. Non-empty denotation*: $[\![p]\!]_{\vec{x}} \neq \emptyset$.*

Careful about the third point: it requires the interpretation to be non-empty—a program typable with the empty multiset $\mathbf{0}$ has a non-empty interpretation. Actually, a term is typable if and only if it is typable with $\mathbf{0}$, as we show next.

Remark 23. By Propositions 1.2 and 8, (weak) evaluations in Plotkin's original CbV λ-calculus λ_v, in the fireball calculus λ_{fire} and in its split variant $\mathsf{Split}\lambda_{\mathsf{fire}}$ coincide on closed terms. So, Corollary 22 says that relational semantics is adequate also for λ_v *restricted to closed terms* (but adequacy for λ_v fails on open terms, see Remark 6).

8   Tight Type Derivations and Exact Bounds

In this section we study a class of minimal type derivations, called *tight*, providing exact bounds for evaluation lengths and sizes of normal forms.

Typing Values and Inert Terms. Values can always be typed with **0** in an empty type context (Lemma 10.3), by means of an axiom for variables or of a λ-rule with zero premises for abstractions. We are going to show that inert terms can also always be typed with **0**. There are differences, however. First, the type context in general is not empty. Second, the derivations typing with **0** have a more complex structure, having sub-derivations for inert terms whose right-hand type might not be **0**. It is then necessary, for inert terms, to consider a more general class of type derivations, that, as a special case, include derivations typing with **0**.

First of all, we define two class of types:

INERT LINEAR TYPES	$L^i ::= \mathbf{0} \multimap N^i$
INERT MULTI TYPES	$M^i, N^i ::= [L_1^i, \dots, L_n^i]$ (with $n \in \mathbb{N}$).

A type context Γ is *inert* if it assigns only inert multi types to variables.

In particular, the empty multi type **0** is inert (take $n = 0$), and hence the empty type context is inert. Note that inert multi types and inert multi contexts are closed under summation ⊎.

We also introduce two notions of type derivations, *inert* and *tight*. The tight ones are those we are actually interested in, but, as explained, for inert terms we need to consider a more general class of type derivations, the inert ones. Formally, given an expression e, a type derivation $\pi \triangleright \Gamma \vdash e : M$ is

- *inert* if Γ is a inert type context and M is a inert multi type;
- *tight* if π is inert and $M = \mathbf{0}$;
- *nonempty* (resp. *empty*) if Γ is a non-empty (resp. empty) type context.

Note that tightness and inertness of type derivations depend only on the judgement in their conclusions. The general property is that inert terms admit a inert type derivation *for every inert multi type M^i*.

Lemma 24 (Inert typing of inert terms). *Let i be a inert term. For any inert multi type M^i there exists a nonempty inert type derivation $\pi \triangleright \Gamma \vdash i : M^i$.*

Lemma 24 holds with respect to *all* inert multi types, in particular **0**, so inert terms can be always typed with a nonempty *tight* derivation. Since values can be always typed with an empty tight derivation (Lemma 10.3), we can conclude:

Corollary 25 (Fireballs are tightly typable). *For any fireball f there exists a tight type derivation $\pi \triangleright \Gamma \vdash f : \mathbf{0}$. Moreover, if f is a inert term then π is nonempty, otherwise f is a value and π is empty.*

By harmony (Proposition 7), it follows that any normal expression is tightly typable (Proposition 26 below). *Terminology:* a *coerced value* is a program of the form (v, ϵ).

Proposition 26 (Normal expressions are tightly typable). *Let e be a normal expression. Then there exists a tight derivation $\pi \triangleright \Gamma \vdash e : \mathbf{0}$. Moreover, e is a value or a coerced value if and only if π is empty.*

Tight Derivations and Exact Bounds. The next step is to show that tight derivations are minimal and provide exact bounds. Again, we have to detour through inert derivations for inert terms. And we need a further property of inert terms: if the type context is inert then the right-hand type is also inert.

Lemma 27 (Inert spreading on inert terms). *Let $\pi \triangleright \Gamma \vdash i : M$ be a type derivation for a inert term i. If Γ is a inert type context then M and π are inert.*

Next, we prove that inert derivations provide exact bounds for inert terms.

Lemma 28 (Inert derivations are minimal and provide the exact size of inert terms). *Let $\pi \triangleright \Gamma \vdash i : M^i$ be a inert type derivation for a inert term i. Then $|i| = |\pi|$ and $|\pi|$ is minimal among the type derivations of i.*

We can now extend the characterisation of sizes to all normal expressions, via tight derivations, refining Proposition 11.

Lemma 29 (Tight derivations are minimal and provide the exact size of normal forms). *Let $\pi \triangleright \Gamma \vdash e : 0$ be a tight derivation and e be a normal expression. Then $|e| = |\pi|$ and $|\pi|$ is minimal among the type derivations of e.*

The bound on the size of normal forms using types rather than type derivations (Proposition 15) can also be refined: *tight* derivations end with judgements whose (inert) *type contexts* provide the *exact* size of normal forms.

Proposition 30 (Inert types and the exact size of normal forms). *Let e be a normal expression and $\pi \triangleright \Gamma \vdash e : 0$ be a tight derivation. Then $|e| = |\underline{\Gamma}|$.*

Tightness and General Programs. Via subject reduction and expansion, exact bounds can be extended to all normalisable programs. Tight derivations indeed induce refined correctness and completeness theorems replacing inequalities with equalities (see Theorems 31 and 32 below and compare them with Theorems 14 and 20 above, respectively): an *exact* quantitative information relates the length $|d|$ of evaluations, the size of normal forms and the size of *tight* type derivations.

Theorem 31 (Tight correctness). *Let $\pi \triangleright \Gamma \vdash p : 0$ be a tight type derivation. Then there is a normalising evaluation $d : p \to^*_{\beta_f} q$ with $|\pi| = |d| + |q| = |d| + |\underline{\Gamma}|$. In particular, if $\mathrm{dom}(\Gamma) = \emptyset$, then $|\pi| = |d|$ and q is a coerced value.*

Theorem 32 (Tight completeness). *Let $d : p \to^*_{\beta_f} q$ be a normalising evaluation. Then there is a tight type derivation $\pi \triangleright \Gamma \vdash p : 0$ with $|\pi| = |d| + |q| = |d| + |\underline{\Gamma}|$. In particular, if q is a coerced value, then $|\pi| = |d|$ and $\mathrm{dom}(\Gamma) = \emptyset$.*

Both theorems are proved analogously to their corresponding non-tight version (Theorems 14 and 20), the only difference is in the base case: here Lemma 29 provides an equality on sizes for normal forms, instead of the inequality given by Proposition 11 and used in the non-tight versions. The proof of tight completeness (Theorem 32) uses also that normal programs are *tightly* typable (Proposition 26).

9   Conclusions

This paper studies multi types for CbV weak evaluation. It recasts in CbV de Carvalho's work for CbN [14,16], building on a type system introduced by Ehrhard [23] for Plotkin's original CbV λ-calculus λ_v [45]. Multi types provide a denotational model that we show to be adequate for λ_v, but only when evaluating *closed* terms; and for Open CbV [3], an extension of λ_v where weak evaluation is on possibly *open* terms. More precisely, our main contributions are:

1. The formalism itself: we point out the issues with respect to subject reduction and expansion of the simplest presentation of Open CbV, the fireball calculus λ_{fire}, and introduce a refined calculus (isomorphic to λ_{fire}) that satisfies them.
2. The characterisation of termination both in a *qualitative* and *quantitative* way. Qualitatively, typable terms and normalisable terms coincide. Quantitatively, types provide bounds on the size of normal forms, and type derivations bound the number of evaluation steps to normal form.
3. The identification of a class of type derivations that provide *exact* bounds on evaluation lengths.

References

1. Accattoli, B.: Proof nets and the call-by-value λ-calculus. Theor. Comput. Sci. **606**, 2–24 (2015)
2. Accattoli, B., Graham-Lengrand, S., Kesner, D.: Tight typings and split bounds. In: ICFP 2018 (2018, to appear)
3. Accattoli, B., Guerrieri, G.: Open call-by-value. In: Igarashi, A. (ed.) APLAS 2016. LNCS, vol. 10017, pp. 206–226. Springer, Cham (2016). https://doi.org/10.1007/978-3-319-47958-3_12
4. Accattoli, B., Guerrieri, G.: Implementing open call-by-value. In: Dastani, M., Sirjani, M. (eds.) FSEN 2017. LNCS, vol. 10522, pp. 1–19. Springer, Cham (2017). https://doi.org/10.1007/978-3-319-68972-2_1
5. Accattoli, B., Guerrieri, G.: Types of Fireballs (Extended Version). CoRR abs/1808.10389 (2018)
6. Accattoli, B., Paolini, L.: Call-by-value solvability, revisited. In: Schrijvers, T., Thiemann, P. (eds.) FLOPS 2012. LNCS, vol. 7294, pp. 4–16. Springer, Heidelberg (2012). https://doi.org/10.1007/978-3-642-29822-6_4
7. Accattoli, B., Sacerdoti Coen, C.: On the relative usefulness of fireballs. In: LICS 2015, pp. 141–155 (2015)
8. Bernadet, A., Graham-Lengrand, S.: Non-idempotent intersection types and strong normalisation. Log. Methods Comput. Sci. **9**(4) (2013). https://doi.org/10.2168/LMCS-9(4:3)2013
9. Bono, V., Venneri, B., Bettini, L.: A typed lambda calculus with intersection types. Theor. Comput. Sci. **398**(1–3), 95–113 (2008)
10. Bucciarelli, A., Ehrhard, T.: On phase semantics and denotational semantics: the exponentials. Ann. Pure Appl. Logic **109**(3), 205–241 (2001)
11. Bucciarelli, A., Ehrhard, T., Manzonetto, G.: A relational semantics for parallelism and non-determinism in a functional setting. Ann. Pure Appl. Logic **163**(7), 918–934 (2012)

12. Bucciarelli, A., Kesner, D., Ventura, D.: Non-idempotent intersection types for the lambda-calculus. Log. J. IGPL **25**(4), 431–464 (2017)
13. Carraro, A., Guerrieri, G.: A semantical and operational account of call-by-value solvability. In: Muscholl, A. (ed.) FoSSaCS 2014. LNCS, vol. 8412, pp. 103–118. Springer, Heidelberg (2014). https://doi.org/10.1007/978-3-642-54830-7_7
14. de Carvalho, D.: Sémantiques de la logique linéaire et temps de calcul. Thèse de doctorat, Université Aix-Marseille II (2007)
15. de Carvalho, D.: The relational model is injective for multiplicative exponential linear logic. In: CSL 2016, pp. 41:1–41:19 (2016)
16. de Carvalho, D.: Execution time of λ-terms via denotational semantics and intersection types. Math. Struct. Comput. Sci. **28**(7), 1169–1203 (2018)
17. de Carvalho, D., Pagani, M., Tortora de Falco, L.: A semantic measure of the execution time in linear logic. Theor. Comput. Sci. **412**(20), 1884–1902 (2011)
18. de Carvalho, D., Tortora de Falco, L.: A semantic account of strong normalization in linear logic. Inf. Comput. **248**, 104–129 (2016)
19. Coppo, M., Dezani-Ciancaglini, M.: A new type assignment for λ-terms. Arch. Math. Log. **19**(1), 139–156 (1978)
20. Coppo, M., Dezani-Ciancaglini, M.: An extension of the basic functionality theory for the λ-calculus. Notre Dame J. Formal Log. **21**(4), 685–693 (1980)
21. Curien, P.L., Herbelin, H.: The duality of computation. In: ICFP, pp. 233–243 (2000)
22. Díaz-Caro, A., Manzonetto, G., Pagani, M.: Call-by-value non-determinism in a linear logic type discipline. In: Artemov, S., Nerode, A. (eds.) LFCS 2013. LNCS, vol. 7734, pp. 164–178. Springer, Heidelberg (2013). https://doi.org/10.1007/978-3-642-35722-0_12
23. Ehrhard, T.: Collapsing non-idempotent intersection types. In: CSL, pp. 259–273 (2012)
24. Ehrhard, T., Guerrieri, G.: The bang calculus: an untyped lambda-calculus generalizing call-by-name and call-by-value. In: PPDP 2016, pp. 174–187. ACM (2016)
25. Fiore, M.P., Plotkin, G.D.: An axiomatization of computationally adequate domain theoretic models of FPC. In: LICS 1994, pp. 92–102 (1994)
26. Gardner, P.: Discovering needed reductions using type theory. In: Hagiya, M., Mitchell, J.C. (eds.) TACS 1994. LNCS, vol. 789, pp. 555–574. Springer, Heidelberg (1994). https://doi.org/10.1007/3-540-57887-0_115
27. Girard, J.Y.: Linear logic. Theor. Comput. Sci. **50**, 1–102 (1987)
28. Girard, J.Y.: Normal functors, power series and the λ-calculus. Ann. Pure Appl. Log. **37**, 129–177 (1988)
29. Grégoire, B., Leroy, X.: A compiled implementation of strong reduction. In: ICFP 2002, pp. 235–246 (2002)
30. Guerrieri, G.: Head reduction and normalization in a call-by-value lambda-calculus. In: WPTE 2015, pp. 3–17 (2015)
31. Guerrieri, G.: Towards a semantic measure of the execution time in call-by-value lambda-calculus. Technical report (2018). Submitted to ITRS 2018
32. Guerrieri, G., Paolini, L., Ronchi Della Rocca, S.: Standardization of a Call-By-Value Lambda-Calculus. In: TLCA 2015, pp. 211–225 (2015)
33. Guerrieri, G., Paolini, L., Ronchi Della Rocca, S.: Standardization and conservativity of a refined call-by-value lambda-calculus. Log. Methods Comput. Sci. **13**(4) (2017). https://doi.org/10.23638/LMCS-13(4:29)2017
34. Guerrieri, G., Pellissier, L., Tortora de Falco, L.: Computing connected proof(-structure)s from their Taylor expansion. In: FSCD 2016, pp. 20:1–20:18 (2016)

35. Honda, K., Yoshida, N.: Game-theoretic analysis of call-by-value computation. Theor. Comput. Sci. **221**(1–2), 393–456 (1999)
36. Kesner, D., Vial, P.: Types as resources for classical natural deduction. In: FSCD 2017. LIPIcs, vol. 84, pp. 24:1–24:17 (2017)
37. Kfoury, A.J.: A linearization of the lambda-calculus and consequences. J. Log. Comput. **10**(3), 411–436 (2000)
38. Krivine, J.L.: λ-calcul, types et modèles. Masson (1990)
39. Lassen, S.: Eager normal form bisimulation. In: LICS 2005, pp. 345–354 (2005)
40. Mazza, D., Pellissier, L., Vial, P.: Polyadic approximations, fibrations and intersection types. PACMPL **2**, 6:1–6:28 (2018)
41. Neergaard, P.M., Mairson, H.G.: Types, potency, and idempotency: why nonlinearity and amnesia make a type system work. In: ICFP 2004, pp. 138–149 (2004)
42. Ong, C.L.: Quantitative semantics of the lambda calculus: Some generalisations of the relational model. In: LICS 2017, pp. 1–12 (2017)
43. Paolini, L., Piccolo, M., Ronchi Della Rocca, S.: Essential and relational models. Math. Struct. Comput. Sci. **27**(5), 626–650 (2017)
44. Paolini, L., Ronchi Della Rocca, S.: Call-by-value solvability. ITA **33**(6), 507–534 (1999)
45. Plotkin, G.D.: Call-by-name, call-by-value and the lambda-calculus. Theor. Comput. Sci. **1**(2), 125–159 (1975)
46. Pottinger, G.: A type assignment for the strongly normalizable λ-terms. In: To HB Curry: Essays on Combinatory Logic, λ-Calculus and Formalism, pp. 561–577 (1980)
47. Pravato, A., Ronchi Della Rocca, S., Roversi, L.: The call-by-value λ-calculus: a semantic investigation. Math. Struct. Comput. Sci. **9**(5), 617–650 (1999)
48. Ronchi Della Rocca, S., Paolini, L.: The Parametric λ-Calculus. Springer, Heidelberg (2004). https://doi.org/10.1007/978-3-662-10394-4
49. Della Rocca, S.R., Roversi, L.: Intersection logic. In: Fribourg, L. (ed.) CSL 2001. LNCS, vol. 2142, pp. 414–429. Springer, Heidelberg (2001). https://doi.org/10.1007/3-540-44802-0_29
50. Sieber, K.: Relating full abstraction results for different programming languages. In: Nori, K.V., Veni Madhavan, C.E. (eds.) FSTTCS 1990. LNCS, vol. 472, pp. 373–387. Springer, Heidelberg (1990). https://doi.org/10.1007/3-540-53487-3_58

Program Analysis

On the Soundness of Call Graph Construction in the Presence of Dynamic Language Features - A Benchmark and Tool Evaluation

Li Sui[1]([⊠]) , Jens Dietrich[2] , Michael Emery[1], Shawn Rasheed[1] ,
and Amjed Tahir[1]

[1] Massey University Institute of Fundamental Sciences,
4410 Palmerston North, New Zealand
{L.Sui,S.Rasheed,A.Tahir}@massey.ac.nz
[2] Victoria University of Wellington School of Engineering and Computer Science,
6012 Wellington, New Zealand
jens.dietrich@ecs.vuw.ac.nz
http://ifs.massey.ac.nz/, https://www.victoria.ac.nz/ecs

Abstract. Static program analysis is widely used to detect bugs and vulnerabilities early in the life cycle of software. It models possible program executions without executing a program, and therefore has to deal with both false positives (precision) and false negatives (soundness). A particular challenge for sound static analysis is the presence of dynamic language features, which are prevalent in modern programming languages, and widely used in practice.

We catalogue these features for Java and present a micro-benchmark that can be used to study the recall of static analysis tools. In many cases, we provide examples of real-world usage of the respective feature. We then study the call graphs constructed with *soot*, *wala* and *doop* using the benchmark. We find that while none of the tools can construct a sound call graph for all benchmark programs, they all offer some support for dynamic language features.

We also discuss the notion of possible program execution that serves as the ground truth used to define both precision and soundness. It turns out that this notion is less straight-forward than expected as there are corner cases where the (language, JVM and standard library) specifications do not unambiguously define possible executions.

Keywords: Static analysis · Call graph construction · Soundness
Benchmark · Java · Dynamic proxies · Reflection
Dynamic class loading · Invokedynamic · sun.misc.Unsafe · JNI

This work was supported by the Science for Technological Innovation (SfTI) National Science Challenge (NSC) of New Zealand (PROP-52515-NSCSEED-MAU). The work of the second author was supported by a faculty gift by Oracle Inc.

S. Ryu (Ed.): APLAS 2018, LNCS 11275, pp. 69–88, 2018.
https://doi.org/10.1007/978-3-030-02768-1_4

1 Introduction

Static analysis is a popular technique to detect bugs and vulnerabilities early in the life cycle of a program when it is still relatively inexpensive to fix those issues. It is based on the idea to extract a model from the program without executing it, and then to reason about this model in order to detect flaws in the program. Superficially, this approach should be sound in the sense that all possible program behaviour can be modelled as the entire program is available for analysis [13]. This is fundamentally different from dynamic analysis techniques that are inherently unsound as they depend on drivers to execute the program under analysis, and for real-world programs, these drivers will not cover all possible execution paths. Unfortunately, it turns out that most static analyses are not sound either, caused by the use of dynamic language features that are available in all mainstream modern programming languages, and prevalent in programs. Those features are notoriously difficult to model.

For many years, research in static analysis has focused on precision [31] - the avoidance of false positives caused by the over-abstraction of the analysis model, and scalability. Only more recently has soundness attracted more attention, in particular, the publication of the soundiness manifesto has brought this issue to the fore [26].

While it remains a major research objective to make static analysis sound (or, to use a quantitative term, to increase its recall), there is value in capturing the state of the art in order to explore and catalogue where existing analysers fall short. This is the aim of this paper. Our contributions are: (1) a micro-benchmark consisting of Java programs using dynamic language features along with a call graph oracle representing possible invocation chains, and (2) an evaluation of the call graphs constructed with *soot*, *wala* and *doop* using the benchmark.

2 Background

2.1 Soundness, Precision and Recall

We follow the soundiness manifesto and define the soundness of a static analysis with respect to possible program executions: "analyses are often expected to be sound in that their result models *all possible executions* of the program under analysis" [26]. Similarly, precision can be defined with respect to possible executions as well – a precise analysis models *only possible executions*.

Possible program executions are the *ground truth* against which both soundness and precision are defined. This can also be phrased as the absence of false negatives (FNs) and false positives (FPs), respectively, adapting concepts widely used in machine learning. In this setting, soundness corresponds to *recall*. Recall has a slightly different meaning as it is measurable, whereas soundness is a quality that a system either does or does not possess.

2.2   Call Graphs

In our study, we focus on a particular type of program behaviour: method invocations, modelled by (static) call graphs [18,32]. The aspect of possible executions to be modelled here are method invocations, i.e. that the invocation of one *source* method triggers the invocation of another *target* method. Another way to phrase this in terms of the Java stack is that the *target* method is above the *source* method on the stack at some stage during program execution. We use the phrases *trigger* and *above* to indicate that there may or may not be intermediate methods between the source and the target method. For instance, in a JVM implemented in Java, the stack may contain intermediate methods between the source and the target method to facilitate dispatch.

Static call graph construction has been used for many years and is widely used to detect bugs and vulnerabilities [32,38,40]. In statically constructed call graphs (from here on, called call graphs for short), methods are represented by vertices, and invocations are represented by edges. Sometimes vertices and edges have additional labels, for instance to indicate the invocation instructions being used. This is not relevant for the work presented here and therefore omitted. A source method invoking a target method is represented by an edge from the (vertex representing the) source method to the (vertex representing the) target method. We are again allowing indirect invocations via intermediate methods, this can be easily achieved by computing the transitive closure of the call graph.

2.3   Java Programs

The scope of this study is Java, but it is not necessarily obvious what this means. One question is which version we study. This study uses Java 8, the version widely used at the time of writing this. Due to Java's long history of ensuring backward compatibility, we are confident that this benchmark will remain useful for future versions of Java.

Another question is whether by Java we mean programs written in the Java language, or compiled into JVM byte code. We use the later, for two reasons: (1) most static analysis tools for Java use byte code as input (2) by using byte code, we automatically widen the scope of our study by allowing programs written in other languages that can be compiled into Java byte code.

By explicitly allowing byte code generated by a compiler other than the (standard) Java compiler, we have to deal with byte code the standard compiler cannot produce. We include some programs in the benchmark that explicitly take advantage of this. We note that even if we restricted our study to byte code that can be produced by the Java compiler we would still have a similar problem, as byte code manipulation frameworks are now widely used and techniques like Aspect-Oriented Programming [21] are considered to be an integral part of the Java technology stack.

2.4   Possible Program Executions

The notion of possible program execution is used as ground truth to assess the soundness and the precision of call graph construction tools. This also requires a clarification. Firstly, we do not consider execution paths that are triggered by JVM or system (platform) errors. Secondly, none of the benchmark programs use random inputs, all programs are deterministic. Their behaviour should therefore be completely defined by their byte code.

It turns out that there are scenarios where the resolution of a reflective method call is not completely specified by the specification[1], and possible program executions depend on the actual JVM. This will be discussed in more detail in Sect. 5.1.

2.5   Dynamic Language Features

Our aim is to construct a benchmark for *dynamic language features* for Java. This term is widely used informally, but some discussion is required what this actually means, in order to define the scope of this study. In general, we are interested in all features that allow the user to customise some aspects of the execution semantics of a program, in particular (1) class and object life cycle (2) field access and (3) method dispatch. There are two categories of features we consider: (1) features built into the language itself, and exposed by official APIs. In a wider sense, those are reflective features, given the ability of a system "to reason about itself" [36]. Java reflection, class loading, dynamic proxies and invokedynamic fit into this category. We also consider (2) certain features where programmers can access extra-linguistic mechanisms. The use of native methods,sun.misc.Unsafe and serialisation are in this category. Java is not the only language with such features, for instance, Smalltalk also has a reflection API, the ability to customise dispatch with doesNotUnderstand, binary object serialisation using the Binary Object Streaming Service (BOSS), and the (unsafe-like) become method [14].

This definition also excludes certain features, in particular the study of exceptions and static initializers (<*clinit*>).

3   Related Work

3.1   Benchmarks and Corpora for Empirical Studies

Several benchmarks and datasets have been designed to assist empirical studies in programming languages and software engineering research. One of the most widely used benchmarks is *DaCapo* [6] - a set of open source, real-world Java programs with non-trivial memory loads. *DaCapo* is executable as it provides a customizable harness to execute the respective programs. The key purpose of this benchmark is to be used to compare results of empirical studies, e.g. to compare the performance of different JVMs. The *Qualitas Corpus* [39] provides

---

[1] Meaning here a combination of the JVM Specification [2] and the documentation of the classes of the standard library.

a larger set of curated Java programs intended to be used for empirical studies on code artefacts. *XCorpus* [10] extends the Qualitas Corpus by adding a (partially synthetic) driver with a high coverage.

SPECjvm2008 [3] is a multi-threaded Java benchmark focusing on core Java functionality, mainly the performance of the JRE. It contains several executable synthetic data sets as well as real-world programs.

Very recently, Reif et al. [30] have published a Java test suite designed to test static analysers for their support for dynamic language features, and evaluated *wala* and *soot* against it. While this is very similar to the approach presented here, there are some significant differences: (1) the authors of [30] assume that the tests (benchmark programs) "provide the ground truth". In this study, we question this assumption, and propose an alternative notion that also take characteristics of the JVM and platform used to execute the tests into account. (2) The study presented here also investigates *doop*, which we consider important as it offers several features for advanced reflection handling. (3) While the construction of both test suites/benchmarks was motivated by the same intention, they are different. Merging and consolidating them is an interesting area for future research.

3.2 Approaches to Handle Dynamic Language Features in Pure Static Analysis

Reflection: reflection [14,36] is widely used in real-world Java programs, but is challenging for static analysis to handle [22,24]. Livshits et al. [27] introduced the first static reflection analysis for Java, which uses points-to analysis to approximate the targets of reflective call sites as part of call graph construction. Landman et al. [22] investigated in detail the challenges faced by static analysers to model reflection in Java, and reported 24 different techniques that have been cited in the literature and existing tool. Li et al. [24] proposed *elf*, a static reflection analysis with the aim to improve the effectiveness of Java pointer analysis tools. This analysis uses a self-inferencing mechanism for reflection resolution. *Elf* was evaluated against *doop*, and as a result it was found that *elf* was able to resolve more reflective call targets than *doop*. Smaragdakis et al. [35] further refined the approach from [27] and [24] in terms of both recall and performance. *Wala* [12] has some built-in support for reflective features like `Class.forName`, `Class.newInstance`, and `Method.invoke`.

invokedynamic: Several authors have proposed support for `invokedynamic`. For example, Bodden [7] provided a *soot* extension that supports reading, representing and writing `invokedynamic` byte codes. The *opal* static analyser also provides support for `invokedynamic` through replacing `invokedynamic` instructions using Java `LambdaMetaFactory` with a standard `invokestatic` instruction [1]. *Wala* provides support for `invokedynamic` generated for Java 8 lambdas[2].

---

[2] https://goo.gl/1LxbSd and https://goo.gl/qYeVTd, both accessed 10 June 2018.

Dynamic Proxies: only recently, at the time of writing this, Fourtounis et al. [15] have proposed support for dynamic proxies in *doop*. This analysis shows that there is a need for the mutually recursive handling of dynamic proxies and other object flows via regular operations (heap loads and stores) and reflective actions. Also, in order to be effective, static modelling of proxies needs full treatment of other program semantics such as flow of string constants.

3.3 Hybrid Analysis

Several studies have focused on improving the recall of static analysis by adding information obtained from a dynamic (pre-)analysis. Bodden et al. proposed *tamiflex* [8]. *Tamiflex* runs a dynamic analyses by on instrumented code. The tool logs all reflective calls and feeds this information into a static analysis, such as *soot*. Grech et al. [17] proposed *heapdl*, a tool similar to *tamiflex* that also uses heap snapshots to further improve recall (compared to *tamiflex*). *Mirror* by Liu et al. [25] is a hybrid analysis specifically developed to resolve reflective call sites while minimising false positives.

Andreasen et al. [4] used a hybrid approach that combines soundness testing, blended analysis, and delta debugging for systematically guiding improvements of soundness and precision of TAJS - a static analyser for JavaScript. Soundness testing is the process of comparing the analysis results obtained from a pure static analysis with the concrete states that are observed by a dynamic analysis, in order to observe unsoundness.

Sui et al. [37] extracted reflective call graph edges from stack traces obtained from GitHub issue trackers and Stack Overflow Q&A forums to supplement statically built call graphs. Using this method, they found several edges *doop* (with reflection analysis enabled) was not able to compute. Dietrich et al. [11] generalised this idea and discuss how to generate *soundness oracles* that can be used to examine the unsoundness of a static analysis.

3.4 Call Graph Construction

Many algorithms have been proposed to statically compute call graphs. A comparative study of some of those algorithms was presented by Tip and Palsberg [40]. Class Hierarchy Analysis (CHA) [18] is a classic call graph algorithm that takes class hierarchy information into account. It assumes that the type of a receiver object (at run time) is possibly any subtype of the declared type of the receiver object at the call site. CHA is imprecise, but fast. Rapid Type Analysis (RTA) extends CHA by taking class instantiation information into consideration, by restricting the possible runtime types to classes that are instantiated in the reachable part of the program [5]. Variable Type Analysis (VTA) models the assignments between different variables by generating subset constraints, and then propagates points-to sets of the specific runtime types of each variable along these constraints [38]. k-CFA analyses [34] add various levels of call site sensitivity to the analysis.

Murphy et al. [29] presented one of the earlier empirical studies in this space, which focused on comparing the results of applying 9 static analysis tools (including tools like GNU cflow) for extracting call graphs from 3 C sample programs. As a results, the extracted call graphs were found to vary in size, which makes them potentially unreliable for developers to use. While this was found for C call graph extractors, it is still likely that the same problem will apply to extractors in other languages. Lhoták [23] proposed tooling and an interchange format to represent and compare call graphs produced by different tools. We use the respective format in our work.

4   The Benchmark

4.1   Benchmark Structure

The benchmark is organised as a Maven[3] project using the standard project layout. The actual programs are organised in name spaces (packages) reflecting their category. Programs are minimalistic, and their behaviour is in most cases easy to understand for an experienced programmer by "just looking at the program". All programs have a `source()` method and one or more other methods, usually named `target(..)`.

Each program has an integrated oracle of expected program behaviour, encoded using standard Java annotations. Methods annotated with `@Source` are call graph sources: we consider the program behaviour triggered by the execution of those methods from an outside client. Methods annotated with `@Target` are methods that may or may not be invoked directly or indirectly from a call site in the method annotated with `@Source`. The expectation whether a target method is to be invoked or not is encoded in the `@Target` annotation's `expectation` attribute that can be one of three values: `Expected.YES` – the method is expected to be invoked , `Expected.NO` – the method is not expected to be invoked, or `Expected.MAYBE` – exactly one of the methods with this annotation is expected to be invoked, but which one may depend on the JVM to be used. For each program, *either* exactly one method is annotated with `@Target(expectation=Expected.YES)`, *or* some methods are annotated with `@Target(expectation=Expected.MAYBE`.

The benchmark contains a `Vanilla` program that defines the base case: a single source method that has a call site where the target method is invoked using a plain `invokevirtual` instruction. The annotated example is shown in Listing 1.1, this also illustrates the use of the oracle annotations.

---

[3] https://maven.apache.org/, accessed 30 August 2018.

```
1  public class Vanilla {
2      public boolean TARGET = false ;
3      public boolean TARGET2 = false ;
4      @Source public void source () {
5              target () ;
6      }
7      @Target ( expectation = YES) public void target () {
8              this .TARGET = true ;
9      }
10     @Target ( expectation = NO) public void target (int o) {
11             this .TARGET2 = true ;
12     }
13 }
```

Listing 1.1. Vanilla program source code (simplified)

The main purpose of the annotations is to facilitate the set up of experiments with static analysers. Since the annotations have a retention policy that makes them visible at runtime, the oracle to test static analysers can be easily inferred from the benchmark program. In particular, the annotations can be used to test for both FNs (soundness issues) and FPs (precision issues).

In Listing 1.1, the target method changes the state of the object by setting the TARGET flag. The purpose of this feature is to make invocations easily observable, and to confirm actual program behaviour by means of executing the respective programs by running a simple client implemented as a junit test. Listing 1.2 shows the respective test for Vanilla – we expect that after an invocation of source() by the test driver, target() will have been called after source() has returned , and we check this with an assertion check on the TARGET field. We also tests for methods that should not be called, by checking that the value of the respective field remains false.

```
1  public class VanillaTest {
2      private Vanilla vanilla ;
3      @Before public void setUp () throws Exception {
4          vanilla = new Vanilla () ;
5          vanilla . source () ;
6      }
7      @Test public void testTargetMethodBeenCalled () {
8          Assert . assertTrue ( vanilla .TARGET) ;
9      }
10     @Test public void testTarget2MethodHasNotBeenCalled () {
11         Assert . assertFalse ( vanilla .TARGET2) ;
12     }
13 }
```

Listing 1.2. Vanilla test case (simplified)

4.2 Dynamic Language Features and Vulnerabilities

One objective for benchmark construction was to select features that are of interest to static program analysis, as there are known vulnerabilities that exploit those features. Since the discussed features allow bypassing Java's security model, which relies on information-hiding, memory and type safety, Java security vulnerabilities involving their use have been reported that have implications ranging from attacks on confidentiality, integrity and the availability of applications. Categorised under the Common Weakness Enumeration (CWE) classification, untrusted deserialisation, unsafe reflection, type confusion, untrusted pointer dereferences and buffer overflow vulnerabilities are the most notable.

CVE-2015-7450 is a well-known serialisation vulnerability in the Apache Commons Collections library. It lets an attacker execute arbitrary commands on a system that uses unsafe Java deserialisation. Use of reflection is common in vulnerabilities as discussed by Holzinger et al. [19] where the authors discover that 28 out of 87 exploits studied utilised reflection vulnerabilities. An example is CVE-2013-0431, affecting the Java JMX API, which allows loading of arbitrary classes and invoking their methods. CVE-2009-3869, CVE-2010-3552, CVE-2013-08091 are buffer overflow vulnerabilities involving the use of native methods. As for vulnerabilities that use the `Unsafe` API, CVE-2012-0507 is a vulnerability in `AtomicReferenceArray` which uses `Unsafe` to store a reference in an array directly that can violate type safety and permit escaping the sandbox. CVE-2016-4000 and CVE-2015-3253 reported for Jython and Groovy are due to serialisable invocation handlers for proxy instances. While we are not aware of vulnerabilities that exploit invokedynamic directly, there are several CVEs that exploit the method handle API used in the invokedynamic bootstrapping process, including CVE-2012-5088, CVE-2013-2436 and CVE-2013-0422.

The following subsections contain a high-level discussion of the various categories of programs in the benchmark. A detailed discussion of each program is not possible within the page limit, the reader is referred to the benchmark repository for more details.

4.3 Reflection

Java's reflection protocol is widely used and it is the foundation for many frameworks. With reflection, classes can be dynamically instantiated, fields can be accessed and manipulated, and methods can be invoked. How easily reflection can be modelled by a static analysis highly depends on the *usage context*. In particular, a reflective call site for *Method.invoke* can be easily handled if the parameter at the method access site (i.e., the call site of `Class.getMethod` or related methods) are known, for instance, if method name and parameter types can be inferred. Existing static analysis support is based on this wider idea.

However, this is not always possible. The data needed to accurately identify an invoked method might be supplied by other methods (therefore, the static analysis must be inter-procedural to capture this), only partially available (e.g., if only the method name can safely be inferred, a static analysis may decide to over-approximate the call graph and create edges for all possible methods with this name), provided through external resources (a popular pattern in enterprise frameworks like spring, service loaders, or JEE web applications), or some custom procedural code. All of those usage patterns do occur in practice [22,24], and while exotic uses of reflection might be rare, they are also the most interesting ones as they might be used in the kind of vulnerabilities static analysis is interested to find.

The benchmark examples reflect this range of usage patterns from trivial to sophisticated. Many programs overload the target method, this is used to test whether a static analysis tool achieves sound reflection handling at the price of precision.

4.4 Reflection with Ambiguous Resolution

As discussed in Sect. 2, we also consider scenarios where a program is (at least partially) not generated by `javac`. Since at byte code level methods are identified by a combination of name and descriptor, the JVM supports return type overloading, and the compiler uses this, for instance, in order to support covariant return types [16, Sect. 8.4.5] by generating bridge methods. This raises the question how the methods in `java.lang.Class` used to locate methods resolve ambiguity as they use only name and parameter types, but not the return type, as parameters. According to the respective class documentation, "If more than one method with the same parameter types is declared in a class, and one of these methods has a return type that is more specific than any of the others, that method is returned; otherwise one of the methods is chosen arbitrarily"[4]. In case of return type overloading used in bridge methods, this rule still yields an unambiguous result, but one can easily engineer byte code where the arbitrary choice clause applies. The benchmark contains a respective example, `dpbbench.ambiguous.ReturnTypeOverloading`. There are two target methods, one returning `java.util.Set` and one returning `java.util.List`. Since neither return type is a subtype of the other type, the JVM is free to choose either. In this case we use the `@Target (expectation=MAYBE)` annotation to define the oracle. We acknowledge that the practical relevance of this might be low at the moment, but we included this scenario as it highlights that the concept of possible program behaviour used as ground truth to assess the soundness of static analysis is not as clear as it is widely believed. Here, possible program executions can be defined either with respect to all or some JVMs.

It turns out that Oracle JRE 1.8.0_144/OpenJDK JRE 1.8.0_40 on the one hand and IBM JRE 1.8.0_171 on the other hand actually do select different methods here. We have also observed that IBM JRE 1.8.0_171 chooses the incorrect method in the related `dpbbench.reflection.invocation.` `ReturnTypeOverloading` scenario (note the different package name). In this scenario, the overloaded target methods return `java.util.Collection` and `java.util.List`, respectively, and the IBM JVM dispatches to the method

---

[4] https://goo.gl/JG9qD2, accessed 24 May 2018.

returning `java.util.Collection` in violation of the rule stipulated in the API specification. We reported this as a bug, and it was accepted and fixed report[5].

A similar situation occurs when the selection of the target method depends on the order of annotations returned via the reflective API. This scenario does occur in practice, for instance, the use of this pattern in the popular *log4j* library is discussed in [37]. The reflection API does not impose constraints on the order of annotations returned by `java.lang.reflect.Method.getDeclaredAnnotations()`, therefore, programs have different possible executions for different JVMs.

```
1  public class Invocation {
2      public boolean TARGET = false;
3      public boolean TARGET2 = false;
4      @Retention(RUNTIME) @Target(METHOD) @interface Method{}
5      @Source public void source() throws Exception {
6          for (Method method: Invocation.class.getDeclaredMethods()){
7              if (method.isAnnotationPresent(Method.class)){
8                  method.invoke(this, null);
9                  return;
10     }   }   } }
11     @Method @Target (expectation=MAYBE) public void target(){
12         this.TARGET =true;
13     }
14     @Method @Target (expectation=MAYBE) public void target2(){
15         this.TARGET2 =true;
16     }
17 }
```

Listing 1.3. Example where the selection of the target method depends on the JVM being used (simplified)

When executing those two examples and recording the actual call graphs, we observe that the call graphs differ depending on the JVM being used. For instance, in the program in Listing 1.3, the target method selected at the call site in `source()` is `target()` for both Oracle JRE 1.8.0_144 and OpenJDK JRE 1.8.0_40 , and `target2()` for IBM JRE 1.8.0_171.

4.5 Dynamic Classloading

Java distinguishes between classes and class loaders. This can be used to dynamically load, or even generate classes at runtime. This is widely used in practice, in particular for frameworks that compile embedded scripting or domain-specific languages "on the fly", such as Xalan[6].

There is a single example in the benchmark that uses a custom classloader to load and instantiate a class. The constructors of the respective class are the expected target methods.

---

[5] https://github.com/eclipse/openj9/pull/2240, accessed 16 August 2018.
[6] https://xalan.apache.org, accessed 4 June 2018.

4.6   Dynamic Proxies

Dynamic proxies were introduced in Java 1.3, they are similar to protocols like Smalltalk's doesNotUnderstand, they capture calls to unimplemented methods via an invocation handler. A major application is to facilitate distributed object frameworks like CORBA and RMI, but dynamic proxies are also used in mock testing frameworks. For example, in the *XCorpus* dataset of 75 real-world programs, 13 use dynamic proxies [10] (implement InvocationHandler and have call sites for Proxy.newProxyInstance). Landman et al. observed that "all [state-of-the-art static analysis] tools assume .. absence of Proxy classes" [22].

The benchmark contains a single program in the dynamicProxy category. In this program, the source method invokes an interface method foo() through an invocation handler. In the invocation handler, target(String) is invoked. The target method is overloaded in order to test the precision of the analysis.

4.7   Invokedynamic

The invokedynamic instruction was introduced in Java 7. It gives the user more control over the method dispatch process by using a user-defined bootstrap method that computes the call target. While the original motivation behind invokedynamic was to provide support for dynamic languages like Ruby, its main (and in the OpenJDK 8, only) application is to provide support for lambdas. In OpenJDK 9, invokedynamic is also used for string concatenation [33].

For known usage contexts, support for invokedynamic is possible. If invokedynamic is used with the LambdaMetafactory, then a tool can rewrite this byte code, for instance, by using an alternative byte code sequence that compiles lambdas using anonymous inner classes. The Opal byte code rectifier [1] is based on this wider idea, and can be used as a standalone pre-processor for static analysis. The rewritten byte code can then be analysed "as usual".

The benchmark contains three examples defined by Java sources with different uses of lambdas. The fourth examples is engineered from byte code and is an adapted version of the dynamo compiler example from [20]. Here, invokedynamic is used for a special compilation of component boundary methods in order to improve binary compatibility. The intention of including this example is to distinguish between invokedynamic for particular usage patterns, and general support for invokedynamic.

4.8   Serialisation

Java serialisation is a feature that is used in order to export object graphs to streams, and vice versa. This is a highly controversial feature, in particular after a large number of serialisation-related vulnerabilities were reported in recent years [9,19].

The benchmark contains a single program in this category that relates to the fact that (de-)serialisation offers an extra-linguistic mechanism to construct objects, avoiding constructors. The scenario constructs an object from a stream, and then invokes a method on this object. The client class is not aware of the actual type of the receiver object, as the code contains no allocation site.

4.9   JNI

The Java Native Interface (JNI) is a framework that enables Java to call and be called by native applications. There are two programs using JNI in the benchmark. The first scenario uses a custom `Runnable` to be started by `Thread.start`. In the Java 8 (OpenJDK 8), `Runnable.run` is invoked by `Thread.start` via an intermediate native method `Thread.start0()`. This is another scenario that can be handled by static analysis tools that can deal with common usage patterns, rather than with the general feature. The second program is a custom example that uses a grafted method implemented in C.

4.10   sun.misc.Unsafe

The class `sun.misc.Unsafe` (unsafe for short) offers several low level APIs that can bypass constraints built into standard APIs. Originally intended to facilitate the implementation of platform APIs, and to provide an alternative for JNI, this feature is now widely used outside the Java platform libraries [28]. The benchmark contains four programs in this category, (1) using unsafe to load a class (`defineClass`), (2) to throw an exception (`throwException`), (3) to allocate an instance (`allocateInstance`) and (4) to swap references (`putObject`, `objectFieldOffset`). leads to an error that was r

5   Experiments

5.1   Methodology

We conducted an array of experiments with the benchmark. In particular, we were interested to see whether the benchmark examples were suitable to differentiate the capabilities of mainstream static analysis frameworks. We selected three frameworks based on (1) their wide use in the community, evidenced by citation counts of core papers, indicating that the respective frameworks are widely used, and therefore issues in those frameworks will have a wider impact on the research community, (2) the respective frameworks claim to have some support for dynamic language features, in particular reflection, (3) the respective projects are active, indicating that the features of those frameworks will continue to have an impact.

Based on those criteria, we evaluated *soot-3.1.0*, *doop*[7] and *wala-1.4.3*. For each tool, we considered a basic configuration, and an advanced configuration to switch on support for advanced language features. All three tools have options

---

[7] As doop does not release versions, we used a version built from commit 4a94ae3bab4edcdba068b35a6c0b8774192e59eb.

to switch those features on. This reflects the fact that advanced analysis is not free, but usually comes at the price of precision and scalability.

Using these analysers, we built call graphs using a mid-precision, context-insensitive variable type analysis. Given the simplicity of our examples, where each method has at most one call site, we did not expect that context sensitivity would have made a difference. To the contrary, a context-sensitive analysis computes a smaller call graph, and would therefore have reduced the recall of the tool further. On the other hand, a less precise method like CHA could have led to a misleading higher recall caused by the accidental coverage of target methods as FPs.

For *wala*, we used the 0-CFA call graph builder. By default, we set `com.ibm.wala.ipa.callgraph.AnalysisOptions.ReflectionOptions` to `NONE`, in the advanced configuration used, it was set to `FULL`.

For *soot*, we used spark (`"cg.spark=enabled,cg.spark=vta"`). For the advanced configuration, we also used the `"safe-forname"` and the `"safe-newinstance"` options. There is another option to support the resolution of reflective call sites, `types-for-invoke`. Enabling this option leads to an error that was reported, but at the time of writing this issue has not yet been resolved[8].

For *doop*, we used the following options: `context-insensitive`, `ignore-mainmethod`, `only-application-classes-fact-gen`. For the advanced configuration, we also enabled `reflection reflection-classic reflection-high-soundness-mode reflection-substring-analysis reflection-invent-unknownobjects reflection-refined-objects` and `reflection-specula tive-use-based-analysis`.

We did not consider any hybrid pre-analysis, such as *tamiflex* [8], this was outside the scope of this study. This will be discussed in more detail in Sect. 5.3.

The experiments were set up as follows: for each benchmark program, we used a lightweight byte code analysis to extract the oracle from the `@Target` annotations. Then we computed the call graph with the respective static analyser using the method annotated as `@Source` as entry point, and stored the result in probe format [23]. Finally, using the call graph, we computed the FPs and FNs of the static call graph with respect to the oracle, using the annotations as the ground truth. For each combination of benchmark program and static analyser, we computed a *result state* depending on the annotations found in the methods reachable from the `@Source`-annotated method in the computed call graph as defined in Table 1. For instance, the state ACC (for accurate) means that in the computed call graph, all methods annotated with `@Target(expectation=YES)` and none of the methods annotated with `@Target(expectation=NO)` are reachable from the method annotated with `@Source`. The FP and FN indicate the presence of false positive (imprecision) and false negatives (unsoundness), respectively, the FN+FP state indicates that the results of the static analysis are both unsound and imprecise. Reachable means that there is a path. This is slightly more gen-

---

[8] https://groups.google.com/forum/m/#!topic/soot-list/xQwsU7DlmqM, accessed 5 June 2018.

eral than looking for an edge and takes the fact into account that a particular JVM might use intermediate methods to implement a certain dynamic invocation pattern.

Table 1. Result state definitions for programs with consistent behaviour across different JVMs

Result	Methods reachable from source by annotation	
State	@Target(expectation=YES)	@Target(expectation=NO)
ACC	All	None
FP	All	Some
FN	None	None
FN+FP	None	Some

Figure 1(a) illustrates this classification. As discussed in Sect. 4.4, there are programs that use the @Target(expectation=MAYBE) annotation, indicating that actual program behaviour is not defined by the specification, and depends on the JVM being used. This is illustrated in Fig. 1(b).

For the programs that use the @Target(expectation=MAYBE) annotation, we had to modify this definition according to the semantics of the annotation: during execution, exactly one of these methods will be invoked, but it is up to the particular JVM to decide which one. We define result states as shown in Table 2. Note that the @Target(expectation=YES) and the @Target(expectation=MAYBE) annotations are never used for the same program, and there is at most one method annotated with @Target(expectation=YES) in a program.

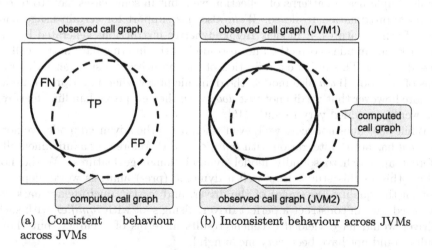

(a) Consistent   behaviour   across JVMs

(b) Inconsistent behaviour across JVMs

Fig. 1. Observed vs computed call graph

This definition is very lenient - we assess the results of a static analyser as sound (ACC or FP) if it does compute a path that links the source with *any* possible target. This means that soundness is defined with respect to the behaviour observed with only *some, but not all*, JVMs.

Table 2. Result state definition for programs with behaviour that depends on the JVM

Result	Methods reachable from source by annotation	
State	`@Target(expectation=MAYBE)`	`@Target(expectation=NO)`
ACC	Some	None
FP	Some	Some
FN	None	None
FN+FP	None	Some

5.2   Reproducing Results

The benchmark and the scripts used to obtain the results can be found in the following public repository: https://bitbucket.org/Li_Sui/benchmark/. Further instructions can be found in the repository `README.md` file.

5.3   Results and Discussion

Results are summarised in Table 3. As expected, none of the static analysers tested handled all features soundly. For *wala* and *doop*, there are significant differences between the plain and the advanced modes. In the advanced mode, both handle simple usage patterns of reflection well, but in some cases have to resort to over-approximation to do so. *Wala* also has support for certain usage patterns of other features: it models `invokedynamic` instructions generated by the compiler for lambdas correctly, and also models the intermediate native call in `Thread.start`. This may be a reflection of the maturity and stronger industrial focus of the tool. *Wala* also models the dynamic proxy when in advanced mode. We note however that we did not test *doop* with the new proxy-handling features that were just added very recently [15].

While *soot* does not score well, even when using the advanced mode, we note that *soot* has better integration with *tamiflex* and therefore uses a fundamentally different approach to soundly model dynamic language features. We did not include this in this study. How well a dynamic (pre-) analysis works depends a lot on the quality (coverage) of the driver, and for the micro-benchmark we have used we can construct a perfect driver. Using soot with *tamiflex* with such a driver would have yielded excellent results in terms of accuracy, but those results would not have been very meaningful.

None of the frameworks handles any of the `Unsafe` scenarios well. There is one particular program where all analysers compute the wrong call graph edge:

the target method is called on a field that is initialised as new Target(), but between the allocation and the invocation of target() the field value is swapped for an instance of another type using Unsafe.putObject. While this scenario appears far-fetched, we note that Unsafe is widely used in libraries [28], and has been exploited (see Sect. 4.2).

Table 3. Static call graph construction evaluation results, reporting the number of programs with the respective result state, format: (number obtained with basic configuration)/(number obtained with advanced configuration)

Category	Analyser	ACC	FN	FP	FN+FP
Vanilla	soot	1/1	0/0	0/0	0/0
	wala	1/1	0/0	0/0	0/0
	doop	1/1	0/0	0/0	0/0
Reflection	soot	0/1	12/11	0/0	0/0
	wala	0/4	12/3	0/5	0/0
	doop	0/0	12/8	0/4	0/0
Dynamic class loading	soot	0/0	1/1	0/0	0/0
	wala	0/0	1/1	0/0	0/0
	doop	0/0	1/1	0/0	0/0
Dynamic proxy	soot	0/0	1/1	0/0	0/0
	wala	0/1	1/0	0/0	0/0
	doop	0/0	1/1	0/0	0/0
Invokedynamic	soot	0/0	4/4	0/0	0/0
	wala	3/3	1/1	0/0	0/0
	doop	0/0	4/4	0/0	0/0
JNI	soot	1/1	1/1	0/0	0/0
	wala	1/1	1/1	0/0	0/0
	doop	0/0	2/2	0/0	0/0
Serialisation	soot	1/1	0/0	0/0	0/0
	wala	1/1	0/0	0/0	0/0
	doop	0/0	1/1	0/0	0/0
Unsafe	soot	0/0	2/2	1/1	1/1
	wala	0/0	2/2	1/1	1/1
	doop	0/0	2/2	1/1	1/1
Reflection-ambiguous	soot	0/0	2/2	0/0	0/0
	wala	0/0	2/0	0/2	0/0
	doop	0/0	2/1	0/1	0/0

6   Conclusion

In this paper, we have presented a micro-benchmark that describes the usage of dynamic language features in Java, and an experiment to assess how popular static analysis tools support those features. It is not surprising that in many cases the constructed call graphs miss edges, or only achieve soundness by compromising on precision.

The results indicate that it is important to distinguish between the actual features, and a usage context for those features. For instance, there is a significant difference between supporting `invokedynamic` as a general feature, and `invokedynamic` as it is used by the Java 8 compiler for lambdas. The benchmark design and the results of the experiments highlights this difference.

We do not expect that static analysis tools will support all of those features and provide a sound and precise call graph in the near future. Instead, many tools will continue to focus on particular usage patterns such as "support for reflection used in the Spring framework", which have the biggest impact on actual programs, and therefore should be prioritised. However, as discussed using examples throughout the paper, more exotic usage patterns do occur, and can be exploited, so they should not be ignored. The benchmark can provide some guidance for tool builders here.

An interesting insight coming out of this study is that notions like *actual programs behaviour* and *possible program executions* are not as clearly defined as widely thought. This is particularly surprising in the context of Java (even in programs that do not use randomness, concurrency or native methods), given the strong focus of the Java platform on writing code once, and run it anywhere with consistent program behaviour. This has implications for the very definitions of soundness and precision. We have suggested a pragmatic solution, but we feel that a wider discussion of these issues is needed.

Acknowledgement. We thank Paddy Krishnan, Francois Gauthier and Michael Eichberg for their comments.

References

1. Invokedynamic rectifier/project serializer. http://www.opal-project.de/Developer Tools.html
2. The Java language specification. https://docs.oracle.com/javase/specs
3. SPECjvm2008 benchmark. www.spec.org/jvm2008
4. Andreasen, E.S., Møller, A., Nielsen, B.B.: Systematic approaches for increasing soundness and precision of static analyzers. In: Proceedings of SOAP 2017. ACM (2017)
5. Bacon, D.F., Sweeney, P.F.: Fast static analysis of c++ virtual function calls. In: Proceedings of the OOPSLA 1996. ACM (1996)
6. Blackburn, S.M., et al.: The DaCapo benchmarks: Java benchmarking development and analysis. In: Proceedings of the OOPSLA 2006. ACM (2006)
7. Bodden, E.: Invokedynamic support in soot. In: Proceedings of the SOAP 2012. ACM (2012)

8. Bodden, E., Sewe, A., Sinschek, J., Oueslati, H., Mezini, M.: Taming reflection: aiding static analysis in the presence of reflection and custom class loaders. In: Proceedings of the ICSE 2011. ACM (2011)

9. Dietrich, J., Jezek, K., Rasheed, S., Tahir, A., Potanin, A.: Evil pickles: DoS attacks based on object-graph engineering. In: Proceedings of the ECOOP 2017. LZI (2017)

10. Dietrich, J., Schole, H., Sui, L., Tempero, E.: XCorpus-an executable corpus of Java programs. JOT 16(4), 1:1–24 (2017)

11. Dietrich, J., Sui, L., Rasheed, S., Tahir, A.: On the construction of soundness oracles. In: Proceedings of the SOAP 2017. ACM (2017)

12. Dolby, J., Fink, S.J., Sridharan, M.: T.J. Watson Libraries for Analysis (2015). http://wala.sourceforge.net

13. Ernst, M.D.: Static and dynamic analysis: synergy and duality. In: Proceedings of the WODA 2003 (2003)

14. Foote, B., Johnson, R.E.: Reflective facilities in Smalltalk-80. In: Proceedings of the OOPSLA 1989. ACM (1989)

15. Fourtounis, G., Kastrinis, G., Smaragdakis, Y.: Static analysis of Java dynamic proxies. In: Proceedings of the ISSTA 2018. ACM (2018)

16. Gosling, J., Joy, B., Steele, G., Bracha, G., Buckley, A.: The Java Language Specification. Java Series, Java SE 8 edn. Addison-Wesley Professional, Boston (2014)

17. Grech, N., Fourtounis, G., Francalanza, A., Smaragdakis, Y.: Heaps don't lie: countering unsoundness with heap snapshots. In: Proceedings of the OOPSLA 2017. ACM (2017)

18. Grove, D., DeFouw, G., Dean, J., Chambers, C.: Call graph construction in object-oriented languages. In: Proceedings of the OOPSLA 1997. ACM (1997)

19. Holzinger, P., Triller, S., Bartel, A., Bodden, E.: An in-depth study of more than ten years of Java exploitation. In: Proceedings of the CCS 2016. ACM (2016)

20. Jezek, K., Dietrich, J.: Magic with dynamo-flexible cross-component linking for Java with invokedynamic. In: Proceedings of the ECOOP 2016. LZI (2016)

21. Kiczales, G., Hilsdale, E., Hugunin, J., Kersten, M., Palm, J., Griswold, W.G.: An overview of AspectJ. In: Knudsen, J.L. (ed.) ECOOP 2001. LNCS, vol. 2072, pp. 327–354. Springer, Heidelberg (2001). https://doi.org/10.1007/3-540-45337-7_18

22. Landman, D., Serebrenik, A., Vinju, J.J.: Challenges for static analysis of Java reflection-literature review and empirical study. In: Proceedings of the ICSE 2017. IEEE (2017)

23. Lhoták, O.: Comparing call graphs. In: Proceedings of the PASTE 2007. ACM (2007)

24. Li, Y., Tan, T., Sui, Y., Xue, J.: Self-inferencing reflection resolution for Java. In: Jones, R. (ed.) ECOOP 2014. LNCS, vol. 8586, pp. 27–53. Springer, Heidelberg (2014). https://doi.org/10.1007/978-3-662-44202-9_2

25. Liu, J., Li, Y., Tan, T., Xue, J.: Reflection analysis for Java: uncovering more reflective targets precisely. In: Proceedings of the ISSRE 2017. IEEE (2017)

26. Livshits, B., Sridharan, M., Smaragdakis, Y., Lhoták, O., Amaral, J.N., Chang, B.Y.E., Guyer, S.Z., Khedker, U.P., Møller, A., Vardoulakis, D.: In defense of soundiness: a manifesto. CACM 58(2), 44–46 (2015)

27. Livshits, B., Whaley, J., Lam, M.S.: Reflection analysis for Java. In: Yi, K. (ed.) APLAS 2005. LNCS, vol. 3780, pp. 139–160. Springer, Heidelberg (2005). https://doi.org/10.1007/11575467_11

28. Mastrangelo, L., Ponzanelli, L., Mocci, A., Lanza, M., Hauswirth, M., Nystrom, N.: Use at your own risk: the Java unsafe API in the wild. In: Proceedings of the OOPSLA 2015. ACM (2015)

29. Murphy, G.C., Notkin, D., Griswold, W.G., Lan, E.S.: An empirical study of static call graph extractors. ACM TOSEM **7**(2), 158–191 (1998)
30. Reif, M., Kübler, F., Eichberg, M., Mezini, M.: Systematic evaluation of the unsoundness of call graph construction algorithms for Java. In: Proceedings of the SOAP 2018. ACM (2018)
31. Rountev, A., Kagan, S., Gibas, M.: Evaluating the imprecision of static analysis. In: Proceedings of the PASTE 2004. ACM (2004)
32. Ryder, B.G.: Constructing the call graph of a program. IEEE TSE **3**, 216–226 (1979)
33. Shipilev, A.: JEP 280: indify string concatenation. http://openjdk.java.net/jeps/280
34. Shivers, O.: Control-flow analysis of higher-order languages. Ph.D. thesis, Carnegie Mellon University (1991)
35. Smaragdakis, Y., Balatsouras, G., Kastrinis, G., Bravenboer, M.: More sound static handling of Java reflection. In: Feng, X., Park, S. (eds.) APLAS 2015. LNCS, vol. 9458, pp. 485–503. Springer, Cham (2015). https://doi.org/10.1007/978-3-319-26529-2_26
36. Smith, B.C.: Reflection and semantics in LISP. In: Proceedings of the POPL 1984. ACM (1984)
37. Sui, L., Dietrich, J., Tahir, A.: On the use of mined stack traces to improve the soundness of statically constructed call graphs. In: Proceedings of the APSEC 2017. IEEE (2017)
38. Sundaresan, V., et al.: Practical virtual method call resolution for Java. In: Proceedings of the OOPSLA 2000. ACM (2000)
39. Tempero, E., Anslow, C., Dietrich, J., Han, T., Li, J., Lumpe, M., Melton, H., Noble, J.: Qualitas corpus: a curated collection of Java code for empirical studies. In: Proceedings of the APSEC 2010 (2010)
40. Tip, F., Palsberg, J.: Scalable propagation-based call graph construction algorithms. In: Proceedings of the OOPSLA 2000. ACM (2000)

Complexity Analysis of Tree Share Structure

Xuan-Bach Le[1]([⊠]), Aquinas Hobor[2,3], and Anthony W. Lin[1]

[1] University of Oxford, Oxford, UK
bachdylan@gmail.com
[2] Yale-NUS College, Singapore, Singapore
[3] National University of Singapore, Singapore, Singapore

Abstract. The tree share structure proposed by Dockins et al. is an elegant model for tracking disjoint ownership in concurrent separation logic, but decision procedures for tree shares are hard to implement due to a lack of a systematic theoretical study. We show that the first-order theory of the full Boolean algebra of tree shares (that is, with all tree-share constants) is decidable and has the same complexity as of the first-order theory of Countable Atomless Boolean Algebras. We prove that combining this additive structure with a constant-restricted unary multiplicative "relativization" operator has a non-elementary lower bound. We examine the consequences of this lower bound and prove that it comes from the combination of both theories by proving an upper bound on a generalization of the restricted multiplicative theory in isolation.

1 Introduction

One general challenge in concurrent program verification is how to specify the ownership of shared resources among threads. A common solution is to tag shared resources with *fractional shares* that track "how much" of a resource is owned by an actor. A *policy* maps ownership quanta with permitted behaviour. For example, a memory cell can be "fully owned" by a thread, permitting both reading and writing; "partially owned", permitting only reading; or "unowned", permitting nothing; the initial model of fractional shares [8] was rationals in $[0, 1]$. Since their introduction, many program logics have used a variety of flavors of fractional permissions to verify programs [2, 3, 7, 8, 14, 15, 18, 24, 26, 33, 37, 38].

Rationals do not mix cleanly with concurrent separation logic [31] because they do not preserve the "disjointness" property of separation logic [32]. Dockins *et al.* [13] proposed a "tree share" model that do preserve this property, and so a number of program logics have incorporated them [2, 18, 19, 26, 37].

In addition to their good metatheoretic properties, tree shares have desirable computational properties, which has enabled several highly-automated verification tools to incorporate them [20, 37] via heuristics and decision procedures [25, 28]. As we shall explain in Sect. 2.2, tree shares have both "additive" and "multiplicative" substructures. All of the verification tools used only

© Springer Nature Switzerland AG 2018
S. Ryu (Ed.): APLAS 2018, LNCS 11275, pp. 89–108, 2018.
https://doi.org/10.1007/978-3-030-02768-1_5

a restricted fragment of the additive substructure (in particular, with only one quantifier alternation) because the general theory's computational structure was not well-understood. These structures are worthy of further study both because even short programs can require hundreds of tree share entailment queries in the permitted formalism [16, Chap. 4: Sects. 2, 6.4, 6.6], and because recent program logics have shown how the multiplicative structures aid program verification [2, 26].

Recently, Le *et al.* did a more systematic analysis of the computational complexity of certain classes of tree share formulae [27]; briefly:

- the additive structure forms a Countable Atomless Boolean Algebra, giving a well-understood complexity for all first-order formulae *so long as they only use the distinguished constants* "empty" **0** and "full" **1**;
- the multiplicative structure has a decidable existential theory but an undecidable first-order theory; and
- the additive theory in conjunction with a weakened version of the multiplicative theory—in particular, only permitting multiplication by constants on the right-hand side—regained first-order decidability.

Contributions. We address significant gaps in our theoretical understanding of tree shares that deter their use in automated tools for more sophisticated tasks.

Section 3. Moving from a restricted fragment of a first-order additive theory to the more general setting of unrestricted first-order formulae over Boolean operations is intuitively appealing due to the increased expressibility of the logic. This expressibility even has computational consequences, as we demonstrate by using it to remove a common source of quantifier alternations. However, verifications in practice often require formulae that incorporate more general constants than **0** and **1**, limiting the application of the analysis from [27] in practice. This is unsurprising since it is true in other settings: many Presburger formulae that arise in engineering contexts, for example, are littered with application-specific constants, *e.g.*, $\forall x.(\exists y.x + y = 7) \Rightarrow (x + 13 < 21)$. A recent benchmark using tree shares for program verification [28] supports this intuition: it made 16k calls in the supported first-order additive fragment, and 21.1% (71k/335k) of the constants used in practice were neither **0** nor **1**. Our main contribution on the additive side is to give a polynomial-time algorithm that reduces first-order additive formulae with arbitrary tree-share constants to first-order formulae using only **0** and **1**, demonstrating that the additive structure's exact complexity is $\mathsf{STA}(*, 2^{n^{O(1)}}, n)$-complete and closing the theory/practice gap between [27, 28].

Section 4. We examine the combined additive/restricted multiplicative theory proved decidable in [27]. We prove a nonelementary lower bound for this theory, via a reduction from the combined theory into the string structure with suffix successors and a prefix relation, closing the complexity gap in the theory.

Section 5. We investigate the reasons for, and mitigants to, the above nonelementary lower bound. First, we show that the first-order restricted-multiplicative theory on its own (*i.e.*, without the Boolean operators) has elementary complexity via an efficient isomorphism with strings equipped with prefix and suffix successors. Thus, the nonelementary behavior comes precisely from the combination of both theories. Lastly, we examine the kinds of formulae that we expect in practice—for example, those coming from biabduction problems discussed in [26]—and notice that they have elementary complexity.

The other sections of our paper support our contributions by (Sect. 2) overviewing tree shares, related work, and several basic complexity results; and by (Sect. 6) discussing directions for future work and concluding.

2   Preliminaries

Here we document the preliminaries for our result. Some are standard (Sect. 2.1) while others are specific to the domain of tree shares (Sects. 2.2, 2.3 and 2.4).

2.1   Complexity Preliminaries

We assume that the readers are familiar with basic concepts in computational complexity such as Turing machine, many-one reduction, space and time complexity classes such as NP and PSPACE. A problem is *nonelementary* if it cannot be solved by any deterministic Turing machine that can be time-bounded by one of the exponent functions $\exp(1) = 2^n, \exp(n + 1) = 2^{\exp(n)}$. Let A, R be complexity classes, a problem P is $\leq_R$-complete for A iff P is in A and every problem in A is many-one reduced into P via Turing machines in R. In addition, we use $\leq_{R\text{-lin}}$ to assert *linear reduction* that belongs to R and only uses linear space with respect to the problem's size. In particular, $\leq_{\log\text{-lin}}$ is linear log-space reduction. Furthermore, we denote $\mathsf{STA}(p(n), t(n), a(n))$ the class of alternating Turing machine [9] that uses at most $p(n)$ space, $t(n)$ time and $a(n)$ alternations between universal states and existential states or vice versa for input of length n. If any of the three bounds is not specified, we replace it with the symbol $*$, *e.g.* $\mathsf{STA}(*, 2^{n^{O(1)}}, n)$ is the class of alternating Turing machines that have exponential time complexity and use at most n alternations.

2.2   Overview of Tree Share Structure

A tree share is a binary tree with Boolean leaves ∘ (white leaf) and • (black leaf). Full ownership is represented by • and no ownership by ∘. For fractional ownership, one can use, *e.g.* $\widehat{\bullet\,\circ}$, to represent the left half-owned resource. Importantly and usefully, $\widehat{\circ\,\bullet}$ is a distinct tree share representing the other right half. We require tree shares are in canonical form, that is, any subtree $\widehat{\tau\,\tau}$ where

$\tau \in \{\bullet, \circ\}$ needs to be rewritten into τ. For example, both $\widehat{\bullet\ \circ}$ and the tree with leaves $\bullet\ \bullet\ \circ\ \circ\ \circ$ represent the same tree share but only the former tree is canonical and thus valid. As a result, the set of tree shares $\mathbb{T}$ is a strict subset of the set of all Boolean binary trees. Tree shares are equipped with Boolean operators $\sqcup$ (union), $\sqcap$ (intersection) and $\bar{\ }$ (complement). When applied to tree shares of height zero, *i.e.* $\{\bullet, \circ\}$, these operators give the same results as in the case of binary BA. Otherwise, our tree shares need to be unfolded and folded accordingly before and after applying the operators leaf-wise, *e.g.*

$$\overline{\widehat{\bullet\ \circ}} = \widehat{\circ\ \bullet} \qquad \widehat{\bullet\ \circ}\,\bullet \sqcup \widehat{\circ\ \circ}\,\bullet \cong \text{tree} \sqcup \text{tree} = \text{tree} \cong \widehat{\bullet\ \circ}\,\bullet.$$

The additive operator $\oplus$ can be defined using $\sqcup$ and $\sqcap$, *i.e.* disjoint union:

$$a \oplus b = c \stackrel{\text{def}}{=} a \sqcup b = c \wedge a \sqcap b = \circ.$$

Tree shares also have a multiplicative operator $\bowtie$ called "bowtie", where $\tau_1 \bowtie \tau_2$ is defined by replacing each black leaf $\bullet$ of τ_1 with an instance of τ_2, *e.g.*

$$\text{tree}(\bullet\ \circ\ \circ\ \bullet) \bowtie \widehat{\circ\ \bullet} = \text{tree}(\circ\ \bullet\ \circ\ \circ\ \circ\ \bullet).$$

While the $\oplus$ operator has standard additive properties such as commutativity, associativity and cancellativity, the $\bowtie$ operator enjoys the unit $\bullet$, is associative, injective over non-$\circ$ arguments, and distributes over $\{\sqcup, \sqcap, \oplus\}$ on the left [13]. However, $\bowtie$ is not commutative, *e.g.*:

$$\widehat{\bullet\ \circ} \bowtie \widehat{\circ\ \bullet} = \text{tree}(\circ\ \bullet\ \circ) \neq \text{tree}(\circ\ \bullet\ \circ) = \widehat{\circ\ \bullet} \bowtie \widehat{\bullet\ \circ}$$

The formalism of these binary operators can all be found in [13].

2.3 Tree Shares in Program Verification

Fractional permissions in general, or tree shares in particular, are integrated into separation logic to reason about ownership. In detail, the mapsto predicate $x \mapsto v$ is enhanced with the permission π, denoted as $x \xmapsto{\pi} v$, to assert that π is assigned to the address x associated with the value v. This notation of fractional mapsto predicate allows us to split and combine permissions conveniently using the additive operator $\oplus$ and disjoint conjunction $\star$:

$$x \xmapsto{\pi_1 \oplus \pi_2} v \dashv\vdash x \xmapsto{\pi_1} v \star x \xmapsto{\pi_2} v. \tag{1}$$

The key difference between tree share model $\langle \mathbb{T}, \oplus \rangle$ and rational model $\langle \mathbb{Q}, + \rangle$ is that the latter fails to preserve the disjointness property of separation logic. For instance, while the predicate $x \mapsto 1 \star x \mapsto 1$ is unsatisfiable, its rational version $x \xmapsto{0.5} 1 \star x \xmapsto{0.5} 1$, which is equivalent to $x \xmapsto{1} 1$ by (1), is satisfiable.

On the other hand, the tree share version $x \longmapsto \widehat{\overset{\bullet\ \circ}{\ \circ}} \star x \longmapsto \widehat{\overset{\bullet\ \circ}{\ \circ}}$ remains unsatisfiable as the sum $\widehat{\overset{\bullet}{\bullet}\circ} \oplus \widehat{\overset{\bullet}{\bullet}\circ}$ is undefined. Such defect of the rational model gives rise to the deformation of recursive structures or elevates the difficulties of modular reasoning, as first pointed out by [32].

Recently, Le and Hobor [26] proposed a proof system for disjoint permissions using the structure $\langle \mathbb{T}, \oplus, \bowtie \rangle$. Their system introduces the notion of predicate multiplication where $\pi \cdot P$ asserts that the permission π is associated with the predicate P. To split the permission, one can apply the following bi-entailment:

$$\pi \cdot P \dashv\vdash (\pi \bowtie \widehat{\overset{\bullet}{\bullet}\circ}) \cdot P \star (\pi \bowtie \widehat{\circ\overset{\bullet}{\bullet}}) \cdot P.$$

which requires the following property of tree shares to hold:

$$\forall \pi.\ \pi = (\pi \bowtie \widehat{\overset{\bullet}{\bullet}\circ}) \oplus (\pi \bowtie \widehat{\circ\overset{\bullet}{\bullet}}). \tag{2}$$

Note that the above property demands a combined reasoning of both $\oplus$ and $\bowtie$. While such property can be manually proved in theorem provers such as Coq [12] using inductive argument, it cannot be handled automatically by known tree share solvers [25,28] due to the shortness of theoretical insights.

2.4 Previous Results on the Computational Behavior of Tree Shares

The first sophisticated analysis of the computational properties of tree shares were done by Le *et al.* [27]. They showed that the structure $\langle \mathbb{T}, \sqcup, \sqcap, \bar{\cdot} \rangle$ is a Countable Atomless BA and thus is complete for the Berman complexity class $\mathsf{STA}(*, 2^{n^{O(1)}}, n)$—problems solved by alternating exponential-time Turing machines with unrestricted space and n alternations—*i.e.* the same complexity as the first-order theory over the reals $\langle \mathbb{R}, +, 0, 1 \rangle$ with addition but no multiplication [4]. However, this result is restrictive in the sense that the formula class only contains $\{\bullet, \circ\}$ as constants, whereas in practice it is desirable to permit arbitrary tree constants, *e.g.* $\exists a \exists b.\ a \sqcup b = \widehat{\overset{\bullet}{\bullet}\circ}$.

When the multiplication operator $\bowtie$ is incorporated, the computational nature of the language becomes harder. The structure $\langle \mathbb{T}, \bowtie \rangle$—without the Boolean operators—is isomorphic to word equations [27]. Accordingly, its first-order theory is undecidable while its existential theory is decidable with continuously improved complexity bounds currently at PSPACE and NP-hard (starting from Makanin's argument [29] in 1977 and continuing with *e.g.* [22]).

Inspired by the notion of "semiautomatic structures" [21], Le *et al.* [27] restricted $\bowtie$ to take only constants on the right-hand side, *i.e.* to a family of unary operators indexed by constants $\bowtie_\tau (x) \overset{\text{def}}{=} x \bowtie \tau$. Le *et al.* then examined $\mathcal{C} \overset{\text{def}}{=} \langle \mathbb{T}, \sqcup, \sqcap, \bar{\cdot}, \bowtie_\tau \rangle$. Note that the verification-sourced sentence (2) from Sect. 2.3 fits perfectly into $\mathcal{C}$: $\forall \pi.\ \pi = \bowtie_{\widehat{\overset{\bullet}{\bullet}\circ}} (\pi) \oplus \bowtie_{\widehat{\circ\overset{\bullet}{\bullet}}} (\pi)$. Le *et al.* encoded $\mathcal{C}$ into *tree-automatic structures* [6], i.e., logical structures whose constants can be encoded as trees, and domains and predicates finitely represented by tree automata. As a result, its first-order theory—with arbitrary tree constants—is decidable [5,6,36], but until our results in Sect. 4 the true complexity of $\mathcal{C}$ was unknown.

3 Complexity of Boolean Structure $\mathcal{A} \overset{\text{def}}{=} \langle \mathbb{T}, \sqcup, \sqcap, \overline{\cdot} \rangle$

Existing tree share solvers [25,28] only utilize the additive operator $\oplus$ in certain restrictive first-order segments. Given the fact that $\oplus$ is defined from the Boolean structure $\mathcal{A} = \langle \mathbb{T}, \sqcup, \sqcap, \overline{\cdot} \rangle$, it is compelling to establish the decidability and complexity results over the general structure $\mathcal{A}$. More importantly, operators in $\mathcal{A}$ can help reduce the complexity of a given formula. For example, consider the following separation logic entailment:

$$a \overset{\tau}{\mapsto} 1 \star a \mapsto \overset{\overset{\frown}{\bullet\,\bullet\,\circ}}{} \;\vdash\; a \mapsto \overset{\overset{\frown}{\bullet\,\circ}}{} 1 \star \top.$$

To check the above assertion, entailment solvers have to extract and verify the following corresponding tree share formula by grouping shares from same heap addresses using $\oplus$ and then applying equality checks:

$$\forall \tau \forall \tau'.\tau \oplus \overset{\overset{\frown}{\bullet\,\bullet\,\circ}}{} = \tau' \rightarrow \exists \tau''.\tau'' \oplus \overset{\overset{\frown}{\bullet\,\circ}}{} = \tau'.$$

By using Boolean operators, the above $\forall\exists$ formula can be simplified into a $\forall$ formula by specifying that either the share in the antecedent is not possible, or the share in the consequent is a 'sub-share' of the share in the antecedent:

$$\forall \tau.\; \neg(\tau \sqcap \overset{\overset{\frown}{\bullet\,\bullet\,\circ}}{} = \circ) \;\vee\; (\overset{\overset{\frown}{\bullet\,\circ}}{} \sqsubseteq \tau \oplus \overset{\overset{\frown}{\bullet\,\bullet\,\circ}}{}).$$

where the 'sub-share' relation $\sqsubseteq$ is defined using Boolean union:

$$a \sqsubseteq b \overset{\text{def}}{=} a \sqcup b = b.$$

In this section, we will prove the following precise complexity of $\mathcal{A}$:

Theorem 1. *The first-order theory of $\mathcal{A}$ is $\leq_{log}$-complete for $\mathsf{STA}(*, 2^{n^{O(1)}}, n)$, even if we allow arbitrary tree constants in the formulae.*

One important implication of the above result is that the same complexity result still holds even if the additive operator $\oplus$ is included into the structure:

Corollary 1. *The Boolean tree share structure with addition $\mathcal{A}_\oplus = \langle \mathbb{T}, \oplus, \sqcup, \sqcap, \overline{\cdot} \rangle$ is $\leq_{log}$-complete for $\mathsf{STA}(*, 2^{n^{O(1)}}, n)$, even with arbitrary tree constants in the formulae.*

Proof. Recall that $\oplus$ can be defined in term of $\sqcup$ and $\sqcap$ without additional quantifier variable:

$$a \oplus b = c \overset{\text{def}}{=} a \sqcup b = c \wedge a \sqcap b = \circ.$$

As a result, one can transform, in linear time, any additive constraint into Boolean constraint using the above definition. Hence the result follows.   □

Theorem 1 is stronger than the result in [27] which proved the same complexity but for restricted tree share constants in the formulae:

Proposition 1 ([27]). *The first-order theory of $\mathcal{A}$, where tree share constants are $\{\bullet, \circ\}$, is $\leq_{log}$-complete for $\mathsf{STA}(*, 2^{n^{O(1)}}, n)$.*

The hardness proof for lower bound of Theorem 1 is obtained directly from Proposition 1. To show that the same complexity holds for upper bound, we construct an $O(n^2)$ algorithm `flatten` (Algorithm 1) that transforms arbitrary tree share formula into an equivalent tree share formula whose constants are $\{\bullet, \circ\}$:

Lemma 1. *Suppose `flatten`$(\Phi) = \Phi'$. Then:*

1. Φ' *only contains $\{\bullet, \circ\}$ as constants.*
2. Φ *and Φ' have the same number of quantifier alternations.*
3. Φ *and Φ' are equivalent with respect to $\mathcal{A}$.*
4. `flatten` *is $O(n^2)$. In particular, if the size of Φ is n then Φ' has size $O(n^2)$.*

Proof of Theorem 1. The lower bound follows from Proposition 1. By Lemma 1, we can use `flatten` in Algorithm 1 to transform a tree formula Φ into an equivalent formula Φ' of size $O(n^2)$ that only contains $\{\bullet, \circ\}$ as constants and has the same number of quantifier alternations as in Φ. By Proposition 1, Φ' can be solved in $\mathsf{STA}(*, 2^{n^{O(1)}}, n)$. This proves the upper bound and thus the result follows. □

It remains to prove the correctness of Lemma 1. But first, we will provide a descriptive explanation for the control flow of `flatten` in Algorithm 1. On line 2, it checks whether the height of Φ, which is defined to be the height of the highest tree constant in Φ, is zero. If it is the case then no further computation is needed as Φ only contains $\{\bullet, \circ\}$ as constants. Otherwise, the shape s (Definition 1) is computed on line 4 to guide the subsequent decompositions. On lines 5–9, each atomic sub-formula Ψ is decomposed into sub-components according to the shape s by the function `split` described on lines 18–26. Intuitively, `split` decomposes a tree τ into subtrees (line 21–22) or a variables v into new variables with appropriate binary subscripts (line 23). On line 8, the formula Ψ is replaced with the conjunction of its sub-components $\bigwedge_{i=1}^{n} \Psi_i$. Next, each quantifier variable Qv in Φ is also replaced with a sequence of quantifier variables $Qv_1 \ldots Qv_n$ (lines 10–13). Finally, the modified formula Φ is returned as the result on line 14. The following example demonstrates the algorithm in action:

Example 1. Let $\Phi: \forall a \exists b.\ a \sqcup b = \overset{\wedge}{\underset{\bullet\ \bullet\ \circ}{}} \vee \neg(\bar{a} = \overset{\wedge}{\underset{\circ\ \bullet\ \circ}{}})$. Then `height`$(\Phi) = 2 > 0$ and its shape s is $\overset{\wedge\quad\wedge}{\underset{*\ *\ *\ *}{}}$. Also, Φ contains the following atomic sub-formulae:

$$\Psi:\ a \sqcup b = \overset{\wedge}{\underset{\bullet\ \circ\ \circ}{}} \quad \text{and} \quad \Psi':\ \bar{a} = \overset{\wedge}{\underset{\circ\ \bullet\ \circ}{}}.$$

After applying the `split` function to Ψ and Ψ' with shape s, we acquire the following components:

Algorithm 1. Flattening a Boolean tree share formula

1: **function** FLATTEN(Φ)
Require: Φ is a Boolean tree sentence
Ensure: Return an equivalent formula of height zero
2:    **if** height(Φ) = 0 **then return** Φ
3:    **else**
4:       let s be the shape of Φ
5:       **for** each atomic formula Ψ in Φ: $t^1 = t^2$ or t^1 op $t^2 = t^3$, op $\in \{\sqcup, \sqcap\}$ **do**
6:          $[t_1^i, \ldots t_n^i] \leftarrow$ SPLIT(t^i, s) for $i = 1 \ldots n$ ▷ n is the number of leaves in s
7:          $\Psi_i \leftarrow t_1^i = t_2^i$ or t_1^i op $t_2^i = t_3^i$ for $i = 1 \ldots n$
8:          $\Phi \leftarrow$ replace Ψ with $\bigwedge_{i=1}^n \Psi_i$
9:       **end for**
10:       **for** each quantifier Qv in Φ **do**
11:          $[v_1, \ldots, v_n] \leftarrow$ SPLIT(v, s)
12:          $\Phi \leftarrow$ replace Qv with $Qv_1 \ldots Qv_n$
13:       **end for**
14:       **return** Φ
15:    **end if**
16: **end function**
17:
18: **function** SPLIT(t, s)
Require: t is either a variable or a constant, s is a shape
Ensure: Return a list of decomposing components of t according to shape s
19:    **if** $s = *$ **then return** $[t]$
20:    **else let** $s = \widehat{s_0 \ s_1}$ **in**
21:       **if** t is • or ∘ **then return** concat(SPLIT(t, s_0), SPLIT(t, s_1))
22:       **else if** let $t = \widehat{t_1 \ t_2}$ **in then return** concat(SPLIT(t_0, s_0), SPLIT(t_1, s_1))
23:       **else** t is a variable **return** concat(SPLIT(t_0, s_0), SPLIT(t_1, s_1))
24:       **end if**
25:    **end if**
26: **end function**

---

1. $\Psi_1 : a_{00} \sqcup b_{00} = \bullet$, $\Psi_2 : a_{01} \sqcup b_{01} = \circ$, $\Psi_3 : a_{10} \sqcup b_{10} = \circ$, $\Psi_4 : a_{11} \sqcup b_{11} = \circ$.
2. $\Psi_1' : \overline{a_{00}} = \circ$, $\Psi_2' : \overline{a_{01}} = \circ$, $\Psi_3' : \overline{a_{10}} = \bullet$, $\Psi_4' : \overline{a_{11}} = \circ$.

The following result formula is obtained by replacing Ψ with $\bigwedge_{i=1}^4 \Psi_i$, Ψ' with $\bigwedge_{i=1}^4 \Psi_i'$, $\forall a$ with $\forall a_{00} \forall a_{01} \forall a_{10} \forall a_{11}$, and $\exists b$ with $\exists b_{00} \exists b_{01} \exists b_{10} \exists b_{11}$:

$$\forall a_{00} \forall a_{01} \forall a_{10} \forall a_{11} \exists b_{00} \exists b_{01} \exists b_{10} \exists b_{11}. \bigwedge_{i=1}^4 \Psi_i \vee \neg(\bigwedge_{i=1}^4 \Psi_i').$$

Definition 1 (Tree shape). *A shape of a tree τ, denoted by $\langle \tau \rangle$, is obtained by replacing its leaves with $*$, e.g. $\langle \widehat{\bullet \ \widehat{\bullet \ \circ}} \rangle = \widehat{* \ \widehat{* \ *}}$. The combined shape $s_1 \sqcup s_2$ is defined by overlapping s_1 and s_2, e.g. $\widehat{\widehat{* \ *} \ *} \sqcup \widehat{* \ \widehat{* \ *}} = \widehat{\widehat{* \ *} \ \widehat{* \ *}}$. The shape of a formula Φ, denoted by $\langle \Phi \rangle$, is the combined shape of its tree constants and $*$.*

Note that tree shapes are not canonical, otherwise all shapes are collapsed into a single shape $*$. We are now ready to prove the first three claims of Lemma 1:

Proof of Lemma 1.1, 1.2 and 1.3. Observe that the shape of each atomic sub-formula Ψ is 'smaller' than the shape of Φ, *i.e.* $\langle\Psi\rangle \sqcup \langle\Phi\rangle = \langle\Phi\rangle$. As a result, each formula in the decomposition of $\mathtt{split}(\Psi, \langle\Phi\rangle)$ always has height zero, *i.e.* its only constants are $\{\bullet, \circ\}$. This proves claim 1.

Next, recall that the number of quantifier alternations is the number of times where quantifiers are switched from $\forall$ to $\exists$ or vice versa. The only place that $\mathtt{flatten}$ modifies quantifiers is on line 12 in which the invariant for quantifier alternations is preserved. As a result, claim 2 is also justified.

We are left with the claim that $\mathtt{flatten}$ is $O(n^2)$ where n is the size of the input formula Φ. By a simple analysis of $\mathtt{flatten}$, it is essentially equivalent to show that the result formula has size $O(n^2)$. First, observe that the formula shape $\langle\Phi\rangle$ has size $O(n)$ and thus we need $O(n)$ decompositions for each atomic sub-formula Ψ and each quantifier variable Qv of Φ. Also, each component in the decomposition of Ψ (or Qv) has size at most the size of Ψ (or Qv). As a result, the size of the formula Φ' only increases by a factor of $O(n)$ compared to the size of Φ. Hence Φ' has size $O(n^2)$. $\qquad\square$

To prove claim 4, we first establish the following result about the $\mathtt{split}$ function. Intuitively, this lemma asserts that one can use $\mathtt{split}$ together with some tree shape s to construct an isomorphic Boolean structure whose elements are lists of tree shares:

Lemma 2. *Let* $\mathtt{split}_s \overset{\mathrm{def}}{=} \lambda\tau.\ \mathtt{split}(\tau, s)$, *e.g.* $\mathtt{split}_{\overset{\frown}{*\ *}}\ (\overset{\frown}{\bullet\ \circ}\ \bullet) = [\overset{\frown}{\bullet\ \circ}, \bullet, \bullet]$.

Then $\mathtt{split}_s$ *is an isomorphism from* $\mathcal{A}$ *to* $\mathcal{A}' = \langle\mathbb{T}^n, \sqcup', \sqcap', \bar{\cdot}'\rangle$ *where* n *is the number of leaves in* s *and each operator in* $\mathcal{M}'$ *is defined component-wise from the corresponding operator in* $\mathcal{A}$, *e.g.* $[a_1, a_2] \sqcup' [b_1, b_2] = [a_1 \sqcup a_2, b_1 \sqcup b_2]$.

Proof. W.l.o.g. we will only prove the case $s = \overset{\frown}{*\ *}$ as similar argument can be obtained for the general case. By inductive arguments, we can prove that $\mathtt{split}_s$ is a bijection from $\mathbb{T}$ to $\mathbb{T} \times \mathbb{T}$. Furthermore:

1. $\mathtt{split}_s(a)\ \diamond\ \underline{\mathtt{split}_s(b)} = \mathtt{split}_s(c)$ iff $a \diamond b = c$ for $\diamond \in \{\sqcup, \sqcap\}$.
2. $\mathtt{split}_s(\bar{\tau}) = \overline{\mathtt{split}_s(\tau)}$.

Hence $\mathtt{split}_s$ is an isomorphism from $\mathcal{A}$ to $\mathcal{A}' = \langle\mathbb{T} \times \mathbb{T}, \sqcup', \sqcap', \bar{\cdot}'\rangle$. $\qquad\square$

Proof of Lemma 1.4. By Lemma 2, the function $\mathtt{split}_s$ allows us to transform formulae in $\mathcal{A}$ into equivalent formulaes over tree share lists in $\mathcal{A}' = \langle\mathbb{T}^n, \sqcup', \sqcap', \bar{\cdot}'\rangle$. On the other hand, observe that formulae in $\mathcal{A}'$ can be rewritten into equivalent formulae in $\mathcal{A}$ using conjunctions and extra quantifier variables, *e.g.* $\exists a \forall b.\ a \sqcup' b = [\overset{\frown}{\circ\ \bullet}, \bullet]$ is equivalent to $\exists a_1 \exists a_2 \forall b_1 \forall b_2.\ a_1 \sqcup b_1 = \overset{\frown}{\circ\ \bullet} \wedge a_2 \sqcup b_2 = \bullet$. Hence the result follows. $\qquad\square$

The correctness of Lemma 1 is now fully justified. We end this section by pointing out a refined complexity result for the existential theory of $\mathcal{A}$, which corresponds to the satisfiability problem of quantifier-free formulae. Note that the number of quantifier alternations for this fragment is zero, and thus Theorem 1 only gives us an upper bound $\mathsf{STA}(*, 2^{n^{O(1)}}, 0)$, which is exponential time complexity. Instead, we can use Lemma 1 to acquire the precise complexity:

Corollary 2. *The existential theory of $\mathcal{A}$, with arbitrary tree share constants, is* NP-*complete.*

Proof. Recall a classic result that existential theory of Countably Atomless BAs is NP-complete [30]. As $\mathcal{A}$ belongs to this class, the lower bound is justified. To see why the upper bound holds, we use the function `flatten` to transform the input formula into standard BA formula and thus the result follows from Lemma 1. □

4   Complexity of Combined Structure $\mathcal{C} \overset{\text{def}}{=} \langle \mathbb{T}, \sqcup, \sqcap, \bar{\cdot}, \bowtie_\tau \rangle$

In addition to the Boolean operators in Sect. 3, recall from Sect. 2.2 that tree shares also possess a multiplicative operator $\bowtie$ that resembles the multiplication of rational permissions. As mentioned in Sect. 2.4, [27] showed that $\bowtie$ is isomorphic to string concatenation, implying that the first-order theory of $\langle \mathbb{T}, \bowtie \rangle$ is undecidable, and so of course the first-order theory of $\langle \mathbb{T}, \sqcup, \sqcap, \bar{\cdot}, \bowtie \rangle$ is likewise undecidable.

By restricting multiplication to have only constants on the right-hand side, however, *i.e.* to the family of unary operators $\bowtie_\tau (x) \overset{\text{def}}{=} x \bowtie \tau$, Le *et al.* showed that decidability of the first-order theory was restored for the combined structure $\mathcal{C} \overset{\text{def}}{=} \langle \mathbb{T}, \sqcup, \sqcap, \bar{\cdot}, \bowtie_\tau \rangle$. However, Le *et al.* were not able to specify any particular complexity class. In this section, we fill in this blank by proving that the first-order theory of $\mathcal{C}$ is nonelementary, *i.e.* that it cannot be solved by any resource-bound (space or time) algorithm:

Theorem 2. *The first-order theory of $\mathcal{C}$ is non-elementary.*

To prove Theorem 2, we reduce the binary string structure with prefix relation [11], which is known to be nonelementary, into $\mathcal{C}$. Here we recall the definition and complexity result of binary strings structure:

Proposition 2 ([11,35]). *Let $\mathcal{K} = \langle \{0,1\}^*, S_0, S_1, \preceq \rangle$ be the binary string structure in which $\{0,1\}^*$ is the set of binary strings, S_i is the successor function s.t. $S_i(s) = s \cdot i$, and $\preceq$ is the binary prefix relation s.t. $x \preceq y$ iff there exists z satisfies $x \cdot z = y$. Then the first-order theory of $\mathcal{K}$ is non-elementary.*

Before going into the technical detail, we briefly explain the many-one reduction from $\mathcal{K}$ into $\mathcal{C}$. The key idea is that the set of binary strings $\{0,1\}^*$ can be bijectively mapped into the set of *unary trees* $\mathcal{U}(\mathbb{T})$, trees that have exactly one black leaf, *e.g.* $\{\bullet, \widehat{\bullet\ \circ}, \widehat{\circ\ \bullet}, \widehat{\circ\ \widehat{\bullet\ \circ}}, \cdots \}$. For convenience, we use the symbol $\mathcal{L}$ to represent the left tree $\widehat{\bullet\ \circ}$ and $\mathcal{R}$ for the right tree $\widehat{\circ\ \bullet}$. Then:

Lemma 3. *Let g map $\langle\{0,1\}^*, S_0, S_1, \preceq\rangle$ into $\langle\mathbb{T}, \sqcup, \sqcap, \bar{\cdot}, \bowtie_r\rangle$ such that:*

1. $g(\epsilon) = \bullet$, $g(0) = \mathcal{L}$, $g(1) = \mathcal{R}$.
2. $g(b_1 \ldots b_n) = g(b_1) \bowtie \ldots \bowtie g(b_n)$, $b_i \in \{0, 1\}$.
3. $g(S_0) = \lambda s. \bowtie_{\mathcal{L}} (g(s))$, $g(S_1) = \lambda s. \bowtie_{\mathcal{R}} (g(s))$.
4. $g(x \preceq y) = g(y) \sqsubseteq g(x)$ where $\tau_1 \sqsubseteq \tau_2 \overset{\text{def}}{=} \tau_1 \sqcup \tau_2 = \tau_2$.

Then g is a bijection from $\{0,1\}^*$ to $\mathcal{U}(\mathbb{T})$, and $x \preceq y$ iff $g(y) \sqsubseteq g(x)$.

Proof. The routine proof that g is bijective is done by induction on the string length. Intuitively, the binary string s corresponds to the path from the tree root in $g(s)$ to its single black leaf, where 0 means 'go left' and 1 means 'go right'. For example, the tree $g(110) = \mathcal{R} \bowtie \mathcal{R} \bowtie \mathcal{L} = \widehat{\circ \bullet} \bowtie \widehat{\circ \bullet} \bowtie \widehat{\bullet \circ} = \overset{\frown}{\underset{\circ \ \ \bullet \ \circ}{\frown}}$ corresponds to the path right→right→left.

Now observe that if τ_1, τ_2 are unary trees then $\tau_1 \sqsubseteq \tau_2$ (*i.e.* the black-leaf path in τ_2 is a sub-path of the black-leaf path in τ_1) iff there exists a unary tree τ_3 such that $\tau_2 \bowtie \tau_3 = \tau_1$ (intuitively, τ_3 represents the difference path between τ_2 and τ_1). Thus $x \preceq y$ iff there exists z such that $xz = y$, iff $g(x) \bowtie g(z) = g(y)$, which is equivalent to $g(y) \sqsubseteq g(x)$ by the above observation. $\square$

In order for the reduction to work, we need to express the type of unary trees using operators from $\mathcal{C}$. The below lemma shows that the type of $\mathcal{U}(\mathbb{T})$ is expressible via a universal formula in $\mathcal{C}$:

Lemma 4. *A tree τ is unary iff it satisfies the following $\forall$-formula:*

$$\tau \neq \circ \land \left(\forall \tau'. \ \tau' \bowtie \mathcal{L} \sqsubset \tau \ \leftrightarrow \ \tau' \bowtie \mathcal{R} \sqsubset \tau\right).$$

where $\tau_1 \sqsubset \tau_2 \overset{\text{def}}{=} \tau_1 \sqcup \tau_2 = \tau_2 \land \tau_1 \neq \tau_2$.

Proof. The $\Rightarrow$ direction is proved by induction on the height of τ. The key observation is that if $\tau_1 \bowtie \tau_2 \sqsubset \tau_3$ and τ_2, τ_3 are unary then τ_1 is also unary, $\tau_1 \sqsubseteq \tau_3$ and thus $\tau_1 \bowtie \bar{\tau_2} \sqsubset \tau_3$. Note that both $\mathcal{L}, \mathcal{R}$ are unary and $\bar{\mathcal{L}} = \mathcal{R}$, hence the result follows.

For $\Leftarrow$, assume τ is not unary. As $\tau \neq \circ$, it follows that τ contains at least two black leaves in its representation. Let τ_1 be the tree that represents the path to one of the black leaves in τ, we have $\tau_1 \sqsubset \tau$ and for any unary tree τ_2, if $\tau_1 \sqsubset \tau_2$ then $\tau_2 \not\sqsubset \tau$. As τ_1 is unary, we can rewrite τ_1 as either $\tau_1' \bowtie \mathcal{L}$ or $\tau_1' \bowtie \mathcal{R}$ for some unary tree τ_1'. The latter disjunction together with the equivalence in the premise give us both $\tau_1' \bowtie \mathcal{L} \sqsubset \tau$ and $\tau_1' \bowtie \mathcal{R} \sqsubset \tau$. Also, we have $\tau_1 \sqsubset \tau_1'$ and thus $\tau_1' \not\sqsubset \tau$ by the aforementioned observation. Hence $\tau_1' = \tau_1 \bowtie \bullet = \tau_1' \bowtie (\mathcal{L} \sqcup \mathcal{R}) \sqsubseteq \tau$ which is a contradiction. $\square$

Proof of Theorem 2. We employ the reduction technique in [17] where formulae in $\mathcal{K}$ are interpreted using the operators from $\mathcal{C}$. The interpretation of constants and operators is previously mentioned and justified in Lemma 3. We then replace each sub-formula $\exists x. \ \Phi$ with $\exists x. \ x \in \mathcal{U}(\mathbb{T}) \land \Phi$ and $\forall x. \ \Phi$ with $\forall x. \ x \in \mathcal{U}(\mathbb{T}) \to \Phi$ using the formula in Lemma 4. It follows that the first-order complexity of $\mathcal{C}$ is bounded below by the first-order complexity of $\mathcal{K}$. Hence by Proposition 2, the first-order complexity of $\mathcal{C}$ is nonelementary. $\square$

5   Causes of, and Mitigants to, the Nonelementary Bound

Having proven the nonelementary lower bound for the combined theory in Sect. 4, we discuss causes and mitigants. In Sect. 5.1 we show that the nonelementary behavior of $\mathcal{C}$ comes from the combination of both the additive and multiplicative theories by proving an elementary upper bound on a generalization of the multiplicative theory, and in Sect. 5.2 we discuss why we believe that verification tools in practice will avoid the nonelementary lower bound.

5.1   Complexity of Multiplicative Structure $\mathcal{B} \stackrel{\text{def}}{=} \langle \mathbb{T}, {}_\tau\bowtie, \bowtie_\tau \rangle$

Since the first-order theory over $\langle \mathbb{T}, \bowtie \rangle$ is undecidable, it may seem plausible that the nonelementary behaviour of $\mathcal{C}$ comes from the $\bowtie_\tau$ subtheory rather than the "simpler" Boolean subtheory $\mathcal{A}$, even though the specific proof of the lower bound given in Sect. 4 used both the additive and multiplicative theories (e.g. in Lemma 4). This intuition, however, is mistaken. In fact, even if we generalize the theory to allow multiplication by constants on either side—i.e., by adding ${}_\tau\bowtie(x) \stackrel{\text{def}}{=} \tau \bowtie x$ to the language—the restricted multiplicative theory $\mathcal{B} \stackrel{\text{def}}{=} \langle \mathbb{T}, {}_\tau\bowtie, \bowtie_\tau \rangle$ is elementary. Specifically, we will prove that the first-order theory of $\mathcal{B}$ is $\mathsf{STA}(*, 2^{O(n)}, n)$-complete and thus elementarily decidable:

Theorem 3. *The first-order theory of $\mathcal{B}$ is $\leq_{log\text{-}lin}$-complete for* $\mathsf{STA}(*, 2^{O(n)}, n)$.

Therefore, the nonelementary behavior of $\mathcal{C}$ arises precisely because of the combination of both the additive and multiplicative subtheories.

    We prove Theorem 3 by solving a similar problem in which two tree shares $\{\bullet, \circ\}$ are excluded from the tree domain $\mathbb{T}$. That is, let $\mathbb{T}^+ = \mathbb{T} \backslash \{\bullet, \circ\}$ and $\mathcal{B}^+ = \langle \mathbb{T}^+, {}_\tau\bowtie, \bowtie_\tau \rangle$, we want:

Lemma 5. *The complexity of* $\mathsf{Th}(\mathcal{B}^+)$ *is* $\leq_{log\text{-}lin}$-*complete for* $\mathsf{STA}(*, 2^{O(n)}, n)$.

    By using Lemma 5, the proof for the main theorem is straightforward:

Proof of Theorem 3. The hardness proof is direct from the fact that membership constraint in $\mathcal{B}^+$ can be expressed using membership constraint in $\mathcal{B}$:

$$\tau \in \mathcal{B}^+ \text{ iff } \tau \in \mathcal{B} \wedge \tau \neq \circ \wedge \tau \neq \bullet.$$

    As a result, any sentence from $\mathcal{B}^+$ can be transformed into equivalent sentence in $\mathcal{B}$ by rewriting each $\forall v.\Phi$ with $\forall v.(v \neq \circ \wedge v \neq \bullet) \rightarrow \Phi$ and each $\exists v.\Phi$ with $\exists v.v \neq \circ \wedge v \neq \bullet \wedge \Phi$.

    To prove the upper bound, we use the guessing technique as in [27]. In detail, we partition the domain $\mathbb{T}$ into three disjoint sets:

$$S_1 = \{\circ\} \qquad S_2 = \{\bullet\} \qquad S_3 = \mathbb{T}^+.$$

Suppose the input formula contains n variables, we then use a ternary vector of length n to guess the partition domain of these variables, *e.g.*, if a variable v is guessed with the value $i \in \{1, 2, 3\}$ then v is assigned to the domain S_i. In particular, if v is assigned to S_1 or S_2, we substitute v for $\circ$ or $\bullet$ respectively. Next, each bowtie term $\bowtie_\tau (a)$ or $_\tau\bowtie(a)$ that contains tree share constants $\bullet$ or $\circ$ is simplified using the following identities:

$$\tau \bowtie \bullet \;=\; \bullet \bowtie \tau \;=\; \tau \qquad\qquad \tau \bowtie \circ \;=\; \circ \bowtie \tau \;=\; \circ.$$

After this step, all the atomic sub-formulae that contain $\circ$ or $\bullet$ are reduced into either variable equalities $v_1 = v_2, v = \tau$ or trivial constant equalities such as $\bullet = \bullet, \widehat{\bullet \circ} = \circ$ that can be replaced by either $\top$ or $\bot$. As a result, the new equivalent formula is free of tree share constants $\{\bullet, \circ\}$ whilst all variables are quantified over the domain $\mathbb{T}^+$. Such formula can be solved using the Turing machine that decides $\mathsf{Th}(\mathcal{B}^+)$. The whole guessing process can be integrated into the alternating Turing machine without increasing the formula size or number of quantifiers (*i.e.* the alternating Turing machine only needs to make two extra guesses $\bullet$ and $\circ$ for each variable and the simplification only takes linear time). Hence this justifies the upper bound. □

The rest of this section is dedicated to the proof of Lemma 5. To prove the complexity $\mathsf{Th}(\mathcal{B}^+)$, we construct an efficient isomorphism from $\mathcal{B}^+$ to the structure of ternary strings in $\{0, 1, 2\}^*$ with prefix and suffix successors. The existence of such isomorphism will ensure the complexity matching between the tree structure and the string structure. Here we recall a result from [34] about the first-order complexity of the string structure with successors:

Proposition 3 ([34]). *Let* $\mathcal{S} = \langle \{0, 1\}^*, P_0, P_1, S_0, S_1 \rangle$ *be the structure of binary strings with prefix successors* P_0, P_1 *and suffix successors* S_0, S_1 *such that:*

$$P_0(s) = 0 \cdot s \qquad P_1(s) = 1 \cdot s \qquad S_0(s) = s \cdot 0 \qquad S_1(s) = s \cdot 1.$$

Then the first-order theory of $\mathcal{S}$ *is* $\leq_{log\text{-}lin}$*-complete for* $\mathsf{STA}(*, 2^{O(n)}, n)$.

The above result cannot be used immediately to prove our main theorem. Instead, we use it to infer a more general result where successors are not only restricted to 0 and 1, but also allowed to be any string s in a finite alphabet:

Lemma 6. *Let* Σ *be a finite alphabet of size* $k \geq 2$ *and* $\mathcal{S}' = \langle \Sigma^*, P_s, S_s \rangle$ *the structure of k-ary strings with infinitely many prefix successors* P_s *and suffix successors* S_s *where* $s \in \Sigma^*$ *such that:*

$$P_s(s') = s \cdot s' \qquad\qquad S_s(s') = s' \cdot s.$$

Then the first-order theory of $\mathcal{S}'$ *is* $\leq_{log\text{-}lin}$*-complete for* $\mathsf{STA}(*, 2^{O(n)}, n)$.

Proof. Although the proof in [34] only considers binary alphabet, the same result still holds even for finite alphabet Σ of size $k \geq 2$ with k prefix and suffix successors. Let $s = a_1 \ldots a_n$ where $a_i \in \Sigma$, the successors P_s and S_s can be defined in linear size from successors in $\mathcal{S}$ as follows:

$$P_s \stackrel{\text{def}}{=} \lambda s'. \, P_{a_1}(\ldots P_{a_n}(s')) \qquad S_s \stackrel{\text{def}}{=} \lambda s'. \, S_{a_n}(\ldots S_{a_1}(s')).$$

These definitions are quantifier-free and thus the result follows. $\qquad\qquad\square$

Next, we recall some key results from [27] that establishes the fundamental connection between trees and strings in word equation:

Proposition 4 ([27]). *We call a tree τ in $\mathbb{T}^+$ prime if $\tau = \tau_1 \bowtie \tau_2$ implies either $\tau_1 = \bullet$ or $\tau_2 = \bullet$. Then for each tree τ in $\mathbb{T}^+$, there exists a unique sequence of prime trees $\{\tau_i\}_{i=1}^n$ such that $\tau = \tau_1 \bowtie \cdots \bowtie \tau_n$. As a result, each tree in $\mathbb{T}^+$ can be treated as a string in a word equation in which the alphabet is $\mathbb{P}$, the countably infinite set of prime trees, and $\bowtie$ is the string concatenation.*

For example, the factorization of is $\bowtie$ $\bowtie$, which

is unique. Proposition 4 asserts that by factorizing tree shares into prime trees, we can effectively transform multiplicative tree share constraints into equivalent word equations. Ideally, if we can represent each prime tree as a unique letter in the alphabet then Lemma 5 would follow from Lemma 6. Unfortunately, the set of prime trees $\mathbb{P}$ are infinite [27] while Lemma 6 requires a finite alphabet. As a result, our tree encoding needs to be more sophisticated than the naïve way. The key observation here is that, as $\mathbb{P}$ is countably infinite, there must be a bijective *encoding function* $I : \mathbb{P} \mapsto \{0,1\}^*$ that encodes each prime tree into binary string, including the empty string ϵ. We need not to know the construction of I in advance, but it is important to keep in mind that I exists and the delay of its construction is intentional. We then extend I into $\hat{I}$ that maps tree shares in $\mathbb{T}^+$ into ternary string in $\{0,1,2\}^*$ where the letter 2 purposely represents the delimiter between two consecutive prime trees:

Lemma 7. *Let $\hat{I} : \mathbb{T}^+ \mapsto \{0,1,2\}^*$ be the mapping from tree shares into ternary strings such that for prime trees $\tau_i \in \mathbb{P}$ where $i \in \{1, \ldots, n\}$, we have:*

$$\hat{I}(\tau_1 \bowtie \ldots \bowtie \tau_n) = I(\tau_1) \cdot 2 \ldots 2 \cdot I(\tau_n).$$

By Proposition 4, $\hat{I}$ is bijective. Furthermore, let $\tau_1, \tau_2 \in \mathbb{T}^+$ then:

$$\hat{I}(\tau_1 \bowtie \tau_2) = \hat{I}(\tau_1) \cdot 2 \cdot \hat{I}(\tau_2).$$

Having the core encoding function $\hat{I}$ defined, it is now routine to establish the isomorphism from the tree structure $\mathcal{B}^+$ to the string structure $\mathcal{S}'$:

Lemma 8. *Let f be a function that maps the tree structure $\langle \mathbb{T}^+, {}_{\tau}\bowtie, \bowtie_{\tau} \rangle$ into the string structure $\langle \{0,1,2\}, P_{s2}, S_{2s} \rangle$ such that:*

1. *For each tree $\tau \in \mathbb{T}^+$, we let $f(\tau) \stackrel{\text{def}}{=} \hat{I}(\tau)$.*

2. *For each function $_\tau\bowtie$, we let $f(_\tau\bowtie) \overset{\text{def}}{=} P_{\hat{I}(\tau)2}$.*

3. *For each function $\bowtie_\tau$, we let $f(\bowtie_\tau) \overset{\text{def}}{=} S_{2\hat{I}(\tau)}$.*

Then f is an isomorphism from $\mathcal{B}^+$ to $\mathcal{S}'$.

Proof of Lemma 5. For the upper bound, observe that the function f in Lemma 8 can be used to transform tree share formulae in $\mathcal{B}^+$ to string formulae in $\mathcal{S}'$. It remains to ensure that the size of the string formula is not exponentially exploded. In particular, it suffices to construct $\hat{I}$ such that if a tree $\tau \in \mathbb{T}^+$ has size n, its corresponding string $\hat{I}(\tau)$ has linear size $O(n)$. Recall that $\hat{I}$ is extended from I which can be constructed in many different ways. Thus to avoid the size explosion, we choose to specify the encoding function I on the fly *after observing the input tree share formula*. To be precise, given a formula Φ in $\mathcal{B}$, we first factorize all its tree constants into prime trees, which can be done in log-space [27]. Suppose the formula has n prime trees $\{\tau_i\}_{i=1}^n$ sorted in the ascending order of their sizes, we choose the most efficient binary encoding by letting $I(\tau_i) = s_i$ where s_i is the ith string in length-lexicographic (shortlex) order of $\{0,1\}^*$, *i.e.* $\{\epsilon, 0, 1, 00, 01, \dots\}$. This encoding ensures that the size of τ_i and the length of s_i only differ by a constant factor. Given the fact that a tree share in its factorized form $\tau_1 \bowtie \dots \bowtie \tau_n$ only requires $O(\sum_{i=1}^n \hat{I}(\tau_i))$ bits to represent, we infer that its size and the length of its string counterpart $\hat{I}(\tau)$ also differ by a constant factor. Hence, the upper bound complexity is justified.

To prove the lower bound, we need to construct the inverse function f^{-1} that maps the string structure $\mathcal{S}'$ into the tree share structure $\mathcal{B}$. Although the existence of f^{-1} is guaranteed since f is isomorphism, we also need to take care of the size explosion problem. It boils down to construct an efficient mapping I^{-1} from binary strings to prime trees by observing the input string formula Φ. For each string constant $s_1 2 \dots 2 s_n$ in Φ where $s_i \in \{0,1\}^*$, we extract all of the binary strings s_i. We then maps each distinct binary string s_i to a unique prime tree τ_i as follows. Let $k(0) = \overset{\frown}{\bullet \, \circ}$, $k(1) = \overset{\frown}{\circ \, \bullet}$ and assume $s_i = a_0 \dots a_m$ for $a_i \in \{0,1\}$, we compute $\tau = k(a_0) \bowtie \dots \bowtie k(a_m)$. Then the mapped tree share for the string s_i is constructed as $\tau_i = \overset{\frown}{\bullet \, \tau}$ (if $s_i = \epsilon$ then $\tau_i = \overset{\frown}{\bullet \, \circ}$). It follows that τ_i is prime and this skewed tree has size $O(n)$ where n is the length of s_i. Thus the result follows. $\square$

Example 2. Consider the tree formula $\forall a \exists b \exists c.\ a = b \bowtie \overset{\frown}{\underset{\circ\,\bullet\,\circ}{}} \wedge b = \overset{\frown}{\underset{\circ\,\bullet\,\circ}{}} \bowtie c$. This formula contains two constants whose factorizations are below:

$$c_1 = \overset{\frown}{\underset{\circ\,\bullet\,\circ}{}} = \overset{\frown}{\bullet\,\circ} \bowtie \overset{\frown}{\circ\,\bullet} \qquad c_2 = \overset{\frown}{\underset{\circ\,\bullet\,\circ}{}} = \overset{\frown}{\circ\,\bullet} \bowtie \overset{\frown}{\bullet\,\circ}.$$

We choose I such that $I(\overset{\frown}{\bullet\,\circ}) = \epsilon$ and $I(\overset{\frown}{\circ\,\bullet}) = 0$. Our encoding gives $s_1 = 20$ and $s_2 = 02$. This results in the string formula $\forall a \exists b \exists c.\ a = S_{220}(b) \wedge b = P_{022}(c)$ whose explicit form is $\forall a \exists b \exists c.\ a = b220 \wedge b = 022c$.

Now suppose that we want to transform the above string formula into equivalent tree formula. Following the proof of Lemma 5, we extract from the formula

104 X.-B. Le et al.

two binary strings $s_1 = \epsilon$ and $s_2 = 0$ which are mapped to the prime trees $\tau_1 = \widehat{\bullet \circ}$ and $\tau_2 = \widehat{\bullet \overset{\frown}{\bullet \circ}}$ respectively. Hence the equivalent tree share formula is $\forall a \exists b \exists c . a =_{\bowtie_{\tau_1 \bowtie \tau_2}} (b) \wedge b =_{\tau_2 \bowtie \tau_1 \bowtie} (c)$. It is worth noticing the difference between this tree formula and the original tree formula, which suggests the fact that the representation of the alphabet (*i.e.* prime trees) is not important.

5.2 Combined $\mathcal{C}$ Formulae in Practice

The source of the nonelementary behavior comes from two factors. First, as proven just above, it comes from the combination of both the additive and multiplicative operations of tree shares. Second, it comes from the number of quantifier alternations in the formula being analyzed, due to the encoding of $\mathcal{C}$ in tree automata [27] and the resulting upper bound (the transformed automata of first-order formulae of tree automatic structures have sizes bounded by a tower of exponentials whose height is the number of quantifier alternations [5,6]).

Happily, in typical verifications, especially in highly-automated verifications such as those done by tools like HIP/SLEEK [28], the number of quantifier alternations in formulae is small, even when carrying out complex verifications or inference. For example, consider the following biabduction problem (a separation-logic-based inference procedure) handled by the ShareInfer tool from [26]:

$$a \overset{\pi}{\mapsto} (b,c,d) \star \widehat{\bullet \circ} \cdot \pi \cdot \mathsf{tree}(c) \star \widehat{\circ \bullet} \cdot \pi \cdot \mathsf{tree}(d) \star [??] \vdash \widehat{\bullet \circ} \cdot \pi \cdot \mathsf{tree}(a) \star [??]$$

ShareInfer will calculate $\widehat{\bullet \circ} \cdot \pi \cdot \mathsf{tree}(d)$ for the antiframe and $a \overset{\pi \bowtie \widehat{\circ \bullet}}{\longmapsto}$ $(b,c,d) \star \widehat{\circ \bullet} \cdot \pi \cdot \mathsf{tree}(d)$ for the inference frame. Although these guesses are a bit sophisticated, verifing them depends on [16] the following quantifier-alternation-free $\mathcal{C}$ sentence: $\forall \pi, \pi'. \ \pi = \pi' \ \Rightarrow \ \bowtie_{\widehat{\bullet \circ}} (\pi) \oplus \bowtie_{\widehat{\bullet \circ}} (\pi) = \pi'$. Even with complex loop invariants, more than one alternation would be surprising because *e.g.* verification tools tend to maintain formulae in well-chosen canonical forms.

Moreover, because tree automata are closely connected to other well-studied domains, we can take advantage of existing tools such as MONA [23]. As an experiment we have hand-translated $\mathcal{C}$ formulae into WS2S, the language of MONA, using the techniques of [10]. The technical details of the translation are provided in Appendix A. For the above formula, MONA reported 205 DAG hits and 145 nodes, with essentially a 0ms running time.

Lastly, heuristics are well-justified both because of the restricted problem formats we expect in practice as well as because of the nonelementary worst-case lower bound we proved in Sect. 4, opening the door to newer techniques like antichain/simulation [1].

6 Future Work and Conclusion

We have developed a tighter understanding of the complexity of the tree share model. As Boolean Algebras, their first-order theory is $\mathsf{STA}(*, 2^{n^{O(1)}}, n)$-

complete, even with arbitrary tree constants in the formulas. Although the first-order theory over tree multiplication is undecidable [27], we have found that by restricting multiplication to be by a constant (on both the left $_r\bowtie$ and right $\bowtie_r$ sides) we obtain a substructure $\mathcal{B}$ whose first-order theory is $\mathsf{STA}(*, 2^{O(n)}, n)$-complete. Accordingly, we have two structures whose first-order theory has elementary complexity. Interestingly, their combined theory is still decidable but nonelementary, even if we only allow multiplication by a constant on the right $\bowtie_r$.

We have several directions for future work. It is natural to investigate the precise complexity of the existential theory with the Boolean operators and right-sided multiplication $\bowtie_r$ (structure $\mathcal{C}$). The encoding into tree-automatic structures from [27] provides only an exponential-time upper bound (because of the result for the corresponding fragment in tree-automatic structures, e.g., see [36]), and there is the obvious NP lower bound that comes from propositional logic satisfiability. We do not know if the Boolean operators ($\sqcup, \sqcap, \bar{\cdot}$) in combination with the left-sided multiplication $_r\bowtie$ is decidable (existential or first order, with or without the right-sided multiplication $\bowtie_r$). Determining if the existential theory with the Boolean operators and *unrestricted* multiplication $\bowtie$ is decidable also seems challenging. We would also like to know if the monadic second-order theory over these structures is decidable.

Acknowledgement. We would like to thank anonymous referees for their constructive reviews. Le and Lin are partially supported by the European Research Council (ERC) under the European Union's Horizon 2020 research and innovation programme (grant agreement no 759969). Le and Hobor are partially supported under Yale-NUS College grant R-607-265-322-121.

A   Appendix

Figure 1 contains the MONA WS2S encoding of the following tree share formula

$$\forall \pi, \pi'. \; \pi = \pi' \; \Rightarrow \; (\pi \bowtie \widehat{_\circ \bullet}) \oplus (\pi \bowtie \widehat{_\bullet \circ}) = \pi'.$$

where lower case letters are for variables of binary strings and upper case letters are for second-order monadic predicates. The last three lines in the code are the formulas with a number of macros defined in the previous lines. Essentially, each tree share is represented by a second-order variable whose elements are *antichains* that describes a single path to one of its black leaves. Roughly speaking, the eqt predicate checks whether two tree shares are equal, leftMul and rightMul correspond to the multiplicative predicates $\bowtie_{\bullet\circ}$ and $\bowtie_{\circ\bullet}$ respectively, and uniont computes the additive operator $\oplus$. Other additional predicates are necessary for the consistent representation of the tree shares. In detail, singleton(X) means that X has exactly one element, ant makes sure any two antichains in the same tree are neither prefix of the other, maxt(X,Y) enforces that X is the maximal antichain of Y, roott(x,X) asserts x is the root of X, subt is a subset-like relation betweens two trees, while `mint` specifies the canonical form. Lastly, we have `sub0` and `sub1` as the intermediate predicates for the multiplicative predicates.

```
ws2s;
pred ant(var2 Y) =
  all1 x,y: (x~=y & x in Y & y in Y) => (~(x<=y) & ~(y<=x));
pred maxt(var2 X,var2 Y) =
  X sub Y & ex1 r:all1 x: x in X =>
  (r <= x & all1 z: r <= z => ex1 x': x' in X & (z <= x' | x' <= z));
pred roott(var1 x,var2 X) =
  all1 y: y in X & x <= y & all1 z:all1 y':y' in X & z <= y' => x <= z;
pred subt(var2 X, var2 Y) =
  all1 x1:all2 X':(maxt(X',X) & roott(x1,X')) =>
  (ex2 Y':maxt(Y',Y) => roott(x1,Y'));
pred eqt(var2 X, var2 Y) =
  subt(X,Y) & subt(Y,X);
pred singleton(var2 X) =
  ex1 x: x in X & (all1 y: y in X => x = y);
pred uniont(var2 X,var2 Y,var2 Z) =
  Z = X union Y & empty(X inter Y);
pred mint(var2 X) =
  all2 Y: maxt(Y,X) => singleton(Y);
pred sub0(var2 X, var2 X0) =
  all1 x:x in X <=> x.0 in X0;
pred sub1(var2 X, var2 X0) =
  all1 x:x in X <=> x.1 in X0;
pred leftMul(var2 X,var2 X') =
  all2 Y:(eqt(X,Y) & mint(Y)) => sub0(Y,X');
pred rightMul(var2 X,var2 X') =
  all2 Y:(eqt(X,Y) & mint(Y)) => sub1(Y,X');

all2 X,X',XL,XR,XU:
  (ant(X) & ant(X') & ant(XL) & ant(XR) & ant(XU) & eqt(X,X') &
  leftMul(X,XL) & rightMul(X,XR) & uniont(XL,XR,XU)) => (eqt(XU,X'));
```

Fig. 1. The transformation of tree share formula in Sect. 5.2 into equivalent WS2S formula.

References

1. Abdulla, P.A., Chen, Y.-F., Holík, L., Mayr, R., Vojnar, T.: When simulation meets antichains. In: Esparza, J., Majumdar, R. (eds.) TACAS 2010. LNCS, vol. 6015, pp. 158–174. Springer, Heidelberg (2010). https://doi.org/10.1007/978-3-642-12002-2_14

2. Appel, A.W., et al.: Program Logics for Certified Compilers. Cambridge University Press, Cambridge (2014)
3. Appel, A.W., Dockins, R., Hobor, A.: Mechanized semantic library (2009)
4. Berman, L.: The complexity of logical theories. Theor. Comput. Sci. **11**(1), 71–77 (1980)
5. Blumensath, A.: Automatic structures. Ph.D. thesis, RWTH Aachen (1999)
6. Blumensath, A., Grade, E.: Finite presentations of infinite structures: automata and interpretations. Theory Comput. Syst. **37**, 641–674 (2004)
7. Bornat, R., Calcagno, C., O'Hearn, P., Parkinson, M.: Permission accounting in separation logic. In: POPL, pp. 259–270 (2005)
8. Boyland, J.: Checking interference with fractional permissions. In: Cousot, R. (ed.) SAS 2003. LNCS, vol. 2694, pp. 55–72. Springer, Heidelberg (2003). https://doi.org/10.1007/3-540-44898-5_4
9. Chandra, A.K., Kozen, D.C., Stockmeyer, L.J.: Alternation. J. ACM **28**(1), 114–133 (1981)
10. Colcombet, T., Löding, C.: Transforming structures by set interpretations. Log. Methods Comput. Sci. **3**(2) (2007)
11. Compton, K.J., Henson, C.W.: A uniform method for proving lower bounds on the computational complexity of logical theories. In: APAL (1990)
12. The Coq Development Team: The Coq proof assistant reference manual. LogiCal Project, version 8.0 (2004)
13. Dockins, R., Hobor, A., Appel, A.W.: A fresh look at separation algebras and share accounting. In: Hu, Z. (ed.) APLAS 2009. LNCS, vol. 5904, pp. 161–177. Springer, Heidelberg (2009). https://doi.org/10.1007/978-3-642-10672-9_13
14. Dohrau, J., Summers, A.J., Urban, C., Münger, S., Müller, P.: Permission inference for array programs. In: CAV (2018)
15. Doko, M., Vafeiadis, V.: Tackling real-life relaxed concurrency with FSL++. In: Yang, H. (ed.) ESOP 2017. LNCS, vol. 10201, pp. 448–475. Springer, Heidelberg (2017). https://doi.org/10.1007/978-3-662-54434-1_17
16. Gherghina, C.A.: Efficiently verifying programs with rich control flows. Ph.D. thesis, National University of Singapore (2012)
17. Grädel, E.: Simple interpretations among complicated theories. Inf. Process. Lett. **35**(5), 235–238 (1990)
18. Hobor, A., Gherghina, C.: Barriers in concurrent separation logic. In: Barthe, G. (ed.) ESOP 2011. LNCS, vol. 6602, pp. 276–296. Springer, Heidelberg (2011). https://doi.org/10.1007/978-3-642-19718-5_15
19. Hobor, A.: Oracle semantics. Ph.D. thesis, Princeton University, Department of Computer Science, Princeton, NJ, October 2008
20. Hobor, A., Gherghina, C.: Barriers in concurrent separation logic: now with tool support! Log. Methods Comput. Sci. **8**(2) (2012)
21. Jain, S., Khoussainov, B., Stephan, F., Teng, D., Zou, S.: Semiautomatic structures. In: Hirsch, E.A., Kuznetsov, S.O., Pin, J.É., Vereshchagin, N.K. (eds.) CSR 2014. LNCS, vol. 8476, pp. 204–217. Springer, Cham (2014). https://doi.org/10.1007/978-3-319-06686-8_16
22. Jez, A.: Recompression: a simple and powerful technique for word equations. J. ACM **63**(1), 4:1–4:51 (2016)
23. Klarlund, N., Møller, A.: MONA version 1.4 User Manual. BRICS, Department of Computer Science, Aarhus University, January 2001
24. Le, D.-K., Chin, W.-N., Teo, Y.M.: Threads as resource for concurrency verification. In: PEPM, pp. 73–84 (2015)

25. Le, X.B., Gherghina, C., Hobor, A.: Decision procedures over sophisticated fractional permissions. In: Jhala, R., Igarashi, A. (eds.) APLAS 2012. LNCS, vol. 7705, pp. 368–385. Springer, Heidelberg (2012). https://doi.org/10.1007/978-3-642-35182-2_26

26. Le, X.-B., Hobor, A.: Logical reasoning for disjoint permissions. In: Ahmed, A. (ed.) ESOP 2018. LNCS, vol. 10801, pp. 385–414. Springer, Cham (2018). https://doi.org/10.1007/978-3-319-89884-1_14

27. Le, X.-B., Hobor, A., Lin, A.W.: Decidability and complexity of tree shares formulas. In: FSTTCS (2016)

28. Le, X.-B., Nguyen, T.-T., Chin, W.-N., Hobor, A.: A certified decision procedure for tree shares. In: Duan, Z., Ong, L. (eds.) ICFEM 2017. LNCS, vol. 10610, pp. 226–242. Springer, Cham (2017). https://doi.org/10.1007/978-3-319-68690-5_14

29. Makanin, G.S.: The problem of solvability of equations in a free semigroup. In: Mat. Sbornik, pp. 147–236 (1977)

30. Marriott, K., Odersky, M.: Negative Boolean constraints. Theor. Comput. Sci. **160**, 365–380 (1996)

31. O'Hearn, P.W.: Resources, concurrency, and local reasoning. Theor. Comput. Sci. **375**(1–3), 271–307 (2007)

32. Parkinson, M.: Local reasoning for Java. Ph.D. thesis, University of Cambridge (2005)

33. Parkinson, M.J., Bornat, R., O'Hearn, P.W.: Modular verification of a non-blocking stack. In: POPL 2007, pp. 297–302 (2007)

34. Rybina, T., Voronkov, A.: Upper bounds for a theory of queues. In: Baeten, J.C.M., Lenstra, J.K., Parrow, J., Woeginger, G.J. (eds.) ICALP 2003. LNCS, vol. 2719, pp. 714–724. Springer, Heidelberg (2003). https://doi.org/10.1007/3-540-45061-0_56

35. Stockmeyer, L.: The complexity of decision problems in automata theory and logic. Ph.D. thesis, M.I.T. (1974)

36. To, A.W.: Model checking infinite-state systems: generic and specific approaches. Ph.D. thesis, LFCS, School of Informatics, University of Edinburgh (2010)

37. Villard, J.: Heaps and Hops. Ph.D. thesis, Laboratoire Spécification et Vérification, École Normale Supérieure de Cachan, France, February 2011

38. Dinsdale-Young, T., da Rocha Pinto, P., Andersen, K.J., Birkedal, L.: Caper: automatic verification for fine-grained concurrency. In: ESOP 2017 (2017)

Relational Thread-Modular Abstract Interpretation Under Relaxed Memory Models

Thibault Suzanne[1,2,3]($\boxtimes$) and Antoine Miné[3]

[1] Département d'informatique de l'ENS, École Normale Supérieure, CNRS,
PSL Research University, 75005 Paris, France
`thibault.suzanne@ens.fr`
[2] Inria, Paris, France
[3] Sorbonne Université, CNRS, Laboratoire d'Informatique de Paris 6, LIP6,
75005 Paris, France
`Antoine.Mine@lip6.fr`

Abstract. We address the verification problem of numeric properties in many-threaded concurrent programs under weakly consistent memory models, especially TSO. We build on previous work that proposed an abstract interpretation method to analyse these programs with relational domains. This method was not sufficient to analyse more than two threads in a decent time. Our contribution here is to rely on a rely-guarantee framework with automatic inference of thread interferences to design an analysis with a thread-modular approach and describe relational abstractions of both thread states and interferences. We show how to adapt the usual computing procedure of interferences to the additional issues raised by weakly consistent memories. We demonstrate the precision and the performance of our method on a few examples, operating a prototype analyser that verifies safety properties like mutual exclusion. We discuss how weak memory models affect the scalability results compared to a sequentially consistent environment.

1 Introduction

Multicore programming is both a timely and challenging task. Parallel architectures are ubiquitous and have significant advantages related to cost effectiveness and performance, yet they exhibit a programming paradigm that makes reasoning about the correctness of the code harder than within sequential systems. Weakly consistent memory models, used to describe the behaviour of distributed systems and multicore CPUs, amplify this fact: by allowing more optimisations, they enable programs to run even faster; however this comes at the cost of counter-intuitive semantic traits that further complicate the understanding of

This work is supported in part by the ITEA 3 project 14014 (ASSUME) and in part by the European Research Council under Consolidator Grant Agreement 681393 – MOPSA.

© Springer Nature Switzerland AG 2018
S. Ryu (Ed.): APLAS 2018, LNCS 11275, pp. 109–128, 2018.
https://doi.org/10.1007/978-3-030-02768-1_6

```
thread /* 1 */ {              thread /* 2 */ {
    x = 1;                        y = 1;
    r1 = y;                       r2 = x;
}                             }
```

Fig. 1. A simple program with counter-intuitive possible results on x86.

these programs, let alone their proof of correctness. These difficulties coupled with the use of such architectures in critical domains call for automatic reasoning methods to ensure correctness properties on concurrent executions.

In a previous work [20], we proposed an abstract interpretation method to verify such programs. However, this method worked by building a global control graph representing all possible interleavings of the threads of the target program. The size of this graph grows exponentially with the number of threads, which makes this method unable to scale. This paper describes a thread-modular analysis that circumvents this problem by analysing each thread independently, propagating through these thread analyses their effect on the execution of other threads. We target in particular the *Total Store Ordering* (TSO) and *Partial Store Ordering* (PSO) memory models.

1.1   Weak Memory Models

A widespread paradigm of concurrent programming is that of shared memory. In this paradigm, the intuitive semantics conforms to sequential consistency (SC) [12]. In SC, the allowed executions of a concurrent program are the interleavings of the instructions of its threads. However, modern multicore architectures and concurrent programming languages do not respect this property: rather, for optimisation reasons, they specify a *weakly consistent memory model* that relaxes sequential consistency and allows some additional behaviors.

We mainly target the TSO (Total Store Ordering) memory model, which is amongst others known for being the base model of x86 CPUs [19]. In this model, a thread cannot immediatly read a store from another thread: they write through a totally ordered *store buffer*. Each thread has its own buffer. Non-deterministically, the oldest entry of a store buffer can be flushed into the memory, writing the store value to the corresponding shared variable. When attempting to read the value of some variable, a thread begins by looking at the most recent entry for this variable in its store buffer. If there is none, it reads from the shared memory.

The program of Fig. 1 exhibits a non-intuitive behaviour. In SC, after its execution from a zeroed memory, either r1 or r2 must be equal to 1. However, when executed on x86, one can observe r1 = 0 && r2 = 0 at the end. This happens when Thread 1 (respectively Thread 2) reads the value of x (respectively y) whereas Thread 2 (respectively Thread 1) has not flushed its store from its buffer yet.

Another related model, PSO (Partial Store Ordering), is strictly more relaxed than TSO, in that its buffers are only partially ordered: stores to a same variable keep their order, but stores to different variables can be flushed in any order into the memory. Another way of expressing it consists in having a totally ordered buffer for each thread and each variable, with no order between different buffers. Both models define a `mfence` instruction that flushes the buffer(s) of the thread that executes it. A systematic insertion of `mfence` allows to get back to sequential consistency, but has a performance cost, thus one should avoid using this instruction when it is not needed for correctness.

As we stated earlier, our main target is TSO, as most previous abstract interpretation works. It acts as a not too complex but real-life model, and fills a sweet spot where relaxed behaviours actually happen but do not always need to be forbidden for programs to be correct. However, to design a computable analysis that stays sound, we were forced to drop completeness by losing some (controlled) precision: this is the foundation of abstract interpretation [5]. Our abstraction ignores the write order between two different variables, to only remember sequences of values written into each variable independently. This design choice makes our analysis sound not only under TSO, but also incidentally under PSO. Therefore we will present it as a PSO analysis since it will simplify the presentation, although the reader should have in mind that it stays sound w.r.t. TSO. The loss of precision, in practice, incurred by a PSO analysis on a TSO program will be discussed in Sect. 4.

We believe our analysis can be extended to more relaxed models such as POWER/ARM by adding "read buffers". This extension could pave the way for the C and Java models, which share some concepts, but we did not have the time to properly study them yet. However we rely on a very operational model: more complex ones are axiomatically defined, so one will need to provide a sound operational overapproximation before doing abstraction.

1.2 Abstraction of Relaxed Memory

To analyse concurrent programs running under PSO, we focus on abstract interpretation [5]. The additional difficulty to design abstractions when considering store-buffer-based memory models lies in buffers: they are unbounded and their size changes dynamically and non-deterministically. This work builds on our previous work [20] that proposed an efficient abstraction for representing buffers.

Our implementation (cf. Sect. 4) targets small algorithms implementable in assembly. Hence the core language of the programs we aim to analyse is a minimal imperative language, whose syntax is defined in Fig. 3, Sect. 2. The program is divided in a fixed number of threads, and they all run simultaneously. Individual instructions run atomically (one can always decompose a non-atomic instruction into atomic ones). We believe that additional features of a realistic programming language, such as data structures and dynamic allocation, are orthogonal to this work on weakly consistent memory: we focus on numerical programs, yet one can combine our abstractions with domains targeting these features to build a more complete analysis.

```
thread /* 0 */ {                    thread /* 1 */ {
    while true {                        while true {
        while x != 1 {}                    while x != 0 {}
        /* Critical start */               /* Critical start */
        ...                                ...
        /* Critical end */                 /* Critical end */
        /* label l1 */                     x = 1;
        x = 0;                         }
        /* label l2 */             }
    }
}
```

Fig. 2. Round-robin: a concurrent program example.

The domain proposed in our previous paper [20] relies on a summarisation technique initially proposed by Gopan et al. [6] to abstract arrays, which they adapt to abstract unbounded FIFO queues. Summarisation consists in grouping together several variables $x_1, \ldots, x_n$ in a numerical domain into a single summarised variable x_{sum}, which retains each possible value of every x_i. For instance, let us consider two possible states over three variables: $(x, y, z) \in \{(1, 2, 3); (4, 5, 6)\}$. If we regroup x and y into a summarised variable v_{xy}, the possible resulting states are $(v_{xy}, z) \in \{(1, 3); (2, 3); (4, 6); (5, 6)\}$. Note that, due to summarisation, these concrete states of (x, y, z) are also described by that abstract element: $(1, 1, 3)$, $(2, 2, 3)$, $(2, 1, 3)$, $(4, 4, 6)$, $(5, 5, 6)$, $(5, 4, 6)$.

We use this technique to summarise the content of each buffer, excluding the most recent entry that plays a special role when reading from the memory. Once summarisation is done, we obtain states with bounded dimensions that can be abstracted with classic numerical domains. This abstraction is described at length in our previous paper [20].

1.3 Interferences: Thread-Modular Abstract Interpretation

The immediate way of performing abstract interpretation over a concurrent program is to build the global control graph, product of the control graph of each thread, that represents each possible interleaving. This graph has a size which is exponential in the number of threads and linear in each thread size: it does not scale up. Thread-modular analyses have been designed to alleviate this combinatorial explosion [8,10,15–17]. Amongst them, we use the formal system of interferences, that has been proposed by Miné [15] to analyse each thread in isolation, generating the effects it can have on the execution of other threads, and taking into account the effects generated by these other threads. Thread-modular analysis scales up better because the analysis is linear in the sum of thread sizes (instead of their product), times the number of iterations needed to stabilise the interferences (which is low in practice, and can always be accelerated by widening [15]).

The effects generated by this analysis are named interferences. Consider the program in Fig. 2, running in sequential consistency from a zeroed memory. This program is a standard round-robin algorithm, whose purpose is to alternate the presence of its threads in the critical section. To analyse it, we first consider Thread 0 and analyse it separately as if it were a sequential program. It cannot enter the critical section since x is initially equal to 0, so the analysis ends here. Then we analyse Thread 1, that immediately exits its inner loop and then enters the critical section, after which it sets x to 1. We then generate the *simple interference* $T1 : x \mapsto 1$, that means that Thread 1 can put 1 in x. Every read from x by a thread can now return 1 instead of the value this thread stored last, in a flow insensitive way. Afterwards, Thread 1 analysis ends: it cannot enter back its critical section, since x is still equal to 1 when it tries again. We go back to Thread 0. The new analysis will take into account the interference from Thread 1 to know that x can now be equal to 1, and thus that Thread 0 can enter its critical section. It will generate the interference $T0 : x \mapsto 0$, and notice that the critical section can be entered several times when applying the interference from Thread 1. Then the second analysis of Thread 1 will also determine that Thread 1 can enter its critical section more than once. No more interference is generated, and the global analysis has ended. It is thread-modular in the sense that it analyses each thread code in isolation from other thread code.

This *simple interference* analysis is provably sound: in particular, it has managed to compute that both threads can indeed enter their critical section. However, it did not succeed in proving the program correct. In general, simple interferences associate to each variable (an abstraction of) the set of its values at each program point. They are non-relational (in particular, there is no relation between the old value of a variable and its new value in an interference) and flow insensitive. To alleviate this problem, previous works [15,16] introduced relational interferences, that model sets of possible state transitions caused by thread instructions between pairs of program points, i.e., they model the effect of the thread in a fully relational and flow-sensitive way, which is more precise and more costly, while still being amenable to classic abstraction techniques. For instance, in the program of Fig. 2, one such interference would be "When x is equal to 1, and Thread 1 is not in its critical section, Thread 0 can write 0 in x; and by doing so it will go from label 11 to label 12". The relational interference framework is complete for reachability properties thus not computable, but Monat and Miné [16] developed precise abstractions of interferences in SC that allow proving this kind of programs in a decidable way.

In this paper, we will combine such abstractions with the domains for weakly consistent memory to get a computable, precise and thread-modular abstract interpretation based analysis under TSO. We implemented this analysis and provided some results on a few examples. We mostly aim to prove relational numerical properties on small albeit complex low-level programs. These programs are regarded as difficult to check—for instance, because they implement a synchronisation model and are thus dependent on some precise thread interaction scenario. We show that our analysis can retain the precision needed to verify their correctness, while taking advantage of the performances of a modular analysis to be able to efficiently analyse programs with more than 2 threads, which is out of reach of most non-modular techniques.

$\langle prog \rangle :: = \langle thread \rangle *$

$\langle thread \rangle ::= \mathbf{thread} \quad \text{‘\{’}$
$\quad \langle stmt \rangle \text{‘\}’}$

$\langle stmt \rangle ::=$
$\quad | \quad \langle var \rangle \text{‘=’} \langle expr \rangle$
$\quad | \quad \mathbf{if} \langle expr \rangle \text{‘\{’} \langle stmt \rangle \text{‘\}’}$
$\quad \quad [\mathbf{else} \text{‘\{’} \langle stmt \rangle \text{‘\}’}]$

$\quad | \quad \mathbf{while} \langle expr \rangle \text{‘\{’}$
$\quad \quad \langle stmt \rangle] \text{‘\}’}$
$\quad | \quad \langle stmt \rangle \text{‘;’} \langle stmt \rangle$

$\langle expr \rangle ::=$
$\quad | \quad \langle var \rangle$
$\quad | \quad n \in \mathbb{Z}$
$\quad | \quad \langle expr \rangle \dagger \langle expr \rangle$

$\quad | \quad \star \langle expr \rangle$
$\quad | \quad \text{‘(’} \langle expr \rangle \text{‘)’}$

$\langle var \rangle ::= \mathbf{x, y, z}...$

$\langle \dagger \rangle ::= \text{‘*’} | \text{‘/’} | \text{‘+’} | \text{‘-’} | \text{‘=’}$
$\quad | \text{‘<’} | \text{‘>’} | \text{‘<=’} | \text{‘>=’} |$
$\quad \text{‘\&\&’} | \text{‘||’}$

$\langle \star \rangle ::= \mathbf{not} | \text{‘-’}$

Fig. 3. Program syntax

Section 2 describes the monolithic and modular concrete semantics of concurrent programs running under the chosen memory model. Section 3 defines a computable modular abstraction for these programs. Section 4 presents experimental results on a few programs using a test implementation of our abstract domains and discusses scaling when considering weakly consistent memories. We present a comparison with related works in Sect. 5. Section 6 concludes.

The monolithic semantics of Sect. 2 has been dealt with in our previous work [20]. Our contribution is composed of the modular semantics of Sects. 2, 3 and 4.

2   Concrete Semantics

2.1   Interleaving Concrete Semantics

Figure 3 defines the syntax of our programs. We specify in Fig. 4 the domain used in the concrete semantics. We consider our program to run under the PSO memory model. Although TSO is our main target, PSO is strictly more relaxed, therefore our PSO semantics stays sound w.r.t. TSO.

Notations. *Shared* is the set of shared variable symbols, *Local* is the set of thread-local variables (or registers). Unless specified, we use the letters x, y, z for *Shared* and r for *Local*. $\mathbb{V}$ is the value space of variables, for instance $\mathbb{Z}$ or $\mathbb{Q}$. e is an arithmetic expression over elements of $\mathbb{V}$ and *Local* (we decompose expressions involving *Shared* variables into reads of these variables into *Local* variables and actually evaluating the expression over these locals). $\circ$ is function composition. $\mathbb{L}$ is a set of *program points* or *control labels*.

Remark 1. $\mathscr{D}$ is isomorphic to a usual vector space. As such, it supports usual operations such as variable assignment ($x := e$) or condition and expression evaluation. We will also use the *add* and *drop* operations, which respectively add an unconstrained variable to the domain, and delete a variable and then project on the remaining dimensions.

As the variables in *Shared* live both in the buffers and the memory, we will use the explicit notation x^{mem} for the bindings of *Mem*. We represent a buffer of length N of the thread T for the variable x by N variables $x_1^T, ..., x_N^T$ containing the buffer entries in order, x_1^T being the most recent one and x_N^T the oldest one.

$$Mem \triangleq Shared \rightarrow \mathbb{V} \qquad \text{Shared memory}$$

$$TLS \triangleq Local \rightarrow \mathbb{V} \qquad \text{Thread Local Storage (registers)}$$

$$\forall x \in Shared, Buf_x^T \triangleq \bigcup_{N \in \mathbb{N}} (\{x_1^T, ..., x_N^T\} \rightarrow \mathbb{V}) \qquad \text{Buffers}$$

$$\mathscr{S} \triangleq Mem \times TLS \times \prod_{\substack{x \in Shared \\ T \in Thread}} Buf_x^T \qquad \text{Program states}$$

$$\mathscr{D} \triangleq \mathcal{P}(\mathscr{S}) \qquad \text{Sets of program states}$$

$$\mathscr{C} \triangleq Thread \rightarrow \mathbb{L} \qquad \text{Control states}$$

Fig. 4. A concrete domain for PSO programs.

This concrete domain has been used by in our previous work [20] to define the concrete non-modular semantics of the programs. For each statement corresponding to a control graph edge *stmt* and for each thread T, they define the operator $[\![stmt]\!]_T : \mathscr{D} \rightarrow \mathscr{D}$ that computes the set of states reachable when T executes *stmt* from any state in an input set. $[\![x := e]\!]_T$ adds the value of e into the buffer of T for the variable x, shifting the already present x_i^T. $[\![r := x]\!]$ reads x_1^T, or, if not defined (the buffer is empty), x^{mem}. $[\![\texttt{flush } x]\!]_T$ removes the oldest entry of x and writes its value in x^{mem}. $[\![\texttt{mfence}]\!]_T$ ensures that all buffers of T are empty before executing subsequent operations. The formal semantics is recalled in Fig. 5. For convenience reasons, we define $[\![.]\!]$ on state singletons $\{S\}$ and then lift it pointwise to any state set.

The standard way of using this semantics consists in constructing the product control graph modeling all interleavings of thread executions of a program from the control graph of each thread it is composed of. The semantics of the program is then computed as the least fixpoint of the equation system described by this graph, whose vertices are control states (elements of $\mathscr{C}$ as defined in Fig. 4) and edges are labelled by operators of Fig. 5. The non-determinism of flushes can be encoded by a self-loop edge of label $[\![\texttt{flush } x]\!]_T$ for each $x \in Shared$, $T \in Thread$ on each vertex in the graph. However, we will now state a lemma that will provide us a new and more efficient computation method.

Lemma 1 (Flush commutation). *Let $x \in Shared$ and $[\![op_{\not{x}}]\!]$ be an operator that neither writes to nor reads from x, that is either $[\![y := expr]\!]$, $[\![r := y]\!]$, $[\![r := expr]\!]$ or $[\![\text{condition}]\!]$, with $\forall y \in Shared, y \neq x \Rightarrow y \notin \text{condition}$. Then:*

$$\forall S \in \mathscr{S}, \forall T \in Thread, [\![\texttt{flush } x]\!]_T \circ [\![op_{\not{x}}]\!]S = [\![op_{\not{x}}]\!] \circ [\![\texttt{flush } x]\!]_T S$$

Proof. We consider S as a numerical point, each variable being a dimension in the state space. We distinguish two cases:

Case 1: $L_S^T(x) = 0$. $[\![\texttt{flush } x]\!]_T S = \emptyset$, thus $[\![op_{\not{x}}]\!]([\![\texttt{flush } x]\!]_T S) = \emptyset$. $[\![op_{\not{x}}]\!]$ does not add any entry to the buffer of x and T, since $[\![x := e]\!]$ is the only operator that does it. Therefore $L_S^T([\![op_{\not{x}}]\!]S) = 0$, which implies $[\![\texttt{flush } x]\!]_T([\![op_{\not{x}}]\!]S) = \emptyset$.

$$\forall T \in \mathit{Thread}, [\![.]\!]_T : \mathcal{D} \rightarrow \mathcal{D}$$

$$[\![x := e]\!]_T\{S\} \triangleq [\![x_1^T := e]\!] \circ [\![x_2^T := x_1^T]\!] \circ \ldots \circ [\![x_{L_S^T(x)+1}^T := x_{L_S^T(x)}^T]\!] \circ [\![\mathit{add}\ x_{L_S^T(x)+1}^T]\!]\{S\}$$

$$[\![r := x]\!]_T\{S\} \triangleq \begin{cases} [\![r := x^{mem}]\!]S & \text{if } L_S^T(x) = 0 \\ [\![r := x_1^T]\!]S & \text{if } L_S^T(x) \geq 1 \end{cases} \qquad [\![\mathtt{mfence}]\!]_T\{S\} \triangleq \begin{cases} S & \text{if } \forall x, L_S^T(x) = 0 \\ \emptyset & \text{otherwise} \end{cases}$$

$$[\![\mathtt{flush}\ x]\!]_T\{S\} \triangleq \begin{cases} \emptyset & \text{if } L_S^T(x) = 0 \\ [\![\mathit{drop}\ x_{L_S^T(x)}^T]\!] \circ [\![x^{mem} := x_{L_S^T(x)}^T]\!]\{S\} & \text{if } L_S^T(x) \geq 1 \end{cases}$$

$$\forall X \in \mathcal{D}, [\![\mathit{stmt}]\!]_T X \triangleq \bigcup_{S \in X} [\![\mathit{stmt}]\!]_T\{S\}$$

Fig. 5. Concrete interleaving semantics in PSO.

Case 2: $L_S^T(x) > 0$. $[\![op_{\neq}]\!]$ does not modify the value of $x_{L_S^T(x)}^T$, and does not use the value of the dimension x^{mem}. Therefore $[\![x^{mem} := x_{L_S^T(x)}^T]\!]$ commutes with $[\![op_{\neq}]\!]$. $[\![op_{\neq}]\!]$ does not use the value of $x_{L_S^T(x)}^T$ either, therefore $[\![op_{\neq}]\!]$ also commutes with $[\![\mathit{drop}\ x_{L_S^T(x)}^T]\!]$. Chaining both commutations makes $[\![op_{\neq}]\!]$ commute with $[\![\mathtt{flush}\ x]\!]_T$. $\qquad\square$

This flush commutation allows us to avoid computing the flush of each variable from each thread at each control state, and to compute only the flush of the variables that have been affected by the statements leading to this control state. Specifically, when computing the result of an edge labelled with $[\![op_x]\!]_T$ (where $[\![op_x]\!]$ denotes an operator that reads from or writes to the *Shared* variable x) from a concrete element X, we do not only compute $[\![op_x]\!]_T X$, but:

$$[\![\mathtt{flush}\ x]\!]^* \circ [\![op_x]\!]_T X$$

where :

$$[\![\mathtt{flush}\ x]\!]^* X \triangleq \mathrm{lfp}(\lambda Y.X \cup \bigcup_{T \in \mathit{Thread}} [\![\mathtt{flush}\ x]\!]_T Y)$$

That is, we compute the result of a *closure by flush* after applying the operator. Note that flushes are computed from all threads, not only the one performing $[\![op_x]\!]$. The lemma states that no other flush is needed. The result $\mathcal{R} : \mathcal{C} \rightarrow \mathcal{D}$ of the analysis can be stated as a fixpoint on the product control graph:

$$\widetilde{[\![op]\!]_T} : \mathcal{D} \rightarrow \mathcal{D} \triangleq \lambda X. \begin{cases} [\![\mathtt{flush}\ x]\!]^* \circ [\![op]\!]_T X & \text{if } [\![op]\!] \text{ acts on } x \in \mathit{Shared} \\ [\![op]\!]_T X & \text{otherwise} \end{cases}$$

$$R_0 : \mathcal{C} \rightarrow \mathcal{D} = \lambda c. \text{ if } c \text{ is initial then } \top \text{ else } \bot$$

$$\mathcal{R} = \mathrm{lfp}\ \lambda R.R_0 \cup \left(\lambda c. \bigcup_{c' \xrightarrow{op}_T c \text{ edges}} \widetilde{[\![op]\!]_T} R(c') \right)$$

This property will prove itself even more useful when going into modular analysis.

Remark 2. As long as we stay in the concrete domain, this computation method has no effect on precision. However, this is no longer necessarily true when going into the abstract, and we found this method to be actually more precise on some examples: the flush abstract operator may induce information loss, and the new method performs less flush operations, thus retaining more precision.

2.2 Modular Concrete Semantics

We rely on Miné's interference system [15] to elaborate a thread-modular semantics from the monolithic previous one, as well as a computation method.

Transition Systems. The interference-based semantics can be expressed in the most general way when resorting to *labelled transition systems* rather than to equation systems (that are described by the control graph based analysis). We follow Cousot and Cousot [5] and express the transition system associated to our concurrent programs as a set $\Sigma = \mathscr{C} \times \mathscr{S}$ of *global states*, a set $I \subseteq \Sigma$ of *initial states*, and a *transition relation* $\tau \subseteq \Sigma \times Thread \times \Sigma$. We write $\sigma \xrightarrow{T}_\tau \sigma'$ for $(\sigma, T, \sigma') \in \tau$, which denotes that executing a step from thread T updates the current global state σ into the state σ'. We refer to Cousot [5] and Miné [15] for the formal definition of such a system, which is quite standard.

The semantics of this transition system specifies that a global state σ is reachable if and only if there exists a finite sequence of states $\sigma_1, ..., \sigma_n$ and some (not necessarily different) threads $T_\alpha, T_\beta, ..., T_\psi, T_\omega \in Thread$ such that $I \xrightarrow{T_\alpha}_\tau \sigma_1 \xrightarrow{T_\beta}_\tau ... \xrightarrow{T_\psi}_\tau \sigma_n \xrightarrow{T_\omega}_\tau \sigma$.

Local States. The monolithic transition system uses as global states a pair of a global control information in $\mathscr{C}$ and a memory state in $\mathscr{S}$. The modular transition system defines the local states of a thread T by reducing the control part to that of T only. By doing so, one retrieves a semantics that has the same structure as when performing a sequential analysis of the thread. However, the control information of the other threads is not lost, but kept in auxiliary variables $pc_{T'}$ for each $T' \in Thread, T' \neq T$. This is needed for staying complete in the concrete, and useful to remain precise in the abstract world. We denote by $\mathscr{S}_T$ the states in $\mathscr{S}$ augmented with these $pc_{T'}$ variables. Local states of $T \in Thread$ thus live in $\Sigma_T = \mathbb{L} \times \mathscr{S}_T$. We define the domain $\mathscr{D}_T \triangleq \mathcal{P}(\mathscr{S}_T)$.

Interferences. Interferences model interaction and communication between threads. The interferences set $\mathscr{I}_T$ caused by a thread T are transitions produced by T: $\mathscr{I}_T \triangleq \left\{ \sigma \xrightarrow{T}_\tau \sigma' \in \tau \mid \sigma \text{ is a state reachable from } I \right\}$.

Computation Method. The method for computing an interference modular semantics works with two least fixpoint iterations:

- The inner fixpoint iteration computes, for a given interference set, the local states result of a thread. It also produces the interferences set generated by this thread executions. It will ultimately compute the program state reachability, one thread at a time.

- The outer fixpoint iteration computes fully the inner fixpoint, using the generated interferences from one inner analysis as an input of the next one. It goes on, computing the inner fixpoint for each thread at each iteration, until the interferences set is stabilised with increasing sets of interferences starting from an empty set.

The outer least fixpoint computation is a standard run-until-stabilisation procedure. The inner fixpoint is alike sequential program fixpoint computation, with the specificity of interference that we will describe. We refer to Miné [15] for the complete development on general transition systems, while we focus here on the specific case of the language of Sect. 2.1 under weak memory models.

This analysis method is thread modular in the sense that it analyses each thread in isolation from other thread code. It must still take into account the interferences from other threads to remain sound. Furthermore, this is a constructive method: we infer the interference set from scratch rather than relying on the user to provide it. This is why we need to iterate the outer fixpoint computation as opposed to analysing each thread separately only once. Practically, we observe that the number of outer iterations until stabilisation is very small (less than 5) on typical programs.

Let us consider the graph representation of the inner fixpoint computation. As already stated, it takes an interference set as an input and works like a sequential program analysis, except when computing the result of an edge transfer operation, the analyser also uses the origin and the resulting local states to build an interference corresponding to the transition associated to the edge. As $\mathscr{S}_T$ holds the control information about other threads, as long as we stay in the concrete domain, all the information needed to build this interference is available. The analyser also needs to take into account the transition from other threads: this is done through an interference application phase that can be performed just after computing the local state attached to a vertex. Amongst all interferences, the analyser picks the ones whose origin global state is compatible with the current local state (which means they model transitions that can happen from this local state); then it updates the local state, adding the destination global states of these interferences as possible elements.

On a thread analysis with a SC model, these two phases are well separated: first, a *generation* phase computes a destination state as well as generated interferences. Then the analyser joins the destination states from all incoming vertices to get the resulting current state at the current label. After this, the *application* phase applies candidate interferences, and the fixpoint engine can move to the next vertex to be computed. However, it works differently in a relaxed memory setting, due to flush self-loop edges: one wants to avoid useless recomputations of incoming edges by computing a flushing fixpoint before applying interferences. These flushes generate interferences themselves, that must be taken into account.

Yet we showed earlier, for the monolithic analysis, that it was equivalent to compute flushes only when needed (which is more efficient), that is after operations on the same variable, with which they do not commute. This works the same way in modular analyses: when applying interferences from other threads, one can in particular apply interferences that interact with a variable in the shared memory. These applications do not commute with flushes of this variable: therefore, one must close by flush with respect to a variable after applying interferences that interact with this variable.

3   Abstract Semantics

3.1   Abstracting Local States

We abstract the local state of a thread T in a similar way to our previous work [20]. We first forget the variables that represent the buffer entries from other threads than T (but we keep their local variables). We define in Fig. 6 this abstraction. The intuition behind this projection is that these entries are not observable by the current thread, yet it will still be aware of them once they are flushed, because they will be found in the accessible shared memory. As a consequence, forgetting them is an abstraction that can lose precision in the long run, but it is necessary for scalability.

We then partition the states with respect to a partial information, for each variable, on the length of the corresponding buffer: either it is empty (we note this information 0), or it contains exactly one entry (we note this 1), or it contains more than one (we note this 1+). The partitioning function, δ_T, is given in Fig. 7a. We use the notation $L_S^T(x)$ as the length of the buffer of the variable x for the thread T in the state S.

We use a state partitioning abstraction [5] with respect to this criterion, the resulting domain being defined in Fig. 7b. We recall that the partitioning itself does not lose any information: $\xleftarrow[\alpha_p]{\gamma_p}$ is a Galois isomorphism.

The intuition behind this particular partitioning is twofold: first, since our operations behave differently depending on the buffer lengths, we regroup together the states with the same abstract lengths in order to get uniform operations on each partition; second, each state in every partition defines the same variables (including buffer variables, as explained in Remark 2), thus the numerical abstraction presented later will benefit from this partitioning: we can use a single numeric abstract element to represent a set of environments over the same variable and buffer variable set.

The next step uses the summarisation technique described by Gopan et al. [6] In each partition, we separate the variables $x_2^T...x_N^T$ (up to the size N of the buffer for x in T) from x_1^T and regroup the former into a single summarised variable x_{bot}^T. The summarisation abstraction is then lifted partition-wise to the partitioned states domain to get a final summarised and partitioned abstract domain. This domain is used through a Galois connection $\mathscr{D}_T^\sharp \xleftarrow[\alpha_S]{\gamma_S} \mathscr{D}_T^{Sum}$, as defined by Gopan et al. [6]

Abstracting the Control. We also need to develop a new abstraction for the control part of the local states. This control part was not present in the states of

$$\mathscr{S}_T^\sharp \triangleq \prod_{\substack{T' \in Thread \\ T' \neq T}} pc_{T'} \times Mem \times TLS \times \prod_{x \in Shared} Buf_x^T \qquad \mathscr{D}_T^\sharp \triangleq \mathcal{P}(\mathscr{S}_T^\sharp)$$

$$\mathscr{D}_T \xleftrightarrow[\alpha_\pi]{\gamma_\pi} \mathscr{D}_T^\sharp$$

$$\gamma_\pi(X_T^\sharp) \triangleq \left\{ PC, M, S, (T, x) \mapsto B_x^T \in \mathscr{S} \mid PC, M, S, x \mapsto B_x^T \in X_T^\sharp \right\}$$

$$\alpha_\pi(X) \triangleq \left\{ PC, M, S, x \mapsto B_x^T \in \mathscr{D}_T^\sharp \mid PC, M, S, (T, x) \mapsto B_x^T \in X \right\}$$

Fig. 6. Forgetting other threads buffers as a first abstraction.

$$\mathscr{B}^\flat \triangleq Shared \to \{0; 1; 1+\} \qquad \text{Abstract buffer lengths}$$

$$\forall T \in Thread, \delta_T : \mathscr{S}_T^\sharp \to \mathscr{B}^\flat$$

$$\delta_T(S_T^\sharp) \triangleq \lambda x. \begin{cases} 0 & \text{if } L_{S_T^\sharp}^T(x) = 0 \\ 1 & \text{if } L_{S_T^\sharp}^T(x) = 1 \qquad \text{State partitioning criterion} \\ 1+ & \text{if } L_{S_T^\sharp}^T(x) > 1 \end{cases}$$

(a) A partial information on states buffers

$$\mathscr{D}_T^\sharp \xleftrightarrow[\alpha_p]{\gamma_p} \left(\mathscr{B}^\flat \to \mathscr{D}_T^\sharp \right)$$

$$\alpha_p(X_T^\sharp) \triangleq \lambda b^\flat. \left\{ S_T^\sharp \in X_T^\sharp \mid \delta_T(S_T^\sharp) = b^\flat \right\}$$

$$\gamma_p(X_T^{part\sharp}) \triangleq \left\{ S_T^\sharp \in \mathscr{S}_T^\sharp \mid S_T^\sharp \in X_T^{part\sharp}(\delta_T(S_T^\sharp)) \right\}$$

(b) The state partitioning abstract domain.

Fig. 7. State-partitioning w.r.t. an abstraction of buffer lengths

the original monolithic semantics [20], which iterated its fixpoint over an explicit product control state. The superiority of the thread-modular analysis lies in the possibility of choosing the control abstraction to be as precise or fast as one wants. In particular, one can emulate the interleaving analysis (the concrete modular semantics being complete).

Several control representations have been proposed by previous authors [14, 16]. Our domain is parametric in the sense that we can choose any control abstraction and plug it into the analysis. However, we tried a few ones and will discuss how they performed as well as our default choice.

No abstraction. The first option is to actually not abstract the control. This emulates the interleaving analysis.

Flow-insensitive abstraction. This abstraction [14] simply forgets the control information about the other threads. The intra-thread analysis remains flow-sensitive regarding the thread itself. Albeit very fast, this is usually too imprecise and does not allow verifying a wide variety of programs.

Control-partitioning abstraction. This technique was explored in sequential consistency by Monat and Miné [16] and consists in selecting a few abstract labels that represent sets of labels, and only distinguishing between different abstract labels and not between two labels mapped to the same abstract label. This is a flexible choice since one can modulate the precision of the analysis by refining at will the abstraction. In particular, one can retrieve the flow-insensitive abstraction by choosing a single abstract label, and the precise representation by mapping each concrete label to itself.

We settled on the general control-partitioning abstraction and manually set our locations program by program. Additional work is needed to propose an automatic method that is both precise enough and does not add too many abstract labels that slow down the analyses.

Formally, we define for each thread T a partition $L_T^\sharp$ of the control points in $\mathbb{L}$ of T. Consider the program of Fig. 2. The partition that splits after the critical section end is $L_T^\sharp = \{[1 \mathrel{..} l_1] ; [l_2 \mathrel{..} end]\}$. Note that this partition does not formally need to be composed of intervals. Once this partition is defined, we denote as $\dot{\alpha}_{\mathbb{L}_T} : \mathbb{L} \to L_T^\sharp$ the mapping from a concrete control label to the partition block to which it belongs: for instance, with the previous example, $\dot{\alpha}_{\mathbb{L}_T}(l_{crit\ start}) = [1 \mathrel{..} l_1]$. With no abstraction, $L_T^\sharp = \mathbb{L}$ and $\dot{\alpha}_{\mathbb{L}_T} = \lambda l.l$, and with a flow-insensitive abstraction, $L_T^\sharp = \{\top\}$ and $\dot{\alpha}_{\mathbb{L}_T} = \lambda l.\top$.

Numerical Abstraction. We eventually regroup the original thread state and the control parts of the local state in a numerical abstraction. Since control information can be represented as an integer, this does not change much from the non-modular abstraction. The partitioning has been chosen so that every summarised state in the same partition defines the same variables (in particular, the buffer ones x_1^T and x_{bot}^T). Thus a well-chosen numerical abstraction can be applied directly to each partition. This abstraction will be denoted as the domain $\mathscr{D}^N$, and defined by a concretisation γ_N (since some common numerical domains, such as polyhedra, do not possess an abstraction α_N that can be used to define a Galois connection).

Our analysis is parametric w.r.t. the chosen numerical abstraction: one can modulate this choice to match some precision or performance goal. In our implementation, we chose numerical domains that allowed us to keep the control information intact after partitioning, since it was usually required to prove our target programs. Namely, we used the Bddapron [9] library, which provides logico-numerical domains implemented as numerical domains (such as octagons or polyhedra) on the leaves of decision diagrams (which can encode bounded integers, therefore control points, with an exact precision). As control information is a finite space, this does not affect the calculability of the semantics.

The resulting global composed domain is recapped in Fig. 8. For convenience, we consider the $\dot{\gamma}_{\mathbb{L}_T}$ concretisation of abstract domains to be integrated to the γ_N definition of the numerical final abstraction, since both are strongly linked.

$$\mathcal{D}_T^\natural \triangleq \mathcal{B}^\flat \to \mathcal{D}^N \qquad\qquad \gamma : \mathcal{D}_T^\natural \to \mathcal{D}_T$$
$$\gamma(X_T^\natural) \triangleq \big\{ S \in \mathcal{S}_T \mid S \in \gamma_\pi \circ \gamma_S \circ \gamma_N(X_T^\natural(\delta(S))) \big\}$$

Fig. 8. Final local states abstraction

3.2   Abstracting Interferences

We recall that interferences in the transition system live in $\Sigma \times Thread \times \Sigma$. They are composed of an origin global state, the thread that generates them, and the destination global state. We group interference sets by thread: one group will thus be an abstraction of $\mathcal{P}(\Sigma \times \Sigma)$. We represent the control part of Σ as a label variable pc_T for each $T \in Thread$.

To represent pairs in $\Sigma \times \Sigma$, we group together the origin and the destination global states in a single numerical environment. We use the standard variable names for the origin state, and use a *primed* version v' of each variable v for the destination domain. This is a common pattern for representing input-output relations over variables, such as function application.

We then apply the same kind of abstractions as in local states: we forget every buffer variable of every thread (including the thread indexing each interference set), and we abstract the control variables of each thread, using the same abstraction as in local states, which is label partitioning.

We partition the interferences with respect to the shared variable they interact with (which can be None for interferences only acting on local variables). This allows us to close-by-flush after interference application considering only the shared variables affected, as we discussed in Sect. 2.2.

After doing that, we use a numerical abstraction for each partition. Although one could theoretically use different numerical domains for local states and interferences, we found that using the same one was more convenient: since interference application and generation use operations that manipulate both local states and interferences (for instance, interferences are generated from local states, then joined to already existing interferences), it is easier to use operations such as join that are natively defined rather than determining similar operators on two abstract elements of different types.

3.3   Abstract Operations

Operators for computing local states and generating interferences can be derived from our abstraction in the usual way: we obtain the corresponding formulas by reducing the equation $f^\sharp = \alpha \circ f \circ \gamma$. The local state ones are practically identical to the monolithic ones [20], we will not restate them here.

We express in Fig. 9 the resulting interference generation operators for flush and shared memory writing. The local state transfer operators are almost the same as in non-modular abstract interpretation, and the other interference generators follow the same general pattern as these two, so we did not write them for space reasons. $\mathcal{D}_T^\sharp$ is the abstract domain of local states, and $\mathcal{I}^\sharp$ are abstract interferences. $\triangleright$ denotes function application ($x \triangleright f \triangleright g$ is $g(f(x))$). We write $l_1[\![stmt]\!]_T^{\sharp l_2}$ for the application of the abstract operator $[\![stmt]\!]_T^\sharp$ between control labels l_1 and l_2. Note that l_1 and l_2 are concrete labels (linked to the location of the statement $stmt$ in the source program, and the corresponding control graph vertices).

We draw the attention of the reader on the $[\![x := r]\!]_T$ interference generator: it does only update the control labels of T. Indeed, the performed write only goes into T's buffer, which is not present in the interferences. The actual write to the memory will be visible by other threads though the flush interference, that will be generated later (during the flush closure).

We refer to Monat and Miné [16] for the interference *application* operator, that does not change from sequential consistency (the difference being that after using *apply*, one will close by *flush*).

Soundness. The soundness proof of this analysis builds upon two results: the soundness of the monolithic analysis [20], and the soundness of the concrete interference analysis [15]. Our pen-and-paper proof is cumbersome, hence we will simply explain its ideas: first, we already gave a formal soundness proof for the monolithic abstract operators [20]. Our local operators being almost the same, their soundness proof is similar. Miné [15] also shows that the interference concrete analysis is both sound and complete. We show that our interference

$$Var \triangleq Shared \cup Local \cup \{pc_T \mid T \in Thread\}$$

$$extend_T \triangleq \begin{cases} \mathscr{D}_T^\sharp \to \mathscr{S}^\sharp \\ X^\sharp \mapsto add(X^\sharp, \{v' \mid v \in Var\} \cup \{pc_T\}) \end{cases}$$

$$x \in Shared \qquad T \in Thread \qquad r \in Local \qquad l_1, l_2 \in \mathbb{L}$$

$$[.]^\sharp : \mathscr{D}_T^\sharp \to \mathscr{S}^\sharp$$

$l_1[\![r := x]\!]_T^{\sharp l_2} X^\sharp =$
$\quad extend_T(X^\sharp)$
$\quad \triangleright [\![\forall v \in Var, v' := v]\!]$
$\quad \triangleright [\![pc_T := \dot{\alpha}_{L_T}(l_1)]\!] \circ [\![pc_T' := \dot{\alpha}_{L_T}(l_2)]\!]$
$\quad \triangleright [\![r' := x_1^T \text{ if } L_S^{T^b} = 1 \text{ else } x^{mem}]\!]$
$\quad \triangleright [\![\forall y \in Shared, drop\{y_1^T, y_{bot}^T\}]\!]$

$l_1[\![x := r]\!]_T^{\sharp l_2} X^\sharp =$
$\quad extend_T(X^\sharp)$
$\quad \triangleright [\![\forall v \in Var, v' := v]\!]$
$\quad \triangleright [\![pc_T := \dot{\alpha}_{L_T}(l_1)]\!] \circ [\![pc_T' := \dot{\alpha}_{L_T}(l_2)]\!]$
$\quad \triangleright [\![\forall y \in Shared, drop\{y_1^T, y_{bot}^T\}]\!]$

$L_S^{T^b}(x) = 0 \implies l_1[\![\text{flush } x]\!]_T^{\sharp l_1} X^\sharp = \perp^\sharp$

$\exists L_S^{T^b}(x) \neq 0 \implies l_1[\![\text{mfence}]\!]_T^{\sharp l_2} X^\sharp = \perp^\sharp$

$\nexists L_S^{T^b}(x) = 0 \implies l_1[\![\text{mfence}]\!]_T^{\sharp l_2} X^\sharp =$
$\quad extend_T(X^\sharp)$
$\quad \triangleright [\![\forall v \in Var, v' := v]\!]$
$\quad \triangleright [\![pc_T := \dot{\alpha}_{L_T}(l_1)]\!] \circ [\![pc_T' := \dot{\alpha}_{L_T}(l_2)]\!]$
$\quad \triangleright [\![\forall y \in Shared, drop\{y_1^T, y_{bot}^T\}]\!]$

$L_S^{T^b}(x) \in \{1, 1+\} \implies l_1[\![\text{flush } x]\!]_T^{\sharp l_1} X^\sharp =$
$\quad extend_T(X^\sharp)$
$\quad \triangleright [\![\forall v \in Var, v' := v]\!]$
$\quad \triangleright [\![pc_T := \dot{\alpha}_{L_T}(l_1)]\!] \circ [\![pc_T' := \dot{\alpha}_{L_T}(l_1)]\!]$
$\quad \triangleright [\![x^{mem'} := x_1^T \text{ if } L_S^{T^b} = 1 \text{ else } x_{bot}^T]\!]$
$\quad \triangleright [\![\forall y \in Shared, drop\{y_1^T, y_{bot}^T\}]\!]$

Fig. 9. Abstract operators for interference generation.

operators soundly compute both the control and the memory part of the concrete transitions: the control part only maps a label to its abstract counterpart, and the memory part also stems from the monolithic analysis.

4 Experimentations

We implemented our method and tested it against a few examples. Our prototype was programmed with the OCaml language, using the BDDApron logico-numerical domain library and contributing a fixpoint engine to ocamlgraph. Our experiments run on a Intel(R) Xeon(R) CPU E3-1505M v5 @ 2.80 GHz computer with 8 GB RAM. We compare against our previous work [20].

Improvements on Scaling. To test the scaling, we used the N-threads version of the program of Fig. 2, and timed both monolithic and modular analyses when N increases. Results are shown in Fig. 10. They show that the modular analysis does indeed scale better than the monolithic one: the performance ratio between both methods is exponential. However, the modular analysis still has an exponential curve, and is slower than in sequential consistency where it was able to analyse hundreds of threads of the same program in a couple of hours [16].

We believe this difference is mainly due to the fact that, in SC, adding a thread only adds so much code for the analyser to go through. This is not the case in relaxed models, where adding a thread also increases the size of program states, due to its buffers. Therefore the 8 threads version of the program has not only 4 times as much code to analyse than the 2 threads version, but this code also deals with a 4 times bigger global state: the analysis difficulty increase is twofold, leading to a greater analysis time augmentation.

Testing the Precision. Modular analysis, after abstraction, provides a more scalable method than a monolithic one. This comes at a cost: the additional abstraction (for instance on control) may lead to precision loss. To assess this precision, we compare with our previous results [20] in Fig. 11.

The analysis of these programs aims to check safety properties expressed as logico-numerical invariants. These properties mostly are mutual exclusions: at some program points (the combinations of at least two thread critical section control points), the abstraction should be $\bot$ (or the property `false` should hold).

The modular analysis was able retain the needed precision to prove the correctness of most of these programs, despite the additional abstraction. However, it does fail on two tests, `kessel` and `bakery`. We believe that it could also pass these ones with a better control partitioning, but our heuristics (see the next paragraph) were not able to determine it.

Note that `bakery` is significantly bigger than the other examples. Although our analysis could not verify it, it did finish (in a few minutes with the most aggressive abstractions), whereas the non-modular one was terminated after running for more than a day. This is not a proper scaling improvement result due to the failure, but it is worth noticing.

All the programs certified correct by our analysis are assumed to run under the PSO model. Yet some programs may be correct under the stronger TSO

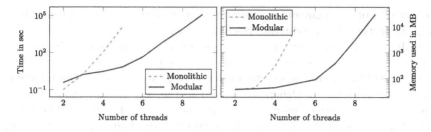

Fig. 10. Scaling results.

Test	abp	concloop	kessel	dekker	peterson	queue	bakery
Non-modular	✓	✓	✓	✓	✓	✓	*timeout after days*
Modular	✓	✓	✗	✓	✓	✓	✗

Fig. 11. Precision results on small programs.

model but not under PSO: for instance, one can sometimes remove some fences (between two writes into different locations) of a PSO valid program and get a TSO (but no longer PSO) valid program. Our prototype will not be able to check these TSO programs, since it is sound w.r.t. PSO.

Our main target being TSO, this can be a precision issue, which one can solve by adding additional fences. However, we observed that all those tests, except peterson, were validated using the minimal set of fences for the program to be actually correct under TSO; this validates our abstraction choice even with TSO as a target. We already proposed a method to handle TSO better by retrieving some precision [20]: this technique could also be implemented within our modular framework if needed.

Leveraging Our Method in Production. For realistic production-ready analyses, one should likely couple this analysis with a less precise, more scalable one, such as a non-relational or flow-insensitive one [11,14]. The precise one should be used on the small difficult parts of the programs, typically when synchronisation happens and precision is needed to model the interaction between threads. Then the scaling method can be used on the other parts, for instance when threads do large computations without interacting much. As, to be scalable, a concurrent program analysis must be thread-modular anyway, we also believe this analysis lays a better ground for this kind of integration than a monolithic one.

We also recall that our method requires the user to manually select the control abstraction. The control partition is specified by adding a label notation at chosen separation points. Most of the time, partitioning at loop heads is sufficient. We believe this could be fully automated but are not able to do it yet. Practically, we found that few trials were needed to find reasonably good abstractions: putting label separations on loops heads and at the control point where the properties must be check was often more than enough. An automatic discovery of a proper control partitioning is left to future work and would be an important feature of a production-ready analyser.

Finally, real-life complex programs feature some additional traits that are not part of our current semantics. Some, such as pointer and heap abstraction or shape analysis, are orthogonal to our work: dedicated domains can be merged with ours to modelise it. Others are linked to the concurrency model, such as atomic operations like `compare-and-swap` and `lock` instructions. The former could be quickly added to our analyser: one needs to evaluate the condition, conditionally perform the affectation, and flush the memory (like `mfence` would); all this without generating or applying interferences inbetween. The latter could also be added with a little more work: the idea would be to generate interferences abstracting a whole `lock/unlock` block transition instead of individual interferences for each statement in the block.

5   Related Work

Thread-modular and weak memory analyses has been investigated by several authors [1,2,4,7,8,10,13,15–17], yet few works combine both. Nonetheless, it was shown [3,14] that non-relational analyses that are sound under sequential consistency remain sound under relaxed models. Thus some of these works can also be used in a weakly consistent memory environment, if one accepts the imprecision that comes with non-relational domains. In particular, Miné [14] proposes a sound yet imprecise (flow-insensitive, non-relational) analysis for relaxed memory.

Ridge [18] has formalised a rely-guarantee logics for x86-TSO. However, his work focuses on a proof system for this model rather than static analysis. Therefore he proposes an expressive approach to express invariants, which is an asset for strong proofs but is less practical for a static analyser which abstracts away this kind of details to build a tractable analysis.

Kusano et al. [11] propose a thread-modular analysis for relaxed memory models, including TSO and PSO. They rely on quickly generating imprecise interference sets and leverage a Datalog solver to remove interferences combinations that can be proved impossible. However, unlike ours, their interferences are not strongly relational in the sense that they do not hold control information and do not link the modification of a variable to its old value. Thus this method will suffer from the same kind of limitations as Miné's flow insensitive one [14].

6   Conclusion

We designed an abstract interpretation based analysis for concurrent programs under relaxed memory models such as TSO that is precise and thread-modular. The specificity of our approach is a relational interference abstract domain that is weak-memory-aware, abstracting away the thread-specific part of the global state to gain performance while retaining enough precision through partitioning to keep the non-deterministic flush computation precise. We implemented this approach, and our experimental results show that this method does scale better than non-modular analysis with no precision loss. We discussed remaining scalability issues and proposed ways to solve them in a production analyser.

Future work should focus on more relaxed memory models such as POWER and C11. We believe that interference-based analysis lays a solid ground to abstract some of these model features that are presented as communication actions between threads. However, besides being more relaxed, these models are also significantly more complex and some additional work needs to be done to propose abstractions that reduce this complexity to get precise yet efficient analyses.

References

1. Abdulla, P.A., Atig, M.F., Jonsson, B., Leonardsson, C.: Stateless model checking for POWER. In: Chaudhuri, S., Farzan, A. (eds.) CAV 2016. LNCS, vol. 9780, pp. 134–156. Springer, Cham (2016). https://doi.org/10.1007/978-3-319-41540-6_8

2. Abdulla, P.A., Atig, M.F., Ngo, T.-P.: The best of both worlds: trading efficiency and optimality in fence insertion for TSO. In: Vitek, J. (ed.) ESOP 2015. LNCS, vol. 9032, pp. 308–332. Springer, Heidelberg (2015). https://doi.org/10.1007/978-3-662-46669-8_13

3. Alglave, J., Kroening, D., Lugton, J., Nimal, V., Tautschnig, M.: Soundness of data flow analyses for weak memory models. In: Yang, H. (ed.) APLAS 2011. LNCS, vol. 7078, pp. 272–288. Springer, Heidelberg (2011). https://doi.org/10.1007/978-3-642-25318-8_21

4. Blackshear, S., Gorogiannis, N., O'Hearn, P.W., Sergey, I.: RacerD: compositional static race detection. Proc. ACM Program. Lang. 1(1) (2018)

5. Cousot, P., Cousot, R.: Abstract interpretation: a unified lattice model for static analysis of programs by construction or approximation of fixpoints. In: Proceedings of the 4th ACM SIGACT-SIGPLAN Symposium on Principles of Programming Languages, pp. 238–252. ACM (1977)

6. Gopan, D., DiMaio, F., Dor, N., Reps, T., Sagiv, M.: Numeric domains with summarized dimensions. In: Jensen, K., Podelski, A. (eds.) TACAS 2004. LNCS, vol. 2988, pp. 512–529. Springer, Heidelberg (2004). https://doi.org/10.1007/978-3-540-24730-2_38

7. Gotsman, A., Berdine, J., Cook, B., Sagiv, M.: Thread-modular shape analysis. In: ACM SIGPLAN Notices, vol. 42, pp. 266–277. ACM (2007)

8. Holík, L., Meyer, R., Vojnar, T., Wolff, S.: Effect summaries for thread-modular analysis. In: Ranzato, F. (ed.) SAS 2017. LNCS, vol. 10422, pp. 169–191. Springer, Cham (2017). https://doi.org/10.1007/978-3-319-66706-5_9

9. Jeannet, B.: The BDDApron logico-numerical abstract domains library (2009)

10. Kusano, M., Wang, C.: Flow-sensitive composition of thread-modular abstract interpretation. In: Proceedings of the 2016 24th ACM SIGSOFT International Symposium on Foundations of Software Engineering, pp. 799–809. ACM (2016)

11. Kusano, M., Wang, C.: Thread-modular static analysis for relaxed memory models. In: Proceedings of the 2017 11th Joint Meeting on Foundations of Software Engineering, ESEC/FSE 2017, pp. 337–348. ACM (2017)

12. Lamport, L.: How to make a multiprocessor computer that correctly executes multiprocess programs. IEEE Trans. Comput. 100(9), 690–691 (1979)

13. Midtgaard, J., Nielson, F., Nielson, H.R.: Iterated process analysis over lattice-valued regular expressions. In: PPDP, pp. 132–145. ACM (2016)
14. Miné, A.: Static analysis of run-time errors in embedded critical parallel C programs. In: Barthe, G. (ed.) ESOP 2011. LNCS, vol. 6602, pp. 398–418. Springer, Heidelberg (2011). https://doi.org/10.1007/978-3-642-19718-5_21
15. Miné, A.: Relational thread-modular static value analysis by abstract interpretation. In: McMillan, K.L., Rival, X. (eds.) VMCAI 2014. LNCS, vol. 8318, pp. 39–58. Springer, Heidelberg (2014). https://doi.org/10.1007/978-3-642-54013-4_3
16. Monat, R., Miné, A.: Precise thread-modular abstract interpretation of concurrent programs using relational interference abstractions. In: Bouajjani, A., Monniaux, D. (eds.) VMCAI 2017. LNCS, vol. 10145, pp. 386–404. Springer, Cham (2017). https://doi.org/10.1007/978-3-319-52234-0_21
17. Mukherjee, S., Padon, O., Shoham, S., D'Souza, D., Rinetzky, N.: Thread-local semantics and its efficient sequential abstractions for race-free programs. In: Ranzato, F. (ed.) SAS 2017. LNCS, vol. 10422, pp. 253–276. Springer, Cham (2017). https://doi.org/10.1007/978-3-319-66706-5_13
18. Ridge, T.: A rely-guarantee proof system for x86-TSO. In: Leavens, G.T., O'Hearn, P., Rajamani, S.K. (eds.) VSTTE 2010. LNCS, vol. 6217, pp. 55–70. Springer, Heidelberg (2010). https://doi.org/10.1007/978-3-642-15057-9_4
19. Sewell, P., Sarkar, S., Owens, S., Francesco, F.Z., Myreen, M.O.: x86-TSO: a rigorous and usable programmer's model for x86 multiprocessors. Commun. ACM 53(7), 89–97 (2010)
20. Suzanne, T., Miné, A.: From array domains to abstract interpretation under store-buffer-based memory models. In: Rival, X. (ed.) SAS 2016. LNCS, vol. 9837, pp. 469–488. Springer, Heidelberg (2016). https://doi.org/10.1007/978-3-662-53413-7_23

Tools

Scallina: Translating Verified Programs from Coq to Scala

Youssef El Bakouny$^{(\boxtimes)}$ ⓘ and Dani Mezher

CIMTI, ESIB, Saint-Joseph University, Beirut, Lebanon
{Youssef.Bakouny,Dany.Mezher}@usj.edu.lb

Abstract. This paper presents the Scallina prototype: a new tool which allows the translation of verified Coq programs to Scala. A typical work-flow features a user implementing a functional program in Gallina, the core language of Coq, proving this program's correctness with regards to its specification and making use of Scallina to synthesize readable Scala components.

This synthesis of readable, debuggable and traceable Scala components facilitates their integration into larger Scala or Java applications; opening the door for a wider community of programmers to benefit from the Coq proof assistant. Furthermore, the current implementation of the Scallina translator, along with its underlying formalization of the Scallina grammar and corresponding translation strategy, paves the way for an optimal support of the Scala programming language in Coq's native extraction mechanism.

Keywords: Formal methods · Functional programming · Compiler
Coq · Scala

1 Introduction

In our modern world, software bugs are becoming increasingly detrimental to the engineering industry. As a result, we have recently witnessed interesting initiatives that use formal methods, potentially as a complement to software testing, with the goal of proving a program's correctness with regards to its specification. A remarkable example of such an initiative is a U.S. National Science Foundation (NSF) expedition in computing project called "the Science of Deep Specification (DeepSpec)" [17].

Since the manual checking of realistic program proofs is impractical or, to say the least, time-consuming; several proof assistants have been developed to provide machine-checked proofs. Coq [12] and Isabelle/HOL [14] are currently two of the world's leading proof assistants; they enable users to implement a program, prove its correctness with regards to its specification and extract a proven-correct implementation expressed in a given functional programming language. Coq has been successfully used to implement CompCert, the world's first formally verified C compiler [8]; whereas Isabelle/HOL has been successfully

© Springer Nature Switzerland AG 2018
S. Ryu (Ed.): APLAS 2018, LNCS 11275, pp. 131–145, 2018.
https://doi.org/10.1007/978-3-030-02768-1_7

used to implement seL4, the world's first formally verified general-purpose operating system kernel [7]. The languages that are currently supported by Coq's extraction mechanism are OCaml, Haskell and Scheme [11], while the ones that are currently supported by Isabelle/HOL's extraction mechanism are OCaml, Haskell, SML and Scala [4].

The Scala programming language [15] is considerably adopted in the industry. It is the implementation language of many important frameworks, including Apache Spark, Kafka, and Akka. It also provides the core infrastructure for sites such as Twitter, Coursera and Tumblr. A distinguishing feature of this language is its practical fusion of the functional and object-oriented programming paradigms. Its type system is, in fact, formalized by the calculus of Dependent Object Types (DOT) which is largely based on path-dependent types [1]; a limited form of dependent types where types can depend on variables, but not on general terms.

The Coq proof assistant, on the other hand, is based on the calculus of inductive constructions; a Pure Type System (PTS) which provides fully dependent types, i.e. types depending on general terms [3]. This means that Gallina, the core language of Coq, allows the implementation of programs that are not typable in conventional programming languages. A notable difference with these languages is that Gallina does not exhibit any syntactic distinction between terms and types [12].[1]

To cope with the challenge of extracting programs written in Gallina to languages based on the Hindley-Milner [5,13] type system such as OCaml and Haskell, Coq's native extraction mechanism implements a theoretical function that identifies and collapses Gallina's logical parts and types; producing untyped λ-terms with inductive constructions that are then translated to the designated target ML-like language, i.e. OCaml or Haskell. During this process, unsafe type casts are inserted where ML type errors are identified [10]. For example, these unsafe type casts are currently inserted when extracting Gallina records with path-dependent types. However, as mentioned in Sect. 3.2 of [11], this specific case can be improved by exploring advanced typing aspects of the target languages. Indeed, if Scala were a target language for Coq's extraction mechanism, a type-safe extraction of such examples could be done by an appropriate use of Scala's path-dependent types.

It is precisely this Scala code extraction feature for Coq that constitutes the primary aim of the Scallina project. Given the advances in both the Scala programming language and the Coq proof assistant, such a feature would prove both interesting and beneficial for both communities. The purpose of this tool demonstration paper is to present the Scallina prototype: a new tool which allows the translation of verified Coq programs to Scala. A typical workflow features a user implementing a functional program in Coq, proving this program's correctness with regards to its specification and making use of Scallina to synthesize readable Scala components which can then be integrated into larger Scala or Java applications. In fact, since Scala is also interoperable with Java, such a feature

---

[1] Except that types cannot start by an abstraction or a constructor.

would open the door for a significantly larger community of programmers to benefit from the Coq proof assistant.

Section 2 of this paper exposes the overall functionality of the tool while Sect. 3 portrays its strengths and weaknesses and Sect. 4 concludes. The source code of Scallina's implementation is available online[2] along with a command line interface, its corresponding documentation and several usage examples.

2 Integrating Verified Components into Larger Applications

Coq's native extraction mechanism tries to produce readable code; keeping in mind that confidence in programs also comes via the readability of their sources, as demonstrated by the Open Source community. Therefore, Coq's extraction sticks, as much as possible, to a straightforward translation and emphasizes the production of readable interfaces with the goal of facilitating the integration of the extracted code into larger developments [9]. This objective of seamless integration into larger applications is also shared by Scallina. In fact, the main goal of Scallina is to extract, from Coq, Scala components that can easily be integrated into existing Scala or Java applications.

Although these Scala components are synthesized from verified Coq code, they can evidently not guarantee the correctness of the larger Scala or Java application. Nevertheless, the appropriate integration of such verified components significantly increases the quality-level of the whole application with regards to its correctness; while, at the same time, reducing the need for heavy testing.

Indeed, even if a purely functional Scala component is verified with regards to its specification, errors caused by the rest of the application can still manifest themselves in the code of this proven-correct component. This is especially true when it comes to the implementation of verified APIs that expose public higher-order functions. Take the case of Listing 1 which portrays a Gallina implementation of a higher-order map function on a binary tree Algebraic Data Type (ADT). A lemma which was verified on this function is given in Listing 2; whereas the corresponding Scala code, synthesized by Scallina, is exhibited in Listing 3.

Listing 1. A Gallina higher-order map function on a binary tree ADT

```
Inductive Tree A := Leaf | Node (v: A) (l r: Tree A).
Arguments Leaf {A}.
Arguments Node {A} _ _ _.
Fixpoint map {A B} (t: Tree A) (f: A → B) : Tree B :=
match t with
  Leaf => Leaf
| Node v l r => Node (f v) (map l f) (map r f)
end.
```

2 https://github.com/JBakouny/Scallina/tree/v0.5.0.

Listing 2. A verified lemma on the higher-order map function

```
Definition compose {A B C} (g : B → C) (f : A → B) := fun x : A => g (f x).
Lemma commute : ∀ {A B C} (t: Tree A) (f: A → B) (g: B → C),
map t (compose g f) = map (map t f) g.
```

Listing 3. The synthesized Scala higher-order map function with the binary tree ADT

```
sealed abstract class Tree[+A]
case object Leaf extends Tree[Nothing]
case class Node[A](v: A, l: Tree[A], r: Tree[A]) extends Tree[A]
object Node {
  def apply[A] =
    (v: A) => (l: Tree[A]) => (r: Tree[A]) => new Node(v, l, r)
}
def map[A, B](t: Tree[A])(f: A => B): Tree[B] =
  t match {
    case Leaf        => Leaf
    case Node(v, l, r) => Node(f(v))(map(l)(f))(map(r)(f))
  }
```

Unlike Gallina, the Scala programming language supports imperative constructs. So, for example, if a user of the map function mistakenly passes a buggy imperative function f as second argument, the overall application would potentially fail. In such a case, the failure or exception would *appear* to be emitted by the verified component, even though the bug was caused by the function f that is passed as second argument, not by the verified component.

To fix such failures, most industrial programmers would first resort to debugging; searching for and understanding the root cause of the failure. Hence, the generation of Scala components that are both readable and debuggable would pave the way for a smoother integration of such formal methods in industry. The synthesized Scala code should also be traceable back to the source Gallina code representing its formal specification in order to clarify and facilitate potential adaptations of this specification to the needs of the overall application.

Therefore, in congruence with Coq's native extraction mechanism, the Scallina translator adopts a relatively straightforward translation. It aims to generate, as much as possible, idiomatic Scala code that is readable, debuggable and traceable; facilitating its integration into larger Scala and Java applications. We hope that this would open the door for Scala and Java programmers to benefit from the Coq proof assistant.

3   Translating a Subset of Gallina to Readable Scala Code

As mentioned in Sect. 1, Gallina is based on the calculus of inductive constructions and, therefore, allows the implementation of programs that are not typable in conventional programming languages. Coq's native extraction mechanism tackles this challenge by implementing a theoretical function that identifies and collapses Gallina's logical parts and types; producing untyped λ-terms with inductive constructions that are then translated to the designated target

ML-like language; namely OCaml or Haskell. During this translation process, a type-checking phase approximates Coq types into ML ones, inserting unsafe type casts where ML type errors are identified [11]. However, Scala's type system, which is based on DOT, significantly differs from that of OCaml and Haskell. For instance, Scala sacrifices Hindley-Milner type inference for a richer type system with remarkable support for subtyping and path-dependent types [1]. So, on the one hand, Scala's type system requires the generation of significantly more type information but, on the other hand, can type-check some constructs that are not typable in OCaml and Haskell.

As previously mentioned, the objective of the Scallina project is not to repeat the extraction process for Scala but to extend the current Coq native extraction mechanism with readable Scala code generation. For this purpose, it defines the Scallina grammar which delimits the subset of Gallina that is translatable to readable and traceable Scala code. This subset is based on an ML-like fragment that includes both inductive types and a polymorphism similar to the one found in Hindley-Milner type systems. This fragment was then augmented by introducing the support of Gallina records, which correspond to first-class modules. In this extended fragment, the support of Gallina dependent types is limited to path-dependent types; which is sufficient to encode system F [1].

The Scallina prototype then implements, for Gallina programs conforming to this grammar, an optimized translation strategy aiming to produce idiomatic Scala code similar to what a Scala programmer would usually write. For example, as exhibited by Listings 1 and 3, ADTs are emulated by Scala case classes. This conforms with Scala best practices [16] and is already adopted by both Isabelle/HOL and Leon [6]. However, note that Scallina optimizes the translation of ADTs by generating a `case object` instead of a `case class` where appropriate; as demonstrated by `Leaf`. Note also that this optimization makes good use of Scala's variance annotations and `Nothing` bottom type. This use of an object instead of a parameterless class improves both the readability and the performance of the output Scala code. Indeed, the use of Scala singleton object definitions removes the performance overhead of instantiating the same parameterless class multiple times. Furthermore, when compared to the use of a parameterless case class, the use of a case object increases the readability of the code by avoiding the unnecessary insertions of empty parenthesis. This optimization, embodied by our translation strategy, is a best practice implemented by Scala standard library data structures such as `List[+A]` and `Option[+A]`.

Since the identification and removal of logical parts and fully dependent types are already treated by Coq's theoretical extraction function, the Scallina prototype avoids a re-implementation of this algorithm but focuses on the optimized translation of the specified Gallina subset to Scala. This supposes that a prior removal of logical parts and fully dependent types was already done by Coq's theoretical extraction function and subsequent type-checking phase; catering for a future integration of the Scallina translation strategy into Coq's native extraction mechanism. In this context, Scallina proposes some modifications to the latter with regards to the typing of records with path-dependent types. These

modifications were explicitly formulated as possible future works through the
aMonoid example in [11]. Listing 4 shows a slight modification of the aMonoid
example which essentially removes its logical parts. While, as explained in [11],
the current extraction of this example produces unsafe type casts in both OCaml
and Haskell; Scallina manages to translate this example to the well-typed Scala
code shown in Listing 5.

Listing 4. The aMonoid Gallina record with its logical parts removed

```
Record aMonoid : Type := newMonoid {
  dom : Type;
  zero : dom;
  op : dom → dom → dom
}.
Definition natMonoid := newMonoid nat 0 (fun (a: nat) (b: nat) => a + b).
```

Listing 5. The Scala translation of the aMonoid Gallina record

```
trait aMonoid {
  type dom
  def zero: dom
  def op: dom => dom => dom
}
def newMonoid[dom](zero: dom)(op: dom => dom => dom): aMonoid = {
  type aMonoid_dom = dom
  def aMonoid_zero = zero
  def aMonoid_op = op
  new aMonoid {
    type dom = aMonoid_dom
    def zero: dom = aMonoid_zero
    def op: dom => dom => dom = aMonoid_op
  }
}
def natMonoid = newMonoid[Nat](0)((a: Nat) => (b: Nat) => a + b)
```

Indeed, Scallina translates Gallina records to Scala functional object-oriented
code which supports path-dependent types. In accordance with their Scala representation given in [1], record definitions are translated to Scala traits and record
instances are translated to Scala objects. When a Gallina record definition explicitly specifies a constructor name, Scallina generates the equivalent Scala object
constructor that can be used to create instances of this record, as shown in Listing 5; otherwise, the generation of the Scala record constructor is intentionally
omitted. In both cases, Gallina record instances can be created using the named
fields syntax {| ... |} , whose translation to Scala produces conventional object
definitions or, where necessary, anonymous class instantiations. A complete and
well-commented example of a significant Gallina record translation to conventional Scala object definitions is available online[3]. This example also contains a

---

[3] https://github.com/JBakouny/Scallina/tree/v0.5.0/packaged-examples/v0.5.0/
list-queue.

proof showing the equivalent behavior, with regards to a given program, of two Scala objects implementing the same trait.

A wide variety of usage examples, available online[4], illustrate the range of Gallina programs that are translatable by Scallina. These examples are part of more than 325 test cases conducted on the current Scallina prototype and persisted by more than 7300 lines of test code complementing 2350 lines of program source code. A significant portion of the aforementioned Scallina usage examples were taken from Andrew W. Appel's Verified Functional Algorithms (VFA) e-book [2] and then adapted according to Scallina's coding conventions.

4   Conclusion and Perspectives

In conclusion, the Scallina project enables the translation of a significant subset of Gallina to readable, debuggable and traceable Scala code. The Scallina grammar, which formalizes this subset, facilitates the reasoning about the fragment of Gallina that is translatable to conventional programming languages such as Scala. The project then defines an optimized Scala translation strategy for programs conforming to the aforementioned grammar. The main contribution of this translation strategy is its mapping of Gallina records to Scala; leveraging the path-dependent types of this new target output language. Furthermore, it also leverages Scala's variance annotations and Nothing bottom type to optimize the translation of ADTs. The Scallina prototype shows how these contributions can be successfully transferred into a working tool. It also allows the practical Coq-based synthesis of Scala components that can be integrated into larger applications; opening the door for Scala and Java programmers to benefit from the Coq proof assistant.

Future versions of Scallina are expected to be integrated into Coq's extraction mechanism by re-using the expertise acquired through the development of the current Scallina prototype. In this context, an experimental patch for the Coq extraction mechanism[5] was implemented in 2012 but has since become incompatible with the latest version of Coq's source code. The implementation of Scallina's translation strategy into Coq's extraction mechanism could potentially benefit from this existing patch; updating it with regards to the current state of the source code. During this process, the external implementation of the Scallina prototype, which relies on Gallina's stable syntax independently from Coq's source code, could be used to guide the aforementioned integration; providing samples of generated Scala code as needed.

Acknowledgements. The authors would like to thank the National Council for Scientific Research in Lebanon (CNRS-L) (http://www.cnrs.edu.lb/) for their funding, as well as Murex S.A.S (https://www.murex.com/) for providing financial support.

---

[4] https://github.com/JBakouny/Scallina/tree/v0.5.0/src/test/resources in addition to https://github.com/JBakouny/Scallina/tree/v0.5.0/packaged-examples/.

[5] http://proofcafe.org/wiki/en/Coq2Scala.

A   Appendix: Demonstration of the Scallina Translator

Scallina's functionalities will be demonstrated through the extraction of Scala programs from source Gallina programs. The fully executable version of the code listings exhibited in this demo are available online[6]. This includes, for both of the exhibited examples: the source Gallina code, the lemmas verifying its correctness and the synthesized Scala code.

A.1   Selection Sort

The selection sort example in Listing 6 is taken from the VFA e-book. It essentially portrays the translation of a verified program that combines Fixpoint, Definition, let in definitions, if expressions, pattern matches and tuples.

The source code of the initial program has been modified in accordance with Scallina's coding conventions. The exact changes operated on the code are detailed in its online version[7] under the Selection.v file.

Listing 6. The VFA selection sort example

```
Require Import Coq.Arith.Arith.
Require Import Coq.Lists.List.
Fixpoint select (x: nat) (l: list nat) : nat * (list nat) :=
match l with
|   nil => (x, nil)
|   h:: t => if x <=? h
                then let (j, l1) := select x t in (j, h:: l1)
                else let (j,l1) := select h t in (j, x:: l1)
end.
Fixpoint selsort (l : list nat) (n : nat) {struct n} : list nat :=
match l, n with
|  x:: r, S n1 => let (y,r1) := select x r
                in y :: selsort r1 n1
|  nil, _ => nil
|  _:: _, 0 => nil
end.
Definition selection_sort (l : list nat) : list nat := selsort l (length l).
```

Listing 7 portrays the theorems developed in the VFA e-book which verify that this is a sorting algorithm. These theorems along with their proofs still hold on the example depicted in Listing 6.

[6] https://github.com/JBakouny/Scallina/tree/v0.5.0/packaged-examples/v0.5.0.
[7] https://github.com/JBakouny/Scallina/tree/v0.5.0/packaged-examples/v0.5.0/selection-sort.

Listing 7. The theorems verifying that selection sort is a sorting algorithm

```
(** Specification of correctness of a sorting algorithm:
it rearranges the elements into a list that is totally ordered. *)
Inductive sorted: list nat → Prop :=
  | sorted_nil: sorted nil
  | sorted_1: ∀ i, sorted (i:: nil)
  | sorted_cons: ∀ i j l, i <= j → sorted (j::l) → sorted (i::j:: l).
Definition is_a_sorting_algorithm (f: list nat → list nat) :=
  ∀ al, Permutation al (f al) ∧ sorted (f al).
Definition selection_sort_correct : Prop :=
  is_a_sorting_algorithm selection_sort.
Theorem selection_sort_perm:
  ∀ l, Permutation l (selection_sort l).
Theorem select_smallest:
  ∀ x al y bl, select x al = (y, bl) →
    Forall (fun z => y <= z) bl.
Theorem selection_sort_sorted: ∀ al, sorted (selection_sort al).
Theorem selection_sort_is_correct: selection_sort_correct.
```

The verified Gallina code in Listing 6 was translated to Scala using Scallina.
The resulting Scala code is exhibited in Listing 8.

Listing 8. The synthesized Scala selection sort algorithm

```scala
import scala.of.coq.lang._
import Nat._
import Pairs._
import MoreLists._
object Selection {
  def select(x: Nat)(l: List[Nat]): (Nat, List[Nat]) =
    l match {
      case Nil => (x, Nil)
      case h :: t => if (x <= h) {
        val (j, l1) = select(x)(t)
        (j, h :: l1)
      }
      else {
        val (j, l1) = select(h)(t)
        (j, x :: l1)
      }
    }
  def selsort(l: List[Nat])(n: Nat): List[Nat] =
    (l, n) match {
      case (x :: r, S(n1)) => {
        val (y, r1) = select(x)(r)
        y :: selsort(r1)(n1)
      }
      case (Nil, _) => Nil
      case (_ :: _, Zero) => Nil
    }
  def selection_sort(l: List[Nat]): List[Nat] = selsort(l)(length(l))
}
```

A.2   List Queue Parametricity

The list queue example in Listing 9 is taken from the test suite of Coq's Parametricity Plugin[8]. It essentially portrays the translation of Gallina record definitions and instantiations to object-oriented Scala code. It also illustrates the use of Coq's Parametricity plugin to prove the equivalence between the behavior of several instantiations of the same record definition; these are then translated to object implementations of the same Scala trait.

The source code of the initial program has been modified in accordance with Scallina's coding conventions. The exact changes operated on the code are detailed in its online version[9] under the `ListQueueParam.v` file.

Listing 9. The parametricity plugin ListQueue example

```
Require Import List.
Record Queue := {
  t : Type;
  empty : t;
  push : nat → t → t;
  pop : t → option (nat * t)
}.
Definition ListQueue : Queue := {|
  t := list nat;
  empty := nil;
  push := fun x l => x ::  l;
  pop := fun l =>
    match rev l with
      | nil => None
      | hd ::  tl => Some (hd, rev tl) end
|}.
Definition DListQueue : Queue := {|
  t := (list nat) * (list nat);
  empty := (nil, nil);
  push := fun x l =>
    let (back, front) := l in
    (x ::  back, front);
  pop := fun l =>
    let (back, front) := l in
    match front with
      | nil =>
        match rev back with
          | nil => None
          | hd ::  tl => Some (hd, (nil, tl))
        end
      | hd ::  tl => Some (hd, (back, tl))
    end
|}.
```

---

[8] https://github.com/parametricity-coq/paramcoq.
[9] https://github.com/JBakouny/Scallina/tree/v0.5.0/packaged-examples/v0.5.0/list-queue.

```
(* A non-dependently typed version of nat_rect. *)
Fixpoint loop {P : Type}
  (op : nat → P → P) (n : nat) (x : P) : P :=
  match n with
  | 0 => x
  | S n0 => op n0 (loop op n0 x)
  end.
(*
This method pops two elements from the queue q and
then pushes their sum back into the queue.
*)
Definition sumElems(Q : Queue)(q: option Q.( t)) : option Q.( t) :=
match q with
| Some q1 =>
  match (Q.( pop) q1) with
  | Some (x, q2) =>
    match (Q.( pop) q2) with
    | Some (y, q3) => Some (Q.( push) (x + y) q3)
    | None => None
    end
  | None => None
  end
| None => None
end.
(*
This programs creates a queue of n+1 consecutive numbers (from 0 to n)
and then returns the sum of all the elements of this queue.
*)
Definition program (Q : Queue) (n : nat) : option nat :=
(* q := 0::1::2::...::n *)
let q :=
  loop Q.( push) (S n) Q.( empty)
in
let q0 :=
  loop
  (fun _ (q0: option Q.( t)) => sumElems Q q0)
  n
  (Some q)
in
match q0 with
| Some q1 =>
  match (Q.( pop) q1) with
  | Some (x, q2) => Some x
  | None => None
  end
| None => None
end.
```

Listing 10 portrays the lemmas verifying the equivalence between the behavior of either ListQueue or DListQueue when used with the given program. The proofs of these lemmas, which were implemented using Coq's Parametricity plugin, still hold on the example depicted in Listing 9. Instructions on how to install the Parametricity plugin to run these machine-checkable proofs are provided online.

Listing 10. The lemmas verifying the ListQueue parametricity example

```
Lemma nat_R_equal : ∀ x y, nat_R x y → x = y.
Lemma equal_nat_R : ∀ x y, x = y → nat_R x y.
Lemma option_nat_R_equal : ∀ x y, option_R nat nat nat_R x y → x = y.
Lemma equal_option_nat_R : ∀ x y, x = y → option_R nat nat nat_R x y.
Notation Bisimilar : = Queue_R.
Definition R (l1 : list nat) (l2 : list nat * list nat) : =
 let (back, front) := l2 in
  l1 = app back (rev front).
Lemma rev_app : ∀ A (l1 l2 : list A),
    rev (app l1 l2) = app (rev l2) (rev l1).
Lemma rev_list_rect A  : ∀ P:list A→ Type,
      P nil →
      (∀ (a:A) (l:list A), P (rev l) → P (rev (a :: l))) →
      ∀ l:list A, P (rev l).
Theorem rev_rect A : ∀ P:list A → Type,
      P nil →
      (∀ (x:A) (l:list A), P l → P (app l (x :: nil))) →
     ∀ l:list A, P l.
Lemma bisim_list_dlist : Bisimilar ListQueue DListQueue.
Lemma program_independent : ∀ n,
    program ListQueue n = program DListQueue n.
```

The verified Gallina code in Listing 9 was translated to Scala using Scallina. The resulting Scala code is exhibited in Listing 11.

Listing 11. The generated Scala ListQueue program

```
import scala.of.coq.lang._
import Nat._
import Pairs._
import MoreLists._
object ListQueueParam {
  trait Queue {
    type t
    def empty: t
    def push: Nat => t => t
    def pop: t => Option[(Nat, t)]
  }
  object ListQueue extends Queue {
    type t = List[Nat]
    def empty: t = Nil
    def push: Nat => t => t = x => l => x :: l
    def pop: t => Option[(Nat, t)] = l => rev(l) match {
      case Nil => None
      case hd :: tl => Some((hd, rev(tl)))
```

```
      }
    }
    object DListQueue extends Queue {
      type t = (List[Nat], List[Nat])
      def empty: t = (Nil, Nil)
      def push: Nat => t => t = x => { l =>
        val (back, front) = l
        (x :: back, front)
      }
      def pop: t => Option[(Nat, t)] = { l =>
        val (back, front) = l
        front match {
          case Nil => rev(back) match {
            case Nil => None
            case hd :: tl => Some((hd, (Nil, tl)))
          }
          case hd :: tl => Some((hd, (back, tl)))
        }
      }
    }
    def loop[P](op: Nat => P => P)(n: Nat)(x: P): P =
      n match {
        case Zero => x
        case S(n0) => op(n0)(loop(op)(n0)(x))
      }
    def sumElems(Q: Queue)(q: Option[Q.t]): Option[Q.t] =
      q match {
        case Some(q1) => Q.pop(q1) match {
          case Some((x, q2)) => Q.pop(q2) match {
            case Some((y, q3)) => Some(Q.push(x + y)(q3))
            case None => None
          }
          case None => None
        }
        case None => None
      }
    def program(Q: Queue)(n: Nat): Option[Nat] = {
      val q = loop(Q.push)(S(n))(Q.empty)
      val q0 = loop(_ => (q0: Option[Q.t]) => sumElems(Q)(q0))(n)(Some(q))
      q0 match {
        case Some(q1) => Q.pop(q1) match {
          case Some((x, q2)) => Some(x)
          case None => None
        }
        case None => None
      }
    }
}
```

References

1. Amin, N., Grütter, S., Odersky, M., Rompf, T., Stucki, S.: The Essence of dependent object types. In: Lindley, S., McBride, C., Trinder, P., Sannella, D. (eds.) A List of Successes That Can Change the World. LNCS, vol. 9600, pp. 249–272. Springer, Cham (2016). https://doi.org/10.1007/978-3-319-30936-1_14
2. Appel, A.W.: Verified Functional Algorithms, Software Foundations, vol. 3 (2017). Edited by Pierce, B.C.
3. Guallart, N.: An overview of type theories. Axiomathes **25**(1), 61–77 (2015). https://doi.org/10.1007/s10516-014-9260-9
4. Haftmann, F., Nipkow, T.: Code generation via higher-order rewrite systems. In: Blume, M., Kobayashi, N., Vidal, G. (eds.) FLOPS 2010. LNCS, vol. 6009, pp. 103–117. Springer, Heidelberg (2010). https://doi.org/10.1007/978-3-642-12251-4_9
5. Hindley, R.: The principle type-scheme of an object in combinatory logic. Trans. Am. Math. Soc. **146**, 29–60 (1969)
6. Hupel, L., Kuncak, V.: Translating scala programs to isabelle/HOL. In: Olivetti, N., Tiwari, A. (eds.) IJCAR 2016. LNCS (LNAI), vol. 9706, pp. 568–577. Springer, Cham (2016). https://doi.org/10.1007/978-3-319-40229-1_38
7. Klein, G., et al.: seL4: formal verification of an OS kernel. In: Matthews, J.N., Anderson, T.E. (eds.) Proceedings of the 22nd ACM Symposium on Operating Systems Principles 2009, SOSP 2009, Big Sky, Montana, USA, 11–14 October 2009, pp. 207–220. ACM (2009). https://doi.org/10.1145/1629575.1629596
8. Leroy, X.: Formal certification of a compiler back-end or: programming a compiler with a proof assistant. In: Morrisett, J.G., Jones, S.L.P. (eds.) Proceedings of the 33rd ACM SIGPLAN-SIGACT Symposium on Principles of Programming Languages, POPL 2006, Charleston, South Carolina, USA, 11–13 January 2006, pp. 42–54. ACM (2006). https://doi.org/10.1145/1111037.1111042
9. Letouzey, P.: A new extraction for Coq. In: Geuvers, H., Wiedijk, F. (eds.) TYPES 2002. LNCS, vol. 2646, pp. 200–219. Springer, Heidelberg (2003). https://doi.org/10.1007/3-540-39185-1_12
10. Letouzey, P.: Programmation fonctionnelle certifiée : L'extraction de programmes dans l'assistant Coq. (Certified functional programming: Program extraction within Coq proof assistant), Ph.D. thesis, University of Paris-Sud, Orsay, France (2004). https://tel.archives-ouvertes.fr/tel-00150912
11. Letouzey, P.: Extraction in Coq: an overview. In: Beckmann, A., Dimitracopoulos, C., Löwe, B. (eds.) CiE 2008. LNCS, vol. 5028, pp. 359–369. Springer, Heidelberg (2008). https://doi.org/10.1007/978-3-540-69407-6_39
12. The Coq development team: The Coq proof assistant reference manual, version 8.0. LogiCal Project (2004). http://coq.inria.fr
13. Milner, R.: A theory of type polymorphism in programming. J. Comput. Syst. Sci. **17**(3), 348–375 (1978). https://doi.org/10.1016/0022-0000(78)90014-4
14. Nipkow, T., Paulson, L.C., Wenzel, M.: Isabelle/HOL - A Proof Assistant for Higher-order Logic. LNCS, vol. 2283. Springer, Heidelberg (2002). https://doi.org/10.1007/3-540-45949-9
15. Odersky, M., Rompf, T.: Unifying functional and object-oriented programming with scala. Commun. ACM **57**(4), 76–86 (2014). https://doi.org/10.1145/2591013

16. Odersky, M., Spoon, L., Venners, B.: Programming in Scala: A Comprehensive Step-by-step Guide, 2nd edn. Artima Incorporation, Walnut Creek (2011)
17. Pierce, B.C.: The science of deep specification (keynote). In: Visser, E. (ed.) Companion Proceedings of the 2016 ACM SIGPLAN International Conference on Systems, Programming, Languages and Applications: Software for Humanity, SPLASH 2016, Amsterdam, Netherlands, 30 October–4 November 2016, p. 1. ACM (2016). https://doi.org/10.1145/2984043.2998388

HoIce: An ICE-Based Non-linear Horn Clause Solver

Adrien Champion[1(✉)], Naoki Kobayashi[1], and Ryosuke Sato[2]

[1] The University of Tokyo, Tokyo, Japan
adrien.champion@email.com
[2] Kyushu University, Fukuoka, Japan

Abstract. The ICE framework is a machine-learning-based technique originally introduced for inductive invariant inference over transition systems, and building on the supervised learning paradigm. Recently, we adapted the approach to non-linear Horn clause solving in the context of higher-order program verification. We showed that we could solve more of our benchmarks (extracted from higher-order program verification problems) than other state-of-the-art Horn clause solvers. This paper discusses some of the many improvements we recently implemented in HoIce, our implementation of this generalized ICE framework.

1 Introduction

Constrained Horn clauses is a popular formalism for encoding program verification problems [4–6], and efficient Horn clause solvers have been developed over the last decade [3, 9, 10]. Recently, we adapted the ICE framework [7, 8] to non-linear Horn clause solving [6]. Our experimental evaluation on benchmarks encoding the verification of higher-order functional programs as (non-linear) Horn clauses showed that our generalized ICE framework outperformed existing solvers in terms of precision. This paper discusses HoIce[1], a Horn clause solver written in Rust [1] implementing the generalized ICE framework from [6]. Let us briefly introduce Horn clause solving before presenting HoIce in more details.

Given a set of unknown predicates Π, a *(constrained) Horn clause* is a constraint of the form

$$\forall v_0, \ldots, v_n \mid \Phi \ \wedge \ \bigwedge_{i \in I} \{\pi_i(\vec{a}_i)\} \models H$$

where Φ is a formula and each $\pi_i(\vec{a}_i)$ is an application of $\pi_i \in \Pi$ to some arguments $\vec{a}_i$. The *head* of the clause H is either the formula *false* (written $\bot$) or a predicate application $\pi(\vec{a})$. Last, $v_0, \ldots, v_n$ are the free variables appearing in Φ, the predicate applications and H. We follow tradition and omit the quantification over $v_0, \ldots, v_n$ in the rest of the paper. To save space, we will occasionally write $\langle \Phi, \ \{\pi_i(\vec{a}_i)\}_{i \in I}, \ H \rangle$ for the clause above.

---

[1] Available at https://github.com/hopv/hoice.

© Springer Nature Switzerland AG 2018
S. Ryu (Ed.): APLAS 2018, LNCS 11275, pp. 146–156, 2018.
https://doi.org/10.1007/978-3-030-02768-1_8

A set of Horn clauses is *satisfiable* if there exist definitions for the predicates in Π that verify all the Horn clauses. Otherwise, it is *unsatisfiable*. A Horn clause solver implements a decision procedure for Horn clauses satisfiability. A solver is also usually expected to be able to yield some definitions of the predicates, when the Horn clauses are satisfiable.

Example 1. Let $\Pi = \{\pi\}$ and consider the following Horn clauses:

$$n > 100 \qquad\qquad \models \pi(n, n - 10) \quad (1)$$
$$\neg(n > 100) \wedge \pi(n + 11, tmp) \wedge \pi(tmp, res) \models \pi(n, res) \quad (2)$$
$$m \le 101 \wedge \neg(res = 91) \wedge \pi(m, res) \models \bot \quad (3)$$

These Horn clauses are satisfiable, for instance with

$$\pi(n, res) \equiv (res = 91) \vee (n > 101 \wedge res = n - 10).$$

Section 2 describes a use-case for Horn clause solving and briefly discusses HoIce's interface. Section 3 provides a succinct description of the generalized ICE framework HoIce relies on. In Sect. 4 we discuss the most important improvements we implemented in HoIce since v1.0.0 [6] for the v1.5.0 release. Next, Sect. 5 evaluates HoIce on our set of benchmarks stemming from higher-order program verification problems, as well as all the benchmarks submitted to the first CHC-COMP Horn clause competition[2] in the linear integer or linear real arithmetic fragments. Finally, Sect. 6 discusses future work.

2   Applications and Interface

As mentioned above, Horn clauses is a popular and well-established formalism to encode program verification, especially imperative program verification [4–6]. HoIce however is developed with (higher-order) functional program verification in mind, in particular through refinement/intersection type inference. We thus give an example of using Horn clauses for refinement type inference.

Example 2. Consider the program using McCarthy's 91 function below (borrowed from [6]). We are interested in proving the assertion in `main` can never fail.

```
let rec mc_91 n = if n > 100 then n - 10
                  else let tmp = mc_91 (n + 11) in mc_91 tmp
let main m = let res = mc_91 m in if m ≤ 101 then assert (res = 91)
```

To prove this program is safe, it is enough to find a predicate π such that `mc_91` has (refinement) type $\{n : \text{int} \mid true\} \rightarrow \{res : \text{int} \mid \pi(n, res)\}$ and π satisfies $\forall m, res \mid m \le 101 \wedge \neg(res = 91) \wedge \pi(n, res) \models \bot$.

The latter is already a Horn clause, and is actually (3) from Example 1. Regarding the constraints for (refinement) typing `mc_91`, we have to consider

---

[2] https://chc-comp.github.io/.

the two branches of the conditional statement in its definition. The first branch yields clause (1). The second one yields clause (2), where *res* corresponds to the result of mc_91 *tmp*.

Horn clause solvers are typically used by program verification tools. Such tools handle the high-level task of encoding the safety of a given program as Horn clauses. The clauses are passed to the solver and the result is communicated back through library calls, process input/output interaction, or files. This is the case, for instance, of r_type [6], which encodes refinement type inference as illustrated in Example 2. It then passes the clauses to HoIce, and rewrites the Horn-clause-level result in terms of the original program. Communication with HoIce is (for now) strictly text-based: either interactively by printing (reading) on its standard input (output), or by passing a file. We give a full example of the SMT-LIB-based [2] input language of HoIce in Appendix A, and refer the reader to Appendix B for a partial description of HoIce's arguments.

3   Generalized ICE

This section provides a quick overview of the generalized ICE framework HoIce is based on. We introduce only the notions we need to discuss, in Sect. 4 the improvements we have recently implemented. ICE, both the original and generalized versions, are supervised learning frameworks, meaning that they consist of a teacher and a learner. The latter is responsible for producing candidate definitions for the predicates to infer, based on ever-growing learning data (defined below) provided by the teacher. The teacher, given some candidates from the learner, checks whether they respect the Horn clauses, typically using an SMT solver[3]. If they do not, the teacher asks for a new candidate after generating more learning data. We are in particular interested in the generation of learning data, discussed below after we introduce Horn clause traits of interest.

A Horn clause $\langle \Phi, \{\pi_i(\vec{a}_i)\}_{i \in I}, H \rangle$ is *positive* if $I = \emptyset$ and $H \neq \bot$, *negative* if $I \neq \emptyset$ and $H = \bot$, and is called an *implication* clause otherwise. A negative clause is *strict* if $|I| = 1$, and *non-strict* otherwise. For all $\pi \in \Pi$, let $C(\pi)$ be the candidate provided by the learner. A *counterexample* for a Horn clause $\langle \Phi, \{\pi_i(\vec{a}_i)\}_{i \in I}, H \rangle$ is a model for

$$\neg(\Phi \wedge \bigwedge_{i \in I} C(\pi_i)(\vec{a}_i) \Rightarrow C(H)),$$

where $C(H)$ is $C(\pi)(\vec{a})$ if H is $\pi(\vec{a})$ and $\bot$ otherwise.

A *sample* for $\pi \in \Pi$ is a tuple of concrete values $\vec{v}$ for its arguments, written $\pi(\vec{v})$. Samples are generated from Horn clause counterexamples, by retrieving the value of the arguments of the clause's predicate applications. The generalized ICE framework maintains *learning data* made of (collections of) samples extracted from Horn clause counterexamples. There are three kinds of learning data depending on the shape of the falsifiable clause.

---

[3] HoIce uses the Z3 [12] SMT solver.

From a counterexample for a positive clause, the teacher extracts a *positive sample*: a single sample $\pi(\vec{v})$, encoding that π must evaluate to true on $\vec{v}$. A counterexample for a negative clause yields a *negative constraint*: a set of samples $\{\pi_i(\vec{v}_i)\}_{i \in I}$ encoding that there must be at least one $i \in I$ such that π_i evaluates to false on $\vec{v}_i$. We say a negative constraint is a *negative sample* if it is a singleton set. An *implication constraint* is a pair $(\{\pi_i(\vec{v}_i)\}_{i \in I}, \pi(\vec{v}))$ and comes from a counterexample to an implication clause. Its semantics is that if all $\pi_i(\vec{v}_i)$ evaluate to true, $\pi(\vec{v})$ must evaluate to true.

Example 3. Say the current candidate is $\pi(v_0, v_1) \equiv \bot$, then (1) is falsifiable and yields, for instance, the positive sample $\pi(101, 91)$. Say now the candidate is $\pi(v_0, v_1) \equiv v_0 = 101$. Then (3) is falsifiable and it might yield the negative sample $\pi(101, 0)$. Last, (2) is also falsifiable and can generate the constraint $(\{\pi(101, 101), \pi(101, 0)\}, \pi(101, 0))$.

We do not discuss in details how the learner generates candidates here and instead highlight its most important features. First, when given some learning data, the learner generates candidates that respect the semantics of all positive samples and implication/negative constraints. Second, the learner has some freedom in how it respect the constraints. Positive/negative samples are *classified* samples in the sense that they force some predicate to be true/false for some inputs. Constraints on the other hand contain *unclassified* samples, meaning that the learner can, to some extent, decide whether the candidates it generates evaluate to true or false on these samples.

4   Improvements

We invested a lot of efforts to improve HoIce since v1.0.0. Besides bug fixes and all-around improvements, HoIce now supports the theories of reals and arrays, as opposed to integers and booleans only previously. The rest of this section presents the improvements which, according to our experiments, are the most beneficial in terms of speed and precision. The first technique extends the notion of sample to capture more than one samples at the same time, while Sect. 4.2 aims at producing more positive/negative samples to better guide the choices in the learning process.

4.1   Partial Samples

Most modern SMT-solvers are able to provide extremely valuable information in the form of *partial models*. By omitting some of the variables when asked for a model, they communicate the fact that the values of these variables are irrelevant (given the values of the other variables). In our context, this information is extremely valuable.

Whenever the teacher retrieves a counterexample for a clause where some variables are omitted, it can generate partial learning data composed of samples where values can be omitted. Each partial sample thus covers many complete samples, infinitely many if the variable's domain is infinite. This of course assumes that the learner is able to handle such partial samples, but in the case of the decision-tree-based approach introduced in [8] and generalized in [6], supporting partial samples is straightforward. Typically, one discards all the qualifiers that mention at least one of the unspecified variables, and proceeds with the remaining ones following the original qualifier selection approach.

4.2   Constraint Breaking

This section deals with the generation of learning data in the teacher part of the ICE framework. Given some candidates, our goal is to generate data *(i)* refuting the current candidate, and *(ii)* the learner will have few (classification) choices to make about.

In the rest of this section, assume that the teacher is working on clause $\langle \Phi, \{\pi_i(\vec{a}_i)\}_{i \in I}, H \rangle$, which is falsifiable *w.r.t.* the current candidate C. Assume also that this clause is either an implication clause or a non-strict negative clause. This means that the teacher will generate either an implication constraint or a non-strict negative one, meaning that the learner will have to classify the samples appearing in these constraints. We are interested in *breaking* these constraints to obtain positive or strict negative samples at best, and smaller constraints at worst. If we can do so, the learner will have fewer choices to make to produce a new candidate. Let us illustrate this idea on an example.

Example 4. Assume that our generalized ICE framework is working on the clauses from Example 1. Assume also that the learning data only consists of positive sample $\pi(101, 91)$, and the current candidate is $\pi(v, v') \equiv v \geq 101 \wedge v' = v - 10$. Implication clause (2) $\langle \neg(n > 100), \{\pi(n + 11, tmp), \pi(tmp, res)\}, \pi(n, res) \rangle$ is falsifiable. Can we force one of the predicate applications in the set to be our positive sample? It turns out $\pi(tmp, res)$ can, yielding constraint ($\{\pi(111, 101), \pi(101, 91)\}, \pi(100, 91))$, which is really ($\{\pi(111, 101)\}, \pi(100, 91))$ since we know $\pi(101, 91)$ must be true.

We could simplify this constraint further if we had $\pi(111, 101)$ as a positive sample. It is indeed safe to add it as a positive sample because it can be obtained from clause (1) by checking whether $n > 100 \wedge n = 111 \wedge (n - 10) = 101$ is satisfiable, which it is. So, instead of generating an implication constraint mentioning three samples the learner would have to make choices on, we ended up generating two new positive samples $\pi(111, 101)$ and $\pi(100, 91)$. (The second sample is the one rejecting the current candidate.)

The rest of this section presents two techniques we implemented to accomplish this goal. The first one takes place during counterexample extraction, while the second one acts right after the extraction. In the following, for all $\pi \in \Pi$, let $\mathcal{P}(\pi)$ (*resp.* $\mathcal{N}(\pi)$) be the positive (*resp.* negative) samples for π. $C(\pi)$ refers to the current candidate for π, and by extension $C(H)$ for the head H of a clause is $C(\pi)(\vec{a})$ if H is $\pi(\vec{a})$ and $\bot$ otherwise.

Improved Counterexample Extraction. This first approach consists in forcing some arguments for a predicate application of π to be in $\mathcal{P}(\pi)$ or $\mathcal{N}(\pi)$. This means that we are interested in models of the following satisfiable formula:

$$\Phi \wedge \bigwedge_{i \in I} \{C(\pi_i)(\vec{a}_i)\} \wedge \neg C(H)(\vec{a}). \tag{4}$$

Positive Reduction. Assume that H is $\pi(\vec{a})$. Let $I_+ \subseteq I$ be the indexes of the predicate applications that can individually be forced to a known positive sample; more formally, $i \in I_+$ if and only if the conjunction of (4) and $P_i \equiv \bigvee_{\vec{v} \in \mathcal{P}(\pi_i)}(\vec{a}_i = \vec{v})$ is satisfiable. Then, if $I_+ \neq \emptyset$ and the conjunction of (4) and $\bigwedge_{i \in I_+} P_i$ is satisfiable, a model for this conjunction refutes the current candidate and yields a smaller constraint than a model for (4) alone would. (This technique was used in the first simplification of Example 4.)

Negative Reduction. Let N be $\bigvee_{\vec{v} \in \mathcal{N}(\pi)}(\vec{a} = \vec{v})$ if H is $\pi(\vec{a})$, and true if H is $\bot$. Assuming $I_+ \neq \emptyset$, we distinguish two cases. If $I_+ = I$, then for all $j \in I_+$, if (4) and N and $\bigwedge_{i \in I_+,\ i \neq j} P_i$ is satisfiable, a model for this conjunction yields a strict negative sample for π_j. Otherwise, if (4) and N and $\bigwedge_{i \in I_+} P_i$ is satisfiable, a model for this conjunction yields a negative sample mentioning the predicates in $I \setminus I_+$.

Post-Extraction Simplification. This second technique applies to implication and non-strict negative constraints right after they are generated from the counterexamples for a candidate. Let us define the predicate $isPos(\pi, \vec{v})$ for all $\pi \in \Pi$, where $\vec{v}$ are concrete input values for π. This predicate is true if and only if there is a positive clause $\langle \Phi, \emptyset, \pi(\vec{a}) \rangle$ such that $\Phi \wedge (\vec{a} = \vec{v})$ is satisfiable. Likewise, let $isNeg(\pi, \vec{v})$ be true if and only if there is a strict negative clause $\langle \Phi, \{\pi(\vec{a})\}, \bot \rangle$ such that $\Phi \wedge (\vec{a} = \vec{v})$ is satisfiable.

Now we can go through the samples appearing in the constraints and check whether we can infer that they should be positive or negative using $isPos$ and $isNeg$. This allows to both discover positive/negative samples, and simplify constraints so that the learner has fewer choices to make. (This technique was used in the second simplification step in Example 4.) Notice in particular that discovering a negative (positive) sample in non-strict negative data or in the antecedents of implication data (consequent of implication data) breaks it completely.

5   Evaluation

We now evaluate the improvements discussed in Sect. 4. The benchmarks we used consist of all 3586 benchmarks submitted to the CHC-COMP 2018 (see footnote 2) that use only booleans and linear integer or real arithmetic. We did not consider benchmarks using arrays as their treatment in the learner part of HoIce is currently quite naïve.

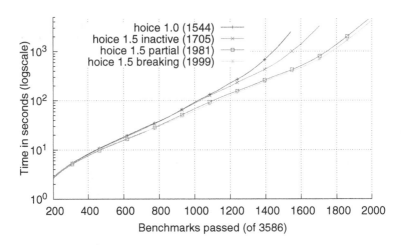

Fig. 1. Cumulative plot over the CHC-COMP 2018 linear arithmetic benchmarks.

Figure 1 compares HoIce 1.0 with different variations of HoIce 1.5 where the techniques from Sect. 4 are activated on top of one another. That is, "hoice inactive" has none of them active, "hoice partial" activates partial samples (Sect. 4.1), and "hoice breaking" activates partial samples *and* constraint breaking (Sect. 4.2). We discuss the exact options used in Appendix B.

We first note that even without the improvements discussed in Sect. 4, HoIce 1.5 is significantly better than HoIce 1.0 thanks to the many optimizations, tweaks and new minor features implemented since then. Next, the huge gain in precision and speed thanks to partial samples cannot be overstated: partial samples allow the framework to represent an infinity of samples with a single one by leveraging information that comes for free from the SMT-solver. Constraint breaking on the other hand does not yield nearly as big an improvement. It was implemented relatively recently and a deeper analysis on how it affects the generalized ICE framework is required to draw further conclusions.

Next, let us evaluate HoIce 1.5 against the state of the art Horn clause solver Spacer [11] built inside Z3 [12]. We used Z3 4.7.1, the latest version at the time of writing. Figure 2a shows a comparison on our benchmarks[4] stemming from higher-order functional programs. The timeout is 30 s, and the solvers are asked to produce definitions which are then verified. The rational behind checking the definitions is that in the context of refinement/intersection type inference, the challenge is to produce types for the function that ensure the program is correct. The definitions are thus important for us, since the program verification tool using HoIce in this context will ask for them.

Spacer clearly outperforms HoIce on the benchmarks it can solve, but fails on 26 of them. While 17 are actual timeouts, Spacer produces definitions that do not verify the clauses on the remaining 9 benchmarks. The problem has

---

[4] Available at https://github.com/hopv/benchmarks/tree/master/clauses.

been reported but is not resolved at the time of writing. Regardless of spurious definitions, HoIce still proves more (all) of our benchmarks.

Last, Fig. 2b compares HoIce and Spacer on the CHC-COMP benchmarks mentioned above. A lot of them are large enough that checking the definitions of the predicates is a difficult problem in itself: we thus did not check the definitions for these benchmarks for practical reasons. There are 632 satisfiable (438 unsatisfiable) benchmarks that Spacer can solve on which HoIce reaches the timeout, and 49 satisfiable (4 unsatisfiable) that HoIce can solve but Spacer times out on. Spacer is in general much faster and solves a number of benchmarks much higher than HoIce. We see several reasons for this. First, some of the benchmarks are very large and trigger bottlenecks in HoIce, which is a very young tool compared to Z3/Spacer. These are problems of the implementation (not of the approach) that we are currently addressing. Second, HoIce is optimized for solving clauses stemming from functional program verification. The vast majority of the CHC-COMP benchmarks come from imperative program verification, putting HoIce out of its comfort zone. Last, a lot of these benchmarks are unsatisfiable, which the Ice framework in general is not very good at. HoIce was developed completely for satisfiable Horn clauses, as we believe proving unsatisfiability (proving programs unsafe) would be better done by a separate engine. Typically a bounded model-checking tool.

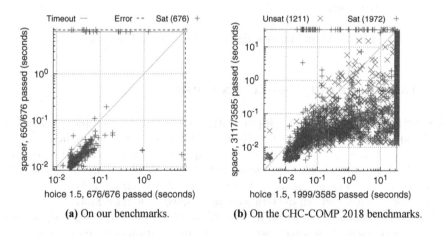

(a) On our benchmarks. (b) On the CHC-COMP 2018 benchmarks.

Fig. 2. Comparison between HoIce and Z3 Spacer.

6   Conclusion

In this paper we discussed the main improvements implemented in HoIce since version 1.0. We showed that the current version outperforms Spacer on our benchmarks stemming from higher-order program verification.

Besides the never-ending work on optimizations and bug fixes, our next goal is to support the theory of Algebraic Data Types (ADT). In our context of higher-order functional program verification, it is difficult to find interesting, realistic use-cases that do not use ADTs.

Acknowledgments. We thank the anonymous referees for useful comments. This work was supported by JSPS KAKENHI Grant Number JP15H05706.

```
(set-logic HORN)

(declare-fun mc_91 ( Int Int ) Bool)

(assert
  (forall ( (n Int) )
    (=> (> n 100)
        (mc_91 n (- n 10))
) ) )
(assert
  (forall ( (n Int) (tmp Int) (res Int) )
    (=> (and (not (> n 100)) (mc_91 (+ n 11) tmp) (mc_91 tmp res))
        (mc_91 n res)
) ) )
(assert
  (forall ( (m Int) (res Int) )
    (=> (and (<= m 101) (mc_91 m res))
        (= res 91)
) ) )

(check-sat)
(get-model)
```

Fig. 3. A legal input script corresponding to Example 1.

A   Input/Output Format Example

This section illustrates HoIce's input/output format. For a complete discussion on the format, please refer to the HoIce wiki https://github.com/hopv/hoice/wiki. HoIce takes special SMT-LIB [2] scripts as inputs such as the one on Fig. 3. A script starts with an optional **set-logic HORN** command, followed by some predicate declarations using the **declare-fun** command. Only predicate declaration are allowed: all declarations must have codomain **Bool**.

The actual clauses are given as assertions which generally start with some universally quantified variables, wrapping the implication between the body and the head of the clause. Negated existential quantification is also supported, for instance the third assertion on Fig. 3 can be written as

```
(assert
  (not
    (exist ( (m Int) (res Int) )
      (and (<= m 101) (mc_91 m res) (not (= res 91)))
) ) )
```

The **check-sat** command asks whether the Horn clauses are satisfiable, which they are, and HoIce answers **sat**. Otherwise, it would have answered **unsat**. Since the clauses are satisifiable, it is legal to ask for a model using the **get-model** command. HoIce provides one in the standard SMT-LIB fashion:

```
(model
  (define-fun mc_91
    ( (v_0 Int) (v_1 Int) ) Bool
    (or
      (and (= (+ v_0 (- 10) (* (- 1) v_1)) 0) (or (= (+ v_1 (- 91)) 0) (>= v_0 102)))
      (and (>= (* (- 1) v_0) (- 100)) (or (= (+ v_1 (- 91)) 0) (>= v_0 102))
           (not (= (+ v_0 (- 10) (* (- 1) v_1)) 0))
) ) ) )
```

Note that hoice can read scripts from files, but also on its standard input in an interactive manner.

B   Arguments

HoIce has no mandatory arguments. Besides options and flags, users can provide a file path argument in which case HoIce reads the file as an SMT-LIB script encoding a Horn clause problem (see Appendix A). When called with no file path argument, HoIce reads the script from its standard input. In both cases, HoIce outputs the result on its standard output.

Running HoIce with -h or --help will display the (visible) options. We do not discuss them here. Instead, let us clarify which options we used for the results presented in Sect. 5. The relevant option for partial samples from Sect. 4.1 is --partial, while --bias_cexs and --assistant activate constraint breaking as discussed in Sect. 4.2. More precisely, --bias_cexs activates constraint breaking during counterexample extraction, while --assistant triggers post-extraction simplification. The commands ran for the variants of Fig. 1 are thus

hoice 1.5 inactive	hoice --partial off --bias_cexs off --assistant off
hoice 1.5 partial	hoice --partial on --bias_cexs off --assistant off
hoice 1.5 breaking	hoice --partial on --bias_cexs on --assistant on

As far as the experiments are concerned, we ran Z3 4.7.1 with only one option, the one activating Spacer: fixedpoint.engine=spacer.

References

1. The Rust language. https://www.rust-lang.org/en-US/
2. Barrett, C., Fontaine, P., Tinelli, C.: The satisfiability modulo theories library (SMT-LIB) (2016). www.SMT-LIB.org
3. Bjørner, N., Gurfinkel, A., McMillan, K., Rybalchenko, A.: Horn clause solvers for program verification. In: Beklemishev, L.D., Blass, A., Dershowitz, N., Finkbeiner, B., Schulte, W. (eds.) Fields of Logic and Computation II. LNCS, vol. 9300, pp. 24–51. Springer, Cham (2015). https://doi.org/10.1007/978-3-319-23534-9_2
4. Bjørner, N., McMillan, K.L., Rybalchenko, A.: Program verification as satisfiability modulo theories. In: SMT@IJCAR. EPiC Series in Computing, vol. 20, pp. 3–11. EasyChair (2012)
5. Bjørner, N., McMillan, K.L., Rybalchenko, A.: Higher-order program verification as satisfiability modulo theories with algebraic data-types. CoRR abs/1306.5264 (2013)

6. Champion, A., Chiba, T., Kobayashi, N., Sato, R.: ICE-based refinement type discovery for higher-order functional programs. In: Beyer, D., Huisman, M. (eds.) TACAS 2018. LNCS, vol. 10805, pp. 365–384. Springer, Cham (2018). https://doi.org/10.1007/978-3-319-89960-2_20

7. Garg, P., Löding, C., Madhusudan, P., Neider, D.: ICE: a robust framework for learning invariants. In: Biere, A., Bloem, R. (eds.) CAV 2014. LNCS, vol. 8559, pp. 69–87. Springer, Cham (2014). https://doi.org/10.1007/978-3-319-08867-9_5

8. Garg, P., Neider, D., Madhusudan, P., Roth, D.: Learning invariants using decision trees and implication counterexamples. In: Proceedings of POPL 2016, pp. 499–512. ACM (2016)

9. Hoder, K., Bjørner, N.: Generalized property directed reachability. In: Cimatti, A., Sebastiani, R. (eds.) SAT 2012. LNCS, vol. 7317, pp. 157–171. Springer, Heidelberg (2012). https://doi.org/10.1007/978-3-642-31612-8_13

10. Hojjat, H., Konečný, F., Garnier, F., Iosif, R., Kuncak, V., Rümmer, P.: A verification toolkit for numerical transition systems. In: Giannakopoulou, D., Méry, D. (eds.) FM 2012. LNCS, vol. 7436, pp. 247–251. Springer, Heidelberg (2012). https://doi.org/10.1007/978-3-642-32759-9_21

11. Komuravelli, A., Gurfinkel, A., Chaki, S., Clarke, E.M.: Automatic abstraction in smt-based unbounded software model checking. CoRR abs/1306.1945 (2013)

12. de Moura, L., Bjørner, N.: Z3: an efficient SMT solver. In: Ramakrishnan, C.R., Rehof, J. (eds.) TACAS 2008. LNCS, vol. 4963, pp. 337–340. Springer, Heidelberg (2008). https://doi.org/10.1007/978-3-540-78800-3_24

Traf: A Graphical Proof Tree Viewer Cooperating with Coq Through Proof General

Hideyuki Kawabata$^{(\boxtimes)}$, Yuta Tanaka, Mai Kimura, and Tetsuo Hironaka

Hiroshima City University,
3-4-1 Ozuka-higashi, Asa-minami, Hiroshima 731-3194, Japan
kawabata@hiroshima-cu.ac.jp

Abstract. Traf is a graphical proof tree viewer that cooperates with the Coq proof assistant and is controlled through Proof General. Among other proof tree viewers and tools for browsing proof scripts, Traf is well suited for daily proving of Coq problems as it is easy to use, non-disturbing, and helpful. Proof trees dynamically updated by Traf during interactive sessions with Proof General are informative and as readable as Gentzen-style natural deduction proofs. Traf facilitates browsing and investigating tactic-based proof scripts, which are often burdensome to read. Traf can also be used for typesetting proof trees with LaTeX. The current version of Traf was developed as an extension to the Prooftree proof tree viewer and makes use of many of its facilities. Traf provides functionalities that are useful to both novice Coq users and experienced Proof General users.

Keywords: Proof tree viewer · Interactive theorem prover · Coq
Proof General · Readability of proof scripts

1 Introduction

Proof assistants are widely used for proving mathematical theorems [14,15] and properties of software [1,4] and for developing dependable software [22]. The power of mechanized verification by using proof assistants has been accepted, and such verification is now thought to be indispensable. Therefore, the readability and maintainability of proof scripts have become major concerns [10].

Among the many proof assistants [26], there are two major styles for writing proof scripts; the tactic-based style and the declarative style [17,25]. Although the former is preferable for writing concise proofs interactively by making use of the theorem prover's automation facilities, it is burdensome to read the proof scripts. Conversely, although proof scripts written in the latter style are informative and readable without tools, writing intermediate formulae could be laborious. To alleviate this situation, several tactic-based systems have been extended to accept declarative proofs [8,13,25], and several systems offer a facility for rendering tactic-based proof scripts in a pseudo-natural language [5,9,12].

© Springer Nature Switzerland AG 2018
S. Ryu (Ed.): APLAS 2018, LNCS 11275, pp. 157–165, 2018.
https://doi.org/10.1007/978-3-030-02768-1_9

Since a proof is not usually in a single-threaded structure, visualizing proofs in graphical representations could be an effective complementary approach for improving the readability of proof scripts. There have been many studies on graphical representations of proofs; IDV [24] can graphically render derivations at various levels of granularity. ProofWeb [18] uses the Coq proof assistant with specialized tactics to help the user learn Gentzen-style natural deduction proofs. ProofTool [11] offers a generic framework for visualizing proofs and is equipped with a method for visualizing large-scale proofs as Sunburst Trees [19]. ViPrS is an interactive visualization tool for large natural deduction proof trees [7]. Mikiβ [20] offers a set of APIs for constructing one's own proof checker with facilities for building proof trees by using a GUI. Pcoq [3] had a GUI for proving lemmas by using a mouse, but it is no longer available. The Prooftree proof tree viewer [23] dynamically draws a proof tree while the user interacts with Coq through Proof General, although the shape of the tree is rather abstract.

In this paper, we present a graphical tool called *Traf* that constructs proof trees automatically while the user is interacting with Coq through Proof General. Traf is different from ordinary proof viewers and proof translators in that it is designed to guide interactive theorem proving by using a full-fledged proof assistant through a standard tactic-based interface. In other words, Traf is a helper tool for enhancing both the writability and readability of proofs. The proof tree shown in Traf's window looks like a readable Gentzen-style natural deduction proof. The user does not have to worry about operating Traf since the tree dynamically grows as the proving process proceeds. Traf reorganizes the layout of the tree adaptively in accordance with changes in the proof structure caused by modifications to the proof script. It can automatically shrink unfocused branches, enabling the user to concentrate on information related to the current subgoal of a potentially large proof tree. Traf's window serves as an informative monitor that displays details of the steps in the proof.

Traf can also be used as a proof script viewer. Arbitrary subtrees can be shrunk so as to enable the entire structure of the proof to be grasped. Detailed information such as the assumptions and the subgoal at each proof step can be examined later. Since no information for the corresponding proof script is lost, the constructed proof tree can be directly used as proof documentation. With Traf the user can obtain a LaTeX description of the tree for documentation.

The rest of the paper is organized as follows. In Sect. 2, we describe the structure of a tree constructed by Traf. We discuss the usages and effectiveness of Traf in Sects. 3 and 4. In Sect. 5, we summarize the strengths and weaknesses of Traf. We conclude in Sect. 6 with a brief summary and mention of future work.

The current version of Traf was constructed based on Prooftree [23] and is available at https://github.com/hide-kawabata/traf.

2   Visualization of a Proof Script as a Proof Tree

Figure 1 shows a proof script for Coq and the corresponding proof tree constructed by Traf. As shown in Fig. 1(b), a proof tree constructed by Traf looks

```
Theorem pq_qp: forall P Q: Prop,
  P \/ Q -> Q \/ P.
Proof.
  intros P Q.
  intros H.
  destruct H as [HP | HQ].
  right. assumption.
  left. assumption.
Qed.
```

(a) Proof script for Coq

$$\cfrac{\cfrac{[H:P\lor Q] \qquad \cfrac{\cfrac{[HP:P]}{P}\text{-assumption.}}{Q\lor P}\text{-right.} \qquad \cfrac{\cfrac{[HQ:Q]}{Q}\text{-assumption.}}{Q\lor P}\text{-left.}}{\cfrac{\cfrac{Q\lor P}{P\lor Q\to Q\lor P}\text{-intros H.}}{\forall P\,Q:\text{Prop},\,P\lor Q\to Q\lor P}\text{-intros P Q.}}}{}$$

(b) Proof tree constructed by Traf

Fig. 1. Proof script for Coq and corresponding proof tree constructed by Traf.

$$\frac{A}{A\lor B}\ (\lor\text{-intro 1}) \qquad \frac{B}{A\lor B}\ (\lor\text{-intro 2}) \qquad \frac{A[y/x]}{\forall x.A}\ (\forall\text{-intro})$$

$$\frac{A\lor B \qquad \begin{matrix}[A]\\ |\\ C\end{matrix} \quad \begin{matrix}[B]\\ |\\ C\end{matrix}}{C}\ (\lor\text{-elim}) \qquad \frac{\begin{matrix}[A]\\ |\\ B\end{matrix}}{A\to B}\ (\to\text{-intro})$$

Fig. 2. Natural deduction inference rules.

like an ordinary proof tree for Gentzen-style natural deduction: it is apparent that the natural deduction inference rules shown in Fig. 2 are combined for constructing the tree shown in Fig. 1(b). However, the details are different. A proof tree used in proof theory is a tree in which each node is a statement (or *subgoal*), and each line with a label indicates the application of the inference rule or axiom identified by the label. In the case of a proof tree constructed by Traf, the label attached to a line is not the name of an inference rule but rather is a *proof command* given to Coq at the proof step. Nodes written over a line are subgoals generated by the application of the proof command to the subgoal written under the line. When a complicated proof command combined by tacticals or a tactic that invokes an automated procedure is applied to a subgoal, the effect might not be as readily understandable as a Gentzen-style proof. However, a proof tree constructed by Traf is much more informative than the corresponding proof script.

Since some commands change only assumptions (and not subgoals), all the subgoals that appear in the course of a proof and all the proof commands used in the proof together and using them to construct a proof tree is not enough to enable the user to mentally reconstruct the proof session by simply looking at the proof tree. For example, the user will not recognize the application of the command "apply H." unless the meaning of H is apparent. Traf makes a proof tree as readable as possible by

1. showing the assumptions used explicitly as branches of the *proven subgoals* over the line when a command refers to assumptions and

2. indicating the steps that do not change subgoals, i.e., the steps that modify only assumptions, by using a line in a specific style, such as bold ones.

The first measure results in proof trees that resemble Gentzen-style natural deduction proofs where the discharged assumptions are explicitly indicated. Although the second measure might not be the best way of illustrating proof scripts, it does ensure that each proof step actually taken is clearly recognizable.

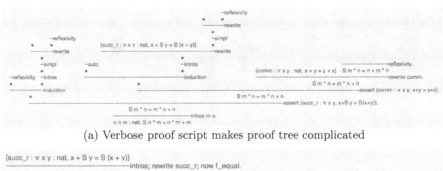

(a) Verbose proof script makes proof tree complicated

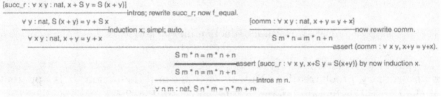

(b) Use of tacticals and automation could simplify proof tree

Fig. 3. Two proof trees constructed by Traf corresponding to two versions of proof for same lemma.

Figure 3 shows two proof trees constructed by Traf corresponding to two versions of proof for the same lemma. In Fig. 3(a), some nodes are shrunk. The proof corresponding to the tree in Fig. 3(b) is essentially the same as that in Fig. 3(a), but the latter tree is smaller due to the use of tacticals. The shape of a proof tree constructed by Traf corresponds exactly to the structure of the proof script.[1] Unlike tools such as Matita [5], which generates descriptions of proofs by analyzing proof terms, Traf simply reflects the structure of a proof script in the proof tree.

The example tree in Fig. 3(b) includes a proof step at which the subgoal does not change. The use of tactics such as `assert` for controlling the flow of a proof can be treated naturally, as shown in Fig. 3.

Figure 4 shows the proof tree for a proof script using SSReflect [16] tactics. As shown in Figs. 1(b), 3, and 4, the major tactics of Coq and SSReflect are recognized by Traf.[2] At each proof step, Traf extracts the identifiers used in

---

[1] Although non-logical tactics such as `cycle` and `swap` can be used in proof scripts, the resulting proof trees are not affected by their use.

[2] The use of goal selectors is currently not supported.

$$[pq : P \rightarrow Q] \qquad [qr : Q \rightarrow R]$$
$$\rule{5cm}{0.4pt} \text{by move /pq /qr.}$$
$$P \rightarrow R$$
$$\rule{7cm}{0.4pt} \text{move=> P Q R pq qr.}$$
$$\forall\, P\, Q\, R : \text{Prop}, (P \rightarrow Q) \rightarrow (Q \rightarrow R) \rightarrow P \rightarrow R$$

Fig. 4. Use of SSReflect [16] tactics.

each proof command, checks whether they exist in the set of local assumptions available at that step, and explicitly displays the assumptions used. Externally defined identifiers are ignored.

3   Traf as a Proving Situation Monitor

Once Traf is enabled, a proof tree is constructed in an external window as shown in Fig. 5. The tree's shape changes as the proving process proceeds. The user does not have to interact with Traf's window while proving a theorem since Traf automatically updates the proof tree by communicating with Proof General.

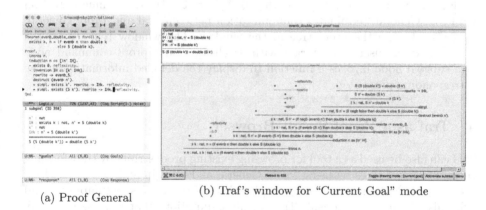

(a) Proof General   (b) Traf's window for "Current Goal" mode

Fig. 5. Screenshots illustrating scene in proving process using Coq through Proof General accompanied by Traf. While user interacts with Coq through Proof General, as shown in (a), Traf automatically updates the corresponding proof tree, as shown in (b). (Color figure online)

The Traf window shows a summary of the situation facing the user during the process of proving a theorem. It has two panes, as shown in Fig. 5(b). The lower pane shows the proof tree as currently constructed. Finished subgoals are shown in green, and the path from the root to the current subgoal is shown in blue. Other subgoals to be proved, if any, are shown in black.[3]

---

[3] Colors can be specified by the user.

The upper pane of the window shows the assumptions and the subgoal at the current state. When the user selects a subgoal on the tree by clicking the mouse, Traf marks the subgoal on the tree as selected and shows the assumptions at the state facing the subgoal in the upper pane. When the user selects a proof command, Traf shows in the upper pane the corresponding raw text string without abbreviation that was entered by the user.[4]

When a proof command is entered, Traf draws a horizontal line segment over the ex-current subgoal and places the input proof command at the right end of the line. Subgoals generated by applying the command are placed over the line. When the user retracts proof steps, the tree's shape is also restored. A proof tree constructed by Traf can be seen as a record of proof step progress.

When an entered command finishes a subgoal, Traf changes the subtree's color to indicate that the branch is finished and switches its focus to one of the remaining subgoals in the proof tree window. At every moment, the current subgoal as well as every node on the path from the root to the subgoal is shown in blue in order to distinguish the current branch from other proven/unproven branches. We call the path from the root to the current subgoal the *current path*. Traf offers "Current Goal" display mode in which nodes that are not on the current path are automatically shrunk, as shown in Fig. 5(b).

Finishing a proof, i.e., entering the "Qed." or "Defined." command to Coq via Proof General, terminates communication between Traf and Proof General. Traf then freezes the proof tree in the window. The window remains on the screen, and the user can interact with it: clicking on a proof command node or a subgoal node invokes a function to display the detailed information at the corresponding proof step.

4   Traf as a Proof Script Browser

Traf can also be used as a tool for browsing existing proof scripts by transforming them into proof trees by using Proof General and Coq. In addition to checking each step by looking at explicitly displayed proof commands, assumptions, and subgoals, the user can consult Traf for all assumptions that were valid at any step in the course of the proof.

If the proof tree becomes very large, the complete tree cannot be seen in Traf's window. Traf thus offers, in addition to scrollbars, a facility for shrinking an arbitrary node, which is helpful for setting off specific portions of the tree. Any subtree can be shrunk/expanded by selecting its root node and pressing a button at the bottom of the window.

Traf can generate LaTeX descriptions of the displayed tree for typesetting by using prftree package.[5] The variation of the details of the tree, i.e., the existence of shrunk branches and/or unproven branches, is reflected in the rendered tree.

---

[4] Command texts that are longer than the predefined length are placed on the tree in an abbreviated form. The threshold length is an adjustable parameter.

[5] https://ctan.org/pkg/prftree.

5   Discussion: Strengths and Weaknesses of Traf

Many tools have been proposed for facilitating proof comprehension. Many of them visualizes proofs graphically [7,11,19,24], and some offer facilities for explaining proofs [6,12,21]. Some have graphical interfaces for interactive theorem proving [3,18,20]. Compared with these systems, Traf's strength is its usefulness as a graphical and informative monitor of the proof states while proving lemmas by using a tactic-based language through a standard interface. In addition, Traf is easy to use and requires no cost for Proof General users. It can be used with the Emacs editor by adding the settings for Traf to the Emacs configuration file.

As a viewer for proof scripts, Traf's approach resembles that of the Coqatoo tool [6] in the sense that both systems enhance the readability of tactic-based proof scripts by presenting the scripts with appropriate information. However, unlike Coqatoo, Traf can be used while proving theorems interactively.

ProofWeb [18] has functionality similar to that of Traf. Although its web interface is promising for educational use, its tree drawing facility is a bit restrictive and not very quick. It therefore would not be a replacement for the combination of Proof General and Traf.

One weakness of Traf mainly stems from its style, i.e., the use of trees for representing proof scripts. Complicated proofs might be better expressed in text format, and other approaches, such as those of Coqatoo [6] and Matita [5], might be more suitable. For browsing extremely large proofs, a method for visualizing large-scale proofs as Sunburst Trees [19] would be preferable. Nevertheless, Traf is appropriate for use as a proving situation monitor.

Another weakness is the environment required. Since the current version of Traf depends on the LablGtk2 GUI library [2], the techniques usable for the graphical representation are restricted. In addition, Traf's implementation depends on that of Proof General.

The current version of Traf is based on Prooftree [23], which was developed by Hendrik Tews. The facilities for communicating with Proof General, many of its basic data structures, and the framework for drawing trees were not changed much. Some of Traf's functionalities, such as those described in Sects. 3 and 4, are based on those in Prooftree. While Traf owes much to Prooftree, it offers added value due to the functionalities introduced for guiding interactive proving sessions by displaying informative proof trees.

6   Conclusion and Future Work

The Traf graphical proof tree viewer cooperates with Coq through Proof General. A user who proves theorems by using Coq through Proof General can thus take advantage of Traf's additional functionalities at no cost.

Future work includes enhancing Traf to enable it to manipulate multiple proofs, to refer to external lemmas and axioms, and to better handle lengthy proof commands.

References

1. The compcert project. http://compcert.inria.fr
2. Lablgtk2. http://lablgtk.forge.ocamlcore.org
3. Pcoq: a graphical user-interface for coq. http://www-sop.inria.fr/lemme/pcoq/
4. The sel4 microkernel. http://sel4.systems
5. Asperti, A., Coen, C.S., Tassi, E., Zacchiroli, S.: User interaction with the matita proof assistant. J. Autom. Reason. **39**(2), 109–139 (2007)
6. Bedford, A.: Coqatoo: generating natural language versions of coq proofs. In: 4th International Workshop on Coq for Programming Languages (2018)
7. Byrnes, J., Buchanan, M., Ernst, M., Miller, P., Roberts, C., Keller, R.: Visualizing proof search for theorem prover development. Electron. Notes Theor. Comput. Sci. **226**, 23–38 (2009)
8. Corbineau, P.: A declarative language for the coq proof assistant. In: Miculan, M., Scagnetto, I., Honsell, F. (eds.) TYPES 2007. LNCS, vol. 4941, pp. 69–84. Springer, Heidelberg (2008). https://doi.org/10.1007/978-3-540-68103-8_5
9. Coscoy, Y., Kahn, G., Théry, L.: Extracting text from proofs. In: Dezani-Ciancaglini, M., Plotkin, G. (eds.) TLCA 1995. LNCS, vol. 902, pp. 109–123. Springer, Heidelberg (1995). https://doi.org/10.1007/BFb0014048
10. Curzon, P.: Tracking design changes with formal machine-checked proof. Comput. J. **38**(2), 91–100 (1995). https://doi.org/10.1093/comjnl/38.2.91
11. Dunchev, C., et al.: Prooftool: a GUI for the GAPT framework. In: Proceedings 10th International Workshop On User Interfaces for Theorem Provers (2013)
12. Fiedler, A.: *P.rex*: an interactive proof explainer. In: Goré, R., Leitsch, A., Nipkow, T. (eds.) IJCAR 2001. LNCS, vol. 2083, pp. 416–420. Springer, Heidelberg (2001). https://doi.org/10.1007/3-540-45744-5_33
13. Giero, M., Wiedijk, F.: MMode, a Mizar Mode for the proof assistant coq. Technical report, Nijmegen Institute for Computing and Information Sciences (2003)
14. Gonthier, G.: A computer-checked proof of the four colour theorem (2006). http://www2.tcs.ifi.lmu.de/~abel/lehre/WS07-08/CAFR/4colproof.pdf
15. Gonthier, G., et al.: A machine-checked proof of the odd order theorem. In: Blazy, S., Paulin-Mohring, C., Pichardie, D. (eds.) ITP 2013. LNCS, vol. 7998, pp. 163–179. Springer, Heidelberg (2013). https://doi.org/10.1007/978-3-642-39634-2_14
16. Gonthier, G., Mahboubi, A.: An introduction to small scale reflection in coq. J. Form. Reason. **3**(2), 95–152 (2010)
17. Harrison, J.: A mizar mode for HOL. In: Goos, G., Hartmanis, J., van Leeuwen, J., von Wright, J., Grundy, J., Harrison, J. (eds.) TPHOLs 1996. LNCS, vol. 1125, pp. 203–220. Springer, Heidelberg (1996). https://doi.org/10.1007/BFb0105406
18. Hendriks, M., Kaliszyk, C., van Raamsdonk, F., Wiedijk, F.: Teaching logic using a state-of-the-art proof assistant. Acta Didact. Napoc. **3**, 35–48 (2010)
19. Libal, T., Riener, M., Rukhaia, M.: Advanced proof viewing in ProofTool. In: Eleventh Workshop on User Interfaces for Theorem Provers (2014)
20. Sakurai, K., Asai, K.: MikiBeta : a general GUI library for visualizing proof trees. In: Alpuente, M. (ed.) LOPSTR 2010. LNCS, vol. 6564, pp. 84–98. Springer, Heidelberg (2011). https://doi.org/10.1007/978-3-642-20551-4_6
21. Tankink, C., Geuvers, H., McKinna, J., Wiedijk, F.: Proviola: a tool for proof re-animation. In: Autexier, S., et al. (eds.) CICM 2010. LNCS (LNAI), vol. 6167, pp. 440–454. Springer, Heidelberg (2010). https://doi.org/10.1007/978-3-642-14128-7_37

22. Tesson, J., Hashimoto, H., Hu, Z., Loulergue, F., Takeichi, M.: Program calculation in coq. In: Johnson, M., Pavlovic, D. (eds.) AMAST 2010. LNCS, vol. 6486, pp. 163–179. Springer, Heidelberg (2011). https://doi.org/10.1007/978-3-642-17796-5_10
23. Tews, H.: Prooftree. https://askra.de/software/prooftree/
24. Trac, S., Puzis, Y., Sutcliffe, G.: An interactive derivation viewer. Electron. Notes Theor. Comput. Sci. **174**(2), 109–123 (2007)
25. Wenzel, M., Wiedijk, F.: A comparison of Mizar and Isar. J. Autom. Reason. **29**, 389–411 (2002)
26. Wiedijk, F. (ed.): The Seventeen Provers of the World. LNCS (LNAI), vol. 3600. Springer, Heidelberg (2006). https://doi.org/10.1007/11542384

The Practice of a Compositional Functional Programming Language

Timothy Jones[1] and Michael Homer[2(✉)]

[1] Montoux, New York, NY, USA
tim@montoux.com
[2] Victoria University of Wellington, Wellington, New Zealand
mwh@ecs.vuw.ac.nz

Abstract. Function composition is a very natural operation, but most language paradigms provide poor support for it. Without linguistic support programmers must work around or manually implement what would be simple compositions. The Kihi language uses only composition, makes all state visible, and reduces to just six core operations. Kihi programs are easily stepped by textual reduction but provide a foundation for compositional design and analysis.

Keywords: Function composition · Concatenative programming

1 Introduction

Programming languages exist in many paradigms split along many different axes. For example, there are imperative languages where each element of the code changes the system state somehow before the next step (C, Java); there are declarative languages where each element of the code asserts something about the result (Prolog, HTML); there are functional languages where each element of the code specifies a transformation from an input to an output (Haskell, ML, Forth). Functional languages can be further divided: there are pure functional languages (Haskell), and those supporting side effects (ML). There are languages based on applying functions (Haskell) and on composing them (Forth).

It is composition that we are interested in here. Forth is a language where the output or outputs of one function are automatically the inputs of the next, so a program is a series of function calls. This family is also known as the *concatenative languages*, because the concatenation of two programs gives the composition of the two: if xyz is a program that maps input A to output B, and pqr is a program that maps B to C, then xyzpqr is a program that maps A to C. Alternatively, they can be analysed as languages where juxtaposition of terms indicates function composition, in contrast with applicative functional languages like Haskell where it indicates function application.

Many concatenative languages, like Forth, are stack-based: operations push data onto the stack, or pull one or more items from it and push results back on.

© Springer Nature Switzerland AG 2018
S. Ryu (Ed.): APLAS 2018, LNCS 11275, pp. 166–177, 2018.
https://doi.org/10.1007/978-3-030-02768-1_10

This is sometimes regarded as an imperative mutation of the stack, but functions in these languages can also be regarded as unary transformations from a stack to another stack. Stack-based languages include Forth, PostScript, RPL, and Joy, and other stack-based systems such as Java bytecode can be (partially) analysed in the same light as well. Most often these languages use a postfix syntax where function calls follow the operations putting their operands on the stack.

Concatenative, compositional languages need not be stack-based. A language can be built around function composition, and allow programs to be concatenated to do so, without any stack either implicit or explicit. One such language is Om [2], which uses a prefix term-rewriting model; we present another here.

In this paper we present Kihi, a compositional prefix concatenative functional language with only six core operations representing the minimal subset to support all computation in this model, and a static type system validating programs in this core. We also present implementations of the core, and of a more user-friendly extension that translates to the core representation at heart.

A Kihi program consists of a sequence of terms. A term is either a (possibly empty) parenthesised sequence of terms (an *abstraction*, the only kind of value), or one of the five core operators:

- **apply**, also written ·: remove the parentheses around the subsequent abstraction, in effect splicing its body in its place.
- **right**, or →: given two subsequent values, insert the rightmost one at the *end* of the body of the left. In effect, partial application of the left abstraction.
- **left**, or ←: given two subsequent values, insert the rightmost one at the *start* of the body of the left. A "partial return" from the first abstraction.
- **copy**, or ×: copy the subsequent value so that it appears twice in succession.
- **drop**, or ↓: delete the subsequent value so that it no longer appears in the program.

These operations form three dual pairs: abstraction and apply; right and left; copy and drop. We consider abstraction an operation in line with these pairings.

At each step of execution, an operator whose arguments are all abstractions will be replaced, along with its arguments, with its output. If no such operator exists, execution is stuck. After a successful replacement, execution continues with a new sequence. If more than one operator is available to be reduced, the order is irrelevant, as Kihi satisfies Church-Rosser (though not the normalisation property), but choosing the leftmost available reduction is convenient.

This minimal core calculus is sufficient to be Turing-complete. We will next present some extensions providing more convenient programmer facilities.

2   Computation

Combined with application, the left and right operators are useful for shuffling data in and out of applications. The left operator in particular is useful for reordering inputs, since each subsequent use of ← moves a value to the left of the value that it used to be to the right of. The swap operation, which consumes two values and returns those values in the opposite order, can be defined from the core operators as · ← ← (). For instance, executing swap x y reduces through the following steps: · ← ← () x y ⟶ · ← (x) y ⟶ · (y x) ⟶ y x.

The under operation · ← executes an abstraction "below" another, preserving its second argument for later use and executing the first with the remaining program as its arguments. The flexibility of under demonstrates the benefit of a compositional style over an applicative one. We do not need to reason about the number of inputs required by the abstraction, nor the number of return values: it is free to consume an arbitrary number of values in the sequence of terms, and to produce many values into that sequence as the result of its execution.

As Kihi is a compositional language, composing two operations together is as simple as writing them adjacently. Defining a composition operator that consumes two abstractions *as inputs* and returns the abstraction representing their composition is more involved, since the resulting abstraction needs to be constructed by consuming the abstractions into the output and then manually applying them. The compose operation is defined as → → (· under (·)). This operation brings two abstractions into the abstraction defined in the operation, which will apply the rightmost first and then the left. The leftmost abstraction can consume outputs from the rightmost, but the right cannot see the left at all.

2.1 Data Structures

Abstractions are the only kind of value in Kihi, but we can build data structures using standard Church-encodings. In the Church-encoding of booleans, true and false both consume two values, with true returning the first and false the second. In Kihi, false is equivalent to (↓): since the drop operation removes the immediately following value, the value that appears after that (in effect, the second argument) is now at the head of the evaluated section of the sequence. The definition of true is the same, but with a swapped input: (↓ swap).

The definition of standard boolean combinators like and and or each involve building a new abstraction and moving the boolean inputs into the abstraction so that, when applied, the resulting abstraction behaves appropriately as either a true or false value. For instance, or can be defined as → → (· · swap true). The result of executing · or x y is · · x true y: if x is true, then the result is an application of true, otherwise the result is an application of y.

In the Church-encoding of the natural numbers, a number n is an abstraction that accepts a function and an initial value, and produces the result of applying that function to its own output n times. In this encoding, zero is equivalent to false, since the function is ignored and the initial value is immediately returned. In Kihi, the Church-encoding of the successor constructor suc is → (· under (·) swap under (×)). For an existing number n and a function f, executing · suc n f produces the sequence · f · n f: apply n to f, then apply f once more to the resulting value. Once again, the function can be flexible in the number of inputs and outputs that it requires and provides: so long as it provides as many as it requires, it will perform a reduction with a constant number of inputs. For an unequal number of inputs to outputs, the function will dynamically consume or generate a number of values proportional to the natural number that is applied.

2.2 Recursion

To be Turing-complete, the language must also support recursion. The recursion operation Y is defined in Kihi as → × → (· under (→ → (·) ×)). For any input f, executing Y f first produces the abstraction (· under (→ → (·) ×) f), and then copies it and partially applies the copy to the original, producing the abstraction (· under (→ → (·) ×) f (· under (→ → (·) ×) f)). Applying this abstraction ultimately produces an application of f to the original abstraction: · f (· under (→ → (·) ×) f (· under (→ → (·) ×) f)). Once again, f is free to consume as many other inputs after its recursive reference as it desires, and can also ignore the recursive abstraction as well.

2.3 Output

Operators cannot access values to their left, so a value preceded by no operators can never be modified or affected later in execution. As a result, any term that moves to the left of all remaining operators is an output of the program. Similarly, any program can be supplied inputs on the right. A stream processor is then an infinite loop, consuming each argument provided on its right, transforming the input, and producing outputs on its left: a traditional transformational pipeline is simply a concatenation of such programs with a data source on the end.

A program (or subprogram) can produce any number of outputs and consume any number of inputs, and these match in an arity-neutral fashion: that is, the composition does not require a fixed correspondence between producer and consumer. It is *not* the case that all outputs of one function must be consumed by the same outer function, as is usually the case when construction a compositional pipeline in imperative or applicative languages.

3 Name Binding

The core calculus of Kihi does not include variables, but the language supports name binding by translation to the core. The bind form takes as its first argument syntax that defines the name to bind.

bind (x) (t ...) value

The name x is bound to the value value inside the term (t ...), which is then applied. For the translation to make sense as a compile-time transformation, the name and body must be present in their parenthesised form in the syntax, but the value does not need to be present; a bind may appear inside an abstraction

$a ::= (t \ ...)$

$t ::= \cdot \mid \leftarrow \mid \rightarrow \mid \downarrow \mid \times \mid a$ $t ::= \ .... \mid$ bind $\mid x$

Fig. 1. Redex language definition   **Fig. 2.** Redex binding extension

$$(t \ ... \cdot (t_t \ ...) \ v \ ...) \longrightarrow (t \ ... \ t_t \ ... \ v \ ...) \qquad \text{[Apply]}$$

$$(t \ ... \leftarrow (t_t \ ...) \ v_t \ v \ ...) \longrightarrow (t \ ... \ (v_t \ t_t \ ...) \ v \ ...) \ \text{[After]}$$

$$(t \ ... \rightarrow (t_t \ ...) \ v_t \ v \ ...) \longrightarrow (t \ ... \ (t_t \ ... \ v_t) \ v \ ...) \ \text{[Before]}$$

$$(t \ ... \downarrow v_d \ v \ ...) \longrightarrow (t \ ... \ v \ ...) \qquad \text{[Drop]}$$

$$(t \ ... \times v_c \ v \ ...) \longrightarrow (t \ ... \ v_c \ v_c \ v \ ...) \qquad \text{[Copy]}$$

Fig. 3. Redex reduction relation

with no input as in (bind (x) (t ...)), in which case the bound value will be the first input of the abstraction.

The transformation brings the bound value leftwards, jumping over irrelevant terms, and leaving a copy behind wherever the bound name occurs. To translate a bind form to the core, for each term t inside (t ...):

1. If t is the name x to be bound, replace it with ×, to leave one copy of the value behind in its place and another to continue moving left.
2. If t is an abstraction v, replace it with swap → (bind (x) v) × and then expand the resulting bind form, to bind a copy of the value in v and swap the original value to the other side of the abstraction.
3. Otherwise replace t with · ← (t), to 'jump' the value leftwards over the operator.

Finally, prepend ↓ to delete the final copy of the value, and remove the parentheses. Translate nested binds innermost-outwards to resolve shadowing.

4   Implementations

Kihi has been implemented as mechanisation of the semantics, a practical Racket language, and a web-based tool that visualises executions.

4.1   Redex

An implementation of Kihi's core calculus in the Redex [3] semantics language is presented in Fig. 1. The syntax corresponds to the syntax we have already presented. The reduction rules for this language are shown in Fig. 3. The semantics presented here proceeds right-to-left: this can easily be made unordered by matching on t instead of v on the right side of each rule. When the semantics are unordered, the Redex procedure `traces` shows every possible choice of reduction at each step, ultimately reducing to the same value (or diverging).

The binding language extension is also encoded into Redex, with syntax defined in Fig. 2. The expand translation from this language to the original calculus is defined in Fig. 4. A malformed bind will produce a term that is not a valid program in the original calculus.

expand : $t \rightarrow t$

expand$[\![(\text{bind } (x) \, v \, t_{tail} \, ...)]\!]$ = $(\downarrow t_{bound} \, ... \, t_{cont} \, ...)$
  where $(t_{bound} \, ...)$ = bind-body$[\![x, \text{expand}[\![v]\!]]\!]$, $(t_{cont} \, ...)$ = expand$[\![(t_{tail} \, ...)]\!]$
expand$[\![(t \, t_{tail} \, ...)]\!]$ = (expand$[\![t]\!] \, t_{cont} \, ...)$
  where $(t_{cont} \, ...)$ = expand$[\![(t_{tail} \, ...)]\!]$
expand$[\![t]\!]$ = t

bind-body : $x \, v \rightarrow v$
bind-body$[\![x, (t \, t_{tail} \, ...)]\!]$ = $(t_{bound} \, ... \, t_{cont} \, ...)$
  where $(t_{bound} \, ...)$ = bind-name$[\![x, t]\!]$, $(t_{cont} \, ...)$ = bind-body$[\![x, (t_{tail} \, ...)]\!]$
bind-body$[\![x, ()]\!]$ = $()$

bind-name : $x \, t \rightarrow (t \, ...)$
bind-name$[\![x, x]\!]$ = (x)

bind-name$[\![x, v]\!]$ = $(\text{swap} \rightarrow (\downarrow t \, ...) \, x)$
  where $(t \, ...)$ = bind-body$[\![x, v]\!]$
bind-name$[\![x, t]\!]$ = $(\cdot \leftarrow (t))$

Fig. 4. Redex binding expansion

Figure 5 presents an extension to the core calculus adding a simple type system. A type $\rightarrow S \, T$ describes the change in *shape* from the given inputs to the resulting outputs of executing a term. A shape is a sequence of types, and describes the type of every value that will be available to the right of a term on execution.

$$S, T, U ::= (A \, ...)$$
$$A, B, C ::= (\Rightarrow S \, T)$$

Fig. 5. Redex type extension

A Kihi program is typed by the shape judgement, defined in Fig. 6. The empty program does not change shape, and a non-empty program composes the changes in shape applied by their terms. Kihi terms are typed by the type judgement, defined in Fig. 7. For instance, the type of $\times$ begins with a shape $(A \, B \, ...)$ and produces a shape $(A \, A \, B \, ...)$, representing the duplication of a value of type A.

The type system does not include a mechanism for polymorphism, and there is no way to abstract over stacks. As a result, every type must include the type of every value to its right, even if it is not relevant to that operation's semantics, so it is difficult to write a type that describes a broad range of possible programs.

The complete Redex implementation is available from https://github.com/zmthy/kihi-redex.

4.2 Racket

Kihi has also been implemented as a practical language in Racket. This version provides access to existing Racket libraries and supports some higher-level constructs directly for efficiency, but otherwise is modelled by the Redex. The Racket implementation is available from https://github.com/zmthy/kihi and operates as a standard Racket language with #lang kihi. The distribution includes some example programs, documentation, and a number of predefined utility functions.

4.3 Web

For ease of demonstration, a web-based deriving evaluator is available. This tool accepts a program as input and highlights each reduction step in its evaluation. At each step, the operation and operands next to be executed are marked in blue, the output of the previous reduction is underlined, and the rule that has been applied is noted. The program can be evaluated using both left- and right-biased choice of term to illustrate the different reduction paths, and Church numerals and booleans can be sugared or not. It supports many predefined named terms which alias longer subprograms for convenience.

The web evaluator can be accessed at http://ecs.vuw.ac.nz/~mwh/kihi-eval/ from any web browser. It includes several sample programs illustrating the tool and language, with stepping back and forth, replay, and reduction highlighting.

As a debugging aid, the evaluator includes two special kinds of term as extensions: for any letter X, ^X is an irreducible labelled marker value, while `X reduces to nothing and has a side effect. These can be used to observe the propagation of values through the program and the order terms are evaluated.

The web evaluator also allows expanding a Kihi program to core terms (that is, using only the six operations of abstraction, application, left, right, copy, and drop). This expansion performs the full reduction of the bind syntax to core,

$$\frac{}{\mathsf{shape}[\![(), S, S]\!]} \text{ [Identity]}$$

$$\frac{\mathsf{type}[\![t_s, T, U]\!] \quad \mathsf{shape}[\![(t \ldots), S, T]\!]}{\mathsf{shape}[\![(t_s\, t \ldots), S, U]\!]} \text{ [Operate]}$$

Fig. 6. Redex shape system

and desugars all predefined named terms. In the other direction, a program can be reduced to the minimal equivalent program (including shrinking unapplied abstractions). Embedded is a command-line JavaScript implementation for node.js that also supports these features.

$$\frac{\text{shape}[\![v, S, T]\!]}{\text{type}[\![v, (A \ ...), ((\Rightarrow S \ T) \ A \ ...)]\!]} \ \text{[Abstraction]}$$

$$\frac{}{\text{type}[\![\cdot, ((\Rightarrow (A \ ...) \ (B \ ...)) \ A \ ...), (B \ ...)]\!]} \ \text{[Apply]}$$

$$\frac{}{\text{type}[\![\leftarrow, ((\Rightarrow S \ (A \ ...)) \ B \ C \ ...), ((\Rightarrow S \ (B \ A \ ...)) \ C \ ...)]\!]} \ \text{[Left]}$$

$$\frac{}{\text{type}[\![\rightarrow, ((\Rightarrow (B \ A \ ...) \ T) \ B \ C \ ...), ((\Rightarrow (A \ ...) \ T) \ C \ ...)]\!]} \ \text{[Right]}$$

$$\frac{}{\text{type}[\![\times, (A \ B \ ...), (A \ A \ B \ ...)]\!]} \ \text{[Copy]}$$

$$\frac{}{\text{type}[\![\downarrow, (A \ B \ ...), (B \ ...)]\!]} \ \text{[Drop]}$$

Fig. 7. Redex type system

5 Related Work

Kihi bears comparison to Krivine machines [9], Post tag system languages [11], and other term-rewriting models. We focus on the compositional nature of execution in Kihi rather than the perspective of these systems and will not address them further in this space.

As a simple Turing-complete language without variables, Kihi also has similar goals to the SK calculus [1]. The core calculus of Kihi has five operators, compared to SK's two, but functions in Kihi are afforded more flexibility in their input and output arities. The K combinator can be implemented in Kihi as ↓ swap, and the S combinator as · under (under (·) swap under (×)). While the reverse is possible, it requires implementing a stack in SK so we do not attempt it here.

Forth [10] is likely the most widely-known concatenative language. Forth programs receive arguments on an implicit stack and push their results to the same stack, following a postfix approach where calls follow their arguments. While generally described in this imperative fashion, a Forth program is also (impurely) functional and compositional when examined from the right perspective: each function takes a single argument (the entire stack to date) and produces a single output (a new stack to be used by the next function); from this point of view functions are composed from left to right, with the inner functions preceding the outer. The library design and nomenclature of the language favour the imperative view, however. The implicit nature of the stack requires the programmer to keep a mental picture of its state after each function mutates it in order to know which arguments will be available to the next, while Kihi's approach allows the stepped semantics of our tools while retaining a valid program at each stage.

The Joy language [12] is similar to Forth and brought the "concatenative" terminology to the fore. Joy incorporates an extensive set of combinators [4] emphasising the more functional elements of the paradigm, but is still fundamentally presented as manipulating the invisible data stack.

5.1   Om

The Om language [2] is closest to Kihi in approach. Described as "prefix concatenative", in an Om program the operator precedes its arguments and the operator plus its arguments are replaced in the program by the result, as in Kihi. The language and implementation focus on embedability and Unicode support and are presented in terms of rewriting and partial programs, rather than composition. Despite some superficial similarity, Om and Kihi do not have similar execution or data models and operate very differently.

Om's brace-enclosed "operand" programs parallel Kihi's abstractions when used in certain ways. In particular, they can be dequoted to splice their bodies into the program, as in Kihi's apply, and Om's quote function would be Kihi ← (). They can also have the *contents* of other operands inserted at the start or end of them: to behave similarly to Kihi's ← and → operators requires double-quoting, because one layer of the operand quoting is always removed, so that ->[expression] {X} {{Y}} is analogous to → (X) (Y); to get the unwrapping effect of ->[expression] in Kihi would be → ← (·). Om has a family of "arrow functions" ->[...], <-[...], [...]->, and [...]<- for manipulating programs interpreted in various ways, but in general these do not relate to Kihi's arrow operators. An operand "program" can be interpreted as a Unicode string, list, dictionary, or function, and Om has distinguished functions for treating the program as each of these interpretations and moving elements in and out, or deconstructing elements (for example, turning {ABC} into {A}{BC}), contrasting with the uniform lower-level treatment in Kihi.

Single-step abstract execution of an Om program results in another Om program with the same result up to side effects. The Om implementation does not provide single-stepping as an option, but a program lacking necessary arguments pauses to wait for them to be supplied after evaluating as far as possible.

6   Future Work

The separation of the six operations in Kihi allows exploration of the subset of programs that omit one or more of the operations. Copy-free programs parallel linear logic, while drop-free programs have similarities with the λ_I calculus and

SCBI calculus, and left-free programs do not reorder terms. These subsets and their equivalences or limitations are worth further investigation.

While Kihi core is Turing-complete, it is impractical for large programs. Building on the core to create a more usable compositional language, building out a useful set of default functions, and extending Kihi with more convenient data structures, is ongoing work. We are currently extending our past work on module systems and code reuse [6–8] to this end, and also on visual programming [5] for novices or end-users. We are interested in exploring domains and tasks where this computational style is beneficial, and integrating it into other systems.

Efficient implementation and representation of Kihi is another live issue. Construction of a suitable virtual machine or compiler for Kihi raises questions of executing the computational model and encoding the operations.

7   Conclusion

Kihi is a compositional functional language with practical higher-level functionality but only six core operations with simple semantics. A key aspect of Kihi's flexibility is the arity-neutral fashion in which functions can compose. We have presented Kihi and the tools we have built to execute and explore the language and the compositional model. These tools are capable of interacting with a broader ecosystem as well as illustrating execution paths and allowing a programmer to explore different facets of computation than most conventional languages and tools provide.

Screenshots and Outline

This appendix provides tool screenshots, identifies various features, and notes points of behaviour that are incorporated in the demonstration.

Overall View of Web Evaluator

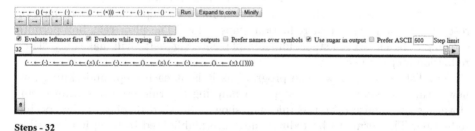

The top row includes, from left to right:

1. A text box for entering a Kihi program to evaluate;
2. A button that executes the program;
3. A button that translates the given program into core operations, expanding binds and named terms;
4. A button that shrinks excess terms inside abstractions.

The second row provides buttons for the operator symbols. The third is the output area, showing the final result value of the program and any values emitted by the evaluation.

The check boxes, from left to right:

1. Select the leftmost available reduction (checked) or the rightmost available reduction (unchecked);
2. Enable evaluation of the program without clicking "Run";
3. Remove values reaching the left-hand edge and move them to the output area;
4. Render operators as names (e.g. `right`) instead of symbols ($\rightarrow$);
5. Sugar outputted Church numerals into textual numbers;
6. Render operators using substitute ASCII symbols (e.g. :) instead of mathematical symbols ($\times$). This mode suits some limited browsers and systems.

The step limit determines the maximum number of reduction steps the evaluator will take before stopping. It also stops if a program becomes too long. These stopping points are to preserve browser resources. In particular, programs with nested binds (as in the provided factorial example program) can expand to many thousands of terms of core Kihi, and creating the list of steps performs very poorly. This is a limitation of the web evaluator.

The fourth row allows manual stepping through the evaluation: jumping to a specific numbered step (left), dragging the slider through steps (middle), or automatically replaying and pausing evaluation (right).

The black box shows the current program being evaluated at this step, depicted and described in more detail in the next section.

The "Steps" heading shows the total number of steps, and acts to hide or restore the complete list of reduction steps below. The filter text box permits showing only a subset of steps: for example, entering "left" will make only "left" reduction steps appear.

The list of steps shows the program as it is at each step, underlining any new terms introduced at that step and marking the rule used to obtain them. Hovering the mouse over the rule will show a detailed display of the specific reduction. The terms to be reduced next are highlighted in blue; it is possible for portions of the program to be both new (underlined) and to-be-reduced (blue) at once. Clicking on a step jumps the display above to that step of the program.

A labelled list of sample programs is below, any of which can be loaded and evaluated by clicking the title.

Single-Step Display of Web Evaluator

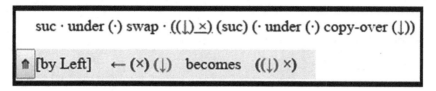

The complete program at this step is displayed at the top, with the rule that produced it displayed below. The underlined text in the program is that on the right-hand side of the rule display, and blue text is the next to be expanded as before. The rule display highlights different elements of the rule (for example, arguments) and matches corresponding elements on each side with the same highlighting.

References

1. Curry, H.B.: Grundlagen der kombinatorischen logik. Am. J. Math. **52**(3), 509–536 (1930)
2. Erb, J.: Om programming language web site. https://sparist.github.io/Om/
3. Felleisen, M., Findler, R.B., Flatt, M.: Semantics Engineering with PLT Redex. MIT Press, Cambridge (2009)
4. Frenger, P.: The JOY of forth. SIGPLAN Not. **38**(8), 15–17 (2003). https://doi.org/10.1145/944579.944583
5. Homer, M., Noble, J.: A tile-based editor for a textual programming language. In: VISSOFT 2013, pp. 1–4, September 2013. https://doi.org/10.1109/VISSOFT.2013.6650546
6. Homer, M., Bruce, K.B., Noble, J., Black, A.P.: Modules as gradually-typed objects. In: DYLA 2013. ACM (2013). https://doi.org/10.1145/2489798.2489799
7. Jones, T., Homer, M., Noble, J.: Brand objects for nominal typing. In: ECOOP 2015. LIPIcs, Dagstuhl, Germany, vol. 37, pp. 198–221 (2015). https://doi.org/10.4230/LIPIcs.ECOOP.2015.198
8. Jones, T., Homer, M., Noble, J., Bruce, K.: Object inheritance without classes. In: ECOOP 2016. LIPIcs, Dagstuhl, Germany , vol. 56, pp. 13:1–13:26 (2016). https://doi.org/10.4230/LIPIcs.ECOOP.2016.13
9. Krivine, J.L.: A call-by-name lambda-calculus machine. Higher Order Symbol. Comput. **20**(3), 199–207 (2007). https://doi.org/10.1007/s10990-007-9018-9
10. Moore, C.: 1x Forth (1999)
11. Post, E.L.: Formal reductions of the general combinatorial decision problem. Am. J. Math. **65**(2), 197–215 (1943)
12. von Thun, M., Thomas, R.: Joy: forth's functional cousin. In: Proceedings of the 17th EuroForth Conference (2001)

Functional Programs and Probabilistic Programs

New Approaches for Almost-Sure Termination of Probabilistic Programs

Mingzhang Huang[1], Hongfei Fu[2(✉)], and Krishnendu Chatterjee[3]

[1] BASICS Lab, Shanghai Jiao Tong University, Shanghai, China
mingzhanghuang@gmail.com
[2] Shanghai Jiao Tong University, Shanghai, China
fuhf@cs.sjtu.edu.cn
[3] IST Austria, Klosterneuburg, Austria
krishnendu.chatterjee@ist.ac.at

Abstract. We study the almost-sure termination problem for probabilistic programs. First, we show that supermartingales with lower bounds on conditional absolute difference provide a sound approach for the almost-sure termination problem. Moreover, using this approach we can obtain explicit optimal bounds on tail probabilities of non-termination within a given number of steps. Second, we present a new approach based on Central Limit Theorem for the almost-sure termination problem, and show that this approach can establish almost-sure termination of programs which none of the existing approaches can handle. Finally, we discuss algorithmic approaches for the two above methods that lead to automated analysis techniques for almost-sure termination of probabilistic programs.

1 Introduction

Probabilistic Programs. Probabilistic programs are classical imperative programs extended with *random value generators* that produce random values according to some desired probability distribution [16,27]. They provide the appropriate model for a wider variety of applications, such as analysis of stochastic network protocols [2,22], robot planning [17], etc. General probabilistic programs induce infinite-state Markov processes with complex behaviours, so that the formal analysis is needed in critical situations. The formal analysis of probabilistic programs is an active research topic across different disciplines, such as probability theory and statistics [21,30,32], formal methods [2,22], artificial intelligence [18], and programming languages [6,9,12,13,33].

Termination Problems. In this paper, we focus on proving termination properties of probabilistic programs. Termination is the most basic and fundamental notion of liveness for programs. For non-probabilistic programs, the proof of termination coincides with the construction of *ranking functions* [14], and many

---

A full version is available in http://arxiv.org/abs/1806.06683.

© Springer Nature Switzerland AG 2018
S. Ryu (Ed.): APLAS 2018, LNCS 11275, pp. 181–201, 2018.
https://doi.org/10.1007/978-3-030-02768-1_11

different approaches exist for such construction [4,11,31,34]. For probabilistic programs the most natural and basic extensions of the termination problem are *almost-sure* termination and *finite* termination. First, the almost-sure termination problem asks whether the program terminates with probability 1. Second, the finite termination problem asks whether the expected termination time is finite. Finite termination implies almost-sure termination, while the converse is not true in general. Here we focus on the almost-sure termination problem.

Previous Results. Below we describe the most relevant previous results on termination of probabilistic programs.

- *finite probabilistic choices.* First, quantitative invariants were used in [23,24] to establish termination for probabilistic programs with non-determinism, but restricted only to finite probabilistic choices.
- *infinite probabilistic choices without non-determinism.* The approach in [23, 24] was extended in [6] to *ranking supermartingales* to obtain a sound (but not complete) approach for almost-sure termination over infinite-state probabilistic programs with infinite-domain random variables, but without non-determinism. For countable state space probabilistic programs without non-determinism, the Lyapunov ranking functions provide a sound and complete method to prove finite termination [3,15].
- *infinite probabilistic choices with non-determinism.* In the presence of non-determinism, the Lyapunov-ranking-function method as well as the ranking-supermartingale method are sound but not complete [13]. Different approaches based on martingales and proof rules have been studied for finite termination [13,20]. The synthesis of linear and polynomial ranking supermartingales have been established [8,9]. Approaches for high-probability termination and non-termination has also been considered [10]. Recently, supermartingales and lexicographic ranking supermartingales have been considered for proving almost-sure termination of probabilistic programs [1,26].

Note that the problem of deciding termination of probabilistic programs is undecidable [19], and its precise undecidability characterization has been investigated. Finite termination of recursive probabilistic programs has also been studied through proof rules [29].

Our Contributions. Now we formally describe our contributions. We consider probabilistic programs where all program variables are integer-valued. Our main contributions are three folds.

- *Almost-Sure Termination: Supermartingale-Based Approach.* We show new results that supermartingales (i.e., not necessarily ranking supermartingales) with lower bounds on conditional absolute difference present a sound approach for proving almost-sure termination of probabilistic programs. Moreover, no previous supermartingale based approaches present explicit (optimal) bounds on tail probabilities of non-termination within a given number of steps.

- *Almost-Sure Termination: CLT-Based Approach.* We present a new approach based on Central Limit Theorem (CLT) that is sound to establish almost-sure termination. The extra power of CLT allows one to prove probabilistic programs where no global lower bound exists for values of program variables, while previous approaches based on (ranking) supermartingales [1,8,9,13,26]. For example, when we consider the program **while** $n \geq 1$ **do** $n := n + r$ **od** and take the sampling variable r to observe the probability distribution $\mathbb{P}$ such that $\mathbb{P}(r = k) = \frac{1}{2^{|k|+1}}$ for all integers $k \neq 0$, then the value of n could not be bounded from below during program execution; previous approaches fail on this example, while our CLT-based approach succeeds.
- *Algorithmic Methods.* We discuss algorithmic methods for the two approaches we present, showing that we not only present general approaches for almost-sure termination, but possible automated analysis techniques as well.

Recent Related Work. In the recent work [26], supermartingales are also considered for proving almost-sure termination. Our results are however different from and independent of the results in [26]. A more elaborate comparison is put in Sect. 7.

Due to lack of space, detailed proofs can be found in the full version at http://arxiv.org/abs/1806.06683.

2 Preliminaries

Below we first introduce some basic notations and concepts in probability theory (see e.g. the standard textbook [35] for details), then present the syntax and semantics of our probabilistic programs.

2.1 Basic Notations and Concepts

In the whole paper, we use $\mathbb{N}$, $\mathbb{N}_0$, $\mathbb{Z}$, and $\mathbb{R}$ to denote the sets of all positive integers, non-negative integers, integers, and real numbers, respectively.

Probability Space. A *probability space* is a triple $(\Omega, \mathcal{F}, \mathbb{P})$, where Ω is a non-empty set (so-called *sample space*), $\mathcal{F}$ is a σ-*algebra* over Ω (i.e., a collection of subsets of Ω that contains the empty set $\emptyset$ and is closed under complementation and countable union) and $\mathbb{P}$ is a *probability measure* on $\mathcal{F}$, i.e., a function $\mathbb{P} \colon \mathcal{F} \to [0, 1]$ such that (i) $\mathbb{P}(\Omega) = 1$ and (ii) for all set-sequences $A_1, A_2, \cdots \in \mathcal{F}$ that are pairwise-disjoint (i.e., $A_i \cap A_j = \emptyset$ whenever $i \neq j$) it holds that $\sum_{i=1}^{\infty} \mathbb{P}(A_i) = \mathbb{P}(\bigcup_{i=1}^{\infty} A_i)$. Elements of $\mathcal{F}$ are usually called *events*. We say an event $A \in \mathcal{F}$ holds *almost-surely* (a.s.) if $\mathbb{P}(A) = 1$.

Random Variables. [35, Chap. 1] A *random variable* X from a probability space $(\Omega, \mathcal{F}, \mathbb{P})$ is an $\mathcal{F}$-measurable function $X \colon \Omega \to \mathbb{R} \cup \{-\infty, +\infty\}$, i.e., a function satisfying the condition that for all $d \in \mathbb{R} \cup \{-\infty, +\infty\}$, the set $\{\omega \in \Omega \mid X(\omega) < d\}$ belongs to $\mathcal{F}$; X is *bounded* if there exists a real number $M > 0$

such that for all $\omega \in \Omega$, we have $X(\omega) \in \mathbb{R}$ and $|X(\omega)| \leq M$. By convention, we abbreviate $+\infty$ as ∞.

Expectation. The *expected value* of a random variable X from a probability space $(\Omega, \mathcal{F}, \mathbb{P})$, denoted by $\mathbb{E}(X)$, is defined as the Lebesgue integral of X w.r.t $\mathbb{P}$, i.e., $\mathbb{E}(X) := \int X \, d\mathbb{P}$; the precise definition of Lebesgue integral is somewhat technical and is omitted here (cf. [35, Chap. 5] for a formal definition). In the case that the range of X ran $X = \{d_0, d_1, \ldots, d_k, \ldots\}$ is countable with distinct d_k's, we have $\mathbb{E}(X) = \sum_{k=0}^{\infty} d_k \cdot \mathbb{P}(X = d_k)$.

Characteristic Random Variables. Given random variables $X_0, \ldots, X_n$ from a probability space $(\Omega, \mathcal{F}, \mathbb{P})$ and a predicate Φ over $\mathbb{R} \cup \{-\infty, +\infty\}$, we denote by $\mathbf{1}_{\phi(X_0,\ldots,X_n)}$ the random variable such that $\mathbf{1}_{\phi(X_0,\ldots,X_n)}(\omega) = 1$ if $\phi(X_0(\omega), \ldots, X_n(\omega))$ holds, and $\mathbf{1}_{\phi(X_0,\ldots,X_n)}(\omega) = 0$ otherwise.

By definition, $\mathbb{E}\left(\mathbf{1}_{\phi(X_0,\ldots,X_n)}\right) = \mathbb{P}(\phi(X_0, \ldots, X_n))$. Note that if ϕ does not involve any random variable, then $\mathbf{1}_\phi$ can be deemed as a constant whose value depends only on whether ϕ holds or not.

Filtrations and Stopping Times. A *filtration* of a probability space $(\Omega, \mathcal{F}, \mathbb{P})$ is an infinite sequence $\{\mathcal{F}_n\}_{n \in \mathbb{N}_0}$ of σ-algebras over Ω such that $\mathcal{F}_n \subseteq \mathcal{F}_{n+1} \subseteq \mathcal{F}$ for all $n \in \mathbb{N}_0$. A *stopping time* (from $(\Omega, \mathcal{F}, \mathbb{P})$) w.r.t $\{\mathcal{F}_n\}_{n \in \mathbb{N}_0}$ is a random variable $R : \Omega \to \mathbb{N}_0 \cup \{\infty\}$ such that for every $n \in \mathbb{N}_0$, the event $R \leq n$ belongs to $\mathcal{F}_n$.

Conditional Expectation. Let X be any random variable from a probability space $(\Omega, \mathcal{F}, \mathbb{P})$ such that $\mathbb{E}(|X|) < \infty$. Then given any σ-algebra $\mathcal{G} \subseteq \mathcal{F}$, there exists a random variable (from $(\Omega, \mathcal{F}, \mathbb{P})$), conventionally denoted by $\mathbb{E}(X|\mathcal{G})$, such that

(E1) $\mathbb{E}(X|\mathcal{G})$ is $\mathcal{G}$-measurable, and
(E2) $\mathbb{E}(|\mathbb{E}(X|\mathcal{G})|) < \infty$, and
(E3) for all $A \in \mathcal{G}$, we have $\int_A \mathbb{E}(X|\mathcal{G}) \, d\mathbb{P} = \int_A X \, d\mathbb{P}$.

The random variable $\mathbb{E}(X|\mathcal{G})$ is called the *conditional expectation* of X given $\mathcal{G}$. The random variable $\mathbb{E}(X|\mathcal{G})$ is a.s. unique in the sense that if Y is another random variable satisfying (E1)–(E3), then $\mathbb{P}(Y = \mathbb{E}(X|\mathcal{G})) = 1$.

Discrete-Time Stochastic Processes. A *discrete-time stochastic process* is a sequence $\Gamma = \{X_n\}_{n \in \mathbb{N}_0}$ of random variables where X_n's are all from some probability space (say, $(\Omega, \mathcal{F}, \mathbb{P})$); and Γ is *adapted to* a filtration $\{\mathcal{F}_n\}_{n \in \mathbb{N}_0}$ of sub-σ-algebras of $\mathcal{F}$ if for all $n \in \mathbb{N}_0$, X_n is $\mathcal{F}_n$-measurable.

Difference-Boundedness. A discrete-time stochastic process $\Gamma = \{X_n\}_{n \in \mathbb{N}_0}$ is *difference-bounded* if there is $c \in (0, \infty)$ such that for all $n \in \mathbb{N}_0$, $|X_{n+1} - X_n| \leq c$ a.s..

Stopping Time Z_Γ. Given a discrete-time stochastic process $\Gamma = \{X_n\}_{n \in \mathbb{N}_0}$ adapted to a filtration $\{\mathcal{F}_n\}_{n \in \mathbb{N}_0}$, we define the random variable Z_Γ by $Z_\Gamma(\omega) := \min\{n \mid X_n(\omega) \leq 0\}$ where $\min \emptyset := \infty$. By definition, Z_Γ is a stopping time w.r.t $\{\mathcal{F}_n\}_{n \in \mathbb{N}_0}$.

Martingales. A discrete-time stochastic process $\Gamma = \{X_n\}_{n \in \mathbb{N}_0}$ adapted to a filtration $\{\mathcal{F}_n\}_{n \in \mathbb{N}_0}$ is a *martingale* (resp. *supermartingale*) if for every $n \in \mathbb{N}_0$, $\mathbb{E}(|X_n|) < \infty$ and it holds a.s. that $\mathbb{E}(X_{n+1}|\mathcal{F}_n) = X_n$ (resp. $\mathbb{E}(X_{n+1}|\mathcal{F}_n) \leq X_n$). We refer to [35, Chap. 10] for more details.

Discrete Probability Distributions over Countable Support. A *discrete probability distribution* over a countable set U is a function $q : U \to [0, 1]$ such that $\sum_{z \in U} q(z) = 1$. The *support* of q, is defined as $\mathrm{supp}(q) := \{z \in U \mid q(z) > 0\}$.

2.2 The Syntax and Semantics for Probabilistic Programs

In the sequel, we fix two countable sets, the set of *program variables* and the set of *sampling variables*. W.l.o.g, these two sets are disjoint. Informally, program variables are the variables that are directly related to the control-flow and the data-flow of a program, while sampling variables reflect randomized inputs to programs. In this paper, we consider integer-valued variables, i.e., every program variable holds an integer upon instantiation, while every sampling variable is bound to a discrete probability distribution over integers. Possible extensions to real-valued variables are discussed in Sect. 5.

The Syntax. The syntax of probabilistic programs is illustrated by the grammar in Fig. 1. Below we explain the grammar.

- *Variables.* Expressions $\langle pvar \rangle$ (resp. $\langle rvar \rangle$) range over program (resp. sampling) variables.
- *Arithmetic Expressions.* Expressions $\langle expr \rangle$ (resp. $\langle pexpr \rangle$) range over arithmetic expressions over both program and sampling variables (resp. program variables), respectively. As a theoretical paper, we do not fix the detailed syntax for $\langle expr \rangle$ and $\langle pexpr \rangle$.
- *Boolean Expressions.* Expressions $\langle bexpr \rangle$ range over propositional arithmetic predicates over program variables.
- *Programs.* A program from $\langle prog \rangle$ could be either an assignment statement indicated by ':=', or '**skip**' which is the statement that does nothing, or a conditional branch indicated by the keyword '**if**', or a while-loop indicated by the keyword '**while**', or a sequential composition of statements connected by semicolon.

$$
\begin{aligned}
\langle prog \rangle ::=\ & \textbf{`skip'} \\
& | \ \langle pvar \rangle \ \text{':='} \ \langle expr \rangle \\
& | \ \langle prog \rangle \ \text{`;'} \langle prog \rangle \\
& | \ \textbf{`if'} \ \langle bexpr \rangle \ \textbf{`then'} \ \langle prog \rangle \ \textbf{`else'} \ \langle prog \rangle \ \textbf{`fi'} \\
& | \ \textbf{`while'} \ \langle bexpr \rangle \ \textbf{`do'} \ \langle prog \rangle \ \textbf{`od'} \\
\langle literal \rangle ::=\ & \langle pexpr \rangle \ \text{`}\leq\text{'} \ \langle pexpr \rangle \ | \ \langle pexpr \rangle \ \text{`}\geq\text{'} \ \langle pexpr \rangle \\
\langle bexpr \rangle ::=\ & \langle literal \rangle \ | \ \neg \langle bexpr \rangle \ | \ \langle bexpr \rangle \ \textbf{`or'} \ \langle bexpr \rangle \ | \ \langle bexpr \rangle \ \textbf{`and'} \ \langle bexpr \rangle
\end{aligned}
$$

Fig. 1. The syntax of probabilistic programs

Remark 1. The syntax of our programming language is quite general and covers major features of probabilistic programming. For example, compared with a popular probabilistic-programming language from [16], the only difference between our syntax and theirs is that they have extra observe statements.   ◄

Single (Probabilistic) While Loops. In order to develop approaches for proving almost-sure termination of probabilistic programs, we first analyze the almost-sure termination of programs with a single while loop. Then, we demonstrate that the almost-sure termination of general probabilistic programs without nested loops can be obtained by the almost-sure termination of all components which are single while loops and loop-free statements (see Sect. 5). Formally, a *single while loop* is a program of the following form:

$$\textbf{while } \phi \textbf{ do } Q \textbf{ od} \tag{1}$$

where ϕ is the loop guard from $\langle bexpr \rangle$ and Q is a loop-free program with possibly assignment statements, conditional branches, sequential composition but without while loops. Given a single while loop, we assign the program counter in to the entry point of the while loop and the program counter out to the terminating point of the loop. Below we give an example of a single while loop.

Example 1. Consider the following single while loop:

in : **while** $x \geq 1$ **do**
            $x := x + r$
        od
out :

where x is a program variable and r is a sampling variable that observes certain fixed distributions (e.g., a two-point distribution such that $\mathbb{P}(r = -1) = \mathbb{P}(r = 1) = \frac{1}{2}$). Informally, the program performs a random increment/decrement on x until its value is no greater than zero.   ◄

The Semantics. Since our approaches for proving almost-sure termination work basically for single while loops (in Sect. 5 we extend to probabilistic programs without nested loops), we present the simplified semantics for single while loops.

We first introduce the notion of valuations which specify current values for program and sampling variables. Below we fix a single while loop P in the form (1) and let X (resp. R) be the set of program (resp. sampling) variables appearing in P. The size of X, R is denoted by $|X|, |R|$, respectively. We impose arbitrary linear orders on both of X, R so that $X = \{x_1, \ldots, x_{|X|}\}$ and $R = \{r_1, \ldots, r_{|R|}\}$. We also require that for each sampling variable $r_i \in R$, a discrete probability distribution is given. Intuitively, at each loop iteration of P, the value of r_i is independently sampled w.r.t the distribution.

Valuations. A *program valuation* is a (column) vector $\mathbf{v} \in \mathbb{Z}^{|X|}$. Intuitively, a valuation $\mathbf{v}$ specifies that for each $x_i \in X$, the value assigned is the i-th coordinate $\mathbf{v}[i]$ of $\mathbf{v}$. Likewise, a *sampling valuation* is a (column) vector $\mathbf{u} \in \mathbb{Z}^{|R|}$.

A *sampling function* Υ is a function assigning to every sampling variable $r \in R$ a discrete probability distribution over $\mathbb{Z}$. The discrete probability distribution $\bar{\Upsilon}$ over $\mathbb{Z}^{|R|}$ is defined by: $\bar{\Upsilon}(\mathbf{u}) := \prod_{i=1}^{|R|} \Upsilon(r_i)(\mathbf{u}[i])$.

For each program valuation $\mathbf{v}$, we say that $\mathbf{v}$ *satisfies* the loop guard ϕ, denoted by $\mathbf{v} \models \phi$, if the formula ϕ holds when every appearance of a program variable is replaced by its corresponding value in $\mathbf{v}$. Moreover, the loop body Q in P encodes a function $F : \mathbb{Z}^{|X|} \times \mathbb{Z}^{|R|} \to \mathbb{Z}^{|X|}$ which transforms the program valuation $\mathbf{v}$ before the execution of Q and the independently-sampled values in $\mathbf{u}$ into the program valuation $F(\mathbf{v}, \mathbf{u})$ after the execution of Q.

Semantics of Single While Loops. Now we present the semantics of single while loops. Informally, the semantics is defined by a Markov chain $\mathcal{M} = (S, \mathbf{P})$, where the state space $S := \{\mathtt{in}, \mathtt{out}\} \times \mathbb{Z}^{|X|}$ is a set of pairs of location and sampled values and the probability transition function $\mathbf{P} : S \times S \to [0, 1]$ will be clarified later. We call states in S *configurations*. A *path* under the Markov chain is an infinite sequence $\{(\ell_n, \mathbf{v}_n)\}_{n \geq 0}$ of configurations. The intuition is that in a path, each $\mathbf{v}_n$ (resp. ℓ_n) is the current program valuation (the current program counter to be executed) right before the n-th execution step of P. Then given an initial configuration $(\mathtt{in}, \mathbf{v}_0)$, the probability space for P is constructed as the standard one for its Markov chain over paths (for details see [2, Chap. 10]). We shall denote by $\mathbb{P}$ the probability measure (over the σ-algebra of subsets of paths) in the probability space for P (from some fixed initial program valuation $\mathbf{v}_0$).

Consider any initial program valuation $\mathbf{v}$. The execution of the single while loop P from $\mathbf{v}$ results in a path $\{(\ell_n, \mathbf{v}_n)\}_{n \in \mathbb{N}_0}$ as follows. Initially, $\mathbf{v}_0 = \mathbf{v}$ and $\ell_0 = \mathtt{in}$. Then at each step n, the following two operations are performed. First, a sampling valuation $\mathbf{u}_n$ is obtained through samplings for all sampling variables, where the value for each sampling variable observes a predefined discrete probability distribution for the variable. Second, we clarify three cases below:

- if $\ell_n = \mathtt{in}$ and $\mathbf{v}_n \models \phi$, then the program enters the loop and we have $\ell_{n+1} := \mathtt{in}$, $\mathbf{v}_{n+1} := F(\mathbf{v}_n, \mathbf{u}_n)$, and thus we simplify the executions of Q as a single computation step;
- if $\ell_n = \mathtt{in}$ and $\mathbf{v}_n \not\models \phi$, then the program enters the terminating program counter $\mathtt{out}$ and we have $\ell_{n+1} := \mathtt{out}$, $\mathbf{v}_{n+1} := \mathbf{v}_n$;
- if $\ell_n = \mathtt{out}$ then the program stays at the program counter $\mathtt{out}$ and we have $\ell_{n+1} := \mathtt{out}$, $\mathbf{v}_{n+1} := \mathbf{v}_n$.

Based on the informal description, we now formally define the probability transition function $\mathbf{P}$:

- $\mathbf{P}((\mathtt{in}, \mathbf{v}), (\mathtt{in}, \mathbf{v}')) = \sum_{\mathbf{u} \in \{\mathbf{u} | \mathbf{v}' = F(\mathbf{v}, \mathbf{u})\}} \bar{\Upsilon}(\mathbf{u})$, for any $\mathbf{v}, \mathbf{v}'$ such that $\mathbf{v} \models \phi$;
- $\mathbf{P}((\mathtt{in}, \mathbf{v}), (\mathtt{out}, \mathbf{v})) = 1$ for any $\mathbf{v}$ such that $\mathbf{v} \not\models \phi$;
- $\mathbf{P}((\mathtt{out}, \mathbf{v}), (\mathtt{out}, \mathbf{v})) = 1$ for any $\mathbf{v}$;
- $\mathbf{P}((\ell, \mathbf{v}), (\ell', \mathbf{v}')) = 0$ for all other cases.

We note that the semantics for general probabilistic programs can be defined in the same principle as for single while loops with the help of transition structures or control-flow graphs (see [8,9]).

Almost-Sure Termination. In the following, we define the notion of *almost-sure termination* over single while loops. Consider a single while loop P. The *termination-time random variable* T is defined such that for any path $\{(\ell_n, \mathbf{v}_n)\}_{n \in \mathbb{N}_0}$, the value of T at the path is $\min\{n \mid \ell_n = \mathtt{out}\}$, where $\min \emptyset := \infty$. Then P is said to be *almost-surely terminating* (from some prescribed initial program valuation $\mathbf{v}_0$) if $\mathbb{P}(T < \infty) = 1$. Besides, we also consider bounds on tail probabilities $\mathbb{P}(T \geq k)$ of non-termination within k loop-iterations. Tail bounds are important quantitative aspects that characterizes how fast the program terminates.

3   Supermartingale Based Approach

In this section, we present our supermartingale-based approach for proving almost-sure termination of single while loops. We first establish new mathematical results on supermartingales, then we show how to apply these results to obtain a sound approach for proving almost-sure termination.

The following proposition is our first new mathematical result.

Proposition 1 (Difference-bounded Supermartingales). *Consider any difference-bounded supermartingale* $\Gamma = \{X_n\}_{n \in \mathbb{N}_0}$ *adapted to a filtration* $\{\mathcal{F}_n\}_{n \in \mathbb{N}_0}$ *satisfying the following conditions:*

1. X_0 *is a constant random variable;*
2. *for all* $n \in \mathbb{N}_0$, *it holds for all* ω *that (i)* $X_n(\omega) \geq 0$ *and (ii)* $X_n(\omega) = 0$ *implies* $X_{n+1}(\omega) = 0$;
3. *Lower Bound on Conditional Absolute Difference (LBCAD). there exists* $\delta \in (0, \infty)$ *such that for all* $n \in \mathbb{N}_0$, *it holds a.s. that* $X_n > 0$ *implies* $\mathbb{E}(|X_{n+1} - X_n||\mathcal{F}_n) \geq \delta$.

Then $\mathbb{P}(Z_\Gamma < \infty) = 1$ *and the function* $k \mapsto \mathbb{P}(Z_\Gamma \geq k) \in \mathcal{O}\left(\frac{1}{\sqrt{k}}\right)$.

Informally, the LBCAD condition requires that the stochastic process should have a minimal amount of vibrations at each step. The amount δ is the least amount that the stochastic process should change on its value in the next step (e.g., $X_{n+1} = X_n$ is not allowed). Then it is intuitively true that if the stochastic process does not increase in expectation (i.e., a supermartingale) and satisfies the LBCAD condition, then we have at some point the stochastic processes will drop below zero. The formal proof ideas are as follows.

Key Proof Ideas. The main idea is a thorough analysis of the martingale

$$Y_n := \frac{e^{-t \cdot X_n}}{\prod_{j=0}^{n-1} \mathbb{E}\left(e^{-t \cdot (X_{j+1} - X_j)}|\mathcal{F}_j\right)} \quad (n \in \mathbb{N}_0)$$

for some sufficiently small $t > 0$ and its limit through Optional Stopping Theorem. We first prove that $\{Y_n\}$ is indeed a martingale. The difference-boundedness ensures that the martingale Y_n is well-defined. Then by letting $Y_\infty := \lim_{n\to\infty} Y_{\min\{n, Z_\Gamma\}}$, we prove that $\mathbb{E}(Y_\infty) = \mathbb{E}(Y_0) = e^{-t\cdot\mathbb{E}(X_0)}$ through Optional Stopping Theorem and the LBCAD condition. Third, we prove from basic definitions and the LBCAD condition that

$$\mathbb{E}(Y_\infty) = e^{-t\cdot\mathbb{E}(X_0)} \leq 1 - \left(1 - \left(1 + \frac{\delta^2}{4} \cdot t^2\right)^{-k}\right) \cdot \mathbb{P}(Z_\Gamma \geq k) \ .$$

By setting $t := \frac{1}{\sqrt{k}}$ for sufficiently large k, one has that

$$\mathbb{P}(Z_\Gamma \geq k) \leq \frac{1 - e^{-\frac{\mathbb{E}(X_0)}{\sqrt{k}}}}{1 - \left(1 + \frac{\delta^2}{4} \cdot \frac{1}{k}\right)^{-k}} \ .$$

It follows that $k \mapsto \mathbb{P}(Z_\Gamma \geq k) \in \mathcal{O}\left(\frac{1}{\sqrt{k}}\right)$.   □

Optimality of Proposition 2. We now present two examples to illustrate two aspects of optimality of Proposition 1. First, in Example 2 we show an application on the classical symmetric random walk that the tail bound $\mathcal{O}(\frac{1}{\sqrt{k}})$ of Proposition 1 is optimal. Then in Example 3 we establish that the always non-negativity condition required in the second item of Proposition 1 is critical (i.e., the result does not hold without the condition).

Example 2. Consider the family $\{Y_n\}_{n\in\mathbb{N}_0}$ of independent random variables defined as follows: $Y_0 := 1$ and each Y_n $(n \geq 1)$ satisfies that $\mathbb{P}(Y_n = 1) = \frac{1}{2}$ and $\mathbb{P}(Y_n = -1) = \frac{1}{2}$. Let the stochastic process $\Gamma = \{X_n\}_{n\in\mathbb{N}_0}$ be inductively defined by: $X_0 := Y_0$. X_n is difference bounded since Y_n is bounded. For all $n \in \mathbb{N}_0$ we have $X_{n+1} := \mathbf{1}_{X_n>0} \cdot (X_n + Y_{n+1})$. Choose the filtration $\{\mathcal{F}_n\}_{n\in\mathbb{N}_0}$ such that every $\mathcal{F}_n$ is the smallest σ-algebra that makes $Y_0,\ldots,Y_n$ measurable. Then Γ models the classical symmetric random walk and $X_n > 0$ implies $\mathbb{E}(|X_{n+1} - X_n| \,||\, \mathcal{F}_n) = 1$ a.s. Thus, Γ ensures the LBCAD condition. From Proposition 1, we obtain that $\mathbb{P}(Z_\Gamma < \infty) = 1$ and $k \mapsto \mathbb{P}(Z_\Gamma \geq k) \in \mathcal{O}\left(\frac{1}{\sqrt{k}}\right)$. It follows from [5, Theorem 4.1] that $k \mapsto \mathbb{P}(Z_\Gamma \geq k) \in \Omega\left(\frac{1}{\sqrt{k}}\right)$. Hence, the tail bound $\mathcal{O}\left(\frac{1}{\sqrt{k}}\right)$ in Proposition 1 is optimal.   ◀

Example 3. In Proposition 1, the condition that $X_n \geq 0$ is necessary; in other words, it is necessary to have $X_{Z_\Gamma} = 0$ rather than $X_{Z_\Gamma} \leq 0$ when $Z_\Gamma < \infty$. This can be observed as follows. Consider the discrete-time stochastic processes $\{X_n\}_{n\in\mathbb{N}_0}$ and $\Gamma = \{Y_n\}_{n\in\mathbb{N}_0}$ given as follows:

- the random variables $X_0,\ldots,X_n,\ldots$ are independent, X_0 is the random variable with constant value $\frac{1}{2}$ and each X_n $(n \geq 1)$ satisfies that $\mathbb{P}(X_n = 1) = e^{-\frac{1}{n^2}}$ and $\mathbb{P}\left(X_n = -4 \cdot n^2\right) = 1 - e^{-\frac{1}{n^2}}$;

- $Y_n := \sum_{j=0}^{n} X_j$ for $n \geq 0$.

Let $\mathcal{F}_n$ be the filtration which is the smallest σ-algebra that makes $X_0, \dots, X_n$ measurable for every n. Then one can show that Γ (adapted to $\{\mathcal{F}_n\}_{n \in \mathbb{N}_0}$) satisfies integrability and the LBCAD condition, but $\mathbb{P}\left(Z_\Gamma = \infty\right) = e^{-\frac{\pi^2}{6}} > 0$. ◄

In the following, we illustrate how one can apply Proposition 1 to prove almost-sure termination of single while loops. Below we fix a single while loop P in the form (1). We first introduce the notion of *supermartingale maps* which are a special class of functions over configurations that subjects to supermartingale-like constraints.

Definition 1 (Supermartingale Maps). *A* (difference-bounded) *supermartingale map (for P) is a function $h : \{in, out\} \times \mathbb{Z}^{|X|} \to \mathbb{R}$ satisfying that there exist real numbers $\delta, \zeta > 0$ such that for all configurations $(\ell, \mathbf{v})$, the following conditions hold:*

(D1) if $\ell = out$ then $h(\ell, \mathbf{v}) = 0$;
(D2) if $\ell = in$ and $\mathbf{v} \models \phi$, then (i) $h(\ell, \mathbf{v}) \geq \delta$ and (ii) $h(\ell, F(\mathbf{v}, \mathbf{u})) \geq \delta$ for all $\mathbf{u} \in \mathrm{supp}(\bar{\Upsilon})$;
(D3) if $\ell = in$ and $\mathbf{v} \models \phi$ then
  (D3.1) $\sum_{\mathbf{u} \in \mathbb{Z}^{|R|}} \bar{\Upsilon}(\mathbf{u}) \cdot h(\ell, F(\mathbf{v}, \mathbf{u})) \leq h(\ell, \mathbf{v})$, and
  (D3.2) $\sum_{\mathbf{u} \in \mathbb{Z}^{|R|}} \bar{\Upsilon}(\mathbf{u}) \cdot |g(\ell, \mathbf{v}, \mathbf{u})| \geq \delta$ where $g(\ell, \mathbf{v}, \mathbf{u}) := h(\ell, F(\mathbf{v}, \mathbf{u})) - h(\ell, \mathbf{v})$;
(D4) (for difference-boundedness) $|g(in, \mathbf{v}, \mathbf{u})| \leq \zeta$ for all $\mathbf{u} \in \mathrm{supp}(\bar{\Upsilon})$ and $\mathbf{v} \in \mathbb{Z}^{|X|}$ such that $\mathbf{v} \models \phi$, and $h(in, F(\mathbf{v}, \mathbf{u})) \leq \zeta$ for all $\mathbf{v} \in \mathbb{Z}^{|X|}$ and $\mathbf{u} \in \mathrm{supp}(\bar{\Upsilon})$ such that $\mathbf{v} \models \phi$ and $F(\mathbf{v}, \mathbf{u}) \not\models \phi$.

Thus, h is a supermartingale map if conditions (D1)–(D3) hold. Furthermore, h is difference bounded if in extra (D4) holds.

Intuitively, the conditions (D1), (D2) together ensure non-negativity for the function h. Moreover, the difference between "$= 0$" in (D1) and "$\geq \delta$" in (D2) ensures that h is positive iff the program still executes in the loop. The condition (D3.1) ensures the supermartingale condition for h that the next expected value does not increase, while the condition (D3.2) says that the expected value of the absolute change between the current and the next step is at least δ, relating to the same amount in the LBCAD condition. Finally, the condition (D4) corresponds to the difference-boundedness in supermartingales in the sense that it requires the change of value both after the loop iteration and right before the termination of the loop should be bounded by the upper bound ζ.

Now we state the main theorem of this section which says that the existence of a difference-bounded supermartingale map implies almost-sure termination.

Theorem 1 (Soundness). *If there exists a difference-bounded supermartingale map h for P, then for any initial valuation $\mathbf{v}_0$ we have $\mathbb{P}(T < \infty) = 1$ and $k \mapsto \mathbb{P}(T \geq k) \in \mathcal{O}\left(\frac{1}{\sqrt{k}}\right)$.*

Key Proof Ideas. Let h be any difference-bounded supermartingale map h for the single while loop program P, $\mathbf{v}$ be any initial valuation and δ, ζ be the parameters in Definition 1. We define the stochastic process $\Gamma = \{X_n\}_{n\in\mathbb{N}_0}$ adapted to $\{\mathcal{F}_n\}_{n\in\mathbb{N}_0}$ by $X_n = h(\ell_n, \mathbf{v}_n)$ where ℓ_n (resp. $\mathbf{v}_n$) refers to the random variable (resp. the vector of random variables) for the program counter (resp. program valuation) at the nth step. Then P terminates iff Γ stops. We prove that Γ satisfies the conditions in Proposition 1, so that P is almost-surely terminating with the same tail bound.

Theorem 1 suggests that to prove almost-sure termination, one only needs to find a difference-bounded supermartingale map.

Remark 2. Informally, Theorem 1 can be used to prove almost-sure termination of while loops where there exists a distance function (as a supermartingale map) that measures the distance of the loop to termination, for which the distance does not increase in expectation and is changed by a minimal amount in each loop iteration. The key idea to apply Theorem 1 is to construct such a distance function.   ◀

Below we illustrate an example.

Example 4. Consider the single while loop in Example 1 where the distribution for r is given as $\mathbb{P}(r = 1) = \mathbb{P}(r = -1) = \frac{1}{2}$ and this program can be viewed as non-biased random walks. The program has infinite expected termination so previous approach based on ranking supermartingales cannot apply. Below we prove the almost-sure termination of the program. We define the difference-bounded supermartingale map h by: $h(\mathtt{in}, x) = x + 1$ and $h(\mathtt{out}, x) = 0$ for every x. Let $\zeta = \delta = 1$. Then for every x, we have that

- the condition (D1) is valid by the definition of h;
- if $\ell = \mathtt{in}$ and $x \geq 1$, then $h(\ell, x) = x + 1 \geq \delta$ and $h(\mathtt{in}, F(x, u)) = F(x, u) + 1 \geq x - 1 + 1 \geq \delta$ for all $u \in \mathrm{supp}(\tilde{\Upsilon})$. Then the condition (D2) is valid;
- if $\ell = \mathtt{in}$ and $x \geq 1$, then $\Sigma_{u\in\mathbb{Z}}\tilde{\Upsilon}(u)\cdot h(\mathtt{in}, F(x, u)) = \frac{1}{2}((x+2)+x) \leq x+1 = h(\mathtt{in}, x)$ and $\Sigma_{u\in\mathbb{Z}}\tilde{\Upsilon}(u) \cdot |g(\mathtt{in}, x, u)| = \frac{1}{2}(1+1) \geq \delta$. Thus, we have that the condition (D3) is valid.
- The condition (D4) is clear as the difference is less than $1 = \zeta$.

It follows that h is a difference-bounded supermartingale map. Then by Theorem 1 it holds that the program terminates almost-surely under any initial value with tail probabilities bounded by reciprocal of square root of the thresholds. By similar arguments, we can show that the results still hold when we consider that the distribution of r in general has bounded range, non-positive mean value and non-zero variance by letting $h(\mathtt{in}, x) = x + K$ for some sufficiently large constant K.   ◀

Now we extend Proposition 1 to general supermartingales. The extension lifts the difference-boundedness condition but derives with a weaker tail bound.

Proposition 2 (General Supermartingales). *Consider any supermartingale $\Gamma = \{X_n\}_{n\in\mathbb{N}_0}$ adapted to a filtration $\{\mathcal{F}_n\}_{n\in\mathbb{N}_0}$ satisfying the following conditions:*

1. X_0 is a constant random variable;
2. for all $n \in \mathbb{N}_0$, it holds for all ω that (i) $X_n(\omega) \geq 0$ and (ii) $X_n(\omega) = 0$ implies $X_{n+1}(\omega) = 0$;
3. (LBCAD). there exists $\delta \in (0, \infty)$ such that for all $n \in \mathbb{N}_0$, it holds a.s. that $X_n > 0$ implies $\mathbb{E}(|X_{n+1} - X_n| | \mathcal{F}_n) \geq \delta$.

Then $\mathbb{P}(Z_\Gamma < \infty) = 1$ and the function $k \mapsto \mathbb{P}(Z_\Gamma \geq k) \in \mathcal{O}\left(k^{-\frac{1}{6}}\right)$.

Key Proof Ideas. The key idea is to extend the proof of Proposition 1 with the stopping times R_M's ($M \in (\mathbb{E}(X_0), \infty)$) defined by $R_M(\omega) := \min\{n \mid X_n(\omega) \leq 0 \text{ or } X_n(\omega) \geq M\}$. For any $M > 0$, we first define a new stochastic process $\{X_n'\}_n$ by $X_n' = \min\{X_n, M\}$ for all $n \in \mathbb{N}_0$. Then we define the discrete-time stochastic process $\{Y_n\}_{n \in \mathbb{N}_0}$ by

$$Y_n := \frac{e^{-t \cdot X_n'}}{\prod_{j=0}^{n-1} \mathbb{E}\left(e^{-t \cdot \left(X_{j+1}' - X_j'\right)} | \mathcal{F}_j\right)}$$

for some appropriate positive real number t. We prove that $\{Y_n\}_{n \in \mathbb{N}_0}$ is still a martingale. Then from Optional Stopping Theorem, by letting $Y_\infty := \lim_{n \to \infty} Y_{\min\{n, R_M\}}$, we also have $\mathbb{E}(Y_\infty) = \mathbb{E}(Y_0) = e^{-t \cdot \mathbb{E}(X_0)}$. Thus, we can also obtain similarly that

$$\mathbb{E}(Y_\infty) = e^{-t \cdot \mathbb{E}(X_0)} \leq 1 - \left(1 - \left(1 + \frac{\delta^2}{16} \cdot t^2\right)^{-k}\right) \cdot \mathbb{P}(R_M \geq k) \ .$$

For $k \in \Theta(M^6)$ and $t = \frac{1}{\sqrt{k}}$, we obtain $\mathbb{P}(R_M \geq k) \in \mathcal{O}(\frac{1}{\sqrt{k}})$. Hence, $\mathbb{P}(R_M = \infty) = 0$. By Optional Stopping Theorem, we have $\mathbb{E}(X_{R_M}) \leq \mathbb{E}(X_0)$. Furthermore, we have by Markov's Inequality that $\mathbb{P}(X_{R_M} \geq M) \leq \frac{\mathbb{E}(X_{R_M})}{M} \leq \frac{\mathbb{E}(X_0)}{M}$. Thus, for sufficiently large k with $M \in \Theta(k^{\frac{1}{6}})$, we can deduce that $\mathbb{P}(Z_\Gamma \geq k) \leq \mathbb{P}(R_M \geq k) + \mathbb{P}(X_{R_M} \geq M) \in \mathcal{O}(\frac{1}{\sqrt{k}} + \frac{1}{\sqrt[6]{k}})$. □

Remark 3. Similar to Theorem 1, we can establish a soundness result for general supermartingales. The result simply says that the existence of a (not necessarily difference-bounded) supermartingale map implies almost-sure termination and a weaker tail bound $\mathcal{O}(k^{-\frac{1}{6}})$. ◀

The following example illustrates the application of Proposition 2 on a single while loop with unbounded difference.

Example 5. Consider the following single while loop program

```
in  :  while  x ≥ 1 do
            x := x + r · ⌊√x⌋
        od
out :
```

where the distribution for r is given as $\mathbb{P}(r = 1) = \mathbb{P}(r = -1) = \frac{1}{2}$. The supermartingale map h is defined as the one in Example 4. In this program, h is not difference-bounded as $\lfloor \sqrt{x} \rfloor$ is not bounded. Thus, h satisfies the conditions except (D4) in Definition 1. We now construct a stochastic process $\Gamma = \{X_n = h(\ell_n, \mathbf{v}_n)\}_{n \in \mathbb{N}_0}$ which meets the requirements of Proposition 2. It follows that the program terminates almost-surely under any initial value with tail probabilities bounded by $\mathcal{O}\left(k^{-\frac{1}{6}}\right)$. In general, if r observes a distribution with bounded range $[-M, M]$, non-positive mean and non-zero variance, then we can still prove the same result as follows. We choose a sufficiently large constant $K \geq \frac{M^2}{4} + 1$ so that the function h with $h(\texttt{in}, x) = x + K$ is still a supermartingale map since the non-negativity of $h(\texttt{in}, x) = x - M \cdot \sqrt{x} + K = (\sqrt{x} - \frac{M}{2})^2 - \frac{M^2}{4} + K \geq -\frac{M^2}{4} + K$ for all $x \geq 0$. ◀

4   Central Limit Theorem Based Approach

We have seen in the previous section a supermartingale-based approach for proving almost-sure termination. However by Example 3, an inherent restriction is that the supermartingale should be non-negative. In this section, we propose a new approach through Central Limit Theorem that can drop this requirement but requires in extra an independence condition.

We first state the well-known Central Limit Theorem [35, Chap. 18].

Theorem 2 (Lindeberg-Lévy's Central Limit Theorem). *Suppose* $\{X_1, X_2, \ldots\}$ *is a sequence of independent and identically distributed random variables with* $\mathbb{E}(X_i) = \mu$ *and* $\mathbf{Var}(X_i) = \sigma^2 > 0$ *is finite. Then as n approaches infinity, the random variables* $\sqrt{n}((\frac{1}{n}\sum_{i=1}^{n} X_i) - \mu)$ *converge in distribution to a normal* $(0, \sigma^2)$. *In the case* $\sigma > 0$, *we have for every real number* z

$$\lim_{n \to \infty} \mathbb{P}(\sqrt{n}((\frac{1}{n}\sum_{i=1}^{n} X_i) - \mu) \leq z) = \Phi(\frac{z}{\sigma}),$$

where $\Phi(x)$ *is the standard normal cumulative distribution functions evaluated at* x.

The following lemma is key to our approach, proved by Central Limit Theorem.

Lemma 1. *Let* $\{R_n\}_{n \in \mathbb{N}}$ *be a sequence of independent and identically distributed random variables with expected value* $\mu = \mathbb{E}(R_n) \leq 0$ *and finite variance* $\mathbf{Var}(R_n) = \sigma^2 > 0$ *for every* $n \in \mathbb{N}$. *For every* $x \in \mathbb{R}$, *let* $\Gamma = \{X_n\}_{n \in \mathbb{N}_0}$ *be a discrete-time stochastic process, where* $X_0 = x$ *and* $X_n = x + \Sigma_{k=1}^{n} R_k$ *for* $n \geq 1$. *Then there exists a constant* $p > 0$, *for any* x, *we have* $\mathbb{P}(Z_\Gamma < \infty) \geq p$.

Proof. According to the Central Limit Theorem (Theorem 2),

$$\lim_{n \to \infty} \mathbb{P}(\sqrt{n}(\frac{X_n - x}{n} - \mu) \leq z) = \Phi(\frac{z}{\sigma})$$

holds for every real number z. Note that

$$\mathbb{P}(\sqrt{n}(\frac{X_n - x}{n} - \mu) \leq z) = \mathbb{P}(X_n \leq \sqrt{n} \cdot z + n \cdot \mu + x) \leq \mathbb{P}(X_n \leq \sqrt{n} \cdot z + x).$$

Choose $z = -1$. Then we have $\mathbb{P}(X_n \leq 0) \geq \mathbb{P}(X \leq -\sqrt{n} + x)$ when $n > x^2$. Now we fix a proper $\epsilon < \Phi(\frac{-1}{\sigma})$, and get $n_0(x)$ from the limit form equation such that for all $n > \max\{n_0(x), x^2\}$ we have

$$\mathbb{P}(X_n \leq 0) \geq \mathbb{P}(X \leq -\sqrt{n} + x) \geq \mathbb{P}(\sqrt{n}(\frac{X_n - X_0}{n} - \mu) \leq -1) \geq \Phi(\frac{-1}{\sigma}) - \epsilon = p > 0.$$

Since $X_n \leq 0$ implies $Z_\Gamma < \infty$, we obtain that $\mathbb{P}(Z_\Gamma < \infty) \geq p$ for every x.   □

Incremental Single While Loops. Due to the independence condition required by Central Limit Theorem, we need to consider special classes of single while loops. We say that a single while loop P in the form (1) is *incremental* if Q is a sequential composition of assignment statements of the form $x := x + \sum_{i=1}^{|R|} c_i \cdot r_i$ where x is a program variable, r_i's are sampling variables and c_i's are constant coefficients for sampling variables. We then consider incremental single while loops. For incremental single while loops, the function F for the loop body Q is incremental, i.e., $F(\mathbf{v}, \mathbf{u}) = \mathbf{v} + \mathbf{A} \cdot \mathbf{u}$ for some constant matrix $\mathbf{A} \in \mathbb{Z}^{|X| \times |R|}$.

Remark 4. By Example 3, previous approaches cannot handle incremental single while loops with unbounded range of sampling variables (so that a supermartingale with a lower bound on its values may not exist). On the other hand, any additional syntax such as conditional branches or assignment statements like $x := 2 \cdot x + r$ will result in an increment over certain program variables that is dependent on the previous executions of the program, breaking the independence condition.   ◀

To prove almost-sure termination of incremental single while loops through Central Limit Theorem, we introduce the notion of *linear progress functions*. Below we fix an incremental single while loop P in the form (1).

Definition 2 (Linear Progress Functions). *A* linear progress function *for P is a function $h : \mathbb{Z}^{|X|} \to \mathbb{R}$ satisfying the following conditions:*

(L1) there exists $\mathbf{a} \in \mathbb{R}^{|X|}$ and $c \in \mathbb{R}$ such that $h(\mathbf{v}) = \mathbf{a}^{\mathrm{T}} \cdot \mathbf{v} + c$ for all program valuations $\mathbf{v}$;
(L2) for all program valuations $\mathbf{v}$, if $\mathbf{v} \models \phi$ then $h(\mathbf{v}) > 0$;
(L3) $\sum_{i=1}^{|R|} a_i \cdot \mu_i \leq 0$ and $\sum_{i=1}^{|R|} a_i^2 \cdot \sigma_i^2 > 0$, where
   • $(a_1, \ldots, a_{|R|}) = \mathbf{a}^{\mathrm{T}} \cdot \mathbf{A}$,
   • μ_i (resp. σ_i^2) is the mean (resp. variance) of the distribution $\Upsilon(r_i)$, for $1 \leq i \leq |R|$.

Intuitively, the condition (L1) says that the function should be linear; the condition (L2) specifies that if the value of h is non-positive, then the program terminates; the condition (L3) enforces that the mean of $\mathbf{a}^{\mathrm{T}} \cdot \mathbf{A} \cdot \mathbf{u}$ should be non-positive, while its variance should be non-zero. The main theorem of this section is then as follows.

Theorem 3 (Soundness). *For any incremental single while loop program P, if there exists a linear progress function for P, then for any initial valuation $\mathbf{v}_0$ we have $\mathbb{P}(T < \infty) = 1$.*

Proof. Let $h(\mathbf{v}) = \mathbf{a}^{\mathrm{T}} \cdot \mathbf{v} + c$ be a linear progress function for P. We define the stochastic process $\Gamma = \{X_n\}_{n \in \mathbb{N}_0}$ by $X_n = h(\mathbf{v}_n)$, where $\mathbf{v}_n$ is the vector of random variables that represents the program valuation at the nth execution step of P. Define $R_n := X_n - X_{n-1}$. We have $R_n = X_n - X_{n-1} = h(\mathbf{v}_n) - h(\mathbf{v}_{n-1}) = h(\mathbf{v}_{n-1} + \mathbf{A} \cdot \mathbf{u}_n) - h(\mathbf{v}_{n-1}) = \mathbf{a}^{\mathrm{T}} \cdot \mathbf{A} \cdot \mathbf{u}_n$ for $n \geq 1$. Thus, $\{R_n\}_{n \in \mathbb{N}}$ is a sequence of independent and identically distributed random variables. We have $\mu := \mathbb{E}(R_n) \leq 0$ and $\sigma^2 := \mathbf{Var}(R_n) > 0$ by the independency of r_i's and the condition (L3) in Definition 2. Now we can apply Lemma 1 and obtain that there exists a constant $p > 0$ such that for any initial program valuation $\mathbf{v}_0$, we have $\mathbb{P}(Z_\Gamma < \infty) \geq p$. By the recurrence property of Markov chain, we have $\{X_n\}$ is almost-surely stopping. Notice that from (L2), $0 \geq X_n = h(\mathbf{v}_n)$ implies $\mathbf{v}_n \not\models \phi$ and (in the next step) termination of the single while loop. Hence, we have that P is almost-surely terminating under any initial program valuation $\mathbf{v}_0$.   □

Theorem 3 can be applied to prove almost-sure termination of while loops whose increments are independent, but the value change in one iteration is not bounded. Thus, Theorem 3 can handle programs which Theorem 1 and Proposition 2 as well as previous supermartingale-based methods cannot.

In the following, we present several examples, showing that Theorem 3 can handle sampling variables with unbounded range which previous approaches cannot handle.

Example 6. Consider the program in Example 1 where we let r be a two-sided geometric distribution sampling variable such that $\mathbb{P}(r = k > 0) = \frac{(1-p)^{k-1}p}{2}$ and $\mathbb{P}(r = k < 0) = \frac{(1-p)^{-k-1}p}{2}$ for some $0 < p < 1$. First note that by the approach in [1], we can prove that this program has infinite expected termination time, and thus previous ranking-supermartingale based approach cannot be applied. Also note that the value that r may take has no lower bound. This means that we can hardly obtain the almost-sure termination by finding a proper supermartingale map that satisfy both the non-negativity condition and the non-increasing condition. Now we apply Theorem 3. Choose $h(x) = x$. It follows directly that both (L1) and (L2) hold. Since $\mathbb{E}(r) = 0$ for symmetric property and $0 < \mathbf{Var}(r) = \mathbb{E}(r^2) - \mathbb{E}^2(r) = \mathbb{E}(r^2) = \mathbb{E}(Y^2) = \mathbf{Var}(Y) - \mathbb{E}^2(Y) < \infty$ where Y is the standard geometric distribution with parameter p, we have (L3) holds. Thus, h is a legal linear progress function and this program is almost-sure terminating by Theorem 3.   ◀

Example 7. Consider the following program with a more complex loop guard.

```
in :  while y > x² do
          x := x + r₁;
          y := y + r₂
      od
out :
```

This program terminates when the point on the plane leaves the area above the parabola by a two-dimensional random walk. We suppose that $\mu_1 = \mathbb{E}(r_1), \mu_2 = \mathbb{E}(r_2)$ are both positive and $0 < \mathbf{Var}(r_1), \mathbf{Var}(r_2) < \infty$. Now we are to prove the program is almost-surely terminating by constructing a linear progress function h. The existence of a linear progress function renders the result valid by Theorem 3. Let $h(x, y) = -\mu_2 \cdot x + \mu_1 \cdot y + \frac{\mu_2^2}{4\mu_1}$. If $y > x^2$, then $h(x, y) > \mu_1 \cdot x^2 - \mu_2 \cdot x + \frac{\mu_2^2}{4\mu_1} = \mu_1(x - \frac{\mu_2}{2\mu_1})^2 \geq 0$. From $\mathbf{a}^T \cdot \mathbf{A} \cdot (\mathbb{E}(r_1), \mathbb{E}(r_2))^T = -\mu_2 \cdot \mu_1 + \mu_1 \cdot \mu_2 = 0$, we have h is a legal linear progress function for P. Thus, P is almost-surely terminating.   ◀

5   Algorithmic Methods and Extensions

In this section, we discuss possible extensions for our results, such as algorithmic methods, real-valued program variables, non-determinism.

Algorithmic Methods. Since program termination is generally undecidable, algorithms for proving termination of programs require certain restrictions. A typical restriction adopted in previous ranking-supermartingale-based algorithms [6, 8–10] is a fixed template for ranking supermartingales. Such a template fixes a specific form for ranking supermartingales. In general, a ranking-supermartingale-based algorithm first establishes a template with unknown coefficients for a ranking supermartingale. The constraints over those unknown coefficients are inherited from the properties of the ranking supermartingale. Finally, constraints are solved using either linear programming or semidefinite programming.

This algorithmic paradigm can be directly extended to our supermartingale-based approaches. First, an algorithm can establish a linear or polynomial template with unknown coefficients for a supermartingale map. Then our conditions from supermartingale maps (namely (D1)–(D4)) result in constraints on the unknown coefficients. Finally, linear or semidefinite programming solvers can be applied to obtain the concrete values for those unknown coefficients.

For our CLT-based approach, the paradigm is more direct to apply. We first establish a linear template with unknown coefficients. Then we just need to find suitable coefficients such that (i) the difference has non-positive mean value and non-zero variance and (ii) the condition (D5) holds, which again reduces to linear programming.

In conclusion, previous algorithmic results can be easily adapted to our approaches.

Real-Valued Program Variables. A major technical difficulty to handle real numbers is the *measurability* condition (cf. [35, Chap. 3]). For example, we need to ensure that our supermartingale map is measurable in some sense. The measurability condition also affects our CLT-based approach as it is more difficult to prove the recurrence property in continuous-state-space case. However, the issue of measurability is only technical and not fundamental, and thus we believe that our approaches can be extended to real-valued program variables and continuous samplings such as uniform or Gaussian distribution.

Non-determinism. In previous works, non-determinism is handled by ensuring related properties in each non-deterministic branch. For examples, previous results on ranking supermartingales [6, 8, 9] ensures that the conditions for ranking supermartingales should hold for all non-deterministic branches if we have demonic non-determinism, and for at least one non-deterministic branch if we have angelic non-determinism. Algorithmic methods can then be adapted depending on whether the non-determinism is demonic or angelic.

Our supermartingale-based approaches can be easily extended to handle non-determinism. If we have demonic non-determinism in the single while loop, then we just ensure that the supermartingale map satisfies the conditions (D1)–(D4) no matter which demonic branch is taken. Similarly, for angelic non-determinism, we just require that the conditions (D1)–(D4) hold for at least one angelic branch. Then algorithmic methods can be developed to handle non-determinism.

On the other hand, we cannot extend our CLT-based approach directly to non-determinism. The reason is that under history-dependent schedulers, the sampled value at the nth step may not be independent of those in the previous step. In this sense, we cannot apply Central Limit Theorem since it requires the independence condition. Hence, we need to develop new techniques to handle non-determinism in the cases from Sect. 4. We leave this interesting direction as a future work.

6 Applicability of Our Approaches

Up till now, we have illustrated our supermartingale based and Central-Limit-Theorem based approach only over single probabilistic while loops. A natural question arises whether our approach can be applied to programs with more complex structures. Below we discuss this point.

First, we demonstrate that our approaches can in principle be applied to all probabilistic programs without nested loops, as is done by a simple compositional argument.

Remark 5 (Compositionality). We note that the property of almost-sure termination for all initial program valuations are closed under sequential composition and conditional branches. Thus, it suffices to consider single while loops, and the results extend straightforwardly to all imperative probabilistic programs without nested loops. Thus, our approaches can in principle handle all probabilistic programs without nested loops. We plan the interesting direction of compositional reasoning for nested probabilistic loops as a future work.   ◄

Second, we show that our approaches cannot be directly extended to nested probabilistic loops. The following remark presents the details.

Remark 6. Consider a probabilistic nested loop

while ϕ **do** P **od**

where P is another probabilistic while loop. On one hand, if we apply super-martingales directly to such programs, then either (i) the value of an appropriate supermartingale may grow unboundedly below zero due to the possibly unbounded termination time of the loop P, which breaks the necessary non-negativity condition (see Example 3), or (ii) we restrict supermartingales to be non-negative on purpose in the presence of nested loops, but then we can only handle simple nested loops (e.g., inner and outer loops do not interfere). On the other hand, the CLT-based approach rely on independence, and cannot be applied to nested loops since the nesting loop will make the increment of the outer loop not independent.   ◄

To summarize, while our approaches apply to all probabilistic programs without nested loops, new techniques beyond supermartingales and Central Limit Theorem are needed to handle general nested loops.

7   Related Works

We compare our approaches with other approaches on termination of probabilistic programs. As far as we know, there are two main classes of approaches for proving termination of probabilistic programs, namely (ranking) supermartingales and proof rules.

Supermartingale-Based Approach. First, we point out the major difference between our approaches and ranking-supermartingale-based approaches [3,6, 8,9,13]. The difference is that ranking-supermartingale-based approaches can only be applied to programs with finite expected termination time. Although in [1] a notion of lexicographic ranking supermartingales is proposed to prove almost-sure termination of compositions of probabilistic while loops, the approach still relies on ranking supermartingales for a single loop, and thus cannot be applied to single while loops with infinite expected termination time. In our paper, we target probabilistic programs with infinite expected termination time, and thus our approaches can handle programs that ranking-supermartingale-based approaches cannot handle.

Then we remark on the most-related work [26] which also considered supermartingale-based approach for almost-sure termination. Compared with our supermartingale-based approach, the approach in [26] relaxes the LBCAD condition in Proposition 1 so that a more general result on almost-sure termination is obtained but the tail bounds cannot be guaranteed, while our results can derive optimal tail bounds. Moreover, the approach in [26] requires that the values taken by the supermartingale should have a lower bound, while our CLT-based approach do not require this restriction and hence can handle almost-sure terminating programs that cannot be handled in [26]. Finally, our supermartingale-based results are independent of [26] (see the arXiv versions [25] and [7, Theorems 5 and 6]).

Proof-Rule-Based Approach. In this paper, we consider the supermartingale based approach for probabilistic programs. An alternative approach is based on the notion of proof rules [20, 29]. In the approach of proof rules, a set of rules is proposes following which one can prove termination. Currently, the approach of proof rules is also restricted to finite termination as the proof rules require certain quantity to decrease in expectation, similar to the requirement of ranking supermartingales.

Potential-Function-Based Approach. Recently, there is another approach through the notion of *potential functions* [28]. This approach is similar to ranking supermartingales that can derive upper bounds for expected termination time and cost. In principle, the major difference between the approaches of ranking supermartingales and potential functions lies in algorithmic details. In the approach of (ranking) supermartingales, the unknown coefficients in a template are solved by linear/semidefinite programming, while the approach of potential functions solves the template through inference rules.

8 Conclusion

In this paper, we studied sound approaches for proving almost-sure termination of probabilistic programs with integer-valued program variables. We first presented new mathematical results for supermartingales which yield new sound approaches for proving almost-sure termination of simple probabilistic while loops. Based on the above results, we presented sound supermartingale-based approaches for proving almost-sure termination of simple probabilistic while loops. Besides almost-sure termination, our supermartingale-based approach is the first to give (optimal) bounds on tail probabilities of non-termination within a given number of steps. Then we proposed a new sound approach through Central Limit Theorem that can prove almost-sure termination of examples that no previous approaches can handle. Finally, we have shown possible extensions of our approach to algorithmic methods, non-determinism, real-valued program variables, and demonstrated that in principle our approach can handle all probabilistic programs without nested loops through simple compositional reasoning.

Acknowledgements. This work was financially supported by NSFC (Grant No. 61772336, 61472239), Notional Key Research and Development Program of China (Grant No. 2017YFB0701900), Austrian Science Fund (FWF) grant S11407-N23 (RiSE/SHiNE) and Vienna Science and Technology Fund (WWTF) project ICT15-003.

References

1. Agrawal, S., Chatterjee, K., Novotný, P.: Lexicographic ranking supermartingales: an efficient approach to termination of probabilistic programs. PACMPL **2**(POPL), 34:1–34:32 (2018). https://doi.org/10.1145/3158122
2. Baier, C., Katoen, J.P.: Principles of Model Checking. MIT Press, Cambridge (2008)

3. Bournez, O., Garnier, F.: Proving positive almost-sure termination. In: Giesl, J. (ed.) RTA 2005. LNCS, vol. 3467, pp. 323–337. Springer, Heidelberg (2005). https://doi.org/10.1007/978-3-540-32033-3_24

4. Bradley, A.R., Manna, Z., Sipma, H.B.: Linear ranking with reachability. In: Etessami, K., Rajamani, S.K. (eds.) CAV 2005. LNCS, vol. 3576, pp. 491–504. Springer, Heidelberg (2005). https://doi.org/10.1007/11513988_48

5. Brázdil, T., Kiefer, S., Kucera, A., Vareková, I.H.: Runtime analysis of probabilistic programs with unbounded recursion. J. Comput. Syst. Sci. **81**(1), 288–310 (2015)

6. Chakarov, A., Sankaranarayanan, S.: Probabilistic program analysis with martingales. In: Sharygina, N., Veith, H. (eds.) CAV 2013. LNCS, vol. 8044, pp. 511–526. Springer, Heidelberg (2013). https://doi.org/10.1007/978-3-642-39799-8_34

7. Chatterjee, K., Fu, H.: Termination of nondeterministic recursive probabilistic programs. CoRR abs/1701.02944, January 2017

8. Chatterjee, K., Fu, H., Goharshady, A.K.: Termination analysis of probabilistic programs through positivstellensatz's. In: Chaudhuri, S., Farzan, A. (eds.) CAV 2016. LNCS, vol. 9779, pp. 3–22. Springer, Cham (2016). https://doi.org/10.1007/978-3-319-41528-4_1

9. Chatterjee, K., Fu, H., Novotný, P., Hasheminezhad, R.: Algorithmic analysis of qualitative and quantitative termination problems for affine probabilistic programs. In: POPL, pp. 327–342 (2016)

10. Chatterjee, K., Novotný, P., Žikelić, Đ.: Stochastic invariants for probabilistic termination. In: POPL, pp. 145–160 (2017)

11. Colón, M.A., Sipma, H.B.: Synthesis of linear ranking functions. In: Margaria, T., Yi, W. (eds.) TACAS 2001. LNCS, vol. 2031, pp. 67–81. Springer, Heidelberg (2001). https://doi.org/10.1007/3-540-45319-9_6

12. Esparza, J., Gaiser, A., Kiefer, S.: Proving termination of probabilistic programs using patterns. In: Madhusudan, P., Seshia, S.A. (eds.) CAV 2012. LNCS, vol. 7358, pp. 123–138. Springer, Heidelberg (2012). https://doi.org/10.1007/978-3-642-31424-7_14

13. Fioriti, L.M.F., Hermanns, H.: Probabilistic termination: soundness, completeness, and compositionality. In: POPL, pp. 489–501 (2015)

14. Floyd, R.W.: Assigning meanings to programs. Math. Aspects Comput. Sci. **19**, 19–33 (1967)

15. Foster, F.G.: On the stochastic matrices associated with certain queuing processes. Ann. Math. Stat. **24**(3), 355–360 (1953)

16. Gordon, A.D., Henzinger, T.A., Nori, A.V., Rajamani, S.K.: Probabilistic programming. In: Herbsleb, J.D., Dwyer, M.B. (eds.) FOSE, pp. 167–181. ACM (2014)

17. Kaelbling, L.P., Littman, M.L., Cassandra, A.R.: Planning and acting in partially observable stochastic domains. Artif. Intell. **101**(1), 99–134 (1998)

18. Kaelbling, L.P., Littman, M.L., Moore, A.W.: Reinforcement learning: a survey. JAIR **4**, 237–285 (1996)

19. Kaminski, B.L., Katoen, J.-P.: On the hardness of almost–sure termination. In: Italiano, G.F., Pighizzini, G., Sannella, D.T. (eds.) MFCS 2015. LNCS, vol. 9234, pp. 307–318. Springer, Heidelberg (2015). https://doi.org/10.1007/978-3-662-48057-1_24

20. Kaminski, B.L., Katoen, J.-P., Matheja, C., Olmedo, F.: Weakest precondition reasoning for expected run–times of probabilistic programs. In: Thiemann, P. (ed.) ESOP 2016. LNCS, vol. 9632, pp. 364–389. Springer, Heidelberg (2016). https://doi.org/10.1007/978-3-662-49498-1_15

21. Kemeny, J., Snell, J., Knapp, A.: Denumerable Markov Chains. D. Van Nostrand Company, Princeton (1966)

22. Kwiatkowska, M., Norman, G., Parker, D.: PRISM 4.0: verification of probabilistic real-time systems. In: Gopalakrishnan, G., Qadeer, S. (eds.) CAV 2011. LNCS, vol. 6806, pp. 585–591. Springer, Heidelberg (2011). https://doi.org/10.1007/978-3-642-22110-1_47

23. McIver, A., Morgan, C.: Developing and reasoning about probabilistic programs in *pGCL*. In: Cavalcanti, A., Sampaio, A., Woodcock, J. (eds.) PSSE 2004. LNCS, vol. 3167, pp. 123–155. Springer, Heidelberg (2006). https://doi.org/10.1007/11889229_4

24. McIver, A., Morgan, C.: Abstraction, Refinement and Proof for Probabilistic Systems. Monographs in Computer Science. Springer, New York (2005). https://doi.org/10.1007/b138392

25. McIver, A., Morgan, C.: A new rule for almost-certain termination of probabilistic and demonic programs. CoRR abs/1612.01091, December 2016

26. McIver, A., Morgan, C., Kaminski, B.L., Katoen, J.: A new proof rule for almost-sure termination. PACMPL **2**(POPL), 33:1–33:28 (2018). https://doi.org/10.1145/3158121

27. van de Meent, J., Yang, H., Mansinghka, V., Wood, F.: Particle gibbs with ancestor sampling for probabilistic programs. In: AISTATS (2015)

28. Ngo, V.C., Carbonneaux, Q., Hoffmann, J.: Bounded expectations: resource analysis for probabilistic programs. In: Foster, J.S., Grossman, D. (eds.) Proceedings of the 39th ACM SIGPLAN Conference on Programming Language Design and Implementation, PLDI 2018, Philadelphia, PA, USA, 18–22 June 2018, pp. 496–512. ACM (2018). https://doi.org/10.1145/3192366.3192394

29. Olmedo, F., Kaminski, B.L., Katoen, J.P., Matheja, C.: Reasoning about recursive probabilistic programs. In: LICS, pp. 672–681 (2016)

30. Paz, A.: Introduction to Probabilistic Automata (Computer Science and Applied Mathematics). Academic Press, Cambridge (1971)

31. Podelski, A., Rybalchenko, A.: A complete method for the synthesis of linear ranking functions. In: Steffen, B., Levi, G. (eds.) VMCAI 2004. LNCS, vol. 2937, pp. 239–251. Springer, Heidelberg (2004). https://doi.org/10.1007/978-3-540-24622-0_20

32. Rabin, M.: Probabilistic automata. Inf. Control **6**, 230–245 (1963)

33. Sankaranarayanan, S., Chakarov, A., Gulwani, S.: Static analysis for probabilistic programs: inferring whole program properties from finitely many paths. In: PLDI, pp. 447–458 (2013)

34. Sohn, K., Gelder, A.V.: Termination detection in logic programs using argument sizes. In: PODS, pp. 216–226 (1991)

35. Williams, D.: Probability with Martingales. Cambridge University Press, Cambridge (1991)

Particle-Style Geometry of Interaction as a Module System

Ulrich Schöpp[✉]

Ludwig-Maximilians-Universität München, Munich, Germany
schoepp@tcs.ifi.lmu.de

Abstract. The Geometry of Interaction (GOI) has its origins in logic, but many of its recent applications concern the interpretation and analysis of functional programming languages. Applications range from hardware synthesis to quantum computation. In this paper we argue that for such programming-language applications it is useful to understand the GOI as a module system. We derive an ML-style module system from the structure of the particle-style GOI. This provides a convenient, familiar formalism for working with the GOI that abstracts from inessential implementation details. The relation between the GOI and the proposed module system is established by a linear version of the F-ing modules elaboration of Rossberg, Russo and Dreyer. It uses a new decomposition of the exponential rules of Linear Logic as the basis for syntax-directed type inference that minimises the scope of exponentials.

1 Introduction

Modularity is very important for software construction. Virtually all programming languages have some kind of module system for the compositional construction of large programs. Modularity is also becoming increasingly important at a much smaller scale, e.g. [3]. For formal verification and program analysis, one wants to decompose programs into as small as possible fragments that can be verified and analysed independently. For the application of formal methods, modularity is essential even when it comes to the low-level implementation of programming languages.

The Geometry of Interaction (GOI) is one approach to the modular decomposition of programming languages. It was originally introduced by Girard [8] in the context of the proof theory of Linear Logic. It has since found many applications in programming languages, especially in situations where one wants to design higher-order programming languages for some restricted first-order model of computation. Examples are hardware circuits [6], LOGSPACE-computation [4], quantum computation [10], distributed systems [5], etc. These applications use the particle-style variant of the GOI, which constructs a model of higher-order programming languages in terms of dialogues between simple interacting entities. These interactive entities are simple enough to be implemented in the first-order computational model. Overall, one obtains a translation of higher-order programs to first-order programs.

© Springer Nature Switzerland AG 2018
S. Ryu (Ed.): APLAS 2018, LNCS 11275, pp. 202–222, 2018.
https://doi.org/10.1007/978-3-030-02768-1_12

In this paper, we connect the Geometry of Interaction to ML-style module systems. Rather than explaining the GOI in terms of interaction dialogues, we explain it as an implementation of a module system with structures, signatures and functors, as in Standard ML and OCaml. Interactive entities can be seen as modules that interact using function calls.

The main motivation of this work is to make the presentation of the GOI more economical and accessible. In programming language applications of the GOI, one usually defines it from scratch. This is not ideal and could be compared to writing a paper on functional programming starting from assembly language. The low-level implementation details are essentially standard, but their explanation can be quite technical and complicated. Since one wants to focus on actual applications, one is led to giving a very concise presentation of an as simplified-as-possible low-level implementation. Such presentations are hard to read for non-experts and thus become an unnecessary hurdle in the way of interesting applications. What is needed is a formalism that abstracts from the low-level implementation and that can be understood informally.

To this end, we propose an ML-style module system as a formalism for the GOI. It captures important constructions of the GOI in terms that are already familiar from programming languages like SML and OCaml. We can use it to study applications of the GOI independently of its efficient low-level implementation.

In the literature, it is common to use variants of System F to abstract from implementation details of the GOI. Indeed, we shall use such a calculus as an intermediate step in Sect. 4. However, while such calculi capture the right structure, they can be quite laborious to work with, especially when it comes to using existential types for abstraction [15,16]. This is much like in SML. Its module system can be seen as a mode of use for System F_ω [14], which is more convenient to use than System F_ω terms themselves. Moreover, a module system directly conveys the computational intention of the GOI. The GOI captures an approach of the compositional construction of larger programs from small independent fragments. This intention is captured well by a module system. With a variant of System F, some explanation is needed to convey it, as is evidenced by Sect. 4.

Readers who are not familiar with the GOI may read the paper as a way of constructing an ML-style module system even for restricted first-order programming languages. The construction requires few assumptions and applies in particular to first-order low-level languages for the restricted models of computation mentioned above. One can think of the GOI as producing a higher-order module system for first-order languages for free. With such a module system it becomes very easy, for example, to implement higher-order programming languages like Idealized Algol efficiently.

The paper is organised as follows. We fix a simple generic notion of core computation in Sect. 2. Then we define a simple first-order programming language for core computation in Sect. 3. It will be the target of the module system. We then construct the module system in two steps. First, we construct a linear type system for the particle-style GOI in Sect. 4, which we then use as the basis of an ML-style module system in Sect. 5. We conclude with examples in Sect. 6.

2   Core Expressions

We fix a very basic language of computational expressions as the basis for all further constructions. Modules will organise these kinds of expressions.

$$
\begin{array}{rcl}
\text{Core types} & A ::= & \texttt{int} \mid \texttt{unit} \mid A \times A \mid \texttt{empty} \mid A + A \\
\text{Core values} & v, w ::= & x \mid n \mid () \mid (v, w) \mid \texttt{inl}\, v \mid \texttt{inr}\, v \\
\text{Core expressions} & e ::= & \texttt{return}\, v \mid op(v) \mid \texttt{let}\ x = e\ \texttt{in}\ e \mid \\
& & \mid \texttt{let}\ (x, y) = v\ \texttt{in}\ e \mid \texttt{case}\ v\ \texttt{of}\ \texttt{inl}(x) \Rightarrow e;\ \texttt{inr}(x) \Rightarrow e
\end{array}
$$

In this grammar, n ranges over integers and op ranges over primitive operations, such as *add*, *sub* and *mul*. It is possible to have effectful operations, such as *print* for I/O, or *put* and *get* for global state. They can be added as needed, but we do not need to assume any specific operations in this paper. The type int is an example of a base type; let us assume that it represents fixed-width integers. The term $\texttt{let}\ (x, y) = v\ \texttt{in}\ e$ is a pattern matching operation for product types.

We use standard syntactic sugar, such as writing $e_1 + e_2$ for expressions.

3   First-Order Programs

We start from a first-order programming language for core expressions. The particular details are not very important for this paper. The first-order language is a stand-in for the first-order models of computation that one uses as a starting point for GOI constructions. It may also be seen as an idealisation of low-level compiler intermediate languages like LLVM-IR.

$$
\begin{array}{rcl}
\text{First-order types} & B ::= & \text{core types} \mid \texttt{raw} \\
\text{First-order expressions} & e ::= & \text{core expressions} \mid f(\overline{v_i}) \mid \texttt{let}\ x = \texttt{coerc}_B(v)\ \texttt{in}\ e \\
& & \mid \texttt{let}\ \texttt{coerc}_B(x) = v\ \texttt{in}\ e \\
\text{First-order programs} & P ::= & \texttt{empty} \mid \texttt{fn}\ f(\overline{x_i{:}\,B_i}) \to B\ \{e\}\ P
\end{array}
$$

The phrase 'core types' means that we include all cases from the grammar for core types, only now with B in place of A. In the syntax, as in the rest of this paper, we use the notation $\overline{a_i}$ for a vector $a_1, \ldots, a_n$.

In contrast to the other calculi in this paper, the type system of first-order programs is not intended to capture interesting correctness properties. Types are nevertheless useful for documentation and implementation purposes, e.g. to statically determine the size of values for efficient compilation.

A program consists of a list of function definitions, which are allowed to be mutually recursive. The new term $f(\overline{v_i})$ is a function call. The syntax is perhaps best explained with a typical example:

```
fn fact_aux(x: int, acc: int) → int
    { if x = 0 then return acc else fact_aux(x - 1, acc * x) }
fn fact(x: int) → int { fact_aux(x, 1) }
```

The new type `raw` is a type of raw, unstructured data. It abstracts from implementation issues that are out of scope for this paper. With the new term `let` $x = \mathsf{coerc}_B(v)$ `in` e one can cast a value v of any type B into its raw underlying data $x\!:\mathsf{raw}$. The term `let` $\mathsf{coerc}_B(y) = w$ `in` e allows one to cast $w\!:\mathsf{raw}$ into a value $y\!:B$. This may produce nonsense. The only guarantee is that if one coerces $v\!:B$ into `raw` and then back into B, then one gets back v.

We consider not just complete programs, but also programs that are incomplete in the sense that they may contain calls to external functions. An *interface* $(I; O)$ for a program consists of two sets I and O of function signatures of the form $f\!: (B_1, \ldots, B_n) \to B$. The functions in I must all be defined in the program. They are considered as its public functions. The set O must contain at least the signatures (of appropriate type) of all functions that are called in the program. Note a program may have more than one interface. The set I need not contain all defined functions and O may contain more functions than are actually called.

Programs can be linked simply by concatenation. If m is a program of interface $(P \uplus I;\ J \uplus O)$ and n is a program of interface $(J;\ P)$, then m, n is a program of interface $(I;\ O)$. Here, $\uplus$ means the disjoint union where no function label may be defined twice. This kind of linking is standard in operating systems.

4   Linear Types for Linking

The particle-style GOI has many presentations, e.g. [1, 2, 6, 11]. Here we present it in the form of a higher-order lambda calculus with the syntax shown below. It will be the basis of the module system in the next section, so we explain it as a calculus for constructing and linking first-order programs. While the calculus is close to previous type systems for the GOI, there are some novelties: a new way of tracking the scope of value variables; a flexible formulation of exponentials that reduces them to value variables; a generalisation to returning functions; a direct elaboration to first-order programs suitable for the elaboration of modules.

Base types	D ::=	first-order types $\mid \alpha$
Interaction types	S, T ::=	$\mathsf{M}D \mid \{\overline{\ell_i\!:S_i}\} \mid D \to S \mid S \multimap T \mid \forall \alpha.\, S \mid \exists \alpha.\, S \mid D{\cdot}S$
Interaction terms	s, t ::=	core expressions $\mid X \mid \{\overline{\ell_i = t_i}\} \mid$ `let` $\{\overline{\ell_i = X_i}\} = s$ `in` t
		$\mid$ `fn` $(x{:}D) \to t \mid t(v) \mid \lambda X{:}S.t \mid s\ t \mid \Lambda \alpha.\, t \mid t\ D$
		$\mid \mathsf{pack}(D, t) \mid$ `let` $\mathsf{pack}(\alpha, X) = s$ `in` t

The syntax uses value variables x, y, z, interactive variables X, Y, Z and type variables α, β. Value variables can appear only in core values, they are bound by core expressions and by the abstraction `fn` $(x{:}C) \to t$. The interactive terms (`let` $\{\overline{\ell_i = X_i}\} = s$ `in` t) and (`let` $\mathsf{pack}(\alpha, X) = s$ `in` t) are pattern matching operations for records and existential types.

The base type $\mathsf{M}D$ represents core computations that return a value of first-order type D. The notation $\mathsf{M}(-)$ signifies the possible presence of the effects from core computations. The type $D \to S$ is a type of functions that take a value of first-order type D as input. The type $\{\overline{\ell_i\!:S_i}\}$ is a record type. A typical use of these three types is to define a list of first-order functions. For example, the term $\{f = \mathtt{fn}\,(x{:}\mathtt{int}) \to \mathtt{return}\,x,\ g = \mathtt{fn}\,(x{:}\mathtt{int}) \to \mathtt{let}\,y = add(x,1)\,\mathtt{in}\,\mathtt{return}\,y\}$ has type $\{f : \mathtt{int} \to \mathtt{Mint},\ g : \mathtt{int} \to \mathtt{Mint}\}$. It represents a list of first-order functions, just like in the first-order programs from the previous section.

The type $S \multimap T$ represents incomplete programs that make use of external definitions of type S that will be linked later. The application of this function type will correspond to first-order program linking. For example, a term of type $\{f_1 : D_1 \to \mathrm{MD}_2, f_2 : D_3 \to \mathrm{MD}_4\} \multimap \{g_1 : D_5 \to \mathrm{MD}_6, g_2 : D_7 \to \mathrm{MD}_8\}$ represents a program that defines the functions g_1 and g_2 and that may call the external functions f_1 and f_2. An application of the $\multimap$-function amounts to linking the missing external definitions.

Of course, any type system with records and functions can represent the examples shown so far. The key point of the type system is that terms of type $\{f_1 : B_1 \to \mathrm{MB}_2, f_2 : B_3 \to \mathrm{MB}_4\}$ and $\{f_1 : B_1 \to \mathrm{MB}_2, f_2 : B_3 \to \mathrm{MB}_4\} \multimap \{g_1 : B_5 \to \mathrm{MB}_6, g_2 : B_7 \to \mathrm{MB}_8\}$ will correspond, respectively, to first-order programs of interfaces $(\{f_1{:}B_1 \to B_2, f_2{:}B_3 \to B_4\}; \emptyset)$ and $(\{g_1{:}B_5 \to B_6, g_2{:}B_7 \to B_8\}; \{f_1{:}B_1 \to B_2, f_2{:}B_3 \to B_4\})$. The application of these terms corresponds to linking these programs. This distinguishes $\multimap$ from the normal function space $\to$. The former is a way of composing programs, while the latter represents value passing as in the first-order language.

The reader should think of an interactive type S as specifying the interface of a first-order program and of terms of this type as denoting particular first-order programs of this interface. This also explains why the type system is linear. A term provides a single implementation of the interface S that is consumed when it is linked to a program of type $S \multimap T$. Once it is linked in one way, it cannot be linked again in a different way.

The types $\forall \alpha.\,S$ and $\exists \alpha.\,S$ allow a weak form of polymorphism. In particular, type variables range only over first-order types.

Finally, the type $D{\cdot}X$ is a slight generalisation of the exponential from Linear Logic. In the present interpretation it can be understood as a type for managing scope and lifetime of a value variable of type D, which is explained below. We write $!X$ for the special case $\mathtt{raw}{\cdot}X$. A reader who prefers to do so, may only consider this special case. The generalisation from $\mathtt{raw}$ to an arbitrary type D allows more precise typing and simplifies technical details.

4.1   Type System

The type system is a linear variant of System F and derives typing judgements of the form $\Gamma \vdash t : T$. The context Γ is a finite list of variable declarations, of which there are three kinds: interaction variable declarations $X{:}S$, value declarations $x{:}D$ and type declarations α. As usual, no variable may be declared twice.

We identify contexts up to the equivalence induced by $\Gamma,\,X{:}S,\,Y{:}T,\,\Delta = \Gamma,\,Y{:}T,\,X{:}S,\,\Delta$. This means that interaction variable declarations may be exchanged. The order of value declarations is important, however. They may not be exchanged with any other variable declaration.

We define a partial operation of joining two contexts Γ and Δ into a single context $\Gamma + \Delta$ as follows.

$$(X{:}S, \Gamma_1) + \Gamma_2 := X{:}S, (\Gamma_1 + \Gamma_2) \qquad \Gamma_1 + (X{:}S, \Gamma_2) := X{:}S, (\Gamma_1 + \Gamma_2)$$
$$(x{:}A, \Gamma_1) + (x{:}A, \Gamma_2) := x{:}A, (\Gamma_1 + \Gamma_2) \qquad (\alpha, \Gamma_1) + (\alpha, \Gamma_2) := \alpha, (\Gamma_1 + \Gamma_2)$$

This is well-defined by the above identification. The typing rules will use $+$ with the effect of treating module variables linearly (i.e. multiplicatively) and all other variables non-linearly (i.e. additively). Moreover, each type S remains in the scope of the same value variables. Indeed, we consider an interactive type S as a different type if it is moved to a context with different value variables. For example, in the empty context, the type $\{f : \mathtt{int} \to \mathtt{Mint}\}$ represents the interface $(\{\Box.f{:}\,\mathtt{int} \to \mathtt{int}\}; \emptyset)$. In context $x{:}\,\mathtt{bool}$, the same type represents the interface $(\{\Box.f{:}\,(\mathtt{bool}, \mathtt{int}) \to \mathtt{int}\}; \emptyset)$. In the elaboration, value variables from the context will become extra arguments.

Given the definition of contexts, most of the typing rules become unsurprising. For example, the rules for $\multimap$ and $\to$ are:

$$\text{\textendash$\circ$-I} \frac{\Gamma, X{:}S \vdash t{:}T}{\Gamma \vdash \lambda X{:}S.t{:}\ S \multimap T} \qquad \text{\textendash$\circ$-E} \frac{\Gamma \vdash s{:}\ S \multimap T \qquad \Delta \vdash t{:}S}{\Gamma + \Delta \vdash s\,t{:}T}$$

$$\text{FN-I} \frac{\Gamma, x{:}D \vdash t{:}S}{\Gamma \vdash \mathbf{fn}\,(x{:}D) \to t{:}\ D \to S} \qquad \text{FN-E} \frac{\Gamma \vdash t{:}\ D \to S \qquad \Gamma \vdash v{:}D}{\Gamma \vdash t(v){:}S}$$

Since the meaning of types depends on the value variables in the context, weakening is available only for interaction variables and the variable rule is restricted to the last variable.

$$\text{WEAK} \frac{\Gamma, \Delta \vdash t{:}T}{\Gamma, X{:}S, \Delta \vdash t{:}T} \qquad \text{VAR} \frac{}{\Gamma, X{:}S \vdash X{:}S}$$

The rules for the exponentials $D{\cdot}S$ are mostly like in Linear Logic (if one thinks of the special case $!S$). For example, there is a contraction rule

$$\text{CONTR} \frac{\Gamma, X_1{:}D_1{\cdot}S, X_2{:}D_2{\cdot}S, \Delta \vdash t{:}T}{\Gamma, X{:}(D_1 + D_2){\cdot}S, \Delta \vdash t[X_1 \mapsto X, X_2 \mapsto X]{:}T} X \notin \{X_1, X_2\}.$$

(The reader who considers only exponentials of the form $!S$, i.e. $D_1 = D_2 = \mathtt{raw}$, may consider also $(D_1 + D_2){\cdot}S$ as an example of $!S$. This is because a value of type $\mathtt{raw} + \mathtt{raw}$ can be cast into one of type $\mathtt{raw}$ and there is a subtyping rule for exponentials.) There are similar structural rules for dereliction and digging.

In the current type system, one may think of $D{\cdot}S$ as the type S, but in an extended context with an additional variable of type D. This is formalised by the following two rules, which refine the promotion rule from Linear Logic.

$$\text{CLOSE-L} \frac{\Gamma, x{:}D, X{:}S, \Delta \vdash t{:}T}{\Gamma, X{:}D{\cdot}S, x{:}D, \Delta \vdash t{:}T} \qquad \text{CLOSE-R} \frac{\Gamma, x{:}D \vdash t{:}S}{\Gamma \vdash t{:}D{\cdot}S} x \notin FV(t)$$

$$\frac{\Gamma \rightsquigarrow \overline{B_i} \qquad \Gamma \vdash D \rightsquigarrow B}{\Gamma \vdash MD \rightsquigarrow \{\square : \overline{B_i} \rightarrow B\}; \emptyset} \qquad \frac{\Gamma \vdash S_k \rightsquigarrow I_k; O_k \text{ for } k = 1, \dots, n}{\Gamma \vdash \{\overline{\ell_i : S_i}\} \rightsquigarrow \bigcup_{i=1}^n I_i[\square.\ell_i]; \bigcup_{i=1}^n O_i[\square.\ell_i]}$$

$$\frac{\Gamma \vdash S \rightsquigarrow I; O \qquad \Gamma \vdash T \rightsquigarrow J; P}{\Gamma \vdash S \multimap T \rightsquigarrow O[\square.\mathbf{arg}] \cup J[\square.\mathbf{res}]; I[\square.\mathbf{arg}] \cup P[\square.\mathbf{res}]} \qquad \frac{\Gamma, x : D \vdash S \rightsquigarrow I; O}{\Gamma \vdash D \cdot S \rightsquigarrow I; O}$$

$$\frac{\Gamma, x : D \vdash S \rightsquigarrow I; \dots \qquad \Gamma \vdash S \rightsquigarrow \dots; O}{\Gamma \vdash D \rightarrow S \rightsquigarrow I; O} \qquad \frac{\Gamma, \alpha \vdash S \rightsquigarrow I; O}{\Gamma \vdash \forall \alpha. S \rightsquigarrow I; O} \qquad \frac{\Gamma, \alpha \vdash S \rightsquigarrow I; O}{\Gamma \vdash \exists \alpha. S \rightsquigarrow I; O}$$

Fig. 1. Interaction types: elaboration

The double line in these rules means that they can be applied both from top to bottom and from bottom to top. A standard promotion rule becomes admissible.

With rule CLOSE-R, it becomes possible to use variables from all positions in the context. For example, the judgement $\Gamma, X : (D \cdot S), x : D, Y : T \vdash X : S$ is derivable using WEAK, CLOSE-R (upside down) and VAR. The exponential in the type of X is necessary to keep the value variable scope unchanged.

4.2 Elaboration into First-Order Programs

The type system can be seen as calculus for first-order programs. In this view, interactive terms and types are abbreviations for programs and their interfaces. The elaboration that expands these abbreviations is defined directly as an annotation on the typing rules.

If one includes the elaboration part, then the type system has the following judgements: $\Gamma \vdash D \rightsquigarrow B$ for the elaboration of base types, $\Gamma \vdash S \rightsquigarrow I; O$ for the elaboration of interactive types, and $\Gamma \vdash t : S \rightsquigarrow m$ for typing and the elaboration of terms. We outline them in turn.

The judgement $\Gamma \vdash D \rightsquigarrow B$ is defined as follows: The base type D is obtained from B by substituting raw for all type variables. Polymorphism is thus implemented by casting any value into its raw representation.

The judgement $\Gamma \vdash S \rightsquigarrow I; O$ expresses that, in context Γ, the interactive type S elaborates to the first-order interface $(I; O)$. The rules appear in Fig. 1. The sets I and O in it contain function labels that are generated by the grammar $L ::= \square \mid X \mid L.\ell$, in which $\square$ represents a hole, X ranges over module variables, and ℓ is a label. We write short $(-)[L]$ for the substitution operation $(-)[\square \mapsto L]$.

To understand the meaning of these labels, it is useful to look at the elaboration judgement for terms $\Gamma \vdash t : S \rightsquigarrow m$ first. It translates the module term t to a first-order program m of interface $(I; O)$ where $\Gamma \vdash S \rightsquigarrow I; O$. The program m defines all the functions in I and it may call the functions from O. But, of course, t may also make use of the modules that are declared in Γ. So, if Γ is $\Delta, X : T, \dots$ and $\Delta \vdash T \rightsquigarrow J; P$, then m may assume that the module X is available as a first-order program with interface $(J[X]; P[X])$. This means that m may also invoke the functions from $J[X]$. In return, it must define all functions from $P[X]$.

The type MD elaborates in context Γ to the interface of a first-order program with a single function $\square\colon (\overline{B_i}) \to B$. The judgement $\Gamma \rightsquigarrow \overline{B_i}$, whose definition is omitted, means that the types $\overline{B_i}$ are the elaboration of the value types in Γ. The function therefore gets the values from the context as input and performs the computation to return a value of type B, the elaboration of D.

The elaboration of type $D \to S$ differs from that of S only in that all functions in the set of entry points I take an additional argument of type D. For example, the term $\mathtt{fn}\,(x{:}\mathtt{int}) \to \mathtt{return}\ x$ of type $\mathtt{int} \to \mathtt{Mint}$ elaborates to the first-order function $\mathtt{fn}\ \square(x{:}\,\mathtt{int}) \to \mathtt{int}\ \{\mathtt{return}\ x\}$ of type $(\mathtt{int}) \to \mathtt{int}$.

The record type $\{\ell_i\colon S_i\}$ elaborates all the S_i and joins their interfaces by prefixing them with the ℓ_i. This explains the informal examples given above.

Type $S \multimap T$ elaborates to the interface of a program that implements T while making use of the interface of some external program with interface S. Suppose S elaborates to $(I; O)$ and T to $(J; P)$. To implement T, such a program must define all functions in J, while it can call the functions in P. To use the external program of interface S, it may additionally call all the functions in I. It must, however, provide the external program all functions that it may need, i.e. it must define all functions in O. This would lead to $(O \cup J; I \cup P)$, but we must take care to avoid name clashes. Therefore we use $(O[\square.\mathtt{arg}] \cup J[\square.\mathtt{res}]; J[\square.\mathtt{arg}] \cup P[\square.\mathtt{res}])$. For example, the type $(\mathtt{Mint} \multimap \mathtt{Mint}) \multimap \mathtt{Mint}$ elaborates to the interface $(\{\square.\mathtt{res}\colon () \to \mathtt{int}, \square.\mathtt{arg}.\mathtt{arg}\colon () \to \mathtt{int}\}; \{\square.\mathtt{arg}.\mathit{res}\colon () \to \mathtt{int}\})$.

Application then becomes linking. Suppose we have a term $t\colon S \multimap T$, which elaborates to a program m of interface $(I[\square.\mathtt{arg}] \cup J[\square.\mathtt{res}]; O[\square.\mathtt{arg}] \cup P[\square.\mathtt{res}])$. An argument $s\colon S$ elaborates to a program n of interface $(I; O)$. By renaming and concatenation, we get the program $n[\square.\mathtt{arg}], m$ of interface $(J[\square.\mathtt{res}]; P[\square.\mathtt{res}])$. From this one gets a program of interface $(J; P)$ by adding forwarding functions, such as $\mathtt{fn}\ f(x)\ \{f[\square.\mathtt{res}](x)\}$.

For a concrete example, consider the following term:

$$\lambda X\colon \{f\colon \mathtt{int} \to \mathtt{Mint}\}.\,\mathtt{let}\ \{f = Y\} = X\ \mathtt{in}\ \{f = \mathtt{fn}\,(x{:}\mathtt{int}) \to Y(x) + 1,\ g = Y(0)\}$$

While the type system treats interaction variables linearly, using Y twice here is justified by rule DUPL explained below. The term has type $\{f\colon \mathtt{int} \to \mathtt{Mint}\} \multimap \{f\colon \mathtt{int} \to \mathtt{Mint},\ g\colon \mathtt{Mint}\}$ and elaborates to (we simplify elaboration examples for readability):

```
fn  □.res.f(x:  int)  →  int  {  □.arg.f(x)+1  }
fn  □.res.g()  →  int  {  □.arg.f(0)  }
```

Suppose we apply it to the actual argument $\{f = \mathtt{fn}\,(x{:}\mathtt{int}) \to \mathtt{return}\ x + x\}$. Elaborating the application has the effect of linking the following definitions.

```
fn  □.arg.f(x:  int)  →  int  {  return  x+x  }
fn  □.f(x:  int)  →  int  {  □.res.f(x)  }
fn  □.g()  →  int  {  □.res.g()  }
```

Finally, the type $D{\cdot}S$ elaborates simply by adding a new value variable to the context. This has the effect of adding a new argument of type D to the elaboration S. In the Linear Logic reading of $!S$ as infinitely many copies of S, this new variable plays the role of storing the number of the copy. The reader should also note that the elaboration of $D \cdot S$ is such that the rules CLOSE-L and CLOSE-R elaborate as the identity. They have no effect on the elaboration and are used just for scope management in the type system.

Consider the elaboration of contraction. We have a term that uses two variables $X_1 \colon (D_1 \cdot S)$ and $X_2 \colon (D_2 \cdot S)$, which we want to replace by a single variable $X \colon ((D_1 + D_2) \cdot S)$. Suppose $(D_1 + D_2) \cdot S$, $D_1 \cdot S$ and $D_2 \cdot S$ elaborate to $(I; O)$, $(I_1; O_1)$ and $(I_2; O_2)$ respectively. These interfaces differ only in the type of the newly added value variable, which is $D_1 + D_2$, D_1 and D_2 respectively. Contraction is then implemented by defining each function in $I[X_1]$ and $I[X_2]$ to invoke the corresponding function in $I[X]$ with the same arguments, except that the new argument of type D_1 or D_2 is injected into $D_1 + D_2$, and by defining each function in $O[X]$ to perform a case distinction on the value of type $D_1 + D_2$ and to call the corresponding functions in $O[X_1]$ and $O[X_2]$. This works because the new variable in $D \cdot S$ is anonymous and may cannot be accessed by a term of this type. It is essentially a callee-save argument.

For a concrete example of contraction, consider first the term $X_1 \colon S,\ X_2 \colon S \vdash X_1(\mathbf{return}\ 1) + X_2(\mathbf{return}\ 2) \colon \mathsf{Mint}$, where S abbreviates $\mathsf{Mint} \multimap \mathsf{Mint}$. Its derivation does not need contraction and elaborates to:

```
fn □() → int { X₁.res() + X₂.res() }
fn X₁.arg() → int { return 1 }
fn X₂.arg() → int { return 2 }
```

One can derive $X \colon (\mathsf{unit} + \mathsf{unit}) \cdot S \vdash X(\mathbf{return}\ 1) + X(\mathbf{return}\ 2) \colon \mathsf{Mint}$ by changing S into $\mathsf{unit} \cdot S$ using dereliction, followed by contraction. The resulting elaboration is:

```
fn □() → int { □.res(inl()) + □.res(inr()) }
fn X₁.arg(x: unit) → int { return 1 }
fn X₂.arg(x: unit) → int { return 2 }
fn X.arg(i: unit + unit) → int
     { case i of inl(x)⇒X₁.arg(x); inr(x)⇒X₂.arg(x) }
```

Note that in the elaboration of contraction, the new argument is only ever used if O is nonempty. Indeed, the following rule is sound:

$$\text{DUPL} \quad \frac{\Gamma,\ X \colon D \cdot S,\ \Delta \vdash t \colon T \qquad \Gamma \vdash S \rightsquigarrow I;\ \emptyset}{\Gamma,\ X \colon S,\ \Delta \vdash t \colon T}$$

This concludes our outline of the elaboration of linear types into first-order programs. With the elaboration of types given, the elaboration of terms becomes essentially straightforward. It is instructive to try to write out the elaboration for some the above rules for terms.

4.3   Relation to Particle-Style Geometry of Interaction

We have presented the linear type system as a calculus for defining and linking first-order programs. Its elaboration procedure is new and is designed to produce a natural, direct implementation of ML-style modules. Nevertheless, it can be seen as a slight generalisation of the particle-style Geometry of Interaction.

The correspondence is most easily explained for the categorical formulation [1,2] of the GOI. It identifies the Int-construction, applied to sets and partial functions, as the core of the particle-style GOI. In this construction, one defines two sets T^- and T^+ for each type T and interprets a term of type $X\colon S \vdash t\colon T$ as a partial function $S^+ + T^- \to S^- + T^+$. Our elaboration implements this function in continuation-passing style. A function $S^+ + T^- \to S^- + T^+$ becomes $((S^- + T^+) \to \bot) \to ((S^+ + T^-) \to \bot)$ in continuation-passing style. Such functions are in one-to-one correspondence to functions $((S^- \to \bot) \times (T^+ \to \bot)) \to ((S^+ \to \bot) \times (T^- \to \bot))$. Such functions can be implemented by first-order programs of interface $(I; O)$ with $I = \{\ell_1\colon S^+ \to \texttt{empty}, \ell_2\colon T^- \to \texttt{empty}\}$ and $O = \{\ell_1\colon S^- \to \texttt{empty}, \ell_2\colon T^+ \to \texttt{empty}\}$.

Our elaboration implements the Int-construction up to this correspondence. The definition of S^- and S^+ for the various types S in the GOI matches our definition of interfaces in Fig. 1. For example, the case for $S \multimap T$ matches the standard definitions $(S \multimap T)^- = S^+ + T^-$ and $(S \multimap T)^+ = S^- + T^+$. The case for records matches $(S \otimes T)^- = S^- + T^-$ and $(S \otimes T)^+ = S^+ + T^+$. The type MD is slightly generalised. In the Int-construction, one would have only $M\texttt{empty}$ and define returning computations in continuation-passing style as e.g. $[D] := (D \to M\texttt{empty}) \multimap M\texttt{empty}$. The generalisation from $M\texttt{empty}$ to MD, i.e. from non-returning functions to returning ones, is useful since this leads to a natural, direct elaboration of ML-modules.

Token-passing formulations of the GOI can be seen as instances of the Int-construction, but it may be helpful to outline the correspondence for them concretely. They are based on viewing proof-net interpretations of proofs as token-passing networks. Recall [7] that in Linear Logic, proofs can be represented by proof-nets. For example, the canonical proof of $Y, X \vdash X \otimes Y$ would lead to the graph on the left below. Its edges are labelled by formulae and the nodes correspond to proof rules. In general, the proof of a Linear Logic judgement $X_1, \ldots, X_n \vdash Y$ leads to proof-net g as on the right.

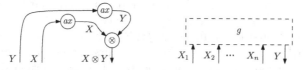

Token-passing formulations of the GOI consider proof-nets as message-passing networks, in which a token travels along edges from node to node. Think of the nodes as stateless processes. An edge label X specifies what messages may be passed along the edge: elements of type X^+ may be passed with the direction of the edge, and elements of type X^- against the direction of the edge. The nodes are passive until they receive a message along one of the edges connected to them. They then process the incoming message, construct a new outgoing message, which they send along a connected edge of their choice before becoming passive again. Nodes have extremely simple, fixed behaviour. For example, if the node $\otimes$ in the example net receives $v \in X^+$ on its left input edge, then it passes $\texttt{inl}(v) \in (X \otimes Y)^+$ along its output edge. The ax-nodes just forward any input on one edge to the other edge. This behaviour is essentially already determined by the type of the token.

Consider now how one can implement token-passing graphs by first-order programs. Message passing may be implemented simply by function calls. To an edge e with label X in the proof-net, we associate two function labels, one for each end of the edge: $\mathtt{send}_e^- : X^- \to \mathtt{empty}$ may be invoked to pass a message against the direction of the edge, and $\mathtt{send}_e^+ : X^+ \to \mathtt{empty}$ may be invoked to pass a message in the other direction. In both cases, the return type is $\mathtt{empty}$, as message passing cedes control to the recipient of the message. With this approach, a node in a proof-net implements the $\mathtt{send}$-functions for the ends of all the edges that are connected to it. The ax-nodes in the above example net would be implemented simply by two functions $\mathtt{fn}\ \mathtt{send}_{e_1}^-(x)\ \{\ \mathtt{send}_{e_2}^+(x)\ \}$ and $\mathtt{fn}\ \mathtt{send}_{e_2}^+(x)\ \{\ \mathtt{send}_{e_1}^-(x)\ \}$, where e_1 is the left edge connected to the node and e_2 is the other. The program for the whole net consists of the (mutually recursive) implementations of all nodes. Its interface is determined by the edges that have an end that is not connected to a node. For each such edge, the program defines a $\mathtt{send}$-function function for sending a message from the environment into the net. The other $\mathtt{send}$-function of this edge is used to return a value to the environment.

The elaboration of the linear type system above can be seen as a direct way of implementing token-passing in this way (with some immediate simplification).

4.4   Correctness

We end this section by outlining in which sense the elaboration provides a correct implementation of the linear type system. We define the intended meaning of the type system by a simple denotational semantics that ignores linearity.

To define the semantics, we assume a monad M on **Sets** that is sufficient to interpret the systems-level language. In the simplest case, this will be just the non-termination monad $MX = X + \{\bot\}$.

The first-order language can be interpreted in a standard way. The interpretation $[\![B]\!]$ of a first-level type B is defined to be the set of closed values of type B. A first-order function $f\colon (B_1, \ldots, B_n) \to B$ is interpreted as a function $[\![B_1]\!] \times \cdots \times [\![B_n]\!] \to M[\![B]\!]$. A first-order program m is interpreted as $[\![m]\!]_\sigma$, where σ is an environment that maps function signatures like $f\colon (B_1, \ldots, B_n) \to B$ to corresponding functions $[\![B_1]\!] \times \cdots \times [\![B_n]\!] \to M[\![B]\!]$. The semantics of the program $[\![m]\!]_\sigma$ is then a mapping from function signatures (the ones defined in m) to corresponding functions (of the same format as in σ).

The denotational semantics of the linear type system interprets types as follows. For any closed interaction type S, we define the set $[\![S]\!]$ as follows:

$$[\![MD]\!] = M[\![D]\!] \qquad [\![\{\overline{\ell_i \colon S_{\ell_i}}\}]\!] = \prod_{\ell \in \{\ell_i\}} [\![S_\ell]\!] \qquad [\![B \cdot S]\!] = [\![S]\!]$$

$$[\![S \multimap T]\!] = [\![S]\!] \to [\![T]\!] \qquad [\![\forall \alpha.\, S]\!] = \prod_B [\![S[\alpha \mapsto B]]\!]$$

$$[\![D \to S]\!] = [\![D]\!] \to [\![S]\!] \qquad [\![\exists \alpha.\, S]\!] = \sum_B [\![S[\alpha \mapsto B]]\!]$$

We omit the interpretations of terms.

Elaboration correctly implements the denotational semantics. To express this, we define a relation $m \sim_S f$, which expresses that the first-order program m implements the semantic value $f \in \llbracket S \rrbracket$. The program m must have the interface $(I; O)$ determined by $\vdash S \rightsquigarrow I; O$. The relation $\sim_S$ is defined by induction on S. On the base type, we let $m \sim_{MD} f$ if, and only if, $\llbracket m \rrbracket (\square.\mathtt{main})() = f$. This is extended to all types in a logical way. For example, $m \sim_{S \multimap T} f$ if, and only if, $n \sim_S g$ implies $\mathtt{app}(m, n) \sim_T f(g)$, where $\mathtt{app}(m, n)$ is the elaboration of application as in rule $\multimap$-E. For a full definition we would need more details of the elaboration than can be included, so we just state the correctness result:

Proposition 1. *If $\vdash t \colon S \rightsquigarrow m$ then $m \sim_S \llbracket t \rrbracket$.*

5   Higher-Order Modules for First-Order Programs

We now capture the structure of the linear type system by a module system. With our explanation of the linear type system as a calculus for the compositional construction of first-order programs, this is a natural step to make. A module system directly conveys this intuition. It also accounts for common application patterns, especially for type declarations and abstraction, in a more usable way.

The module system is intentionally kept fairly standard in order to express the GOI in terms that are familiar to anyone familiar with ML. It is implemented by elaboration into the linear type system and has the following syntax.

$$
\begin{array}{rll}
\text{Paths} & p ::= & X \mid p.\ell \\
\text{Base types} & C ::= & \text{core types} \mid p \\
\text{Module types} & \Sigma ::= & MC \mid \mathbf{type} \mid \mathbf{type} = C \mid \mathbf{sig}\ \overline{\ell_i(X_i)\colon \Sigma_i}\ \mathbf{end} \\
& & \mid \mathbf{functor}(X\colon \Sigma) \to \Sigma \mid C \to \Sigma \mid B \cdot \Sigma \\
\text{Module terms} & M ::= & p \mid \mathbf{type}\ C \mid \mathbf{struct}\ \overline{\ell_i(X_i) = M_i}\ \mathbf{end} \mid \mathbf{functor}(X\colon \Sigma) \to M \\
& & \mid M\ X \mid M \mathrel{:\!\!>} \Sigma \mid \mathbf{fn}\,(x\colon C) \to M \mid M(v) \mid \text{core expressions}
\end{array}
$$

In paths, X ranges over an infinite supply of module variables. These variables are distinct from the value variables that may appear in core values. Base types are core types with an additional base case for paths, as usual, so that one can write types like $\mathtt{int} \times X.t$.

The type MC is a base case for computations that return a value of type C. Again, one should think of $M(-)$ as a type of core computations. We make it explicit to make clear where computational effects may happen. Note that the module system does *not* allow value declarations like $\mathtt{val\ x{:}A}$ in ML. This simplifies the development, as we do not need to think about the evaluation order of modules, which is essential in the presence of effects. Without value declarations, all possible effects are accounted for by the type MC.

Type declarations come in two forms: $\mathbf{type}$ and $\mathbf{type} = C$. The former declares *some* base type, while the latter is a *manifest type* [13] that is known to be the same as C. For example, one can write $\mathtt{sig\ t{:}type\ =\ int,\ f{:}Mt\ end}$, which means that t is the type $\mathtt{int}$. We shall allow ourselves to write both $\mathtt{type\ t}$ and $\mathtt{type\ t\ =\ int}$ as syntactic sugar for $t\colon \mathtt{type}$ and $t\colon \mathtt{type=int}$.

Signatures have the form $\mathtt{sig}\ \ell_1(X_1)\colon \Sigma_1, \ldots, \ell_n(X_n)\colon \Sigma_n\ \mathtt{end}$. In such a signature, the ℓ_i are *labels* for referring to the components from the outside using paths. The X_i are *identifiers* for referring to the components from within the signature. In a programming language, one would typically write only labels, i.e. write $\mathtt{sig}\ \ell_1\colon \Sigma_1, \ldots, \ell_n\colon \Sigma_n\ \mathtt{end}$. However, since labels may be used to access parts of the signature from the outside, they cannot be α-renamed. For this reason, one introduces the additional identifiers, which can be α-renamed without harm [9].

While the module system does not allow value declarations, it allows parameterisation over values with the type $C \to \Sigma$. In ML notation, $C \to \Sigma$ would be written as $\mathtt{functor(X\colon sig\ val\ x}\colon C\ \mathtt{end}) \to \Sigma$. The typical use here is for first-order function types of the form $C_1 \to MC_2$.

Most module terms should be familiar from other module systems, particularly type declarations, signatures, functors and type sealing. For example, if M has type $\mathtt{sig\ type\ t\ =\ int,\ f\colon Mt\ end}$, then sealing $M :> \Sigma$ allows one to abstract the signature to $\Sigma = \mathtt{sig\ type\ t,\ f\colon Mt\ end}$.

The terms for the value-passing function $C \to \Sigma$ are an abstraction over value variables $\mathtt{fn}\,(x\colon C) \to M$ and a corresponding application $M(v)$, in which v is a core value. They have the same meaning as in the linear type system.

The module terms are also closed under the term formers for core expressions. Core expressions may not only be used for terms of type MC. One can use the terms $\mathtt{let}\ (x, y) = v\ \mathtt{in}\ M$ and $\mathtt{case}\ v\ \mathtt{of}\ \mathtt{inl}(x) \Rightarrow M_1;\ \mathtt{inr}(y) \Rightarrow M_2$ for M, M_1 and M_2 of arbitrary module type. We give examples in the next section.

5.1   Examples

We give a few very simple examples to illustrate that the module system is close to standard ML-like module systems. The signature $\mathtt{Stream}$ defines an interface for infinite streams. The structure $\mathtt{Nats}$ implements the stream $0, 1, 2, \ldots$.

```
Stream := sig                    Nats := struct
            t: type,                       t = type int,
            init: Mt,                      init = return 0,
            next: t → M(int*t)             next = fn(x: t) →
          end                                     return (x, x+1)
                                         end :> Stream
```

Without sealing, one could also write $\mathtt{t\colon type=int}$ in the type of $\mathtt{Nats}$. An example of a functor is a module that multiplies a given stream with $1, -1, 1, -1, \ldots$

```
A := functor(X: Stream) →
        struct
          t = type (int × X.t),
          init = let x = X.init in return (1, x),
          next = fn ((s, x): t) → let (i, x') = X.next(x) in
                                  return (s * i, (-s, x'))
        end :> Stream
```

The following example shows how modules can be defined by case-distinction.

```
G := fn(b: unit+unit) → case b of inl_⇒A(Nats); inr_⇒Nats
```

It has type (unit + unit)→ Stream. The elaboration of case distinction translates this term into a form of dynamic dispatch. A call to G(v).next(x) will first perform a case distinction on v and then dispatch to either of the two implementations of next from the two branches.

The following example shows that higher-order functors are available. In it, Σ_1 and Σ_2 abbreviate sig f: int → Mint end and sig g: int → Mint end.

```
functor(F: (unit + unit)·(functor(X:Σ₁) → Σ₂)) →
   struct
     A1 = struct f = fn(x:int) → int { return x+1 } end,
     A2 = struct f = fn(x:int) → int { return x+2 } end,
     h = fn (x:int) → int { F(A1).g(x) + F(A2).g(x) }
   end
```

The exponential (unit + unit)·− in the argument is essential because F is being used twice. We make exponentials explicit in the module systems, because they are visible in the public interface of first-order programs after elaboration.

5.2   Elaboration

The type system for modules is defined by elaboration into the linear type system. Most parts of the module system have corresponding types in the linear type system. In particular, structures and functors elaborate to records and −∘ respectively. The main difficulty is to account for type declarations, their abstraction and the use of paths to access them.

To address this, we follow the approach of F-ing modules [14], which elaborates an ML-style module system into System F_ω. Here we adapt it to translate our module system into the linear type system. Module types translate to interaction types and module terms translate to interaction terms. In short, structures translate to records, functors translate to −∘, and any type declaration type or type = D in a module type is replaced by the unit type {} (the empty record). As unit types elaborate to an empty first-order interface, this means that type declarations are compiled out completely and are only relevant for type checking.

While one wants to remove type declarations in the elaboration process, type information is needed for type checking. In order to be able to express elaboration and type-checking in one step, it is useful to use labelled unit types that still record the erased type information. We define the type $[=D]$ as a copy of the unit type {}, labelled with D. This type could be made a primitive type, but it can also be defined as the type $[=D] := D \to \{\}$ with inhabitant $\star_D := \mathtt{fn}\,(x{:}D) \to \{\}$. Note that $[=D]$ elaborates to an empty first-order interface. The labelling can now be used to track the correct usage of types: type = D becomes $[=D]$ and type becomes $[=\alpha]$ for a new, existentially quantified, type variable α. For example, sig s: type, t: type, f: Mt, g: Ms end becomes $\exists \alpha, \beta.\,\{s{:}[=\alpha],\ t{:}[=\beta],\ f{:}M\beta,\ g{:}M\alpha\}$. The elaborated type contains the information that f returns a value of type t, which would have been lost had we used {} instead of $[=\beta]$. Elaborated types thus contain all information that is needed for type-checking.

$$\frac{}{\Gamma, X\colon[=D], \Delta \vdash X \rightsquigarrow D} \qquad \frac{}{\Gamma \vdash \mathtt{int} \rightsquigarrow \mathtt{int}} \qquad \frac{\Gamma \vdash C_1 \rightsquigarrow D_1 \quad \Gamma \vdash C_2 \rightsquigarrow D_2}{\Gamma \vdash C_1 \times C_2 \rightsquigarrow D_1 \times D_2}$$

Fig. 2. Base type elaboration (selection)

Elaboration is defined by five judgements, which we describe next and in which S and Ξ are interaction types defined by the following grammar.

$$\Xi\colon\colon = \exists \overline{\alpha}.\, S \qquad S\colon\colon = [=D] \mid MD \mid \{\overline{\ell_i\colon S}\} \mid \forall \alpha.\, S \multimap \Xi \mid D \rightarrow \Xi \mid D{\cdot}S$$

The elaboration judgements use the same kind of contexts Γ as the linear type system. However, all module variable declarations in it must have the form $X\colon S$, where S is generated by the above grammar.

The judgement $\Gamma \vdash C \rightsquigarrow D$ in Fig. 2 elaborates base types. The variable case is where the labelled unit types are being used.

The judgement $\Gamma \vdash \Sigma \rightsquigarrow \Xi$ in Fig. 3 formalises module type elaboration. For example, $\Sigma = \mathtt{sig\ t\colon type,\ f\colon Mt\ end}$ elaborates to $\Xi = \exists \alpha.\, \{\mathtt{t}\colon[=\alpha], \mathtt{f}\colon M\alpha\}$.

The judgement $\Gamma \vdash M\colon \Xi \rightsquigarrow t$ in Fig. 4 expresses that M is a module term whose type elaborates to Ξ and that the module itself elaborates to the interaction term t with $\Gamma \vdash t\colon \Xi$.

The judgement $\Gamma \vdash \Xi \leq \Xi' \rightsquigarrow t$ in Fig. 5 is for subtyping. In it, t is a coercion term from Ξ to Ξ' that satisfies $\Gamma, X\colon\Xi \vdash t\ X\colon \Xi'$.

Finally, $\Gamma \vdash S \leq \Xi \rightsquigarrow \overline{D}, t$ in Fig. 5 is a matching judgement. By definition, Ξ has the form $\exists \overline{\alpha}.\, S'$. The matching judgement produces a list of types $\overline{D}$ and a term t, such that $\Gamma \vdash S \leq S'[\overline{\alpha} \mapsto \overline{D}] \rightsquigarrow t$.

In all judgements, the context records the already elaborated type of variables. Labelled unit types record enough information for type checking.

Module type elaboration in Fig. 3 implements the idea of translating structures to records, functors to $\multimap$-functions and to replace type declarations by labelled unit types. Functors are modelled generatively. If the argument and result elaborate to $\exists \alpha.\, S$ and $\exists \beta.\, T$ respectively, then the functor elaborates to $\forall \alpha.\, S \multimap \exists \beta.\, T$. The type β may therefore be different for each application of the functor. To cover existing applications, such as [17], generative functors were a natural choice (indeed, types of the form $\forall \alpha.\, S \multimap \exists \beta.\, T$ already appear in [15,17]); in the future, applicative functors may also be useful.

A selection of elaboration rules for terms is shown in Fig. 4. These rules are subject to the same linearity restrictions as the linear type system. The structural rules are the same. Indeed, the new form of contexts in the linear type system was designed to support a direct elaboration of modules.

To capture a suitable notion of linearity, the elaboration of paths is different from other approaches [13,14]. In rule VAR, the base case of term elaboration is defined only for variables, not for arbitrary paths. However, rule SIG-E allows one to reduce paths beforehand. To derive $X\colon\{f\colon S, g\colon T\} \vdash X.f\colon S \rightsquigarrow \ldots$, one can first use SIG-E to reduce the goal to $Y\colon S, Z\colon T \vdash Y\colon S \rightsquigarrow \ldots$, for example. This approach is more general than syntactic linearity. For example, if $X\colon\{f\colon S, g\colon T\}$

$$\frac{\Gamma \vdash C \rightsquigarrow D}{\Gamma \vdash MC \rightsquigarrow MD} \qquad \frac{}{\Gamma \vdash \text{type} \rightsquigarrow \exists \alpha.\, [=\alpha]} \qquad \frac{\Gamma \vdash C \rightsquigarrow D}{\Gamma \vdash \text{type} = C \rightsquigarrow [=D]}$$

$$\frac{\Gamma \vdash \Sigma \rightsquigarrow \exists \overline{\alpha}.\, S \quad \Gamma, \overline{\alpha}, X:S \vdash \text{sig } \overline{d} \text{ end} \rightsquigarrow \exists \overline{\beta}.\, \{\overline{E}\}}{\Gamma \vdash \text{sig } \ell(X): \Sigma, \overline{d} \text{ end} \rightsquigarrow \exists \overline{\alpha}, \overline{\beta}.\, \{\ell: S, \overline{E}\}} \qquad \frac{\Gamma \vdash \Sigma \rightsquigarrow \exists \overline{\alpha}.\, S}{\Gamma \vdash B{\cdot}\Sigma \rightsquigarrow \exists \overline{\alpha}.\, B{\cdot}S}$$

$$\frac{\Gamma \vdash \Sigma \rightsquigarrow \exists \overline{\alpha}.\, S \quad \Gamma, \overline{\alpha}, X:S \vdash T \rightsquigarrow \exists \overline{\beta}.\, T}{\Gamma \vdash \text{functor}(X: \Sigma) \rightarrow T \rightsquigarrow \forall \overline{\alpha}.\, S \multimap \exists \overline{\beta}.\, T} \qquad \frac{\Gamma, x:D \vdash \Sigma \rightsquigarrow \Xi \quad \Gamma \vdash C \rightsquigarrow D}{\Gamma \vdash C \rightarrow \Sigma \rightsquigarrow D \rightarrow \Xi}$$

Fig. 3. Module type elaboration (selection)

$$\text{VAR} \ \frac{}{\Gamma, X:S \vdash X: S \rightsquigarrow X} \qquad \text{TYPE} \ \frac{\Gamma \vdash C \rightsquigarrow D}{\Gamma \vdash \text{type } C: [=D] \rightsquigarrow \star_D}$$

$$\text{SIG-I2} \ \frac{\Gamma \vdash M: \exists \overline{\alpha}.\, S \rightsquigarrow t \quad \Delta, \overline{\alpha}, X:S \vdash \text{struct } \overline{d} \text{ end}: \exists \overline{\beta}.\, \{\overline{E}\} \rightsquigarrow s \quad \ell \text{ not defined in } \overline{d}}{\Gamma + \Delta \vdash \text{struct } \ell(X) = M, \overline{d} \text{ end}: \exists \overline{\alpha}, \overline{\beta}.\, \{\ell: S, \overline{E}\}}$$

$$\rightsquigarrow \text{let pack}(\overline{\alpha}, x) = t \text{ in let pack}(\overline{\beta}, \{\overline{b}\}) = s \text{ in pack}(\overline{\alpha}\overline{\beta}, \{\ell = x, \overline{b}\})$$

$$\text{SIG-E} \ \frac{\Gamma, \overline{Y_i: S_i}, \Delta \vdash M: \Xi \rightsquigarrow t}{\Gamma, X:\{\overline{\ell_i: S_i}\}, \Delta \vdash M[Y_i \mapsto X.\ell_i]: \Xi \rightsquigarrow \text{let } \{\overline{\ell_i = Y_i}\} = X \text{ in } t}$$

$$\text{FUN-I} \ \frac{\Gamma \vdash \Sigma \rightsquigarrow \exists \overline{\alpha}.\, S \quad \Gamma, \overline{\alpha}, X:S \vdash M: \Xi \rightsquigarrow t}{\Gamma \vdash \text{functor}(X: \Sigma) \rightarrow M: \forall \overline{\alpha}.\, S \multimap \Xi \rightsquigarrow \lambda \overline{\alpha}.\, \lambda X: S.\, t}$$

$$\text{FUN-E} \ \frac{\Gamma \vdash M: \forall \overline{\alpha}.\, S \multimap \Xi \rightsquigarrow t \quad \Delta \vdash Y: S' \rightsquigarrow s \quad \Gamma + \Delta \vdash S' \leq \exists \overline{\alpha}.\, S \rightsquigarrow \overline{D}, f}{\Gamma + \Delta \vdash M\, Y: \Xi[\overline{\alpha} \mapsto \overline{D}] \rightsquigarrow t\, \overline{D}\, (f\, s)}$$

$$\text{SEAL} \ \frac{\Gamma \vdash M: \Xi \rightsquigarrow t \quad \Gamma \vdash \Sigma \rightsquigarrow \Xi' \quad \Gamma \vdash \Xi \leq \Xi' \rightsquigarrow c}{\Gamma \vdash M :> \Sigma: \Xi' \rightsquigarrow c\, t}$$

Fig. 4. Module term elaboration (selection)

then one can give a type to the module struct $Y = X.f$, $Z = X.g$ end. The use of X counts as linear because the two uses pertain to different parts of the structure. However, the module struct $Y = X.f$, $Z = X$ end cannot (in general) be given a type, as both Y and Z contain $X.f$.

Finally, the rules for subtyping and matching appear in Fig. 5. From a technical point of view, they are very similar to the rules in [14]. However, type variables only range over base types, which means that subtyping can be decided simply using unification.

Elaboration is defined to maintain the following invariant.

Proposition 2. *If $\Gamma \vdash M: \Xi \rightsquigarrow m$ then $\Gamma \vdash m: \Xi$ in the linear type system.*

5.3 Examples

To give an example for elaboration, consider the module Nats from above. The struct in it elaborates to: $\{t = \star_{\text{int}}, \text{init} = \text{return } 0, \text{next} = \text{fn}\,(x{:}\text{int}) \rightarrow (x, x+1)\}$ of type $\{t: [=\text{int}], \text{init}: M\text{int}, \text{next}: \text{int} \rightarrow M(\text{int} \times \text{int})\}$. Sealing packs it into $\exists \alpha.\, \{t: [=\alpha], \text{init}: M\alpha, \text{next}: \alpha \rightarrow M(\text{int} \times \alpha)\}$, which is the elaboration of Stream. The first-order elaboration of Nats is:

$$\frac{}{\Gamma \vdash S \leq S \rightsquigarrow \lambda X.\, X} \qquad \frac{\Gamma, x{:}D \vdash S \leq T \rightsquigarrow c \quad D \times D_2 \lhd D_1}{\Gamma \vdash D_1 \cdot (D \to S) \leq D_2 \cdot (D \to T) \rightsquigarrow \lambda F.\, \mathtt{fn}\,(x{:}D) \to c\,(F(x))}$$

$$\frac{\Gamma, x{:}D \vdash S \leq T \rightsquigarrow c}{\Gamma \vdash D{\cdot}S \leq D{\cdot}T \rightsquigarrow \lambda X.\, c\, X}$$

$$\frac{\Gamma, \overline{\beta} \vdash S_2 \leq \exists \overline{\alpha}.\, S_1 \rightsquigarrow \overline{D}, c \quad \Gamma, \overline{\beta} \vdash \Xi_1[\overline{\alpha} \mapsto \overline{D}] \leq \Xi_2 \rightsquigarrow d}{\Gamma \vdash (\forall \overline{\alpha}.\, S_1 \multimap \Xi_1) \leq (\forall \overline{\beta}.\, S_2 \multimap \Xi_2) \rightsquigarrow \lambda F.\, \Lambda \overline{\beta}.\, \lambda X.\, d\,(F\,\overline{D}\,(c\,X))}$$

$$\frac{\Gamma \vdash S \leq T[\overline{\alpha} \mapsto \overline{D}] \rightsquigarrow c}{\Gamma \vdash S \leq \exists \overline{\alpha}.\, T \rightsquigarrow \overline{D}, c} \qquad \frac{\Gamma, \overline{\alpha} \vdash S \leq \Xi \rightsquigarrow \overline{D}, c}{\Gamma \vdash \exists \overline{\alpha}.\, S \leq \Xi \rightsquigarrow \lambda X.\, \mathtt{let}\, \mathtt{pack}(\overline{\alpha}, Y) = X \,\mathtt{in}\, \mathtt{pack}(\overline{D}, c\, Y)}$$

Fig. 5. Module subtyping and matching (selection)

```
fn □.init() → raw { let x = coerc_int(0) in return x }
fn □.next(x:raw) → int { let coerc_int(y) = x in
                         let z = coerc_int(y + 1) in return (y,z) }
```

It is a direct first-order implementation of the module. The use of raw in it is an idealisation for simplicity. In practice, one would like to use a more precise type. To this end, one may refine the quantifiers from $\exists \alpha.\, S$ to $\exists \alpha \lhd D.S$, much like we have refined $!S$ into $D{\cdot}S$. The annotation D can be computed by type inference. In this case, one can use int instead of raw and coercions are not needed at all.

The example higher-order functor from Sect. 5.1 elaborates to:

```
fn □.res.A1.f(x: int) → int { return x+1 }
fn □.res.A2.f(x: int) → int { return x+2 }
fn □.res.h(x:int) → int
    { □.arg.res.g(inl(),x) + □.arg.res.g(inr(),x) }
fn □.arg.arg.f(i: unit + unit, x: int) → int
    { case i of inl(x) ⇒ □.res.A1.f(x); inr(x) ⇒ □.res.A2.f(x) }
```

5.4   Type Checking

For practical type checking, it is possible to bring the type system into an algorithmic form. This is necessary because rules like CONTR and SIG-E can be applied in many ways and there are many possible ways to place exponentials.

The choice of derivation in such an algorithmic formulation is important. In the elaboration to first-order programs, it is desirable to minimise the scope of the value variables introduced by exponentials. For example, suppose we have a module term that contains a module variable X such that $X.\ell_1$ is used once and $X.\ell_2$ is used twice. It can be typed with $X{:}(\mathtt{unit} + \mathtt{unit}){\cdot}\{\ell_1{:}\Sigma_1,\ \ell_2{:}\Sigma_2\}$, but it would be better to use $X{:}\{\ell_1{:}\Sigma_1,\ \ell_2{:}(\mathtt{unit} + \mathtt{unit}){\cdot}\Sigma_2\}$, as first-order elaboration produces functions with fewer arguments. We have found the standard rules for exponentials to be inconvenient for developing a typing strategy that achieves such an innermost placement of exponentials. If one wants to derive the goal $\Gamma \vdash t\colon D{\cdot}\Sigma$, then one cannot always apply the standard promotion rule right away. In contrast, rule CLOSE-R can be always be applied immediately.

The elaboration rules can be brought into a syntax-directed form as follows: Of the structural rules, we only keep CLOSE-R (from top to bottom). Rules —∘-I and SIG-I2 are modified to integrate SIG-E, CONTR and DUPL. One applies SIG-E as often as possible to the newly introduced variable and uses CONTR as needed to the newly introduced variables. This eliminates the non-syntax-directed rules SIG-E and CONTR. Finally, one shows that a rule deriving $\Gamma, X : D_1 \cdot S, \Delta \vdash X : D_2 \cdot S$ for suitable D_2 (depending on Δ and D_1) can be derived using VAR, WEAK, CLOSE-R (upside down) and digging. The remaining rules are all syntax-directed.

Proposition 3. *There is an algorithm, which, given Γ and M, computes Ξ and m such that $\Gamma \vdash M : \Xi \rightsquigarrow m$, if such Ξ and m exist, and rejects otherwise.*

As it is stated, the statement of the proposition quite weak, since Ξ is allowed to contain full exponentials $!S$ everywhere. In practice, one would like to optimise the placement of exponentials. There is an easy approach to doing so. One inserts exponentials of the form $\alpha \cdot (-)$ for a fresh variable α in all possible places and treats them like $!(-)$. This leads to constraints for the α, which are not hard to solve. In places where no exponential is needed, one can solve the constraints with $\alpha := \texttt{unit}$, which effectively removes the exponential.

6   Intended Applications

Having motivated the module system as a convenient formalism for programming language applications of the GOI, we ought to outline intended applications of the module system and potential benefits of its use. Since we intend exponentials to be computed automatically during type checking, we do not show them here and treat them as if they were written with invisible ink.

The GOI is often used to interpret functional programming languages, e.g. [4–6,10]. Let us outline the implementation of the simply-typed λ-calculus with the types $X, Y :: = \mathbb{N} \mid X \to Y$. With a call-by-name evaluation strategy, an encoding is easy. One translates types by letting $[\![\mathbb{N}]\!] := \texttt{sig eval: Mint end}$ and $[\![X \to Y]\!] := \texttt{functor}(\_ : [\![X]\!]) \to [\![Y]\!]$. The translation of terms is almost the identity. This translation is used very often in applications of the GOI.

The case for call-by-value is more interesting and shows the value of the module system. One can reduce it to the call-by-name case by CPS-translation, but the resulting implementation would be unsatisfactory because of its inefficient use of stack space [15]. A more efficient GOI-interpretation is possible, but quite technical and complicated [15,17]. With the module system, its definition becomes easy. To make the evaluation strategy observable, let us assume that the λ-calculus has a constant $\texttt{print}: \mathbb{N} \to \mathbb{N}$ for printing numbers.

To implement call-by-value evaluation, one can translate a closed λ-term $t : X$ to a module of type $\mathcal{M}[\![X]\!] := \texttt{sig T}: \mathcal{I}[\![X]\!], \texttt{eval}: \texttt{M(T.t) end}$, where:

```
        I[[N]]    := sig  t:  type=int  end
I[[X → Y]]  :=  sig  t:  type ,  /* abstract */
                    T:  functor (X:  I[[X]]) → sig
```

```
⟦ ⊢ print: ℕ → ℕ⟧ := struct          ⟦ ⊢ t₁ t₂: Y⟧ := struct
   t = type unit,                        T1 = ⟦ ⊢ t₁: X → Y⟧,
   T = functor (X: 𝓘⟦ℕ⟧) → struct        T2 = ⟦ ⊢ t₂: X⟧,
       T = struct t = type int end,      S  = T1.T(T2),
       apply = fn(f:t, x:int) →          T  = S.T,
               print(x)                  eval = let f = T1.eval in
   end,                                         let x = T2.eval in
   eval = return ()                             S.apply(f, x)
end :> 𝓜⟦ℕ → ℕ⟧                         end :> 𝓜⟦Y⟧
```

Fig. 6. Example cases for the translations of terms

$$
\begin{aligned}
&\text{T: } 𝓘⟦Y⟧, \\
&\text{apply: } t \times X.t \to M(T.t) \\
&\quad\text{end}
\end{aligned}
$$
$$\text{end}$$

In effect, a closed term $t: ℕ$ translates to a computation eval: Mint that computes the number and performs the effects of term t. A term of type $ℕ \to ℕ$ translates to a computation eval: Mt that computes the abstract function value and a function apply: t × int → Mint for function application. In the higher-order case, where X is a function type, the function apply can make calls to X.apply. If Y is also a function type, then the module T: $𝓘⟦Y⟧$ defines the apply-function for the returned function, see [17].

Defining the translation of terms is essentially straightforward. Examples for application and the constant print: $ℕ \to ℕ$ are shown in Fig. 6. It should not be hard for a reader familiar with ML-like languages to fill in the rest of the details. The result is a compositional, modular translation to the first-order language. By adding a fixed-point combinator to the module system, this approach can be extended to a full programming language.

For comparison, a direct definition of the above translation appears in [17]. It is also possible to use a type system as in Sect. 4 directly [16,17]. But, in effect, F-ing is performed manually in this. For example, $𝓜⟦X \to Y⟧$ elaborates to $\exists\alpha. \{\text{eval}: M\alpha, \text{T}: \{t: [=\alpha], \text{T}:! (\forall\beta. S_\beta \multimap \exists\gamma. \{\text{T}: T_\gamma, \text{apply}:!(\alpha \times \beta \to M\gamma)\})\}$ if $𝓜⟦X⟧$ and $𝓜⟦Y⟧$ elaborate to $\exists\beta. S_\beta$ and $\exists\gamma. T_\gamma$ respectively. In [16,17], the authors work directly with types of this form. This is unsatisfactory, however, as one needs to pack and unpack existentials often. Here, the module system does this job for us. Also, we hope that the module type $𝓜⟦X \to Y⟧$ is easier to understand for programmers who are not familiar with the GOI.

7 Conclusion

We have shown how the GOI constructs an ML-style module system for first-order programming languages. The module system can be seen as a natural higher-order generalisation of systems-level linking. In contrast to other higher-order module systems, its elaboration does not need a higher-order target language.

The module system captures the central structure of the GOI in familiar terms. This makes the constructions of the GOI more accessible. It may also help to clarify the GOI. For example, computational effects are standard in ML-like module systems, but their role has only recently been studied in the GOI [11].

The module system also helps to separate implementation from application concerns. Especially for programming-language applications of the GOI, where one is interested in efficient implementations, the amount of low-level detail needed for efficient implementation can become immense. A module system encapsulates implementation aspects. We believe that the module system is a good basis to investigate it separately from higher-level applications of the GOI. Examples of implementation issues that were out of the scope of this paper are the elimination of the idealised use of **raw** and the separate compilation with link-time optimisations, such as [12].

We have adapted the F-ing to a linear type system. This has required us to develop a more flexible way of handling the scope of value variables. Decomposing the promotion rule into the CLOSE-rules has allowed us to define a simple syntax-directed type checking method that minimises the scope of values.

Acknowledgments. Bernhard Pöttinger provided much helpful feedback on technical details. I also want thank the anonymous reviewers for their feedback.

References

1. Abramsky, S., Haghverdi, E., Scott, P.J.: Geometry of interaction and linear combinatory algebras. Math. Struct. Comput. Sci. **12**(5), 625–665 (2002)
2. Abramsky, S., Jagadeesan, R.: New foundations for the geometry of interaction. Inf. Comput. **111**(1), 53–119 (1994)
3. Chen, H., Wu, X.N., Shao, Z., Lockerman, J., Gu, R.: Toward compositional verification of interruptible OS kernels and device drivers. J. Autom. Reason. **61**(1–4), 141–189 (2018)
4. Dal Lago, U., Schöpp, U.: Computation by interaction for space bounded functional programming. Inf. Comput. **248**(C), 150–194 (2016)
5. Fredriksson, O., Ghica, D.R.: Seamless distributed computing from the geometry of interaction. In: Palamidessi, C., Ryan, M.D. (eds.) TGC 2012. LNCS, vol. 8191, pp. 34–48. Springer, Heidelberg (2013). https://doi.org/10.1007/978-3-642-41157-1_3
6. Ghica, D.R.: Geometry of synthesis: a structured approach to VLSI design. In: Hofmann, M., Felleisen, M. (eds.) Principles of Programming Languages, POPL 2007, pp. 363–375. ACM (2007)
7. Girard, J.Y.: Linear logic. Theor. Comput. Sci. **50**(1), 1–101 (1987)
8. Girard, J.Y.: Towards a geometry of interaction. In: Gray, J.W., Scedrov, A. (eds.) Categories in Computer Science and Logic, pp. 69–108. American Mathematical Society (1989)
9. Harper, R., Lillibridge, M.: A type-theoretic approach to higher-order modules with sharing. In: Boehm, H., Lang, B., Yellin, D.M. (eds.) Principles of Programming Languages, POPL 1994, pp. 123–137. ACM (1994)
10. Hasuo, I., Hoshino, N.: Semantics of higher-order quantum computation via geometry of interaction. In: Dawar, A., Grädel, E. (eds.) Logic in Computer Science, LICS 2011, pp. 237–246. IEEE (2011)

11. Hoshino, N., Muroya, K., Hasuo, I.: Memoryful geometry of interaction: from coalgebraic components to algebraic effects. In: Henzinger, T.A., Miller, D. (eds.) Computer Science Logic - Logic in Computer Science, CSL-LICS 2014. ACM (2014)
12. Johnson, T., Amini, M., Li, X.D.: ThinLTO: scalable and incremental LTO. In: Reddi, V.J., Smith, A., Tang, L. (eds.) Code Generation and Optimization, CGO 2017, pp. 111–121 (2017)
13. Leroy, X.: A modular module system. J. Funct. Program. **10**(3), 269–303 (2000)
14. Rossberg, A., Russo, C.V., Dreyer, D.: F-ing modules. J. Funct. Program. **24**(5), 529–607 (2014)
15. Schöpp, U.: Call-by-value in a basic logic for interaction. In: Garrigue, J. (ed.) APLAS 2014. LNCS, vol. 8858, pp. 428–448. Springer, Cham (2014). https://doi.org/10.1007/978-3-319-12736-1_23
16. Schöpp, U.: From call-by-value to interaction by typed closure conversion. In: Feng, X., Park, S. (eds.) APLAS 2015. LNCS, vol. 9458, pp. 251–270. Springer, Cham (2015). https://doi.org/10.1007/978-3-319-26529-2_14
17. Schöpp, U.: Defunctionalisation as modular closure conversion. In: Pientka, B. (ed.) Principles and Practice of Declarative Programming, PPDP 2017. ACM (2017)

Automated Synthesis of Functional Programs with Auxiliary Functions

Shingo Eguchi, Naoki Kobayashi$^{(\boxtimes)}$, and Takeshi Tsukada

The University of Tokyo, Tokyo, Japan
koba@is.s.u-tokyo.ac.jp

Abstract. Polikarpova et al. have recently proposed a method for synthesizing functional programs from specifications expressed as refinement types, and implemented a program synthesis tool SYNQUID. Although SYNQUID can generate non-trivial programs on various data structures such as lists and binary search trees, it cannot automatically generate programs that require auxiliary functions, unless users provide the specifications of auxiliary functions. We propose an extension of SYNQUID to enable automatic synthesis of programs with auxiliary functions. The idea is to prepare a template of the target function containing unknown auxiliary functions, infer the types of auxiliary functions, and then use SYNQUID to synthesize the auxiliary functions. We have implemented a program synthesizer based on our method, and confirmed through experiments that our method can synthesize several programs with auxiliary functions, which SYNQUID is unable to automatically synthesize.

1 Introduction

The goal of program synthesis [2–4,6,7,9,11] is to automatically generate programs from certain program specifications. The program specifications can be examples (a finite set of input/output pairs) [2,3], validator code [11], or refinement types [9]. In the present paper, we are interested in the approach of synthesizing programs from refinement types [9], because refinement types can express detailed specifications of programs, and synthesized programs are guaranteed to be correct by construction (in that they indeed satisfy the specification given in the form of refinement types).

Polikarpova et al. [9] have formalized a method for synthesizing a program from a given refinement type, and implemented a program synthesis tool called SYNQUID. It can automatically generate a number of interesting programs such as those manipulating lists and trees. SYNQUID, however, suffers from the limitation that it cannot automatically synthesize programs that require auxiliary functions (unless the types of auxiliary functions are given as hints).

In the present paper, we propose an extension of SYNQUID to enable automatic synthesis of programs with auxiliary functions. Given a refinement type specification of a function, our method proceeds as follows.

© Springer Nature Switzerland AG 2018
S. Ryu (Ed.): APLAS 2018, LNCS 11275, pp. 223–241, 2018.
https://doi.org/10.1007/978-3-030-02768-1_13

$sort :: l$:List Int

$\quad \rightarrow \{$List $Int\ \langle \lambda x.\lambda y.x \leq y\rangle \mid$ len $\nu =$ len $l \wedge$ elems $\nu =$ elems $l\}$

Fig. 1. The type of a sorting function

$sort = \lambda l.$ match l with

$\quad \mid$ Nil $\mapsto \square_1$

$\quad \mid$ Cons $x\ xs \mapsto \square_2\ x\ (sort\ xs\ )$

Fig. 2. A template for list-sorting function

Step 1: Prepare a template of the target function with unknown auxiliary functions. The template is chosen based on the simple type of the target function. For example, if the function takes a list as an argument, a template that recurses over the list is typically selected.

Step 2: Infer the types of auxiliary functions from the template.

Step 3: Synthesize the auxiliary functions by passing the inferred types to SYN-QUID. (If this fails, go back to Step 1 and choose another template.)

We sketch our method through an example of the synthesis of a list-sorting function. Following SYNQUID [9], a specification of the target function can be given as the refinement type shown in Fig. 1. Here, "List $Int\ \langle \lambda x.\lambda y.x \leq y\rangle$" is the type of a sorted list of integers, where the part $\lambda x.\lambda y.x \leq y$ means that $(\lambda x.\lambda y.x \leq y)v_1 v_2$ holds for any two elements v_1 and v_2 such that v_1 occurs before v_2 in the list. Thus, the type specification in Fig. 1 means that the target function $sort$ should take a list of integers as input, and returns a sorted list that is of the same length and has the same set of elements as the input list.

In Step 1, we generate a template of the target function. Since the argument of the function is a list, a default choice is the "fold template" shown in Fig. 2. The template contains the holes $\square_1$ and $\square_2$ for unknown auxiliary functions. Thus, the goal has been reduced to the problem of finding appropriate auxiliary functions to fill the holes.

In Step 2, we infer the types of auxiliary functions, so that the whole function has the type in Fig. 2. This is the main step of our method and consists of a few substeps. First, using a variation of the type inference algorithm of SYNQUID, we obtain type judgments for the auxiliary functions. For example, for $\square_2$, we infer:

$l :$ List $Int, x : Int, xs : \{$List $Int \mid$ len $\nu =$ len $l - 1 \wedge$ elems $\nu + [x] =$ elems $l\}$
$\vdash \square_2::x' : \{Int \mid \nu = x\}$
$\quad \rightarrow l' : \{$List $Int\ \langle \lambda x.\lambda y.x \leq y\rangle \mid$ len $\nu =$ len $xs \wedge$ elems $\nu =$ elems $xs\}$
$\quad \rightarrow \{$List $Int\ \langle \lambda x.\lambda y.x \leq y\rangle \mid$ len $\nu =$ len $l \wedge$ elems $\nu =$ elems $l\}$.

Here, for example, the type of the second argument of $\square_2$ comes from the type of the target function $sort$. Since we wish to infer a *closed* function for $\square_2$

$\square_1 :: \{\text{List } Int \; \langle \lambda x \lambda y.x \leq y \rangle \mid \text{len } \nu = 0 \; \wedge \; \text{elems } \nu = \emptyset\}$

$\square_2 :: x : Int \rightarrow l : \text{List } Int$

$\qquad \rightarrow \{\text{List } Int \; \langle \lambda x \lambda y.x \leq y \rangle \mid \text{len } \nu = \text{len } l + 1 \; \wedge \; \text{elems } \nu = \text{elems } l + [x]\}$

Fig. 3. The type of the auxiliary function

$g = \lambda x.\lambda l.\text{match } l \text{ with}$

$\qquad \mid \text{Nil} \mapsto \text{Cons} x \text{Nil}$

$\qquad \mid \text{Cons } y \; ys \mapsto \text{if } x \leq y \text{ then} \text{Cons } x \; (\text{Cons } y \; ys)$

$\qquad\qquad\qquad\qquad\qquad \text{else } \text{Cons } y \; (g \; x \; ys)$

$sort = \lambda l.\text{match } l \text{ with}$

$\qquad \mid \text{Nil} \mapsto \text{Nil}$

$\qquad \mid \text{Cons } x \; xs \mapsto g \; x \; (sort \; xs)$

Fig. 4. A synthesized list-sorting function

(that does not contain l, x, xs), we then convert the above judgment to a closed type using quantifiers. For example, the result type becomes:

$$\{\text{List } Int \; \langle \lambda x.\lambda y.x \leq y \rangle \mid$$
$$\forall l, x, xs.(\text{len } xs = \text{len } l - 1 \wedge \text{elems } xs + [x] = \text{elems } l$$
$$\wedge \text{len } l' = \text{len } xs \; \wedge \; \text{elems } l' = \text{elems } xs)$$
$$\Rightarrow \text{len } \nu = \text{len } l \; \wedge \; \text{elems } \nu = \text{elems } l\}.$$

Here, the lefthand side of the implication comes from the constraints in the type environment and the type of the second argument. We then eliminate quantifiers (in a sound but incomplete manner), and obtain the types shown in Fig. 3.

Finally, in Step 3, we just pass the inferred types of auxiliary functions to SYNQUID. By filling the holes of the template with the auxiliary functions synthesized by SYNQUID, we get a complete list-sorting function as shown in Fig. 4.

We have implemented a prototype program synthesis tool, which uses SYN-QUID as a backend, based on the proposed method. We have tested it for several examples, and confirmed that our method is able to synthesize programs with auxiliary functions, which SYNQUID alone fails to synthesize automatically.

The rest of the paper is structured as follows. Section 2 defines the target language. Section 3 describes the proposed method. Section 4 reports an implementation and experimental results. Section 5 discusses related work and Sect. 6 concludes the paper. Proofs omitted in the paper are available in the longer version [10].

2 Target Language

This section defines the target language of program synthesis. Since the language is essentially the same as the one used in SYNQUID [9], we explain it only briefly.

$$t \text{ (program terms)} ::= e \mid b \mid f$$
$$e \text{ (E-terms)} ::= x \mid e\, e \mid e\, f$$
$$b \text{ (branching)} ::= \texttt{if } e \texttt{ then } t \texttt{ else } t \mid (\texttt{match } e \texttt{ with } \mathtt{C}_1 \widetilde{x}_1 \mapsto t_1 \mid \cdots \mid \mathtt{C}_k \widetilde{x}_k \mapsto t_k)$$
$$f \text{ (functions)} ::= \lambda x.t \mid \texttt{fix } x.t$$

Fig. 5. Syntax of programs

For the sake of simplicity, we omit polymorphic types in the formalization below, although they are supported by the implementation reported in Sect. 4.

Figure 5 shows the syntax of program terms. Following [9], we classify terms into E-terms, branching, and function terms; this is for the convenience of formalizing the synthesis algorithm. Apart from it, the syntax is that of a standard functional language. In the figure, x and $\mathtt{C}$ range over the sets of variables and data constructors respectively. Data constructors are also treated as variables (so that $\mathtt{C}$ is also an E-term). The match expression first evaluates e, and if the value is of the form $\mathtt{C}_i \, \widetilde{v}$, evaluates $[\widetilde{v}/\widetilde{x}_i]t_i$; here we write $\widetilde{}$ for a sequence. The function term $\texttt{fix } x.t$ denotes the recursive function defined by $x = t$.

The syntax of types is given in Fig. 6. A type is either a refinement type $\{B \mid \psi\}$ or a function type $x : T_1 \to T_2$. The type $\{B \mid \psi\}$ describes the set of elements ν of ground type B that satisfies ψ; here, ψ is a formula that may contain a special variable ν, which refers to the element. For example, $\{Int \mid \nu > 0\}$ represents the type of an integer ν such that $\nu > 0$. For a technical convenience, we assume that ψ always contains ν as a free variable, by considering $\psi \wedge (\nu = \nu)$ instead of ψ if necessarily. The function type $x : T_1 \to T_2$ is dependent, in that x may occur in T_2 when T_1 is a refinement type. A ground type B is either a base type (*Bool* or *Int*), or a data type $D\, T_1 \cdots T_n$, where D denotes a type constructor. For the sake of simplicity, we consider only covariant type constructors, i.e., $D\, T_1 \cdots T_n$ is a subtype of $D\, T_1' \cdots T_n'$ if T_i is a subtype of T_i' for every $i \in \{1, \ldots, n\}$. The type $\texttt{List } Int \, \langle \lambda x.\lambda y.x \le y \rangle$ of sorted lists in Sect. 1 is expressed as $(\texttt{List}\langle \lambda x.\lambda y.x \le y \rangle) Int$, where $\texttt{List}\langle \lambda x.\lambda y.x \le y \rangle$ is the D-part. The list constructor *Cons* is given a type of the form:

$$z : \{B \mid \psi'\} \to w : (\texttt{List}\langle \lambda x.\lambda y.\psi \rangle)\{B \mid \psi' \wedge [z/x, \nu/y]\psi\}$$
$$\to \{(\texttt{List}\langle \lambda x.\lambda y.\psi \rangle)\{B \mid \psi'\} \mid \texttt{len } \nu = \texttt{len } w + 1 \wedge \texttt{elems } \nu = \texttt{elems } w + [z]\}$$

for each ground type B and formulas ψ, ψ'. Here, $\texttt{len}$ and $\texttt{elems}$ are uninterpreted function symbols. In a contextual type $\texttt{let } C \texttt{ in } T$, the context C binds some variables in T and impose constraints on them; for example, $\texttt{let } x : \{Int \mid \nu > 0\} \texttt{ in } \{Int \mid \nu = 2x\}$ denotes the type of positive even integers.

A *type environment* Γ is a sequence consisting of bindings of variables to types and formulas (called *path conditions*), subject to certain well-formedness conditions. We write $\Gamma \vdash T$ to mean that T is well formed under Γ; see Appendix A for the well-formedness conditions on types and type environments. Figure 7 shows the typing rules. The typing rules are fairly standard ones for a refinement type system, except that, in rule T-APP, contextual types are used

$$T \text{ (types) } ::= \{B \mid \psi\} \mid x : T_1 \rightarrow T_2$$
$$B \text{ (ground types) } ::= Bool \mid Int \mid D\, T_1 \cdots T_n$$
$$C \text{ (contexts) } ::= \cdot \mid x : T; C$$
$$\hat{T} \text{ (contextual types) } ::= \texttt{let } C \texttt{ in } T$$

Fig. 6. Syntax of types

to avoid substituting program terms for variables in types; this treatment of contextual types follows the formalization of SYNQUID [9].

In the figure, $\mathsf{FV}(\psi)$ represents the set of free variables occurring in ψ. In rule T-MATCH, $\widetilde{x}_i : \widetilde{T}_i \rightarrow T$ represents $x_{i,1} : T_{i,1} \rightarrow \cdots x_{i,k_i} : T_{i,k_i} \rightarrow T$.

We write $[\![\Gamma]\!]_{vars}$ for the formula obtained by extracting constraints on the variables $vars$ from Γ. It is defined by:

$$[\![\Gamma; \psi]\!]_{vars} = \psi \wedge [\![\Gamma]\!]_{vars \cup \mathsf{FV}(\psi)}$$
$$[\![\Gamma; x : \{B \mid \psi\}]\!]_{vars} = \begin{cases} [x/\nu]\psi \wedge [\![\Gamma]\!]_{vars \cup \mathsf{FV}(\psi)} & \text{if } x \in vars \\ [\![\Gamma]\!]_{vars} & \text{otherwise} \end{cases}$$
$$[\![\Gamma; x : T_1 \rightarrow T_2]\!]_{vars} = [\![\Gamma]\!]_{vars}$$
$$[\![\cdot]\!]_{vars} = \top.$$

The goal of our program synthesis is, given a type environment Γ (that represents the types of constants and already synthesized functions) and a type T, to find a program term t such that $\Gamma \vdash t :: T$.

3   Our Method

This section describes our method for synthesizing programs with auxiliary functions. As mentioned in Sect. 1, the method consists of the following three steps:

Step 1: Generate a program template with unknown auxiliary functions.
Step 2: Infer the types of the unknown auxiliary functions.
Step 3: Synthesize auxiliary functions of the required types by using SYNQUID.

3.1   Step 1: Generating Templates

In this step, program templates are generated based on the (simple) type of an argument of the target function. Figure 8 shows the syntax of templates. It is an extension of the language syntax described in Sect. 2 with unknown auxiliary functions $\square_i$. We require that for each i, $\square_i$ occurs only once in a template.

We generate multiple candidates of templates automatically, and proceed to Steps 2 and 3 for each candidate. If the synthesis fails, we backtrack and try another candidate.

In the current implementation (reported in Sect. 4), we prepare the following templates.

Subtyping $\boxed{\Gamma \vdash T <: T'}$

$$\frac{\Gamma \vdash B <: B' \qquad \mathsf{valid}(\llbracket \Gamma \rrbracket_{\mathsf{FV}(\psi \to \psi')} \wedge \psi \to \psi')}{\Gamma \vdash \{B \mid \psi\} <: \{B' \mid \psi'\}} \tag{<:-G}$$

$$\frac{\Gamma \vdash T_1 <: T_1' \qquad (\Gamma; y : T_1) \vdash [y/x]T_2' <: T_2}{\Gamma \vdash x : T_1' \to T_2' <: y : T_1 \to T_2} \tag{<:-Fun}$$

$$\frac{}{\Gamma \vdash \mathit{Int} <: \mathit{Int}} \; (\text{<:-Int}) \qquad\qquad \frac{}{\Gamma \vdash \mathit{Bool} <: \mathit{Bool}} \; (\text{<:-Bool})$$

$$\frac{\Gamma \vdash T_i <: T_i' \text{ for each } i \in \{1, \ldots, n\}}{\Gamma \vdash D \; T_1 \; \cdots \; T_n <: D \; T_1' \; \cdots \; T_n'} \tag{<:-DT}$$

Typing with contextual types $\boxed{\Gamma \vdash e :: \hat{T}}$

$$\frac{\Gamma(x) = \{B \mid \psi\}}{\Gamma \vdash x :: \mathtt{let} \; \cdot \; \mathtt{in} \; \{B \mid \nu = x\}} \tag{T-VarG}$$

$$\frac{\Gamma(x) = T \qquad \Gamma \vdash T}{\Gamma \vdash x :: \mathtt{let} \; \cdot \; \mathtt{in} \; T} \tag{T-Var}$$

$$\frac{\begin{array}{c}\Gamma \vdash e :: \mathtt{let} \; C_1 \; \mathtt{in} \; x : T_x \to T \\ \Gamma; C_1 \vdash t :: \mathtt{let} \; C_2 \; \mathtt{in} \; T_x' \\ \Gamma; C_1; C_2 \vdash T_x' <: T_x\end{array}}{\Gamma \vdash e \; t :: \mathtt{let} \; C_1; C_2; x : T_x' \; \mathtt{in} \; T} \tag{T-App}$$

Context-free typing $\boxed{\Gamma \vdash t :: T}$

$$\frac{\Gamma \vdash e :: \mathtt{let} \; C \; \mathtt{in} \; T' \qquad \Gamma; C \vdash T' <: T}{\Gamma \vdash e :: T} \tag{T-Sub}$$

$$\frac{\Gamma \vdash x : T_x \to T \qquad \Gamma; x : T_x \vdash t :: T}{\Gamma \vdash \lambda x.t :: x : T_x \to T} \tag{T-Abs}$$

$$\frac{\begin{array}{c}\Gamma \vdash e :: \mathtt{let} \; C \; \mathtt{in} \; \{\mathtt{Bool} \mid \psi\} \qquad \Gamma \vdash T \\ \Gamma; C; [\top/\nu]\psi \vdash t_1 :: T \qquad \Gamma; C; [\bot/\nu]\psi \vdash t_2 :: T\end{array}}{\Gamma \vdash \mathtt{if} \; e \; \mathtt{then} \; t_1 \; \mathtt{else} \; t_2 :: T} \tag{T-If}$$

$$\frac{\begin{array}{c}\Gamma \vdash e :: \mathtt{let} \; C \; \mathtt{in} \; \{D \; T_1' \; \cdots \; T_n' \mid \psi\} \qquad \Gamma \vdash T \\ \Gamma(\mathsf{C}_i) = \widetilde{x}_i : \widetilde{T}_i \to \{D \; T_1' \; \cdots \; T_n' \mid \psi_i'\} \qquad \Gamma_i = \widetilde{x}_i : \widetilde{T}_i; [z/\nu]\psi_i' \\ \Gamma; C; z : \{D \; T_1' \; \cdots \; T_n' \mid \psi\}; \Gamma_i \vdash t_i :: T \; (\text{for each } i)\end{array}}{\Gamma \vdash \mathtt{match} \; e \; \mathtt{with} \; \mathsf{C}_1 \widetilde{x}_1 \; \mapsto t_1 \mid \cdots \mid \mathsf{C}_k \widetilde{x}_k \; \mapsto t_k :: T} \tag{T-Match}$$

$$\frac{\Gamma; x : T \vdash t :: T}{\Gamma \vdash \mathtt{fix} \; x.t :: T} \tag{T-Fix}$$

Fig. 7. Typing rules

$$t_\square \text{ (program terms with holes) } ::= e \mid b \mid f \mid e_\square \mid b_\square \mid f_\square$$
$$e_\square \text{ (E-terms with a hole) } ::= \square_i \mid e_\square \, e \mid e_\square \, f$$
$$b_\square \text{ (branching with holes) } ::= \texttt{if } e \texttt{ then } t_\square \texttt{ else } t_\square$$
$$\mid (\texttt{match } e \texttt{ with } C_1 \widetilde{x}_1 \mapsto t_\square^1 \mid \cdots \mid C_k \widetilde{x}_k \mapsto t_\square^k)$$
$$f_\square \text{ (functions with holes) } ::= \lambda x.t_\square \mid \texttt{fix } x.t_\square$$

Fig. 8. The syntax of templates

- Fold-style (or, catamorphism) templates: These are templates of functions that recurse over an argument of algebraic data type. For example, the followings are templates for unary functions on lists (shown on the lefthand side) and those on binary trees (shown on the righthand side).

$$f = \lambda l. \texttt{ match } l \texttt{ with} \qquad\qquad f = \lambda t. \texttt{ match } t \texttt{ with}$$
$$\texttt{Nil} \mapsto \square_1 \qquad\qquad\qquad\qquad \texttt{Empty} \mapsto \square_1$$
$$\mid \texttt{Cons } x \; xs \mapsto \square_2 \, x \, (f \; xs) \qquad \mid \texttt{Node } v \, l \, r \mapsto \square_2 \, x \, (f \; l) \, (f \; r)$$

- Divide-conquer-style templates: These are templates for functions on lists (or other set-like data structures). The following is a template for a function that takes a list as the first argument.

$$f = \lambda l. \texttt{ match } l \texttt{ with}$$
$$\texttt{Nil} \mapsto \square_1$$
$$\mid \texttt{Cons } x \; \texttt{Nil} \mapsto \square_2 \, x$$
$$\mid \texttt{Cons } x \; xs \mapsto (\texttt{match } (\mathit{split} \; l) \texttt{ with Pair } l_1 \; l_2 \mapsto \square_3 \, (f \; l_1) \, (f \; l_2))$$

The function f takes a list l as an input; if the length of l is more than 1, it splits l into two lists l_1 and l_2, recursively calls itself for l_1 and l_2, and combines the result with the unknown auxiliary function $\square_3$. A typical example that fits this template is the merge sort function, where $\square_3$ is the merge function.

Note that the rest of our method (Steps 2 and 3) does not depend on the choice of templates; thus other templates can be freely added.

3.2   Step 2: Inferring the Types of Auxiliary Functions

This section describes a procedure to infer the types of auxiliary functions from the template generated in Step 1. This procedure is the core part of our method, which consists of the following three substeps.

Step 2.1: Extract type constraints on each auxiliary function.
Step 2.2: From the type constraints, construct closed types of auxiliary functions that may contain quantifiers in refinement formulas.
Step 2.3: Eliminate quantifiers from the types of auxiliary functions.

Step 2.1: Extraction of Type Constraints. Given a type T of a program to synthesize and a program template $t_\square$ with n holes, this step derives a set $\{\Gamma_1 \vdash \square_1 :: T_1, \ldots, \Gamma_n \vdash \square_n :: T_n\}$ of constraints for each hole $\square_i$. The constraints mean that, if each hole $\square_i$ is filled by a closed term of type stronger than T_i, then the resulting program has type T.

The procedure is shown in Fig. 9, obtained based on the typing rules in Sect. 2. It is similar to the type checking algorithm used in SYNQUID [9]; the main difference from the corresponding type inference algorithm of SYNQUID is that, when a template of the form $\square_i\, e_1 \ldots e_n$ is encountered (the case for $e_\square$ in the procedure step2.1, processed by the subprocedure extractConst), we first perform type inference for the arguments $e_1, \ldots, e_n$, and then construct the type for $\square_i$. To see this, observe that the template $\square_i\, e_1 \ldots e_n$ matches the first pattern $e_\square :: T$ of the match expression in step2.1, and the subprocedure extractConst is called. In extractConst, $\square_i\, e_1 \ldots e_n$ (with $n > 0$) matches the second pattern $e'_\square\, e$ (where $e'_\square$ and e are bound to $\square_i\, e_1 \ldots e_{n-1}$ and e_n respectively), and the type T_n of e_n is first inferred. Subsequently, the procedure extractConst is recursively called and the types $T_{n-1}, \ldots, T_1$ of $e_{n-1}, \ldots, e_1$ (along with contexts $C_{n-1}, \ldots, C_1$) are inferred in this order, and then $y_1 : T_1 \to \cdots \to y_n : T_n \to T$ (along with a context) is obtained the type of $\square_i$. In contrast, for an application $e_1 e_2$, SYNQUID first performs type inference for the function part e_1, and then propagates the resulting type information to the argument e_2.

Example 1. Given the type T of a sorting function in Fig. 1 and the template $t_\square$ in Fig. 2, step2.1($\Gamma \vdash t_\square :: T$) (where Γ contains types for constants such as Nil) returns the following constraint for the auxiliary function $\square_2$ (we omit types for constants).

$$l : \text{List } Int \,;\, x : Int;\; xs : \text{List } \langle \lambda x. \lambda y. x \le y \rangle \, \{Int \mid x \le \nu\}\,;$$
$$z : \{\text{List } Int \mid \nu = l\}; \text{len } xs + 1 = \text{len } z \wedge \text{elems } xs + [x] = \text{elems } z$$
$$\vdash$$
$$\square_i :: y : \{Int \mid \nu = x\}$$
$$\to ys : \{\text{List}\langle \lambda x \lambda y. x \le y\rangle \, \{Int \mid x \le \nu\}$$
$$\mid \text{len } \nu = \text{len } xs \wedge \text{elems } \nu = \text{elems } xs\}$$
$$\to \{\text{List}\langle \lambda x \lambda y. x \le y\rangle \, Int \mid \text{len } \nu = \text{len } l \wedge \text{elems } \nu = \text{elems } l\}.$$

$\square$

The theorem below states the soundness of the procedure. Intuitively, it claims that a target program of type T can indeed be obtained from a given template $t_\square$, by filling the holes $\square_1, \ldots, \square_n$ with terms $t_1, \ldots, t_n$ of the types inferred by the procedure step2.1.

Theorem 1. *Let Γ be a well-formed environment, $t_\square$ a program template and T a type well-formed under Γ. Suppose that* step2.1($\Gamma \vdash t_\square :: T$) *returns*

$$\{\Delta_1 \vdash \square_1 :: U_1, \ldots, \Delta_n \vdash \square_n :: U_n\}.$$

If $\emptyset \vdash S_i$ and $\Delta_i \vdash S_i <: U_i$ for each $i \in \{1, \ldots, n\}$, then

$$\Gamma; \square_1 : S_1, \ldots, \square_n : S_n \vdash t_\square :: T.$$

$\text{step2.1}(\Gamma \vdash t_\square :: T) =$

$\text{match } (t_\square :: T) \text{ with}$

$\quad | \; e_\square :: T \quad \Rightarrow \quad \text{extractConst}(\Gamma, e_\square, T, \emptyset)$

$\quad | \; e :: T \quad \text{when} \quad \Gamma \vdash e :: T \quad \Rightarrow \emptyset$

$\quad | \; \text{fix } x.t_\square :: T \quad \Rightarrow \quad \text{step2.1}((\Gamma; x : T) \vdash t_\square : T)$

$\quad | \; \lambda y.t_\square :: (x : T_x \to T') \quad \Rightarrow \quad \text{step2.1}((\Gamma; y : T_x) \vdash t_\square :: [y/x]T') \qquad (1)$

$\quad | \; \text{if } e_1 \text{ then } t'_\square \text{ else } t''_\square \; : T$

$\qquad \text{when} \quad \Gamma \vdash e_1 :: \text{let } C \text{ in } \{\text{Bool} \mid \psi\} \Rightarrow$

$\qquad\qquad \text{step2.1}((\Gamma; C; [\text{true}/\nu]\psi) \vdash t'_\square : T) \cup \text{step2.1}((\Gamma; C; [\text{false}/\nu]\psi) \vdash t''_\square : T)$

$\quad | \; (\text{match } e \text{ with } \texttt{C}_1 \widetilde{x}_1 \mapsto t_\square^{(1)} \mid \cdots \mid \texttt{C}_k \widetilde{x}_k \mapsto t_\square^{(k)}) : T$

$\qquad \text{when} \quad \Gamma \vdash e :: \text{let } C \text{ in } \{D \, \widetilde{T} \mid \psi\}$

$\qquad\qquad \Gamma(\texttt{C}_i) = \widetilde{x}_i : \widetilde{T}_i \to \{D \, \widetilde{T} \mid \psi'_i\} \Rightarrow$

$\qquad\qquad \bigcup_i \text{step2.1}((\Gamma; C; z : \{D \, \widetilde{T} \mid \psi\} \vdash t_\square^{(i)} : T) \; (\text{where } z \text{ is fresh})$

$\quad | \; \_ \Rightarrow \textit{fail}$

$\text{extractConst}(\Gamma, e_\square, T, C) =$

$\quad \text{match } e_\square \text{ with}$

$\qquad | \; \square_i \Rightarrow \{\Gamma; C \vdash \square_i :: T\}$

$\qquad | \; e'_\square \, e \Rightarrow$

$\qquad\qquad \text{infer } C' \text{ and } T' \text{ such that}$

$\qquad\qquad\qquad \Gamma \vdash e :: \text{let } C' \text{ in } T'$

$\qquad\qquad\qquad \text{where all variables bounded in } C' \text{ occur only in } T'$

$\qquad\qquad \text{extractConst}(\Gamma, e'_\square, y : T' \to T, C; C') \; (\text{where } y \text{ is fresh})$

$\qquad | \; e'_\square \, f \Rightarrow$

$\qquad\qquad \text{infer } T' \text{ such that}$

$\qquad\qquad\qquad \Gamma \vdash f :: T'$

$\qquad\qquad \text{extractConst}(\Gamma, e'_\square, y : T' \to T, C) \; (\text{where } y \text{ is fresh})$

Fig. 9. The algorithm for Step 2.1

Step 2.2: Construction of Closed Types. We have obtained a constraint $\Gamma_i \vdash \square_i :: T_i$ for each hole $\square_i$, and now it suffices to find an auxiliary function (i.e. a closed term) of type T_i for each i. We shall use SYNQUID [9] to synthesize a desired function but the type T_i itself cannot be an input of SYNQUID since it is not closed in general. The goal of Step 2.2 is, thus, to calculate a closed type S_i such that $\Gamma \vdash S_i <: T_i$, using universal and existential quantifiers.

In order to solve the problem above by induction on T_i, we generalize the problem as follows: Given a well-formed type $\Gamma \vdash T$ and a set var of variables,

(a) find a type S such that $\Gamma \vdash S <: T$ and $\text{FV}(S) \subseteq var$, and

(b) find a type S such that $\Gamma \vdash T <: S$ and $\text{FV}(S) \subseteq var$.

Let us first consider the simplest but most important case, where T is a scalar type $\{B \mid \psi\}$ with $B = Bool$ or Int. Suppose that ψ has free variables $\{\nu\} \cup var \cup \{y_1, \ldots, y_n\}$, where y_i $(1 \leq i \leq n)$ comes from the environment Γ and $y_i \notin var$. Let $var = \{x_1, \ldots, x_k\}$ and $\boldsymbol{x}$ be the sequence of variables $x_1, \ldots, x_k$. The goal is to find a formula $\psi_0(\nu, \boldsymbol{x})$ with free variable $\{\nu, x_1, \ldots, x_k\}$ such that

$$\Gamma \vdash \{B \mid \psi_0(\nu, \boldsymbol{x})\} <: \{B \mid \psi(\nu, \boldsymbol{x}, \boldsymbol{y})\}.$$

By the subtyping rule, this subtyping judgment holds if and only if

$$[\![\Gamma]\!]_{\boldsymbol{x}, \boldsymbol{y}}(\boldsymbol{x}, \boldsymbol{y}, \boldsymbol{z}) \wedge \psi_0(\nu, \boldsymbol{x}) \Rightarrow \psi(\nu, \boldsymbol{x}, \boldsymbol{y})$$

is valid. The weakest formula $\psi_0(\nu, \boldsymbol{x})$ that satisfies the above condition can be given by using the universal quantifier, namely,

$$\psi_0(\nu, \boldsymbol{x}) \quad := \quad \forall \boldsymbol{y} \boldsymbol{z}. \left([\![\Gamma]\!]_{\boldsymbol{x}, \boldsymbol{y}}(\boldsymbol{x}, \boldsymbol{y}, \boldsymbol{z}) \Rightarrow \psi(\nu, \boldsymbol{x}, \boldsymbol{y})\right).$$

The dual problem can be solved in a similar way: the formula $\psi_0'(\nu)$ defined by

$$\psi_0'(\nu, \boldsymbol{x}) \quad := \quad \exists \boldsymbol{y} \boldsymbol{z}. \left([\![\Gamma]\!]_{\boldsymbol{x}, \boldsymbol{y}}(\boldsymbol{x}, \boldsymbol{y}, \boldsymbol{z}) \wedge \psi(\nu, \boldsymbol{x}, \boldsymbol{y})\right)$$

satisfies the subtyping judgment $\Gamma \vdash \{B \mid \psi(\nu, \boldsymbol{x}, \boldsymbol{y})\} <: \{B \mid \psi_0'(\nu, \boldsymbol{x})\}$.

The case $T = \{D\, U_1 \ldots U_\ell \mid \psi\}$ is similar to the above case, except that we should replace each U_i with a closed type S_i. We recursively call the procedure to construct such a S_i.

When $T = (x : T_1 \to T_2)$, we simply invoke the procedures recursively. Every solution S must be of the form $S = (x : S_1 \to S_2)$, and the requirements are $\Gamma \vdash T_1 <: S_1$ (with $\mathsf{FV}(S_1) \subseteq var$) and $\Gamma; x : T_1 \vdash S_2 <: T_2$ (with $\mathsf{FV}(S_2) \subseteq var \cup \{x\}$). These subproblems can be solved by recursively calling the procedure.

Figure 10 gives a formal definition of the procedures; necessType($\Gamma \vdash T$, var) solves the problem (a) and suffType($\Gamma \vdash T$, var) does (b).

Example 2. We continue discussing the example of the list sorting function. So far, the following constraint for the hole $\square_2$ is derived. (Γ is same as the environment shown in Example 1)

$$\Gamma \vdash \square_2 :: y : \{Int \mid \nu = x\}$$
$$\to ys : \{\mathtt{List}\langle\lambda x \lambda y. x \leq y\rangle \{Int \mid x \leq \nu\}$$
$$\mid \mathtt{len}\ \nu = \mathtt{len}\ xs \wedge \mathtt{elems}\ \nu = \mathtt{elems}\ xs\}$$
$$\to \{\mathtt{List}\langle\lambda x \lambda y. x \leq y\rangle\ Int \mid \mathtt{len}\ \nu = \mathtt{len}\ l \wedge \mathtt{elems}\ \nu = \mathtt{elems}\ l\}$$

In this step, we construct a closed type from the above constraint. The result is shown in Fig. 11.

The type returned by the procedure indeed satisfies the requirement.

Theorem 2. *Let $\Gamma \vdash T$ be a well-formed type and var be a set of variables.*

- *If $S = \mathsf{necessType}(\Gamma \vdash T, var)$, then $\Gamma \vdash S <: T$ and $\mathsf{FV}(S) \subseteq var$.*
- *If $S = \mathsf{suffType}(\Gamma \vdash T, var)$, then $\Gamma \vdash T <: S$ and $\mathsf{FV}(S) \subseteq var$.*

Hence, if $S = \mathsf{necessType}(\Gamma \vdash T, \emptyset)$, then $\Gamma \vdash S <: T$ and S is closed.

Step 2.3: Elimination of Quantifiers. By Step 2.2, closed types of auxiliary functions have been obtained, but these types cannot be passed to SYNQUID yet because SYNQUID can handle only types with quantifier-free refinement formulas. Therefore, in Step 2.3, we eliminate quantifiers from the types derived by Step 2.2. Depending on the underlying logic, there may not exist a sound and complete quantifier elimination procedure. For example, in our running example, we use a combination of uninterpreted function symbols, linear integer arithmetic, and sets, for which a complete procedure does not exist. We thus apply a sound but incomplete procedure, so that, given the type T obtained by Step 2.2, produces a subtype T' of T that does not contain quantifiers.

An important observation in designing a sound procedure is that, by the definition of the procedure for Step 2.2, existential quantifiers may occur in the form $\exists \tilde{x}.(\psi_1 \wedge \cdots \wedge \psi_k)$ only in *negative* positions of types, and universal quantifiers may occur in the form $\forall \tilde{x}.(\psi_1 \wedge \cdots \wedge \psi_k \Rightarrow \psi)$ only in *positive* positions. Here, as usual, we say that ψ occurs positively in $\{B \mid \psi\}$, and that ψ occurs positively (resp. negatively) in $x{:}T_1 \to T_2$ if ψ occurs positively (resp. negatively) in T_2 or negatively (resp. positively) in T_1. Thus, it suffices to replace each existential formula ψ with a quantifier-free formula ψ' weaker than ψ (i.e., $\psi \Rightarrow \psi'$), and each universal formula ψ with a quantifier-free formula ψ' stronger than ψ. We discuss two procedures below.

The first procedure, which is naive but was adopted in our implementation and effective in the experiments reported in Sect. 4, just propagates equality information so that quantified variables are removed as much as possible. Given an existentially-quantified formula $\exists \tilde{x}.(\psi_1 \wedge \cdots \wedge \psi_\ell)$, we collect the subset of $\{\psi, \ldots, \psi_\ell\}$ consisting of equality constraints, orient the equations (so that terms containing quantified variables tend to be replaced by those that do not contain quantified variables), and rewrite each ψ_i to ψ_i' using the equations. We then collect the subset $\{\psi_i'\}_{i \in I}$ of $\{\psi_1', \ldots, \psi_k'\}$ that do not contain quantified variables, and replace $\exists \tilde{x}.(\psi_1 \wedge \cdots \wedge \psi_\ell)$ with $\wedge_{i \in I} \psi_i'$. Similarly, given a universally quantified formula $\forall \tilde{x}.(\psi_1 \wedge \cdots \wedge \psi_k \Rightarrow \psi)$, we rewrite ψ by using the equality constraints in $\psi_1, \ldots, \psi_k$. If the resulting formula ψ' contains no quantified variables, we return ψ'; otherwise the whole formula is replaced by $\bot$.

Example 3. We continue Example 2. The type obtained in Step 2.2 is shown in Fig. 11. Here,

$P_5 \equiv \forall\, x, xs, z, l.$
$(z = l \wedge \mathtt{len}\ xs + 1 = \mathtt{len}\ z \wedge \mathtt{elems}\ xs + [x] = \mathtt{elems}\ z \wedge x = y$
$\wedge \mathtt{len}\ ys = \mathtt{len}\ xs \wedge \mathtt{elems}\ ys = \mathtt{elems}\ xs$
$\Rightarrow\ \mathtt{len}\ \nu = \mathtt{len}\ l \wedge \mathtt{elems}\ \nu = \mathtt{elems}\ l\ )$

$\mathsf{step2.2}(\Gamma \vdash T) \;=\; \mathsf{necessType}(\Gamma \vdash T,\; \emptyset)$

$\mathsf{necessType}(\Gamma \vdash T,\; var) \;=$
$\mathbf{match}\ T\ \mathbf{with}$
  $|\ \{B \mid \psi\}\quad \Rightarrow$
      $\{B \mid \forall X.([\![\Gamma]\!]_{\mathsf{FV}(\psi)\cup var} \to \psi)\}$ where $X = \mathsf{FV}([\![\Gamma]\!]_{\mathsf{FV}(\psi)\cup var} \to \psi) \setminus var$
  $|\ \{D\ T_1 \cdots T_n \mid \psi\}\quad \Rightarrow$
      $\mathbf{let}\ T'_{k,} = \mathsf{necessType}(\Gamma \vdash T_k\ var)\ (\text{for each } k)\ \mathbf{in}$
      $\{D\ T'_1 \cdots T'_n \mid \forall X.([\![\Gamma]\!]_{\mathsf{FV}(\psi)\cup var} \to \psi)\}$
           $\text{where } X = \mathsf{FV}([\![\Gamma]\!]_{\mathsf{FV}(\psi)\cup var} \to \psi) \setminus var$
  $|\ x : T_1 \to T_2\quad \Rightarrow$
      $\mathbf{let}\ T'_1 = \mathsf{suffType}(\Gamma \vdash T_1,\; var)\ \mathbf{in}$
      $\mathbf{let}\ T'_2 = \mathsf{necessType}((\Gamma; x : T_1) \vdash T_2,\; var \cup \{x\})\ \mathbf{in}$
      $x : T'_1 \to T'_2$

$\mathsf{suffType}(\Gamma \vdash T,\; var) \;=$
$\mathbf{match}\ T\ \mathbf{with}$
  $|\ \{B \mid \psi\}\quad \Rightarrow$
      $\{B \mid \exists X.([\![\Gamma]\!]_{\mathsf{FV}(\psi)\cup var} \land \psi)\}$ where $X = \mathsf{FV}([\![\Gamma]\!]_{\mathsf{FV}(\psi)\cup var} \land \psi) \setminus var$
  $|\ \{D\ T_1 \cdots T_n \mid \psi\}\quad \Rightarrow$
      $\mathbf{let}\ T'_k = \mathsf{suffType}(\Gamma \vdash T_k\ var)\ (\text{for each } k)\ \mathbf{in}$
      $\{D\ T_1 \cdots T_n \mid \exists X.([\![\Gamma]\!]_{\mathsf{FV}(\psi)\cup var} \land \psi)\}$
           $\text{where } X = \mathsf{FV}([\![\Gamma]\!]_{\mathsf{FV}(\psi)\cup var} \land \psi) \setminus var$
  $|\ x : T_1 \to T_2\quad \Rightarrow$
      $\mathbf{let}\ T'_{1,} = \mathsf{necessType}(\Gamma \vdash T_1,\; var)\ \mathbf{in}$
      $\mathbf{let}\ T'_{2,} = \mathsf{suffType}((\Gamma; x : T'_1) \vdash T_2,\; var \cup \{x\})\ \mathbf{in}$
      $x : T'_1 \to T'_2$

Fig. 10. The algorithm for Step 2.2

Using the equations on the lefthand side of $\Rightarrow$, the righthand side can be rewritten as follows.

$$\mathtt{len}\ \nu = \mathtt{len}\ l \land \mathtt{elems}\ \nu = \mathtt{elems}\ l$$
$$\leadsto \mathtt{len}\ \nu = \mathtt{len}\ z \land \mathtt{elems}\ \nu = \mathtt{elems}\ z \qquad (\text{by } z = l)$$
$$\leadsto \mathtt{len}\ \nu = \mathtt{len}\ xs + 1 \land \mathtt{elems}\ \nu = \mathtt{elems}\ xs + [x]$$
$$(\text{by } \mathtt{len}\ xs + 1 = \mathtt{len}\ z, \mathtt{elems}\ xs + [x] = \mathtt{elems}\ z)$$
$$\leadsto \mathtt{len}\ \nu = \mathtt{len}\ ys + 1 \land \mathtt{elems}\ \nu = \mathtt{elems}\ ys + [y]$$
$$(\text{by } x = y, \mathtt{len}\ ys = \mathtt{len}\ xs, \mathtt{elems}\ ys = \mathtt{elems}\ xs)$$

$y : \{Int \mid P_1\}$
$\rightarrow ys : \{\texttt{List}\langle \lambda x \lambda y.x \leq y\rangle \ \{Int \mid P_2\} \mid P_3\}$
$\rightarrow \{\texttt{List}\langle \lambda x \lambda y.x \leq y\rangle \ \{Int \mid P_4\} \mid P_5\}$

$P_1 \equiv \exists x, xs, z.(\llbracket \Gamma_1 \rrbracket_{\{x\}} \wedge \nu = x), \ P_2 \equiv \exists x, xs, z, l.(\llbracket \Gamma_2 \rrbracket_{\{x,y\}} \wedge x \leq \nu),$
$P_3 \equiv \exists x, xs, z, l.(\llbracket \Gamma_2 \rrbracket_{\{xs,y\}} \wedge \texttt{len } \nu = \texttt{len } xs \wedge \texttt{elems } \nu = \texttt{elems } xs),$
$P_4 \equiv \forall x, xs, z, l.(\llbracket \Gamma_3 \rrbracket_{\{y,ys\}} \Rightarrow \texttt{True})$
$P_5 \equiv \forall x, xs, z, l.(\llbracket \Gamma_3 \rrbracket_{\{l,y,ys\}} \Rightarrow \texttt{len } \nu = \texttt{len } l \wedge \texttt{elems } \nu = \texttt{elems } l)$
where
$\Gamma_1 \equiv \Gamma, \ \Gamma_2 \equiv \Gamma; \ y : \{Int \mid \nu = x\}$
$\Gamma_3 \equiv \Gamma_2; \ ys : \{\texttt{List}\langle \lambda x \lambda y.x \leq y\rangle \ \{Int \mid \nu \leq x\} \mid$
$\qquad \texttt{len } \nu = \texttt{len } xs \wedge \texttt{elems } \nu = \texttt{elems } xs\}$

$\llbracket \Gamma_1 \rrbracket_{\{x\}} \equiv z = l \wedge \texttt{ len } xs + 1 = \texttt{len } z \wedge \texttt{elems } xs + [x] = \texttt{elems } z$
$\llbracket \Gamma_2 \rrbracket_{\{x,y\}} \equiv \llbracket \Gamma_2 \rrbracket_{\{xs,y\}} \equiv$
$\qquad z = l \wedge \texttt{ len } xs + 1 = \texttt{len } z \wedge \texttt{elems } xs + [x] = \texttt{elems } z \wedge y = x$
$\llbracket \Gamma_3 \rrbracket_{\{y,ys\}} \equiv \llbracket \Gamma_3 \rrbracket_{\{l,y,ys\}} \equiv$
$\qquad z = l \wedge \texttt{ len } xs + 1 = \texttt{len } z \wedge \texttt{elems } xs + [x] = \texttt{elems } z \wedge y = x$
$\qquad \wedge \texttt{len } ys = \texttt{len } xs \wedge \texttt{elems } ys = \texttt{elems } xs$

Fig. 11. An example output of Step 2.2

Since the resulting formula does not contain quantified variables, we obtain $\texttt{len } \nu = \texttt{len } ys + 1 \wedge \texttt{elems } \nu = \texttt{elems } ys + [y]$ as a sound approximation of P_5. We can eliminate quantifiers from $P_1, \ldots, P_4$ in a similar manner, and obtain the following type for auxiliary function $\Box_2$.

$\Box_2 :: y : Int \rightarrow ys : \texttt{List}\langle \lambda x \lambda y.x \leq y\rangle \ Int \rightarrow$
$\qquad \{\texttt{List}\langle \lambda x \lambda y.x \leq y\rangle \ Int \mid \texttt{len } \nu = \texttt{len } ys + 1 \wedge \texttt{elems } \nu = \texttt{elems } ys + [y]\}$

$\Box$

Though the naive algorithm above may be effective for formulas consisting of equality constraints, it is not so for formulas containing other constraints. For example, $\exists y.(\texttt{len } x \leq 1 + \texttt{len } y \wedge 2 \times \texttt{len } y \leq z)$ is equivalent to $2 \times \texttt{len } x \leq 2 + z$, but the naive algorithm obviously fails to output it, as there is no equality information available. The second method we discuss below first eliminates uninterpreted function symbols, and then applies quantifier elimination to the formula without uninterpreted function symbols. Consider the following formula (which is a twisted version of the formula above):

$$\exists y, w.(\texttt{len } x \leq 1 + \texttt{len } y \wedge y = w \wedge 2 \times \texttt{len } w \leq z).$$

We first pick equality constraints; $y = w$ in the case above. For each equality constraint $v_1 = v_2$, we add equalities of the form

$$E[v_1] = E[v_2]$$

$$\begin{aligned}
&\texttt{infer\_aux\_types}(\Gamma \vdash t_\Box :: T)\{ \\
&\quad \{\Gamma_1 \vdash \Box_1 :: T_1, \ldots, \Gamma_k \vdash \Box_k :: T_k\} \leftarrow \texttt{step2.1}(\Gamma \vdash t_\Box :: T); \\
&\quad \texttt{foreach } \Gamma_i \vdash \Box_i :: T_i \texttt{ do } \{ \\
&\qquad T_i' \leftarrow \texttt{step2.2}(\Gamma_i \vdash T_i); \\
&\qquad T_{\Box_i} \leftarrow \texttt{step2.3}(T_i')\}; \\
&\quad \texttt{return } \{\Box_1 : T_{\Box_1}, \ldots, \Box_k : T_{\Box_k}\}; \\
&\}
\end{aligned}$$

Fig. 12. Step 2

whenever the term $E[v_1]$ or $E[v_2]$ occurs in the formula. In the example above, we obtain

$$\exists y, w.(\texttt{len}\, x \leq 1 + \texttt{len}\, y \wedge y = w \wedge 2 \times \texttt{len}\, w \leq z \wedge \texttt{len}\, y = \texttt{len}\, w)).$$

We then replace each term t constructed by uninterpreted function symbols with a fresh variable v_t.

$$\exists y, w, v_{\texttt{len}\, y}, v_{\texttt{len}\, w}.(v_{\texttt{len}\, x} \leq 1 + v_{\texttt{len}\, y} \wedge y = w \wedge 2 \times v_{\texttt{len}\, w} \leq z \wedge v_{\texttt{len}\, y} = v_{\texttt{len}\, w}).$$

Note that the resulting formula is weaker than the original formula, because we have lost correlations between, e.g., x and $v_{\texttt{len}\, x}$. In general, an existential formula (a universal formula, resp.) may be replaced by a weaker (a stronger, resp.) formula, but this is what we need for the soundness of our quantifier elimination. In the example above, we can now apply quantifier elimination for linear integer arithmetic, and obtain $2 \times v_{\texttt{len}\, x} \leq 2 + z$. Finally, by recovering terms containing uninterpreted function symbols, we obtain $2 \times \texttt{len}\, x \leq 2 + z$, as required. This approach would be effective in particular when the underlying logic is a logic L extended with uninterpreted function symbols, such that a complete quantifier elimination procedure exists for L.

Soundness of Step 2. The whole procedure for Step 2 is summarized in Fig. 12; step-2.3 is one of the sound but incomplete quantifier procedures discussed above. Theorem 3 below states soundness of the procedure. The first property states that the inferred types are closed (so that they can be passed to SYNQUID), and the second one implies that if we can find auxiliary functions of the inferred types, we can obtain a target function of type T by filling the template t with the auxiliary functions.

Theorem 3. *Given* $\{\Box_i : T_{\Box_i}\} = \mathsf{infer\_aux\_types}(\Gamma \vdash t :: T)$, *the following properties hold.*

1. $\mathsf{FV}(T_{\Box_i}) = \emptyset$
2. $(\Gamma; \Box_i : T_{\Box_i}) \vdash t :: T$

3.3   Step 3: Synthesizing Auxiliary Function Using Synquid

Finally, we pass to SYNQUID the types of auxiliary functions inferred in Step 2 (Sect. 3.2). By filling the template with the auxiliary functions, we obtain a required target function. If SYNQUID fails to discover auxiliary functions (this can happen either if the types inferred in Step 2 are not inhabited by any programs, or if they are inhabited but SYNQUID is not powerful enough to find inhabitants), we go back to Step 1 and try another template.

$$f = \lambda l. \; \mathtt{match} \; l \; \mathtt{with}$$
$$\mathtt{Nil} \mapsto \square_1$$
$$| \; \mathtt{Cons} \; x \; \mathtt{Nil} \mapsto \square_2 \; x$$
$$| \; \mathtt{Cons} \; x \; xs \mapsto (\mathtt{match} \; (\square_3 \; l) \; \mathtt{with} \; \mathtt{Pair} \; l_1 \; l_2 \mapsto append \; (f \; l_1) \; (f \; l_2))$$

Fig. 13. An invalid divide-and-conquer template

3.4   Limitations

Our procedure for program synthesis may fail for various reasons, due to limitations of each step. First, the syntax of templates in Fig. 8 is rather restricted. For example, consider another divide-conquer template shown in Fig. 13, which is obtained by replacing *split* of the divide-and-conquer template in Sect. 3.1 with a hole, and instead instantiating $\square_3$ to the append function. This template is invalid due to the position in which $\square_3$ occurs; if it were valid, we would be able to obtain a quick sort function, by instantiating $\square_3$ with the partition function. Unfortunately allowing this (invalid) template is problematic for type inference in Step 2.1. A problem is that, in order to conclude that the subterm $append \; (f \; l_1) \; (f \; l_2)$ returns a sorted list, we need to infer that all the elements of l_1 are no greater than those of l_2. It is not clear at all how to infer such information from the specification of f.

The other sources of failures of our program synthesis include the incompleteness of the quantifier elimination procedure in Step 2.3, and limitations of the backend tool SYNQUID used in Step 3.

4   Implementation and Experiments

We have implemented a prototype program synthesis tool based on our method. The tool is written in OCaml and uses SYNQUID [8,9] for the final step of our method.

We have run our tool and compared it with SYNQUID for several problems of synthesizing programs that manipulate lists and binary search trees. We have checked the standard libraries of functional languages such as the list library of Haskell, and chosen, as the benchmark problems, library functions whose specifications can be expressed by refinement types and whose implementations are expected to require auxiliary functions. In all the problems, no information

Table 1. Experimental results (times are in seconds).

Programs	Our method			SYNQUID	SYNQUID + foldr
	Total	Type-infer	Synquid	Total	Total
list-intersect	1.290	0.166	1.103	-	-
list-sub	0.603	0.110	0.478	-	-
list-to-bst	1.934	0.059	1.860	-	-
list-sort	0.910	0.105	0.791	-	3.931
list-reverse	0.574	0.104	0.457	-	-
list-unique	0.568	0.101	0.455	-	2.937
list-concat	0.466	0.052	0.400	-	-
bst-to-list	2.752	0.091	2.644	-	-
list-mergeSort	5.865	0.207	5.655	-	N/A

about auxiliary functions was given to our tool and SYNQUID. Our tool uses the fold-style templates and the divide-conquer template discussed in Sect. 3.1. The experiment was conducted on a machine with 1.8 GHz Intel Core i5 (8 GB of memory).

The experimental results are summarized in Table 1. The column "programs" shows the names of functions to synthesize. We briefly describe them below.

- list-intersect: given two sets (represented as lists), returns the intersection.
- list-sub: given two sets (represented as lists), returns the difference.
- list-to-bst: converts a list to a binary search tree.
- list-sort: sorts a list.
- list-reverse: reverses a list.
- list-unique: removes duplicate elements in a list.
- list-concat: flattens a list of lists.
- bst-to-list: converts a binary search tree to a list.
- list-mergeSort: sorts a list; the divide-conquer pattern is used as the default template.

The fold-style template was used as the default template, except for the last one. The three sub-columns in the column "our method" respectively show the total execution time, the time spent for the inference of the types of auxiliary functions (in Steps 1 and 2 in Sect. 3), and the time spent by SYNQUID (in Step 3 in Sect. 3). The cell "-" represents a failure. The column "SYNQUID" shows the result of running SYNQUID with no hints, and "SYNQUID+foldr" shows the result of running SYNQUID with the type of the fold-right function (shown in Fig. 14) as a hint (so that SYNQUID can use the fold-right function in the target functions). The latter is based on the method for discovering auxiliary functions as proposed by Polikarpova [9]. The result "N/A" for list-mergeSort means "non-applicable"; given the type of the fold-right function, SYNQUID synthesizes an insertion sort program instead of a merge sort program.

$foldr :: \langle p :: \text{List } \beta \to \gamma \to \text{Bool} \rangle.$

$\quad f : (t : \text{List } \beta \to h : \beta \to acc : \{\gamma \mid p\ t\ \nu\} \to \{\gamma \mid p\ (\text{Cons } h\ t)\ \nu\})$

$\quad \to seed : \{\gamma \mid p\ \text{Nil}\ \nu\} \to ys : \text{List } \beta \to \{\gamma \mid p\ ys\ \nu\}$

Fig. 14. The type of the fold-right function [9]

As the table shows, our tool could successfully synthesize all the programs. In contrast, SYNQUID could synthesize none of the benchmark programs; it is as expected, because the benchmark programs require auxiliary functions. It may come as a surprise that, even given the type of the fold-right function, SYNQUID could synthesize only two of the benchmark programs. This is because of the limitation that the full behavior of the fold-right function is not expressed by its type, The type in Fig. 14 is quite general: roughly, it describes that, for any predicate p on a list of elements of type β and a value of type γ, *foldr f seed ys* returns a value r such that $p\ ys\ r$, provided that p Nil *seed* holds and the accumulation function f preserves the invariant p between an input list and the corresponding output. The type still fails to describe certain information about the behavior of fold-right; for example, the type of the first argument f does not directly express the relationship between the accumulation parameter *acc* and the return value.

5   Related Work

We have already discussed the work of Polikarpova et al. [9], which we have extended to enable synthesis of programs with auxiliary functions. There are other studies of automated synthesis of functional programs [2,6,7,9,11], but we are not aware of previous methods that can automatically synthesize auxiliary functions from the specification of a main function alone. Kneuss et al. [6] discuss the synthesis of a merge sort function from a user-supplied template similar to our divide-and-conquer template, but they also require that the specification of the auxiliary function "merge" be provided by a user.

To express precise specifications of target functions, we have borrowed the type system of Polikarpova et al. [9], which is in turn based on Vazou et al.'s type system with abstract refinement types [12].

In the context of automated theorem proving, there have been studies on techniques for automated discovery of lemmas [1,5]. Through the Curry-Howard correspondence between proofs and programs, lemmas correspond to auxiliary functions; thus, we plan to investigate the techniques for lemma discovery to refine our method.

6   Conclusion

We have proposed a method for automatically synthesizing functional programs that require auxiliary functions. We have implemented a prototype synthesis tool that uses SYNQUID as a backend, and confirmed that it is able to synthesize several functions with auxiliary functions. Overcoming the limitations discussed in Sect. 3.4 is left for future work.

Acknowledgments. We would like to thank anonymous referees for useful comments. This work was supported by JSPS KAKENHI Grant Number JP15H05706 and JP16K16004.

Appendix

A   Well-Formedness of Types and Type Environments

A formula ψ is *well formed* in the environment Γ, written $\Gamma \vdash \psi$, when it has a boolean sort under the assumption that each free variable in ψ has the sort declared in Γ.

The well-formedness relations on types and type environments, $\Gamma \vdash T$ and $\vdash \Gamma$ respectively, are defined by the rules given below.

$$\frac{\Gamma; \nu : B \vdash \psi}{\Gamma \vdash \{B \mid \psi\}} \ (\text{WFT-Sc}) \qquad\qquad \frac{\Gamma; C \vdash T}{\Gamma \vdash \texttt{let } C \texttt{ in } T} $$
$$(\text{WFT-Ctx})$$

$$\frac{\Gamma \vdash \{B \mid \psi\} \qquad \Gamma; x : \{B \mid \psi\} \vdash T}{\Gamma \vdash x : \{B \mid \psi\} \to T} \quad (\text{WFT-Fun1})$$

$$\frac{T_x \text{ is not of the form } \{B \mid \psi\} \qquad \Gamma \vdash T_x \qquad \Gamma \vdash T}{\Gamma \vdash x : T_x \to T}$$
$$(\text{WFT-Fun2})$$

$$\frac{}{\vdash \emptyset} \qquad (\text{WFTE-Emp})$$

$$\frac{\vdash \Gamma \qquad \Gamma \vdash T \qquad x \text{ does not occur in } \Gamma}{\vdash \Gamma; x : T} \quad (\text{WFTE-T})$$

$$\frac{\vdash \Gamma \qquad \Gamma \vdash \psi}{\vdash \Gamma; \psi} \qquad (\text{WFTE-P})$$

References

1. Aoto, T.: Sound lemma generation for proving inductive validity of equations. In: Hariharan, R., Mukund, M., Vinay, V. (eds.) IARCS Annual Conference on Foundations of Software Technology and Theoretical Computer Science, FSTTCS 2008, Bangalore, India, 9–11 December 2008. LIPIcs, vol. 2, pp. 13–24. Schloss Dagstuhl - Leibniz-Zentrum fuer Informatik (2008)

2. Frankle, J., Osera, P., Walker, D., Zdancewic, S.: Example-directed synthesis: a type-theoretic interpretation. In: Bodík, R., Majumdar, R. (eds.) Proceedings of the 43rd Annual ACM SIGPLAN-SIGACT Symposium on Principles of Programming Languages, POPL 2016, St. Petersburg, FL, USA, 20–22 January 2016, pp. 802–815. ACM (2016)
3. Gulwani, S., Harris, W.R., Singh, R.: Spreadsheet data manipulation using examples. Commun. ACM **55**(8), 97–105 (2012)
4. Gulwani, S., Jha, S., Tiwari, A., Venkatesan, R.: Synthesis of loop-free programs. In: Hall, M.W., Padua, D.A. (eds.) Proceedings of the 32nd ACM SIGPLAN Conference on Programming Language Design and Implementation, PLDI 2011, San Jose, CA, USA, 4–8 June 2011, pp. 62–73. ACM (2011)
5. Kapur, D., Subramaniam, M.: Lemma discovery in automating induction. In: McRobbie, M.A., Slaney, J.K. (eds.) CADE 1996. LNCS, vol. 1104, pp. 538–552. Springer, Heidelberg (1996). https://doi.org/10.1007/3-540-61511-3_112
6. Kneuss, E., Kuraj, I., Kuncak, V., Suter, P.: Synthesis modulo recursive functions. In: Hosking, A.L., Eugster, P.T., Lopes, C.V. (eds.) Proceedings of the 2013 ACM SIGPLAN International Conference on Object Oriented Programming Systems Languages & Applications, OOPSLA 2013, part of SPLASH 2013, Indianapolis, IN, USA, 26–31 October 2013, pp. 407–426. ACM (2013)
7. Osera, P., Zdancewic, S.: Type-and-example-directed program synthesis. In: Grove, D., Blackburn, S. (eds.) Proceedings of the 36th ACM SIGPLAN Conference on Programming Language Design and Implementation, Portland, OR, USA, 15–17 June 2015, pp. 619–630. ACM (2015)
8. Polikaropova, N.: Synquid. https://bitbucket.org/nadiapolikarpova/synquid/
9. Polikarpova, N., Kuraj, I., Solar-Lezama, A.: Program synthesis from polymorphic refinement types. ACM SIGPLAN Not. **51**(6), 522–538 (2016)
10. Shingo, E., Kobayashi, N., Tsukada, T.: Automated synthesis of functional programs with auxiliary functions. http://www-kb.is.s.u-tokyo.ac.jp/~koba/papers/aplas18-long.pdf
11. Solar-Lezama, A.: Program synthesis by sketching. Ph.D. thesis, University of California, Berkeley (2008)
12. Vazou, N., Rondon, P.M., Jhala, R.: Abstract refinement types. In: Felleisen, M., Gardner, P. (eds.) ESOP 2013. LNCS, vol. 7792, pp. 209–228. Springer, Heidelberg (2013). https://doi.org/10.1007/978-3-642-37036-6_13

Verification

Modular Verification of SPARCv8 Code

Junpeng Zha[1], Xinyu Feng[2(✉)], and Lei Qiao[3]

[1] University of Science and Technology of China, Hefei, China
[2] State Key Laboratory for Novel Software Technology, Nanjing University,
Nanjing, China
xyfeng@nju.edu.cn
[3] Beijing Institute of Control Engineering, Beijing, China

Abstract. Inline assembly code is common in system software to interact with the underlying hardware platforms. Safety and correctness of
the assembly code is crucial to guarantee the safety of the whole system. In this paper we propose a practical Hoare-style program logic for
verifying SPARC assembly code. The logic supports modular reasoning about the main features of SPARCv8 ISA, including delayed control
transfers, delayed writes to special registers, and register windows. We
have applied it to verify the main body of a context switch routine in a
realistic embedded OS kernel. All of the formalization and proofs have
been mechanized in Coq.

1 Introduction

Operating system kernels are at the most foundational layer of computer software
systems. To interact directly with hardware, many important components in OS
kernels are implemented in assembly, such as the context switch code or the
code that manages interrupts. Their correctness is crucial to ensure the safety
and security of the whole system. However, assembly code verification remains a
challenging task in existing work on OS kernel verification (*e.g.* [8,9,18]), where
the assembly code is either unverified or verified based on operational semantics
without a general program logic.

SPARC (Scalable Processor ARChitecture) is a CPU instruction set architecture (ISA) with high-performance and great flexibility [2]. It has been widely used
in various processors for workstations and embedded systems. The SPARCv8
ISA has some interesting features, which make it a non-trivial task to design a
Hoare-style program logic for assembly code.

- *Delayed control transfers.* SPARCv8 has two program counters pc and npc.
  The npc register points to the next instruction to run. Control-transfer
  instructions in SPARCv8 change npc instead of pc to the target program
  point, while pc takes the original value of npc. This makes the control transfer
  to happen one cycle later than the execution of the control transfer instructions.

This work is supported in part by grants from National Natural Science Foundation
of China (NSFC) under Grant Nos. 61632005, 61502442 and 61502031.

S. Ryu (Ed.): APLAS 2018, LNCS 11275, pp. 245–263, 2018.
https://doi.org/10.1007/978-3-030-02768-1_14

```
      CALLER :                              ChangeY :

           . . .                            5    rd   Y, %l₀
      1    mov   1, %o₀                     6    wr   %i₀, 0, Y
      2    call  ChangeY                    7    nop
      3    save  %sp, −64, %sp              8    nop
      4    mov   %o₀, %l₀                   9    nop
           . . .                            10   ret
                                            11   restore  %l₀, 0, %o₀
```

Fig. 1. An example for SPARC code

- *Delayed writes.* The wr instruction that writes a special class of registers does not take effect immediately. Instead the write operation is buffered and then executed X cycles later, where X is a predefined system parameter which usually ranges from 0 to 3.
- *Register windows.* SPARCv8 uses register windows and the window rotation mechanism to avoid saving contexts in the stack directly and achieves high performance in context management.

We use a simple example in Fig. 1 to show these three features. The function CALLER calls ChangeY, which updates the special register Y and returns its original value.

ChangeY requires an input parameter as the new value for the special register Y. CALLER calls ChangeY at line 2, and pc and npc point to line 2 and 3 respectively at this moment. The call instruction changes the value of pc to npc and let npc points to ChangeY at line 5, which means the control-flow will not transfer to ChangeY in the next cycle, but in the cycle after the execution of the save instruction following the call. Similarly, when ChangeY returns (at line 10), the control is transferred back to the caller after executing the restore instruction at line 11. We call this feature "delayed control transfers".

SPARCv8 uses the save instruction (at line 3 in the example) to save the current context and restore (at line 10) to restore it. Its 32 general registers are split into four logic groups as global (r_0–r_7), out (r_8–r_{15}), local (r_{16}–r_{23}) and in (r_{24}–r_{31}) registers. Correspondingly, we give aliases "%g₀–%g₇", "%o₀–%o₇", "%l₀–%l₇" and "%i₀–%i₇" for these groups respectively. The out, local and in registers form the *current register window*. The local registers are for private use in the current context. The in and out registers are shared with adjacent register windows for parameters passing. The save instruction rotates the register window from the current one to the next. Then the local and in registers in the original window are no longer accessible, and the original out registers becomes the in registers in the current window. The restore instruction does the inverse. The arguments taken by the save and restore instructions are irrelevant here and can be ignored.

At line 6, the wr instruction tries to update the special register Y with the value of $\%i_0 \oplus 0$ (bitwise exclusive OR). However, the write is delayed for X cycles, where X is some predefined system parameter that ranges from 0 to 3. For portability, programmers usually do not rely on the exact value of X and assume it takes the maximum value 3. Therefore three nop instructions are inserted. Reading of Y earlier than line 9 may give us the old value. This feature is called "delayed writes".

These features make the semantics of the SPARCv8 code context-dependent. For instance, a read of a special register (*e.g.* the register Y in the above example) needs to make sure there are enough instructions executed since the most recent *delayed* write. As another example, the instruction following the call can be any instruction in general, but it is not supposed to update the register r_{15}, which contains the return address saved by the call instruction. In addition, the delayed control transfer and the register windows also allow highly flexible calling conventions. Together, they make it a challenging task to have a Hoare-style program logic for local and modular reasoning of SPARCv8 assembly code.

Working towards a fully certified OS kernel for aerospace crafts whose inline assembly is written in SPARCv8, we try to address these challenges and propose a practical program logic for realistically modelled SPARCv8 code. We have applied our logic to verify the main body of the task context switch routine in the kernel. Our work is based on earlier work on assembly code verification but makes the following contributions:

- Our logic supports all the above features of SPARCv8. We redefine basic blocks to include the instruction following the jump or return as the tail of a block, which models the delayed control transfer. To reason about delayed writes, we introduce a modal assertion $\triangleright_t \mathtt{sr} \mapsto w$, saying that the special register sr will hold the value w in up to t cycles. We also give logic rules for save and restore instructions that do register window rotation.
- Following SCAP [7], our logic supports modular reasoning of function calls in a direct-style. We use the standard pre- and post-conditions as function specifications, instead of the binary assertion g used in SCAP. This allows us to reuse existing techniques (*e.g.* Coq tactics) to simplify the program verification process. The logic rules for function call and return is general and independent of any specific calling convention.
- We give direct-style semantic interpretation for the logic judgments, based on which we establish the soundness. This is different from previous work, which either does syntactic-based soundness proof (*e.g.* SCAP [7]) or treats return code pointers as first-class code pointers and gives CPS-style semantics. Those approaches for soundness make it difficult to verify the interaction between the inline assembly and the C code in the kernel, the latter being verified following a direct-style program logic.
- Context switch of concurrent tasks is an important component in OS kernels. It is usually implemented as inline assembly because of the need to access registers and the stack. We verify the main body of the context switch routine in a realistic embedded OS kernel for aerospace crafts, which consists of around 250 lines of SPARCv8 code.

(Word)	w, $\mathtt{f}$, l	$\in$	Int32				
(Prog)	P	$::=$	$(C, S, \mathtt{pc}, \mathtt{npc})$	(CodeHeap)	C	$\in$	Word $\rightharpoonup$ Comm
(State)	S	$::=$	(M, Q, D)	(RState)	Q	$::=$	(R, F)
(Memory)	M	$\in$	Word $\rightharpoonup$ Word	(ProgCount)	$\mathtt{pc}$, $\mathtt{npc}$	$\in$	Word
(OpExp)	o	$::=$	$\mathtt{r} \mid w$	(AddrExp)	a	$::=$	$\mathtt{o} \mid \mathtt{r} + \mathtt{o}$

(Comm)	c	$::=$	$\mathtt{i} \mid \mathtt{call}\ \mathtt{f} \mid \mathtt{jmp}\ \mathtt{a} \mid \mathtt{retl} \mid \mathtt{be}\ \mathtt{f}$
(SimpIns)	i	$::=$	$\mathtt{ld}\ \mathtt{a}\ \mathtt{r}_d \mid \mathtt{st}\ \mathtt{r}_s\ \mathtt{a} \mid \mathtt{nop} \mid \mathtt{save}\ \mathtt{r}_s\ \mathtt{o}\ \mathtt{r}_d \mid \mathtt{restore}\ \mathtt{r}_s\ \mathtt{o}\ \mathtt{r}_d$
			$\mid\ \mathtt{add}\ \mathtt{r}_s\ \mathtt{o}\ \mathtt{r}_d \mid \mathtt{rd}\ \mathtt{sr}\ \mathtt{r}_d \mid \mathtt{wr}\ \mathtt{r}_s\ \mathtt{o}\ \mathtt{sr} \mid \ldots$
(InstrSeq)	$\mathbb{I}$	$::=$	$\mathtt{i};\ \mathbb{I} \mid \mathtt{jmp}\ \mathtt{a};\ \mathtt{i} \mid \mathtt{call}\ \mathtt{f};\ \mathtt{i}; \mathbb{I} \mid \mathtt{retl};\ \mathtt{i} \mid \mathtt{be}\ \mathtt{f};\ \mathtt{i};\ \mathbb{I}$

Fig. 2. Machine states and language for SPARCv8 code

The program logic, its soundness proof and the verification of the context switch module have been mechanized in Coq [1].

In the rest of paper, we present the program model and operational semantics of SPARCv8 in Sect. 2. Then we propose the program logic in Sect. 3, including the inference rules and the soundness proof. We show the verification of the main body of the context switch routine in Sect. 4. Finally we discuss more on related work and conclude in Sect. 5.

2   The SPARCv8 Assembly Language

We introduce the key SPARCv8 instructions, the model of machine states, and the operational semantics in this section.

2.1   Language Syntax and States

The machine model and syntax of SPARCv8 assembly language are defined in Fig. 2. The whole program configuration P consists of the code heap C, the machine state S, and the program counters $\mathtt{pc}$ and $\mathtt{npc}$. The code heap C is a partial function from labels $\mathtt{f}$ to commands c. Labels are 32-bit integers (called *words*), which can be viewed as memory addresses where the commands are saved. Commands in SPARCv8 can be classified into two categories, the simple instructions $\mathtt{i}$ and the control-transfer instructions like $\mathtt{call}$ and $\mathtt{jmp}$.

The machine state S consists of three parts: the memory M, the register state Q which is a pair of register file R and frame list F, and the delay buffer D. As defined in Fig. 3, R is a partial mapping from register names to words. Registers include the general registers $\mathtt{r}$, the processor state register $\mathtt{psr}$ and the special registers $\mathtt{sr}$. The processor state register $\mathtt{psr}$ contains the integer condition code fields $\mathtt{n}$, $\mathtt{z}$, $\mathtt{v}$ and $\mathtt{c}$, which can be modified by the arithmetic and logical instructions and used for conditional control-transfer, and $\mathtt{cwp}$ recording the id of the current register window. We explain the frame list F and the delay buffer D below.

(RegFile) $R \in \text{RegName} \rightharpoonup \text{Word}$ (RegName) $\text{rn} ::= r_0 \mid \ldots \mid r_{31} \mid \text{psr} \mid \text{sr}$

(PsrReg) $\text{psr} ::= \text{n} \mid \text{z} \mid \text{v} \mid \text{c} \mid \text{cwp}$ (SpeReg) $\text{sr} ::= \text{wim} \mid \text{Y} \mid \text{asr}_0 \mid \ldots \mid \text{asr}_{31}$

(FrameList) $F ::= \text{nil} \mid \text{fm}::F$ (Frame) $\text{fm} := [w_0, \ldots, w_7]$

(DelayBuff) $D ::= \text{nil} \mid (t, \text{sr}, w)::D$ (DelayCycle) $t \in \{0, 1, \ldots, X\}$

Fig. 3. Register file, frame list and DelayBuffer

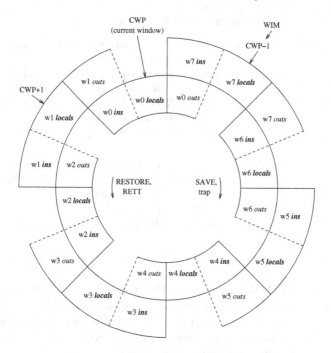

Fig. 4. Register windows (figure taken from [2])

Register Windows and Frame List. SPARCv8 provides 32 general registers, which are split into four groups as global (r_0–r_7), out (r_8–r_{15}), local(r_{16}–r_{23}) and in (r_{24}–r_{31}) registers. The latter three groups (out, local and in) form the current *register window*.

At the entry and exit of functions and traps, one may need to save and restore some of the general registers as execution contexts. Instead of saving them into stacks in memory, SPARCv8 uses multiple register windows to form a circular stack, and does window rotation for efficient context save and restore. As shown in Fig. 4, there are N register windows ($N = 8$ here) consisting of $2 \times N$ groups of registers (each group containing 8 registers). The cwp register (part of psr) records the id number of the current window (cwp = 0 in this example).

The in and out registers of each window are shared with its adjacent windows for parameter passing. For example, the in registers of the w_0 is the out registers of the w_1, and the out registers of the w_0 is the in registers of the w_7. This explains why we need only $2 \times N$ groups of registers for N windows, while each window consisting of three groups (out, local and in).

$$\text{out} \triangleq [\mathtt{r_8}, \ldots, \mathtt{r_{15}}] \qquad \text{local} \triangleq [\mathtt{r_{16}}, \ldots, \mathtt{r_{23}}] \qquad \text{in} \triangleq [\mathtt{r_{24}}, \ldots, \mathtt{r_{31}}]$$

$$R([\mathtt{r}_i, \ldots, \mathtt{r}_{i+k}]) \triangleq [R(\mathtt{r}_i), \ldots, R(\mathtt{r}_{i+k})]$$

$$R\{[\mathtt{r}_i, \ldots, \mathtt{r}_{i+7}] \rightsquigarrow \text{fm}\} \triangleq R\{\mathtt{r}_i \rightsquigarrow w_0\} \ldots \{\mathtt{r}_{i+7} \rightsquigarrow w_7\}$$
$$\text{where} \quad \text{fm} = [w_0, \ldots, w_7]$$

$$\mathbf{win\_valid}(w_{id}, R) \triangleq 2^{w_{id}} \,\&\, R(\mathtt{wim}) = 0$$
$$\text{where \& is the bitwise AND operation.}$$

$$\mathbf{next\_cwp}(w_{id}) \triangleq (w_{id} + N - 1)\%N \qquad \mathbf{prev\_cwp}(w_{id}) \triangleq (w_{id} + 1)\%N$$

$$\mathbf{save}(R, F) \triangleq \begin{cases} (R', F') & \text{if } w'_{id} = \mathbf{next\_cwp}(R(\mathtt{cwp})),\, \mathbf{win\_valid}(w'_{id}, R), \\ & F = F'' \cdot \text{fm}_1 \cdot \text{fm}_2,\; F' = R(\text{local}) :: R(\text{in}) :: F'', \\ & R'' = R\{\text{in} \rightsquigarrow R(\text{out}), \text{local} \rightsquigarrow \text{fm}_2, \text{out} \rightsquigarrow \text{fm}_1\}, \\ & R' = R''\{\mathtt{cwp} \rightsquigarrow w'_{id}\}, \\ \bot & \text{if } \neg\mathbf{win\_valid}(\mathbf{next\_cwp}(R(\mathtt{cwp})), R) \end{cases}$$

$$\mathbf{restore}(R, F) \triangleq \begin{cases} (R', F') & \text{if } w'_{id} = \mathbf{prev\_cwp}(R(\mathtt{cwp})),\, \mathbf{win\_valid}(w'_{id}, R), \\ & F = \text{fm}_1 :: \text{fm}_2 :: F'',\; F' = F'' \cdot R(\text{out}) \cdot R(\text{local}), \\ & R'' = R\{\text{in} \rightsquigarrow \text{fm}_2, \text{local} \rightsquigarrow \text{fm}_1, \text{out} \rightsquigarrow R(\text{in})\}, \\ & R' = R''\{\mathtt{cwp} \rightsquigarrow w'_{id}\}, \\ \bot & \text{if } \neg\mathbf{win\_valid}(\mathbf{prev\_cwp}(R(\mathtt{cwp})), R) \end{cases}$$

Fig. 5. Auxiliary definitions for instruction save and restore

To save the context, the save instruction rotates the window by decrements the cwp pointer (modulo N). So w_7 becomes the current window. The out registers of w_0 becomes the in registers of w_7. The in and local registers of w_0 become inaccessible. This is like pushing them onto the circular stack. The restore instruction does the inverse, which is like a stack pop.

The wim register is used as a bit vector to record the end of the stack. Each bit in wim corresponds to a register window. The bit corresponding to the last available window is set to 1, which means *invalid*. All other bits are 0 (*i.e. valid*). When executing save (and restore), we need to ensure the next window is valid. We use the assertion $\mathbf{win\_valid}(w_{id}, R)$ defined in Fig. 5 to say the window pointed to by w_{id} is valid, given the value of wim in R.

We use the frame list F to model the circular stack consisting of register windows. As defined in Fig. 3, a frame is an array of 8 words, modeling a group of 8 registers. F consists of a sequence of frames corresponding to all the register windows except the out, local and in registers in the current window. Then save saves the local and in registers onto the head of F and loads the two groups of register at the *tail* of F to the local and out registers (and the original out registers becomes the in group). The restore instruction does the inverse. The operations are defined formally in Fig. 5.

The Delay Buffer. The delay buffer D is a sequence of delayed writes. Because the wr instruction does not update the target register immediately, we put the write operation onto the delay buffer. A delayed write is recorded as a triple consisting of the remaining cycles t to be delayed, the target special register sr and the value w to be written.

Instruction Sequences. We use an instruction sequence $\mathbb{I}$ to model a basic block, *i.e.* a sequence of commands ending with a control transfer. As defined in Fig. 2, we require that a delayed control-transfer instruction must be followed by a simple instruction i, because the actual control-transfer occurs after the execution of i. The end of each instruction sequence can only be jmp or retl followed by a simple instruction i. Note that we do not view the call instruction as the end of a basic block, since the callee is expected to return, following our direct-style semantics for function calls. We define $C[\mathtt{f}]$ to extract an instruction sequence starting from f in C below.

$$
C[\mathtt{f}] =
\begin{cases}
\mathtt{i}; \mathbb{I} & C(\mathtt{f}) = \mathtt{i} \text{ and } C[\mathtt{f} + 4] = \mathbb{I} \\
c; \mathtt{i} & c = C(\mathtt{f}) \text{ and } c = \mathtt{jmp}\ \mathtt{a} \text{ or } \mathtt{retl} \\
& \text{and } C(\mathtt{f} + 4) = \mathtt{i} \\
c; \mathtt{i}; \mathbb{I} & c = C(\mathtt{f}) \text{ and } c = \mathtt{call}\ \mathtt{f} \text{ or } \mathtt{be}\ \mathtt{f} \\
& \text{and } C(\mathtt{f} + 4) = \mathtt{i} \text{ and } C[\mathtt{f} + 8] = \mathbb{I} \\
\mathbf{undefined} & \text{otherwise}
\end{cases}
$$

2.2   Operational Semantics

The operational semantics is taken from Wang et al. [17], but we omit features like interrupts and traps. We show the selected rules in Fig. 6. The program transition relation $C \vdash (S, \mathtt{pc}, \mathtt{npc}) \longmapsto (S', \mathtt{pc}', \mathtt{npc}')$ is defined in Fig. 6(a). Before the execution of the instruction pointed by pc, the delayed writes in D with 0 delay cycles are executed first. The execution of the delayed writes are defined in the form of $(R, D) \rightrightarrows (R', D')$, as shown below:

$$
\frac{}{(R, \mathtt{nil}) \rightrightarrows (R, \mathtt{nil})}
\qquad
\frac{(R, D) \rightrightarrows (R', D')}{(R, (t{+}1, \mathtt{sr}, w) :: D) \rightrightarrows (R', (t, \mathtt{sr}, w) :: D')}
$$

$$
\frac{(R, D) \rightrightarrows (R', D') \qquad \mathtt{sr} \in \mathrm{dom}(R)}{(R, (0, \mathtt{sr}, w) :: D) \rightrightarrows (R'\{\mathtt{sr} \rightsquigarrow w\}, D')}
\qquad
\frac{(R, D) \rightrightarrows (R', D') \qquad \mathtt{sr} \notin \mathrm{dom}(R)}{(R, (0, \mathtt{sr}, w) :: D) \rightrightarrows (R', D')}
$$

Note that the write of sr has no effect if sr is not in the domain of R. Since R is defined as a partial map, we can prove the following lemma.

Lemma 2.1. $(R, D) \rightrightarrows (R', D')$ and $R = R_1 \uplus R_2$, if and only if there exists R_1' and R_2', such that $(R_1, D) \rightrightarrows (R_1', D')$, $(R_2, D) \rightrightarrows (R_2', D')$, and $R' = R_1' \uplus R_2'$.

Here the disjoint union $R_1 \uplus R_2$ represents the union of R_1 and R_2 if they have disjoint domains, and undefined otherwise. This lemma is important to give sound semantics to delay buffer related assertions, as discussed in Sect. 3.

The transition steps for individual instructions are classified into three categories: the control transfer steps ($\_ \vdash \_ \circ\!\longrightarrow \_$), the steps for save, restore and

$$\frac{\begin{array}{c}(R, D) \rightrightarrows (R', D') \\ C \vdash ((M, (R', F), D'), \mathrm{pc}, \mathrm{npc}) \circ\!\!\longrightarrow ((M', (R'', F'), D''), \mathrm{pc}', \mathrm{npc}')\end{array}}{C \vdash ((M, (R, F), D), \mathrm{pc}, \mathrm{npc}) \longmapsto ((M', (R'', F'), D''), \mathrm{pc}', \mathrm{npc}')}$$

(a) Program Transistion

$$\frac{C(\mathrm{pc}) = \mathtt{i} \qquad (M, (R, F), D) \bullet\!\!\xrightarrow{\;\mathtt{i}\;} (M', (R', F'), D')}{C \vdash ((M, (R, F), D), \mathrm{pc}, \mathrm{npc}) \circ\!\!\longrightarrow ((M', (R', F'), D'), \mathrm{npc}, \mathrm{npc} + 4)}$$

$$\frac{C(\mathrm{pc}) = \mathtt{jmp\ a} \qquad [\![\mathtt{a}]\!]_R = \mathtt{f}}{C \vdash ((M, (R, F), D), \mathrm{pc}, \mathrm{npc}) \circ\!\!\longrightarrow ((M, (R, F), D), \mathrm{npc}, \mathtt{f})}$$

$$\frac{C(\mathrm{pc}) = \mathtt{call\ f} \qquad \mathtt{r}_{15} \in \mathrm{dom}(R)}{C \vdash ((M, (R, F), D), \mathrm{pc}, \mathrm{npc}) \circ\!\!\longrightarrow ((M, (R\{\mathtt{r}_{15} \rightsquigarrow \mathrm{pc}\}, F), D), \mathrm{npc}, \mathtt{f})}$$

$$\frac{C(\mathrm{pc}) = \mathtt{retl} \qquad R(\mathtt{r}_{15}) = \mathtt{f}}{C \vdash ((M, (R, F), D), \mathrm{pc}, \mathrm{npc}) \circ\!\!\longrightarrow ((M, (R, F), D), \mathrm{npc}, \mathtt{f} + 8)}$$

(b) Control Transfer Instruction Transition

$$\frac{(M, R) \xrightarrow{\;\mathtt{i}\;} (M', R')}{(M, (R, F), D) \bullet\!\!\xrightarrow{\;\mathtt{i}\;} (M', (R', F), D)} \qquad \frac{\begin{array}{c}R(\mathtt{r}_s) = w_1 \quad [\![\mathtt{o}]\!]_R = w_2 \quad w = w_1 \oplus w_2 \\ \mathtt{sr} \in \mathrm{dom}(R) \quad D' = \mathbf{set\_delay}(\mathtt{sr}, w, D)\end{array}}{(M, (R, F), D) \bullet\!\!\xrightarrow{\;\mathtt{wr\ r_s\ o\ sr}\;} (M, (R, F), D')}$$

$$\frac{\mathbf{save}(R, F) = (R', F') \quad [\![\mathtt{o}]\!]_R = w \quad R'' = R'\{\mathtt{r}_d \rightsquigarrow R(\mathtt{r}_s) + w\}}{(M, (R, F), D) \bullet\!\!\xrightarrow{\;\mathtt{save\ r_s\ o\ r_d}\;} (M, (R'', F'), D)}$$

$$\frac{\mathbf{restore}(R, F) = (R', F') \quad [\![\mathtt{o}]\!]_R = w \quad R'' = R'\{\mathtt{r}_d \rightsquigarrow R(\mathtt{r}_s) + w\}}{(M, (R, F), D) \bullet\!\!\xrightarrow{\;\mathtt{restore\ r_s\ o\ r_d}\;} (M, (R'', F'), D)}$$

(c) Save, Restore and Wr instruction Transition

$$\frac{R(\mathtt{sr}) = w \qquad \mathtt{r}_d \in \mathrm{dom}(R)}{(M, R) \xrightarrow{\;\mathtt{rd\ sr\ r_d}\;} (M, R\{\mathtt{r}_d \rightsquigarrow w\})} \qquad \frac{R(\mathtt{r}_s) = w_1 \quad [\![\mathtt{o}]\!]_R = w_2 \quad \mathtt{r}_d \in \mathrm{dom}(R)}{(M, R) \xrightarrow{\;\mathtt{add\ r_s\ o\ r_d}\;} (M, R\{\mathtt{r}_d \rightsquigarrow w_1 + w_2\})}$$

$$\frac{[\![\mathtt{a}]\!]_R = w \quad M(w) = w' \quad \mathtt{r}_d \in \mathrm{dom}(R)}{(M, R) \xrightarrow{\;\mathtt{ld\ a\ r_d}\;} (M, R\{\mathtt{r}_d \rightsquigarrow w'\})}$$

(d) Simple Instruction Transition

$$[\![\mathtt{o}]\!]_R \triangleq \begin{cases} R(r) & \text{if } \mathtt{o} = r \\ w & \text{if } \mathtt{o} = w, \\ & -4096 \le w \le 4095 \\ \bot & \text{otherwise} \end{cases} \qquad [\![\mathtt{a}]\!]_R \triangleq \begin{cases} [\![\mathtt{o}]\!]_R & \text{if } \mathtt{a} = \mathtt{o} \\ w_1 + w_2 & \text{if } \mathtt{a} = r + \mathtt{o},\ R(r) = w_1 \\ & \text{and } [\![\mathtt{o}]\!]_R = w_2 \\ \bot & \text{otherwise} \end{cases}$$

(e) Expression Semantics

Fig. 6. Selected operational semantics rules

wr instructions ($\_\bullet\xrightarrow{\quad}\_$), and the steps for other simple instructions ($\_\xrightarrow{\quad}\_$). The corresponding step transition relations are defined inductively in Fig. 6(b), (c) and (d) respectively.

Note that, after the control-transfer instructions, pc is set to npc and npc contains the target address. This explains the one cycle delay for the control transfer. The call instruction saves pc into the register r_{15}, while retl uses $r_{15}+8$ as the return address (which is the address for the second instruction following the call). Evaluation of expressions a and o is defined as $[\![a]\!]_R$ and $[\![o]\!]_R$ in Fig. 6(e).

The wr wants to save the bitwise exclusive OR of the operands into the special register sr, but it puts the write into the delay buffer D instead of updating R immediately. The operation $\textbf{set\_delay}(\textbf{sr}, w, D)$ is defined below:

$$\textbf{set\_delay}(\textbf{sr}, w, D) \triangleq (X, \textbf{sr}, w) :: D$$

where X ($0 \le X \le 3$) is a predefined system parameter for the delay cycle.

The save and restore instruction rotate the register windows and update the register file. Their operations over F and R are defined in Fig. 5.

3   Program Logic

In this section, we introduce the assertion language and program logic designed for SPARCv8 program.

3.1   Assertions

We define syntax of assertions in Fig. 7, and their semantics in Fig. 8. We extend separation logic assertions with specifications of delay buffers and register windows. Registers are like variables in separation logic, but are treated as resources. The assertion emp says that the memory and the register file are both empty. $l \mapsto w$ specifies a singleton memory cell with value w stored in the address l. $\textbf{rn} \mapsto w$ says that rn is the only register in the register file and it contains the value w. Also rn is *not* in the delay buffer. Separating conjunction $p * q$ has the standard semantics as in separation logic.

$$(Asrt)\ p, q \triangleq \textbf{emp} \mid l \mapsto w \mid \textbf{rn} \mapsto w \mid \rhd_t \textbf{sr} \mapsto w \mid p{\downarrow} \mid \textbf{cwp} \mapsto (\!|w_{id}, F|\!)$$
$$\mid p \wedge q \mid p \vee q \mid p * q \mid \textbf{a} =_a w \mid \textbf{o} = w \mid \forall x.\, p \mid \exists x.\, p \mid \dots$$

Fig. 7. Syntax of assertions

The assertion $\rhd_t \textbf{sr} \mapsto w$ describes a delayed write in the delay buffer D. It describes the uncertainty of sr's value in R, which is unknown for now but will become w in up to $t+1$ cycles. We use $\_ \Rightarrow^k \_$ to represent k-step execution of the delayed writes in D. It also requires that there be at most one delayed write

$$S \models \mathsf{emp} \quad \overset{\triangle}{=} S.M = \emptyset \wedge S.Q.R = \emptyset$$

$$S \models l \mapsto w \quad \overset{\triangle}{=} S.M = \{l \leadsto w\} \wedge S.Q.R = \emptyset$$

$$S \models \mathsf{rn} \mapsto w \quad \overset{\triangle}{=} S.Q.R = \{\mathsf{rn} \leadsto w\} \wedge \mathsf{rn} \notin \mathrm{dom}(S.D) \wedge S.M = \emptyset$$

$$S \models \rhd_t \mathsf{sr} \mapsto w \quad \overset{\triangle}{=} \exists k, R', D'. 0 \le k \le t+1 \wedge (R, D) \rightrightarrows^k (R', D') \wedge$$
$$((M, (R', F), D') \models \mathsf{sr} \mapsto w) \wedge \mathbf{noDup}(D, \mathsf{sr})$$
$$\text{where } S = (M, (R, F), D)$$

$$S \models p \downarrow \quad \overset{\triangle}{=} \exists R', D'. ((M, (R', F), D') \models p) \wedge (R', D') \rightrightarrows (R, D)$$
$$\text{where } S = (M, (R, F), D)$$

$$S \models \mathsf{cwp} \mapsto (\!| w_{id}, F |\!) \overset{\triangle}{=} (S \models \mathsf{cwp} \mapsto w_{id}) \wedge \exists F'. F \cdot F' = S.Q.F$$

$$S \models \mathsf{a} =_a w \quad \overset{\triangle}{=} [\![\mathsf{a}]\!]_{S.Q.R} = w \wedge \mathbf{word\_align}(w)$$

$$S \models \mathsf{o} = w \quad \overset{\triangle}{=} [\![\mathsf{o}]\!]_{S.Q.R} = w$$

$$S \models p_1 * p_2 \quad \overset{\triangle}{=} \exists S_1, S_2. S_1 \models p_1 \wedge S_2 \models p_2 \wedge S = S_1 \uplus S_2$$

$$S_1 \uplus S_2 \overset{\triangle}{=} \begin{cases} (M_1 \cup M_2, (R_1 \cup R_2, F), D) & \text{if } M_1 \perp M_2 \wedge R_1 \perp R_2 \wedge \\ & \quad S_1 = (M_1, (R_1, F), D) \wedge S_2 = (M_2, (R_2, F), D) \\ \mathbf{undefined} & \text{otherwise} \end{cases}$$

$$\mathrm{dom}(D) \overset{\triangle}{=} \begin{cases} \{\mathsf{sr}\} \cup \mathrm{dom}(D') & \text{if } D = (t, \mathsf{sr}, w) :: D' \\ \emptyset & \text{if } D = \mathrm{nil} \end{cases}$$

$$\mathbf{noDup}(D, \mathsf{sr}) \overset{\triangle}{=} \begin{cases} \mathsf{sr} \notin \mathrm{dom}(D') & \text{if } D = (t, \mathsf{sr}, w) :: D' \\ \mathsf{sr} \neq \mathsf{sr}' \wedge \mathbf{noDup}(D', \mathsf{sr}) & \text{if } D = (t, \mathsf{sr}', w) :: D' \\ \mathbf{True} & \text{if } D = \mathrm{nil} \end{cases}$$

Fig. 8. Semantics of assertions

for a specific special register sr in D (*i.e.* $\mathbf{noDup}(\mathsf{sr}, D)$). This prevents more than one delayed writes to the same register within 4 instruction cycles, which practically have no restrictions on programming. By the semantics we have

$$\mathsf{sr} \mapsto w \implies \rhd_t \mathsf{sr} \mapsto w \qquad \rhd_t \mathsf{sr} \mapsto w \implies \rhd_{t+k} \mathsf{sr} \mapsto w$$

The assertion $p \downarrow$ allows us to reduce the uncertainty by executing one step of the delayed writes. It specifies states reachable after executing one step of delayed writes from those states satisfying p. Therefore we know:

$$(\rhd_0 \mathsf{sr} \mapsto w) \downarrow \implies \mathsf{sr} \mapsto w \qquad (\rhd_{t+1} \mathsf{sr} \mapsto w) \downarrow \implies \rhd_t \mathsf{sr} \mapsto w$$

Also it's easy to see that if p syntactically does not contain sub-terms in the form of $\rhd_t \mathsf{sr} \mapsto w$, then $(p \downarrow) \iff p$.

The following lemma shows $(\_) \downarrow$ is distributive over separating conjunction.

Lemma 3.1. $(p * q) \downarrow \iff (p \downarrow) * (q \downarrow)$.

The lemma can be proved following Lemma 2.1.

We use $\mathsf{cwp} \mapsto (\!| w_{id}, F |\!)$ to describe the pointer cwp of the current register window and the frame list as a circular stack. Note that F is just a prefix of the

- {(fp, fq)}
  add   %i$_0$, %i$_1$, %l$_7$
  add   %l$_7$, %i$_2$, %l$_7$
  retl
  nop

$$\text{fp} \triangleq \lambda \, lv. \, (\%\text{i}_0 \mapsto lv[0]) * (\%\text{i}_1 \mapsto lv[1]) * (\%\text{i}_2 \mapsto lv[2])$$
$$* \%\text{l}_7 \mapsto \_ * (\text{r}_{15} \mapsto lv[3])$$

$$\text{fq} \triangleq \lambda \, lv. \, (\%\text{i}_0 \mapsto lv[0]) * (\%\text{i}_1 \mapsto lv[1]) * (\%\text{i}_2 \mapsto lv[2])$$
$$* (\%\text{l}_7 \mapsto lv[0] + lv[1] + lv[2]) * (\text{r}_{15} \mapsto lv[3])$$

Fig. 9. Example for function specification

frame list, since usually we do not need to know contents of the full list. Here we use $F \cdot F'$ to represent the concatenation of lists F and F'. Therefore we have $\text{cwp} \mapsto (\!| w_{id}, F \cdot F' |\!) \implies \text{cwp} \mapsto (\!| w_{id}, F |\!)$.

The assertions $\text{a} =_a w$ and $\text{o} = w$ describe the value of a and o respectively. They are intuitionistic assertions. Since a is used as an address, we also require it to be properly aligned on a 4-byte boundary (*i.e.* **word_align**, whose definition is omitted here).

3.2   Inference Rules

The code specification θ and code heap specification Ψ are defined below:

(valList)	$\iota \in$ list value	(pAsrt)	$\text{fp}, \text{fq} \in$ valList $\rightarrow$ *Asrt*
(CdSpec)	$\theta ::= (\text{fp}, \text{fq})$	(CdHpSpec)	$\Psi ::= \{\text{f} \rightsquigarrow \theta\}^*$

The code heap specification Ψ maps the code labels for basic blocks to their specifications θ, which is a pair of pre- and post-conditions. Instead of using normal assertions, the pre- and post-conditions are assertions parameterized over a list of values $lgvl$. They play the role of auxiliary variables—Feeding the pre- and the post-conditions with the same $lgvl$ allows us to establish relationship of states specified in the pre- and post-conditions.

Although we assign a θ to each basic block, the post-condition does not specify the states reached at the end of the block. Instead, it specifies the condition that needs to be specified in the future when the *current function* returns. This follows the idea developed in SCAP [7], but we use the standard unary state assertion instead of the binary state assertions used in SCAP, so that existing proof techniques (such as Coq tactics) for standard Hoare-triples can be applied to simplify the verification process.

We give a simple example in Fig. 9 to show a specification for a function, which simply sums the values of the registers %i$_0$, %i$_1$ and %i$_2$ and writes the result into the register %l$_7$. The specification (fp, fq) says that, when provided with the same lv as argument, the function preserves the value of %i$_0$, %i$_1$ and %i$_2$, %l$_7$ at the end contains the sum of %i$_0$, %i$_1$ and %i$_2$, and the function also preserves the value of r_{15}, which it uses as the return address. To verify the function, we need to prove that it satisfies (fp lv, fq lv) for all lv.

Figure 10 shows selected inference rules in our logic. The top rule **CDHP** verifies the code heap C. It requires that every basic block specified in Ψ can be verified with respect to the specification, with any argument ι used to instantiate the pre- and post-conditions.

$\boxed{\vdash C : \Psi}$ **(Well-Formed Code Heap)**

$$\frac{\text{for all } \mathtt{f} \in \text{dom}(\Psi),\ \iota :\ \ \Psi(\mathtt{f}) = (\text{fp}, \text{fq})\quad \Psi \vdash \{(\text{fp } \iota, \text{fq } \iota)\}\ \mathtt{f} : C[\mathtt{f}]}{\vdash C : \Psi}\ \text{(CDHP)}$$

$\boxed{\Psi \vdash \{(p, q)\}\ \mathtt{f} : \mathbb{I}}$ **(Well-Formed Instruction Sequences)**

$$\frac{\vdash \{p\downarrow\}\,\mathtt{i}\,\{p'\}\quad \Psi \vdash \{(p', q)\}\ \mathtt{f}+4 : \mathbb{I}}{\Psi \vdash \{(p, q)\}\ \mathtt{f} : \mathtt{i}; \mathbb{I}}\ \text{(SEQ)}$$

$$\frac{\begin{array}{c}p\downarrow \Rightarrow (\mathtt{a} =_a \mathtt{f}')\quad \mathtt{f}' \in \text{dom}(\Psi)\quad \Psi(\mathtt{f}') = (\text{fp}, \text{fq})\\ \vdash \{p\downarrow\downarrow\}\,\mathtt{i}\,\{p'\}\quad \exists \iota, p_r.\ (p' \Rightarrow \text{fp } \iota * p_r) \wedge (\text{fq } \iota * p_r \Rightarrow q)\end{array}}{\Psi \vdash \{(p, q)\}\ \mathtt{f} : \mathtt{jmp\ a}; \mathtt{i}}\ \text{(JMP)}$$

$$\frac{\begin{array}{c}\mathtt{f}' \in \text{dom}(\Psi)\quad \Psi(\mathtt{f}') = (\text{fp}, \text{fq})\quad \Psi \vdash \{(p', q)\}\ \mathtt{f}+8 : \mathbb{I}\\ p\downarrow \Rightarrow (\mathtt{r}_{15} \mapsto \_) * p_1\quad \vdash \{(\mathtt{r}_{15} \mapsto \mathtt{f} * p_1)\downarrow\}\,\mathtt{i}\,\{p_2\}\\ \exists \iota, p_r.\ (p_2 \Rightarrow \text{fp } \iota * p_r) \wedge (\text{fq } \iota * p_r \Rightarrow p') \wedge (\text{fq } \iota \Rightarrow \mathtt{r}_{15} = \mathtt{f})\end{array}}{\Psi \vdash \{(p, q)\}\ \mathtt{f} : \mathtt{call\ f'}; \mathtt{i}; \mathbb{I}}\ \text{(CALL)}$$

$$\frac{p\downarrow\downarrow \Rightarrow (\mathtt{r}_{15} \mapsto \mathtt{f}') * p_1\quad \vdash \{p_1\}\,\mathtt{i}\,\{p_2\}\quad (\mathtt{r}_{15} \mapsto \mathtt{f}') * p_2 \Rightarrow q}{\Psi \vdash \{(p, q)\}\ \mathtt{f} : \mathtt{retl}; \mathtt{i}}\ \text{(RETL)}$$

$\boxed{\vdash \{p\}\,\mathtt{i}\,\{q\}}$ **(Well-Formed Instructions)**

$$\frac{\mathtt{sr} \mapsto \_ * p \Rightarrow (\mathtt{r}_s = w_1 \wedge \mathtt{o} = w_2)}{\vdash \{\mathtt{sr} \mapsto \_ * p\}\,\mathtt{wr}\ \mathtt{r}_s\ \mathtt{o}\ \mathtt{sr}\,\{(\triangleright_3 \mathtt{sr} \mapsto (w_1 \oplus w_2)) * p\}}\ \text{(WR)}$$

$$\frac{}{\vdash \{\mathtt{sr} \mapsto w * \mathtt{r}_d \mapsto \_\}\,\mathtt{rd}\ \mathtt{sr}\ \mathtt{r}_d\,\{\mathtt{sr} \mapsto w * \mathtt{r}_d \mapsto w\}}\ \text{(RD)}$$

$$\frac{\begin{array}{c}p \Rightarrow (\mathtt{r}_s = w_1 \wedge \mathtt{o} = w_2)\quad w'_{id} = \mathbf{next\_cwp}(w_{id})\quad w\ \&\ 2^{w'_{id}} = 0\\ p \Rightarrow (\mathtt{cwp} \mapsto (\!|w_{id}, F \cdot \_ \cdot \_|\!)) * (\mathtt{out} \mapsto \text{fm}_o) * (\mathtt{local} \mapsto \text{fm}_l) * (\mathtt{in} \mapsto \text{fm}_i) * p_1\\ (\mathtt{cwp} \mapsto (\!|w'_{id}, \text{fm}_l :: \text{fm}_i :: F|\!)) * (\mathtt{out} \mapsto \_) * (\mathtt{local} \mapsto \_) * (\mathtt{in} \mapsto \text{fm}_o) * p_1 \Rightarrow \mathtt{r}_d \mapsto \_ * p_2\end{array}}{\vdash \{(\mathtt{wim} \mapsto w) * p\}\,\mathtt{save}\ \mathtt{r}_s\ \mathtt{o}\ \mathtt{r}_d\,\{(\mathtt{wim} \mapsto w) * (\mathtt{r}_d \mapsto w_1 + w_2) * p_2\}}\ \text{(SAVE)}$$

where $[\mathtt{r}_i, \dots, \mathtt{r}_{i+7}] \mapsto [w_0, \dots, w_7] \overset{\triangle}{=} \mathtt{r}_i \mapsto w_0 * \cdots * \mathtt{r}_{i+7} \mapsto w_7$
and out, local and in are defined in Fig. 5.

$$\frac{\begin{array}{c}p \Rightarrow (\mathtt{r}_s = w_1 \wedge \mathtt{o} = w_2)\quad w'_{id} = \mathbf{prev\_cwp}(w_{id})\quad w\ \&\ 2^{w'_{id}} = 0\\ p \Rightarrow (\mathtt{cwp} \mapsto (\!|w_{id}, \text{fm}_1 :: \text{fm}_2 :: F|\!)) * (\mathtt{out} \mapsto \_) * (\mathtt{local} \mapsto \_) * (\mathtt{in} \mapsto \text{fm}_i) * p_1\\ (\mathtt{cwp} \mapsto (\!|w'_{id}, F \cdot \_ \cdot \_|\!)) * (\mathtt{out} \mapsto \text{fm}_i) * (\mathtt{local} \mapsto \text{fm}_1) * (\mathtt{in} \mapsto \text{fm}_2) * p_1 \Rightarrow \mathtt{r}_d \mapsto \_ * p_2\end{array}}{\vdash \{(\mathtt{wim} \mapsto w) * p\}\,\mathtt{restore}\ \mathtt{r}_s\ \mathtt{o}\ \mathtt{r}_d\,\{(\mathtt{wim} \mapsto w) * (\mathtt{r}_d \mapsto w_1 + w_2) * p_2\}}\ \text{(RESTORE)}$$

Fig. 10. Selected inference rules

The **SEQ** rule is applied when meeting an instruction sequence starting with a simple instruction $\mathtt{i}$. The instruction $\mathtt{i}$ is verified by the corresponding well-formed instruction rules, with the precondition $p\downarrow$ and some post-condition p'. We use $p\downarrow$ because there is an implicit step executing delayed writes before executing every instruction. The post-condition p' for $\mathtt{i}$ is then used as the precondition to verify the remaining part of the instruction sequence.

Delayed Control Transfers. We distinguish the $\mathtt{jmp}$ and $\mathtt{call}$ instructions—The former makes an *intra-function* control transfer, while the latter makes function calls. The **JMP** rule requires that the target address is a valid one specified in Ψ. Starting from the precondition p, after executing the instruction i following **JMP** and the corresponding delayed writes, the post-condition p' of i should satisfy the precondition of the target instruction sequence, with some instantiation ι of the logical variables and a frame assertion p_r. Since the target instruction sequence of jmp is in the same function as the jmp instruction itself, the post-condition fq specified at the target address (with the same instantiation ι of the logical variables and the frame assertion p_r) should meet the post-condition q of the current function. As we explained before, the post-condition q does not specify the states reached at the end of the instruction sequence (which are specified by p' instead).

The **CALL** rule is similar to the **JMP** rule in that it also requires the post-condition p_2 of the instruction i following the call satisfy the precondition of the target instruction sequence, with some instantiation ι of the logical variables and a frame assertion p_r. Here we need to record that the code label f is saved in r_{15} by the call instruction. When the callee returns, its post-condition fq (with the same instantiation of auxiliary variables ι) needs to ensure r_{15} still contains f, so that the callee returns to the correct address. Also the fq with the frame p_r needs to satisfy the precondition p' for the remaining instruction sequences of the caller.

The **RETL** rule simply requires that the post-condition q holds at the end of the instruction i following retl. Also i cannot touch the register r_{15}, therefore r_{15} specified in p must be the same as in q. Since at the calling point we already required that the post-condition of the callee guarantees r_{15} contains the correct return address, we know r_{15} contains the correct value before retl.

Delayed Writes and Register Windows. The bottom layer of our logic is for well-formed instructions. The **WR** rule requires the ownership of the target register sr in the precondition $(sr \mapsto \_)$. Also it implies there is no delayed writes to sr in the delay buffer (see the semantics defined in Fig. 8). At the end of the delayed write, we use $\triangleright_3 sr \mapsto w_1 \oplus w_2$ to indicate the new value will be ready in up to 3 cycles. Since the maximum delay cycle X cannot be bigger than 3 and the value of X may vary in different systems, programmers usually take a conservative approach to assume $X = 3$ for portability of code. Our rule reflects this conservative view. The **RD** rule says the special register can be read only if it is not in the delay buffer. The **SAVE** and **RESTORE** rules reflect the save and recovery of the execution contexts, which is consistent with the operational semantics of the save and restore instructions given in Figs. 5 and 6.

3.3   Semantics and Soundness

We first define the safety of instruction sequences, $\mathsf{safe\_insSeq}(C, S, pc, npc, q, \Psi)$. It says C can execute safely from S, pc and npc until reaching the end of the current instruction sequence ($C[pc]$), and q holds if $C[pc]$ ends with the return instruction. It is formally defined in Definition 3.2. Here we use "$\_ \longmapsto^n \_$" to represent n-step execution.

Definition 3.2 (Safety of Instruction Sequences). safe_insSeq($C, S, \text{pc},$ npc, q, Ψ) holds if and only if the following are true (we omit the case for be here, which is similar to jmp):

- if $C(\text{pc}) = \mathtt{i}$ then:
  - there exist $S', \text{pc}, \text{npc}'$, such that $C \vdash (S, \text{pc}, \text{npc}) \longmapsto (S', \text{pc}', \text{npc}')$,
  - for any $S', \text{pc}', \text{npc}'$, if $C \vdash (S, \text{pc}, \text{npc}) \longmapsto (S', \text{pc}', \text{npc}')$, then
    safe_insSeq $(C, S', \text{pc}', \text{npc}', q, \Psi)$
- if $C(\text{pc}) = \mathtt{jmp\ a}$ then:
  - there exist $S', \text{pc}', \text{npc}'$, such that $C \vdash (S, \text{pc}, \text{npc}) \longmapsto^2 (S', \text{pc}', \text{npc}')$,
  - for any $S', \text{pc}', \text{npc}'$, if $C \vdash (S, \text{pc}, \text{npc}) \longmapsto^2 (S', \text{pc}', \text{npc}')$, then there exist fp, fq, ι and p_r, such that the following hold:
    (1) $\text{npc}' = \text{pc}'+4$, $\Psi(\text{pc}') = (\text{fp}, \text{fq})$,
    (2) $S' \models (\text{fp}\ \iota) * p_r$, $(\text{fq}\ \iota) * p_r \Rightarrow q$.
- if $C(\text{pc}) = \mathtt{be\ f}$ then ...
- if $C(\text{pc}) = \mathtt{call\ f}$ then:
  - there exist $S', \text{pc}', \text{npc}'$, such that $C \vdash (S, \text{pc}, \text{npc}) \longmapsto^2 (S', \text{pc}', \text{npc}')$,
  - for any S', pc' and npc', if $C \vdash (S, \text{pc}, \text{npc}) \longmapsto^2 (S', \text{pc}', \text{npc}')$, then there exist fp, fq, ι and p_r, such that the following hold:
    (1) $\text{npc}' = \text{pc}'+4$, $\Psi(\text{pc}') = (\text{fp}, \text{fq})$,
    (2) $S' \models (\text{fp}\ \iota) * p_r$,
    (3) for any S', if $S' \models (\text{fq}\ \iota) * p_r$, then safe_insSeq $(C, S', \text{pc} + 8, \text{pc} + 12, q, \Psi)$,
    (4) for any S', if $S' \models (\text{fq}\ \iota)$, then $S'.Q.R(\mathtt{r}_{15}) = \text{pc}$.
- if $C(\text{pc}) = \mathtt{retl}$ then:
  - there exist $S', \text{pc}', \text{npc}'$, such that $C \vdash (S, \text{pc}, \text{npc}) \longmapsto^2 (S', \text{pc}', \text{npc}')$,
  - for any S', pc' and npc', if $C \vdash (S, \text{pc}, \text{npc}) \longmapsto^2 (S', \text{pc}', \text{npc}')$, then $S' \models q$, $\text{pc}' = S'.Q.R(\mathtt{r}_{15})+8$, and $\text{npc}' = S'.Q.R(\mathtt{r}_{15})+12$.

Then we can define the semantics for well-formed instruction sequences and well-formed code heap.

Definition 3.3 (Judgment Semantics)

- $\Psi \models \{(p, q)\}\ \mathtt{f} : \mathbb{I}$ if and only if, for all C and S such that $C[\mathtt{f}] = \mathbb{I}$ and $S \models p$, we have safe_insSeq$(C, S, \mathtt{f}, \mathtt{f}+4, q, \Psi)$.
- $\models C : \Psi$ if and only if, for all $\mathtt{f}$, fp and fq such that $\Psi(\mathtt{f}) = (\text{fp}, \text{fq})$, we have $\Psi \models \{(\text{fp}\ \iota, \text{fq}\ \iota)\}\ \mathtt{f} : C[\mathtt{f}]$ for all ι.

Next we define the safety $\mathsf{safe}^n(C, S, \text{pc}, \text{npc}, q, k)$ of whole program execution. It says that, starting with pc, npc and the state S, and with the depth k of function calls, the code C either *halts* in less than n steps, with the final state satisfies q, or it executes at least n steps safely. Here we say C halts if it reaches the return point of the topmost function (when the depth k of the function call is 0). In the definition below, the depth k increases by the call instruction and decreases by retl (unless $k = 0$).

Definition 3.4 (Program Safety). $\text{safe}^0(C, S, \text{pc}, \text{npc}, q, k)$ always holds. $\text{safe}^{n+1}(C, S, \text{pc}, \text{npc}, q, k)$ holds if and only if the following are true:

1. if $C(\text{pc}) \in \{\text{i}, \text{jmp a}, \text{be f}\}$, then:
   - there exist $S', \text{pc}', \text{npc}'$, such that $C \vdash (S, \text{pc}, \text{npc}) \longmapsto (S', \text{pc}', \text{npc}')$;
   - for any $S', \text{pc}', \text{npc}'$, if
     $C \vdash (S, \text{pc}, \text{npc}) \longmapsto (S', \text{pc}', \text{npc}')$, then $\text{safe}^n (C, S', \text{pc}', \text{npc}', q, k)$;
2. if $C(\text{pc}) = \text{call f}$, then:
   - there exist $S', \text{pc}', \text{npc}'$ such that $C \vdash (S, \text{pc}, \text{npc}) \longmapsto^2 (S', \text{pc}', \text{npc}')$;
   - for any $S', \text{pc}', \text{npc}'$, if $C \vdash (S, \text{pc}, \text{npc}) \longmapsto^2 (S', \text{pc}', \text{npc}')$,
     then $\text{safe}^n(C, S', \text{pc}', \text{npc}', q, k + 1)$;
3. if $C(\text{pc}) = \text{retl}$, then:
   - there exist $S', \text{pc}', \text{npc}'$ such that $C \vdash (S, \text{pc}, \text{npc}) \longmapsto^2 (S', \text{pc}', \text{npc}')$;
   - for any $S', \text{pc}', \text{npc}'$, if $C \vdash (S, \text{pc}, \text{npc}) \longmapsto^2 (S', \text{pc}', \text{npc}')$, then
     if $k = 0$ then
     $$S' \models q$$
     else
     $$\text{safe}^n(C, S', \text{pc}', \text{npc}', q, k-1).$$

Then the following theorem and corollary show the soundness of our logic.

Theorem 3.5 (Soundness). $\vdash C : \Psi \Longrightarrow \models C : \Psi$

Corollary 3.6 (Function Safety). If $\Psi \models \{(p, q)\} \text{pc} : C[\text{pc}]$, $S \models p$, and $\models C : \Psi$, then $\forall n. \text{safe}^n(C, S, \text{pc}, \text{pc}+4, q, 0)$.

4   Verifying a Realistic Context Switch Module

We apply our program logic to verify the main body of a context switch routine implemented in SPARCv8, which is used to save the current task's context and restore the new task's context. Figure 11 shows the structure of the code.

- SwitchEntry is the entry of the module. It checks SwitchFlag to see if a context switch is needed. If yes, it enters the Window_OK block.
- Window_OK checks if the current task is null (which may happen if the switch follows the delete of the current task). If yes, it jumps to Adjust_CWP, which resets the pointer cwp of the current register window so that it points to the last valid window. It essentially pops all the frames to empty the circular stack of register windows. If the current task is *not* null, it calls reg_save to save the general registers into the TCB, and then enter the code block Save_UsedWindows to save other register windows (F in our state model).
- Save_UsedWindows saves the register windows (except the current one) into the current task's stack in memory.
- Switch_NewContext restores the general registers and other register windows from the new task's TCB and its stack in memory, respectively. Then it sets the new task as the current one.

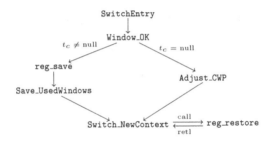

Fig. 11. The structure of context switch module

The main complexity of the verification lies in the code manages the register windows. To save all the register windows, `Save_UsedWindows` repetitively restores the next window into general registers (as the current window) and then saves them into memory, until all the windows are saved.

Specification. Below we give the pre- and post-conditions (a_{pre} and a_{post}) of the verified module. Each of them takes 5 arguments, the id of the current task t_c, the id of the new task t_n, the value *flag* of the SwitchFlag, the values *env* of general registers and all other register windows, and the new task's context *nst* that needs to be restored.

$$a_{pre}(t_c, t_n, \mathit{flag}, \mathit{env}, \mathit{nst}) \triangleq \mathsf{Env}(\mathit{env}) * (\mathsf{SwitchFlag} \mapsto \mathit{flag}) * (\mathsf{TaskNew} \mapsto t_n) *$$
$$(\mathit{flag} = \mathrm{false} \vee \mathsf{CurT}(t_c, \_, \mathit{env}) * \mathsf{NoCurT}(t_n, \mathit{nst}))$$

$$a_{post}(t_c, t_n, \mathit{flag}, \mathit{env}, \mathit{nst}) \triangleq \exists \mathit{env}'.\ \mathsf{Env}(\mathit{env}') * (\mathsf{SwitchFlag} \mapsto \mathrm{false}) * (\mathsf{TaskNew} \mapsto t_n) *$$
$$(\mathit{flag} = \mathrm{false} \wedge \mathsf{p\_env}(\mathit{env}) = \mathsf{p\_env}(\mathit{env}')$$
$$\vee (\mathsf{CurT}(t_n, \mathit{nst}, \mathit{env}') \wedge \mathsf{p\_env}(\mathit{env}') = \mathit{nst}) *$$
$$\mathsf{NoCurT}(t_c, \mathsf{p\_env}(\mathit{env})))$$

In the specification, we use $\mathsf{Env}(\mathit{env})$ to specify the values of general registers and the register windows. The variable TaskNew records the identifier of the new task. If SwitchFlag is false, we do not need any knowledge about the current and the new tasks since there is no context switch. Otherwise we describe the state of the current task (its TCB and stack in memory) using $\mathsf{CurT}(t_c, \_, \mathit{env})$, and the saved context of the new task using $\mathsf{NoCurT}(t_n, \mathit{nst})$. Due to space limitation we omit the detailed definitions here.

If we compare a_{pre} and a_{post}, we can see that t_n becomes the current task ($\mathsf{CurT}(t_n, \mathit{nst}, \mathit{env}')$), and its general registers and stack, specified by $\mathsf{Env}(\mathit{env}')$, are loaded from the saved context *nst* (*i.e.* $\mathsf{p\_env}(\mathit{env}') = \mathit{nst}$). Here $\mathsf{p\_env}(\mathit{env}')$ refers to the part of the environment that we want to save or restore as context. Correspondingly, t_c becomes non-current-thread, and part of its environment *env* at the entry of the context switch is saved, as specified by $\mathsf{NoCurT}(t_c, \mathsf{p\_env}(\mathit{env}))$.

We omit the code that manages interrupt and float registers in the original system, which are not supported in our logic. The segment we verify has around 250 lines of assembly code, and we verify it by 6690 lines of Coq proof scripts.

5   Related Work and Conclusion

There has been much work on assembly or machine code verification. Most of them do not support function calls or simply treat function calls in the continuation-passing style where return addresses are viewed as first class code pointers [3,10,11,13,14,16,20]. SCAP [7] supports assembly code verification with various stack-based control abstractions, including function call and return. We follow the same idea here. However, SCAP gives a syntactic-based soundness proof by establishing the preservation of the syntactic judgment, which makes it difficult to interact with other modules verified in different logic. Since our goal is to verify inline assembly and link the verified code with the verified C programs, we give a direct-style semantic model of the logic judgments. Also SCAP is based on a simplified subset of assembly instructions, while our work is focused on a realistically modeled subset of SPARCv8 instructions.

In terms of the support of realistic instruction sets, previous work on proof-carrying code (PCC) and typed assembly language (TAL) mostly supports subsets of x86. Myreen's work [12] presents a framework for ARM verification based on a realistic model (but it doesn't support function call and return).

As part of the Foundational Proof-Carrying Code (FPCC) project [3], Tan and Appel present a program logic $\mathcal{L}_c$ for reasoning about control flow in assembly code [16]. Although $\mathcal{L}_c$ is implemented on top of SPARC machine language, the underlying logic is a type system instead of a full-blown program logic for functional correctness. It reasons about functions in the continuation-passing style. Also handling SPARC features such as delayed writes or delayed control transfers is not the focus of $\mathcal{L}_c$. There has been work on mechanized semantics of the SPARCv8 ISA. Hou et al. [21] model the SPARCv8 ISA in Isabelle/HOL. Wang et al. [17] formalize its semantics in Coq. Our operational semantics of SPARCv8 follows Wang et al. [17].

Ni et al. [15] verify a context switch module of 19 lines in x86 code to show case the support of embedded code pointers (ECP) in XCAP [14]. The context switch module we verify comes from a practical OS kernel, which is more realistic and consists of more than 250 lines of assembly code, but our logic does not really support the switch of return addresses, which requires further extension like OCAP [6]. Our focus is to verify the code manages the register windows, and the function calls made internally.

Yang and Hawblitzel [19] verify Verve, an x86 implementation of an experimental operating system. Verve has two levels, the high-level TAL code and the low-level "Nucleus" that provides primitive access to hardware and memory. The Nucleus code is verified automatically using the Z3 SMT solver, while the goal of our work is to generate machine checkable proofs. Another key difference is the use of different ISAs. Here we give details to verify specific features of SPARCv8 programs.

There have been many techniques and tools proposed for automated program verification (e.g. [4,5]). It is possible to adapt them to verify SPARCv8 code. We propose a new program logic and do the verification in Coq mainly because the work is part of a big project for a fully certified OS kernel for aerospace crafts whose inline assembly is written in SPARCv8. We already have a program logic implemented in Coq for C programs, which allows us to verify C code with Coq proofs. Therefore we want to have a program logic for SPARCv8 so that it can be linked with the logic for C and can generate machine-checkable Coq proofs too. That said, many of the automated verification techniques can be applied to reduce the manual efforts to write Coq proofs, which we would like to study in the future work.

Conclusion. We present a program logic for SPARCv8. Our logic is based on a realistic semantics model and supports main features of SPARCv8, including delayed control transfer, delayed writes, and register windows. We have applied the program logic to verify the main body of the context switch routine in a realistic embedded OS kernel. Our current work can only handle sequential SPARCv8 program verification for partial correctness. We will extend it for concurrency and refinement verification in the future. Also we would like to link the verified inline assembly with verified C code for whole system verification.

References

1. Program logic for SPARCv8 implementation in Coq (project code). https://github.com/jpzha/VeriSparc
2. SPARC. https://gaisler.com/doc/sparcv8.pdf
3. Appel, A.W.: Foundational proof-carrying code. In: Proceedings of 16th Annual IEEE Symposium on Logic in Computer Science, pp. 85–97, January 1998
4. Berdine, J., Calcagno, C., O'Hearn, P.W.: Smallfoot: modular automatic assertion checking with separation logic. In: de Boer, F.S., Bonsangue, M.M., Graf, S., de Roever, W.-P. (eds.) FMCO 2005. LNCS, vol. 4111, pp. 115–137. Springer, Heidelberg (2006). https://doi.org/10.1007/11804192_6
5. Berdine, J., Calcagno, C., O'Hearn, P.W.: Symbolic execution with separation logic. In: Yi, K. (ed.) APLAS 2005. LNCS, vol. 3780, pp. 52–68. Springer, Heidelberg (2005). https://doi.org/10.1007/11575467_5
6. Feng, X., Ni, Z., Shao, Z., Guo, Y.: An open framework for foundational proof-carrying code. In: TLDI, pp. 67–78 (2007)
7. Feng, X., Shao, Z., Vaynberg, A., Xiang, S., Ni, Z.: Modular verification of assembly code with stack-based control abstractions. In: PLDI, June 2006
8. Gu, R., et al.: Deep specifications and certified abstraction layers. In: POPL, pp. 595–608, January 2015
9. Klein, G., et al.: seL4: formal verification of an OS kernel. In: SOSP, pp. 207–220, October 2009
10. Morrisett, G.: TALx86: a realistic typed assembly language. In: 1999 ACM SIGPLAN Workshop on Compiler Support for System Software, pp. 25–35, May 1996
11. Morrisett, G., Walker, D., Crary, K., Glew, N.: From system F to typed assembly language. In: POPL, pp. 85–97, January 1998
12. Myreen, M.O., Gordon, M.J.C.: Hoare logic for realistically modelled machine code. In: Grumberg, O., Huth, M. (eds.) TACAS 2007. LNCS, vol. 4424, pp. 568–582. Springer, Heidelberg (2007). https://doi.org/10.1007/978-3-540-71209-1_44
13. Necula, G.C., Lee, P.: Safe kernel extensions without run-time checking. In: Proceedings of 2nd USENIX Symposium on Operating System Design and Implementation, pp. 229–243 (1996)

14. Ni, Z., Shao, Z.: Certified assembly programming with embedded code pointers. In: POPL, pp. 320–333 (2006)
15. Ni, Z., Yu, D., Shao, Z.: Using XCAP to certify realistic systems code: machine context management. In: Schneider, K., Brandt, J. (eds.) TPHOLs 2007. LNCS, vol. 4732, pp. 189–206. Springer, Heidelberg (2007). https://doi.org/10.1007/978-3-540-74591-4_15
16. Tan, G., Appel, A.W.: A compositional logic for control flow. In: Emerson, E.A., Namjoshi, K.S. (eds.) VMCAI 2006. LNCS, vol. 3855, pp. 80–94. Springer, Heidelberg (2005). https://doi.org/10.1007/11609773_6
17. Wang, J., Fu, M., Qiao, L., Feng, X.: Formalizing SPARCv8 instruction set architecture in Coq. In: Larsen, K.G., Sokolsky, O., Wang, J. (eds.) SETTA 2017. LNCS, vol. 10606, pp. 300–316. Springer, Cham (2017). https://doi.org/10.1007/978-3-319-69483-2_18
18. Xu, F., Fu, M., Feng, X., Zhang, X., Zhang, H., Li, Z.: A practical verification framework for preemptive OS kernels. In: Chaudhuri, S., Farzan, A. (eds.) CAV 2016. LNCS, vol. 9780, pp. 59–79. Springer, Cham (2016). https://doi.org/10.1007/978-3-319-41540-6_4
19. Yang, J., Hawblitzel, C.: Safe to the last instruction: automated verification of a type-safe operating system. In: PLDI, pp. 99–110 (2010)
20. Yu, D., Nadeem, A.H., Shao, Z.: Building certified libraries for PCC: dynamic storage allocation. Sci. Comput. Program. 50(1–3), 101–127 (2004)
21. Hou, Z., Sanan, D., Tiu, A., Liu, Y., Hoa, K.C.: An executable formalisation of the SPARCv8 instruction set architecture: a case study for the LEON3 processor. In: Fitzgerald, J., Heitmeyer, C., Gnesi, S., Philippou, A. (eds.) FM 2016. LNCS, vol. 9995, pp. 388–405. Springer, Cham (2016). https://doi.org/10.1007/978-3-319-48989-6_24

Formal Small-Step Verification of a Call-by-Value Lambda Calculus Machine

Fabian Kunze$^{(\boxtimes)}$, Gert Smolka$^{(\boxtimes)}$, and Yannick Forster$^{(\boxtimes)}$

Saarland University, Saarbrücken, Germany
{kunze,smolka,forster}@ps.uni-saarland.de

Abstract. We formally verify an abstract machine for a call-by-value λ-calculus with de Bruijn terms, simple substitution, and small-step semantics. We follow a stepwise refinement approach starting with a naive stack machine with substitution. We then refine to a machine with closures, and finally to a machine with a heap providing structure sharing for closures. We prove the correctness of the three refinement steps with compositional small-step bottom-up simulations. There is an accompanying Coq development verifying all results.

1 Introduction

The call-by-value λ-calculus is a minimal functional programming language that can express recursive functions and inductive data types. Forster and Smolka [12] employ the call-by-value λ-calculus as the basis for a constructive theory of computation and formally verify elaborate programs such as step-indexed self-interpreters. Dal Lago and Martini [8] show that Turing machines and the call-by-value λ-calculus can simulate each other within a polynomial time overhead (under a certain cost model). Landin's SECD machine implements the call-by-value λ-calculus with closures eliminating the need for substitution [14,18].

In this paper we consider the call-by-value λ-calculus L from [12]. L comes with de Bruijn terms and simple substitution, and restricts β-reduction to terms of the form $(\lambda s)(\lambda t)$ that do not appear within abstractions. This is in contrast to Plotkin's call-by-value λ-calculus [18], which employs terms with named argument variables and substitution with renaming, and β-reduces terms of the forms $(\lambda x.s)(\lambda y.t)$ and $(\lambda x.s)y$. L and Plotkin's calculus agree for closed terms, which suffice for functional computation.

The subject of this paper is the formal verification of an abstract machine for L with closures and structure sharing. Our machine differs from the SECD machine in that it operates on programs rather than terms, has two flat stacks rather than one stack of frames, and provides structure sharing through a heap. Our goal was to come up with a transparent machine design providing for an elegant formal verification. We reach this goal with a stepwise refinement approach starting with a naive stack machine with programs and substitution. We then refine to a machine with closures, and finally to a machine with a heap. As

© Springer Nature Switzerland AG 2018
S. Ryu (Ed.): APLAS 2018, LNCS 11275, pp. 264–283, 2018.
https://doi.org/10.1007/978-3-030-02768-1_15

it comes to difficulty of verification, the refinement to the naive stack machine is by far the most substantial.

We prove the correctness of the three refinement steps with compositional small-step bottom-up simulations (i.e., L is above the machines and simulates machine transitions). While L has only β-steps, our machines have β- and τ-steps. L simulates a machine by following β-steps and ignoring τ-steps, and a machine simulates a lower-level machine by following β-steps with β-steps and τ-steps with τ-steps. To obtain bisimulations, we require progress conditions: Reducibility must propagate downwards and machines must stop after finitely many τ-steps.

The first verification step establishes the naive stack machine as a correct implementation of L, the second verification step establishes the closure machine as a correct implementation of the naive stack machine, and the third verification step establishes the heap machine as a correct implementation of the closure machine. The second and third verification step are relatively straightforward since they establish strict simulations (no silent steps). Strict simulations suffice since the programs of the naive stack machine already provide the right granularity for the structure sharing heap machine.

The entire development is formalised with the Coq proof assistant [22]. Coq's type theory provides an ideal foundation for the various inductive constructions needed for the specification and verification of the machines. All reasoning is naturally constructive. In the paper we don't show Coq code but use mathematical notation and language throughout. While familiarity with constructive type theory is helpful for reading the paper, technical knowledge of Coq is not required. For the expert and the curious reader, the definitions and theorems in the paper are hyperlinked with their formalisations in an HTML rendering of the Coq development. The Coq formalisation is available at https://www.ps.uni-saarland.de/extras/cbvlcm2/.

Related Work

We review work concerning the verification of abstract machines for call-by-value λ-calculus.

Plotkin [18] presents the first formalisation and verification of Landin's SECD machine [14]. He considers terms and closures with named variables and proves that his machine computes normal forms of closed terms using a step-indexed evaluation semantics for terms and top-down arguments (from λ-calculus to machine). He shows that failure of term evaluation for a given bound entails failure of machine execution for this bound. Plotkin does not prove his substitution lemmas. Ramsdell [19] reports on a formalisation of a Plotkin-style verification of an SECD machine optimising tail calls using the Boyer-Moore theorem prover. Ramsdell employs de Bruijn terms and de Bruijn substitution.

Felleisen and Friedman [10] study Plotkin's call-by-value λ-calculus extended with control operators like J and call/cc. They prove correctness properties relating abstract machines, small-step reduction systems, and algebraic theories. Like Plotkin, they use terms and closures with named variables.

Rittri [20] seems to be the first who verifies an abstract machine for a call-by-value λ-calculus using a small-step bottom up simulation. Rittri's work is also similar to ours in that he starts from a λ-calculus with simple substitution reducing closed terms, and in that his machine uses a control and an argument stack. Rittri gives detailed informal proofs using terms with named variables. He does not consider a naive intermediate machine nor a heap realisation.

Hardin et al. [13] verify several abstract machines with respect to a fine-grained λ-calculus with de Bruijn terms and explicit substitution primitives. Like us, they simulate machine steps with reduction steps of the calculus and disallow infinitely many consecutive silent steps. They consider the Krivine machine [7] (call-by-name), the SECD machine [14, 18] (call-by-value), Cardelli's FAM [5] (call-by-value), and the categorical abstract machine [6] (call-by-value).

Accattoli et al. [1] verify several abstract machines for the linear substitution calculus with explicit substitution primitives. They simulate machine steps with reduction steps of the calculus and model internal steps of the calculus with a structural congruence. They employ a global environment acting as heap. Among other machines, they verify a simplified variant of the ZINC machine [15].

Leroy [16, 17] verifies the Modern SECD machine for call-by-value λ-calculus specified with de Bruijn terms and an environment-based evaluation semantics in Coq. The modern SECD machine has programs and a single stack. Leroy's semantic setup is such that neither substitution nor small-step reduction of terms have to be considered. He uses top-down arguments and compiles terms into machine states. Using coinductive divergence predicates, Leroy shows that the machine diverges on states obtained from diverging terms. Leroy's proofs are pleasantly straightforward.

Danvy and Nielsen [9] introduce the refocusing technique, a general procedure transforming small-step reduction systems defined with evaluation contexts into abstract machines operating on the same syntax. Biernacka and Danvy [4] extend refocusing and obtain environment-based abstract machines. This yields a framework where the derived machines are provably correct with respect to small-step bisimulation. Biernacka et al. [3] formalise a generalisation of the framework in Coq.

Swierstra [21] formally verifies the correctness of a Krivine machine for simply typed λ-calculus in the dependently typed programming language Agda. Also following Biernacka and Danvy [4], Swierstra does this by showing the correctness of a Krivine-style evaluator for an iterative and environment-based head reduction evaluator. This way substitution does not appear. Swierstra's dependently typed constructions also provide normalisation proofs for simply typed λ-calculus. Swierstra's approach will not work for untyped λ-calculus.

Contribution of the Paper

We see the main contribution of the paper in the principled formal verification of a heap machine for a call-by-value λ-calculus using a small-step bottom-up simulation. A small-step bottom-up verification is semantically more informative than the usual evaluation-based top-down verification in that it maps every reachable machine state to a term of L. The entire Coq development consists of 500 lines of proof plus 750 lines of specification. The decomposition of the verification in three refinement steps provides for transparency and reusability.

The use of the naive stack machine as an intermediate machine appears to be new. We also think that our simple formalisation of structure sharing with code and heap is of interest.

We envision a formal proof showing that Turing machines can simulate L with polynomial overhead in time and constant overhead in space (under a suitable cost model) [11]. The verifications in this paper are one step into this direction.

Plan of the Paper

After some preliminaries fixing basic notions in Coq's type theory, we specify the call-by-value λ-calculus L and present our abstract framework for machines and refinements. We then introduce programs and program substitution and prove a substitution lemma. Next we specify and verify the naive stack machine for L. This is the most complex refinement step as it comes to proofs. Next we specify the closure machine and verify that it is an implementation of the naive stack machine and hence of L (by compositionality). Finally, we define abstractions for codes and heaps and verify that the heap machine is an implementation of the closure machine and hence of L.

2   Preliminaries

Everything in this paper is carried out in Coq's type theory and all reasoning is constructive. We use the following inductive types: N providing the *numbers* $n ::= 0 \mid \mathsf{S}n$, and $\mathcal{O}(X)$ providing the *options* $\emptyset$ and $°x$, and $\mathcal{L}(X)$ providing the *lists* $A ::= [] \mid x :: A$.

For lists $A, B : \mathcal{L}(X)$ we use the functions *length* $|A| : \mathsf{N}$, *concatenation* $A + B : \mathcal{L}(X)$, *map* $f@A : \mathcal{L}(Y)$ where $f : X \to Y$, and *lookup* $A[n] : \mathcal{O}(X)$ where $(x :: A)[0] = °x$, and $(x :: A)[\mathsf{S}n] = A[n]$, and $[][n] = \emptyset$. When we define functions that yield an option, we will omit equations that yield $\emptyset$ (e.g., the third equation $[][n] = \emptyset$ defining lookup $A[n] : \mathcal{O}(X)$ will be omitted).

We write $\mathbf{P}$ for the universe of propositions and $\bot$ for the proposition falsity. A *relation on X and Y* is a predicate $X \to Y \to \mathbf{P}$, and a *relation on X* is a predicate $X \to X \to \mathbf{P}$. A relation R is *functional* if $y = y'$ whenever Rxy and Rxy'. A relation R on X and Y is *computable* if there is a function $f : X \to \mathcal{O}(Y)$ such that $\forall x. (\exists y. fx = °y \land Rxy) \lor (fx = \emptyset \land \neg\exists y. Rxy)$.

We use a recursive *membership* predicate $x \in A$ such that $(x \in []) = \bot$ and $(x \in y :: A) = (x{=}y \lor x \in A)$.

We define an inductive predicate $\mathsf{ter}_R\, x$ identifying the *terminating points* of a relation R on X:

$$\frac{\forall x'.\ Rxx' \to \mathsf{ter}_R\, x'}{\mathsf{ter}_R\, x}$$

If x is a terminating point of R, we say that R *terminates on x* or that x *terminates for R*. We call a relation *terminating* if it terminates on every point.

Let R be a relation on X. The *span of R* is the inductive relation $\rhd_R$ on X defined as follows:

$$\frac{\neg \exists y.\ Rxy}{x \rhd_R x} \qquad\qquad \frac{Rxx' \qquad x' \rhd_R y}{x \rhd_R y}$$

If $x \rhd_R y$, we say that *y is a normal form of x for R*.

Fact 1. *1. If R is functional, then $\rhd_R$ is functional.*
2. If R is functional and x has a normal form for R, then R terminates on x.
3. If R is computable, then every terminating point of R has a normal form for R.

A *reduction system* is a structure consisting of a type X and a relation R on X. Given a reduction system $A = (X, R)$, we shall write A for the type X and $\succ_A$ for the relation of A. We say that *a reduces to b in A* if $a \succ_A b$.

3   Call-by-Value Lambda Calculus L

The call-by-value λ-calculus we consider in this paper employs de Bruijn terms with simple substitution and admits only abstractions as values.

We provide *terms* with an inductive type

$$s, t, u, v\ :\ \mathsf{Ter} :: = \ n \mid st \mid \lambda s \qquad (n : \mathsf{N})$$

and define a recursive function s_u^k providing *simple substitution*:

$$
\begin{aligned}
k_u^k &:= u & (st)_u^k &:= (s_u^k)(t_u^k) \\
n_u^k &:= n \quad \text{if } n \neq k & (\lambda s)_u^k &:= \lambda(s_u^{\mathsf{S}k})
\end{aligned}
$$

We define an inductive *reduction relation* $s \succ t$ on terms:

$$\frac{}{(\lambda s)(\lambda t) \succ s_{\lambda t}^0} \qquad\qquad \frac{s \succ s'}{st \succ s't} \qquad\qquad \frac{t \succ t'}{(\lambda s)t \succ (\lambda s)t'}$$

Fact 2. *$s \succ t$ is functional and computable.*

We define an *inductive bound predicate* $s < k$ for terms:

$$\frac{n < k}{n < k} \qquad\qquad \frac{s < k \qquad t < k}{st < k} \qquad\qquad \frac{s < \mathsf{S}k}{\lambda s < k}$$

Informally, $s < k$ holds if every free variable of s is smaller than k. A term is *closed* if $s < 0$. A term is *open* if it is not closed.

For closed terms, reduction in L agrees with reduction in the λ-calculus. For open terms, reduction in L is ill-behaved since L is defined with simple substitution. For instance, we have $(\lambda\lambda 1)(\lambda 1)(\lambda 0) \succ (\lambda\lambda 1)(\lambda 0) \succ \lambda\lambda 0$. Note that the second 1 in the initial term is not bound and refers to the De Bruijn index 0. Thus the first reduction step is capturing.

We define *stuck terms* inductively:

$$\frac{}{\text{stuck } n} \qquad \frac{\text{stuck } s}{\text{stuck } (st)} \qquad \frac{\text{stuck } t}{\text{stuck } ((\lambda s)t)}$$

Fact 3 (Trichotomy). *For every term s, exactly one of the following holds: (1) s is reducible. (2) s is an abstraction. (3) s is stuck.*

4 Machines and Refinements

We model machines as reduction systems. Recall that L is also a reduction system. We relate a machine M with L with a relation $a \gg s$ we call *refinement*. If $a \gg s$ holds, we say that a (a state of M) refines s (a term of L). Correctness means that L can simulate steps of M such that refinement between states and terms is preserved. Concretely, if a refines s and a reduces to a' in M, then either a' still *refines* s or s reduces to some s' in L such that a' refines s'. Steps where the refined term stays unchanged are called *silent*.

The general idea is now as follows. Given a term s, we compile s into a refining state a. We then run the machine on a. If the machine terminates with a normal form b of a, we decompile b into a term t such that b refines t and conclude that t is a normal form of s. We require that the machine terminates for every state refining a term that has a normal form.

Definition 4. *A* machine *is a structure consisting of a type A of states and two relations $\succ_\tau$ and $\succ_\beta$ on A. When convenient, we consider a machine A as a reduction system with the relation $\succ_A := \succ_\tau \cup \succ_\beta$.*

The letter X ranges over reduction systems and A and B range over machines.

Definition 5. *A refinement A to X is a relation $\gg$ on A and X such that:*

1. *If $a \gg x$ and x is reducible with $\succ_X$, then a is reducible with $\succ_A$.*
2. *If $a \gg x$ and $a \succ_\tau a'$, then $a' \gg x$.*
3. *If $a \gg x$ and $a \succ_\beta a'$, then there exists x' such that $a' \gg x'$ and $x \succ x'$.*
4. *If $a \gg x$, then a terminates for $\succ_\tau$.*

We say that a refines x if $a \gg x$.

Figure 1 illustrates refinements with a diagram. Transitions in X appear in the upper line and transitions in A appear in the lower line. The dotted lines represent the refinement relation. Note that conditions (2) and (3) of Definition 5 ensure that refinements are bottom up simulations (i.e., X can simulate A). Conditions (1) and (4) are progress conditions. They suffice to ensure that refinements also act as top-down simulations (i.e. A can simulate X), given mild assumptions that are fulfilled by L and all our machines.

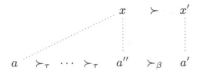

Fig. 1. Refinement diagram

Fact 6 (Correctness). *Let* $\gg$ *be a refinement A to X and $a \gg x$. Then:*

1. *If $a \triangleright_A a'$, there exists x' such that $a' \gg x'$ and $x \triangleright_X x'$.*
2. *If $a \triangleright_A a'$, $a' \gg x'$, and $\gg$ is functional, then $x \triangleright_X x'$.*
3. *If x terminates for $\succ_X$, then a terminates for $\succ_A$.*
4. *If x terminates for $\succ_X$ and $\succ_A$ is computable, then there exists a' such that $a \triangleright_A a'$.*

Proof. (1) follows by induction on $a \triangleright_A x$. (2) follows with (1) and Fact 1. (3) follows by induction on the termination of x for $\succ_X$ and the termination of a for $\succ_\tau$. (4) follows by induction on the termination of x.   □

We remark that the concrete reduction systems we will consider in this paper are all functional and computable. Moreover, all concrete refinements will be functional and, except for the heap machine, also be computable.

A refinement may be seen as the combination of an invariant and a decompilation function. We speak of an invariant since the fact that a state is a refinement of a term is preserved by the reduction steps of the machine.

Under mild assumptions fulfilled in our setting, the inverse of a refinement is a stuttering bisimulation [2]. The following fact asserts the necessary top-down simulation.

Fact 7. *Let $\gg$ be a refinement A to X where $\succ_X$ is functional and $\succ_\tau$ is computable.*

1. *If $a \gg x \succ_X x'$, then there exist a' and a'' such that $a \triangleright_\tau a'' \succ_\beta a' \gg x'$.*
2. *If $a \gg x \triangleright_X x'$, then there exists a' such that $a \triangleright_A a' \gg x'$.*

Proof. (1) follows with Fact 1. (2) follows by induction on $x \triangleright_X x'$ using (1). □

We will also refine machines with machines and rely on a composition theorem that combines two refinements A to B and B to X to a refinement A to X. We define refinement of machines with strict simulation.

Definition 8. *A refinement A to B is a relation $\gg$ on A and B such that:*

1. *If $a \gg b$ and b is reducible with $\succ_B$, then a is reducible with $\succ_A$.*
2. *If $a \gg b$ and $a \succ_\tau a'$, then there exists b' such that $a' \gg b'$ and $b \succ_\tau b'$.*
3. *If $a \gg b$ and $a \succ_\beta a'$, then there exists b' such that $a' \gg b'$ and $b \succ_\beta b'$.*

Fact 9 (Composition). *Let $\gg_1$ be a refinement A to B and $\gg_2$ be a refinement B to X. Then the composition $\lambda ac. \exists b. a \gg_1 b \wedge b \gg_2 c$ is a refinement A to X.*

5 Programs

The machines we will consider execute programs. Programs may be seen as lists of commands to be executed one after the other. Every term can be compiled into a program, and programs that are images of terms can be decompiled. There are commands for variables, abstractions, and applications. We represent *programs* with a tree-recursive inductive type so that the command for abstractions can nest programs:

$$P, Q, R \; : \; \mathsf{Pro} \; ::= \; \mathsf{ret} \mid \mathsf{var}\, n; P \mid \mathsf{lam}\, Q; P \mid \mathsf{app}; P \qquad (n : \mathsf{N})$$

We define a tail recursive *compilation function* $\gamma : \mathsf{Ter} \to \mathsf{Pro} \to \mathsf{Pro}$ translating terms into programs:

$$\gamma n P \; := \; \mathsf{var}\, n; P \qquad\qquad \gamma(\lambda s)P \; := \; \mathsf{lam}(\gamma s\mathsf{ret}); P$$
$$\gamma(st)P \; := \; \gamma s(\gamma t(\mathsf{app}; P))$$

The second argument of γ may be understood as a continuation.

We also define a *decompilation function* δPA of type $\mathsf{Pro} \to \mathcal{L}(\mathsf{Ter}) \to \mathcal{O}(\mathcal{L}(\mathsf{Ter}))$ translating programs into terms. The function executes the program over a stack of terms. The optional result acknowledges the fact that not every program represents a term. We write A and B for lists of terms. Here are the equations defining the decompilation function:

$$\delta \,\mathsf{ret}\, A \; := \; {}^{\circ}A$$
$$\delta(\mathsf{var}\, n; P)A \; := \; \delta P(n :: A)$$
$$\delta(\mathsf{lam}\, Q; P)A \; := \; \delta P(\lambda s :: A) \qquad \text{if } \delta Q\,[] = {}^{\circ}[s]$$
$$\delta(\mathsf{app}; P)A \; := \; \delta P(st :: A') \qquad \text{if } A = t :: s :: A'$$

Decompilation inverts compilation:

Fact 10. $\delta(\gamma s P)A = \delta P(s :: A)$.

Fact 11. *Let* $\delta PA = {}^{\circ}A'$. *Then* $\delta P(A \mathbin{+\!\!+} A'') = {}^{\circ}(A' \mathbin{+\!\!+} A'')$.

We define a predicate $P \gg s := \delta P[] = {}^{\circ}[s]$ read as P *represents* s.

The naive stack machine will use a *substitution operation* P_R^k for programs:

$$\mathsf{ret}\,{}_R^{\,k} \; := \; \mathsf{ret} \qquad\qquad (\mathsf{lam}\, Q; P)_R^k \; := \; \mathsf{lam}(Q_R^{\mathsf{S}k}); P_R^k$$
$$(\mathsf{var}\, k; P)_R^k \; := \; \mathsf{lam}\, R; P_R^k \qquad\qquad (\mathsf{app}; P)_R^k \; := \; \mathsf{app}; P_R^k$$
$$(\mathsf{var}\, n; P)_R^k \; := \; \mathsf{var}\, n; P_R^k \qquad \text{if } n \neq k$$

Note the second equation for the variable command that replaces a variable command with a lambda command. The important thing to remember here is the fact that the program R is inserted as the body of a lambda command.

For the verification of the naive stack machine we need a substitution lemma relating term substitution with program substitution. The lemma we need appears as Corollary 13 below. We prove the fact with a generalised version that can be shown by induction on programs. We use the notation $A_u^k := (\lambda s.s_u^k)@A$.

$$\mathsf{ret} :: T, \ V \ \succ_\tau \ T, \ V$$
$$(\mathsf{lam}\, Q; P) :: T, \ V \ \succ_\tau \ P :: T, \ Q :: V$$
$$(\mathsf{app}; P) :: T, \ R :: Q :: V \ \succ_\beta \ Q_R^0 :: P :: T, \ V$$

Fig. 2. Reduction rules of the naive stack machine

Lemma 12 (Substitution). *Let* $R \gg t$ *and* $\delta QA = {}^\circ B$. *Then* $\delta\, Q_R^k\, A_{\lambda t}^k = {}^\circ B_{\lambda t}^k$.

Corollary 13 (Substitution). *If* $P \gg s$ *and* $Q \gg t$, *then* $P_Q^k \gg s_{\lambda t}^k$.

We define a *bound predicate* $P < k$ for programs that is analogous to the bound predicate for terms and say that a program P is *closed* if $P < 0$:

$$\frac{}{\mathsf{ret} < k} \qquad \frac{n < k \qquad P < k}{\mathsf{var}\, n; P < k} \qquad \frac{Q < \mathsf{S}k \qquad P < k}{\mathsf{lam}\, Q; P < k} \qquad \frac{P < k}{\mathsf{app}; P < k}$$

Fact 14. *If* $s < k$ *and* $P < k$, *then* $\gamma s P < k$.

It follows that $\gamma s P$ is closed whenever s and P are closed.

6   Naive Stack Machine

The naive stack machine executes programs using two stacks of programs called *control stack* and *argument stack*. The control stack holds the programs to be executed, and the argument stack holds the programs computed so far. The machine executes the first command of the first program on the control stack until the control stack is empty or execution of a command fails.

The *states of the naive stack machine* are pairs

$$(T, V) \ : \ \mathcal{L}(\mathsf{Pro}) \times \mathcal{L}(\mathsf{Pro})$$

consisting of two lists T and V representing the control stack and the argument stack. We use the letters T and V since we think of the items on T as tasks and the items on V as values. The *reduction rules of the naive stack machine* appear in Fig. 2. The parentheses for states are omitted for readability. We will refer to the rules as *return rule*, *lambda rule*, and *application rule*. The return rule removes the trivial program from the control stack. The lambda rule pushes a program representing an abstraction on the argument stack. Note that the programs on the control stack are executed as they are. This is contrast to the programs on the argument stack that represent bodies of abstractions. The application rule takes two programs from the argument stack and pushes an instantiated program obtained by β-reduction on the control stack. This way control is passed from the calling program to the called program. There is no reduction rule for the variable command since we will only consider states that represent closed terms.

Fact 15. *The relations* $\succ_\tau$, $\succ_\beta$, *and* $\succ_\tau \cup \succ_\beta$ *are functional and computable. Moreover, the relations* $\succ_\tau$ *and* $\succ_\beta$ *are terminating.*

We decompile machine states by executing the task stack on the stack of terms obtained by decompiling the programs on the value stack. To this purpose we define two decompilation functions. The *decompilation function* δV *for argument stacks* has type $\mathcal{L}(\mathsf{Pro}) \rightarrow \mathcal{O}(\mathcal{L}(\mathsf{Ter}))$ and satisfies the equations

$$\delta[] := {}^\circ[]$$
$$\delta(P :: V) := {}^\circ(\lambda s :: A) \qquad \text{if } P \gg s \text{ and } \delta V = {}^\circ A$$

Note that the second equation turns the term s obtained from a program on the argument stack into the abstraction λs. This accounts for the fact that programs on the argument stack represent bodies of abstractions. The *decompilation function* δTA *for control stacks* has type $\mathcal{L}(\mathsf{Pro}) \rightarrow \mathcal{L}(\mathsf{Ter}) \rightarrow \mathcal{O}(\mathcal{L}(\mathsf{Ter}))$ and satisfies the equations

$$\delta[]A := {}^\circ A$$
$$\delta(P :: T)A := \delta T A' \qquad \text{if } \delta P A = {}^\circ A'$$

We now define the *refinement relation* between states of the naive stack machine and terms as follows:

$$(T, V) \gg s := \exists A.\ \delta V = {}^\circ A \ \wedge\ \delta T A = {}^\circ[s]$$

We will show that $(T, V) \gg s$ is in fact a refinement.

Fact 16. $(T, V) \gg s$ *is functional and computable.*

Fact 17 (τ-Simulation). *If* $(T, V) \gg s$ *and* $T, V \succ_\tau T', V'$, *then* $(T', V') \gg s$.

Proof. We prove the claim for the second τ-rule, the proof for the first τ-rule is similar. Let $\mathsf{lam}\, Q; P :: T,\ V\ \succ_\tau\ P :: T,\ Q :: V$. We have

$$\delta(\mathsf{lam}\, Q; P :: T)(\delta V) = \delta T(\delta(\mathsf{lam}\, Q; P)(\delta V))$$
$$= \delta T(\delta P(\lambda s :: \delta V)) \qquad Q \gg s$$
$$= \delta(P :: T)(\delta(Q :: V)) \qquad \qquad \square$$

Note that the equational part of the proof nests optional results to avoid cluttering with side conditions and auxiliary names.

Proving that L can simulate β-steps of the naive stack machine takes effort.

Fact 18. *If* $\delta V = {}^\circ A$, *then every term in A is an abstraction.*

Fact 19. $\delta(\mathsf{app}; P :: T)(t :: s :: A) = \delta(P :: T)(st :: A)$.

Fact 20. $\delta(P :: T)A = \delta T(s :: A)$ *if* $P \gg s$.

Proof. Follows with Fact 11.   □

Lemma 21 (Substitution). $\delta(Q_R^0 :: T)A = \delta T(s_{\lambda t}^0 :: A)$ *if* $Q \gg s$ *and* $R \gg t$.

Proof. By Corollary 13 we have $Q_R^0 \gg s_{\lambda t}^0$. The claim follows with Fact 20.   □

We also need a special reduction relation $A \succ A'$ for term lists:

$$\frac{s \succ s' \qquad \forall t \in A. \; t \text{ is an abstraction}}{s :: A \succ s' :: A} \qquad\qquad \frac{A \succ A'}{s :: A \succ s :: A'}$$

Informally, $A \succ A'$ holds if A' can be obtained from A by reducing the term in A that is only followed by abstractions.

Lemma 22. *Let* $A \succ A'$ *and* $\delta PA = {}^{\circ}B$. *Then* $\exists B'. \; B \succ B' \wedge \delta PA' = {}^{\circ}B'$.

Proof. By induction on P. We consider the case $P = \mathsf{app}; P$.
    Let $\delta(\mathsf{app}; P)(t :: s :: A) = {}^{\circ}B$ and $t :: s :: A \succ t' :: s' :: A'$. Then $\delta P(st :: A) = {}^{\circ}B$ and $st :: A \succ s't' :: A'$ (there are three cases: (1) $t = t'$, $s = s'$, and $A \succ A'$; (2) $t = t'$, $s \succ s'$, $A = A'$, and A contains only abstractions; (3) $t \succ t'$, $s :: A = s' :: A'$, and $s :: A$ contains only abstractions). By the inductive hypothesis we have $B \succ B'$ and $\delta P(s't' :: A') = {}^{\circ}B'$ for some B'. Thus $\delta(\mathsf{app}; P)(t' :: s' :: A') = {}^{\circ}B'$.   □

Fact 23 (β-Simulation).   *If* $(T, V) \gg s$ *and* $T, V \succ_{\beta} T', V'$, *then* $\exists s'. \; (T', V') \gg s' \wedge s \succ s'.]$

Proof. Let $\mathsf{app}; P :: T, \; R :: Q :: V \succ_{\beta} Q_R^0 :: P :: T, V$. Moreover, let $R \gg t$, $Q \gg u$, and $\delta V = {}^{\circ}A$. We have:

$$
\begin{aligned}
{}^{\circ}[s] &= \delta(\mathsf{app}; P :: T)(\delta(R :: Q :: V)) \\
&= \delta(\mathsf{app}; P :: T)(\lambda t :: \lambda u :: A) \\
&= \delta(P :: T)((\lambda u)(\lambda t) :: A) &&\text{Fact 19}\\
&\succ \delta(P :: T)(u_{\lambda t}^0 :: A) &&\text{Lemma 22 and Fact 18}\\
&= \delta(Q_R^0 :: P :: T)A &&\text{Lemma 21}\\
&= {}^{\circ}[s'] &&\text{for some } s'
\end{aligned}
$$

Note that s' exists since $\succ$ preserves the length of a list. We now have $s \succ s'$ by the definition of $\succ$ and $(Q_R^0 :: P :: T, V) \gg s'$, which concludes the proof.   □

It remains to show that states are reducible if they refine reducible terms. For this purpose, we define *stuck term lists*:

$$\frac{\mathsf{stuck}\; s \qquad \forall t \in A. \; t \text{ is an abstraction}}{\mathsf{stuck}\,(s :: A)} \qquad\qquad \frac{\mathsf{stuck}\; A}{\mathsf{stuck}\,(s :: A)}$$

Note that s is stuck iff $[s]$ is stuck.

Lemma 24. *Let A be stuck and $\delta PA = {}^\circ B$. Then B is stuck.*

Lemma 25. *Let A be stuck and $\delta TA = {}^\circ B$. Then B is stuck.*

Fact 26 (Trichotomy). *Let $T, V \gg s$. Then exactly one of the following holds:*

1. (T, V) is reducible.
2. $(T, V) = ([], [P])$ and $P \gg s'$ with $s = \lambda s'$ for some P, s'.
3. $T = \mathsf{var}\, x; P :: T'$ for some x, P, T' and s is stuck.

Proof. Let $\delta V = {}^\circ A$ and $\delta TA = {}^\circ[s]$, and s be reducible. By Fact 18 we know that A contains only abstractions. Case analysis on T.

$T = []$. Then $A = [s]$ and the second case holds by definition of δ.

$T = \mathsf{ret} :: T'$. Then (T, V) is reducible.

$T = \mathsf{var}\, n; P :: T'$. We have

$$ {}^\circ[s] = \delta(\mathsf{var}\, n; P :: T')A = \delta T'(\delta(\mathsf{var}\, n; P)A) = \delta T'(\delta P(n :: A)) $$

Since $n :: A$ is stuck, we know by Lemmas 24 and 25 that $[s]$ is stuck. Thus the third case holds.

$T = \mathsf{lam}\, Q; P :: T'$. Then (T, V) is reducible.

$T = \mathsf{app}; P :: T'$. Then ${}^\circ[s] = \delta(\mathsf{app}; P :: T')A = \delta T'(\delta(\mathsf{app}; P)A)$ and hence $A = t :: s :: A'$. Thus $V = R :: Q :: V'$. Thus (T, V) is reducible. $\qquad\square$

Corollary 27 (Progress). *If $T, V \gg s$ and s is reducible, then (T, V) is reducible.*

Proof. Follows from Fact 26 using Fact 3. $\qquad\square$

Theorem 28 (Naive Stack Machine to L). *The relation*

$$ (T, V) \gg s \ := \ \exists A.\ \delta V = {}^\circ A \ \wedge \ \delta TA = {}^\circ[s] $$

is a functional and computable refinement. Moreover, $([\gamma\, s\, \mathsf{ret}], []) \gg s$ holds for every term s.

Proof. The first claim follows with Facts 16, 27, 17, 23, and 15. The second claim follows with Fact 10. $\qquad\square$

7   Closures

A closure is a pair consisting of a program and an environment. An environment is a list of closures representing a delayed substitution. With closures we can refine the naive stack machine so that no substitution operation is needed.

$$ e \ : \ \mathsf{Clo} \ ::= \ P/E \qquad\qquad closure $$
$$ E, F, T, V \ : \ \mathcal{L}(\mathsf{Clo}) \qquad\qquad environment $$

$$(\mathsf{ret}/E) :: T,\ V \ \succ_\tau\ T,\ V$$
$$(\mathsf{var}\,n; P/E) :: T,\ V \ \succ_\tau\ (P/E) :: T,\ e :: V \qquad\qquad \text{if } E[n] = {}^\circ e$$
$$(\mathsf{lam}\,Q; P/E) :: T,\ V \ \succ_\tau\ (P/E) :: T,\ (Q/E) :: V$$
$$(\mathsf{app}; P/E) :: T,\ e :: (Q/F) :: V \ \succ_\beta\ (Q/e :: F) :: (P/E) :: T,\ V$$

Fig. 3. Reduction rules of the closure machine

For the decompilation of closures into plain programs we define a *parallel substitution operation* P_W^k for programs (W ranges over lists of programs):

$$\mathsf{ret}\,_W^k \ := \ \mathsf{ret}$$
$$(\mathsf{app}; P)_W^k \ := \ \mathsf{app}; P_W^k$$
$$(\mathsf{lam}\,Q; P)_W^k \ := \ \mathsf{lam}(Q_W^{\mathsf{S}k}); P_W^k$$
$$(\mathsf{var}\,n; P)_W^k \ := \ \text{if } n \geq k \wedge W[n-k] = {}^\circ Q \text{ then } \mathsf{lam}\,Q; P_W^k \text{ else } \mathsf{var}\,n; P_W^k$$

We will use the notation $W < 1 := \forall P \in W.\ P < 1$.

Fact 29 (Parallel Substitution)

1. $P_{[]}^k = P$.
2. If $P < k$ and $k \leq k'$, then $P < k'$.
3. If $P < k$, then $P_Q^k = P$.
4. If $W < 1$, then $P_{Q::W}^k = (P_W^{\mathsf{S}k})_Q^k$.
5. If $W < 1$ and $P < |W| + k$, then $P_W^k < k$.

Note that Fact 29 (4) relates parallel substitution to single substitution.

We define a function $\delta_1 e$ of type $\mathsf{Clo} \to \mathsf{Pro}$ translating closures into programs:

$$\delta_1(P/E) \ := \ P_{\delta @ E}^1$$

We also define an inductive *bound predicate* $e < 1$ for closures:

$$\frac{P < \mathsf{S}|E| \qquad E < 1}{P/E < 1} \qquad\qquad E < 1 \ := \ \forall e \in E.\ e < 1$$

Note the recursion through environments via the map function and via the membership predicate in the last two definitions.

Fact 30. *If $e < 1$, then $\delta_1 e < 1$.*

8 Closure Machine

We now refine the naive stack machine by replacing all programs on the control stack and the argument stack with closures, eliminating program substitution.

States of the closure machine are pairs

$$(T, V) \; : \; \mathcal{L}(\mathsf{Clo}) \times \mathcal{L}(\mathsf{Clo})$$

consisting of a *control stack* T and an *argument stack* V.

The *reduction rules of the closure machine* appear in Fig. 3. The *variable rule* (second τ-rule) is new. It applies if the environment provides a closure for the variable. In this case the closure is pushed on the argument stack. We see this as delayed substitution of the variable. The variable rule will be simulated with the lambda rule of the naive stack machine.

The *application rule* (β-rule) takes two closures e and Q/F from the argument stack and pushes the closure $Q/e :: F$ on the control stack, which represents the result of β-reducing the abstraction represented by Q/F with the argument e.

We will show that the closure machine implements the naive stack machine correctly provided there are no free variables.

There is the complication that the closures on the control stack must be closed while the closures on the argument stack are allowed to have the free variable 0 representing the argument to be supplied by the application rule.

We define *closed states* of the closure machine as follows:

$$P/E < 0 \; := \; P < |E| \; \wedge \; E < 1$$
$$T < 0 \; := \; \forall e \in T. \, e < 0$$
$$\mathsf{closed}\,(T, V) \; := \; T < 0 \; \wedge \; V < 1$$

We define a function $\delta_0 e$ of type $\mathsf{Clo} \to \mathsf{Pro}$ for decompiling closures on the task stack:

$$\delta_0(P/E) \; := \; P^0_{\delta @ E}$$

We can now define the *refinement relation* between states of the closure machine and states of the naive stack machine:

$$(T, V) \gg \sigma \; := \; \mathsf{closed}\,(T, V) \; \wedge \; (\delta_0 @ T, \delta_1 @ V) = \sigma$$

We show that $(T, V) \gg \sigma$ is a refinement.

Fact 31. $(T, V) \gg \sigma$ *is functional and computable.*

Fact 32 (Progress). *Let* $(\delta_0 @ T, \delta_1 @ V)$ *be reducible. Then* (T, V) *is reducible.*

Fact 33. *Let* (T, V) *be closed and* $(T, V) \succ (T', V')$. *Then* (T', V') *is closed.*

Fact 34 (τ-Simulation). *Let* $(T, V) \succ_\tau (T', V')$.
Then $(\delta_0 @ T, \delta_1 @ V) \succ_\tau (\delta_0 @ T', \delta_1 @ V')$.

Fact 35 (β-Simulation). *Let* (T, V) *be closed and* $(T, V) \succ_\beta (T', V')$.
Then $(\delta_0 @ T, \delta_1 @ V) \succ_\beta (\delta_0 @ T', \delta_1 @ V')$.

Proof Follows with Facts 29 (4) and 30. □

Theorem 36 (Closure Machine to Naive Stack Machine). *The relation*

$$(T, V) \gg \sigma := \mathsf{closed}\,(T, V) \wedge (\delta_0 @ T, \delta_1 @ V) = \sigma$$

is a functional and computable refinement. Moreover, $([P/[]], []) \gg ([P], [])$ *holds for every closed program* P.

Proof. The first claim follows with Facts 31, 32, 33, 34, and 35. The second claim follows with Fact 29 (1). □

Note that Theorems 28 and 36 Facts 9 and 14 yield a refinement to L.

9   Codes

If a state is reachable from an initial state in the closure machine, all its programs are subprograms of programs in the initial state. We can thus represent programs as addresses of a fixed code, providing structure sharing for programs.

A code represents a program such that the commands and subprograms of the program can be accessed through addresses. We represent codes abstractly with a type Code, a type PA of program addresses, and two functions $\#$ and φ as follows:

$$
\begin{aligned}
C &: \mathsf{Code} & & code \\
p, q, r &: \mathsf{PA} & & program\ address \\
\# &: \mathsf{PA} \to \mathsf{PA} \\
\mathsf{Com} &:= \mathsf{ret} \mid \mathsf{var}\,n \mid \mathsf{lam}\,p \mid \mathsf{app} & & command \\
\varphi &: \mathsf{Code} \to \mathsf{PA} \to \mathcal{O}(\mathsf{Com})
\end{aligned}
$$

Note that commands are obtained with a nonrecursive inductive type Com. The function $\#$ increments a program address, and the φ yields the command for a valid program address. We will use the notation $C[p] := \varphi C p$. We fix the semantics of codes with a relation $p \gg_C P$ relating program addresses with programs:

$$\frac{C[p] = {}^\circ\mathsf{ret}}{p \gg_C \mathsf{ret}} \qquad \frac{C[p] = {}^\circ\mathsf{var}\,n \qquad \#p \gg_C P}{p \gg_C \mathsf{var}\,n;\, P}$$

$$\frac{C[p] = {}^\circ\mathsf{lam}\,q \qquad q \gg_C Q \qquad \#p \gg_C P}{p \gg_C \mathsf{lam}\,Q;\, P} \qquad \frac{C[p] = {}^\circ\mathsf{app} \qquad \#p \gg_C P}{p \gg_C \mathsf{app};\, P}$$

Fact 37. *The relation $p \gg_C P$ is functional.*

We obtain one possible implementation of codes as follows:

$$\mathsf{PA} \;:=\; \mathsf{N} \qquad\qquad \varphi C n \;:=\; \mathsf{lam}\,(n + k) \qquad \text{if } C[n] = \mathsf{lam}\,k$$
$$\mathsf{Code} \;:=\; \mathcal{L}(\mathsf{Com}) \qquad \varphi C n \;:=\; C[n] \qquad\qquad \text{otherwise}$$
$$\#n \;:=\; \mathsf{S}\,n$$

For this realisation of codes we define a function $\psi : \mathsf{Pro} \to \mathcal{L}(\mathsf{Com})$ compiling programs into codes as follows:

$$\psi\,\mathsf{ret} \;:=\; [\mathsf{ret}] \qquad\qquad \psi(\mathsf{lam}\,Q; P) \;:=\; \mathsf{lam}\,(\mathsf{S}|\psi P|) :: \psi P + \psi Q$$
$$\psi(\mathsf{var}\,n; P) \;:=\; \mathsf{var}\,n :: \psi P \qquad\qquad \psi(\mathsf{app}; P) \;:=\; \mathsf{app} :: \psi P$$

The linear representation of a program $\mathsf{lam}\,Q; P$ provided by ψ is as follows: First comes a command $\mathsf{lam}\,k$, then the commands for P, and finally the commands for Q (i.e., the commands for the body Q come after the commands for the continuation P). The number k of the command $\mathsf{lam}\,k$ is chosen such that $n + \mathsf{S}k$ is the address of the first command for Q if n is the address of the command $\mathsf{lam}\,k$.

Fact 38. $|C_1| \gg_{C_1 + \psi P + C_2} P$. *In particular,* $0 \gg_{\psi P} P$.

10 Heaps

A heap contains environments accessible through addresses. This opens the possibility to share the representation of environments.

We model heaps abstractly based on an assumed code structure. We start with types for heaps and heap addresses and a function **get** accessing heap addresses:

$$
\begin{array}{rll}
H &: \mathsf{Heap} & \qquad\qquad\qquad heap \\
a, b, c &: \mathsf{HA} & \qquad\qquad heap\ address \\
g &: \mathsf{HC} := \mathsf{PA} \times \mathsf{HA} & \qquad\quad heap\ closure \\
& \mathsf{HE} := \mathcal{O}(\mathsf{HC} \times \mathsf{HA}) & \quad heap\ environment \\
\mathsf{get} &: \mathsf{Heap} \to \mathsf{HA} \to \mathcal{O}(\mathsf{HE}) &
\end{array}
$$

We will use the notation $H[a] := \mathsf{get}\,H\,a$. We fix the semantics of heaps with an inductive relation $a \gg_H E$ relating heap addresses with environments:

$$
\frac{H[a] = {}^{\circ}\emptyset}{a \gg_H []} \qquad\qquad
\frac{H[a] = {}^{\circ\circ}((p, b), c) \quad p \gg_C P \quad b \gg_H F \quad c \gg_H E}{a \gg_H (P/F) :: E}
$$

Fact 39. *The relation $a \gg_H E$ is functional.*

We also need an operation put $:$ Heap $\to$ HC $\to$ HA $\to$ Heap $\times$ HA extending a heap with an environment. Note that put yields the extended heap and the address of the extending environment. We use the notation

$$H \subseteq H' \ := \ \forall a. \ H[a] \neq \emptyset \ \to \ H[a] = H'[a]$$

to say that H' is an *extension* of H. We fix the semantics of put with the following requirement:

HR. If put $H \, g \, a = (H', b)$, then $H'[b] = (g, a)$ and $H \subseteq H'$.

Fact 40. *If $H \subseteq H'$ and $a \gg_H E$, then $a \gg_{H'} E$.*

We define a relation $g \gg_H e$ relating heap closures with proper closures:

$$(p, a) \gg_H (P, E) \ := \ p \gg_C P \wedge a \gg_H E$$

Fact 41. *If $H \subseteq H'$ and $g \gg_H e$, then $g \gg_{H'} e$.*

We define a *lookup function* $H[a, n] : \mathcal{O}(\mathsf{HC})$ yielding the heap closure appearing at position n of the heap environment designated by a in H:

$$
\begin{aligned}
H[a, 0] &:= \ {}^\circ(p, b) && \text{if } H[a] := {}^\circ((p, b), c) \\
H[a, \mathsf{S}\,n] &:= \ H[c, n] && \text{if } H[a] := {}^\circ((p, b), c)
\end{aligned}
$$

Fact 42. *Let $a \gg_H E$. Then:*

1. *If $E[n] = {}^\circ e$, then $H[a, n] = {}^\circ g$ and $g \gg_H e$ for some g.*
2. *If $H[a, n] = {}^\circ g$, then $E[n] = {}^\circ e$ and $g \gg_H e$ for some e.*

Here is one possible implementation of heaps:

$$
\begin{aligned}
\mathsf{HA} &:= \ \mathsf{N} \\
\mathsf{Heap} &:= \ \mathcal{L}(\mathsf{HC} \times \mathsf{HA}) \\
\mathsf{get}\ H\, 0 &:= \ {}^\circ\emptyset \\
\mathsf{get}\ H\,(\mathsf{S}\,n) &:= \ {}^{\circ\circ}(g, a) && \text{if } H[n] = {}^\circ(g, a) \\
\mathsf{put}\ H\, g\, a &:= \ (H + [(g, a)], \ \mathsf{S}\,|H|)
\end{aligned}
$$

Note that with this implementation the address 0 represents the empty environment in every heap.

Given that Coq admits only structurally recursive functions, writing a function computing $a \gg_H E$ is not straightforward. The problem goes away if we switch to a step-indexed function computing $a \gg_H E$.

$$(p,a) :: T, \ V, \ H \ \succ_\tau \ T, \ V, \ H \qquad\qquad \text{if } C[p] = {}^\circ\text{ret}$$

$$(p,a) :: T, \ V, \ H \ \succ_\tau \ (\#p,a) :: T, \ g :: V, \ H \qquad \text{if } C[p] = {}^\circ\text{var } n$$
$$\text{and } H[a,n] = {}^\circ g$$

$$(p,a) :: T, \ V, \ H \ \succ_\tau \ (\#p,a) :: T, \ (q,a) :: V, \ H \quad \text{if } C[p] = {}^\circ\text{lam } q$$

$$(p,a) :: T, \ g :: (q,b) :: V, \ H \ \succ_\beta \ (q,c) :: (\#p,a) :: T, \ V, \ H' \quad \text{if } C[p] = {}^\circ\text{app}$$
$$\text{and put } H\, g\, b = {}^\circ(H',c)$$

Fig. 4. Reduction rules of the heap machine

11   Heap Machine

The heap machine refines the closure machine by representing programs as addresses into a fixed code and environments as addresses into heaps that reside as additional component in the states of the heap machine.

We assume a code structure providing types Code and PA, a code C : Code, and a heap structure providing types Heap and HA. *States of the heap machine are triples*

$$(T, V, H) \ : \ \mathcal{L}(\text{HC}) \times \mathcal{L}(\text{HC}) \times \text{Heap}$$

consisting of a control stack, an argument stack, and a heap. The *reduction rules of the heap machine* appear in Fig. 4. They refine the reduction rules of the closure machine as one would expect.

Note that the application rule is the only rule that allocates new environments on the heap. This is at first surprising since with practical machines (e.g., FAM and ZINC) heap allocation takes place when lambda commands are executed. The naive allocation policy of our heap machine is a consequence of the naive realisation of the lambda command in the closure machine, which is common in formalisations of the SECD machine. Given our refinement approach, smart closure allocation would be prepared at the level of the naive stack machine with programs that have explicit commands for accessing and constructing closure environments.

Proving correctness of the heap machine is straightforward:

Theorem 43 (Heap Machine to Closure Machine). *Let a code structure, a code C, and a heap structure be fixed. Let $T \gg_H \dot{T}$ and $V \gg_H \dot{V}$ denote the pointwise extension of $g \gg_H E$ to lists. Then the relation*

$$(T, V, H) \gg (\dot{T}, \dot{V}) \ := \ T \gg_H \dot{T} \ \wedge \ V \gg_H \dot{V}$$

is a functional refinement. Moreover, $([(p,a)], [], H) \gg ([P/[]], [])$ for all p, a, H, and P such that $p \gg_C P$ and $a \gg_H []$.

Proof. Follows with Facts 37, 39, 40, 41, and 42. Straightforward.   □

Using the refinement from the closure machine to L, Theorem 43 and Fact 9 we obtain a refinement from the Heap Machine to L.

If we instantiate the heap machine with the realisation of codes from Sect. 9 and the realisation of heaps from Sect. 10 we obtain a function compiling closed terms into initial states. Moreover, given a function computing $a \gg_H E$, we can obtain a decompiler for the states of the heap machine.

12   Final Remarks

The tail call optimisation can be realised in our machines and accommodated in our verifications. For this subprograms app; ret are executed such that no trivial continuation (i.e., program ret) is pushed on the control stack.

The control stack may be merged with the argument stack. If this is done with explicit frames as in the SECD machine, adapting our verification should be straightforward. There is also the possibility to leave frames implicit as in the modern SECD machine. This will require different decompilation functions and concomitant changes in the verification.

We could also switch to a λ-calculus with full substitution. This complicates the definition of substitution and the basic substitution lemmas but has the pleasant consequence that we can drop the closedness constraints coming with the correctness theorems for the closure and heap machines. The insight here is that a closure machine implements full substitution. With full substitution we may reduce β-redexes where the argument is a variable and show a substitutivity property for small-step reduction.

References

1. Accattoli, B., Barenbaum, P., Mazza, D.: Distilling abstract machines. In: Proceedings of the 19th ACM SIGPLAN International Conference on Functional Programming, pp. 363–376 (2014)
2. Baier, C., Katoen, J.-P.: Principles of Model Checking. MIT Press, Cambridge (2008)
3. Biernacka, M., Charatonik, W., Zielinska, K.: Generalized refocusing: from hybrid strategies to abstract machines. In: LIPIcs, vol. 84. Schloss Dagstuhl-Leibniz-Zentrum für Informatik (2017)
4. Biernacka, M., Danvy, O.: A concrete framework for environment machines. ACM Trans. Comput. Logic (TOCL) **9**(1), 6 (2007)
5. Cardelli, L.: Compiling a functional language. In: Proceedings of the 1984 ACM Symposium on LISP and Functional Programming, pp. 208–217. ACM (1984)
6. Cousineau, G., Curien, P.-L., Mauny, M.: The categorical abstract machine. Sci. Comput. Program. **8**(2), 173–202 (1987)
7. Crégut, P.: An abstract machine for lambda-terms normalization. In: Proceedings of the 1990 ACM Conference on LISP and Functional Programming, pp. 333–340 (1990)
8. Dal Lago, U., Martini, S.: The weak lambda calculus as a reasonable machine. Theor. Comput. Sci. **398**(1–3), 32–50 (2008)

9. Danvy, O., Nielsen, L.R.: Refocusing in reduction semantics. BRICS Rep. Ser. **11**(26) (2004)
10. Felleisen, M., Friedman, D.P.: Control Operators, the SECD-machine, and the λ-calculus. Indiana University, Computer Science Department (1986)
11. Forster, Y., Kunze, F., Roth, M.: The strong invariance thesis for a λ-calculus. In: Workshop on Syntax and Semantics of Low-Level Languages (LOLA) (2017)
12. Forster, Y., Smolka, G.: Weak call-by-value lambda calculus as a model of computation in Coq. In: Ayala-Rincón, M., Muñoz, C.A. (eds.) ITP 2017. LNCS, vol. 10499, pp. 189–206. Springer, Cham (2017). https://doi.org/10.1007/978-3-319-66107-0_13
13. Hardin, T., Maranget, L., Pagano, B.: Functional runtime systems within the lambda-sigma calculus. J. Funct. Programm. **8**(2), 131–176 (1998)
14. Landin, P.J.: The mechanical evaluation of expressions. Comput. J. **6**(4), 308–320 (1964)
15. Leroy, X.: The ZINC experiment: an economical implementation of the ML language. Technical report, INRIA (1990)
16. Leroy, X.: Functional programming languages, Part II: Abstract machines, the Modern SECD. Lectures on Functional Programming and Type Systems, MPRI course 2-4, slides and Coq developments (2016). https://xavierleroy.org/mpri/2-4/
17. Leroy, X., Grall, H.: Coinductive big-step operational semantics. Inf. Comput. **207**(2), 284–304 (2009)
18. Plotkin, G.D.: Call-by-name, call-by-value and the λ-calculus. Theor. Comput. Sci. **1**(2), 125–159 (1975)
19. Ramsdell, J.D.: The tail-recursive SECD machine. J. Autom. Reason. **23**(1), 43–62 (1999)
20. Rittri, M.: Proving the correctness of a virtual machine by a bisimulation. Licentiate thesis, Chalmers University and University of Göteborg (1988)
21. Swierstra, W.: From mathematics to abstract machine: a formal derivation of an executable Krivine machine. In: Proceedings Fourth Workshop on Mathematically Structured Functional Programming, pp. 163–177 (2012)
22. The Coq Proof Assistant (2018). http://coq.inria.fr

Automated Modular Verification for Relaxed Communication Protocols

Andreea Costea[1]([✉]), Wei-Ngan Chin[1], Shengchao Qin[2,3], and Florin Craciun[4]

[1] School of Computing, National University of Singapore, Singapore, Singapore
{andreeac,chinwn}@comp.nus.edu.sg
[2] School of Computing, Teesside University, Middlesbrough, UK
s.qin@tees.ac.uk
[3] Shenzhen University, Shenzhen, China
[4] Faculty of Mathematics and Computer Science, Babes-Bolyai University,
Cluj-Napoca, Romania
craciunf@cs.ubbcluj.ro

Abstract. Ensuring software correctness and safety for communication-centric programs is important but challenging. In this paper we introduce a solution for writing communication protocols, for checking protocol conformance and for verifying implementation safety. This work draws on ideas from both multiparty session types, which provide a concise way to express communication protocols, as well as from separation-style logics for shared-memory concurrency, which provide strong safety guarantees for resource sharing. On the one hand, our proposal improves the expressiveness and precision of session types, without sacrificing their conciseness. On the other hand, it increases the applicability of software verification as well as its precision, by making it protocol aware. We also show how to perform the verification of such programs in a modular and automatic fashion.

1 Introduction

Asynchronous distributed systems are ubiquitous in digital applications, yet achieving their safe design and implementation is notoriously hard. The difficulties in building such systems are many-fold. First, these systems are normally described in the designing phase using communication protocols. The problem at this phase is that, because of the lack of formal, yet easy-to-use specification languages for communication protocols, designers prefer to draft the communication using RFC documents. But these drafts lack mathematical rigorosity, and, therefore, lead to ambiguous interpretations of the communication. Secondly, a developer often validates a system's correct implementation via testing. However, in the case of distributed systems, where reproductibility of execution is challenging, testing is rarely exhaustive. This kind of behavior commonly harbors difficult-to-detect bugs. Thirdly, the safe coordination of independent entities interacting with each other is problematic: on the one hand, the developer must

© Springer Nature Switzerland AG 2018
S. Ryu (Ed.): APLAS 2018, LNCS 11275, pp. 284–305, 2018.
https://doi.org/10.1007/978-3-030-02768-1_16

ensure exclusive access to shared resources in the case of tightly coupled entities, and, on the other hand, it must offer safe communication guarantees for the loosely coupled ones. Lastly, it is often the case that the code refactoring of one of the communicating entities requires the re-validation of the entire system. Since validation might be expensive, or difficult to achieve if the source code of certain components is not available, it is desirable for the developer to be able to only validate her changes locally, rather than at the global level.

Over the last decades, behavioral types [26,35] have been studied as specifications of the interactions in communicating systems. In particular, multiparty session types [23], or MPSTs, provide a user-friendly syntax for writing choreographic specifications of distributed systems, and a lightweight mechanism for enforcing communication safety. Communication is considered correct when the system's constituent processes are statically type-checked against the endpoint projections of the MPST. This formalism and its numerous extensions are attractive in checking if the implementation follows the intended communication pattern, but it lacks the strong safety and correctness guarantees normally provided by the resource-aware verification systems. Specifically, the MPST approach checks if a transmission's exchanged type is the expected one. However, in their most common form, MPSTs are unable to assert something about the message's numerical properties, and even less so about its carried resources in the case of tightly coupled systems. All these, while numerical properties and resource sharing constitute the pièce de résistance for separation logic [38], a logic for reasoning about resource sharing. In this work, we attach a communication logic in the user-friendly style of MPST, to a separation logic for program verification. Even though we draw on ideas from MPST, the proposed logic differs from MPST in a number of features which yield a more expressive communication specification - without compromising its friendly syntax. The current proposal ultimately leads to stronger guarantees w.r.t. the safety and correctness of distributed system. We shall next highlight these differences.

Writing Multiparty Communication Protocols. The language we propose for writing communication protocols is described in Fig. 1a. Similar to MPST, the language contains the terminal notation $S{\rightarrow}R : c\langle v{\cdot}\Delta\rangle$ to describe a transmission from sender S to receiver R, over channel c. Different from type approaches where a message abstracts a type, the exchanged message v is expressed in the logical form Δ (defined in Fig. 1b). Do note that $v{\cdot}\Delta$ is in fact a shorthand for the lambda function $(\lambda v . \Delta)$. This language uses $G_1 * G_2$ for the concurrency of global protocols G_1 and G_2, and $G_1 \vee G_2$ for disjunctive choice between either G_1 or G_2, and finally $G_1 ; G_2$ on the implicit sequentialization of G_1 before G_2 for either the same party or the same channel. Let us next consider a series of examples to introduce this language and to highlight the benefits over MPST.

Example 1: We consider a cloud service for video editing, where a client sends to the cloud a file of some video format, and expects back an enhanced version of the original file, see Fig. 2a. A client-server protocol to describe this simple interaction is written as follows:

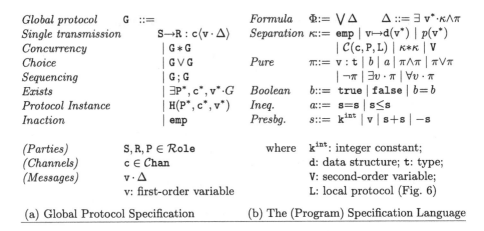

Global protocol	G ::=		Formula	$\Phi ::= \bigvee \Delta$ $\Delta ::= \exists\, v^* \cdot \kappa \wedge \pi$
Single transmission	$S{\to}R : c\langle v \cdot \Delta\rangle$		Separation	$\kappa ::= \texttt{emp} \mid v{\mapsto}d(v^*) \mid p(v^*)$
Concurrency	$\mid$ G $*$ G			$\mid \mathcal{C}(c,P,L) \mid \kappa *\kappa \mid V$
Choice	$\mid$ G $\vee$ G		Pure	$\pi ::= v : t \mid b \mid a \mid \pi\wedge\pi \mid \pi\vee\pi$
Sequencing	$\mid$ G $;$ G			$\mid \neg\pi \mid \exists v \cdot \pi \mid \forall v \cdot \pi$
Exists	$\mid \exists P^*, c^*, v^* \cdot G$		Boolean	$b ::= \texttt{true} \mid \texttt{false} \mid b{=}b$
Protocol Instance	$\mid$ H(P^*, c^*, v^*)		Ineq.	$a ::= s{=}s \mid s{\leq}s$
Inaction	$\mid \texttt{emp}$		Presbg.	$s ::= k^{int} \mid v \mid s{+}s \mid -s$

(Parties)	$S, R, P \in \mathcal{R}ole$	where	k^{int}: integer constant;
(Channels)	$c \in \mathcal{C}han$		d: data structure; t: type;
(Messages)	$v \cdot \Delta$		V: second-order variable;
	v: first-order variable		L: local protocol (Fig. 6)

(a) Global Protocol Specification	(b) The (Program) Specification Language

Fig. 1. Mercurius

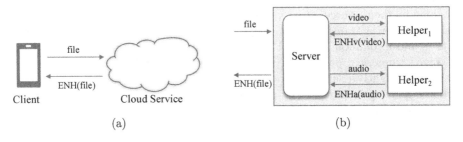

Client   Cloud Service

(a)   (b)

Fig. 2. A multimedia cloud service: A client requests the server for a video file enhancement (a). The server engages two helpers to process the desired enhancement (b)

$$CS_a \triangleq C{\to}S : c\langle v \cdot v : \texttt{file}\rangle\,;\, S{\to}C : c\langle v \cdot v : \texttt{file}\rangle.$$

The CS_a lightweight protocol suffices to describe the order of communication and the exchanged message type. A rigorous specification though, also emphasizes that the server applies some filter on the original file:

$$CS_b \triangleq \exists \texttt{fd} : \texttt{file} \cdot (C{\to}S : c\langle \texttt{fd}\rangle\,;\, S{\to}C : c\langle \texttt{ENH}(\texttt{fd})\rangle).$$

where $C{\to}S : c\langle \texttt{fd}\rangle$ is a prettyprint for $C{\to}S : c\langle v \cdot v : \texttt{file} \wedge v{=}\texttt{fd}\rangle$, and $\texttt{ENH}(\texttt{fd})$ is a logical predicate describing the enhanced file, e.g. such as applying a brightness, or a slow motion filter. For the simplicity of this explanation we do not define ENH, keeping it abstract, however a user can always attach a definition to ENH to reflect the changes over the file referenced by fd. To note that this protocol not only highlights that the server returns an enhanced file, but that it actually returns the enhancement of the original file since both transmissions reference the same file via fd.

Moreover, the protocol could also be instrumented to capture the server's enhancement action:

$$\texttt{CS}_\texttt{c} \triangleq \exists \texttt{fd} : \texttt{file} \cdot (\texttt{C} \rightarrow \texttt{S} : \texttt{c}\langle\texttt{fd}\rangle \, ; \, \texttt{FILTER} \, ; \, \texttt{S} \rightarrow \texttt{C} : \texttt{c}\langle\texttt{ENH(fd)}\rangle).$$

If the server were to delegate its task to some helper processes - Fig. 2b, where, for example, one processes the video and one handles the audio component of the original media file, the enhancement protocol could be defined as follows:

$$\texttt{FILTER} \triangleq \exists \texttt{H}_1, \texttt{H}_2, \texttt{c}_1, \texttt{c}_2 \cdot (\texttt{S} \rightarrow \texttt{H}_1 : \texttt{c}_1\langle\texttt{fd.vid}\rangle \, ; \, \texttt{H}_1 \rightarrow \texttt{S} : \texttt{c}_1\langle\texttt{ENHv(fd.vid)}\rangle) *$$
$$(\texttt{S} \rightarrow \texttt{H}_2 : \texttt{c}_2\langle\texttt{fd.aud}\rangle \, ; \, \texttt{H}_2 \rightarrow \texttt{S} : \texttt{c}_2\langle\texttt{ENHa(fd.aud)}\rangle).$$

where $\texttt{ENHv}$ and $\texttt{ENHa}$ describe some video and audio effects, respectively. The $*$ operator which denotes concurrent interactions, intentionally resembles the separating conjunction of separation logic to express a clear separation of communication. In this context, all of the following four possible C-like implementations of the server faithfully follow the $\texttt{FILTER}$ protocol:

(i)
```
send(c1,fd.vid);
send(c2,fd.aud);
fd.vid = receive(c1);
fd.aud = receive(c2);
```

(ii)
```
send(c1,fd.vid);
fd.vid = receive(c1);
send(c2,fd.aud);
fd.aud = receive(c2);
```

(iii)
```
(send(c1,fd.vid); fd.vid = receive(c1);)
              ||
(send(c2,fd.aud); fd.aud = receive(c2);)
```

(iv)
```
(send(c1,fd.vid); send(c2,fd.aud);)
              ||
(fd.vid = receive(c1); fd.aud = receive(c2);)
```

and the combinations could continue with the sequential permutations between sends or receives in *(i)* and *(iv)*, or the parallelization of selected pairs of interactions in *(i)* and *(ii)* as long as the sending on a certain channel precedes the local receive on the same channel. To the best of our knowledge, the current state of the art in formalizing communication protocols does not allow such permissive protocols, where the *relaxed order of transmissions* is explicitly captured by the communication protocol. We stress on the fact that the relaxed order of transmissions is not restricted to just inter-party parallel composition specific to MPST, but also comprises the intra-party parallel composition as exemplified above. There is an attempt to tackle the arbitrary order of transmissions in MPST [10], but instead of writing a relaxed protocol, the authors engage a swap relation to check whether the interleaving of transmissions should be allowed at the implementation level. The approach of [10] only checks against cases *(i)* and *(ii)* though, and fail to recognize *(iii)* and *(iv)* as correct implementations of the server described by the $\texttt{FILTER}$ protocol. Any other MPST extension would require four different global types to capture the four different kinds of implementation exemplified earlier.

Another subtle point of this example is the *careful usage of the resources,* the file in this case. The file pointed by `fd` is split into its two components, `fd.vid` and `fd.aud`, respectively, and exclusively shared between helpers H_1 and H_2. The server gains back the ownership of the two components only after the two helpers have finished their job and return the resources back to the server. Any attempt to access a resource before the helper returns its ownership to the server is regarded as unsafe in our approach. To the best of our knowledge, this is the first such approach where the safe resource usage is captured in a lightweight, yet expressive multiparty protocol even in the case of hybrid communication, with both loosely (`C` and `S`) and tightly (S, H_1 and H_2) coupled communicating entities. Better yet, the communication protocol does not need to distinguish between the loosely and the tightly coupled scenarios, consigning the choice of the coupling degree to the developer.

Example 2: In the cloud service examples we described the interaction between exactly one client and a cloud server. Clearly this is too restrictive, since a server should be allowed to serve multiple clients. To support a dynamic number of participants, we describe the protocol using recursive parameterized protocols:

$$\texttt{CLOUD(S,c)} \triangleq \exists \texttt{C}, \texttt{c}' \cdot \texttt{C} \rightarrow \texttt{S} : \texttt{c}\langle \texttt{c}' \rangle \,; (\texttt{CS}_\texttt{d}(\texttt{C}, \texttt{S}, \texttt{c}') * \texttt{CLOUD(S,c)}).$$
$$\texttt{CS}_\texttt{d}(\texttt{C}, \texttt{S}, \texttt{c}) \triangleq \exists \texttt{fd} : \texttt{file} \cdot (\texttt{C} \rightarrow \texttt{S} : \texttt{c}\langle \texttt{fd} \rangle \,; \texttt{FILTER} \,; \texttt{S} \rightarrow \texttt{C} : \texttt{c}\langle \texttt{ENH(fd)} \rangle).$$

where the client-server CS_d protocol is similar to CS_c, except that it is now parameterized with the communicating entities and corresponding channel. The client first sends the server a private channel c', which is then used for the communication within the CS_d protocol. The $*$ between CS_d and the recursive instance of `CLOUD` servers two purposes. On the one hand, it denotes exclusive resource usage between the two protocols. On the other hand, it permits a *relaxed* implementation of the cloud application, where the server could either (1) serve one client at a time, or it could (2) serve multiple clients concurrently spawning a new process once it receives the private channel of some client.

Contributions and Outline. The contributions of this paper are as follows:

- An *expressive session logic* called Mercurius, that is both precise (supports logical message) and concise (in the style of session types) for modelling multi-party protocols. Through its support for relaxed protocols, Mercurius offers wider communication design choices than the current state of the art.
- A deductive verification system which embeds Mercurius for automatically checking protocol conformance and safe implementation. This system copes with both distributed as well as tightly coupled systems.
- A projection mechanism for each communicating party such that each party follows its local specification. This enables modular verification, where each party is verified independently from the other communication participants.
- A projection mechanism for each communication channel w.r.t. a party. The verifier is instructed to manipulate channel specifications, exploiting thus the possibility to delegate the communication to third parties in a natural way,

without breaking locality and without the need of additional communication primitives, except for the usual send/receive, open/close.

After formalizing the global protocol in Sect. 2, we describe the projection rules in Sect. 3, and then embed the logic into a verification system in Sect. 4.

2   Global Protocols

We now formalize Mercurius, whose syntax is depicted in Fig. 1a. We first describe the communication model, and then list down the elements of the protocol and discuss their properties.

Communication Model. To support a wide range of communication interfaces, the current session logic is designed for a permissive communication model, where:

- The transfer of a message dissolves *asynchronously*, that is to say that sending is non-blocking while receiving is blocking.
- The communication interface of choice manipulates *linear FIFO channels* in the style of [3] (i.e. a message is delivered without interference from other participants: the receiver is able to determine who the sender is without any ambiguity).
- For simplicity, the communication assumes unbounded buffers.

Transmission. As described in Sect. 1, a *transmission* $S \to R : c\langle v \cdot \Delta \rangle$ involves a sender S and a receiver R transmitting a message v expressed in logical form Δ over a buffered channel c. To access the components of a transmission we define the following auxiliary functions: $\mathtt{send}(S \to R : c\langle v \cdot \Delta \rangle) \stackrel{\text{def}}{=} S$, $\mathtt{recv}(S \to R : c\langle v \cdot \Delta \rangle) \stackrel{\text{def}}{=} R$, $\mathtt{chan}(S \to R : c\langle v \cdot \Delta \rangle) \stackrel{\text{def}}{=} c$ and $\mathtt{msg}(S \to R : c\langle v \cdot \Delta \rangle) \stackrel{\text{def}}{=} v \cdot \Delta$. We shall often quantify over the existing transmissions using the literal i. Transmissions are irreflexive, $\mathtt{send}(i) \neq \mathtt{recv}(i)$. We define a function $\mathtt{TR}(G)$ which decomposes a given protocol G to collect a set of all its constituent transmissions, and a function $\mathtt{TR}^{\mathrm{fst}}(G)$ to return the set of all possible first transmissions.

Two messages are said to be *disjoint*, denoted by $v_1 \cdot \Delta_1 \# v_2 \cdot \Delta_2$, if $\mathrm{UNSAT}(\Delta_1 \wedge [v_1/v_2]\Delta_2)$. We next abuse the set membership symbol, $\in$, to denote the followings (and, correspondingly, $\notin$ to denote their negation):

$(\in_{\text{transm.}})\ i \in G \Leftrightarrow i \in \mathtt{TR}(G)$
$(\in_{\text{channel}})\ c \in i \Leftrightarrow \mathtt{chan}(i) = c$
$(\in_{\text{channel}})\ c \in G \Leftrightarrow \exists i \in G \cdot c \in i$

$(\in_{\text{party}})\ P \in i \Leftrightarrow \mathtt{send}(i) = P$ or $\mathtt{recv}(i) = P$
$(\in_{\text{party}})\ P \in G \Leftrightarrow \exists i \in G \cdot P \in i$

The parallel composition of global protocols forms a commutative monoid $(G, *, \mathtt{emp})$ with $\mathtt{emp}$ as identity element, while disjunction and sequence form semigroups, $(G, \vee)$ and $(G, ;)$, with the former also satisfying commutativity. $\mathtt{emp}$ acts as the left identity element for sequential composition:

$$(G_1 \; ; \; G_2) \; ; \; G_3 \equiv G_1 \; ; \; (G_2 \; ; \; G_3)$$
$$(G_1 * G_2) * G_3 \equiv G_1 * (G_2 * G_3)$$
$$(G_1 \vee G_2) \vee G_3 \equiv G_1 \vee (G_2 \vee G_3)$$

$$G_1 * G_2 \equiv G_2 * G_1$$
$$G_1 \vee G_2 \equiv G_2 \vee G_1$$

$$G * emp \equiv G$$
$$emp \; ; \; G \equiv G$$

Sequential composition is not commutative, unless it satisfies certain disjointness properties:

$$G_1 \; ; \; G_2 \equiv G_2 \; ; \; G_1 \quad when \quad \forall c_1 \in G_1, c_2 \in G_2 \Rightarrow c_1 \neq c_2 \text{ and } \forall P_1 \in G_1, P_2 \in G_2 \Rightarrow P_1 \neq P_2.$$

The equivalence of protocols could be reduced to that of graph isomorphism, by interpreting the protocol as a graph whose vertexes are actions (message sending or receiving), and whose directed edges are transmissions from a sending to a receiving action. For lack of space and since these proofs are not of interest for the current work, we treat the above equivalences as axioms.

2.1 Well-Formedness

Concurrency. The $*$ operator offers support for arbitrary-ordered (concurrent) transmissions, where the order of their completion is not important for the final outcome.

Definition 1 (Well-Formed Concurrency). *A protocol specification, $G_1 * G_2$, is said to be well-formed w.r.t. $*$ if and only if $\forall c \in G_1 \Rightarrow c \notin G_2$, and vice versa.*

This restriction avoids non-determinism of concurrent communications over the same channel.

Choice. The $\vee$ operator is essential for the expressiveness of Mercurius, but its usage must be carefully controlled:

Definition 2 (Well-Formed Choice). *A disjunctive protocol specification, $G_1 \vee G_2$, is said to be well-formed with respect to $\vee$ if and only if all of the following conditions hold, where T_1 and T_2 account for all first transmissions of G_1 and G_2, respectively, namely $T_1 = TR^{fst}(G_1)$ and $T_2 = TR^{fst}(G_2)$:*

(a) (same first channel) $\forall i_1, i_2 \in T_1 \cup T_2 \Rightarrow chan(i_1) = chan(i_2)$;
(b) (same first sender) $\forall i_1, i_2 \in T_1 \cup T_2 \Rightarrow send(i_1) = send(i_2)$;
(c) (same first receiver) $\forall i_1, i_2 \in T_1 \cup T_2 \Rightarrow recv(i_1) = recv(i_2)$;
(d) (mutually exclusive "first" messages).

$$\forall i_1, i_2 \in T_1 \cup T_2 \Rightarrow msg(i_1) \# msg(i_2) \vee i_1 = i_2;$$

(e) (same pattern) Except for the parties in T_1 and T_2, the rest of the participants must have a uniform local view of the communications across all disjuncts (to avoid informing all the participants of the choice being made).
(f) (recursive well-formedness) G_1 and G_2 are well-formed with respect to $\vee$.

Definition 3 (Well-Formed Protocol). *A protocol G is said to be well-formed, if and only if G contains only well-formed concurrent transmissions, and well-formed choices.*

To ensure the correctness of our approach, Mercurius disregards as unsound any usage of $*$ or $\vee$ which is not well-formed.

3   Local Projection

Based on the communication interface, but also on the verifier's requirements, the projection of the global protocol to local specifications goes through a couple of automatic projection phases before being used by the verification process. This way, the projections of phase one (we call them *per-party projections*) describe how each party is contributing to the communication. More granularly, the projections in the second phase (called *per-channel projections*) describe how each communication channel is used by their respective communicating parties.

Projection Overview and Protocol Refinement

Example 3: Consider the following protocol between some parties C_1, C_2 and P, communicating via channels c_1 and c_2:

$$G \triangleq C_1{\rightarrow}P : c_1\langle v{\cdot}\Delta_1\rangle; C_2{\rightarrow}P : c_2\langle v{\cdot}\Delta_2\rangle; C_2{\rightarrow}P : c_2\langle v{\cdot}\Delta_3\rangle; C_1{\rightarrow}P : c_1\langle v{\cdot}\Delta_4\rangle.$$

We visually represent the protocol G using sequence diagrams, as per Fig. 3, where the arrows show the direction of transmission, and its labels show the engaged channel and/or the transmitted message. The per-party projection (middle diagram) only highlights the view of party P, and the per-channel projection (rightmost diagram) highlights the views of channels c_1 and c_2, respectively, w.r.t. party P (ignoring the dashed arrows for now).

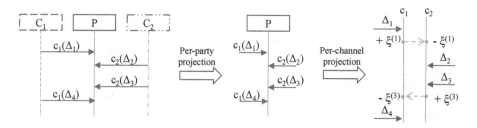

Fig. 3. A visual representation of protocol G (left sequenced diagram) projected onto party P (middle diagram), and then projected over channel c_1 and c_2, respectively (right diagram).

The specification of channel c_1 features only the transmissions over this channel, loosing thus the information that Δ_1 should be transmitted before Δ_2. Similarly for channel c_2, Δ_3 should be transmitted before Δ_4. To support such fine granularity, namely the per-channel specification, without breaking the sequence of transmissions when a party is engaging multiple channels, we propose the usage of a fencing mechanism. The fencing mechanism enforces a party to respect the correct order of transmissions across multiple channels (fences are represented by dashed arrows in the rightmost diagram of Fig. 3).

A fence is introduced w.r.t. a set of parties and a channel, say $\{C_1, P\}$ and c_1 for the first transmission of G, and must be proved to hold, locally, before P

can engage channel c_2 and before C_1 can engage any other channel . Generally, a fence is denoted by $\xi(\{P^*\}, c, n)$, and is uniquely identified by the id n. We employ a refinement mechanism which introduces fences after each transmission of a global protocol, and assume from now on that each global protocol is refined. The details of this refinement are trivial, and therefore omitted. For the ongoing example, protocol G is refined to:

$$C_1 \rightarrow P : c_1 \langle v \cdot \Delta_1 \rangle; \xi(\{C_1, P\}, c_1, 1); C_2 \rightarrow P : c_2 \langle v \cdot \Delta_2 \rangle; \xi(\{C_2, P\}, c_2, 2);$$

$$C_2 \rightarrow P : c_2 \langle v \cdot \Delta_3 \rangle; \xi(\{C_2, P\}, c_2, 3); C_1 \rightarrow P : c_1 \langle v \cdot \Delta_4 \rangle; \xi(\{C_1, P\}, c_1, 4).$$

Projection Language. Figure 4 describes the two kinds of specification mentioned above. The per party specification language is depicted in Fig. 4a. Here, each send and receive specification refers to the communication instrument c along with a message v described by a formula Δ. The congruence of all the compound terms described in Sect. 2 holds for the projected languages as well, with the exception of sequential commutativity since the disjointness conditions for the latter do not hold (e.g. either the peer or the channel are implicitly the same for the entire projected specification). To note that, for brevity of this presentation, we denote the fences in the endpoint specification by the shorter notation $\xi^{(n)}$ since the party and the channel are implicit. Moreover, to note the notation for fence assumption, $\oplus \xi^{(n)}$, and that for fence guard, $\ominus \xi^{(n)}$, where the former is assumed to hold, and the latter needs to be proved to hold.

	$\Upsilon ::=$		$L ::=$
Local protocol			
Send/Receive/Transmission	$c!v \cdot \Delta \mid c?v \cdot \Delta$		$!v \cdot \Delta \mid ?v \cdot \Delta$
HO variable	$\mid V$		$\mid V$
Concurrency	$\mid \Upsilon * \Upsilon$		
Choice	$\mid \Upsilon \vee \Upsilon$		$\mid L \vee L$
Sequence	$\mid \Upsilon ; \Upsilon$		$\mid L ; L$
Exists	$\mid \exists c^*, v^* \cdot \Upsilon$		$\mid \exists v^* \cdot L$
Fence	$\mid \xi(\{P\}, c, n)$		$\mid \oplus \xi^{(n)} \mid \ominus \xi^{(n)}$
Inaction	$\mid$ emp		$\mid$ emp
	(a) Per party		(b) Per channel

Fig. 4. Mercurius: the projection language

Automatic Projection. Using different projection granularities should not permit event re-orderings (modulo $*$ composed events).

Proposition 1 (Projection Fidelity). *The projection to a decomposed specification, such as global protocol to per party, or per party to per channel, does not alter the communication pattern specified before the projection.*

$$(S{\rightarrow}R : c\langle\Delta\rangle)\!\downharpoonright_P := \begin{cases} c!v \cdot \Delta & \text{if } P{=}S \\ c?v \cdot \Delta & \text{if } P{=}R \\ emp & \text{otherwise} \end{cases}$$

$$(G_1 * G_2)\!\downharpoonright_P := (G_1)\!\downharpoonright_P * (G_2)\!\downharpoonright_P$$

$$(G_1 \vee G_2)\!\downharpoonright_P := (G_1)\!\downharpoonright_P \vee (G_2)\!\downharpoonright_P$$

$$(G_1 ; G_2)\!\downharpoonright_P := (G_1)\!\downharpoonright_P ; (G_2)\!\downharpoonright_P$$

$$(\exists P_0^*, c^*, v^* \cdot G)\!\downharpoonright_P := \exists c^*, v^* \cdot (G)\!\downharpoonright_P$$

$$(emp)\!\downharpoonright_P := emp$$

$$(c_0!v \cdot \Delta)\!\downharpoonright_c := \begin{cases} !v \cdot \Delta & \text{if } c{=}c_0 \\ emp & \text{otherwise} \end{cases}$$

$$(c_0?v \cdot \Delta)\!\downharpoonright_c := \begin{cases} ?v \cdot \Delta & \text{if } c{=}c_0 \\ emp & \text{otherwise} \end{cases}$$

$$(\Upsilon_1 * \Upsilon_2)\!\downharpoonright_c := \begin{cases} (\Upsilon_j)\!\downharpoonright_c & \text{if } c{\in}\Upsilon_j, j{=}1,2 \\ emp & \text{otherwise} \end{cases}$$

$$(\Upsilon_1 \vee \Upsilon_2)\!\downharpoonright_c := (\Upsilon_1)\!\downharpoonright_c \vee (\Upsilon_2)\!\downharpoonright_c$$

$$(\Upsilon_1 ; \Upsilon_2)\!\downharpoonright_c := (\Upsilon_1)\!\downharpoonright_c ; (\Upsilon_2)\!\downharpoonright_c$$

$$(\exists c_0^*, v^* \cdot \Upsilon)\!\downharpoonright_c := \exists v^* \cdot (\Upsilon)\!\downharpoonright_c$$

$$(emp)\!\downharpoonright_c := emp$$

(a) global spec $\rightarrow$ per party spec   (b) per party spec $\rightarrow$ per endpoint spec

Fig. 5. Projection rules

To support the above proposition, we have designed a set of structural projection rules, described in Fig. 5. The rules Fig. 5a, describing per party projection rules, are standard, with the exception of disjunction and fences. As opposed to MPST, which projects the choice constructs to branching and selection, respectively, Mercurius maintains the disjunction through all the projection phases. It is able to do that since it relies on the verification system to reason about the underlying conditional constructs, verifying them against the disjunctive specification: sending expects a disjunctive abstract state, while receiving is creating a disjunctive abstract state. As expected, the per channel projection rules, Fig. 5b, strips the channel information from the per party specifications, since it will be implicitly available.

The projection of fences is a bit more subtle, and it obeys the following rules for per party and per channel projection, respectively:

$$(\xi(\{P^*\}, c, n))\!\downharpoonright_P := \begin{cases} \xi(\{P\}, c, n) & \text{if } P \in \{P^*\} \\ emp & \text{otherwise} \end{cases}$$

$$(\xi(\{P\}, c_0, n))\!\downharpoonright_c := \begin{cases} \oplus \xi^{(n)} & \text{if } c{=}c_0 \\ \ominus \xi^{(n)} & \text{if } c{\neq}c_0 \end{cases}$$

Inserting a fence guard $\ominus \xi^{(n)}$ between adjacent transmissions on different channels on the same party ensures that the order of transmissions is accurately inherited from the corresponding per party specification across different channels. Fences are assumed to hold $\oplus \xi^{(n)}$, after consuming the transmission which introduced this fence.

Example 4: To emphasize the behavior of fences we consider the following sequence of receiving events captured by a per party specification, say $(G)\!\downharpoonright_P$:

$(G)\!\downharpoonright_P$	$: c_1?v \cdot \Delta_1 ;$	$\xi(\{P\}, c_1, 1) ;$	$c_2?v \cdot \Delta_2$	$; \xi(\{P\}, c_2, 2) ;$	$c_2?v \cdot \Delta_3 ;$	$\xi(\{P\}, c_2, 3) ;$	$c_1?v \cdot \Delta_4$
$(G)\!\downharpoonright_{P,c_1}$	$: ?v \cdot \Delta_1 ;$	$\oplus \xi^{(1)}$	$;$ emp	$;$	$\ominus \xi^{(2)} ;$	emp $;$	$\ominus \xi^{(3)} ;$	$\boxed{?v \cdot \Delta_4}$
$(G)\!\downharpoonright_{P,c_2}$	$:$ emp	$; \ominus \xi^{(1)}$	$; \boxed{?v \cdot \Delta_2} ;$	$\oplus \xi^{(2)}$	$; ?v \cdot \Delta_3 ;$	$\oplus \xi^{(3)}$	$;$ emp

The above local specification snapshot highlights how local fidelity is secured: the events marked with red boxes are guarded by their immediately preceding events, since they are handled by different channels. A subsequent refinement removes redundant guards, grayed in the example above, since adjacent same channel events need to guard only the last event on the considered channel.

Given the congruence of global protocols and local specifications, the projection is an isomorphism (closed under all operators). Specifically, given two protocols G_1 and G_2, with $P_1..P_n \in G_1$ such that $\forall P \in G_1 \Rightarrow P \in \{P_1..P_n\}$, and $\forall P \in G_2 \Rightarrow P \in \{P_1..P_n\}$, and $\forall P \in \{P_1..P_n\} \Rightarrow P \in G_2$, and with $c_1..c_m \in G_1$ such that $\forall c \in G_1 \Rightarrow c \in \{c_1..c_m\}$, and $\forall c \in G_2 \Rightarrow c \in \{c_1..c_m\}$, and $\forall c \in \{c_1..c_m\} \Rightarrow c \in G_2$ the following isomorphism holds:

$$G_1 \equiv G_2 \Leftrightarrow \{(G_1)\lfloor_{P_j}\}_{j=1..n} \equiv \{(G_2)\lfloor_{P_j}\}_{j=1..n}$$

$$G_1 \equiv G_2 \Leftrightarrow \{(G_1)\lfloor_{P_j,c_k}\}_{j=1..n,k=1..m} \equiv \{(G_2)\lfloor_{P_j,c_k}\}_{j=1..n,k=1..m}$$

4   Verification of C-Like Programs

The user provides the global protocol which is then automatically refined according to the methodology described in Sect. 3. The refined protocol is then automatically projected onto a per party specification, followed by a per channel endpoint basis. Using such a modular approach where we provide a specification for each channel endpoint adds natural support for delegation, where a channel (as well as its specification) could be delegated to a third party in the style of binary session logic [14]. These communication specifications are made available in the program abstract state using a combination of ghost assertions and release lemmas (detailed in the subsequent). The verification could then automatically check whether a certain implementation follows the global protocol, after it had first bounded the *program elements* (processes and channel endpoints) to the *logical ones* (parties and channels).

Language. Figure 6 depicts the syntax of a core language with support for communication primitives, where a program contains data and method definitions. Each method is decorated with a set of pre-/postconditions meant to guide the verification process. All of the program constructs are standard, with the exception of `open()` with (c, P^*), which binds a logical channel c and parties P^* to the channel reference returned by `open()`.

Concurrent Separation Logics. Due to its expressive power and elegant proofs, we choose to integrate our session logic on top of concurrent separation logic. Separation logic is an attractive extension of Hoare logic in which assertions are interpreted w.r.t. some relevant portion of the heap. Spatial conjunction, the core operator of separation logic, $P * Q$ divides the heap between two disjoint heaps described by assertions P and Q, respectively. The main benefit of this approach is the local reasoning: the specifications of a program code need

Program	$\mathcal{P}$	$::=$ $datat^*$ $meth^*$
Data Struct.	$datat$	$::=$ struct d { $(t\,f)^*$ }
Method Definitions	$meth$	$::=$ $t\ mn\ ((t\ v)^*)$ $requires$ $\Phi, ensures$ Φ {e}
Types	t	$::=$ $d \mid \tau$ τ $::=$ int $\mid$ bool $\mid$ float $\mid$ void
Expressions	e	$::=$ NULL $\mid k^\tau \mid v \mid$ new $d(v^*) \mid t\ v;\ e \mid v.f \mid mn(v^*) \mid$ skip
		$\mid v{:=}e \mid v.f{:=}e \mid e;e \mid e\|e \mid$ if (b) e else $e \mid$ return e
		$\mid$ open() with (c,P*) $\mid$ close$(v) \mid$ receive$(v) \mid$ send(v,e)
Boolean Expressions b		$::= e{=}{=}e \mid\ !(b) \mid b\&b \mid b|b$

where k^τ is a type τ constant, v is a program variable, f denotes a field

Fig. 6. A core imperative language

only mention the portion of the resources which it uses, the rest are assumed unchanged. The details of the model and the semantics of the state assertions can be found in [12].

Verification. To check whether a user program follows the stipulated communication scenario, a traditional analysis would need to reason about the behaviour of a program using the operational semantics of the primitives' implementation. Since our goal is to emphasize on the benefits of implementing a protocol guided communication, rather than deciding the correctness of the primitives machinery, we adopt a specification strategy using abstract predicates [17,37] to describe the behavior of the program's primitives. Provided that the primitives respect their abstract specification, developers could then choose alternative communication libraries, without the need to re-construct the correctness proof of their underlying program.

The verification process follows the traditional forward verification rules, where the pre-conditions are checked for each method call, and if the check succeeds it adds their corresponding postcondition to the poststate. The verification of the method definition starts by assuming its precondition as the initial abstract state, and then inspects whether the postcondition holds after progressively checking each of the method's body instructions.

Abstract Specification. We define a set of abstract predicates to support session specification of different granularity. Some of these predicates have been progressively introduced across the paper, but for brevity we have omitted certain details. We resume their presentation here with more details:

$$[\text{OPEN}]$$
$$\{\text{init}(c)\} \ \text{open}() \ \text{with} \ (c, P^*) \ \{\text{opened}(c, P^*, \text{res})\}$$

$$[\text{CLOSE}]$$
$$\{ \ \text{empty}(c, \tilde{c})\} \ \text{close}(\tilde{c}) \ \{ \ \text{emp} \ \}$$

$$[\text{SEND}]$$
$$\frac{\mathcal{I} \triangleq \text{Peer}(P) * \text{opened}(c, P^*, \tilde{c}) \wedge P \in P^*}{\{\mathcal{C}(c, P, !v \cdot V(v); L) * V(x) * \mathcal{I}\} \ \text{send}(\tilde{c}, x) \ \{\mathcal{C}(c, P, L) * \mathcal{I}\}}$$

$$[\text{RECV}]$$
$$\frac{\mathcal{I} \triangleq \text{Peer}(P) * \text{opened}(c, P^*, \tilde{c}) \wedge P \in P^*}{\{\mathcal{C}(c, P, ?v \cdot V(v); L) * \mathcal{I}\} \ \text{recv}(\tilde{c}) \ \{\mathcal{C}(c, P, L) * V(\text{res}) * \mathcal{I}\}}$$

(a) Annotated communication primitives.

$$G(\{P_1..P_n\}, c^*) \qquad \Rightarrow \text{Party}(P_1, c^*, (G)\!\downharpoonleft_{P_1}) * ... * \text{Party}(P_n, c^*, (G)\!\downharpoonleft_{P_n}) * \text{initall}(c^*).$$
$$\text{Party}(P, \{c_1..c_m\}, (G)\!\downharpoonleft_{P}) \Rightarrow \mathcal{C}(c_1, P, (G)\!\downharpoonleft_{P,c_1}) * ... * \mathcal{C}(c_m, P, (G)\!\downharpoonleft_{P,c_m}) * \text{bind}(P, \{c_1..c_m\}).$$
$$\text{initall}(\{c_1..c_m\}) \qquad \Rightarrow \text{init}(c_1) * ... * \text{init}(c_m).$$

(b) Splitting lemmas

$$\mathcal{C}(c, P_1, \text{emp}) * ... * \mathcal{C}(c, P_n, \text{emp}) \backslash * \ \text{opened}(c, \{P_1..P_n\}, \tilde{c}) \ \Rightarrow \ \text{empty}(c, \tilde{c})$$
$$\mathcal{C}(c_1, P, \text{emp}) * ... * \mathcal{C}(c_m, P, \text{emp}) \backslash * \ \text{bind}(P, \{c_1..c_m\}) \ \Rightarrow \ \text{Party}(P, c^*, \text{emp})$$

(c) Joining simpagation rules

$$\mathcal{C}(c, P, \oplus \xi^{(n)}; L) \Rightarrow \mathcal{C}(c, P, L) \wedge \xi^{(n)}$$
$$\mathcal{C}(c, P, \ominus \xi^{(n)}; L) \wedge \xi^{(n)} \Rightarrow \mathcal{C}(c, P, L)$$

(d) Lemmas to handle fences

Fig. 7. Communication primitives

$\text{Party}(P, c^*, \Upsilon)$	associates a local protocol projection Υ to its corresponding party P and the set of channels c^* used by P to communicate with its peers;
$\text{Peer}(P)$	flow-sensitively tracks the executing party, since the execution of parties can either be in parallel or sequentialized;
$\mathcal{C}(c, P, L)$	associates an endpoint specification L to its corresponding party P and channel c;
$\text{initall}(c^*)/$ $\text{init}(c)$	hold only when the specifications corresponding to logical channels c^*/c are available (have been released into the abstract program state - Fig. 7b);
$\text{bind}(P, c^*)$	binds a party P to all the channels c^* it uses;
$\text{opened}(c, P^*, \tilde{c})$	binds a program channel $\tilde{c}$ to a logical one c and to the peers sharing $\tilde{c}$;
$\text{empty}(c, \tilde{c})$	holds only when all the transmissions on $\tilde{c}$ have been consumed (Fig. 7c).

To cater for each verification phase, the session specifications with the required granularity are made available in the program's abstract state via the lemmas in Fig. 7.

Channel endpoint creation and closing described by the [OPEN] and [CLOSE] triples in Fig. 7, have mirrored specification: open associates the specification of a channel c to its corresponding program endpoint c̃. The keyword res is a dedicated ghost variable denoting the result returned by open in this particular case, and the result of evaluating the underlying expression in the general case. close regards the closing of a channel endpoint as safe only when all the parties have finished their communication w.r.t. the closing endpoint.

To support send and receive operations, we decorate the corresponding methods with dual generic specifications. The precondition of [SEND] ensures that indeed a send operation is expected, $!v \cdot V(v)$, with the transmitted message v being described using a higher-order relation over v, namely $V(v)$. To ensure memory safety, the verifier also checks whether the program state indeed owns the message to be transmitted and that it adheres to the properties described by the freshly discovered relation, $V(x)$. Dually, [RECV] ensures that the receiving state gains the ownership of the transmitted message. Both specifications guarantee that the transmission is consumed by the expected party, $\text{Peer}(P)$.

The proof obligations generated by this verifier are discharged to a Separation Logic solver in the form of enatailment checks, detailed in the subsequent.

Entailment. Traditionally, the logical entailment between formalae written in the symbolic heap fragment of separation logic is expressed as follows: $\Delta_a \vdash \Delta_c * \Delta_r$, where Δ_r comprises those residual resources described by Δ_a, but not by Δ_c. Intuitively, a valid entailment suggests that the resource models described by Δ_a are sufficient to conclude the availability of those described by Δ_c.

Since the proposed logic is tailored to support reasoning about communication primitives with generic protocol specifications, the entailment should also be able to interpret and instantiate such generic specifications. Therefore we equip the entailment checker to reason about formulae which contain second-order variables. Consequently, the proposed entailment is designed to support the instantiation of such variables. However, the instantiation might not be unique, so we collect the candidate instantiations in a set of residual states. The entailment has thus the following form: $\Delta_a \vdash \Delta_c \leadsto S$, where S is the set of possible residual states. Note that S is derived and its size should be of at least 1 in order to consider the entailment as valid. The entailment rules needed to accommodate session reasoning are given in Fig. 8. Other rules used for the manipulation of general resource predicates are adapted from Separation Logic [38].

To note also how [ENT-RECV] and [ENT-SEND] are soundly designed to be the dual of each other: while the former checks for covariant subsumption of the communication models, the latter enforces contravarinat subsumption since the information should only flow from a stronger constraint towards a weaker one. Considering the example below, a context expecting to read an integer greater than or equal to 1 could engage a channel designed with a more relaxed

$$\boxed{\textbf{ENT-CHAN–MATCH}}$$
$$\Delta_a \Rightarrow c_1 = c_2 \quad \mathcal{C}(c_1, P_1, L_a) \vdash \mathcal{C}(c_2, P_2, L_c) \leadsto S_1$$
$$S_2 = \{\pi_i^e \mid \pi_i^e \in S_1 \text{ and } \mathrm{SAT}(\Delta_a \wedge \pi_i^e) \text{ and } \mathrm{SAT}(\Delta_c \wedge \pi_i^e)\} \quad \bigvee_{\pi^e \in S_2} (\Delta_a \wedge \pi^e) \vdash \Delta_c \leadsto S$$

$$\overline{\mathcal{C}(v_1, P, L_a) * \Delta_a \vdash \mathcal{C}(v_2, P, L_c) * \Delta_c \leadsto S}$$

$$\boxed{\textbf{ENT-SEND}} \qquad\qquad\qquad \boxed{\textbf{ENT-RECV}}$$
$$\frac{[v_1/v_2]\Delta_c \vdash \Delta_a \leadsto S' \quad S = \{\pi_i^e \mid \pi_i^e \in S'\}}{!v_1 \cdot \Delta_a \vdash !v_2 \cdot \Delta_c \leadsto S} \qquad \frac{\Delta_a \vdash [v_1/v_2]\Delta_c \leadsto S' \quad S = \{\pi_i^e \mid \pi_i^e \in S'\}}{?v_1 \cdot \Delta_a \vdash ?v_2 \cdot \Delta_c \leadsto S}$$

$$\boxed{\textbf{ENT-SEQ}} \qquad\qquad\qquad\qquad\qquad \boxed{\textbf{ENT-RHS–PVAR}}$$
$$\frac{\Box_a \vdash \Box_c \leadsto S_1 \quad L_a \vdash L_c \leadsto S_2 \quad \text{where } \Box := ?v \cdot \Delta \mid !v \cdot \Delta}{\Box_a;L_a \vdash \Box_c;L_c \leadsto \{\text{emp}\wedge\pi_1\wedge\pi_2 \mid \pi_1 \in S_1 \text{ and } \pi_2 \in S_2\}} \qquad \frac{S = \{\text{emp}\wedge V = L_a\}}{L_a \vdash V \leadsto S}$$

$$\boxed{\textbf{ENT-CHAN}}$$
$$\frac{P_1 = P_2 \quad L_a \vdash L_c \leadsto S' \quad S = \{\pi_i^e \mid \pi_i^e \in S'\}}{\mathcal{C}(c, P_1, L_a) \vdash \mathcal{C}(c, P_2, L_c) \leadsto S}$$

$$\boxed{\textbf{ENT-LHS–OR}} \qquad\qquad\qquad\qquad \boxed{\textbf{ENT-RHS–OR}}$$
$$\frac{L_i;L_a \vdash L_c \leadsto S_i \quad S = \{\bigvee_i \Delta_i \mid \Delta_i \in S_i\}}{(\bigvee_i L_i);L_a \vdash L_c \leadsto S} \qquad \frac{L_a \vdash L_i;L_c \leadsto S_i \quad S = \bigcup S_i}{L_a \vdash (\bigvee_i L_i);L_c \leadsto S}$$

$$\boxed{\textbf{ENT-LHS–HO–VAR}}$$
$$\frac{V \notin \mathrm{fv}(\Delta_c) \quad \mathrm{SAT}(\Delta_c) \quad \text{fresh } w \quad S = \{\text{emp}\wedge V(w) = [w/v]\Delta_c\}}{V(v) \vdash \Delta_c \leadsto S}$$

$$\boxed{\textbf{ENT-RHS–HO–VAR}}$$
$$\frac{V \notin \mathrm{fv}(\Delta_a) \quad \Delta_a \vdash \Delta_c \leadsto S' \quad \text{fresh } w \quad S = \{\text{emp}\wedge V(w) = [w/v]\Delta_i \mid \Delta_i \in S'\}}{\Delta_a \vdash V(v) * \Delta_c \leadsto S}$$

Fig. 8. Selected entailment rules: π^e is a shorthand for $\text{emp}\wedge\pi$, $\mathrm{fv}(\Delta)$ returns all free variables in Δ, and `fresh` denotes a fresh variable.

specification *(i)*. However, a context expecting to transmit an integer greater than or equal to 1 should only be allowed to engage a more specialized channel, such as one which designed to transmit solely 1 *(ii)*.

(i)

$$\cfrac{\cfrac{v_1 \geq 1 \vdash [v_1/v_2]v_2 \geq 0}{?v_1 \cdot v_1 \geq 1 \vdash ?v_2 \cdot v_2 \geq 0}\text{ ENT-RECV}}{\mathcal{C}(c, P, ?v_1 \cdot v_1 \geq 1) \vdash \mathcal{C}(c, P, ?v_2 \cdot v_2 \geq 0)}\text{ ENT-CHAN}$$

(ii)

$$\cfrac{\cfrac{[v_1/v_2]v_2 = 1 \vdash v_1 \geq 1}{!v_1 \cdot v_1 \geq 1 \vdash !v_2 \cdot v_2 = 1}\text{ ENT-SEND}}{\mathcal{C}(c, P, !v_1 \cdot v_1 \geq 1) \vdash \mathcal{C}(c, P, !v_2 \cdot v_2 = 1)}\text{ ENT-CHAN}$$

Soundness. The soundness of our verification rules is defined with respect to the operational semantics of [13] by proving progress and preservation. For lack of space we omit the soundness statement and its corresponding proofs, but their full details can be found in [13].

5   Implementation

We have implemented Mercurius in OCaml and attached it to a well established software verifier [12] for C-like languages. Even though this prototype implementation was build to tackle C-like programs, its design may be used to handle other languages as well, provided that this languages support communication primitives in the style of send/receive/open/close.

Moreover, the implementation is highly modular treating the communication primitives as function definitions annotated with generic specifications. On the one hand, thanks to the support for higher order variables, the send/receive functions exhibit a polymorphic behavior being used to transmit different types of values and different kinds of resources. On the other hand, the abstract behavior of the communication primitives may be changed by simply changing its abstract specification rather than changing the verifier's behavior. Using lemmas to handle the auxiliary predicates allows us to support changes to the logic by simply introducing new lemmas or changing the existing ones, lifting thus the burden of changing the underlying verifier. The prototype comprises about 6 K lines of OCaml code, excluding the communication primitives (30 lines) and lemmas (103 lines), considered specifications and given as input files to the verifier.

We run the verifier to check the cloud service discussed in Sect. 1 for protocol conformance and communication safety. The results are depicted in Table 1. We checked the client-sever protocol against different implementations of the server, which are either purely sequential (Server-seq[1–3]) or contain some parallelism (Server-par[1–3]). No verification time took more than 8 s, despite the high number of generated proofs. The reason why the solver needs to handle so many proofs is that for each implementation, the verifier needs to re-check for well-formedness all the specifications and predicates decorating the program, as well as those within the configuration files for the primitives and lemmas.

Moreover we experimented both with the version of the cloud service which handles only one client (CS), as well as the one which supports multiple clients (CLOUD) sequentially (Server-seq) or in parallel (Server-par). For the (CLOUD) protocol, we picked only the implementation of the CS which communicates with the helpers concurrently, namely Server-par1. The verification worked seamlessly in both cases, without the need to tweak the specification in any way irrespective of the underlying implementation.

We also report our results on verifying a simple calculator adopted from [39]. As opposed to [39] though, Mercurius is unable to handle a memoizing calculator, since our lightweight approach did not instrument the global protocol to assert anything about how the communication affects the local state of each party. The changes in local states are only reflected by the generic specifications of the communication primitives (not by the protocol itself) indicating what is released into or consumed from the local state.

Lastly, we also report our results w.r.t. the "Rock, Paper, Scissors" protocol adopted from [15]. In [15] the authors claim that this kind of protocol and its logical pitfalls are common when building smart contracts - a form of distributed programs often engaged in cryptocurrency transactions. The logical bugs mentioned in [15], such as imprecise payments and inaccessible resources, may be avoided with a rigorous verification system. More examples and their detailed proofs can be found online [1], where the interested reader can also test Mercurius with her own protocols.

Example 5: In the subsequent we show how the specification of party P from example 4, guides the verification process to identify a buggy implementation:

```
//C(c1,P,?v·Δ₁;⊕ξ⁽¹⁾;⊖ξ⁽³⁾;?v·Δ₄) * C(c2,P,⊖ξ⁽¹⁾;?v·Δ₂;⊕ξ⁽²⁾;?v·Δ₃;⊕ξ⁽³⁾)
1 x = receive(c1);
//C(c1,P,⊕ξ⁽¹⁾;⊖ξ⁽³⁾;?v·Δ₄) * C(c2,P,⊖ξ⁽¹⁾;?v·Δ₂;⊕ξ⁽²⁾;?v·Δ₃;⊕ξ⁽³⁾) * Δ₁
//============ fire assume lemma to release ξ⁽¹⁾============
//C(c1,P,⊖ξ⁽³⁾;?v·Δ₄) * C(c2,P,⊖ξ⁽¹⁾;?v·Δ₂;⊕ξ⁽²⁾;?v·Δ₃;⊕ξ⁽³⁾) * Δ₁ * ξ⁽¹⁾
//============ fire guard lemma on ξ⁽¹⁾============
//C(c1,P,⊖ξ⁽³⁾;?v·Δ₄) * C(c2,P,?v·Δ₂;⊕ξ⁽²⁾;?v·Δ₃;⊕ξ⁽³⁾) * Δ₁ * ξ⁽¹⁾
2 y = receive(c2);
//C(c1,P,⊖ξ⁽³⁾;?v·Δ₄) * C(c2,P,⊕ξ⁽²⁾;?v·Δ₃;⊕ξ⁽³⁾) * Δ₁ * ξ⁽¹⁾ * Δ₂
//============ fire assume lemma to release ξ⁽²⁾============
//C(c1,P,⊖ξ⁽³⁾;?v·Δ₄) * C(c2,P,?v·Δ₃;⊕ξ⁽³⁾) * Δ₁ * ξ⁽¹⁾ * Δ₂ * ξ⁽²⁾
//FAIL to verify the next receive on c1 since ξ⁽³⁾ is not available
3 t = receive(c1);
5 z = receive(c2);
```

where program's statements are numbered 1–4, and the program's abstract state is prefixed by //. A correct implementation expects lines 3 and 4 to be swapped such that fence $\xi^{(3)}$ required by c1 is available in the program's abstract state. $\xi^{(3)}$ is only released in the after the second receive on c2 is consumed.

6 Related Work

Behavioral Types. The behavioral types specify the expected interaction pattern of communicating entities. Most of seminal works develop type systems on the π-calculus [26] for deadlock [27] and livelock [25] detection. However, these system do not account for communication protocols, nor do they express messages in a logical form. To improve on the latter, Igarashi and Kobayashi propose an abstraction of the behavior of pi-calculus processes as generic types [24]. However, the generic type system finally throws away the information about base values such as integers, as opposed to our proposal which uses the messages' logical description to guide the verification of the implementation.

The session types [22,23] proposed by Honda et al. are probably the most intensely studied refinement of the behavioral type systems, since they offer the means of writing formal communication protocols in a concise and user-friendly manner. Extensions of session types add support for: exception handling [8,9], multithreaded functional languages [30,33,36], for MPI [31], for OO languages [16,18], and, similar to our approach, for C-like languages [34]. However, none of

Table 1. Evaluation of Mercurius

Component	LOC	Proofs.	Verification time (sec)
Multimedia Cloud Service **(CS)** - **29 lines of spec**			
Client	2	958	1.1
Server-seq1	23	3987	6.7
Server-seq2	23	3987	6.7
Server-seq3	23	3987	6.7
Server-par1	38	3162	7.1
Server-par2	38	3345	7.2
Server-par3	34	3848	7.0
Multimedia Cloud Service **(CLOUD)** - **32 lines of spec**			
Client	3	1342	1.4
Server-seq	40	4569	7.7
Server-par	45	4348	7.9
Simple Calculator - **6 lines of spec**			
Client	3	575	0.8
Server-seq	4	1534	1.6
Server-par	7	933	1.4
"Rock, Paper, Scissors" - **11 lines of spec**			
Client	2	728	1.0
Server-seq	6	2252	2.3
Server-par	8	1774	3.0

these approaches exploit the possibility of expressing messages in a more precise manner, since the type system constraints the messages to be abstracted to just types. Expressing the messages in logical form could uncover implementation bugs that would otherwise easily bypass a simple type check. Works such as [6,11,29,42] draw a correspondence between linear logic and different session types, while [4,40] combine session types with dependent type. While these works have the potential to exploit their results in linear logic, they solely tackle the type and numerical properties of the exchanged data. Our proposal goes beyond numerical properties to resources sharing.

Closer to our goal, Caires and Seco [7] propose behavioral separation for disciplining the interference of higher-order programs in the presence of concurrency, sharing and aliasing. Behavioural separation types build upon the knowledge of behavioural type theories, behavioral-spatial types [5], and separation logic. More recently, [2] also promotes non-determinism and shared channels in an extension of linear logic-based session types. Even though these works permit inter-party resource sharing, they do not explore the idea of relaxed protocols in the sense described in this paper, where $*$ permits intra-party concurrency, adding thus less constraints over the underlying protocol implementation.

Concurrent Logics for Message Passing. The idea of coupling together the model theory of concurrent separation logic with that of Communicating Sequential Processes [20] is studied in [21]. The processes are modeled by using trace semantics, drawing an analogy between channels and heap cells, and distinguishing between separation in space from separation in time. Our proposal shares the same idea of distinguishing between separation in space and separation in time, by using the * and ; operators, respectively. However, their model relies on process algebras, while we propose an expressive logic based on separation logic able to also tackle memory management.

Heap-Hop [32,41] is a sound proof system for copyless message passing managed by contracts. The system is integrated within a static analyzer which checks whether messages are safely transmitted. Similar with our proposal, this work is also based on separation logic. As opposed to ours, its communication model is limited to solely two party communication.

IronFleet [19], embedded in Dafny [28], supports the verification of large system focusing on their liveness and safety properties, and going as far as being able to tackle consensus protocols. However, though important, their verification efforts are not reusable, using highly specialized primitives and predicates to express each verified system. We propose a lighter, yet more generic, verification mechanisms, where the same communication primitives and predicates can be reused for most of the verification scenarios. Moreover, our specification language is designed to be accessible to less specialized system designers and developers, while still offering safety guarantees.

Designed concurrently with out logic, DISEL [39] is a domain specific language for describing, implementing and verifying distributed systems. The protocols are described in DISEL using state-transition systems, as opposed to the more concise protocols of session types. The authors have also exploited the benefits of separation logic for providing strong safety guarantees, embedding their proofs in Coq. On contrast, we promote automated verification, where instead of using mechanized proofs, we rely on our verifier to automatically find the proof or correctness or to identify bugs.

7   Discussions and Final Remarks

We have designed a multi-party session logic that goes beyond the traditional type checking system, by embedding the communication protocols as guiding tools for verification systems. We have shown how the messages can be described in the more precise and expressive logical form, without sacrificing the conciseness of type approaches. We have shown how to write relaxed protocols that offer wider design choices for the implementation of protocols. Moreover, we have shown how a lightweight specification system in the style of session types can be embedded into a deductive verification system to offer stronger correctness and safety guarantees than those offered by type-checking. Moreover, automation is achieved without sacrificing modularity. [1,13] discuss deadlock checking, delegation and recursion in Mercurius.

As part of future work, we investigate how to improve the expressiveness further such that Mercurius is able to handle more distributed properties, such as consensus. Moreover, we intend to extend this work to other less mainstream, yet important communication models, such as those using non-linear channels. We also intend to go beyond the current limits of our well-formed disjunctions.

References

1. Mercurius. http://loris-5.d2.comp.nus.edu.sg/Mercurius
2. Balzer, S., Pfenning, F.: Manifest sharing with session types. PACMPL 1(ICFP), 37 (2017)
3. Bettini, L., Coppo, M., D'Antoni, L., De Luca, M., Dezani-Ciancaglini, M., Yoshida, N.: Global progress in dynamically interleaved multiparty sessions. In: van Breugel, F., Chechik, M. (eds.) CONCUR 2008. LNCS, vol. 5201, pp. 418–433. Springer, Heidelberg (2008). https://doi.org/10.1007/978-3-540-85361-9_33
4. Bocchi, L., Honda, K., Tuosto, E., Yoshida, N.: A theory of design-by-contract for distributed multiparty interactions. In: Gastin, P., Laroussinie, F. (eds.) CONCUR 2010. LNCS, vol. 6269, pp. 162–176. Springer, Heidelberg (2010). https://doi.org/10.1007/978-3-642-15375-4_12
5. Caires, L.: Spatial-behavioral types for concurrency and resource control in distributed systems. Theor. Comput. Sci. 402(2–3), 120–141 (2008)
6. Caires, L., Pfenning, F.: Session types as intuitionistic linear propositions. In: Gastin, P., Laroussinie, F. (eds.) CONCUR 2010. LNCS, vol. 6269, pp. 222–236. Springer, Heidelberg (2010). https://doi.org/10.1007/978-3-642-15375-4_16
7. Caires, L., Seco, J.C.: The type discipline of behavioral separation. In: ACM SIGPLAN Notices, pp. 275–286. ACM (2013)
8. Capecchi, S., Giachino, E., Yoshida, N.: Global escape in multiparty sessions. MSCS 26, 156–295 (2014)
9. Carbone, M., Honda, K., Yoshida, N.: Structured interactional exceptions in session types. In: van Breugel, F., Chechik, M. (eds.) CONCUR 2008. LNCS, vol. 5201, pp. 402–417. Springer, Heidelberg (2008). https://doi.org/10.1007/978-3-540-85361-9_32
10. Carbone, M., Montesi, F.: Deadlock-freedom-by-design: multiparty asynchronous global programming. SIGPLAN Not. 48(1), 263–274 (2013)
11. Carbone, M., Montesi, F., Schürmann, C., Yoshida, N.: Multiparty session types as coherence proofs. In: CONCUR, vol. 42, pp. 412–426 (2015)
12. Chin, W.N., David, C., Nguyen, H.H., Qin, S.: Automated verification of shape, size and bag properties via user-defined predicates in separation logic. Sci. Comput. Program. 77(9), 1006–1036 (2012)
13. Costea, A.: A session logic for relaxed communication protocols. Ph.D. dissertation, School of Computing, National University of Singapore (2017)
14. Craciun, F., Kiss, T., Costea, A.: Towards a session logic for communication protocols. In: ICECCS, pp. 140–149 (2015)
15. Delmolino, K., Arnett, M., Kosba, A., Miller, A., Shi, E.: Step by step towards creating a safe smart contract: lessons and insights from a cryptocurrency lab. In: Clark, J., Meiklejohn, S., Ryan, P.Y.A., Wallach, D., Brenner, M., Rohloff, K. (eds.) FC 2016. LNCS, vol. 9604, pp. 79–94. Springer, Heidelberg (2016). https://doi.org/10.1007/978-3-662-53357-4_6

16. Dezani-Ciancaglini, M., Mostrous, D., Yoshida, N., Drossopoulou, S.: Session types for object-oriented languages. In: Thomas, D. (ed.) ECOOP 2006. LNCS, vol. 4067, pp. 328–352. Springer, Heidelberg (2006). https://doi.org/10.1007/11785477_20

17. Dinsdale-Young, T., Dodds, M., Gardner, P., Parkinson, M.J., Vafeiadis, V.: Concurrent abstract predicates. In: D'Hondt, T. (ed.) ECOOP 2010. LNCS, vol. 6183, pp. 504–528. Springer, Heidelberg (2010). https://doi.org/10.1007/978-3-642-14107-2_24

18. Gay, S.J., Vasconcelos, V.T., Ravara, A., Gesbert, N., Caldeira, A.Z.: Modular session types for distributed object-oriented programming. In: POPL, pp. 299–312 (2010)

19. Hawblitzel, C., et al.: IronFleet: proving practical distributed systems correct. In: SOSP, pp. 1–17 (2015)

20. Hoare, C.A.R.: Communicating sequential processes. In: Hansen, P.B. (ed.) The Origin of Concurrent Programming, pp. 413–443. Springer, New York (1978). https://doi.org/10.1007/978-1-4757-3472-0_16

21. Hoare, T., O'Hearn, P.: Separation logic semantics for communicating processes. Electron. Notes Theor. Comput. Sci. **212**, 3–25 (2008)

22. Honda, K., Vasconcelos, V.T., Kubo, M.: Language primitives and type discipline for structured communication-based programming. In: Hankin, C. (ed.) ESOP 1998. LNCS, vol. 1381, pp. 122–138. Springer, Heidelberg (1998). https://doi.org/10.1007/BFb0053567

23. Honda, K., Yoshida, N., Carbone, M.: Multiparty asynchronous session types. J. ACM **63**, 1–67 (2016)

24. Igarashi, A., Kobayashi, N.: A generic type system for the pi-calculus. Theor. Comput. Sci. **311**(1), 121–163 (2004)

25. Kobayashi, N.: Type systems for concurrent processes: from deadlock-freedom to livelock-freedom, time-boundedness. In: van Leeuwen, J., Watanabe, O., Hagiya, M., Mosses, P.D., Ito, T. (eds.) TCS 2000. LNCS, vol. 1872, pp. 365–389. Springer, Heidelberg (2000). https://doi.org/10.1007/3-540-44929-9_27

26. Kobayashi, N.: A type system for lock-free processes. IC **177**(2), 122–159 (2002)

27. Kobayashi, N., Laneve, C.: Deadlock analysis of unbounded process networks. IC **252**, 48–70 (2017)

28. Leino, K.R.M., Müller, P.: A basis for verifying multi-threaded programs. In: Castagna, G. (ed.) ESOP 2009. LNCS, vol. 5502, pp. 378–393. Springer, Heidelberg (2009). https://doi.org/10.1007/978-3-642-00590-9_27

29. Lindley, S., Morris, J.G.: A semantics for propositions as sessions. In: Vitek, J. (ed.) ESOP 2015. LNCS, vol. 9032, pp. 560–584. Springer, Heidelberg (2015). https://doi.org/10.1007/978-3-662-46669-8_23

30. Lindley, S., Morris, J.G.: Embedding session types in Haskell. In: Proceedings of the 9th International Symposium on Haskell, pp. 133–145. ACM (2016)

31. Lopez, H.A., et al.: Protocol-based verification of message-passing parallel programs. In: OOPSLA 2015. ACM (2015)

32. Lozes, É., Villard, J.: Shared contract-obedient channels. Sci. Comput. Program. **100**, 28–60 (2015)

33. Neubauer, M., Thiemann, P.: An implementation of session types. In: Jayaraman, B. (ed.) PADL 2004. LNCS, vol. 3057, pp. 56–70. Springer, Heidelberg (2004). https://doi.org/10.1007/978-3-540-24836-1_5

34. Ng, N., Yoshida, N., Honda, K.: Multiparty session C: safe parallel programming with message optimisation. In: Furia, C.A., Nanz, S. (eds.) TOOLS 2012. LNCS, vol. 7304, pp. 202–218. Springer, Heidelberg (2012). https://doi.org/10.1007/978-3-642-30561-0_15

35. Nielson, F., Nielson, H.R.: From CML to its process algebra. Theor. Comput. Sci. **155**(1), 179–219 (1996)
36. Orchard, D., Yoshida, N.: Effects as sessions, sessions as effects. In: POPL, pp. 568–581. ACM, New York (2016)
37. Parkinson, M., Bierman, G.: Separation logic and abstraction. In: ACM SIGPLAN Notices, pp. 247–258. ACM (2005)
38. Reynolds, J.C.: Separation logic: a logic for shared mutable data structures. In: LICS, pp. 55–74 (2002)
39. Sergey, I., Wilcox, J.R., Tatlock, Z.: Programming and proving with distributed protocols. POPL **2**, 28:1–28:30 (2018)
40. Toninho, B., Caires, L., Pfenning, F.: Dependent session types via intuitionistic linear type theory. In: PPDP, pp. 161–172. ACM (2011)
41. Villard, J., Lozes, É., Calcagno, C.: Proving copyless message passing. In: Hu, Z. (ed.) APLAS 2009. LNCS, vol. 5904, pp. 194–209. Springer, Heidelberg (2009). https://doi.org/10.1007/978-3-642-10672-9_15
42. Wadler, P.: Propositions as sessions. In: ICFP, pp. 273–286. ACM (2012)

Logic

Automated Proof Synthesis for the Minimal Propositional Logic with Deep Neural Networks

Taro Sekiyama[1](✉) and Kohei Suenaga[2,3] (iD)

[1] National Institute of Informatics, Tokyo, Japan
sekiyama@nii.ac.jp
[2] Kyoto University, Kyoto, Japan
[3] JST PRESTO, Tokyo, Japan

Abstract. This work explores the application of *deep learning*, a machine learning technique that uses *deep neural networks (DNN)* in its core, to an automated theorem proving (ATP) problem. To this end, we construct a statistical model which quantifies the likelihood that a proof is indeed a correct one of a given proposition. Based on this model, we give a proof-synthesis procedure that searches for a proof in the order of the likelihood. This procedure uses an estimator of the likelihood of an inference rule being applied at each step of a proof. As an implementation of the estimator, we propose a *proposition-to-proof* architecture, which is a DNN tailored to the automated proof synthesis problem. To empirically demonstrate its usefulness, we apply our model to synthesize proofs of the minimal propositional logic. We train the proposition-to-proof model using a training dataset of proposition–proof pairs. The evaluation against a benchmark set shows the very high accuracy and an improvement to the recent work of neural proof synthesis.

Keywords: Automated theorem proving · Deep learning
Neural networks

1 Introduction

Automated theorem proving (ATP) [5], a set of techniques that prove logical formulas automatically, is becoming important as the realm of the areas that rely on theorem proving is expanding beyond mathematics to, e.g., system verification [20,22]. We are concerned with the following form of ATP called *automated proof synthesis (APS)*: Given a logical formula P, if P holds, return a proof M of P. In the light of the importance of theorem proving, APS serves as a useful tool for activities based on formal reasoning. For example, from the perspective of the aforementioned system verification, APS serves for automating system verification; indeed, various methods for (semi)automated static program verification [3,7,9] can be seen as APS procedures. We also remark another important application of APS: automated program synthesis. An APS algorithm can

© Springer Nature Switzerland AG 2018
S. Ryu (Ed.): APLAS 2018, LNCS 11275, pp. 309–328, 2018.
https://doi.org/10.1007/978-3-030-02768-1_17

be seen as an automated program synthesis procedure via the Curry–Howard isomorphism [32], in which M can be seen as a program and P can be seen as a specification. Not only is APS interesting from the practical viewpoint, it is also interesting from the algorithmic perspective of theorem proving.

Traditionally, the main weapon from the programming-language community to tackle APS has been *symbolic* methods; an APS algorithm inspects the syntactic structure of the formula P and, using the obtained information, tries to construct a proof derivation of P. A seminal work in this regard is by Ben-Yelles [4]; they proposed a sound and complete APS algorithm for an implicational fragment of the propositional logic.

This paper tackles the APS problem using another emerging technology: *statistical machine learning*. In particular, we explore an application of *deep neural networks (DNN)* [12]. DNNs have seen a great success in recent years for solving various tasks; to name a few, image recognition [14], speech recognition [15], and natural language processing [2].

To this end, we build a rigorous statistical model of the APS problem; this statistical model gives a specification of our DNN-based APS procedure by quantifying how a partially constructed proof is likely to lead to a correct proof of the given proposition P. Based on this statistical model, we define a proof-synthesis procedure that searches for a proof of given proposition P in the order of the likelihood. This proof-synthesis procedure requires a function to estimate the likelihood of an inference rule being applied at a specific step of a proof (or, equivalently, a specific position of a partially constructed proof). For this estimation, we propose a novel DNN architecture named *proposition-to-proof* network, which is tailored to the APS problem.[1] We empirically evaluate the performance of our network in proof synthesis of the minimal propositional logic and confirm that it can predict the inference rules that fill the rest of a partially constructed proof with 96.79% accuracy.

The contributions of this work are summarized as follows.

- We construct a statistical model for the APS problem to formally quantify the likelihood of a partially constructed proof leading to a correct one of a given proposition. Based on this statistical model, we design a proof-synthesis procedure that searches for a proof of a given proposition in the descending order of the likelihood.
- We propose a novel DNN architecture which we call *proposition-to-proof* architecture that estimates the above likelihood.
- We implement the proof-synthesis procedure with a trained network and empirically confirm its effectiveness with the minimal propositional logic. In addition to measuring the accuracy of the trained proposition-to-proof model, we conduct in-depth analyses of the performance of the model. We confirm that our model estimates the inference rule that should be applied at each step of a proof with 96.79% accuracy, which outperforms a previous DNN-based APS procedure by Sekiyama et al. [29].

---

[1] Following the convention of neural network research, we use the word "model" both for a statistical model and for a trained DNN.

Currently, we do not claim that our procedure outperforms the state-of-the-art APS method for propositional logic. Rather, our contribution consists in the statistical reformulation of the APS problem and application of deep learning, which exposes superhuman performance in many areas. We believe that deep learning is also useful in the APS problem and that the present work opens up a new research direction in this regard.

The rest of this paper is organized as follows: Sect. 2 defines the logic and the proof system that we use in this paper; Sect. 3 gives a statistical model of proof synthesis and defines the proof-synthesis procedure based on the statistical model; Sect. 4 introduces the proposition-to-proof architecture; Sect. 5 describes the result of the experiments; Sect. 6 discusses related work; and Sect. 7 concludes.

Due to the page limitation, we put several detailed discussions in the full version [30].

2   The Simply Typed Lambda Calculus as the Minimal Propositional Logic

In this work, we identify the simply typed lambda calculus with the minimal propositional logic via the Curry–Howard isomorphism [32]. This view is indeed beneficial for us: (1) a term of the simply typed lambda calculus is the concise representation of a derivation tree, which is essentially the proof of a proposition and (2) we can express a partially constructed proof as a term with *holes*, which denote positions in a proof that needs to be filled. In the rest of this section, we introduce the simply typed lambda calculus extended with product types and sum types. The Curry–Howard isomorphism allows us to identify a product type with the conjunction of propositions and a sum type with the disjunction. We sometimes abuse the terminologies in the simply typed lambda-calculus for those of the proof theory of the propositional logic.

The top of Fig. 1 shows the syntax of the simply typed lambda calculus. *Types* (or *propositions*) are represented by the metavariables P, Q, and R; *terms* (or *proofs*) are represented by the metavariables L, M, and N; and *typing contexts* (or *collections of assumptions*) are represented by the metavariable Γ. The definition of types is standard: they consist of *type variables* (or *propositional variables*), *function types* $P \to Q$, *product types* $P \times Q$, and *sum types* $P + Q$. We use the metavariables a, b, c, and d for type variables. The syntax of *terms* is that of the simply typed lambda calculus. Products are constructed by pair (M, N) and destructed by case M of $(x, y) \to M$; sums are constructed by injection Left M and Right N and destructed by case L of { Left $x \to M$; Right $y \to N$}. The term syntax is equipped with a *hole* [ ] to express partially constructed terms. A hole denotes a position in a term that needs to be filled (see below). We use metavariables x, y, and z for term variables.

A term that contains holes represents a partially constructed term. Our proof-synthesis procedure introduced in Sect. 3 maintains a set of partially constructed terms and fills a hole inside a term in the set at each step. We assume that holes

Types

$$P, Q, R ::= a \mid P \to Q \mid P \times Q \mid P + Q$$

Terms

$$L, M, N ::= [\,] \mid x \mid \lambda x.M \mid M\,N \mid (M, N) \mid \mathsf{case}\ M\ \mathsf{of}\ (x, y) \to N \mid$$
$$\mathsf{Left}\ M \mid \mathsf{Right}\ M \mid \mathsf{case}\ L\ \mathsf{of}\ \{\ \mathsf{Left}\ x \to M;\ \mathsf{Right}\ y \to N\}$$

Typing contexts

$$\Gamma ::= \emptyset \mid \Gamma, x{:}P$$

$$\boxed{\Gamma \vdash M\ :\ P}$$

$$\frac{}{\Gamma \vdash [\,]\ :\ P}\ \text{HOLE} \qquad\qquad \frac{x{:}P\ \in\ \Gamma}{\Gamma \vdash x\ :\ P}\ \text{VAR}$$

$$\frac{\Gamma, x{:}P \vdash M\ :\ Q}{\Gamma \vdash \lambda x.M\ :\ P \to Q}\ \text{ABS} \qquad \frac{\Gamma \vdash M\ :\ P \to Q \quad \Gamma \vdash N\ :\ P}{\Gamma \vdash M\,N\ :\ Q}\ \text{APP}$$

$$\frac{\Gamma \vdash M\ :\ P \quad \Gamma \vdash N\ :\ Q}{\Gamma \vdash (M, N)\ :\ P \times Q}\ \text{PAIR} \qquad \frac{\Gamma \vdash M\ :\ P \times Q \quad \Gamma, x{:}P, y{:}Q \vdash N\ :\ R}{\Gamma \vdash \mathsf{case}\ M\ \mathsf{of}\ (x, y) \to N\ :\ R}\ \text{CASEPAIR}$$

$$\frac{\Gamma \vdash M\ :\ P}{\Gamma \vdash \mathsf{Left}\ M\ :\ P + Q}\ \text{LEFT} \qquad \frac{\Gamma \vdash M\ :\ Q}{\Gamma \vdash \mathsf{Right}\ M\ :\ P + Q}\ \text{RIGHT}$$

$$\frac{\Gamma \vdash L\ :\ P + Q \quad \Gamma, x{:}P \vdash M\ :\ R \quad \Gamma, y{:}Q \vdash N\ :\ R}{\Gamma \vdash \mathsf{case}\ L\ \mathsf{of}\ \{\ \mathsf{Left}\ x \to M;\ \mathsf{Right}\ y \to N\}\ :\ R}\ \text{CASESUM}$$

Fig. 1. Syntax and inference rules.

in a term are uniquely identified by natural numbers. We write $[\,]_i$ for a hole with number i. We write $M[N]_i$ for the term obtained by filling the hole $[\,]_i$ in M with N.

We also define the typing relation $\Gamma \vdash M\ :\ P$ as the least relation that satisfies the inference rules in the bottom of Fig. 1. This relation means that term M is typed at P under Γ or, equivalently, M is a proof of P under assumptions Γ. We write $\Gamma \nvdash M\ :\ P$ to denote that $\Gamma \vdash M\ :\ P$ does not hold. The rules in Fig. 1 are standard except for the rule HOLE for holes. This rule allows any type to be given to a hole. We call the inference rules except for the rule HOLE *proof inference rules*. We say that M is a *(complete) proof* of P if $\emptyset \vdash M\ :\ P$ is derived and M has no holes. M is said to be *partial* or *partially constructed* if $\emptyset \vdash M\ :\ P$ but M contains holes.

3   Proof-Synthesis Procedure with Statistical Model

3.1   Statistical Model of Automated Proof Synthesis

The strategy of our proof-synthesis procedure is to incrementally construct a proof term M of a given proposition P so that the likelihood of M leading to a correct proof of P is as high as possible. In order to quantify the likelihood, we introduce a statistical model of proof synthesis.

We assume an oracle that returns a complete proof M given a provable proposition P; our aim is to mimic the behavior of this oracle. To build the statistical model, we designate two random variables: M that evaluates to a complete proof and P that evaluates to a proposition. For a proposition P and a complete proof M, we can consider a probability $p(M = M|P = P)$ that quantifies how M is likely to be a term returned by the oracle as a proof of P; this probability is one if M is returned by the oracle; zero otherwise. If we could compute M that makes this probability one for a given P, we are done. However, this is not possible because (1) we cannot precisely compute $p(M = M|P = P)$ without the oracle and (2) even if we could compute $p(M = M'|P = P)$ for any M' and P, it would not be trivial to find M that makes $p(M = M|P = P)$ one.

We solve this difficulty by approximating the probability distribution $p(M|P = P)$ from data. We could directly learn the probability distribution $p(M \mid P = P)$ from the training dataset using a certain machine leaning technique; this is the strategy taken by Sekiyama et al. [29]. However, such monolithic approximation of the probabilistic distribution often leads to a bad approximation; indeed, the accuracy of the automated proof synthesizer by Sekiyama et al. was around 50% at best.

We, instead, convert the probability distribution $p(M \mid P = P)$ to a product of easier-to-approximate ones. In order to derive this decomposition, we first introduce several notions.

Definition 1 (One-depth contexts). *The set of* one-depth contexts *is defined by the following BNF:*

$$C \in \mathbf{Ctx} ::= \lambda x.\,[]\mid[]\mid[]\,[]\mid([]\,,[])\mid \mathsf{case}\;[]\;\mathsf{of}\;(x,y)\to[]\mid$$
$$\mathsf{Left}\;[]\mid \mathsf{Right}\;[]\mid \mathsf{case}\;[]\;\mathsf{of}\;\{\,\mathsf{Left}\,x\to[]\,;\,\mathsf{Right}\,y\to[]\}.$$

We assume that each hole in a one-depth context is equipped with a unique natural number. We write $C\overline{[M_i]}_i$ for the term obtained by filling holes $[]_0,...,[]_n$ in C with terms $M_0,...,M_n$, respectively.

Definition 2 (Paths). *A path ρ is a finite sequence of pairs (C,i) where i is a natural number that identifies a hole in C. We write $\langle \rho,(C,i)\rangle$ for the path obtained by postpending (C,i) to path ρ.*

One-depth contexts represent term constructors other than variables. Using one-depth contexts, $\rho = \langle(C_0,i_0),(C_1,i_1),...,(C_n,i_n)\rangle$ specifies a path in a term, whose top-level constructor is identical to C_0, from its root node in the following way: C_0; the hole in C_0 with the natural number i_0; C_1; the hole in C_1 with the natural number i_1; and so on. For example, let M be a term $\lambda x.\mathsf{case}\;x\;\mathsf{of}\;(y,z)\to (z,y)$. Then, a path from the root of M to the reference to variable y is represented by the path $\langle(\lambda x.\,[]_0,0),\;(\mathsf{case}\;[]_0\;\mathsf{of}\;(y,z)\to[]_1,1),\;(([]_0,[]_1),1)\rangle$.

We compute the probability $p(M = M \mid P = P)$ by using the following two probability expressions: $p(x = x \mid P = P, Q = Q, \rho = \rho)$ and $p(C = C \mid$

$P = P, Q = Q, \rho = \rho$). In both probability expressions, P is the final goal proposition to be proved by the entire proof procedure. The former probability quantifies how x is likely to be a correct proof of the proposition Q that appears under the path ρ. The latter quantifies how the one-depth context C is likely to be a correct proof constructor to be chosen to prove the proposition Q that appears under the path ρ. These two probabilities are easier to approximate by using data compared to approximating $p(M = M \mid P = P)$ monolithically. The experimental result presented in Sect. 5 also indicates that our strategy leads to a better proof synthesizer than learning M directly.

Formally, we show that the function $\phi_P(x, \rho)$ defined below computes the probability $p(M = M \mid P = P)$ for a hole-free term M; see the full version for the detail of the proof.

Definition 3. *For any term M, let* typeof(M) *be the type of M.[2] Let P be a proposition, M be a hole-free term, and ρ be a path. Then, $\phi_P(M, \rho)$ is defined by induction on the structure of M as follows:*

$$\phi_P(x, \rho) = p(\boldsymbol{x} = x \mid \boldsymbol{P} = P, \boldsymbol{Q} = \mathsf{typeof}(x), \boldsymbol{\rho} = \rho)$$
$$\phi_P(C\overline{[M_i]_i}, \rho) = p(\boldsymbol{C} = C \mid \boldsymbol{P} = P, \boldsymbol{Q} = \mathsf{typeof}(C\overline{[M_i]_i}), \boldsymbol{\rho} = \rho) \times$$
$$\textstyle\prod_i \phi_P(M_i, \langle \rho, (C, i)\rangle),$$

where the random variable $\boldsymbol{x}$ evaluates to a term variable; $\boldsymbol{C}$ evaluates to a one-depth context; $\boldsymbol{Q}$ evaluates to a type to be proved by M; and $\boldsymbol{\rho}$ evaluates to a path that specifies the position where x or C is placed. Note that $\boldsymbol{P}$ evaluates to a type that is supposed to be proved by the root node, not by M. The probability $p(\boldsymbol{x} = x \mid \boldsymbol{P} = P, \boldsymbol{Q} = Q, \boldsymbol{\rho} = \rho)$ is that of x being a proof of Q under the condition that it appears at the position specified by ρ; and $p(\boldsymbol{C} = C \mid \boldsymbol{P} = P, \boldsymbol{Q} = Q, \boldsymbol{\rho} = \rho)$ is the probability of C being the top-level constructor of a proof term of Q if it appears at the position specified by ρ.

For proposition P, term M, and path ρ, the function $\phi_P(M, \rho)$ computes the product of (1) $p(\boldsymbol{C} = C \mid \boldsymbol{P} = P, \boldsymbol{Q} = \mathsf{typeof}(C\overline{[M_i]_i}), \boldsymbol{\rho} = \rho)$ for each subterm $C\overline{[M_i]_i}$ of M whose path from the root node is ρ and (2) $p(\boldsymbol{x} = x \mid \boldsymbol{P} = P, \boldsymbol{Q} = Q, \boldsymbol{\rho} = \rho)$ for each occurrence of variable x in M whose path from the root node is ρ. Therefore, we can compute the value of $\phi_P(M, \rho)$ if we can approximate $p(\boldsymbol{x} = x \mid \boldsymbol{P} = P, \boldsymbol{Q} = \mathsf{typeof}(x), \boldsymbol{\rho} = \rho)$ and $p(\boldsymbol{C} = C \mid \boldsymbol{P} = P, \boldsymbol{Q} = \mathsf{typeof}(C\overline{[M_i]_i}), \boldsymbol{\rho} = \rho)$. We show how we approximate these probabilities in Sect. 4. Once we approximate these probabilities, we can synthesize M that maximizes $p(M = M \mid P = P)$ using the procedure that we present below.

3.2   Proof Synthesis Procedure

Based on the discussion in Sect. 3.1, we design a proof-synthesis procedure. Procedure 1 shows the definition of our procedure PROOFSYNTHESIZE, which takes

---

[2] We can annotate typeof(M) by applying a standard type-inference algorithm for the simply typed lambda calculus to M.

Procedure 1 Proof synthesis

1: **procedure** PROOFSYNTHESIZE(P)
2:     Initialize priority queue $\mathcal{Q}$ that contains partial proofs constructed so far.
3:     Push $[\,]$ to $\mathcal{Q}$ with priority 1.0.
4:     **while** $\mathcal{Q}$ is not empty **do**
5:         Pop M with the highest priority $\mathcal{P}$ from $\mathcal{Q}$.
6:         Let $\rho = \arg\max_{\rho \in \mathsf{hole}\,(M)} \max_r p^*(r = r \mid \boldsymbol{P} = P, \boldsymbol{Q} = Q, \boldsymbol{\rho} = \rho)$
            where Q is a proof obligation to be discharged at $[\,]_\rho$.
7:         **for each** $C_x \in \mathbf{Ctx} \cup \mathsf{BV}\,(M, \rho)$ such that $\emptyset \vdash M[C_x]_\rho : P$ **do**
8:             **if** $\mathsf{hole}\,(M[C_x]_\rho) = \emptyset$ **then**
9:                 **return** $M[C_x]_\rho$
10:            **else**
11:                Let Q be a proof obligation to be discharged at $[\,]_\rho$.
12:                Let q be probability $p^*(r = r_{C_x} \mid \boldsymbol{P} = P, \boldsymbol{Q} = Q, \boldsymbol{\rho} = \rho)$.
13:                Push $M[C_x]_\rho$ to $\mathcal{Q}$ with priority $q \times \mathcal{P}$
14:            **end if**
15:        **end for**
16:    **end while**
17: **end procedure**

---

proposition P to be proved. This procedure maintains a priority queue $\mathcal{Q}$ of partially constructed terms. The priority associated with M by $\mathcal{Q}$ denotes the likelihood of M forming a proof of P. In each iteration of Lines 4–6, PROOFSYN-THESIZE picks a term M with the highest likelihood and fills a hole in M with a one-depth context or a variable. It returns a proof if it encounters a correct proof of P. We write $p^*(\varphi_1 \mid \varphi_2)$ for an approximation of $p(\varphi_1 \mid \varphi_2)$ for predicates φ_1 and φ_2.

Before going into the detail, we remark a gap between the procedure PROOF-SYNTHESIZE and the statistical model in Sect. 3.1. In that statistical model, we defined the likelihood of a variable $p(\boldsymbol{x} \mid \boldsymbol{P} = P, \boldsymbol{Q} = Q, \boldsymbol{\rho} = \rho)$ and that of a one-depth context $p(\boldsymbol{C} \mid \boldsymbol{P} = P, \boldsymbol{Q} = Q, \boldsymbol{\rho} = \rho)$ as separate probability distributions. Although this separation admits the inductive definition of the function ϕ_P, it is not necessarily plausible from the viewpoint of proof synthesis since, in filling a hole, we do not know whether it should be filled with a variable or with a one-depth context.

In order to solve this problem, we assume that we have an approximation of the likelihood of a *proof inference rule* that should be applied at the position of a hole. Concretely, we assume that we can approximate the probability distribution $p(\boldsymbol{r} \mid \boldsymbol{P}, \boldsymbol{Q}, \boldsymbol{\rho})$, where $\boldsymbol{r}$ is a random variable that evaluates to the name of a proof inference rule in Fig. 1. This assumption requires that we estimate the likelihood of VAR being applied for a hole, which can be done in the same way as the estimation of those of other inference rules.

Let us explain the inside of the procedure in more detail. A proof is synthe-sized by the while loop, where the procedure fills the hole $[\,]_\rho$ pointed by ρ in the partial proof M that has the highest likelihood $\mathcal{P}$ (Lines 4–16). We write $\mathsf{hole}\,(M)$ for the set of paths to holes in M. We select path ρ such that the inference rule applied at the position pointed by the path has the highest probability. After finding the hole to be filled, we replace it with C_x, which denotes one-depth contexts or variables. $\mathsf{BV}(M, \rho)$ is the set of bound variables that can be referred to at $[\,]_\rho$ and $M[C_x]_\rho$ is the term obtained by filling $[\,]_\rho$ in M with C_x. Note that **Ctx** is the set of all one-depth contexts. If $M[C_x]_\rho$ is a proof of P, which can be checked using an off-the-shelf type checker, then the procedure returns it as the synthesis result (Line 9). Otherwise, $M[C_x]_\rho$ is added to $\mathcal{Q}$ with priority $p^*(\boldsymbol{r} = r_{C_x} \mid \boldsymbol{P} = P, \boldsymbol{Q} = Q, \boldsymbol{\rho} = \rho) \times \mathcal{P}$, which is the likelihood of $M[C_x]_\rho$ leading to a correct proof (Line 13). r_{C_x} is the proof inference rule corresponding to C_x. Q is a proof obligation at $[\,]_\rho$; how to find it is discussed in Sect. 5.2.

We make a few remarks about the procedure:

- In the current implementation, we have not implemented the approximator of $p(\boldsymbol{x} \mid \boldsymbol{P}, \boldsymbol{Q}, \boldsymbol{\rho})$; instead, in filling a hole with a variable, we assume that $p(\boldsymbol{x} \mid \boldsymbol{P}, \boldsymbol{Q}, \boldsymbol{\rho})$ is the uniform distribution on the set of variables that are available at this scope. Although this assumption may look naive, our implementation still works well for many propositions; see Sect. 5.2. The problem of estimating the likelihood of a variable is similar to the *premise selection problem*, for which various work has been done [16,18,23,35]. Combining our synthesizer with such a technique is an interesting future direction.
- In the current implementation, we assume that the type checking conducted in Line 7 infers the type of each subexpression of $M[C_x]_\rho$ and annotates these types to them; this is indeed how we handle the typeof (M) in Sect. 3.1. This is a reasonable assumption as far as we are concerned with the propositional logic. For more expressive logics, we may need some auxiliary methods to guess the type of each expression.
- The procedure PROOFSYNTHESIZE is not an algorithm. If it is fed with an invalid (unprovable) proposition, then it does not terminate. Even if it is fed with a valid (provable) proposition, it may not be able to discover a proof of the proposition depending on the performance of the estimator of p^*.

4   Neural Proposition-to-Proof Architecture

In order to implement PROOFSYNTHESIZE, we are to approximate the probability distribution $p(\boldsymbol{r} \mid \boldsymbol{P}, \boldsymbol{Q}, \boldsymbol{\rho})$ that produces the likelihood of a proof inference rule being applied at a given position in a proof. To this end, we design a new DNN architecture, which we call a *proposition-to-proof architecture*, tailored to the classification task of inference rules. See, e.g., Goodfellow et al. [12] for an overview of deep learning.

4.1   Proposition-to-Proof Architecture

We design a DNN architecture that takes three arguments, proposition P to be proved, path ρ pointing to the hole to be filled, and proof obligation Q a

AST representation   Feature vectors in AST

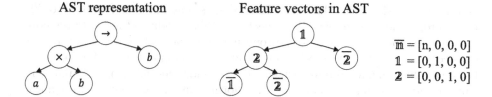

$$\overline{m} = [n, 0, 0, 0]$$
$$\mathbb{1} = [0, 1, 0, 0]$$
$$\mathbb{2} = [0, 0, 1, 0]$$

Fig. 2. Representation of $a \times b \to b$ in our proposition-to-proof architecture.

term of which should be placed in the hole, and approximates the likelihood of a proof inference rule being applied at the position specified by ρ in a proof of P. Following the standard style in deep learning, our architecture converts these three arguments to real vectors and then approximates the likelihood of each proof inference rule with them. We first explain how we translate P and Q to real vectors. The vector representation of a path is computed by using that of P. We finally concatenate vectors of Q and ρ into a single vector and use it to estimate a proof inference rule that should be applied.

Proposition Encoder. The vector representation of P is computed from the abstract syntax tree (AST) representation of P. Each node of the AST is equipped with a proposition constructor ($\to$, $\times$, or $+$) or a propositional variable. Each of these proposition constructors and propositional variables are associated with a vector described below. From these assigned vectors, the architecture computes the vector representation of the entire P.

One possible way to provide vectors that distinguish nodes of an AST is to use so-called one-hot vectors, which are used broadly in natural language processing. A one-hot vector for a word is an n-dimensional vector, where n is the size of the vocabularies, that only the element corresponding to the word has scalar value 1 and the others have 0. In this work, the information of a proposition constructor is embedded into a vector as in one-hot vectors, while a propositional variable a is embedded as a vector $[f(a), 0, 0, 0]$ where $f(a)$ is a postive number that identifies the variable a.

Definition 4 (Vector representation of proposition node). *Let f be a bijective function that maps propositional variables to positive numbers. Then, Enc gives a vector to node t as follows.*

$$Enc(a) = [f(a), 0, 0, 0] \qquad Enc(\to) = [0, 1, 0, 0]$$
$$Enc(\times) = [0, 0, 1, 0] \qquad Enc(+) = [0, 0, 0, 1]$$

Figure 2 illustrates vectors given by Enc, which are similar to one-hot vectors in that each dimension of them represents a class of a node. We consider that all propositional variables belong to the same class; therefore, Enc assigns their numerical values to the same dimension. On the other hand, different propositional variables should be distinguished; if $a \neq b$, proofs generated for $a \to b \to a$

and $a \to b \to b$ should be different. Thus, Enc assigns different numbers to different propositional variables. We expect that this encoding of nodes to be more informative especially for unknown propositional variables (i.e., variables that do not occur in a training dataset) than encoding by one-hot vectors, because one-hot vector encoding maps unknown entities to a single special symbol "unknown" whereas our encoding does not drop the information on the identity of unknown propositional variables.

After computing $\mathsf{Enc}(t)$ for each node t in a proposition P, we compute the vector representation of P in two steps. The first step is *AST convolution*, which updates the vector for each node t using those of the nodes around t by using *AST convolution layers*. The second step aggregates the vectors of the nodes into a single vector by an *aggregation layer*. The function of these two kinds of layers parallels the convolution layer used in image processing [10,12]; a convolution layer in image processing works as an image filter by transforming each pixel of an image with the weighted sum of its neighborhoods. Our AST-convolutional and aggregation layers transform an AST by transforming each node with the weighted sum of its neighboring nodes. We benefit from this transformation since our DNN can recognize the knowledge about the structure of AST.

AST Convolution Layer. An AST convolution layer updates a vector of each node t in an AST by using the vectors of the nodes around t. Suppose that $\mathsf{parent}\,(t)$ is the parent and $\mathsf{child}\,(t,i)$ is the i-th child of t. Let v_t be an n-dimensional vector of t. Then, the AST convolution layer updates all vectors of nodes in a given AST simultaneously as follows. Let ς_t be a class of node t, that is, a proposition constructor ($\to$, $\times$, or $+$) or a class to denote propositional variables. We write Wv for the matrix product of real matrix W in $\mathbb{R}^{m \times n}$ and the real column vector $v \in \mathbb{R}^n$, $v_1 + v_2$ for the element-wise addition of real vectors v_1 and v_2, and $F(v)$ for the element-wise application of function F over reals to real vector v. Then, the computation conducted by a convolution layer is defined by

$$
v_t \leftarrow F^{\mathrm{conv}} \left(\sum_i W^{\mathrm{conv}}_{\varsigma_t, i} \, v_{\mathsf{child}\,(t,i)} + W^{\mathrm{conv}}_{\varsigma_t} v_t + W^{\mathrm{conv}}_{\varsigma_t, p} \, v_{\mathsf{parent}\,(t)} + b^{\mathrm{conv}}_{\varsigma_t} \right) \quad (1)
$$

where $W^{\mathrm{conv}}_{\varsigma_t, i} \in \mathbb{R}^{m \times n}$ is a weight parameter which is a coefficient of the vector of the i-th child, $W^{\mathrm{conv}}_{\varsigma_t} \in \mathbb{R}^{m \times n}$ is for t, $W^{\mathrm{conv}}_{\varsigma_t, p} \in \mathbb{R}^{m \times n}$ is for the parent, $b^{\mathrm{conv}}_{\varsigma_t} \in \mathbb{R}^m$ is a bias parameter for ς_t, and F^{conv} is an activation function. Each parameter is shared among the nodes with the same ς_t. If t is the root node, then $v_{\mathsf{parent}\,(t)}$ denotes the zero vector. We use multiple AST convolution layers to update the vector for each node.

The update (1) is inspired by tree-based convolution proposed by Mou et al. [25]. Our definition, however, differs from theirs in the following aspects. First, our update rule involves the vector of a parent node to capture the context where a node is used, whereas Mou et al. do not. Second, the convolution by Mou et al. deals with only binary trees; they require an AST is represented by a binary tree before convolution is applied, which is essentially possible by, for example, representing an AST as a left-child right-sibling binary trees.[3] They require the binary-tree representation in order to fix the number of weight parameters for children to be only two. However, a different tree representation may affect a vector representation learned by DNNs and may not preserve the locality of the original AST representation. Thus, instead of requiring a proposition to be expressed as a binary tree, we design our network so that it can deal with an AST as it is. Fortunately, the syntax of propositions is defined so that the number of children of each node is fixed. Hence, we can fix the number of learnable weight parameters for children: two for each proposition constructor.

Aggregation Layer. An aggregation layer integrates vectors of nodes in an AST to a single vector.

Definition 5 (Aggregation layer). *Let t be a node of an AST where nodes are augmented with n-dimensional vectors. Function $Agg(t)$ produces an n-dimensional vector from t as follows:*

$$Agg(t) = F^{\mathrm{agg}} \left(\sum_i W_{\varsigma_t,i}^{\mathrm{agg}} \, Agg(child(t,i)) + W_{\varsigma_t}^{\mathrm{agg}} v_t + b_{\varsigma_t}^{\mathrm{agg}} \right)$$

where $W_{\varsigma_t}^{\mathrm{agg}}$ and $W_{\varsigma_t,i}^{\mathrm{agg}} \in \mathbb{R}^{n \times n}$ are weight parameters which are coefficients of vectors of t and its i-th child, respectively, $b_{\varsigma_t}^{\mathrm{agg}} \in \mathbb{R}^n$ is a bias for ς_t, and F^{agg} is an activation function. Each parameter is shared among the nodes with the same ς_t.

Another way to produce a single vector from an AST is a max-pool [25], which, for each dimension, takes the maximum scalar value among all the vectors in the AST. While max-pools are used by usual convolutional neural networks [21], for our purpose, it is not clear whether only the maximum value describes the characteristic of the whole AST well. Our aggregation layer can be considered as "fold" on trees with vectors; we expect that $Agg(t)$ learns a vector representation of the AST that fits better for our purpose because it takes not only the maximum values but also the other elements of vectors of all nodes into account.

In what follows, we write v_P for the vector produced from P by applying Enc, one or more AST convolution layers, and an aggregation layer sequentially.

Path Encoder. To achieve good performance, we have to know what assumptions are available at the position for which an inference rule is estimated. For example, suppose we are to prove b at a certain hole of a partially constructed term. If we know that there is a variable x of type $a \to b$ that is available at this position, then we could use the rules APP and VAR to fill the hole with $x\ [\ ]$; then the remaining task is to fill the newly generated hole with a term of

---

[3] It is not clear from Mou et al. [25] how they express an AST as a binary tree in their implementation.

type a. In our setting, the information of the available assumptions is accessible via proposition P and path ρ. To make P available to the proposition-to-proof architecture, we use v_P; for ρ we use $\mathsf{Extract}\,(\rho, v_P)$ defined as follows.

Definition 6 (Extraction). $\mathsf{Extract}(\rho, v)$ *extracts a vector in the position to which ρ points from v.*

$$
\begin{aligned}
\mathsf{Extract}\,(\langle\rangle, v) &= W^{\mathrm{ext}}\, v + b^{\mathrm{ext}} \\
\mathsf{Extract}\,(\langle(C, i), \rho\rangle, v) &= \mathsf{Extract}\,(\rho, v') \quad \text{where } v' = F^{\mathrm{ext}}\left(W^{\mathrm{ext}}_{C,i}\, v + b^{\mathrm{ext}}_{C,i}\right)
\end{aligned}
$$

where $W^{\mathrm{ext}}, W^{\mathrm{ext}}_{C,i} \in \mathbb{R}^{n\times n}$ and $b^{\mathrm{ext}}, b^{\mathrm{ext}}_{C,i} \in \mathbb{R}^n$ are learnable parameters and F^{ext} is an activation function. $\langle(C, i), \rho\rangle$ is the addition of (C, i) to path ρ at the beginning.

We write $v_{P,\rho}$ for $\mathsf{Extract}\,(\rho, v_P)$. The weight parameters in Definition 6 have a role of extracting vectors necessary to capture assumptions from v_P. The biases are expected to capture information of the context around the node to which the path points.

Classification. We estimate what proof inference rule is most likely to be applied by using two vectors $v_{P,\rho}$, which is the extracted vector from P along ρ, and v_Q, which is the vector of proof obligation Q. For this estimation, we apply multiple fully connected layers to the vector obtained by concatenating $v_{P,\rho}$ and v_Q. The number of the dimensions of the final output v_o is equal to the number of proof inference rules; eight in our logic. Each index in the vector v_o corresponds to an inference rule.

We use the values obtained by applying a softmax to v_o as the approximation of the likelihood of each inference rule. Concretely, the approximated probability $p^*(\boldsymbol{r} = r \mid \boldsymbol{P} = P, \boldsymbol{Q} = Q, \boldsymbol{\rho} = \rho)$ is calculated by:

$$
\frac{exp(v_o[n_r])}{\sum_{j=1}^{8} exp(v_o[j])},
$$

where $v[i]$ is the value of the i-th dimension of v and $n_r \in \{1, ..., 8\}$ is the index corresponding to the proof inference rule r in v_o.

5 Experiments

This section reports the performance of our proposition-to-proof model and the proof-synthesis procedure combined with the model. We train the proposition-to-proof architecture on a dataset that contains pairs of a proposition and its proof by supervised learning. After explaining the details of our architecture, we detail the configuration of the experiments including the dataset and hyperparameters. We evaluate the trained model on the basis of accuracy; given a proposition, a partially constructed proof, and a hole from a validation dataset, we check how

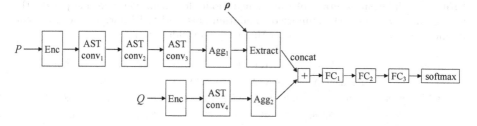

Fig. 3. The architecture used in experiments. P is a proposition to be proved, ρ is a path specifying the hole to be filled, and Q is a proof obligation to be discharged at the hole.

accurately the model estimates the inference rule to be applied at the hole. We also conduct in-depth analyses of the performance of the model; we especially evaluate the influence of the depth of a hole to the accuracy. Finally, we evaluate the proof-synthesis procedure given in Sect. 3.2.

We implemented the procedure PROOFSYNTHESIZE and our model on Python 3 (version 3.6.3) with the deep learning framework Chainer [34] (version 2.1.0). We use the Haskell interpreter GHCi (version 8.0.1) as the type checker used in PROOFSYNTHESIZE. All the experiments are conducted on a machine equipped with 12 CPU cores (Intel i7-6850K 3.60 GHz), 32 GB RAM, and NVIDIA GPUs (Quadro P6000).

5.1   Configuration

Figure 3 shows the proposition-to-proof architecture used in the experiments. For the role of each layer, see Sect. 4. We use three AST convolution layers to encode proposition P to be proved and one to encode proof-obligation proposition Q. The concatenation of $v_{P,\rho}$ computed by Extract and v_Q by Agg$_2$ is fed to three fully connected layers. The detailed specification of each layer is shown in the full version [30]. We use a rectified linear unit (ReLU) [11] as activation functions throughout the architecture.

The power of deep learning rests on datasets used to train DNNs. In this work, we need a dataset of pairs of a proposition and its proof. We make dataset D_{all} by generating proofs of sizes 2 through 9 exhaustively (their number is 136877) and about 30000 proofs of sizes 10 through 50 at random. The dataset consists of tuples of proposition P to be proved by a proof, proof obligation Q to be discharged at a hole, a path ρ which specifies the hole, and inference rule r which should be applied at the position of the hole; note that P, Q, and ρ are inputs to the proposition-to-proof architecture and r is an expected output from it. We use 90% of D_{all} as the training dataset D_t and the remaining 10% as the validation dataset D_v. See the full version [30] for details of the dataset.

Table 1. Validation accuracy of the trained model for each inference rule per depth. The column "#" shows the number of validation data and "All" does the accuracy for all inference rules. "N/A" means that there are no validation data.

Depth	#	All	VAR	ABS	APP	PAIR	CASEPAIR	LEFT	RIGHT	CASESUM
1	16774	100.0	N/A	100.0	N/A	100.0	N/A	100.0	100.0	N/A
5	27262	96.92	97.36	99.30	90.95	98.82	62.87	97.50	97.75	82.08
9	7616	92.57	97.90	96.16	30.51	92.46	34.10	93.88	95.86	33.00
14	1221	90.17	98.08	97.06	12.00	89.39	21.88	93.97	89.92	17.14
16–20	1158	90.50	97.91	95.75	19.05	91.11	8.33	95.05	86.79	3.70
1–26	193108	96.79	98.03	99.27	78.21	98.50	57.25	98.05	97.95	67.34

We train the proposition-to-proof architecture on dataset D_t by stochastic gradient descent with a mini-batch size of 1000 for 20 epochs.[4] Weights in each layer of the architecture are initialized by the values independently drawn from the Gaussian distribution with mean 0 and standard deviation $\sqrt{\frac{1}{n}}$ where n is the number of dimensions of vectors in the input to the layer. The biases are initialized with 0. We use the softmax cross entropy as the loss function. As an optimizer, we use Adam [19] with parameters $\alpha = 0.001$, $\beta_1 = 0.9$, $\beta_2 = 0.999$, and $\epsilon = 10^{-8}$. We lower α, which controls the learning rate, by 10 times when the training converges. We regularize our model by a weight decay with penalty rate $\lambda = 0.0001$. The training takes 50 hours per epoch in our environment.

5.2   Evaluation

Accuracy. Table 1 shows the accuracy of the trained model on the validation dataset D_v, that is, the ratio of the number of tuples (P, Q, ρ, r) in D_v such that the trained model estimates r successfully given P, Q, and ρ. The bottom row in the table reports the summarized accuracy. It shows that the trained model achieves 96.79% accuracy in total. Looking at results per inference rule, we achieve the very high accuracy for VAR, ABS, PAIR, LEFT, and RIGHT. It is interesting that the trained model chooses either of LEFT or RIGHT appropriately according to problem instances. It means that, given proposition $P + Q$, the proof-synthesis procedure combined with our trained model can predict which of P and Q to be proved correctly with high probability. The accuracy for APP, CASEPAIR, and CASESUM are not as high as that for the other rules. One of the reasons for this relatively low accuracy for these rules seems to be the characteristic of the dataset; the numbers of training data that involves APP, CASEPAIR, and CASESUM are much smaller than those of the other rules.[5] Since

---

[4] Epoch is the unit that means how many times the dataset is scanned during the training.

[5] See the full version [30] for the detail. The low accuracy of these rules does not influence the overall accuracy much because the validation dataset does not contain many applications of them either.

the model is trained so that inference rules that often occur in the training dataset are more likely to be estimated in order to minimize the loss, the trained model may prefer to choose inference rules other than APP, CASEPAIR, and CASESUM. Furthermore, it may be possible that the training data for those rules are insufficient to learn vector representation of the likelihood of them being applied. In either case, data augmentation would be useful, though we need to establish effective augmentation of proofs.

Our model is supposed to access the assumptions via the P and ρ. Since ρ becomes larger as the position of the hole does deeper, the depth of the hole is expected to affect the performance of the model. To evaluate how large the influence is, we measure the relation between accuracy and the depths of holes in the validation data, which is shown in Table 1; see the full version for the complete results. The column "All" shows that the accuracy at a greater depth tends to be lower. The accuracy of ABS, PAIR, LEFT, and RIGHT is still high even if holes are at deep positions. We consider that this is because, rather than assumptions, proof obligations play an important role to choose those inference rules. By contrast, the accuracy of APP, CASEPAIR, and CASESUM decreases as the depth of the holes becomes greater. This is because these rules need information about assumptions to judge whether they should be applied. We expect that we can improve the accuracy of these rules by improving the vector representation of assumptions. The accuracy of VAR is very high at any depth, though whether we can apply VAR should depend on assumptions. This may be due to the large number of training data for VAR (the detail is in the full version [30]), which may make it possible to learn vector representations of assumptions only for VAR.

To confirm the power of explicit use of proof obligations, we train a DNN architecture that does *not* use the vector of a proof obligation in the same way as Sect. 5.1. The total accuracy of the trained obligation-free model is 83.90%. The accuracy per inference rule/depth is also lower than the proposition-to-proof architecture that uses proof obligations explicitly; see the full version [30] for the detail.

Proof Synthesis. We also conduct experiments to evaluate PROOFSYNTHESIZE (Procedure 1) executed with the trained proposition-to-proof model. We make two test datasets for evaluation by choosing 500 propositions from D_v respectively. One dataset D_{small} consists of propositions that have proofs whose sizes are not larger than 9. The other dataset D_{large} includes propositions that are generated at random so that the sizes of their proofs are larger than 9. We abort the proof synthesis if a proof is not generated within three minutes. We use the principal type [24] for a proof obligation that is required by PROOFSYNTHESIZE.

We compare our procedure with an existing method of APS with deep learning by Sekiyama et al. [29]. They view proof generation as a machine-translation task from a proposition language to a proof language and apply a so-called sequence-to-sequence architecture [33], which is a popular network in DNN-based machine translation, in order to produce a token sequence expected to be a proof from a token sequence of a proposition. They find that, though the response

Table 2. The evaluation result of the proof-synthesis procedures: Rows "Number of successes" show the number of propositions to which correct proofs are generated; Rows "Average time (sec.) in success" show the average of elapsed time spent for a successful proof synthesis.

		PROOFSYNTHESIZE	Sekiyama et al. [29]
D_{small}	Number of successes	500	500
	Average time (sec.) in success	0.45	1.85
D_{large}	Number of successes	466	157
	Average time (sec.) in success	4.56	29.03

from the sequence-to-sequence model may not be a proof of the proposition, the response is often "close" to a correct proof and, based on this observation, propose a proof-synthesis procedure that uses the response from the sequence-to-sequence model as a guide of proof search. We train the sequence-to-sequence model on D_t for 200 epochs in the same way as Sekiyama et al. and apply their proof-synthesis procedure to propositions in D_{small} and D_{large}.

Table 2 shows the number of propositions for which the proof synthesis succeeds. This figure also shows the average of the elapsed times spent by the procedure for the successful propositions. Both procedures succeed in generating proofs for all propositions in D_{small}, which indicates that they work well, at least, for propositions that have small proofs. As for D_{large}, PROOFSYNTHESIZE successfully generates proofs for 93.2% of propositions in D_{large}, while the procedure of Sekiyama et al. does for only 31.4%. Since PROOFSYNTHESIZE calculates the likelihood of a proof being a correct one by the joint probability of inference rules in the proof, we can generate a correct proof even in a case that the likelihoods of a few instances of inference rules in the correct proof are estimated to be low, if the likelihoods of other instances are to be high. By contrast, the procedure of Sekiyama et al. uses only a single term as a guide, so it is hard to recover the mistake of the estimation by the sequence-to-sequence model. This would also lead to a difference of elapsed times taken by two proof-synthesis procedures—the procedure of Sekiyama et al. takes four times and six times as long as PROOFSYNTHESIZE for propositions in D_{small} and D_{large}, respectively.

Finally, we remark the comparison of our DNN-based APS technique with an existing theorem prover. For comparison, we evaluate PITPINV [1], a theorem prover for propositional intuitionistic logic that solves the highest number of problems of the ILTP [26], on D_{small} and D_{large}.[6] PITPINV solves all problems of D_{small} and D_{large} and the average times to solve one problem of D_{small} and D_{large} is 0.0035 and 0.0038 seconds, respectively. PITPINV is faster than our approach because, while our approach involves many expensive matrix operations for use of neural networks, PITPINV exploits domain knowledge of

---

[6] The source code is at http://www2.disco.unimib.it/fiorino/pitp.html; accessed on 26/8/2018.

intuitionistic theorem proving effectively. It is left as future work how to make the DNN-based approach cooperate with these traditional methods.

6 Related Work

Application of deep learning to ATP is becoming in trend recently. Roughly speaking, there have been two research directions for ATP with deep learning: *enhancing existing solvers with deep learning* and *implementing ATP procedures using deep learning*. We discuss these two lines of work in the following.

6.1 Enhancing Existing Provers

Existing automated theorem provers rely on many heuristics. Applying deep learning to improve these hand-crafted heuristics, aiming at enhancing them, is an interesting direction. *Premise selection*, a task to select premises needed to prove a given conjecture, is an important heuristic to narrow the search space of proofs. Irving et al. [16] show the possibility of the application of deep learning to this area using various DNN models to encode premises and a conjecture to be proved in first-order logic. Kaliszyk et al. [18] make a dataset in the HOL Light theorem prover [13] for several tasks, including premise selection, related to ATP. Wang et al. [35] tackles the premise selection problem in higher-order logic. Their key idea is to regard logical formulas as graphs by connecting a propositional variable to its binder, while the other work such as Irving et al. [16] and Kaliszyk et al. [18] deals with them as token sequences. This idea allows a DNN model to utilize structural information of formulas and be invariant to names of bound variables.

Loos et al. [23] apply several off-the-shelf DNNs to guide *clause selection* of a saturation-based first-order logic prover E [28]. Given a conjecture to be proved, E generates a set of clauses from logical formulas including the negated conjecture and investigates whether a contradiction is derivable by processing the clauses one by one; if a contradiction is found, the conjecture holds; otherwise, it does not. If E processes clauses that derive a contradiction early, the proof search finishes in a small number of steps. Hence, clause selection is an important task in saturation-based theorem provers including E. Loos et al. use DNNs to rank clauses that are not processed yet and succeed in accelerating the proof search by combining the DNN-guided clause selection with existing heuristics.

This direction of enhancing the existing provers is orthogonal to our present work. Although our goal is to generate proofs directly with deep learning, rather than focusing on specific subproblems that are important in theorem proving, we expect (as we discussed in Sect. 3.2) that the combination of our approach with these techniques is also beneficial to our technique.

6.2 Formula Proving

Solving the Boolean satisfiability (SAT) problem by encoding problem instances into neural networks has been attempted in early days [17]. Recent work uses

DNNs as a binary classifier of Boolean logical formulas. Bünz and Lamm [6] represent a Boolean formula in conjunctive normal form (CNF) as a graph where variable nodes are connected to nodes that represent disjunctive clauses referring to the variables and apply a graph neural network [27] to classify the satisfiability of the formula. Similarly NeuroSAT [31] regards CNF formulas as graphs, but it adopts a message passing architecture and can often (not always) produce a Boolean assignment, which makes it possible to check that the formula is truly satisfied. Evans et al. [8] tackle the entailment problem in the propositional logic, that is, whether a propositional conjecture can be proved under considered assumptions. They also develop a new DNN architecture that classifies whether a given entailment holds. These lines of work do not guarantee the correctness of the solution. Our work, although the procedure may not terminate, guarantees the correctness of the returned proof.

Sekiyama et al. [29] applied deep learning to proof synthesis. Their key idea is that the task of proof synthesis can be seen as a translation task from propositions to proofs. Based on this idea, they use a sequence-to-sequence architecture [33], which is widely used in machine translation with deep learning, in order to translate a proposition to its proof. As shown in Sect. 2, our proposition-to-proof model outperforms their model from the perspectives of (1) the number of propositions that are successfully proved and (2) the time spent by the proof-synthesis procedures.

7   Conclusion

We present an approach to applying deep learning to the APS problem. We formulate the APS problem in terms of statistics so that we can quantify the likelihood of a term being a correct proof of a proposition. From this formulation, we show that this likelihood can be calculated by using the likelihood of an inference rule being applied at a specified position in a proof, which enables us to synthesize proofs gradually. To approximate this likelihood, we develop a DNN that we call a proposition-to-proof architecture. Our DNN architecture encodes the tree representation of a proposition and decodes it to estimate an inference rule to be applied by using the proof obligation to be discharged effectively.

We train the DNN architecture on a dataset of automatically generated proposition-proof pairs and confirmed that the trained model achieves 96.79% accuracy in the inference-rule estimation, though there is still room for improvement. We also develop a proof-synthesis procedure with the trained DNN model and show that it can synthesize many proofs of a proposition faster compared to the existing DNN-based proof-syntehsis work [29].

Acknowledgments. We are grateful to Akifumi Imanishi, Kensuke Kojima, and Takayuki Muranushi for the discussion and the contribution to the earlier version of the present work. Kohei Suenaga is supported by JST PRESTO Grant Number JPMJPR15E5, Japan. Taro Sekiyama is supported by ERATO HASUO Metamathematics for Systems Design Project (No. JPMJER1603), JST.

References

1. Avellone, A., Fiorino, G., Moscato, U.: A new $O(n \log n)$-space decision procedure for propositional intuitionistic logic. Kurt Gödel Society Collegium Logicum VIII, 17–33 (2004)
2. Bahdanau, D., Cho, K., Bengio, Y.: Neural machine translation by jointly learning to align and translate. CoRR abs/1409.0473 (2014)
3. Barnett, M., et al.: The Spec# programming system: challenges and directions. In: Meyer, B., Woodcock, J. (eds.) VSTTE 2005. LNCS, vol. 4171, pp. 144–152. Springer, Heidelberg (2008). https://doi.org/10.1007/978-3-540-69149-5_16
4. Ben-Yelles, C.: Type assignment in the lambda-calculus: syntax and semantics. Ph.D. thesis, University College of Swansea, September 1979
5. Bibel, W.: Automated Theorem Proving. Springer, Heidelberg (2013)
6. Bünz, B., Lamm, M.: Graph neural networks and boolean satisfiability. CoRR abs/1702.03592 (2017)
7. Chalin, P., James, P.R., Karabotsos, G.: An integrated verification environment for JML: architecture and early results. In: Proceedings of SAVCBS, pp. 47–53. ACM, New York (2007)
8. Evans, R., Saxton, D., Amos, D., Kohli, P., Grefenstette, E.: Can neural networks understand logical entailment? CoRR abs/1802.08535 (2018)
9. Filliâtre, J.-C., Paskevich, A.: Why3 — where programs meet provers. In: Felleisen, M., Gardner, P. (eds.) ESOP 2013. LNCS, vol. 7792, pp. 125–128. Springer, Heidelberg (2013). https://doi.org/10.1007/978-3-642-37036-6_8
10. Fukushima, K.: Neocognitron: a self-organizing neural network for a mechanism of pattern recognition unaffected by shift in position. Biol. Cybern. **36**, 193–202 (1980)
11. Glorot, X., Bordes, A., Bengio, Y.: Deep sparse rectifier neural networks. In: Proceedings of AISTATS, pp. 315–323 (2011)
12. Goodfellow, I., Bengio, Y., Courville, A.: Deep Learning. MIT Press, Cambridge (2016)
13. Harrison, J.: HOL light: an overview. In: Berghofer, S., Nipkow, T., Urban, C., Wenzel, M. (eds.) TPHOLs 2009. LNCS, vol. 5674, pp. 60–66. Springer, Heidelberg (2009). https://doi.org/10.1007/978-3-642-03359-9_4
14. He, K., Zhang, X., Ren, S., Sun, J.: Deep residual learning for image recognition. In: Proceedings of CVPR, pp. 770–778 (2016)
15. Hinton, G., et al.: Deep neural networks for acoustic modeling in speech recognition: the shared views of four research groups. IEEE Sig. Process. Mag. **29**(6), 82–97 (2012)
16. Irving, G., Szegedy, C., Alemi, A.A., Eén, N., Chollet, F., Urban, J.: DeepMath - deep sequence models for premise selection. In: Proceedings of NIPS, pp. 2235–2243 (2016)
17. Johnson, J.L.: A neural network approach to the 3-satisfiability problem. J. Parallel Distrib. Comput. **6**(2), 435–449 (1989)
18. Kaliszyk, C., Chollet, F., Szegedy, C.: HolStep: a machine learning dataset for higher-order logic theorem proving. CoRR abs/1703.00426 (2017)
19. Kingma, D.P., Ba, J.: Adam: a method for stochastic optimization. CoRR abs/1412.6980 (2014)
20. Klein, G., et al.: seL4: formal verification of an OS kernel. In: Proceedings of SOSP, pp. 207–220 (2009)

21. Krizhevsky, A., Sutskever, I., Hinton, G.E.: Imagenet classification with deep convolutional neural networks. In: Proceedings of NIPS, pp. 1106–1114 (2012)
22. Leroy, X.: Formal verification of a realistic compiler. Commun. ACM **52**(7), 107–115 (2009)
23. Loos, S.M., Irving, G., Szegedy, C., Kaliszyk, C.: Deep network guided proof search. In: Proceedings of LPAR, pp. 85–105 (2017)
24. Milner, R.: A theory of type polymorphism in programming. J. Comput. Syst. Sci. **17**(3), 348–375 (1978)
25. Mou, L., Li, G., Zhang, L., Wang, T., Jin, Z.: Convolutional neural networks over tree structures for programming language processing. In: Proceedings of AAAI, pp. 1287–1293 (2016)
26. Raths, T., Otten, J., Kreitz, C.: The ILTP problem library for intuitionistic logic. J. Autom. Reason. **38**(1–3), 261–271 (2007)
27. Scarselli, F., Gori, M., Tsoi, A.C., Hagenbuchner, M., Monfardini, G.: The graph neural network model. IEEE Trans. Neural Netw. **20**(1), 61–80 (2009)
28. Schulz, S.: System description: E 1.8. In: McMillan, K., Middeldorp, A., Voronkov, A. (eds.) LPAR 2013. LNCS, vol. 8312, pp. 735–743. Springer, Heidelberg (2013). https://doi.org/10.1007/978-3-642-45221-5_49
29. Sekiyama, T., Imanishi, A., Suenaga, K.: Towards proof synthesis guided by neural machine translation for intuitionistic propositional logic. CoRR abs/1706.06462 (2017)
30. Sekiyama, T., Suenaga, K.: Automated proof synthesis for propositional logic with deep neural networks. CoRR abs/1805.11799 (2018). http://arxiv.org/abs/1805.11799
31. Selsam, D., Lamm, M., Bünz, B., Liang, P., de Moura, L., Dill, D.L.: Learning a SAT solver from single-bit supervision. CoRR abs/1802.03685 (2018)
32. Sørensen, M.H., Urzyczyn, P.: Lectures on the Curry-Howard Isomorphism. Studies in Logic and the Foundations of Mathematics, vol. 149. Elsevier Science Inc., Amsterdam (2006)
33. Sutskever, I., Vinyals, O., Le, Q.V.: Sequence to sequence learning with neural networks. In: Proceedings of NIPS, pp. 3104–3112 (2014)
34. Tokui, S., Oono, K., Hido, S., Clayton, J.: Chainer: a next-generation open source framework for deep learning. In: Proceedings of workshop on LearningSys (2015)
35. Wang, M., Tang, Y., Wang, J., Deng, J.: Premise selection for theorem proving by deep graph embedding. In: Proceedings of NIPS, pp. 2783–2793 (2017)

On the Complexity of Pointer Arithmetic in Separation Logic

James Brotherston[1($\boxtimes$)] and Max Kanovich[1,2]

^{1} University College London, London, UK
J.Brotherston@ucl.ac.uk
^{2} National Research University Higher School of Economics,
Moscow, Russian Federation

Abstract. We investigate the complexity consequences of adding pointer arithmetic to separation logic. Specifically, we study an extension of the points-to fragment of symbolic-heap separation logic with sets of simple "difference constraints" of the form $x \leq y + k$, where x and y are pointer variables and k is an integer offset. This extension can be considered a practically minimal language for separation logic with pointer arithmetic.

Most significantly, we find that, even for this minimal language, polynomial-time decidability is already impossible: satisfiability becomes NP-complete, while quantifier-free entailment becomes coNP-complete and quantified entailment becomes Π_2^P-complete (where Π_2^P is the second class in the polynomial-time hierarchy).

However, the language does satisfy the small model property, meaning that any satisfiable formula has a model, and any invalid entailment has a countermodel, of polynomial size, whereas this property fails when richer forms of arithmetical constraints are permitted.

Keywords: Separation logic · Pointer arithmetic · Complexity

1 Introduction

Separation logic (SL) [23] is a well-known and popular Hoare-style framework for verifying the memory safety of heap-manipulating programs. Its power stems from the use of *separating conjunction* in its assertion language, where $A * B$ denotes a portion of memory that can be split into two disjoint fragments satisfying A and B respectively. Using separating conjunction, the *frame rule* becomes sound [27], capturing the fact that any valid Hoare triple can be extended with the same separate memory in its pre- and postconditions and remain valid, which empowers the framework to scale to large programs (see e.g. [26]). Indeed, separation logic now forms the basis for verification tools used in industrial practice, notably Facebook's INFER [8] and Microsoft's SLAYER [3].

Most separation logic analyses and tools restrict the form of assertions to a simple propositional structure known as *symbolic heaps* [2]. Symbolic heaps are

© Springer Nature Switzerland AG 2018
S. Ryu (Ed.): APLAS 2018, LNCS 11275, pp. 329–349, 2018.
https://doi.org/10.1007/978-3-030-02768-1_18

(possibly existentially quantified) pairs of so-called "pure" and "spatial" assertions, where pure assertions mention only equalities and disequalities between variables and spatial formulas are $*$-conjoined lists of pointer formulas $x \mapsto y$ and data structure formulas typically describing (segments of) *linked lists* ($\mathsf{ls}\, x\, y$) or sometimes binary trees. This fragment of the logic enjoys decidability in polynomial time [11] and is therefore highly suitable for use in large-scale analysers. However, in recent years, various authors have investigated the computational complexity of (and/or developed prototype analysers for) many other fragments employing various different assertion constructs, including user-defined inductive predicates [1,5,7,10,18], pointers with *fractional permissions* [13,22], arrays [6,19], separating *implication* ($-*$) [4,9], reachability predicates [14] and arithmetic [20,21].

It is with this last feature, arithmetic, and more specifically *pointer arithmetic*, with which we are concerned in this paper. Although most programming languages do not allow the explicit use of pointer arithmetic (with the exception of C, where it is nevertheless discouraged), it nevertheless occurs *implicitly* in many programming situations, of which the most common are array indexing and structure/union member selection. For example, a C expression like `ptr[i]` implicitly generates an address expression of the form `ptr+(sizeof(*ptr)*i)`. Thus a program analysis performing bounds checking for C arrays or strings, say, must account for such implicit pointer arithmetic. We therefore set out by asking the following question: *How much pointer arithmetic can one include in separation logic and remain within polynomial time?*

Unfortunately, and perhaps surprisingly, the answer turns out to be: essentially none at all.

We study the complexity of symbolic-heap separation logic with points-to formulas, but no other data structure predicates, when pure formulas are extended by a minimal form of pointer arithmetic. Specifically, we permit only conjunctions of "difference constraints" $x \leq y + k$, where x and y are pointer variables and k is an integer. We certainly do *not* claim that this fragment is appropriate for practical program verification; clearly, lacking constructs for lists or other data structures, and using only a very weak form of arithmetic, it will be insufficiently expressive for most purposes (although it might *possibly* be practical e.g. for some concurrent programs that deal only with shared memory buffers of a small fixed size). The point is that any practical fragment of separation logic employing pointer arithmetic will almost inevitably include our minimal language and thus inherit its computational lower bounds.

We establish precise complexity bounds for the satisfiability and entailment problems, in both quantified and quantifier-free forms, for our SL with minimal pointer arithmetic. Perhaps our most striking result is that the satisfiability problem is already NP-complete; the entailment problem becomes coNP-complete for quantifier-free entailments, and Π_2^P-complete for existentially quantified entailments (where Π_2^P is the second class in the *polynomial-time hierarchy* [25]). However, the language does at least enjoy the *small model property*, meaning that any satisfiable symbolic heap A has a model of size polynomial in A, and any invalid entailment $A \models B$ has a countermodel of size polynomial in A and B—a property that fails when richer forms of arithmetical constraints are permitted in the language. In all cases, the lower bounds follow by reduction from the 3-colourability problem or its 2-round variant [15]. The upper bounds are by straightforward encodings into Presburger arithmetic, but the Π_2^P upper bound for quantified entailments is *not* trivial, as it requires us to show that all quantified variables in the resulting Presburger formula can be polynomially bounded; this follows from the small model property.

The remainder of this paper is structured as follows. In Sect. 2 we define symbolic-heap separation logic with minimal pointer arithmetic. Sections 3 and 4 study the satisfiability and quantifier-free entailment problems, respectively, for this language, and Sects. 5 and 6 establish the lower and upper complexity bounds, respectively, for the general entailment problem. Section 7 concludes.

2   Separation Logic with Minimal Pointer Arithmetic

Here, we introduce a minimal language for *separation logic with pointer arithmetic* (SL$_{\mathsf{MPA}}$ for short), a simple variant of the well-known "symbolic heap" fragment over pointers [2].

Our choice of language is influenced primarily by the need to 'balance' the arithmetical part of the language against the spatial part. To show lower complexity bounds, we have to challenge the fact that Σ_1^0 Presburger arithmetic is already NP-hard by itself; thus, to reveal the true memory-related nature of the problem, we restrict the language to a minimal form of pointer arithmetic, which is simple enough that it can be processed in polynomial time. This leads us to consider only conjunctions of "difference constraints", of the form $x = y + k$ and $x \leq y + k$ where x and y are variables and k is an integer (even disequality $x \neq y$ is not permitted). We write bold vector notation to denote sequences of variables, e.g. $\mathbf{x}$ for $x_1, \ldots, x_n$.

Definition 2.1 (Syntax). *A symbolic heap is given by*

$$\exists \mathbf{z}.\ \Pi : F$$

where $\mathbf{z}$ is a tuple of variables from an infinite set Var, *and Π and F are respectively* pure *and* spatial *formulas, defined along with terms t by:*

$$t ::= x \mid x + k$$
$$\Pi ::= x = t \mid x \leq t \mid \Pi \wedge \Pi$$
$$F ::= \mathsf{emp} \mid t \mapsto t \mid t \mapsto \mathsf{nil} \mid F * F$$

where x ranges over Var *and k over integers $\mathbb{Z}$. If Π is empty in a symbolic heap $\exists \mathbf{z}.\ \Pi : F$, we omit the colon. We sometimes abbreviate $*$-conjunctions of spatial formulas using "big star" notation:*

$$\text{\Large$*$}_{i=1}^{n} F_i =_{def} F_1 * \ldots * F_n,$$

which is interpreted as emp if $n < 1$.

In our SL$_{\mathsf{MPA}}$, the pure part of a symbolic heap is a conjunction of *difference constraints* of the form $x = y + k$ or $x \leq y + k$, where x and y are variables, and k is a fixed offset in $\mathbb{Z}$ (we disallow equalities of the form $x = $ nil for technical convenience). Thus $x < y + k$ can be encoded as $x \leq y + (k - 1)$, $x \leq y - k$ as $x \leq y + (-k)$ and $x + k \leq y$ as $x \leq y - k$; however, note that unlike the conventional symbolic heap fragment in [2], we *cannot* express disequality $x \neq y$. The satisfiability of such formulas can be decided in polynomial time; see [12]. The crucial observation for polynomial-time decidability is:

Proposition 2.2. *A 'circular' system of difference constraints $x_1 \leq x_2 + k_{12}$, ..., $x_{m-1} \leq x_m + k_{m-1,m}$, $x_m \leq x_1 + k_{m,m+1}$ implies that $x_1 - x_1 \leq \sum_{i=1}^{m} k_{i,i+1}$, which is a contradiction iff the latter sum is negative.*

Semantics. As usual, we interpret symbolic heaps in a stack-and-heap model of the standard type, as given, e.g., in Reynolds' seminal paper on separation logic [23] (which similarly permits unrestricted pointer arithmetic). For convenience we consider the addressable locations to be the set $\mathbb{N}$ of natural numbers, and values to be either natural numbers or a non-addressable null value *nil*. Thus a *stack* is a function $s \colon \mathsf{Var} \to \mathbb{N} \cup \{nil\}$. We extend stacks to terms by $s(\mathsf{nil}) = nil$ and, insisting that any pointer-offset sum should always be non-negative: $s(x + k) = s(x) + k$ if $s(x) + k \geq 0$, and undefined otherwise. If s is a stack, $z \in \mathsf{Var}$ and v is a value, we write $s[z \mapsto v]$ for the stack defined as s except that $s[z \mapsto v](z) = v$. We extend stacks pointwise over term tuples.

A *heap* is a finite partial function $h \colon \mathbb{N} \rightharpoonup_{\mathrm{fin}} \mathbb{N} \cup \{nil\}$ mapping finitely many locations to values; we write $\mathrm{dom}\,(h)$ for the domain of h, and e for the empty heap that is undefined on all locations. We write $\circ$ for *composition* of domain-disjoint heaps: if h_1 and h_2 are heaps, then $h_1 \circ h_2$ is the union of h_1 and h_2 when $\mathrm{dom}\,(h_1)$ and $\mathrm{dom}\,(h_2)$ are disjoint, and undefined otherwise.

Definition 2.3. *The* satisfaction relation $s, h \models A$, *where s is a stack, h a heap and A a symbolic heap, is defined by structural induction on A.*

$$
\begin{aligned}
s, h &\models x = t &&\Leftrightarrow s(x) = s(t) \\
s, h &\models x \leq t &&\Leftrightarrow s(x) \leq s(t) \\
s, h &\models \Pi_1 \wedge \Pi_2 &&\Leftrightarrow s, h \models \Pi_1 \text{ and } s, h \models \Pi_2 \\
s, h &\models \mathsf{emp} &&\Leftrightarrow h = e \\
s, h &\models t_1 \mapsto t_2 &&\Leftrightarrow \mathrm{dom}\,(h) = \{s(t_1)\} \text{ and } h(s(t_1)) = s(t_2) \\
s, h &\models F_1 * F_2 &&\Leftrightarrow \exists h_1, h_2.\ h = h_1 \circ h_2 \text{ and } s, h_1 \models F_1 \text{ and } s, h_2 \models F_2 \\
s, h &\models \exists \mathbf{z}.\ \Pi : F &&\Leftrightarrow \exists \mathbf{m} \in \mathbb{N}^{|\mathbf{z}|}.\ s[\mathbf{z} \mapsto \mathbf{m}], h \models \Pi \text{ and } s[\mathbf{z} \mapsto \mathbf{m}], h \models F
\end{aligned}
$$

We remark that the satisfaction of pure formulas Π does not depend on the heap, which justifies writing $s \models \Pi$ rather than $s, h \models \Pi$.

Remark 2.4. Although our language allows unbounded integer offsets k to be added to pointer variables, we would have exactly the same expressivity even if offsets were restricted to 1 and -1. Namely, a difference constraint $x \leq y + k$ for $k > 0$ can be encoded by introducing k auxiliary variables and k equalities:

$$z_1 = y + 1 \wedge z_2 = z_1 + 1 \wedge \ldots \wedge z_k = z_{k-1} + 1 \wedge x \leq z_k.$$

3 Satisfiability and the Small Model Property

In this section we investigate the *satisfiability* problem for our $\mathsf{SL_{MPA}}$, defined formally as follows:

Satisfiability Problem for $\mathsf{SL_{MPA}}$. *Given a symbolic heap A, decide whether there is a stack s and heap h with $s, h \models A$.*

(Without loss of generality, we may consider A to be quantifier-free in the above problem, because A and $\exists \mathbf{z}.A$ are equisatisfiable.)

We establish three main results about this problem: (a) an NP upper bound; (b) an NP lower bound; and (c) the small model property, meaning that any satisfiable formula has a model of polynomial size.

In fact, the NP upper bound is fairly trivial; there is a simple encoding of the satisfiability problem into Σ_1^0 *Presburger arithmetic* (as is also done for a more complicated *array separation logic* in [6]). Nevertheless, we include the details here, since they will be useful in setting up later results.

Definition 3.1. Presburger arithmetic *(PbA) is defined as the first-order theory of the natural numbers $\mathbb{N}$ over the signature $\langle 0, s, +, = \rangle$, where s is the successor function, and $0, +, =$ have their usual interpretations. The relations $\neq$, $\leq$ and $<$ can be straightforwardly encoded (possibly introducing an existential quantifier).*

Note that a stack is just a first-order valuation, and a pure formula in $\mathsf{SL_{MPA}}$ is also a formula of PbA, with exactly the same interpretation. Thus we overload $\models$ to include the standard first-order satisfaction relation of PbA.

Definition 3.2. *Let A be a quantifier-free symbolic heap, of the general form*

$$\Pi : \bigstar_{i=1}^{m} t_i \mapsto u_i.$$

We define a corresponding PbA formula γ_A by enriching the pure part Π with the constraints that the allocated addresses t_i must be distinct:

$$\gamma_A =_{def} \Pi \wedge \bigwedge_{1 \leq i < j \leq m} t_i \neq t_j.$$

The above γ_A can be easily rewritten as a Boolean combination of elementary formulas of the form $x \leq y + k$ where the 'offset' k is an integer.

Lemma 3.3. *For any symbolic heap A in $\mathsf{SL_{MPA}}$, we have*

$$(\exists h.\ s, h \models A) \Leftrightarrow s \models \gamma_A.$$

Proof. We assume A of the general form given by Definition 3.2.

($\Rightarrow$) By assumption, we have $s \models \Pi$ and $\text{dom}\,(h) = \{s(t_1), \ldots, s(t_m)\}$, which implies that all the t_i are distinct. Hence $s \models \gamma_A$ as required.

($\Leftarrow$) By assumption, we have $s \models \Pi$ and all of $s(t_1), \ldots, s(t_m)$ are distinct. Hence, defining a heap h by $\text{dom}\,(h) = \{s(t_1), \ldots, s(t_m)\}$ and $h(s(t_i)) = u_i$ for each i, we have $s, h \models A$ as required.   □

Proposition 3.4. *Satisfiability for* SL$_{\text{MPA}}$ *is in* NP.

Proof. Follows from Lemma 3.3 and the fact that satisfiability for quantifier-free Presburger arithmetic belongs to NP [24].   □

Next, we tackle the lower bound. Satisfiability is shown NP-hard by reduction from the 3-*colourability problem* [15].

3-Colourability Problem. *Given an undirected graph with $n \geq 4$ vertices, decide whether there is a "perfect" 3-colouring of the vertices, such that no two adjacent vertices share the same colour.*

Definition 3.5. *Let $G = (V, E)$ be a graph with n vertices $v_1, \ldots, v_n$. We encode a perfect 3-colouring of G with the following symbolic heap A_G.*

First, we introduce n variables $c_1, \ldots, c_n$ to represent the colour (1, 2, or 3) assigned to each vertex. The fact that no two adjacent vertices v_i and v_j share the same colour will be encoded by allocating two cells with base address $e_{ij} \in \mathbb{N}$ and offsets c_i and c_j respectively in A_G. To ensure that all such pairs of cells are disjoint, the base addresses e_{ij} are defined by:

$$e_{ij} = i \cdot n^2 + j \cdot n \quad (1 \leq i < j \leq n) \tag{1}$$

We then define A_G to be the following quantifier-free symbolic heap:

$$\bigwedge_{i=1}^{n}(a + 1 \leq c_i \wedge c_i \leq a + 3) : \mathop{\text{\Large$*$}}_{(v_i, v_j) \in E} (c_i + e_{ij} \mapsto \text{nil} * c_j + e_{ij} \mapsto \text{nil})$$

where a is a "dummy" variable (ensuring that A_G adheres to the strict formatting of pure assertions in SL$_{\text{MPA}}$*).*

The relevant fact concerning our definition of the base addresses e_{ij} in Definition 3.5 is the following.

Proposition 3.6. *For distinct pairs of numbers (i, j) and (i', j'), with $1 \leq i, i', j, j' \leq n$, we have $|e_{i'j'} - e_{ij}| \geq n$.*

Although for the present purposes we *could* have used a simpler definition of the e_{ij}, such that they are all spaced 4 cells apart, the definition by Eq. (1) is convenient as it will be re-used later on; see Definition 5.1.

Lemma 3.7. *Let G be an instance of the 3-colouring problem. Then A_G from Definition 3.5 is satisfiable iff there is a perfect 3-colouring of G.*

Proof. Let $G = (V, E)$ have vertices $v_1, \ldots, v_n$, where $n \geq 4$.

($\Leftarrow$) Suppose G has a perfect 3-colouring given by assigning a colour b_i to each vertex v_i, with each $b_i \in \{1, 2, 3\}$. We define a stack s by $s(a) = 0$ and $s(c_i) = b_i$ for each $1 \leq i \leq n$. Note that since $b_i \in \{1, 2, 3\}$ we have $s(a + 1) \leq s(c_i) \leq s(a + 3)$ for each i, and so s satisfies the pure part of A_G. Now define heap h by

$$\mathrm{dom}\,(h) =_{\mathrm{def}} \bigcup_{(v_i, v_j) \in E} (\{s(c_i) + e_{ij}\} \cup \{s(c_j) + e_{ij}\})$$

and $h(\ell) = nil$ for all $\ell \in \mathrm{dom}\,(h)$. Clearly, by construction, $s, h \models A_G$ provided that none of the singleton sets involved in the definition of $\mathrm{dom}\,(h)$ are overlapping.

Since we have a perfect 3-colouring of G, for any edge $(v_i, v_j) \in E$ we have $s(c_i) \neq s(c_j)$, so the subsets $\{s(c_i) + e_{ij}\}$ and $\{s(c_j) + e_{ij}\}$ of $\mathrm{dom}\,(h)$ do not overlap. Furthermore, by Proposition 3.6, for any two distinct edges (v_i, v_j) and $(v_{i'}, v_{j'})$ in E, the base addresses e_{ij} and $e_{i'j'}$ are at least 4 cells apart (because $n \geq 4$). Since $1 \leq s(c_i) \leq 3$ for any i, we cannot have $s(c_i) + e_{ij} = s(c_{i'}) + e_{i'j'}$ either. Thus all involved singleton sets are non-overlapping as required.

($\Rightarrow$) Supposing that $s, h \models A_G$, we define a 3-colouring of G by $b_i = s(c_i) - s(a)$ for each $1 \leq i \leq n$. Since $s \models a + 1 \leq c_i \wedge c_i \leq a + 3$ by assumption, we have $b_i \in \{1, 2, 3\}$ for each i, so this is indeed a 3-colouring. To see that it is a *perfect* 3-colouring, let $(v_i, v_j) \in E$. By construction, we have that $s, h' \models c_i + e_{ij} \mapsto nil * c_j + e_{ij} \mapsto nil$ for some subheap h' of h. Using the definition of $*$, this means that $s(c_i) + e_{ij} \neq s(c_j) + e_{ij}$, i.e. $s(c_i) \neq s(c_j)$, and so $b_i \neq b_j$ as required. $\square$

In fact, given a graph G with m edges, one can see that the proof above still works by taking the numbers e_{ij} to be $\{0, 4, 8, \ldots, 4(m-1)\}$. Thus Definition 3.5 encodes the 3-colouring problem for G inside a heap region of size roughly $4m$, i.e., only a linear size expansion.

Theorem 3.8. *Satisfiability for* SL$_{\mathrm{MPA}}$ *is* NP-*hard.*

Proof. From Lemma 3.7 and the fact that 3-colourability is NP-hard [15]. $\square$

Corollary 3.9. *Satisfiability in* SL$_{\mathrm{MPA}}$ *is* NP-*complete.*

Proof. From Proposition 3.4 and Theorem 3.8. $\square$

Finally, we tackle the *small model property* for SL$_{\mathrm{MPA}}$; that is, any satisfiable formula A has a model (s, h) of size polynomial w.r.t. A (see e.g. [1]). Note that, by "size", we do not mean here the number of allocated cells in h (since clearly any model of A only allocates as many cells as there are $\mapsto$-assertions in A) but the sizes of the addresses and/or values involved in their definition. Indeed, this property breaks if we increase the expressivity of our system only slightly.

Remark 3.10. The small model property fails if we allow our symbolic heaps to contain constraints of the form $x \leq y \pm z$ where x, y and z are *all* variables. In that case, we could define, e.g.,

$$A_n =_{\mathrm{def}} \bigwedge_{i=0}^{n-1} x_{i+1} > x_i + x_i : \ \underset{i=1}{\overset{n}{\text{\Large *}}} \ x_i \mapsto nil$$

(Note that the constraint $x_{i+1} > x_i + x_i$ can be expressed in our syntax, e.g., as $x_i \leq x_{i+1} - y_i \wedge y_i = x_i + 1$.) Then, for any model (s, h) of A_n, and for any $i < n$, we have that $s(x_{i+1}) > 2s(x_i)$, which implies $s(x_{i+1}) > 2^{i+1}$. Thus, (the distances between) at least half the addresses in h must be of exponential size.

In order to prove the small model property for our $\mathsf{SL_{MPA}}$, we need a more workable specification of γ_A:

Definition 3.11. *Given a symbolic heap A, we rewrite the Presburger formula γ_A by replacing every formula $x = y + k$ by $x \leq y + k \wedge y \leq x - k$, and every formula $t_i \neq t_j$ by $t_i \leq t_j - 1 \vee t_j \leq t_i - 1$. Then γ_A can be viewed as*

$$\gamma_A \equiv f_A(Z_1, Z_2, \ldots, Z_m) \tag{2}$$

where $f_A(z_1, z_2, \ldots, z_m)$ is a Boolean function, and within (2) the Boolean variable z_i is substituted with a difference constraint Z_i of the form $x_i \leq y_i + k_i$ (where k_i is an integer).

Proposition 3.12. *Any model s of γ_A for a symbolic heap A can be conceived of as a non-negative integer solution to the system $\gamma_{A,\bar{\zeta}}$ given by*

$$Z_1 \equiv \zeta_1, \ldots, Z_m \equiv \zeta_m \tag{3}$$

where $(\zeta_1, \ldots, \zeta_m)$ is a tuple of Boolean values ($\top$ or $\bot$) with $f_A(\zeta_1, \ldots, \zeta_m) = \top$, where $f_A(Z_1, \ldots, Z_m)$ is γ_A as a Boolean function over difference constraints, as in Definition 3.11.

Proof. Rewriting γ_A as $f_A(Z_1, \ldots, Z_m)$ as in Definition 3.11, we can evaluate each difference constraint Z_i as $\top$ or $\bot$ under s, which gives an appropriate value for each ζ_i such that s is a solution to (3). Clearly, $f_A(\zeta_1, \ldots, \zeta_m) = \top$.

Conversely, given a non-negative solution to (3), we can view this solution as a stack s and observe that, since $f_A(\zeta_1, \ldots, \zeta_m) = \top$, we have $s \models \gamma_A$.   □

Definition 3.13. *Given a model (s, h) for symbolic heap A, we further encode the equation system $\gamma_{A,\bar{\zeta}}$ (3) in Proposition 3.12 as a constraint graph $G_{A,\bar{\zeta}}$, constructed as follows.*

- *For each variable x in $\gamma_{A,\bar{\zeta}}$, we will associate a vertex $\hat{x}$;*

- *An equation of the form $(x \leq y + k) \equiv \top$ in (3) is encoded as an edge from $\hat{y}$ to $\hat{x}$ labelled by k: $\hat{y} \xrightarrow{k} \hat{x}$.*

- *An equation of the form $(x \leq y + k) \equiv \bot$ in (3), meaning that $y \leq x - k - 1$, is encoded as an edge from $\hat{x}$ to $\hat{y}$ labelled by $(-k - 1)$: $\hat{x} \xrightarrow{-k-1} \hat{y}$.*

- *Finally, to provide the connectivity we need for models, we always add, if necessary, a "maximum node" $\hat{x_0}$, with the constraint $x_i \leq x_0$, i.e. edges $\hat{x_0} \xrightarrow{0} \hat{x_i}$, for all x_i.*

Example 3.14. Let A be the symbolic heap $y \leq x \colon x \mapsto \text{nil} * y \mapsto \text{nil}$. We have:

$$\gamma_A = (y \leq x) \wedge ((x \leq y - 1) \vee (y \leq x - 1)).$$

Following Definition 3.11, we can view γ_A as $f_A(Z_0, Z_1, Z_2)$, where $f_A(z_0, z_1, z_2)$ is the Boolean function $z_0 \wedge (z_1 \vee z_2)$, and $Z_0 = (y \leq x)$, $Z_1 = (x \leq y - 1)$ and $Z_2 = (y \leq x - 1)$ are difference constraints.

Since Z_1 and Z_2 are mutually exclusive, there are essentially two Boolean vectors $\bar{\zeta} = \zeta_0, \zeta_1, \zeta_2$ such that $f_A(\bar{\zeta}) = \top$:

(a) $\bar{\zeta} = \top, \top, \bot$, giving us difference constraints $\gamma_1 =_{\text{def}} (y \leq x) \wedge (x \leq y - 1)$.
(b) $\bar{\zeta} = \top, \bot, \top$, giving us difference constraints $\gamma_2 =_{\text{def}} (y \leq x) \wedge (y \leq x - 1)$.

Figure 1 shows the respective constraint graphs for γ_1 and γ_2. Notice that, because of $y \leq x$, the node $\hat{x}$ is a "maximum node" in both cases, and so we do not need to add one.

In the case of (a), we have no solution. Namely, there is a negative cycle of the form $\hat{x} \xrightarrow{0} \hat{y} \xrightarrow{-1} \hat{x}$, which encodes the contradictory $x \leq x - 1$.

In the case of (b), the minimal weighted path from $\hat{x}$ to $\hat{y}$ has weight -1, which guarantees that $y = x - 1$ is a model for γ_A and thereby for A.

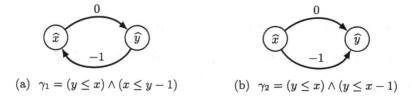

(a) $\gamma_1 = (y \leq x) \wedge (x \leq y - 1)$ (b) $\gamma_2 = (y \leq x) \wedge (y \leq x - 1)$

Fig. 1. The constraint graphs for γ_1 and γ_2 from Example 3.14.

Theorem 3.15 (Small model property). *Let A be a satisfiable symbolic heap in minimal pointer arithmetic. Then we can find a model (s, h) for A in which all values are bounded by $M = \sum_i (|k_i| + 1)$, where k_i ranges over all occurrences of integers in A.*

Proof. According to Proposition 3.12, there is a Boolean vector $\bar{\zeta} = \zeta_1, \zeta_2, \ldots, \zeta_m$ such that the corresponding system, $\gamma_{A,\bar{\zeta}}$, has a solution. Hence, the associated constraint graph $G_{A,\bar{\zeta}}$ has no negative cycles (see Proposition 2.2).

We define our small model with the following mapping s over all variables x_i in A, such that $s \models \gamma_A$. First we define $s(x_0) = M$ for the "maximum node" $\widehat{x_0}$. Then, $s(x_i)$ is defined as $M + d_i$, where d_i is the *minimal weighted path* from $\widehat{x_0}$ to $\hat{x_i}$; this is well-defined since $G_{A,\bar{\zeta}}$ has no negative-weight cycles. Note that d_i can never be positive, as there is always, trivially, a path from $\widehat{x_0}$ to $\hat{x_i}$ of weight 0 by construction. Thus s is indeed "small". To see that it is a model of $\gamma_{A,\bar{\zeta}}$, consider e.g. the difference constraint $x \leq y + k$; thus there is an edge from $\hat{y}$ to $\hat{x}$ with weight k in the graph, and so d_x cannot be greater than $d_y + k$, meaning $s(x) \leq s(y) + k$. Hence s satisfies $\gamma_{A,\bar{\zeta}}$ and, by Proposition 3.12, $s \models \gamma_A$. Thus by Lemma 3.3 there is an h such that $s, h \models A$; note that h only uses values given by $s(x_i)$ and thus is also "small'. $\qquad\square$

Remark 3.16. In addition, the corresponding polytime sub-procedures are the shortest path procedures with negative weights allowed (e.g., the Bellman-Ford algorithm), which provides polynomials of low degrees.

4   Quantifier-Free Entailment

We now turn to the *entailment* problem for our SL$_{MPA}$, given as follows:

Entailment in SL$_{MPA}$. Given symbolic heaps A and B, decide whether $s, h \models A$ implies $s, h \models B$ for all stacks s and heaps h (we say $A \models B$ is *valid*).

   Without loss of generality, A may be assumed quantifier-free, and any quantified variables in B assumed disjoint from the free variables in A and B.

   In this section, we focus on the case of (entirely) quantifier-free entailments, for which we establish both an upper and a lower bound of coNP.

Definition 4.1. *Let $A \models B$ be an SL$_{MPA}$ entailment, where A and B are symbolic heaps of the form*

$$A \ = \ \Pi_A \colon \mbox{\Large$*$}_{i=1}^{\ell} \ t_i \mapsto t_i' \quad and \quad B \ = \ \exists \mathbf{y} . \Pi_B \colon \mbox{\Large$*$}_{j=1}^{\ell'} \ u_j \mapsto u_j'$$

We define a corresponding PbA formula $\varepsilon_{A,B}$ by:

$$\gamma_A \rightarrow \exists \mathbf{y} \left(\gamma_B \wedge \bigwedge_i \bigvee_j (t_i = u_j \wedge t_i' = u_j') \wedge \bigwedge_j \bigvee_i (u_j = t_i \wedge u_j' = t_i') \right) \quad (4)$$

where γ_- is given by Definition 3.2.

Lemma 4.2. *For any SL$_{MPA}$ entailment $A \models B$ and stack s, we have*

$$(\exists h. \ s, h \models A \ implies \ s, h \models B) \ \Leftrightarrow \ s \models \varepsilon_{A,B} \ .$$

Proof. We assume A and B of the general form given by Definition 4.1, and assume w.l.o.g. that $\mathbf{y}$ is disjoint from all free variables in A and B. We write $\mathsf{qf}(B)$ for the quantifier-free part of B.

($\Rightarrow$) Assume that $s \models \gamma_A$, the antecedent of (4). By Lemma 3.3 we have h with $s, h \models A$. By assumption, $s, h \models B$; i.e., for some values $\mathbf{v}$ with $|\mathbf{v}| = |\mathbf{y}|$, and defining $s' = s[\mathbf{y} \mapsto \mathbf{v}]$, we have $s', h \models \mathsf{qf}(B)$. Thus $s' \models \gamma_B$ by Lemma 3.3, and $\mathrm{dom}\,(h) = \{s'(u_1), \ldots, s'(u_{\ell'})\}$ (all of which are disjoint), with $h(s'(u_j)) = s'(u_j')$ for each $1 \leq j \leq \ell'$. Since no variable in $\mathbf{y}$ occurs in A and $s, h \models A$, we also have $s', h \models A$, and so $\mathrm{dom}\,(h) = \{s'(t_1), \ldots, s'(t_\ell)\}$ (all disjoint), with $h(s'(t_i)) = s'(t_i')$ for each $1 \leq i \leq \ell$. Thus $\ell' = \ell$ and each pair $(s'(t_i), s'(t_i'))$ is equal to some pair $(s'(u_j), s'(u_j'))$. Thus s' satisfies the quantifier-free consequent of (4), meaning that s satisfies the entire consequent, as required.

($\Leftarrow$) Suppose that $s, h \models A$ for some heap h. We have $s \models \gamma_A$ by Lemma 3.3, so, for some $s' = s[\mathbf{y} \mapsto \mathbf{v}]$, we have that s' satisfies the quantifier-free consequent of (4). That is, $s' \models \gamma_B$, so that $s', h' \models \mathsf{qf}(B)$ for some h' by Lemma 3.3. Moreover, for each pair $(s'(t_i), s'(t_i'))$ with $1 \leq i \leq \ell$, there is an equal pair

$(s'(u_j), s'(u'_j))$ with $1 \leq j \leq \ell'$, and vice versa. Now, since no variable in **y** occurs in A and $s, h \models A$, we also have $s', h \models A$, and so dom $(h) = \{s'(t_1), \ldots, s'(t_\ell)\}$ (all disjoint), with $h(s'(t_i)) = s'(t'_i)$ for each $1 \leq i \leq \ell$. Simultaneously, since $s', h' \models \mathsf{qf}(B)$, we have dom $(h') \{s'(u_1), \ldots, s'(u_{\ell'})\}$ (all disjoint), with $h'(s'(u_j)) = s'(u'_j)$ for each $1 \leq j \leq \ell'$. Thus $\ell' = \ell$ and, because of the isomorphism between the pairs $(s'(t_i), s'(t'_i))$ and $(s'(u_j), s'(u'_j))$, we deduce that in fact $h' = h$. Thus $s', h \models \mathsf{qf}(B)$ and so $s, h \models B$, as required.   □

As an immediate consequence of Lemma 4.2, the general entailment problem for SL$_{\mathsf{MPA}}$ is in Π_2^0 Presburger arithmetic, which corresponds to Π_1^{EXP} in the *exponential-time hierarchy* [17]. However, as it turns out, this bound is exponentially overstated; as we show in Theorem 6.7, the problem also belongs to the much smaller class Π_2^P, the second class in the polynomial time hierarchy [25]. The crucial difference between Presburger Π_2^0 and polynomial Π_2^P is that, in the latter, all variables must be *polynomially bounded*.

However, the construction above does yield an optimal upper bound for the quantifier-free version of the problem.

Theorem 4.3. *The quantifier-free entailment problem for* SL$_{\mathsf{MPA}}$ *is in* coNP.

Proof. According to Lemma 4.2, deciding whether $A \models B$ is valid is equivalent to deciding whether the PbA formula $\forall \mathbf{x}.\ \varepsilon_{A,B}$ is valid (where **x** is the set of all free variables in A and B). Although the latter is in general a Π_2^0 formula, it becomes a Π_1^0 formula when B is quantifier-free; the validity of such formulas can be decided in coNP time.   □

We now turn to the small model property. We note that this property is sensitive to the exact form of our arithmetical constraints, and, similar to Remark 3.10, it fails when we allow the addition of two pointer variables.

Theorem 4.4 (Small model property). *Suppose that the quantifier-free entailment $A \models B$ is not valid. Then we can find a counter-model (s, h) such that $(s, h) \models A$ but $(s, h) \not\models B$, in which all values are bounded by $M = \sum_i (|k_i| + 1)$, where k_i ranges over all occurrences of numbers in A and B.*

Proof. (Sketch) The proof follows the structure of the small model property for satisfiability (Theorem 3.15), noting first that we can rewrite the PbA formula $\forall \mathbf{x}.\ \varepsilon_{A,B}$ as a Π_2^0 Boolean combination of difference constraints $x \leq y + k$, similar to Definition 3.11.   □

As for the coNP *lower* bound, we use a construction similar to Definition 3.5, based on the complement of 3-colourability.

Definition 4.5. *Given a graph G with n vertices, and reusing notation from Definition 3.5, we introduce a satisfiable symbolic heap A'_G by:*

$$\bigwedge_{i=1}^n (a + 1 \leq c_i \wedge c_i \leq d) : \text{\Large$*$}_{(v_i, v_j) \in E}\ c_i + e_{ij} \mapsto \mathsf{nil} * c_j + e_{ij} \mapsto \mathsf{nil}$$

and a satisfiable symbolic heap B'_G by $d \geq a + 4 : A'_G$.

Lemma 4.6. *Let G be an instance of the 3-colouring problem, and let A'_G and B'_G be given by Definition 4.5 above. Then $A'_G \models B'_G$ is not valid iff there is a perfect 3-colouring of G.*

Proof. Let $G = (V, E)$ have n vertices $v_1, \ldots, v_n$, where $n \geq 4$.

($\Leftarrow$) Suppose G has a perfect 3-colouring given by assigning colours $b_i \in \{1, 2, 3\}$ to vertices v_i. By the argument in the ($\Leftarrow$) case of the proof of Lemma 3.7, if we define $s(a) = 0$, $s(c_i) = b_i$ and (new here) $s(d) = 3$ then there is a heap h such that $s, h \models A'_G$. However, we do not have $s, h \models B'_G$ because $s \not\models d \geq a + 4$. Thus $A'_G \models B'_G$ is not valid, as required.

($\Rightarrow$) Conversely, suppose $s, h \models A'_G$ but $s, h \not\models B'_G$ for some (s, h). By construction of B'_G, this implies that $s \not\models a \leq d - 4$, which implies $s(d) \leq s(a) + 3$. We can then use this fact together with the fact that $s, h \models A'_G$ to obtain a 3-colouring of G exactly as in the ($\Rightarrow$) case of the proof of Lemma 3.7. □

Theorem 4.7. *The quantifier-free entailment problem for* SL$_{\mathsf{MPA}}$ *is* coNP-*hard, even when both symbolic heaps are satisfiable.*

Proof. Lemma 4.6 gives a reduction from the complement of the 3-colourability problem, which is coNP-hard, using only satisfiable symbolic heaps. □

Corollary 4.8. *The quantifier-free entailment problem for* SL$_{\mathsf{MPA}}$ *is* coNP-*complete (even when both symbolic heaps are satisfiable).*

Proof. Theorems 4.3 and 4.7 give the upper and lower bounds respectively. □

5   Quantified Entailment: Π_2^P Lower Bound

In this section, and the following one, we investigate the general form of the entailment problem $A \models B$ for our SL$_{\mathsf{MPA}}$, where B may contain existential quantifiers. Here, we establish a lower bound for this problem of Π_2^P in the *polynomial-time hierarchy* (see [25]); in the next section we shall establish an identical upper bound.

To prove Π_2^P-hardness, we build a reduction from the so-called *2-round* version of the 3-colourability problem, defined as follows.

2-Round 3-Colourability Problem. *Let $G = (V, E)$ be an undirected graph with $n \geq 4$ vertices and k leaves (vertices of degree 1). The problem is to decide whether every 3-colouring of the leaves can be extended to a perfect 3-colouring of the entire graph, such that no two adjacent vertices share the same colour.*

Definition 5.1 *Let $G = (V, E)$ be an instance graph with n vertices and k leaves. In addition to the variables c_i and a and the numbers e_{ij} which we reuse from Definition 3.5, to each edge (v_i, v_j) we also associate a new variable $\widetilde{c_{ij}}$, representing the colour "complementary" to c_i and c_j.*

To encode the fact that no two adjacent vertices v_i and v_j share the same colour, we shall use c_i, c_j, and $\widetilde{c_{ij}}$ as the addresses, relative to the base-offset

e_{ij}, *for three consecutive cells within a memory chunk of length* 3, *which forces* c_i, c_j, *and* $\widetilde{c_{ij}}$ *to form a* permutation *of* $(1, 2, 3)$.
Formally, we define A_G'' *to be the following quantifier-free symbolic heap:*

$$\bigwedge_{i=1}^{k}(a + 1 \leq c_i \wedge c_i \leq a + 3): \quad \mathbin{\text{\Large\reflectbox{\rotatebox[origin=c]{90}{\ensuremath{*}}}}}_{(v_i, v_j) \in E}^{\ell \in \{1,2,3\}} \; a + (e_{ij} + \ell) \mapsto \mathsf{nil}$$

and B_G'' *to be the following quantified symbolic heap:*

$$\exists \mathbf{z}. \; \bigwedge_{i=1}^{n}(a + 1 \leq c_i \leq a + 3) \wedge \bigwedge_{(v_i, v_j) \in E}(a + 1 \leq \widetilde{c_{ij}} \leq a + 3):$$
$$\mathbin{\text{\Large$*$}}_{(v_i, v_j) \in E} \; c_i + e_{ij} \mapsto \mathsf{nil} * c_j + e_{ij} \mapsto \mathsf{nil} * \widetilde{c_{ij}} + e_{ij} \mapsto \mathsf{nil} \tag{5}$$

where the existentially quantified variables $\mathbf{z}$ *are all variables occurring in* B_G''
that are not mentioned explicitly in A_G''; *namely, the variables* c_i *for* $k+1 \leq i \leq n$,
and the "complementary colour" variables $\widetilde{c_{ij}}$. *Note that both* A_G'' *and* B_G'' *are*
satisfiable.

Lemma 5.2. *Let* G *be an instance of the 2-round 3-colouring problem, and let*
A_G'' *and* B_G'' *be given by Definition 5.1 above. Then* $A_G'' \models B_G''$ *is valid iff there*
is a perfect 3-colouring of G *given any 3-colouring of its leaves.*

Proof. Let $G = (V, E)$ have vertices $v_1, \ldots, v_n$ of which the first k are leaves.
We assume $n \geq 4$.

($\Leftarrow$) Let (s, h) be a stack-heap pair satisfying $s, h \models A_G''$; we have to show that
$s, h \models B_G''$. The spatial part of A_G'' yields

$$\mathrm{dom}\,(h) = \bigcup_{(v_i, v_j) \in E}^{\ell = 1, 2, 3} \{ s(a) + e_{ij} + \ell \} \tag{6}$$

where these locations are all disjoint (and h maps each of them to *nil*); furthermore, $s(a) + 1 \leq s(c_i) \leq s(a) + 3$ for each $1 \leq i \leq k$. Take the 3-colouring of
the leaves obtained by assigning colours $b_i = s(c_i) - s(a)$ to each of the leaves
$v_1, \ldots, v_k$. According to the winning strategy, we can assign colours b_i to the
remaining vertices $v_{k+1}, \ldots, v_n$, obtaining a 3-colouring of the whole G such
that no two adjacent vertices share the same colour. In addition, we mark each
edge (v_i, v_j) by $\tilde{b}_{ij}$, the colour complementary to b_i and b_j.
    We extend the stack s to interpret the existentially quantified variables in B_G''
as follows:
$$s(c_i) = s(a) + b_i \qquad \text{for each } k + 1 \leq i \leq n$$
$$s(\widetilde{c_{ij}}) = s(a) + 6 - b_i - b_j \text{ for each } (v_i, v_j) \in E$$

The fact that no adjacent vertices v_i and v_j share the same colour means that

$$(s(c_i), s(c_j), s(\widetilde{c_{ij}})) \text{ is a } permutation \text{ of } (s(a) + 1, \, s(a) + 2, \, s(a) + 3),$$

and, as a result, (s, h) is also a model for B_G''; in particular,

$$s, h \models \mathbin{\text{\Large$*$}}_{(v_i, v_j) \in E} \; s(c_i) + e_{ij} \mapsto \mathsf{nil} * s(c_j) + e_{ij} \mapsto \mathsf{nil} * s(\widetilde{c_{ij}}) + e_{ij} \mapsto \mathsf{nil}. \tag{7}$$

($\Rightarrow$) As for the opposite direction, let $A_G'' \models B_G''$. Since A_G'' is satisfiable, there is a model (s, h) for A_G'' so that, in particular, h satisfies (6).

We will construct the required winning strategy in the following way. Assume a 3-colouring of the leaves is given by assigning colours b_i to the leaves $v_1, \ldots, v_k$. We modify our original s to a stack s' by defining $s'(c_i) = s(a) + b_i$ for each $1 \le i \le k$. This does not change the heap h, but provides

$$s(a) + 1 \le s'(c_i) \le s(a) + 3 \quad \text{for each } 1 \le i \le k.$$

It is clear that the modified (s', h) is still a model for A_G'', and, hence, a model for B_G''. Then for some stack s_B, an extension of s' to the existentially quantified variables in B, we get $s_B, h \models B_G''$.

For each $1 \le i \le k$, we have $s_B(c_i) = s'(c_i) = s_B(a) + b_i$, which means that these $s_B(c_i)$ represent correctly the original 3-colouring of the leaves. By assigning the colours $b_i = s_B(c_i) - s_B(a)$ to each of the remaining vertices $v_{k+1}, \ldots, v_n$, we obtain a 3-colouring of the whole G.

The spatial part of B_G'', cf. (7), provides that $s_B(c_i) \neq s_B(c_j)$, which implies that no adjacent vertices v_i and v_j can share the same colours b_i and b_j. This means that we have a perfect 3-colouring of G, as required. □

Theorem 5.3. *The general entailment problem for* SL$_{\mathsf{MPA}}$ *is* Π_2^P-*hard, even when both symbolic heaps are satisfiable.*

Proof. Definition 5.1 and Lemma 5.2 give a reduction from the 2-round 3-colourability problem, which is Π_2^P-hard [15]. □

6 Quantified Entailment: Π_2^P Upper Bound

Following the Π_2^P lower bound for quantified entailments in SL$_{\mathsf{MPA}}$ given in the previous section, we show here that the upper bound is also Π_2^P, as well as establishing the small model property. Indeed, we shall see that the former result follows from the latter one.

Theorem 6.1 (Small model property). *Suppose that $A \models B$, encoded as $\epsilon_{A,B}$ in Definition 4.1, is not valid. Let $x_1, \ldots, x_n$ be the free variables in A and B, and let $y_1, \ldots, y_m$ be the existentially quantified variables in B.*

Then we can find a counter-model (s, h) such that $s, h \models A$ but $s, h \not\models B$, in which all values of $s(x_i)$ are bounded by $(n+1) \cdot M$ and all values of $s(y_j)$ by $(n + m + 2) \cdot M$, where $M = \sum_i(|k_i| + 1)$, with k_i ranging over all occurrences of 'offset' integers in A and B.

Proof Sketch. Let (s, h) be a counter-model for $A \models B$. For convenience (but without loss of generality) we assume that s orders the variables as follows: $s(x_1) = 0$, and $s(x_1) < s(x_2) < \cdots < s(x_n)$, and $s(x_n) \le s(y_m)$, and, for all y_j, $s(x_1) \le s(y_j) \le s(y_m)$. In particular, note that x_1 is a "zero" variable and y_m a "maximum" variable under the valuation s.

Note that, being a model for A, (s, h) is fully determined by the system:

$$\gamma_{A,s} = \bigwedge_{i=1}^{n-1}(x_{i+1} = x_i + d_{i,i+1}) \tag{8}$$

where for all $1 \leq i < j \leq n$, the d_{ij} is defined as: $d_{ij} = s(x_j) - s(x_i)$.

Following Proposition 3.12, the fact that $s, h \not\models B$ means that for a certain Boolean function $f_{A,B}$, whatever Boolean vector $\bar{\zeta} = \zeta_1, .., \zeta_\ell$ such that $f_{A,B}(\zeta_1, .., \zeta_\ell) = \top$ we take, the following system, $G_{A,B,s,\bar{\zeta}}$, has no integer solution for fixed $s(x_1), .., s(x_n)$ given by $\gamma_{A,s}$ from (8):

$$G_{A,B,s,\bar{\zeta}} = \gamma_{A,s} \wedge Z_1 \equiv \zeta_1 \wedge \cdots \wedge Z_\ell \equiv \zeta_\ell \tag{9}$$

This constraint system can be seen as a graph, in exactly the same way as is done in Definition 3.13.

Example 6.2 (A running example). Let A and B be the following symbolic heaps:

A : $\qquad x_1 < x_2 < x_3 < x_4 : x_1 \mapsto \text{nil} * x_4 \mapsto \text{nil}$
B : $\qquad \exists y_1 \exists y_4. \, x_2 \leq y_1 - 3 \wedge x_3 \leq y_4 + 7 : y_1 \mapsto \text{nil} * y_4 \mapsto \text{nil}$

As a 'large' counter-model for $A \models B$, we take (s, h), where s is defined by

$$\begin{cases} s(x_2) = s(x_1) + 3D, \\ s(x_3) = s(x_2) + 2, \\ s(x_4) = s(x_3) + D, \end{cases}$$

where D is a very large number (say 2^{1024}). To show that (s, h) is not a model for B, the spatial parts provide two cases to be considered: $y_1 = x_1 \wedge y_4 = x_4$ and $y_1 = x_4 \wedge y_4 = x_1$.

(a) In case of $y_1 = x_1 \wedge y_4 = x_4$, the corresponding system $G_{A,B,s,\bar{\zeta}}$ in (9) has no solution, e.g., because of the negative cycle:

$$\widehat{x_1} \xrightarrow{0} \widehat{y_1} \xrightarrow{-3} \widehat{x_2} \xrightarrow{-3D} \widehat{x_1} \tag{10}$$

(b) In case of $y_1 = x_4 \wedge y_4 = x_1$, the corresponding system $G_{A,B,s,\bar{\zeta}}$ in (9) has no solution, e.g., because of the negative cycle:

$$\widehat{x_4} \xrightarrow{0} \widehat{y_1} \xrightarrow{-3} \widehat{x_2} \xrightarrow{-3D} \widehat{x_1} \xrightarrow{0} \widehat{y_4} \xrightarrow{7} \widehat{x_3} \xrightarrow{D} \widehat{x_4} \tag{11}$$

□

The intuitive idea of constructing a small counter-model is as follows.

Definition 6.3. *Given a 'large' counter-model (s, h) and a small M, we construct a small counter-model (s', h') by simply replacing all large gaps $d_{i,i+1}$ in (8) with M, as follows:*

$$s'(x_{i+1}) := \begin{cases} s'(x_i) + d_{i,i+1}, & \text{if } d_{i,i+1} \leq M \\ s'(x_i) + M, & \text{otherwise} \end{cases}$$

(The heap h' is then obtained simply by updating h to use values given by s' rather than s, in the evident way.)

Lemma 6.4. *We can check that (s', h') is still a model for A.*

A real challenge is to prove that our (s', h') is not a model for B.

Example 6.5 (continuing Example 6.2). To show that $s', h' \not\models B$, we have two cases to be considered: $y_1 = x_1 \wedge y_4 = x_4$, and $y_1 = x_4 \wedge y_4 = x_1$.

(a) In case of $y_1 = x_1 \wedge y_4 = x_4$, the updated $G_{A,B,s',\bar{\zeta}}$ has no solution. E.g., by replacing the large $3D$ in the negative cycle (10) with our modest M, we get a negative cycle in terms of (s', h'):

$$\widehat{x_1} \xrightarrow{\ 0\ } \widehat{y_1} \xrightarrow{\ -3\ } \widehat{x_2} \xrightarrow{\ -M\ } \widehat{x_1}$$

(b) In case of $y_1 = x_4 \wedge y_4 = x_1$, however, the same strategy *fails*. Namely, by replacing the large D and $3D$ in the negative cycle (11) with M, we get a cycle in terms of (s', h'):

$$\widehat{x_4} \xrightarrow{\ 0\ } \widehat{y_1} \xrightarrow{\ -3\ } \widehat{x_2} \xrightarrow{\ -M\ } \widehat{x_1} \xrightarrow{\ 0\ } \widehat{y_4} \xrightarrow{\ 7\ } \widehat{x_3} \xrightarrow{\ M\ } \widehat{x_4}$$

but now with *positive* weight. $\square$

The challenge to our construction can be resolved by the following lemma.

Lemma 6.6. *Having got a negative cycle $\mathcal{C}$ for (9), we can extract a smaller negative cycle which is good for (s', h') as well.*

Proof. (Sketch) We introduce the following *reductions* on negative cycles $\mathcal{C}$. We write $\widehat{x}_j \overset{\sigma}{\Longrightarrow}_Y \widehat{x}_i$ to denote a subpath of $\mathcal{C}$ from $\widehat{x}_j$ to $\widehat{x}_i$ with total weight σ and whose intermediate nodes are all of the form $\widehat{y}_k$. Then, assuming $i < j$, we distinguish two cases:

Case: $\mathcal{C}$ contains $\widehat{x}_j \overset{\sigma}{\Longrightarrow}_Y \widehat{x}_i$. We note that $d_{ij} > 0$, because $s(x_j) > s(x_i)$ by assumption. We distinguish two subcases:

Subcase (a1): $-d_{ij} \leq \sigma$. In this subcase, we replace the above path with the single labelled edge $\widehat{x}_j \xrightarrow{-d_{ij}} \widehat{x}_i$, which ensures that the updated $\mathcal{C}$ still has negative weight, but now also contains *fewer nodes of the form $\widehat{y}_k$*.

E.g., within Example 6.5, replacing $\widehat{x_4} \xrightarrow{\ 0\ } \widehat{y_1} \xrightarrow{\ -3\ } \widehat{x_2}$, the cycle (11) can be transformed into the negative cycle:

$$\widehat{x_4} \xrightarrow{-D-2} \widehat{x_2} \xrightarrow{-3D} \widehat{x_1} \xrightarrow{\ 0\ } \widehat{y_4} \xrightarrow{\ 7\ } \widehat{x_3} \xrightarrow{\ D\ } \widehat{x_4} \tag{12}$$

Subcase (a2): $-d_{ij} > \sigma$. We identify the negative cycle:

$$\widehat{x}_j \overset{\sigma}{\Longrightarrow}_Y \widehat{x}_i \xrightarrow{d_{ij}} \widehat{x}_j$$

Since $d_{ij} < -\sigma \leq M$, we have $d'_{ij} = d_{ij}$, and hence this smaller negative cycle is good for (s', h') as well. This completes the case.

Case: $\mathcal{C}$ contains $\widehat{x}_i \overset{\sigma}{\Longrightarrow}_Y \widehat{x}_j$. In that case, $d_{ij} < 0$, again because $s(x_j) > s(x_i)$, and we again distinguish two subcases:

Subcase (b1): $d_{ij} \leq \sigma$. In this subcase, we replace this path with the edge $\widehat{x}_i \overset{d_{ij}}{\longrightarrow} \widehat{x}_j$, which ensures that the updated $\mathcal{C}$ remains negative, *but has fewer nodes of the form* $\widehat{y}_k$.

Subcase (b2): $d_{ij} > \sigma$. We identify the negative cycle:

$$\widehat{x}_i \overset{\sigma}{\Longrightarrow}_Y \widehat{x}_j \overset{-d_{ij}}{\longrightarrow} \widehat{x}_i$$

If $d_{k,k+1} \leq M$ for all k such that $i \leq k < j$, then $d'_{ij} = d_{ij}$, and hence this smaller negative cycle is good for (s', h'), as well. Otherwise, for some k, $d_{k,k+1} > M$, and thereby by construction $d'_{k,k+1} = M$, and, hence, $d'_{ij} \geq M$. Then the following cycle defined in terms of (s', h'),

$$\widehat{x}_i \overset{\sigma}{\Longrightarrow}_Y \widehat{x}_j \overset{-d'_{ij}}{\longrightarrow} \widehat{x}_i$$

is of negative weight, since $\sigma - d'_{ij} \leq \sigma - M < 0$.

E.g., within Example 6.5 with: $\widehat{x_1} \overset{0}{\longrightarrow} \widehat{y_4} \overset{7}{\longrightarrow} \widehat{x_3}$, in (12), we obtain the following cycle in terms of (s', h'):

$$\widehat{x_1} \overset{0}{\longrightarrow} \widehat{y_4} \overset{7}{\longrightarrow} \widehat{x_3} \overset{-2-M}{\longrightarrow} \widehat{x_1}$$

which is guaranteed to be of negative weight.

Finally, we show that any chain of reductions must terminate in one of the subcases (a2) and (b2). To see this, suppose otherwise. Then, having eliminated all nodes of the form $\widehat{y}_k$ in $\mathcal{C}$ via reductions (a1) and (b1), we would obtain a negative cycle $\mathcal{C}$ (by Lemma 6.6) consisting only of nodes of the form $\widehat{x}_i$, e.g.:

$$\widehat{x}_i \overset{d_{ij}}{\longrightarrow} \widehat{x}_j \overset{-d_{ij}}{\longrightarrow} \widehat{x}_i$$

However, such a cycle necessarily has weight 0, and is therefore non-negative; contradiction. This concludes the proof of the lemma, and thereby of Theorem 6.1. □

Theorem 6.7. *The entailment problem in* SL$_{\mathsf{MPA}}$ *is in* Π_2^P.

Moreover, given A and B, for a certain Boolean combination of difference constraints $R(\mathbf{x}, \mathbf{y})$ defined by A and B as in Definition 4.1, $A \models B$ is equivalent to

$$\forall \mathbf{x}. \ (\gamma_A(\mathbf{x}) \rightarrow \exists \mathbf{y}. \ R(\mathbf{x}, \mathbf{y}))$$

where all x_i in $\mathbf{x}$ and all y_j in $\mathbf{y}$ are bounded in accordance with Theorem 6.1.

Proof. This follows from the small model property provided by Theorem 6.1. □

Remark 6.8. The proof of Theorem 6.1 provides quite efficient procedures for the entailment problem in Theorem 6.7, in which the corresponding polytime sub-procedures are the usual shortest paths procedures with negative weights allowed, providing polynomials of low degrees. Alternatively, Theorem 5.3 and Definition 4.1 give an encoding of entailment as a Π_2^0 sentence of PbA and a polynomial bound for all variables, which could be passed directly to an arithmetic constraint solver.

In fact we prove that the entailment problem is Π_2^P-complete, and enjoys the small model property, even if we allow *any* Boolean combination of difference constraints $x \leq y + k$ in the pure part of our symbolic heaps.

7   Conclusions and Future Work

In this paper, we study the points-to fragment of symbolic-heap separation logic extended with pointer arithmetic, in a minimal form allowing only conjunctions of difference constraints $x \leq y + k$ for $k \in \mathbb{Z}$.

Perhaps surprisingly, we find that polynomial time algorithms are out of reach even in this minimal case: satisfiability is already NP-complete, quantifier-free entailment is coNP-complete, and quantified entailment is Π_2^P-complete. However, a small consolation is that the *small model property* holds for all three problems.

We note that our upper bound complexity results for satisfiability and quantifier-free entailment can be seen as following already from our earlier results for *array separation logic* [6], where we allow array predicates array(x, y) as well as pointers and arithmetic constraints. Of course, pointer arithmetic is often an essential feature in reasoning about array-manipulating programs. The main value of our findings, we believe, is in our *lower* bound complexity results, which show that NP-hardness or worse is an inevitable consequence of admitting pointer arithmetic of almost any kind. Moreover, the exact upper bound of Π_2^P for entailment in SL$_{\mathsf{MPA}}$ is new, and not straightforward to obtain.

We remark that our lower-bound results do however rely on the presence of *pointer* arithmetic, as opposed to arithmetic *per se*. Where pointers and data values are strictly distinguished and arithmetic is permitted only over data, as is done e.g. in [16], then polynomial-time algorithms may still be achievable in that case. Another possibility might be to impose further restrictions on the version of pointer arithmetic used here by adopting a different memory model, e.g. one that only allows pointers to be compared within specified memory regions (similar to the way pointers are intended to be used in C). To stand any chance of yielding a complexity improvement, such regions would need to be bounded "in advance", since, as we point out in Sect. 3, one can encode a 3-colourability graph with m edges as a satisfiability problem in SL$_{\mathsf{MPA}}$ within a heap region of only linear size in m. In any case, however, we are not aware of any such region-aware models in the literature on separation logic.

It is worth mentioning the existence of software security measures that combat attacks like "stack smashing" by deliberately reordering the heap memory.

For programs employing such obfuscatory defensive measures, one typically cannot say anything definitive about the relative ordering of pointers in memory, in which case pointer arithmetic may be of limited utility as a reasoning tool.

Finally, we believe that our complexity results might well extend to the full first-order version of SL_{MPA}. For the entailment lower bound, the natural approach would be to develop a reduction from the k-round 3-colourability problem to Π_k^0 entailments, building on the reduction from 2-round 3-colourability to Π_2^0 entailments[1] with one alternation in Sect. 5. For the upper bound, the translation into an equivalent PbA formula in Definition 4.1 extends to quantifiers in the obvious way; but, moreover, we believe that our small-model technique in Sect. 6 might be also extended to alternating quantifiers, thus obtaining polynomial bounds for all variables. If so, then this would result in Π_k^P-completeness for Π_k^0 entailments in SL_{MPA}, i.e., the standard polynomial-time hierarchy; but, of course, that remains to be seen.

Acknowledgements. Many thanks to Josh Berdine and Nikos Gorogiannis for a number of illuminating discussions on pointer arithmetic, and to our anonymous reviewers for their comments, which have helped us to improve the presentation of this paper.

References

1. Antonopoulos, T., Gorogiannis, N., Haase, C., Kanovich, M., Ouaknine, J.: Foundations for decision problems in separation logic with general inductive predicates. In: Muscholl, A. (ed.) FoSSaCS 2014. LNCS, vol. 8412, pp. 411–425. Springer, Heidelberg (2014). https://doi.org/10.1007/978-3-642-54830-7_27
2. Berdine, J., Calcagno, C., O'Hearn, P.W.: A decidable fragment of separation logic. In: Lodaya, K., Mahajan, M. (eds.) FSTTCS 2004. LNCS, vol. 3328, pp. 97–109. Springer, Heidelberg (2004). https://doi.org/10.1007/978-3-540-30538-5_9
3. Berdine, J., Cook, B., Ishtiaq, S.: SLAYER: memory safety for systems-level code. In: Gopalakrishnan, G., Qadeer, S. (eds.) CAV 2011. LNCS, vol. 6806, pp. 178–183. Springer, Heidelberg (2011). https://doi.org/10.1007/978-3-642-22110-1_15
4. Brochenin, R., Demri, S., Lozes, E.: On the almighty wand. Inf. Comput. **211**, 106–137 (2012)
5. Brotherston, J., Fuhs, C., Gorogiannis, N., Navarro Pérez, J.: A decision procedure for satisfiability in separation logic with inductive predicates. In: Proceedings of the CSL-LICS, pp. 25:1–25:10. ACM (2014)
6. Brotherston, J., Gorogiannis, N., Kanovich, M.: Biabduction (and related problems) in array separation logic. In: de Moura, L. (ed.) CADE 2017. LNCS (LNAI), vol. 10395, pp. 472–490. Springer, Cham (2017). https://doi.org/10.1007/978-3-319-63046-5_29
7. Brotherston, J., Gorogiannis, N., Kanovich, M., Rowe, R.: Model checking for symbolic-heap separation logic with inductive predicates. In: Proceedings of the POPL-43, pp. 84–96. ACM (2016)
8. Calcagno, C., et al.: Moving fast with software verification. In: Havelund, K., Holzmann, G., Joshi, R. (eds.) NFM 2015. LNCS, vol. 9058, pp. 3–11. Springer, Cham (2015). https://doi.org/10.1007/978-3-319-17524-9_1

---

[1] Here we view the complexity of $A \models \exists \mathbf{z}.B$ as Π_2^0, noting that the entailment is, implicitly, universally quantified at the outermost level.

9. Calcagno, C., Yang, H., O'Hearn, P.W.: Computability and complexity results for a spatial assertion language for data structures. In: Hariharan, R., Vinay, V., Mukund, M. (eds.) FSTTCS 2001. LNCS, vol. 2245, pp. 108–119. Springer, Heidelberg (2001). https://doi.org/10.1007/3-540-45294-X_10

10. Chen, T., Song, F., Wu, Z.: Tractability of separation logic with inductive definitions: beyond lists. In: Proceedings of the CONCUR-28, pp. 33:1–33:16. Dagstuhl (2017)

11. Cook, B., Haase, C., Ouaknine, J., Parkinson, M., Worrell, J.: Tractable reasoning in a fragment of separation logic. In: Katoen, J.-P., König, B. (eds.) CONCUR 2011. LNCS, vol. 6901, pp. 235–249. Springer, Heidelberg (2011). https://doi.org/10.1007/978-3-642-23217-6_16

12. Cormen, T.H., Leiserson, C.E., Rivest, R.L., Stein, C.: Introduction to Algorithms, 3rd edn. MIT Press, Cambridge (2009)

13. Demri, S., Lozes, E., Lugiez, D.: On symbolic heaps modulo permission theories. In: Proceedings of the FSTTCS-37, pp. 25:1–25:13. Dagstuhl (2017)

14. Demri, S., Lozes, É., Mansutti, A.: The effects of adding reachability predicates in propositional separation logic. In: Baier, C., Dal Lago, U. (eds.) FoSSaCS 2018. LNCS, vol. 10803, pp. 476–493. Springer, Cham (2018). https://doi.org/10.1007/978-3-319-89366-2_26

15. Garey, M.R., Johnson, D.S.: Computers and Intractability: A Guide to the Theory of NP-Completeness. W. H. Freeman, New York (1979)

16. Gu, X., Chen, T., Wu, Z.: A complete decision procedure for linearly compositional separation logic with data constraints. In: Olivetti, N., Tiwari, A. (eds.) IJCAR 2016. LNCS (LNAI), vol. 9706, pp. 532–549. Springer, Cham (2016). https://doi.org/10.1007/978-3-319-40229-1_36

17. Haase, C.: Subclasses of Presburger arithmetic and the weak EXP hierarchy. In: Proceedings of CSL-LICS, pp. 47:1–47:10. ACM (2014)

18. Iosif, R., Rogalewicz, A., Simacek, J.: The tree width of separation logic with recursive definitions. In: Bonacina, M.P. (ed.) CADE 2013. LNCS (LNAI), vol. 7898, pp. 21–38. Springer, Heidelberg (2013). https://doi.org/10.1007/978-3-642-38574-2_2

19. Kimura, D., Tatsuta, M.: Decision procedure for entailment of symbolic heaps with arrays. In: Chang, B.-Y.E. (ed.) APLAS 2017. LNCS, vol. 10695, pp. 169–189. Springer, Cham (2017). https://doi.org/10.1007/978-3-319-71237-6_9

20. Le, Q.L., Sun, J., Chin, W.-N.: Satisfiability modulo heap-based programs. In: Chaudhuri, S., Farzan, A. (eds.) CAV 2016. LNCS, vol. 9779, pp. 382–404. Springer, Cham (2016). https://doi.org/10.1007/978-3-319-41528-4_21

21. Le, Q.L., Tatsuta, M., Sun, J., Chin, W.-N.: A decidable fragment in separation logic with inductive predicates and arithmetic. In: Majumdar, R., Kunčak, V. (eds.) CAV 2017. LNCS, vol. 10427, pp. 495–517. Springer, Cham (2017). https://doi.org/10.1007/978-3-319-63390-9_26

22. Le, X.B., Gherghina, C., Hobor, A.: Decision procedures over sophisticated fractional permissions. In: Jhala, R., Igarashi, A. (eds.) APLAS 2012. LNCS, vol. 7705, pp. 368–385. Springer, Heidelberg (2012). https://doi.org/10.1007/978-3-642-35182-2_26

23. Reynolds, J.C.: Separation logic: a logic for shared mutable data structures. In: Proceedings of the LICS-17, pp. 55–74. IEEE (2002)

24. Scarpellini, B.: Complexity of subcases of Presburger arithmetic. Trans. Am. Math. Soc. **284**(1), 203–218 (1984)

25. Stockmeyer, L.J.: The polynomial-time hierarchy. Theor. Comput. Sci. **3**, 1–22 (1977)

26. Yang, H., et al.: Scalable shape analysis for systems code. In: Gupta, A., Malik, S. (eds.) CAV 2008. LNCS, vol. 5123, pp. 385–398. Springer, Heidelberg (2008). https://doi.org/10.1007/978-3-540-70545-1_36
27. Yang, H., O'Hearn, P.: A semantic basis for local reasoning. In: Nielsen, M., Engberg, U. (eds.) FoSSaCS 2002. LNCS, vol. 2303, pp. 402–416. Springer, Heidelberg (2002). https://doi.org/10.1007/3-540-45931-6_28

A Decision Procedure for String Logic with Quadratic Equations, Regular Expressions and Length Constraints

Quang Loc Le$^{(\boxtimes)}$ and Mengda He

Teesside University, Middlesbrough, UK
`Q.Le@tees.ac.uk`

Abstract. In this work, we consider the satisfiability problem in a logic that combines word equations over string variables denoting words of unbounded lengths, regular languages to which words belong and Presburger constraints on the length of words. We present a novel decision procedure over two decidable fragments that include quadratic word equations (i.e., each string variable occurs at most twice). The proposed procedure reduces the problem to solving the satisfiability in the Presburger arithmetic. The procedure combines two main components: (i) an algorithm to derive a complete set of all solutions of conjunctions of word equations and regular expressions; and (ii) two methods to precisely compute relational constraints over string lengths implied by the set of all solutions. We have implemented a prototype tool and evaluated it over a set of satisfiability problems in the logic. The experimental results show that the tool is effective and efficient.

1 Introduction

The problem of solving word algebras has been studied since the early stage of mathematics and computer science [16]. Solving word equation (which includes concatenation operation, equalities and inequalities on string variables) was an intriguing problem and initially investigated due to its ties to Hilbert's 10th problem. The major result was obtained in 1977 by Makanin [37] who showed that the satisfiability of word equations with constants is, indeed, decidable. In recent years, due to considerable number of security threats over the Internet, there has been much renewed interest in the satisfiability problem involving the development of formal reasoning systems to either verify safety properties or to detect vulnerability for web and database applications. These applications often require a reasoning about string theories that combines word equations, regular languages and constraints on the length of words.

Providing a decision procedure for the satisfiability problem on a string logic including word equations and length constraints has been difficult to achieve. One main challenge is how to support an inductive reasoning about the combination of unbounded strings and the *infinite* integer domain. Indeed, the satisfiability of word equations combined with length constraints of the form $|x| = |y|$

© Springer Nature Switzerland AG 2018
S. Ryu (Ed.): APLAS 2018, LNCS 11275, pp. 350–372, 2018.
https://doi.org/10.1007/978-3-030-02768-1_19

is open [11,22] (where $|x|$ denotes the length of the string variable x). So far, very few decidability results in this logic are known; the most expressive result is restricted within the straight-line fragment (SL) which is based on *acyclic* word equations [7,12,22,23,36]. This SL fragment excludes constraints combining *quadratic* word equations, the equations in which each string variable occurs at most twice. For instance, the following constraint is beyond the SL fragment: $e_c \equiv x \cdot a \cdot a \cdot y = y \cdot b \cdot a \cdot x$ where x and y are string variables, a and b are letters, and $\cdot$ is the string concatenation operation. Hence, one research goal is to identify decidable logics combining quadratic word equations (and beyond), based on which we can develop an efficient decision procedure.

There have been efforts to deal with the cyclic string constraints in Z3str2 [50,51], CVC4 [34] and S3P [48]. While Z3str2 presented a mechanism to detect overlapping variables to avoid non-termination, CVC4 proposed *refutation complete* procedure to generate a refutation for any unsatisfiable input problem and S3P [48] provided a method to identify and prune non-progressing scenarios. However, none is both complete and terminating over quadratic word equations. For instance, Z3str2, CVC4 and S3P (and all the state-of-the-art string solving techniques [6–9,12,23]) is not able to decide the satisfiability of the word equation e_c above.

In this work, we propose a novel cyclic proof system within a satisfiability procedure for the string theory combining word equations, regular memberships and Presburger constraints over the length functions. Moreover, we identify decidable fragments with quadratic word equations (e.g., the constraint e_c above) where the proposed procedure is complete and terminating. To the best of our knowledge, our proposal is the first decision procedure for string constraints beyond the straight-line word equations. Our proposal has two main components. First, we present a novel algorithm to construct a cyclic *reduction* tree which finitely represents all solutions of a conjunction of word equations and regular membership predicates. Secondly, we describe two procedures to infer the length constraints implied by the set of all solutions.

Contributions. We make the following technical contributions.

- We develop a algorithm, called ω-SAT, to derive a cyclic reduction tree as a finite representation for all solutions of a conjunction of word equations and regular expressions. We show that if ω-SAT terminates with a reduction tree, the tree forms a finite-index *EDT0L* system [41].
- We present a decision procedure, called Kepler$_{22}$, with two decidable fragments and provide a complexity analysis of our approach. This is the first decidable result for the string theory combining *quadratic* word equations with length constraints.
- We have implemented a prototype solver and evaluated it over a set of handdrafted benchmarks in the decidable fragments. The experimental results show that when compared with the state-of-the-art solvers, our proposal is both effective and efficient in solving string constraints with quadratic equations and length constraints.

Organization. The rest of the paper is organized as follows. Section 2 presents relevant definitions. Section 3 shows an overview of our approach through an example. We show how to compute a cyclic reduction tree to finitely represent all solutions of a conjunction of word equations and regular memberships in Sect. 4. Section 5 presents the proposed decision procedure. Sections 6 and 7 describe the two decidable fragments. Section 8 presents an implementation and evaluation. Section 9 reviews related work and concludes.

2   Preliminaries

Concrete string models assume a finite alphabet Σ whose elements are called *letters*, set of finite words over Σ^* including ϵ - the empty word, and a set of integer numbers $\mathbb{Z}$. We work with a set U of string variables denoting words in Σ^*, and a set I of arithmetical variables. We use $|w|$ to denote the length of $w \in \Sigma^*$ and $\bar{v}$ a sequence of variables. A language L over the alphabet Σ is a set $L \subseteq \Sigma^*$. A language L is a set of words generated by a grammar system. We use $\mathcal{L}(L)$ to denote the class of all languages L.

disj formula	$\pi ::= \phi \mid \pi_1 \vee \pi_2$		formula	$\phi ::= \mathbf{e} \mid \alpha \mid s \in \mathcal{R} \mid \neg\phi_1 \mid \phi_1 \wedge \phi_2$	
(dis)equality	$\mathbf{e} ::= s_1 = s_2$		term	$s ::= \epsilon \mid c \mid x \mid s_1 \cdot s_2$	
regex	$\mathcal{R} ::= \emptyset \mid \epsilon \mid c \mid w \mid \mathcal{R}_1 \cdot \mathcal{R}_2 \mid \mathcal{R}_1 + \mathcal{R}_2 \mid \mathcal{R}_1 \cap \mathcal{R}_2 \mid \mathcal{R}_1^C \mid \mathcal{R}_1^*$				
Arithmetic	$\alpha ::= a_1 = a_2 \mid a_1 > a_2 \mid \alpha_1 \wedge \alpha_2 \mid \alpha_1 \vee \alpha_2 \mid \exists v.\alpha_1$				
	$a ::= 0 \mid 1 \mid v \mid |u| \mid i \times a_1 \mid -a_1 \mid a_1 + a_2$				

Fig. 1. Syntax

Syntax. The syntax of quantifier-free string formulas, called STR, is presented in Fig. 1. π is a disjunction formula where each disjunct ϕ is a conjunction of word equations $\mathbf{e}$, arithmetic constraints α and regular memberships $s \in \mathcal{R}$. A word equation $\mathbf{e}$ is an equality of string terms s. (We use either s or tr to denote a string term.) A string term is a concatenation of the empty word ϵ, letters $c \in \Sigma$ and string variables x. We often write $s_1 s_2$ to denote $s_1 \cdot s_2$ if it is not ambiguous. Regular expression $\mathcal{R}$ over Σ is built over $c \in \Sigma$, $w \in \Sigma^*$, ϵ, and closing under union $+$, intersection $\cap$, complement C, concatenation $\cdot$, and the Kleene star operator $*$. Regular expressions $\mathcal{R}$ does not contain any string variables.

We use $\mathcal{E}$ to denote a conjunction (a.k.a system) of word equations. $\pi[t_1/t_2]$ denotes a substitution of all occurrences of t_2 in π to t_1. We use function $FV(\pi)$ to return all free variables of π. We inductively define length function of a string term s, denoted as $|s|$, as: $|\epsilon| = 0$, $|c| = 1$, and $|s_1 \cdot s_2| = |s_1| + |s_2|$. Notational length of the word equation $\mathbf{e}$, denoted by $\mathbf{e}(N)$, is the number of its symbols.

A word equation is called *acyclic* if each variable occurs at most once. A word equation is called *quadratic* if each variable occurs at most twice. Similarly, a

$$\begin{aligned}
&\eta, \beta_\eta \models \pi_1 \vee \pi_2 \ \texttt{iff} \ \eta, \beta_\eta \models \pi_1 \text{ or } \eta, \beta_\eta \models \pi_2\\
&\eta, \beta_\eta \models \pi_1 \wedge \pi_2 \ \texttt{iff} \ \eta, \beta_\eta \models \pi_1 \text{ and } \eta, \beta_\eta \models \pi_2\\
&\eta, \beta_\eta \models \neg\pi_1 \quad\ \, \texttt{iff} \ \eta, \beta_\eta \not\models \pi_1\\
&\eta, \beta_\eta \models s \in \mathcal{R} \quad \texttt{iff} \ \exists w \in \mathcal{L}(\mathcal{R}) \cdot \eta, \beta_\eta \models s = w\\
&\eta, \beta_\eta \models s_1 = s_2 \ \texttt{iff} \ \eta(s_1) = \eta(s_2) \text{ and } \beta_\eta(s_1) = \beta_\eta(s_2)\\
&\eta, \beta_\eta \models s_1 \neq s_2 \ \texttt{iff} \ \eta, \beta_\eta \models \neg(s_1 = s_2)\\
&\eta, \beta_\eta \models a_1 \oslash a_2 \ \texttt{iff} \ \eta(a_1) \oslash \eta(a_2), \text{ where } \oslash \in \{=, \leq\}
\end{aligned}$$

Fig. 2. Semantics

system of word equations is called quadratic if each variable occurs at most twice.

A word equation system is said to be straight-line [7,22,36] if it can be rewritten (by reordering the conjuncts) as the form $\bigwedge_{i=1}^{n} x_i = s_i$ such that: (i) $x_1, ..., x_n$ are different variables; and (ii) $FV(s_i) \subseteq \{x_1, x_2, .., x_{i-1}\}$. A formula $\pi \equiv e_1 \wedge e_2 \wedge ... \wedge e_n \wedge \Upsilon$ is called in straight-line fragment (SL) if $e_1 \wedge e_2 \wedge ... \wedge e_n$ is straight-line and the regular expression Υ is of the conjunction of regular memberships $x_j \in \mathcal{R}_j$ where $x_j \in \{x_1, ..., x_n\}$.

Semantics. Every regular expression $\mathcal{R}$ is evaluated to the language $\mathcal{L}(\mathcal{R})$. We define:

$$SStacks \overset{\text{def}}{=} (U \cup \Sigma) \to \Sigma^* \qquad ZStacks \overset{\text{def}}{=} I \to \mathbb{Z}.$$

The semantics is given by a satisfaction relation: $\eta, \beta_\eta \models \pi$ that forces the interpretation on both string η and arithmetic β_η to satisfy the constraint π where $\eta \in SStacks$, $\beta_\eta \in ZStacks$, and π is a formula. We remark that $\forall \eta \in SStacks$: $\eta(c) = c$ for all $c \in \Sigma$ and $\eta(t_1 t_2) = \eta(t_1)\eta(t_2)$. The semantics of our language is formalized in Fig. 2. If $\eta, \beta_\eta \models \pi$, we use the pair $\langle \eta, \beta_\eta \rangle$ to denote a solution of the formula π. Let $e \equiv x_1 \cdot ... \cdot x_l = x_{l+1} \cdot ... \cdot x_n$ be a word equation. If e is satisfied with the solution $\langle \eta, \beta_\eta \rangle$, we also refer $\eta(x_1) \cdot ... \cdot \eta(x_l)$ as a solution word of e. A solution word is minimal if the length of the solution word $(|\eta(x_1)| + ... + |\eta(x_l)|)$ is minimal. e_1 is referred as a suffix of e_2 if they are satisfied and the solution word of e_1 is a suffix of the solution word of e_2.

Formal Language. A deterministic finite automaton (DFA) A is a tuple: $A = \langle Q, \Sigma, \delta, q_0, Q_F \rangle$, where Q is a finite set of states, $\delta \subseteq Q \times (\Sigma \cup \{\epsilon\}) \times Q$ is a finite set of transitions, $q_0 \in Q$ is the initial state and $Q_F \subseteq Q$ is a set of accepting states. We use $\mathcal{L}(A)$ to denote the (regular) language generated by a DFA A. It is known that the languages generated by regular expressions are also in the class of regular languages [26].

A context-free grammar (CFG) G is defined by the quadruple: $G = \langle V, \Sigma, P, S \rangle$ where V is a finite nonempty set of nonterminals, Σ is a finite set of terminals and disjoint from V, and $P \subseteq V \times (V \cup \Sigma)^*$ is a finite relation. For any strings $u, v \in (V \cup \Sigma)^*$, v is a result of applying the rule (α, β)

to u $u \Rightarrow_G v$ if $\exists (\alpha, \beta) \in P$ $u_1, u_2 \in (V \cup \Sigma)^*$ such that $u = u_1 \alpha u_2$ and $v = u_1 \beta u_2$. $\mathcal{L}(G) = \{w \in \Sigma^* \mid S \Rightarrow_G^* w\}$ to denote a language produced by the CFG G. Given a CFG $G = \langle V, \Sigma, P, S \rangle$, we use G_X (where $X \in V$) to denote a sub-language of $\mathcal{L}(G)$, defined by $\mathcal{L}(G_X) = \{w \in \Sigma^* \mid X \Rightarrow_G^* w\}$.

Normal Form. $\pi \equiv \mathcal{E} \wedge \Upsilon \wedge \alpha$ is called in the normal form if it is of the form: $\mathcal{E}$ is a system of word equations, Υ is a conjunction of regular memberships (e.g., $X \in \mathcal{R}$) and α is a Presburger formula. (For the transformation of a formula presented in Fig. 1 into the normal form, [15, 29] described how to eliminate negation over word equations, and disjunction of word equations and [7] showed how to remove the negation and the concatenation operator over regular expressions.)

Problem Definition. Throughout this work, we consider the following problem.

PROBLEM: SAT−STR.
INPUT: A string constraint π in normal form over Σ.
QUESTION: Is π satisfiable?

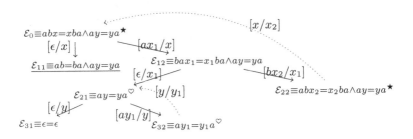

Fig. 3. Reduction tree $\mathcal{T}_3$.

3   Overview and Illustration

The overall of our idea is an algorithm to reduce an input constraint to a set of solvable constraints. In this section, we first define the reduction tree (Subsect. 3.1). After that, we illustrate the proposed decision procedure through an example (Subsect. 3.2).

3.1   Cyclic Reduction Tree

Formally, a cyclic reduction tree $\mathcal{T}_i$ is a tuple $(V, E, \mathcal{C})$ where

- V is a finite set of nodes where each node represents a conjunction of word equations $\mathcal{E}$.
- E is a set of labeled and directed edges $(\mathcal{E}, \sigma, \mathcal{E}') \in E$ where $\mathcal{E}'$ is a child of $\mathcal{E}$. This edge means we can reduce $\mathcal{E}$ to $\mathcal{E}'$ via the label σ, a substitution, s.t.: $\mathcal{E}' \equiv \mathcal{E}\sigma$.

- And $\mathcal{C}$ is a back-link (partial) function which captures virtual cycles in the tree. A cycle, e.g. $\mathcal{C}(\mathcal{E}_c \rightarrow \mathcal{E}_b, \sigma)$, in $\mathcal{C}$ means the leaf $\mathcal{E}_b$ is linked back to its ancestor $\mathcal{E}_c$ and $\mathcal{E}_c \equiv \mathcal{E}_b\sigma$. In this back-link, $\mathcal{E}_b$ is referred as a *bud* and $\mathcal{E}_c$ is referred as a *companion*.

A path (v_s, v_e) is a sequence of nodes and edges connecting node v_s with node v_e. A leaf node is either unsatisfiable, or satisfiable or linked back to an interior node, or not-yet-reduced. If a leaf node is not-yet-reduced, it is marked as open. Otherwise, it is marked as closed. A trace of a tree is a sequence of edge labels of a path in the tree. We refer a trace as solution trace if it corresponds to a path (v_s, v_e) where v_s is the root and v_e is a satisfiable leaf. This trace represents a (infinite) family solutions of the equation at the root.

3.2 Illustrative Example

We consider the following constraint: $\pi \equiv abx = xba \wedge ay = ya \wedge |x| = 2|y|$ where x, y are string variables and a, b are letters. This constraint is beyond the straight-line fragment [7,12,22,23,36]. Moreover, as the length constraint $|x| = 2|y|$ is not regular-based, the automata-based translation proposed in [12] cannot be applied.

The proposed solver Kepler22 could solve the constraint π above through the following three steps. First, it invokes procedure ω-SAT to construct a cyclic reduction tree to capture all solutions of the word equations $\mathcal{E}_0 \equiv abx = xba \wedge ay = ya$. Next, it infers a precise constraint α_{xy} implied by string lengths of all solutions. Lastly, it solves the conjunction: $\alpha_{xy} \wedge \alpha$ where α is the arithmetic constraint in the input π.

The Representation of All Solutions. ω-SAT derives the reduction tree $\mathcal{T}_3$ (V, E, C), shown in Fig. 3, as the finite presentation of all solutions for $\mathcal{E}_0$. In particular, the root of the tree is $\mathcal{E}_0$. $\mathcal{E}_0$ has two children $\mathcal{E}_{11}$ and $\mathcal{E}_{12}$, which are obtained by reducing x into two *complete* cases: $x = \epsilon$ and $x = ax_1$ where x_1 is fresh. Note that $\mathcal{E}_{12}$ is obtained by first applying the substitution: $\mathcal{E}'_{12} \equiv \mathcal{E}_0[ax_1/x] \equiv abax_1 = ax_1ba \wedge ay = ya$ prior to subtracting the letter a at the heads of the two sides of the first word equation. Next, while $\mathcal{E}_{11}$ is classified as unsatisfiable, (underlined) and marked closed, $\mathcal{E}_{12}$ is further reduced into two children, $\mathcal{E}_{21}$ and $\mathcal{E}_{22}$. They are obtained by reducing x_1 at the head of the right-hand side (RHS) of $\mathcal{E}_{12}$ into two complete cases: $x_1 = \epsilon$ to generate $\mathcal{E}'_{21} \equiv \mathcal{E}'_{12}[\epsilon/x_1] \equiv ab = ab \wedge ay = ya$ and $x_1 = bx_2$ (where x_2 is a fresh variable) to generate $\mathcal{E}'_{22} \equiv e'_{12}[bx_2/x_1] \equiv babx_2 = bx_2ba$. Next, $\mathcal{E}'_{21}$ is further reduced into $\mathcal{E}_{21}$ by matching a, b letters; and $\mathcal{E}'_{22}$ is further reduced into $\mathcal{E}_{22}$ by matching b letters at the heads of its two sides. Lastly, $\mathcal{E}_{22}$ is linked back to $\mathcal{E}_0$ to form the back-link $\mathcal{C}(\mathcal{E}_0 \rightarrow \mathcal{E}_{22}, [x/x_2])$. Similarly, $\mathcal{E}_{21}$ is reduced until all leaf nodes are marked closed.

A path (v_s, v_e) with trace σ represents for $v_e \equiv v_s\sigma$. If v_e is satisfiable, then σ represents for a family of solutions (or valid assignments). For instance, in Fig. 3, the path $(\mathcal{E}_0, \mathcal{E}_{31})$ has the trace $\sigma_{31} = [ax_1/x, \epsilon/x_1, \epsilon/y]$. As $\mathcal{E}_{31}$ is satisfiable, we can derive a solution of $\mathcal{E}_0$ based on σ_{31} as: $x = a$ and $y = \epsilon$. Moreover, trace solution that is involved in cycles represents a set of infinite solutions, since we can construct infinitely many solution traces by iterating through the cycles an unbounded number of times. For example, all solution traces σ_{ij} obtained from the path $(\mathcal{E}_0, \mathcal{E}_{31})$ above is as:

$$\sigma_{ij} \equiv [ax_1/x] \circ [bx_2/x_1, x/x_2, ax_1/x]^i \circ [ay_1/y, y_1/y]^j \circ [\epsilon/x_1 \circ \epsilon/y]$$

where $\circ$ is the substitution composition operation, σ^k means σ is repeatedly composed zero, one or more times, and $i \geq 0$, $j \geq 0$.

Computing α_{xy} Constraint. Based on the solution trace σ_{ij} above, Kepler$_{22}$ first generates a conjunctive set of constrained Horn clauses to define the relational assumptions over lengths of x and y in the set of all solutions. After that it infers the length constraint as: $\alpha_{xy} \equiv \exists i. |x| = 2i + 1 \wedge i \geq 0 \wedge |y| \geq 0$. Now, the satisfiability of π is equi-satisfiable to the following formula: $\pi' \equiv (\exists i. |x| = 2i + 1 \wedge i \geq 0 \wedge |y| \geq 0) \wedge |x| = 2|y|$. As π' is unsatisfiable, so is π.

4   The Representation of All Solutions

In this section, we first present procedure ω-SAT which constructs a cyclic reduction tree for a conjunction of word equations $\mathcal{E}$ (Subsect. 4.1). After that, we describe how to combine the tree with regular membership predicates Υ (Subsect. 4.2). Finally, we discuss the correctness in Subsect. 4.3.

4.1   Constructing Cyclic Reduction Tree

ω-SAT transforms a conjunction of word equations $\mathcal{E}$ into a cyclic reduction tree $\mathcal{T}_n$ which represents all its solutions. This procedure starts with the tree $\mathcal{T}_0$ with only the input $\mathcal{E}$ at the root. After that, in each iteration it chooses one leaf node to reduce (using function reduce) or to make a back-link (using function link_back) until every leaf node is either irreducible or linked back. A leaf node is irreducible if it either trivially true (i.e., $w_1 = w_1 \wedge ... \wedge w_i = w_i$ where $w_1, ..., w_i \in \Sigma^*$) or trivially false (i.e., either it is of the form: $c_1 tr_1 = c_2 tr_2 \wedge \mathcal{E}$ where c_1, c_2 are different letters or its over-approximation over the length functions is unsatisfiable). Function reduce takes a leaf node $\mathcal{E}_i$ as input and produces a set L_i each element of which is a pair of a node $\mathcal{E}_{i_j}$ and a corresponding substitution σ_j such that $\mathcal{E}_{i_j} = \mathcal{E}_i \sigma_j$. For each pair $(\mathcal{E}_{i_j}, \sigma_j) \in L_i$, it adds an new open node $\mathcal{E}_{i_j}$ and a new edge $(\mathcal{E}_i, \sigma_j, \mathcal{E}_{i_j})$. As a result, reduce extends the current tree with the new nodes and new edges. In particular, function reduce is implemented as: $L_i = \bigcup \{\text{matchs}(\mathcal{E}_{i_j}) \mid \mathcal{E}_{i_j} \in \text{complete}(\mathcal{E}_i)\}$ where function matchs exhaustively matches and subtracts identical letters and string variables at the heads of left-hand side (LHS) and right-hand side (RHS) of each word equation using function match. In the following, we describe the details of the functions used by ω-SAT.

Matching. `match(e)` matches two terms at the heads of LHS and RHS of e as follows.

$$\mathtt{match}(u_1 \cdot tr_1 = u_2 \cdot tr_2) = \begin{cases} \mathtt{match}(tr_1 = tr_2) & \text{if } u_1, u_2 \text{ are identical} \\ u_1 \cdot tr_1 = u_2 \cdot tr_2 & \text{otherwise} \end{cases}$$

where u_1, u_2 are either letters or string variables.

Procedure `complete`. The overall goal of our reduction is to transform every word equation, say $e \equiv u_1 tr_1 = u_2 tr_2$ where $\mathcal{E}_i = e \wedge \mathcal{E}$, into a set of "smaller" string equation e_i such that if e is satisfied, e_i is a suffix of e. Word equations in a node are reduced in a depth-first manner. Intuitively, our reduction over the word equation e is based on the possible arrangements of two carrier terms, the terms at the heads of LHS and RHS of e. Suppose that e is satisfied. Let l_1, r_1 be the starting and ending positions of u_1 in the solution word of e. Similarly, let l_2, r_2 be the starting and ending positions of u_1 in the solution word of e. Obviously, $l_1 = l_2$. Our reduction, function `complete`, considers all possible arrangements based on these positions. For arrangements in one-side (LHS or RHS), it considers the cases: $l_1 = r_1$ (i.e., $u_1 = \epsilon$), $l_1 < r_1$ and $l_2 = r_2$ (i.e., $u_2 = \epsilon$), $l_2 < r_2$. For arrangements between the two sides, it considers the cases: $r_1 \geq r_2$ and $r_2 \geq r_1$. In particular, function `complete` considers the following two scenarios of the carrier terms.

Case 1: One term is a letter and another term is a string variable, e.g. $x_1 tr_1 = c_2 tr_2$. `complete` generates the set L_i as $L_i \equiv \{(\mathcal{E}_{i_1}, \sigma_1); (\mathcal{E}_{i_2}, \sigma_2)\}$ where

- (1a) $\sigma_1 = [\epsilon/x_1]$
- (1b) $\sigma_2 = [c_2 x_1'/x_1]$, x_1' is a fresh variable and referred as a subterm of x_1.

Case 2: These terms are two different string variables, e.g. $x_1 tr_1 = x_2 tr_2$. `complete` generates the set L_i as: $L_i \equiv \{(\mathcal{E}_{i_1}, \sigma_1); (\mathcal{E}_{i_2}, \sigma_2); (\mathcal{E}_{i_3}, \sigma_3); (\mathcal{E}_{i_4}, \sigma_4)\}$ where

- (2a) $\sigma_1 = [\epsilon/x_1]$,
- (2b) $\sigma_3 = [x_2 x_1'/x_1]$, x_1' is a fresh variable and referred as a subterm of x_1,
- (2c) $\sigma_2 = [\epsilon/x_2]$
- (2d) $\sigma_4 = [x_1 x_2'/x_2]$, x_2' is a fresh variable and referred as a subterm of x_2.

As both Case 2b and Case 2d include the scenario where $x_1 = x_2$, the reduction tree generated represents a *complete* but *not minimal* set of all solution.

Linking Back. `link_back` links a leaf node $\mathcal{E}_b$ to an interior node $\mathcal{E}_c$ if after some substitution σ_{cyc}, two nodes are identical: $\mathcal{E}_c \equiv \mathcal{E}_b \sigma_{cyc}$. In addition, for every entry $X/X' \in \sigma_{cyc}$ where X and X' are string variables, X' is a subterm of X. σ_{cyc} can be considered as a permutation function on both U and the alphabet Σ. We recap that we refer to this cycle as a triple $\mathcal{C}(\mathcal{E}_c \rightarrow \mathcal{E}_b, \sigma_{cyc})$ where $\mathcal{E}_c$ is called a companion, $\mathcal{E}_b$ is called a bud.

4.2   Combining with Regular Memberships

We propose to derive a finite representation of all solutions of a conjunction of word equations and regular expressions. using procedure `widentree`. Procedure `widentree` takes a pair of a reduction tree $\mathcal{T}_n$ of $\mathcal{E}_0$ (generated by ω-SAT) and a conjunction of regular expressions Υ as inputs and manipulates the reduction tree $\mathcal{T}_n$ through the following three steps. First, it constructs a DFA $A = \langle Q, \Sigma, \delta, q_0, Q_F \rangle$ which generates the same language with Υ. Let m be the number states in Q and $M = m!$. Intuitively, $m+1$ is the minimal times of a cycle to obtain the minimal solutions of $\mathcal{E}_0 \wedge \Upsilon$. M is the periodic of the sets of all solutions. Secondly, it unfolds every cycles $\mathcal{C}(\mathcal{E}_c \to \mathcal{E}_b, \sigma)$ of $\mathcal{T}_n$ $m+M$ times. It updates `link_back` functions by eliminating the old back-link between $\mathcal{E}_b$ and $\mathcal{E}_c$ prior to generating a new back-link between $\mathcal{E}_{b_{m+M}}$ and $\mathcal{E}_{c_m}$ as well as marking $\mathcal{E}_{b_{m+M}}$ as closed. We note that a solution corresponding to a trace which visits the companion $\mathcal{E}_{c_m}$ $l+1$ times (i.e., including k new cycles above) has the form: $S \equiv u_1 w^{m+1+lM} u_2$. Lastly, it collects label σ_j for every path

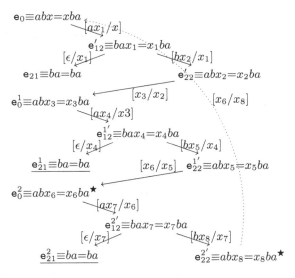

Fig. 4. Extending tree $\mathcal{T}_2$ with $x \in a^*$.

$(\mathcal{E}_0, \mathcal{E}_j)$ in the new tree where $\mathcal{E}_0$ is the root, $\mathcal{E}_j$ is a leaf node that is neither unsatisfiable nor a bud prior to evaluating $\mathcal{E}_j$. From σ_j, it generates the following formula: $\pi_j \equiv \bigwedge\{X_i = s_i | (s_i/X_i) \in \sigma_j\} \wedge \Upsilon$. π_j is in a *straight-line* fragment where the satisfiability problem `SAT-STR` is decidable [36].

Example 1. To illustrate our first decidable fragment, we use the following word equation as a running example: $abx = xba$ where x is string variable and a, b are letters. This is the first equation in the motivating example (Sect. 3.2). Its reduction tree $\mathcal{T}_2$ is presented in Fig. 5. We now illustrate how to use procedure

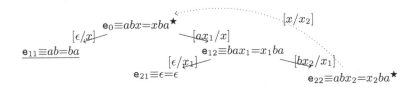

Fig. 5. Reduction tree $\mathcal{T}_2$.

`widentree` above to extend the tree to represent all solutions of $\pi_1 \equiv abx = xba \wedge$ $x \in a^*$. To do that, `widentree` first derives for the regular expression $x \in a^*$ a DFA as: $A = \langle \{q_0\}, \{a\}, \{((q_0, a), a)\}, q_0, \{q_0\} \rangle$, and then identifies $m=1$ and $M = m! = 1$. Secondly, it clones the cycle of $\mathcal{T}_2$ $m + M = 1 + 1 = 2$ more times. The resulting tree is described in Fig. 4. Lastly, it discharges the satisfiability of solutions corresponding to the paths which start from the root and end at leaf nodes e_{21}, e_{21}^1 or e_{21}^2. The evaluation is as follows.

path	formula	outcome
(e_0, e_{21})	$x = ax_1 \wedge x_1 = \epsilon \wedge x \in a^*$	SAT
(e_0, e_{21}^1)	$x = ax_1 \wedge x_1 = bx_2 \wedge x_2 = x_3 \wedge x_3 = ax_4 \wedge x_4 = \epsilon \wedge x \in a^*$	UNSAT
(e_0, e_{21}^2)	$x = ax_1 \wedge x_1 = bx_2 \wedge x_2 = x_3 \wedge x_3 = ax_4 \wedge x_4 = bx_5 \wedge$ $x_5 = x_6 \wedge x_6 = ax_7 \wedge x_7 = \epsilon \wedge x \in a^*$	UNSAT

4.3 Correctness

In the following, we formalize the correctness of the proposed procedures and show the relationship between the derived reduction tree with $EDT0L$ system [41].

Proposition 1. *Suppose that ω-SAT takes a conjunction $\mathcal{E}$ as input, and produces a cyclic reduction graph $\mathcal{T}_n$ in a finite time. Then, $\mathcal{T}_n$ represents all solutions of $\mathcal{E}$.*

Proposition 2. *Suppose that $\Upsilon \equiv X_1 \in \mathcal{R}_1 \wedge ... \wedge X_n \in \mathcal{R}_n$ $(X_i \in FV(\mathcal{E}_0), \forall 1 \leq i \leq n)$ is a conjunction of regular memberships and $\mathcal{T}_n$ be the reduction tree derived for $\mathcal{E}_0$. Then, `widentree`$(\mathcal{T}_n, \Upsilon)$ produces a reduction tree representing all solutions of $\mathcal{E}_0 \wedge \Upsilon$.*

An *interactionless Lindenmayer system* (0L system) [41] is a parallel rewriting system which was introduced in 1968 to model the development of multicellular system. The class of $EDT0L$ languages forms perhaps the central class in the theory of L systems. The acronym EDT0L refers to Extended, Deterministic, Table, 0 interaction, and Lindenmayer. In the following, we give a formal definition of $EDT0L$ system.

Definition 1. *An ET0L system is a quadruple $G = \langle V, \Sigma, \mathcal{P}, S \rangle$ where V is a finite nonempty set of nonterminals (or variables), Σ is a finite set of terminals and disjoint from V, $S \in V$ is the start variable (or start symbol), $\mathcal{P}$ is a finite set each element of which (called a table) is a finite binary relation included in $V \times (V \cup \Sigma)^*$. It is assumed that $\forall P \in \mathcal{P}, \forall x \in V, \exists tr \in (V \cup \Sigma)^*$ such that $(x, tr) \in P$. An EDT0L system is a deterministic ET0L system in which $\forall P \in \mathcal{P}, \forall x \in V, \exists! tr \in (V \cup \Sigma)^*$ s.t. $(x, tr) \in P$.*

For a production (x,tr) of P in $\mathcal{P}$, we often write: $x \to tr$. We also write $x \to_P tr$ for "$x \to tr$ is in $\mathcal{P}$". Let $G = \langle V, \Sigma, \mathcal{P}, S \rangle$ be an $ET0L$ system.

1. Let $x, y \in (V \cup \Sigma)^*$, and x contains k nonterminals $v_1, ..., v_k$ in V. We say that x directly derives y (in G), denoted as $x \Rightarrow_G y$, if there is a $P \in \mathcal{P}$ such that y is obtained by substituting v_i by s_i, respectively for all $i \in \{1, ..., k\}$, where $v_1 \to_P s_1, ..., v_k \to_P s_k$. In this case, we also write $x \Rightarrow_P y$.
2. Let $\Rightarrow_G^*$ be the reflexive transitive closure of the relation $\Rightarrow$. If $x \Rightarrow_G^* y$ then we say that x derives y (in G).
3. The language of G, denoted by $\mathcal{L}(G)$, defined by $\mathcal{L}(G) = \{w \in \Sigma^* \mid S \Rightarrow_G^* w\}$.

A grammar system that is k-$index$ is restricted so that, for every word generated by the grammar, there is some successful derivation where at most k nonterminals appear in every sentential form of the derivation [42]. A system is finite-index if it is k-index for some k. We use $\mathcal{L}(L)_{FIN}$ to denote the class of all L languages of finite-index.

Corollary 4.1. *A reduction tree derived by ω-SAT forms a finite-index EDT0L system.*

Example 2. The tree in the Fig. 5 above forms the following finite-index $EDT0L$. $G = \langle \{S, x, x_1, x_2\}, \Sigma, \{P_1, P_2\}, S \rangle$ where $P_1 = \{(S, abx), (x, ax_1), (x_1, \epsilon)\}$ and $P_2 = \{(S, abx), (x, ax_1), (x_1, bx_2), (x_2, x)\}$.

5   Decision Procedure

We present decision procedure $\texttt{Kepler}_{22}$ to handle SAT-STR. $\texttt{Kepler}_{22}$ takes a constraint, say $\mathcal{E} \wedge \Upsilon \wedge \alpha$, as input and returns SAT or UNSAT. It works as follows. First, it invokes ω-SAT to construct a reduction tree $\mathcal{T}_n$ as a finite representation of all solutions of $\mathcal{E}$. After that, $\mathcal{T}_n$ is post-processed using procedure $\texttt{postpro}$ as below to explicate all free variables. This step is critical to the next step. Secondly, it uses

Decision Procedure: $\texttt{Kepler}_{22}(\mathcal{E} \wedge \Upsilon \wedge \alpha)$
1 $\mathcal{T}_n \leftarrow \texttt{postprotrim}(\omega\text{-SAT}(\mathcal{E}))$;
2 **if** $(\text{is\_false}(\mathcal{T}_n))$ **return** UNSAT;
3 $\mathcal{T}_{n+1} \leftarrow \texttt{widentree}(\mathcal{T}_n, \Upsilon)$
4 **if** $(\text{is\_false}(\mathcal{T}_{n+1}))$ **return** UNSAT;
5 $\alpha_w \leftarrow extract\_pres(\mathcal{T}_{n+1})$;
6 **return** $\text{SAT}_{\texttt{pres}}(\alpha_w \wedge \alpha)$;

Fig. 6. Satisfiability solving.

procedure $\texttt{widentree}$ to extend $\mathcal{T}_n$ with membership predicates Υ and obtains $\mathcal{T}_{n+1}$. Note that unsatisfiable nodes in the reduction tree are eliminated. Thirdly, it computes the length constraints which are precisely implied by all solutions generated through procedure $extract\_pres(\mathcal{T}_{n+1})$. These length constrains, say α_w, are computed as an existentially quantified Presburger formula. Lastly, $\texttt{Kepler}_{22}$ solves that satisfiability of the conjunction $\alpha_w \wedge \alpha$ which is in the Presburger arithmetic and decidable [21] (Fig. 6).

Post-processing. Given a path from the root e_0 to a satisfiable leaf node e_i, a variable x appearing in this path is called *free* if it has not been reduced yet. This means x can be assigned any value in Σ^* in a solution. Procedure `postpro` aims to replace a free variable by a sub-tree which represents for arbitrary values in Σ^*. The sub-tree is presented in Fig. 7. This tree has a *base*

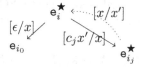

Fig. 7. Free variable x.

leaf node (with substitution $[\epsilon/x]$) and k cycles (k is the size of the alphabet Σ) one of which represents for a letter $c_i \in \Sigma$. If a satisfiable leaf node has more than one free variable, each variable is replaced by such sub-tree and these sub-trees are connected together at base nodes.

Correctness. The correctness of step 1 and step 2 have been shown in the previous section. Thus, the remaining tasks to show `Kepler`$_{22}$ is a decision procedure in a fragment are the termination of ω-`SAT` as well as the decidability of $extract\_pres(\mathcal{T}_{n+1})$.

6 STR$_{\text{EDT0L}}$ Decidable Fragment

Computing length constraint in this fragment is based on Parikh's Theorem [38], one of the most celebrated theorem in automata theory. The Parikh image (a.k.a. letter-counts) of a word over a given alphabet counts the number of occurrences of each symbol in the word without regard to their order. The Parikh image of a language is the set of Parikh images of the words in the language. A language is Parikh-definable if its Parikh image precisely coincides with semilinear sets which, in turn, can be computed as a Presburger formula. In particular, Parikh's Theorem [38] states that context-free languages (and regular languages, of course) are Parikh-definable. In fact, given a context-free grammar, we can compute its Parikh image in polynomial time [19,49]. Moreover, the authors in [42] show that finite-index EDT0L languages [41] are also Parikh-definable. In our work, we use $Par(L)$ to denote the Parikh images computed for the language L.

A given constraint, say $\mathcal{E} \wedge \Upsilon \wedge \pi$, is said to be in the fragment if the following two conditions hold. First, ω-`SAT` terminates on $\mathcal{E}$. Secondly, $\pi \equiv \alpha_1 \wedge .. \wedge \alpha_n$ where $FV(\alpha_i)$ contains at most one string length $\forall i \in \{1...n\}$. By the first condition, `Kepler`$_{22}$ can derive for $\mathcal{E}$ a finite-index $EDT0L$ system (Corollary 4.1). Moreover, finite-index $EDT0L$ can be translated into a Parikh-equivalent DFA (by Parikh's Theorem [38,42]). This means length of each string variable in the set of all solutions can be computed as a DFA. By the second condition, each constraint α_1 is based on the length of one string variable. Hence, this constraint can be translated into another DFA. As regular languages are closed under intersection. Therefore, the satisfiability of π is decidable.

`Kepler`$_{22}$ uses $extract\_pres(\mathcal{T}_{n+1})$ to compute the length constraints represented for all solutions of $\mathcal{E} \wedge \Upsilon$ as follows. Firstly, it transforms $\mathcal{T}_{n+1}$ into a finite-index $EDT0L$ system. Secondly, it transforms the $EDT0L$ grammar into a Parikh-equivalent CFG G (see [42]). Lastly, it computes the length constraints α_w for every string variables as: $\alpha_w \equiv \bigwedge\{Par(\mathcal{L}(G_x)) \mid x \in FV(\mathcal{E} \wedge \Upsilon)\}$.

6.1   Parikh Image of CFG

In order to infer the Parikh image for a given CFG, we first transform the CFG into a Parikh equivalent communication-free Petri net and then compute the Parikh image of the communication-free Petri net [49]. The correctness was presented in [18, 45, 49]. Procedure Par takes a CFG $G = \langle V, \Sigma, P, s_0 \rangle$ as input and produces a Presburger formula to represents the Parikh image of all words derived from the start symbol s_0. In particular, it first transforms the CFG into a communication-free Petri net and then generates a Presburger formula α_G for this net.

A net N is a quadruple $N = \langle S, T, W, s_0 \rangle$ where S is a set of places, T is a set of transitions, W is a weight function: $(S \times T) \cup (T \times S) \rightarrow \mathbb{N}$, and s_0 is the start place in the net. If $W(x, y) > 0$, there is an edge from x to y of weight $W(x, y)$. A net is communication-free if for each transition t there is at most one place s with $W(s, t) > 0$ and furthermore $W(s, t) = 1$. A marking M, a function $S \rightarrow \mathbb{N}$, associates a number of tokens with each place. A communication-free Petri net is a pair (N, M) where N is a communication-free net and M is a marking.

The CFG G is transformed into a communication-free Petri net (N_G, M_G) as: $N_G = \langle V \cup \Sigma, P, W, s_0 \rangle$. If $A \rightarrow s$ is a production $p \in P$ then $W(A, p) = 1$ and $W(B, p)$ is the number occurrences of B in s, for each $B \in V \cup \Sigma$. Finally, $M_G(s_0) = 1$ and $M_G(X) = 0$ for all other $X \in V \cup \Sigma$ and $X \neq s_0$. Let x_c be a new integer variable for each letter $c \in \Sigma$, y_p be a new integer variable for each rule $p \in P$, and z_s be a new integer variable for each symbol $s \in V \cup \Sigma$. We assume that we have m variables $y_{p_1}, .., y_{p_m}$ and n variables $z_{s_1}, .., z_{s_n}$. We note that x_c is used to count the number occurrences of the letter $c \in \Sigma$ in a word derived by the grammar G. The output α_G is generated through the following two steps. Firstly, the procedure generates a quantifier-free Presburger formula α_{count} which constrains the occurrences of letters in words derived by the grammar G. In particular, α_{count} is a conjunction of the four following kinds of subformulas.

- $x_c \geq 0$ for all $c \in \Sigma$.
- For each $X \in V$, let $p_1, ..., p_k$ be all productions which X is on the left-hand side. And we recap $W(X, p)$ denotes the number occurrences of X on the right-hand side of the production rule p. Then, α_{count} contains the following conjunct:

$$M_G(X) + \Sigma_{p \in P} W(X, p) y_p - \Sigma_{i=1}^k y_{p_i} = 0$$

- For each $c \in \Sigma$, α_{count} contains the following conjuncts:

$$x_c = \Sigma_{p \in P} W(c, p) y_p \wedge (x_c = 0 \vee z_c > 0)$$

- For each $s \in V \cup \Sigma$, let $p_1, ..., p_l$ be the productions where s is on the right-hand side and $X_1, ... X_l$ are their corresponding left-hand sides. Then, α_{count} contains the following conjunct: $(z_s = 0 \lor \bigvee_{i=1}^{l}(z_s = z_{X_i} + 1 \land y_{p_i} > 0 \land z_{X_i} > 0))$. If one of the X_i is the start symbol s_0, the corresponding disjunct is replaced by $z_s = 1 \land y_{p_i} > 0$.

Secondly, α_G is generated as: $\alpha_G \equiv \exists y_{p_1}, .., y_{p_m}, z_{s_1}, .., z_{s_n} . |s_0| = \Sigma_{c \in \Sigma} x_c \land \alpha_{count}$.

Example 3. For the *EDT0L* in Example 2, we generate the following Parikh-equivalent CFG G_1 $\langle V_1, \Sigma, P_1, S_1 \rangle$ where the start symbol S_1 is fresh, $V_1 = \{S_1, x, x_1, x_2, x_3\}$ and $P_1 \equiv \{(S_1, abx), (x, ax_1), (x_1, bx_2), (x_2, x), (x, x_3), (x_3, ax_1), (x_1, \epsilon)\}$.

Next, we show how to compute $Par(\mathcal{L}(G_{1_x}))$, Parikh image of CFG G_{1_x}. Let x_a and x_b be integer variables which count the occurrences of letters a and b, resp., of every word. Let $y_1, y_2, ..., y_7$ be integer variables representing for the each production in P_1 following the left-right order. And let $z_a, z_b, z_{S_1}, z_x, z_{x_1}, z_{x_2}$ and z_{x_3} be integer variables which reflect the distance of the corresponding symbols to the start symbol x in a spanning tree on the subgraph of the transformed net induced by those p with $y_p > 0$. The first kind of conjuncts in α_{count} is: $x_a \geq 0 \land x_b \geq 0$. The second is:

Variable	conjunct	Variable	conjunct
x	$1 + (y_4 + y_1) - (y_2 + y_5) = 0$	x_2	$0 + y_3 - y_4 = 0$
S_1	$0 + 0 - y_1 = 0$	x_3	$0 + y_5 - y_6 = 0$
x_1	$0 + (y_2 + y_6) - (y_3 + y_7) = 0$		

The third kind of conjuncts in α_{count} corresponding to letter a and b is: $x_a = y_1 + y_2 + y_6 \land (x_a = 0 \lor z_a > 0)$ and $x_b = y_1 + y_3 \land (x_b = 0 \lor z_b > 0)$, respectively. The fourth is as follows.

x $z_x = 0 \lor (z_x = z_{x_2} + 1 \land y_4 > 0 \land z_{x_2} > 0) \lor (z_x = z_{S_1} + 1 \land y_1 > 0 \land z_{S_1} > 0)$
S_1 $z_{S_1} = 0$
x_1 $z_{x_1} > 0 \lor (z_{x_1} = 1 \land y_2 > 0) \lor (z_{x_1} = z_{x_3} + 1 \land y_6 > 0 \land z_{x_3} > 0)$
x_2 $z_{x_2} > 0 \lor (z_{x_2} = z_{x_1} + 1 \land y_3 > 0 \land z_{x_1} > 0)$
x_3 $z_{x_3} > 0 \lor (z_{x_3} = 1 \land y_5 > 0)$
a $z_a > 0 \lor (z_a = z_{S_1} + 1 \land y_1 > 0 \land z_{S_1} > 0) \lor (z_a = 1 \land y_2 > 0) \lor (z_a = z_{x_3} + 1 \land y_6 > 0 \land z_a > 0)$
b $z_b > 0 \lor (z_b = z_S + 1 \land y_1 > 0 \land z_{S_1} > 0) \lor (z_a = z_{x_1} + 1 \land y_3 > 0 \land z_a > 0)$

Then, the length constraint of x is inferred as:

$$\alpha_{G_{1_x}} \equiv \exists y_1, .., y_7, z_a, z_b, z_x, z_{S_1}, z_{x_1}, z_{x_2}, z_{x_3} . |x| = x_a + x_b \land \alpha_{count}$$
$$\equiv \exists y_1, .., y_7, z_a, z_b, z_x, z_{S_1}, z_{x_1}, z_{x_2}, z_{x_3} . |x| = 2y_3 + 1 \land x_a = y_3 + 1 \land x_b = y_3 \land \alpha_{count}$$

6.2 STR$_{EDTOL}$: A Syntactic Decidable Fragment

Definition 2 (STR$_{EDTOL}$ Formulas). $\mathcal{E} \land \Upsilon \land \alpha_1 \land .. \land \alpha_n$ *is called in fragment* STR$_{EDTOL}$ *if $\mathcal{E}$ is a quadratic system and $FV(\alpha_i)$ contains at most one string length $\forall i \in \{1...n\}$.*

For example, $e_c \equiv xaby = ybax$ is in STR$_{\text{EDT0L}}$. But $\pi \equiv abx = xba \wedge ay = ya \wedge |x| = 2|y|$ (Sect. 3.2) is *not* in STR$_{\text{EDT0L}}$ as the arithmetic constraint includes two string lengths.

The decidability relies on the termination of ω-SAT over quadratic systems.

Proposition 3. ω-SAT *runs in factorial time in the worst case for quadratic systems.*

Let SAT-STR[STR$_{\text{EDT0L}}$] be the satisfiability problem in this fragment. The following theorem immediately follows from Proposition 3, Corollary 4.1, Parikh image of finite-index *EDT0L* systems [42].

Theorem 1. SAT-STR[STR$_{\text{EDT0L}}$] *is decidable.*

7   STR$_{\text{flat}}$ Decidable Fragment

We first describe STR$_{\text{flat}}^{\text{dec}}$ fragment through a semantic restriction and then show the computation of the length constraints. After that, we syntactically define STR$_{\text{flat}}$.

Definition 3. *The normalized formula* $\mathcal{E} \wedge \Upsilon \wedge \alpha$ *is called in the* STR$_{\text{flat}}^{\text{dec}}$ *fragment if* ω-SAT *takes* $\mathcal{E}$ *as input, and produces a tree* $\mathcal{T}_n$ *in a finite time. Furthermore, for every cycle* $\mathcal{C}(\mathcal{E}_c \rightarrow \mathcal{E}_b, \sigma_{cyc})$ *of* $\mathcal{T}_n$, *every label along the path* $(\mathcal{E}_c, \mathcal{E}_b)$ *is of the form:* $[cY/X]$ *where* X, Y *are string variables and* c *is a letter.*

This restriction implies that every node in a $\mathcal{T}_n$ belongs to *at most one cycle* and $\mathcal{T}_n$ does not contain any nested cycles. We refer such $\mathcal{T}_n$ as a *flat(able)* tree. It further implies that σ_{cyc} is of the form $\sigma_{cyc} \equiv [X_1/X_1', ..., X_k/X_k']$ and X_j' is a (direct or indirect) subterm of X_j for all $j \in \{1...k\}$. We refer the variables X_j for all $j \in \{1...k\}$ as extensible variables and such cycle as $\mathcal{C}(\mathcal{E}_c \rightarrow \mathcal{E}_b, \sigma_{cyc})^{[X_1,...,X_k]}$.

Procedure Extract_pres. From a reduction tree, we propose to extract a system of inductive predicates which precisely capture the length constraints of string variables.

First, we extend the syntax of arithmetical constraints in Fig. 1 with inductive definitions as: $\alpha ::= a_1 = a_2 \mid a_1 > a_2 \mid \alpha_1 \wedge \alpha_2 \mid \alpha_1 \vee \alpha_2 \mid \exists v. \alpha_1 \mid P(\bar{v})$. In intuition, α may contain occurrences of predicates $P(\bar{v})$ whose definitions are inductively defined. Inductive predicate is interpreted as a least fixed-point of values [46]. We notice that inductive predicates are restricted within arithmetic domain only. We assume that the system $\mathcal{P}$ includes n *unknown* (a.k.a. uninterpreted) predicates and $\mathcal{P}$ is defined by a set of constrained Horn clauses. Every clause is of the form: $\phi_{i_j} \Rightarrow P_i(\bar{v}_i)$ where $P_i(\bar{v}_i)$ is the head and ϕ_{i_j} is the body. A clause without head is called a query. A formula without any inductive predicate is referred as a *base* formula and denoted as ϕ^b. We now introduce Γ to denote an interpretation over unknown predicates such that for every $P_i \in \mathcal{P}$, $\Gamma(P_i(\bar{v}_i)) \equiv \phi^b_i$. We use $\phi(\Gamma)$ to denote a formula obtained by replacing all unknown predicates in ϕ with their definitions in Γ. We say a clause $\phi_b \Rightarrow \phi_h$

satisfies if there exists Γ and for all stacks $\eta \in Stacks$, we have $\eta \models \phi_b(\Gamma)$ implies $\eta \models \phi_h(\Gamma)$. A conjunctive set of Horn clauses (CHC for short), denoted by $\mathcal{R}$, is satisfied if every constraints in $\mathcal{R}$ is satisfied under the same interpretation of unknown predicates.

We maintain a one to one function that maps every string variable $x \in U$ to its respective length variable $n_x \in I$. We further distinguish U into two disjoint sets: G a set of global variables and E a set of local (existential) variables. While G includes those variables from the root of a reduction tree, E includes those fresh variables generated by ω-SAT. Given a tree $\mathcal{T}_{n+1}$ $(V, E, \mathcal{C})$ (where $\mathcal{E}_0 \in V$ be the root of the tree) deduced from an input $\mathcal{E}_0 \wedge \Upsilon$, we generate a system of inductive predicates and CHC $\mathcal{R}$ as follows.

1. For every node $\mathcal{E}_i \in V$ s.t. $\bar{v}_i = FV(\mathcal{E}_i) \neq \emptyset$, we generate an inductive predicate $P_i(\bar{v}_i)$.
2. For every edge $(\mathcal{E}_i, \sigma, \mathcal{E}_j) \in E$, $\bar{v}_i = FV(\mathcal{E}_i) \neq \emptyset$, $\bar{v}_j = FV(\mathcal{E}_j)$, $\bar{w}_j = FV(\mathcal{E}_j) \cap E$, we generate the clause: $\exists \bar{w}_j.\ \mathbf{gen}(\sigma) \wedge P_j(\bar{v}_j) \Rightarrow P_i(\bar{v}_i)$ where $\mathbf{gen}(\sigma)$ is defined as:

$$\mathbf{gen}(\sigma) == \begin{cases} n_x = 0 & \text{if } \sigma \equiv [\epsilon/x] \\ n_x = n_y + 1 & \text{if } \sigma \equiv [cy/x] \\ n_x = n_y + n_z & \text{if } \sigma \equiv [yz/x] \end{cases}$$

3. For every cycle $\mathcal{C}(\mathcal{E}_c \to \mathcal{E}_b, \sigma_{cyc}) \in \mathcal{C}$, we generate the following clause:

$$\bigwedge \{ v_{b_i} = v_{c_i} \mid [v_{c_i}/v_{b_i}] \in \sigma_{cyc} \} \wedge P_c(\bar{v}_c) \Rightarrow P_b(\bar{v}_b)$$

The length constraint of all solutions of $\mathcal{E}_0 \wedge \Upsilon$ is captured by the query: $P_0(FV(\mathcal{E}_0))$.

In the following, we show that if $\mathcal{T}_n$ is a flat tree, the satisfiability of the generated CHC is decidable. This decidability relies on the decidability of inductive predicates in DPI fragment which is presented in [46]. In particular, a system of inductive predicates is in DPI fragment if every predicate P is defined as follows. Either it is constrained by one base clause as: $\phi^b \Rightarrow P(\bar{v})$ or it is defined by two clauses as:

$$\phi^b{}_1 \wedge .. \wedge \phi^b{}_m \Rightarrow P(\bar{v}) \qquad \exists \bar{w}. \bigwedge \{ \bar{v}_i \pm \bar{t}_i = k \} \wedge P(\bar{t}) \Rightarrow P(\bar{v})$$

where $FV(\phi^b{}_j) \in \bar{v}$ (for all $i \in 1..m$) and has at most one variable; $\bar{t} \subseteq \bar{v} \cup \bar{w}$, $\bar{v}_i$ is the variable at i^{th} position of the sequence $\bar{v}$, and $k \in \mathbb{Z}$.

To solve the generated clauses $\mathcal{R}$, we infer definitions for the unknown predicates in a bottom-up manner. Under assumption that $\mathcal{T}_n$ does not contain any mutual cycles, all mutual recursions can be eliminated and predicates are in the DPI fragment.

Proposition 4. *The length constraint implied by a flat tree is Presburger-definable.*

Example 4 (Motivating Example Revisited). We generate the following CHC for the tree $\mathcal{T}_3$ in Fig. 3.

$$\exists n_{x_1}.\, n_x = n_{x_1} + 1 \wedge P_{12}(n_{x_1}, n_y) \quad \Rightarrow P_0(n_x, n_y)$$
$$n_{x_1} = 0 \wedge P_{21}(n_y) \qquad\qquad\qquad \Rightarrow P_{12}(n_{x_1}, n_y)$$
$$\exists n_{x_2}.\, n_{x_1} = n_{x_2} + 1 \wedge P_{22}(n_{x_2}, n_y) \Rightarrow P_{12}(n_{x_1}, n_y)$$
$$n_{x_2} = n_x \wedge P_0(n_x, n_y) \qquad\quad \Rightarrow P_{22}(n_{x_2}, n_y)$$
$$n_y = 0 \qquad\qquad\qquad\qquad\qquad \Rightarrow P_{21}(n_y)$$
$$\exists n_{y_1}.\, n_y = n_{y_1} + 1 \wedge P_{32}(n_{y_1}) \quad \Rightarrow P_{21}(n_y)$$
$$n_{y_1} = n_y \wedge P_{21}(n_y) \qquad\qquad \Rightarrow P_{32}(n_{y_1})$$
$$P_0(n_x, n_y) \wedge (\exists k.\, n_x = 4k + 3) \wedge n_x = 2n_y$$

After eliminating the mutual recursion, predicate P_{21} is in the DPI fragment and generated a definitions as: $P_{21}(n_y) \equiv n_y \geq 0$. Similarly, after substituting the definition of P_{21} into the remaining clauses and eliminating the mutual recursion, predicate P_0 is in the DPI fragment and generated a definitions as: $P_0(n_x, n_y) \equiv \exists i.\, n_x = 2i + 1 \wedge n_y \geq 0$.

STR$_{\texttt{flat}}$ *Decidable Fragment.* A quadratic word equation is called *regular* if it is either acyclic or of the form $X w_1 = w_2 X$ where X is a string variable and $w_1, w_2 \in \Sigma^*$. A quadratic word equation is called *phased-regular* if it is of the form: $s_1 \cdot \ldots \cdot s_n = t_1 \cdot \ldots \cdot t_n$ where $s_i = t_i$ is a regular equation for all $i \in \{1 \ldots n\}$.

Definition 4 (STR$_{\texttt{flat}}$ Formulas). $\pi \equiv \mathcal{E} \wedge \Upsilon \wedge \alpha$ *is called in the* STR$_{\texttt{flat}}$ *fragment if either $\mathcal{E}$ is both quadratic and phased-regular or $\mathcal{E}$ is in SL fragment.*

For example, $\pi \equiv abx = xba \wedge ay = ya \wedge |x| = 2|y|$ is in STR$_{\texttt{flat}}$. But $e_c \equiv xaby = ybax$ is *not* in STR$_{\texttt{flat}}$.

Proposition 5. ω-SAT *constructs a flat tree for a* STR$_{\texttt{flat}}$ *constraint in linear time.*

Let SAT-STR[STR$_{\texttt{flat}}$] be the satisfiability problem in this fragment.

Theorem 2. SAT-STR[STR$_{\texttt{flat}}$] *is decidable.*

8   Implementation and Evaluation

We have implemented a prototype for Kepler$_{22}$, using OCaml, to handle the satisfiability problem in theory of word equations and length constraints over the Presburger arithmetic. It takes a formula in SMT-LIB format version as input and produces SAT or UNSAT as output. For the problem beyond the decidable fragments, ω-SAT may not terminate and Kepler$_{22}$ may return UNKNOWN. We made use of Z3 [14] as a back-end SMT solver for the linear arithmetic.

Evaluation. As noted in [12,22], all constraints in the standard Kaluza benchmarks [43] with 50,000+ test cases generated by symbolic execution on JavaScript applications satisfy the straight-line conditions. Therefore, these

Table 1. Experimental results

	#√SAT	#√UNSAT	#✗SAT	#✗UNSAT	#UNKNOWN	#timeout	ERR	Time
Trau [4]	8	73	8	0	354	117	40	713 min33 s
S3P [3]	55	110	1	0	100	253	81	801 min55 s
CVC4 [1]	120	143	0	69	0	268	0	795 min49 s
Norn [2]	67	98	0	3	432	0	0	336 min20 s
Z3str3 [5]	69	102	0	0	292	24	113	77 min4 s
Z3str2 [51]	136	66	0	0	380	18	0	54 min35 s
Kepler$_{22}$	298	302	0	0	0	0	0	18 min58 s

benchmarks are not be suitable to evaluate our proposal that focuses on the
cyclic constraints. We have generated and experimented Kepler$_{22}$ over a new
set of 600 hand-drafted benchmarks each of which is in the the proposed decidable fragments. The set of benchmarks includes 298 satisfiable queries and 302
unsatisfiable queries. For every benchmark which is a *phased-regular* constraint
in STR$_{\texttt{flat}}$, it has from one to three phases. We have also compared Kepler$_{22}$
against the existing state-of-the-art string solvers: Z3-str2 [51,52], Z3str3 [9],
CVC4 [34], S3P [48], Norn [7,8] and Trau [6]. All experiments were performed
on an Intel Core i7 3.6Gh with 12GB RAM. Experiments on Trau were performed in the VirtualBox image provided by the Trau's authors.

The experiments are shown in Table 1. The first column shows the solvers.
The column #√SAT (resp., #√UNSAT) indicates the number of benchmarks for
which the solvers decided SAT (resp., UNSAT) correctly. The column #✗SAT (resp.,
#✗UNSAT) indicates the number of benchmarks for which the solvers decided
UNSAT on satisfiable queries (resp., SAT on unsatisfiable queries). The column
#UNKNOWN indicates the number of benchmarks for which the solvers returned
unknown, *timeout* for which the solvers were unable to decide within 180 s, ERR
for internal errors. The column *Time* gives CPU running time (m for minutes
and s for seconds) taken by the solvers.

The experimental results show that among the existing techniques that deal
with cyclic scenarios, the method presented by Z3-str2 performed the most effectively and efficiently. It could detect the overlapping variables in 380 problems
(63.3%) without any wrong outcomes in a short running time. Moreover, it could
decide 202 problems (33.7%) correctly. CVC4 produced very high number of correct outcome (43.8% - 263/600). However, it returned both false positives and
false negatives. Finally, non-progressing detection method in S3P worked not
very well. It detected non-progressing reasoning in only 98 problems (16.3%)
but produced false negatives and high number of timeouts and internal errors
(crashes). Surprisingly, Norn performed really well. It could detect the highest
number of the cyclic reasoning (432 problems - 72%). Trau was able to solve
a small number of problems with 8 false negatives. The results also show that
Kepler$_{22}$ was both effective and efficient on these benchmarks. It decided correctly all queries within a short running time. These results are encouraging us

to extend the proposed cyclic proof system to support inductive reasoning over other string operations (like `replaceAll`).

To highlight our contribution, we revisit the problem $e_c \equiv xaay = ybax$ (highlighted in Sect. 1) which is contained in file `quad−004−2 − unsat` of the benchmarks. $Kepler_{22}$ generates a cyclic proof for e_c with the base case $e_c^1 \vee e_c^2$ where $e_c^1 \equiv e_c[\epsilon/x] \equiv aay = yba$ and $e_c^2 \equiv e_c[\epsilon/y] \equiv xaa = bax$. It is known that for certain words w_1, w_2 and a variable z the word equation $z \cdot w_1 = w_2 \cdot z$ is satisfied if there exist words A, B and a natural number i such that $w_1 = A \cdot B$, $w_2 = B \cdot A$ and $z = (A \cdot B)^i \cdot A$. Therefore, both e_c^1 and e_c^2 are unsatisfiable. The soundness of the cyclic proof implies that e_c is unsatisfiable. For this problem, while $Kepler_{22}$ returned UNSAT within 1 s, Z3str2 and Z3str3 returned UNKNOWN, S3P, Norn and CVC4 were unable to decide within 180 s.

9 Related Work and Conclusion

Makanin notably provides a mathematical proof for the satisfiability problem of word equation [37]. In the sequence of papers, Plandowski *et al.* showed that the complexity of this problem is PSPACE [39]. The proposed procedure ω-SAT is closed to the (more general) problem in computing the set of all solutions for a word equation [13, 20, 27, 28, 40]. The algorithm presented in [27] which is based on Makanin's algorithm does not terminate if the set is infinite. Moreover, the length constraints derived by [28, 40] may not be in a finite form. In comparison, due to the consideration of cyclic solutions, ω-SAT terminates even for infinite sets of all solutions. ω-SAT is relevant to the Nielsen transform [17, 44] and cyclic proof systems [10, 30–32]. Our work extends the Nielsen transform to the set of all solution to handle the string constraints beyond the word equations. Furthermore, in contrast to the cyclic systems our soundness proof is based on the fact that solutions of a word equation must be finite. The description of the sets of all solutions as EDT0L languages was known [13, 20]. For instance, authors in [20] show that the languages of quadratic word equations can be recognized by some pushdown automaton of level 2. Although [28] did not aim at giving such a structural result, it provided *recompression* method which is the foundation for the remarkable procedure in [13] which prove that languages of solution sets of arbitrary word equations are EDT0L. In this work, we propose a decision procedure which is based on the description of solution sets as *finite-index* EDT0L languages. Like [20], we also show that sets of all solutions of quadratic word equation are EDT0L languages. In contrast to [20], we give a concrete procedure to construct such languages for a solvable equation such that an implementation of the decision procedure for string constraints is feasible. As shown in this work, finite-index feature is the key to obtain a decidability result when handling a theory combining word equations with length constraints over words. It is unclear whether the description derived by the procedure in [13] is the language of finite index. Furthermore, node of the graph derived by [13] is an extended equation which is an element in a free partially commutative monoid rather than a word equation.

Decision procedures for quadratic word equations are presented in [17,44]. Moreover, Schulz [44] also extends Makanin's algorithm to a theory of word equations and regular memberships. Recently, [24,25] presents a decision procedure for subset constraints over regular expressions. [35] presents a decision procedure for regular memberships and length constraints. [7,22] presents a decidable fragment of *acyclic* word equations, regular expressions and constraints over length functions. It can be implied that this fragment is subsumed by ours. [12,23,36] presents a straight-line fragment including word equations and transducer-based functions (e.g., `replaceAll`) which is incomparable to our decidable fragments. Z3str [52] implements string theory as an extension of Z3 SMT solver through string plug-in. It supports unbounded string constraints with a wide range of string operations. Intuitively, it solves string constraints and generates string lemmas to control with Z3's congruence closure core. Z3str2 [51] improves Z3str by proposing a detection of those constraints beyond the tractable fragment, i.e. overlapping arrangement, and pruning the search space for efficiency. Similar to Z3str, CVC4-based string solver [33] communicates with CVC4's equality solver to exchange information over string. S3P [47,48] enhances Z3str to incrementally interchange information between string and arithmetic constraints. S3P also presented some heuristics to detect and prune non-minimal subproblems while searching for a proof. While the technique in S3P was able to detect non-progressing scenarios of satisfiable formulas, it would not terminate for unsatisfiable formulas due to presence of multiple occurrences of each string variable. Our solver can support well for both classes of queries in case of less than or equal to two occurrences of each string variable.

Conclusion. We have presented the solver $\texttt{Kepler}_{22}$ for the satisfiability of string constraints combining word equations, regular expressions and length functions. We have identified two decidable fragments including quadratic word equations. Finally, we have implemented and evaluated $\texttt{Kepler}_{22}$. Although our solver is only a prototype, the results are encouraging for their coverage as well as their performance. For future work, we plan to support other string operations (e.g., replaceAll). Deriving the length constraint implied by more expressive word equations would be another future work.

Acknowledgments. Anthony W. Lin and Vijay Ganesh for the helpful discussions. Cesare Tinelli and Andrew Reynolds for useful comments and testing on the benchmarks over CVC4. We thank Bui Phi Diep for his generous help on Trau experiments. We are grateful for the constructive feedback from the anonymous reviewers.

References

1. CVC4-1.5. http://cvc4.cs.stanford.edu/web/. Accessed 14 Jun 2018
2. Norn. http://user.it.uu.se/jarst116/norn/. Accessed 14 June 2018
3. S3P. http://www.comp.nus.edu.sg/trinhmt/S3/S3P-bin-090817.zip. Accessed 20 Jan 2018
4. TRAU. https://github.com/diepbp/fat. Accessed 10 June 2018

5. Z3str3. https://sites.google.com/site/z3strsolver/getting-started. Accessed 14 June 2018
6. Abdulla, P.A., et al.: Flatten and conquer: a framework for efficient analysis of string constraints. In: PLDI (2017)
7. Abdulla, P.A., et al.: String constraints for verification. In: Biere, A., Bloem, R. (eds.) CAV 2014. LNCS, vol. 8559, pp. 150–166. Springer, Cham (2014). https://doi.org/10.1007/978-3-319-08867-9_10
8. Abdulla, P.A., et al.: Norn: an SMT solver for string constraints. In: Kroening, D., Păsăreanu, C.S. (eds.) CAV 2015. LNCS, vol. 9206, pp. 462–469. Springer, Cham (2015). https://doi.org/10.1007/978-3-319-21690-4_29
9. Berzish, M., Ganesh, V., Zheng, Y.: ZSstrS: a string solver with theory-aware heuristics. In: 2017 Formal Methods in Computer Aided Design (FMCAD), pp. 55–59, October 2017
10. Brotherston, J.: Cyclic proofs for first-order logic with inductive definitions. In: Beckert, B. (ed.) TABLEAUX 2005. LNCS (LNAI), vol. 3702, pp. 78–92. Springer, Heidelberg (2005). https://doi.org/10.1007/11554554_8
11. Büchi, J.R., Senger, S.: Definability in the existential theory of concatenation and undecidable extensions of this theory. In: Mac Lane, S., Siefkes, D. (eds.) The Collected Works of J. Richard Büchi, pp. 671–683. Springer, New York (1990). https://doi.org/10.1007/978-1-4613-8928-6_37
12. Chen, T., Chen, Y., Hague, M., Lin, A.W., Wu, Z.: What is decidable about string constraints with the replaceall function. In: POPL (2018)
13. Ciobanu, L., Diekert, V., Elder, M.: Solution sets for equations over free groups are EDT0L languages. In: Halldórsson, M.M., Iwama, K., Kobayashi, N., Speckmann, B. (eds.) ICALP 2015. LNCS, vol. 9135, pp. 134–145. Springer, Heidelberg (2015). https://doi.org/10.1007/978-3-662-47666-6_11
14. de Moura, L., Bjørner, N.: Z3: an efficient SMT solver. In: Ramakrishnan, C.R., Rehof, J. (eds.) TACAS 2008. LNCS, vol. 4963, pp. 337–340. Springer, Heidelberg (2008). https://doi.org/10.1007/978-3-540-78800-3_24
15. Diekert, V.: Makanin's Algorithm. Cambridge University Press, Cambridge (2002)
16. Diekert, V.: More than 1700 years of word equations. In: Maletti, A. (ed.) CAI 2015. LNCS, vol. 9270, pp. 22–28. Springer, Cham (2015). https://doi.org/10.1007/978-3-319-23021-4_2
17. Diekert, V., Robson, J.M.: Quadratic word equations. In: Karhumäki, J., Maurer, H., Păun, G., Rozenberg, G. (eds.) Jewels are Forever, pp. 314–326. Springer, Heidelberg (1999). https://doi.org/10.1007/978-3-642-60207-8_28
18. Esparza, J.: Petri nets, commutative context-free grammars, and basic parallel processes. In: Reichel, H. (ed.) FCT 1995. LNCS, vol. 965, pp. 221–232. Springer, Heidelberg (1995). https://doi.org/10.1007/3-540-60249-6_54
19. Esparza, J., Ganty, P., Kiefer, S., Luttenberger, M.: Parikh's theorem: a simple and direct automaton construction. Inf. Process. Lett. 111(12), 614–619 (2011)
20. Ferté, J., Marin, N., Sénizergues, G.: Word-mappings of level 2. Theory Comput. Syst. 54(1), 111–148 (2014)
21. Fischer, M.J., Rabin, M.O.: Super-exponential complexity of presburger arithmetic. Technical report, Cambridge, MA, USA (1974)
22. Ganesh, V., Minnes, M., Solar-Lezama, A., Rinard, M.: Word equations with length constraints: what's decidable? In: Biere, A., Nahir, A., Vos, T. (eds.) HVC 2012. LNCS, vol. 7857, pp. 209–226. Springer, Heidelberg (2013). https://doi.org/10.1007/978-3-642-39611-3_21
23. Holik, L., Janku, P., Lin, A.W., Ruemmer, P., Vojnar, T.: String constraints with concatenation and transducers solved efficiently. In: POPL (2018)

24. Hooimeijer, P., Weimer, W.: A decision procedure for subset constraints over regular languages. In: Proceedings of the 30th ACM SIGPLAN Conference on Programming Language Design and Implementation, PLDI 2009, pp. 188–198. ACM, New York (2009)
25. Hooimeijer, P., Weimer, W.: Solving string constraints lazily. In: Proceedings of the IEEE/ACM International Conference on Automated Software Engineering, ASE 2010, pp. 377–386 (2010)
26. Hopcroft, J.E., Motwani, R., Ullman, J.D.: Introduction to Automata Theory, Languages, and Computation 3rd edn. Addison-Wesley Longman Publishing Co., Inc. (2006)
27. Jaffar, J.: Minimal and complete word unification. J. ACM **37**(1), 47–85 (1990)
28. Jez, A.: Recompression: a simple and powerful technique for word equations. J. ACM **63**(1), 4:1–4:51 (2016)
29. Khmelevskii, I.: Equations in free semigroups, issue 107 of Proceedings of the Steklov Institute of Mathematics (1971). English Translation in Proceedings of American Mathematical Society (1976)
30. Le, Q.L., Sun, J., Chin, W.-N.: Satisfiability modulo heap-based programs. In: Chaudhuri, S., Farzan, A. (eds.) CAV 2016. LNCS, vol. 9779, pp. 382–404. Springer, Cham (2016). https://doi.org/10.1007/978-3-319-41528-4_21
31. Le, Q.L., Sun, J., Qin, S.: Frame inference for inductive entailment proofs in separation logic. In: Beyer, D., Huisman, M. (eds.) TACAS 2018. LNCS, vol. 10805, pp. 41–60. Springer, Cham (2018). https://doi.org/10.1007/978-3-319-89960-2_3
32. Le, Q.L., Tatsuta, M., Sun, J., Chin, W.-N.: A decidable fragment in separation logic with inductive predicates and arithmetic. In: Majumdar, R., Kunčak, V. (eds.) CAV 2017. LNCS, vol. 10427, pp. 495–517. Springer, Cham (2017). https://doi.org/10.1007/978-3-319-63390-9_26
33. Liang, T., Reynolds, A., Tinelli, C., Barrett, C., Deters, M.: A DPLL(T) theory solver for a theory of strings and regular expressions. In: Biere, A., Bloem, R. (eds.) CAV 2014. LNCS, vol. 8559, pp. 646–662. Springer, Cham (2014). https://doi.org/10.1007/978-3-319-08867-9_43
34. Liang, T., Reynolds, A., Tsiskaridze, N., Tinelli, C., Barrett, C., Deters, M.: An efficient smt solver for string constraints. Form. Methods Syst. Des. **48**(3), 206–234 (2016)
35. Liang, T., Tsiskaridze, N., Reynolds, A., Tinelli, C., Barrett, C.: A decision procedure for regular membership and length constraints over unbounded strings. In: Lutz, C., Ranise, S. (eds.) FroCoS 2015. LNCS (LNAI), vol. 9322, pp. 135–150. Springer, Cham (2015). https://doi.org/10.1007/978-3-319-24246-0_9
36. Lin, A.W., Barceló, P.: String solving with word equations and transducers: towards a logic for analysing mutation XSS. In: POPL, pp. 123–136. ACM (2016)
37. Makanin, G.: The problem of solvability of equations in a free semigroup. Math. USSR-Sbornik **32**(2), 129–198 (1977)
38. Parikh, R.J.: On context-free languages. J. ACM **13**(4), 570–581 (1966)
39. Plandowski, W.: Satisfiability of word equations with constants is in PSPACE. J. ACM **51**(3), 483–496 (2004)
40. Plandowski, W.: An efficient algorithm for solving word equations. In: STOC, pp. 467–476. ACM, New York (2006)
41. Rozenberg, G., Salomaa, A.: Handbook of Formal Lanuages: Volume 1 Word, Language, Grammar. Springer, Heidelberg (1997). https://doi.org/10.1007/978-3-642-59136-5
42. Rozenberg, G., Vermeir, D.: On ETOL systems of finite index. Inf. Control **38**(1), 103–133 (1978)

43. Saxena, P., Akhawe, D., Hanna, S., Mao, F., McCamant, S., Song, D.: A symbolic execution framework for javascript. In: Proceedings of the 2010 IEEE Symposium on Security and Privacy, SP 2010, pp. 513–528, Washington, DC, USA. IEEE Computer Society (2010)
44. Schulz, K.U.: Makanin's algorithm for word equations-two improvements and a generalization. In: Schulz, K.U. (ed.) IWWERT 1990. LNCS, vol. 572, pp. 85–150. Springer, Heidelberg (1992). https://doi.org/10.1007/3-540-55124-7_4
45. Seidl, H., Schwentick, T., Muscholl, A., Habermehl, P.: Counting in trees for free. In: Díaz, J., Karhumäki, J., Lepistö, A., Sannella, D. (eds.) ICALP 2004. LNCS, vol. 3142, pp. 1136–1149. Springer, Heidelberg (2004). https://doi.org/10.1007/978-3-540-27836-8_94
46. Tatsuta, M., Le, Q.L., Chin, W.-N.: Decision procedure for separation logic with inductive definitions and Presburger arithmetic. In: Igarashi, A. (ed.) APLAS 2016. LNCS, vol. 10017, pp. 423–443. Springer, Cham (2016). https://doi.org/10.1007/978-3-319-47958-3_22
47. Trinh, M.T., Chu, D.H., Jaffar, J.: S3: asymbolic string solver for vulnerability detection in web applications. In: CCS, pp. 1232–1243. ACM, New York (2014)
48. Trinh, M.-T., Chu, D.-H., Jaffar, J.: Progressive reasoning over recursively-defined strings. In: CAV (2016)
49. Verma, K.N., Seidl, H., Schwentick, T.: On the complexity of equational horn clauses. In: Nieuwenhuis, R. (ed.) CADE 2005. LNCS (LNAI), vol. 3632, pp. 337–352. Springer, Heidelberg (2005). https://doi.org/10.1007/11532231_25
50. Zheng, Y., et al.: Z3str2: an efficient solver for strings, regular expressions, and length constraints. Form. Methods Syst. Des. 50(2–3), 249–288 (2017)
51. Zheng, Y., Ganesh, V., Subramanian, S., Tripp, O., Dolby, J., Zhang, X.: Effective search-space pruning for solvers of string equations, regular expressions and length constraints. In: Kroening, D., Păsăreanu, C.S. (eds.) CAV 2015. LNCS, vol. 9206, pp. 235–254. Springer, Cham (2015). https://doi.org/10.1007/978-3-319-21690-4_14
52. Zheng, Y., Zhang, X., Ganesh, V.: Z3-str: a z3-based string solver for web application analysis. In: Proceedings of the 2013 9th Joint Meeting on Foundations of Software Engineering, ESEC/FSE 2013, pp. 114–124. ACM, New York (2013)

Continuation and Model Checking

Certifying CPS Transformation of Let-Polymorphic Calculus Using PHOAS

Urara Yamada[✉] and Kenichi Asai

Ochanomizu University, Tokyo, Japan
{yamada.urara,asai}@is.ocha.ac.jp

Abstract. This paper formalizes the correctness of a one-pass CPS transformation for the lambda calculus extended with let-polymorphism. We prove in Agda that equality is preserved through the CPS transformation. Parameterized higher-order abstract syntax is used to represent binders both at the term level and the type level. Unlike the previous work based on denotational semantics, we use small-step operational semantics to formalize the equality. Thanks to the small-step formalization, we can establish the correctness without any hypothesis on the well-formedness of input terms. The resulting formalization is simple enough to serve as a basis for more complex CPS transformations such as selective one for a calculus with delimited control operators.

Keywords: One-pass CPS transformation
Parameterized higher-order abstract syntax · Let-polymorphism · Agda

1 Introduction

Continuation-passing style (CPS) transformations are important not only as an intermediate language in compilers [1], but also as a solid foundation for control operators [9]. In particular, the one-pass CPS transformation presented by Danvy and Filinski [10] produces compact results by reducing administrative redexes *during* the transformation.

However, formalizing a CPS transformation is not easy. Minamide and Okuma [12] formalized the correctness of CPS transformations including the one by Danvy and Filinski in Isabelle/HOL, but had to axiomatize alpha conversion of bound variables. Handling of bound variables in formalizing programming languages is known to be non-trivial and the POPLMARK Challenge [4] was presented to overcome the problem. A standard technique to avoid the formalization of alpha conversion is to use de Bruijn indices [5]. However, for the one-pass CPS transformation, it is hard to determine the indices in general, because the result of the CPS transformation is intervened by static abstractions that are reduced at transformation time.

One of the promising directions to avoid the binding problem is to use parameterized higher-order abstract syntax (PHOAS) by Chlipala [6,7]. He proves the

© Springer Nature Switzerland AG 2018
S. Ryu (Ed.): APLAS 2018, LNCS 11275, pp. 375–393, 2018.
https://doi.org/10.1007/978-3-030-02768-1_20

correctness of one-pass CPS transformations for the simply-typed lambda calculus and System F in Coq, keeping the proof manageable using PHOAS.

In this paper, we prove the correctness of a one-pass CPS transformation for the lambda calculus extended with let-polymorphism using PHOAS. Specifically, we show that if a source term e_1 reduces to a term e_2, then their CPS transforms are equal in the target calculus. Thanks to the use of PHOAS, the proof is simple and reflects manual proofs. In the presence of let-polymorphism, it becomes nontrivial both to define the CPS transformation and to prove its correctness. We do so by making precise correspondence between types before and after the CPS transformation. Unlike Chlipala's work where a denotational approach is taken, we use small-step operational semantics to formalize equality. The use of small-step formalization avoids instantiation of variable parameters, making it possible to show the correctness without assuming the well-formedness condition on terms.

The contributions of this paper are summarized as follows.

- We prove the correctness of the one-pass CPS transformation for the lambda calculus extended with let-polymorphism in Agda, without assuming any well-formedness condition on terms.
- We show how to represent let-polymorphism naturally in PHOAS. We describe the difficulty that occurs in defining the CPS transformation of polymorphic values and present a solution that makes exact type correspondence before and after the CPS transformation.
- We identify where reduction is *not* preserved during the CPS transformation and thus we need to fall back to equality. This is in contrast to Danvy and Filinski [10] who show exact correspondence between reductions before and after the CPS transformation.

The paper is organized as follows. In Sect. 2, we define polymorphic types, source terms that contain let-polymorphism, typing rules and reduction rules, before we attempt to define the CPS transformation. Since there is a problem with this definition of the CPS transformation, in Sect. 3, we define target terms, typing rules, reduction rules to avoid the problem, and define the CPS transformation from source terms to target terms. In Sect. 4, we prove the correctness of the CPS transformation. We discuss related work in Sect. 5 and conclude in Sect. 6.

The complete Agda code is available from http://pllab.is.ocha.ac.jp/~asai/papers/aplas18.agda.

2   Direct-Style Terms

In this section, we introduce source terms of the CPS transformation, the typed lambda calculus extended with let-polymorphism, and show how to represent them using PHOAS.

2.1   Types and Type Schemes

We use the standard types and type schemes, informally defined as follows:

$$\tau := \alpha \mid \mathsf{Nat} \mid \tau \to \tau \quad \text{(types)} \quad \sigma := \tau \mid \forall \alpha.\sigma \quad \text{(type schemes)}$$

To represent a type variable α and a binder $\forall \alpha.\sigma$, we use parameterized higher-order abstract syntax (PHOAS) proposed by Chlipala [6,7]. Using PHOAS, types and type schemes are formally defined in Fig. 1.

$$
\begin{aligned}
\mathsf{typ}(T) &: * \\
|\cdot| &: T \to \mathsf{typ}(T) \\
\mathsf{Nat} &: \mathsf{typ}(T) \\
\cdot \Rightarrow \cdot &: \mathsf{typ}(T) \to \mathsf{typ}(T) \to \mathsf{typ}(T)
\end{aligned}
\qquad
\begin{aligned}
\mathsf{ts}(T) &: * \\
\mathsf{ty}(\cdot) &: \mathsf{typ}(T) \to \mathsf{ts}(T) \\
\forall \cdot &: (T \to \mathsf{ts}(T)) \to \mathsf{ts}(T)
\end{aligned}
$$

$$
\begin{aligned}
\mathsf{Typ} &: * \\
\mathsf{Typ} &= \hat{\forall} T : *.\, \mathsf{typ}(T)
\end{aligned}
\qquad
\begin{aligned}
\mathsf{Ts} &: * \\
\mathsf{Ts} &= \hat{\forall} T : *.\, \mathsf{ts}(T)
\end{aligned}
$$

Fig. 1. Definition of types and type schemes

The type of types, $\mathsf{typ}(T)$, and the type of type schemes, $\mathsf{ts}(T)$, are both parameterized over the type T of type variables. A type variable is represented by $|\alpha|$ which is bound by the constructor $\forall \cdot$ in $\mathsf{ts}(T)$. The dot $\cdot$ shows the position of arguments.[1] Note that the argument to $\forall \cdot$ is higher order: it receives a value of type $T \to \mathsf{ts}(T)$ which is a function in the metalanguage (in our case, Agda). In other words, we represent the binder using the binder of Agda. For example, the type informally written as $\forall \alpha.\alpha \to \alpha$ is represented formally as $\forall (\hat{\lambda}\alpha.|\alpha| \Rightarrow |\alpha|)$, where $\hat{\lambda}\alpha.\sigma$ is a function in the metalanguage.

In this section, we explicitly distinguish the informal notation (such as $\forall \alpha.\,\sigma$, $\lambda x.\,e$, and let $x = v$ in e, the letter two of which appear in the next substitution) and its formal definition (such as $\forall (\hat{\lambda}\alpha.\sigma)$, $\lambda(\hat{\lambda}x.\,e)$, and let $v\,(\hat{\lambda}x.\,e)$), respectively). We use the informal notation to explain ideas and examples, but all the technical development in this paper is performed using the formal definition. The reader could regard the former as an abbreviation of the latter.

Unlike higher-order abstract syntax, PHOAS employs the type T of type variables. The use of T instead of $\mathsf{ts}(T)$ in the definition of $\forall \cdot$ avoids negative occurrences of $\mathsf{ts}(T)$ and thus makes it possible to define $\mathsf{ts}(T)$ in Agda at all, without spoiling most of the merits of higher-order abstract syntax.

Since variables are all bound by the binder in the metalanguage, there is no way to define an open type, such as $\forall \alpha.\alpha \to \beta \to \alpha$. We will formalize all these open types (and type schemes, terms, etc.) under a suitable binder in the metalanguage.

Finally, we close $\mathsf{typ}(T)$ and $\mathsf{ts}(T)$ by quantifying over T using $\hat{\forall}$ in the metalanguage to obtain Typ and Ts. We require that T can be instantiated to any type. Typ and Ts are the definition of types and type schemes that we use in the final theorem.

---

[1] We follow the notation employed by Chlipala [6].

$\mathsf{value}(T, V)$: $\mathsf{typ}(T) \to *$
$\qquad | \cdot |.$: $\hat{\forall}\sigma : \mathsf{ts}(T). V(\sigma) \to \hat{\forall}\tau : \mathsf{typ}(T). \sigma > \tau \to \mathsf{value}(T, V)\, \tau$
$\qquad n$: $\mathsf{value}(T, V)\, \mathsf{Nat}$
$\qquad \lambda \cdot$: $\hat{\forall}\tau_1, \tau_2 : \mathsf{typ}(T). (V(\mathsf{ty}(\tau_2)) \to \mathsf{term}(T, V)\, \tau_1) \to \mathsf{value}(T, V)\, (\tau_2 \Rightarrow \tau_1)$

$\quad\mathsf{Value}$: $\mathsf{Typ} \to *$
$\quad\mathsf{Value}\, \tau = \hat{\forall}T : *. \hat{\forall}V : \mathsf{ts}(T) \to *. \mathsf{value}(T, V)\, (\tau\, T)$

$\mathsf{term}(T, V)$: $\mathsf{typ}(T) \to *$
$\qquad \mathsf{Val}(\cdot)$: $\hat{\forall}\tau : \mathsf{typ}(T). \mathsf{value}(T, V)\, \tau \to \mathsf{term}(T, V)\, \tau$
$\qquad \cdot @ \cdot$: $\hat{\forall}\tau_1, \tau_2 : \mathsf{typ}(T). \mathsf{term}(T, V)\, (\tau_2 \Rightarrow \tau_1) \to \mathsf{term}(T, V)\, \tau_2 \to \mathsf{term}(T, V)\, \tau_1$
$\qquad \mathsf{let} \cdot \cdot$: $\hat{\forall}\sigma_1 : \mathsf{ts}(T). \hat{\forall}\tau_2 : \mathsf{typ}(T). (\hat{\forall}\tau_1 : \mathsf{typ}(T). \sigma_1 > \tau_1 \to \mathsf{value}(T, V)\, \tau_1) \to$
$\qquad\qquad\qquad (V(\sigma_1) \to \mathsf{term}(T, V)\, \tau_2) \to \mathsf{term}(T, V)\, \tau_2$

$\quad\mathsf{Term}$: $\mathsf{Typ} \to *$
$\quad\mathsf{Term}\, \tau = \hat{\forall}T : *. \hat{\forall}V : \mathsf{ts}(T) \to *. \mathsf{term}(T, V)\, (\tau\, T)$

Fig. 2. Definition of terms and values

2.2 Values and Terms

Values and terms are informally defined as follows:

$$v := x \mid n \mid \lambda x. e \quad \text{(values)} \qquad e := v \mid e @ e \mid \mathsf{let}\ x = v\ \mathsf{in}\ e \quad \text{(terms)}$$

We employ the value restriction in let terms so that only values are allowed to have polymorphic types. Since our calculus is pure, the value restriction is not strictly necessary. We employ the value restriction, because we want to extend the calculus with control operators, shift and reset [9], in the future, where some kind of restriction is necessary.

Values and terms are formally defined in Fig. 2. We represent them with type families, $\mathsf{value}(T, V)\, \tau$ and $\mathsf{term}(T, V)\, \tau$, indexed by the type τ of values and terms, respectively. They are parameterized over T and V, latter of which represents the type of (term) variables. In a calculus with let-polymorphism, a variable has a type scheme rather than a monomorphic type. Thus, V is parameterized over $\mathsf{ts}(T)$ and has the type $\mathsf{ts}(T) \to *$. In the definition of $\mathsf{value}(T, V)$ and $\mathsf{term}(T, V)$, types and type schemes bound by $\hat{\forall}$ are assumed to be implicit and are inferred automatically.

The values and terms are defined in a typeful manner. Namely, typing rules are encoded in their definitions and we can construct only well-typed values and terms. A (term) variable is represented as $|x|_p$, where p represents a type instantiation relation for x. Remember that if a variable x has a type scheme σ, the type of x can be any τ that is an instantiation of σ (see Fig. 3 for the standard typing rules [14]). We encode this relationship by p of type $\sigma > \tau$ to be introduced later.

An abstraction is formally represented by λe, where e is a function in the metalanguage. The type $V(\mathsf{ty}(\tau_2))$ of the domain of the function is restricted to

$$\Gamma \vdash n : \mathsf{Nat} \qquad \frac{(x : \sigma) \in \Gamma \qquad \sigma > \tau}{\Gamma \vdash x : \tau} \qquad \frac{\Gamma, x : \tau_2 \vdash e : \tau_1}{\Gamma \vdash \lambda x.\, e : \tau_2 \to \tau_1}$$

$$\frac{\Gamma \vdash e_1 : \tau_2 \to \tau_1 \qquad \Gamma \vdash e_2 : \tau_2}{\Gamma \vdash e_1 @ e_2 : \tau_1} \qquad \frac{\Gamma \vdash v_1 : \tau_1 \qquad \Gamma, x : Gen(\tau_1, \Gamma) \vdash e_2 : \tau_2}{\Gamma \vdash \mathsf{let}\ x = v_1\ \mathsf{in}\ e_2 : \tau_2}$$

Fig. 3. Standard typing rules (in informal notation)

$$\mathsf{ty}(\tau_1) > \tau_1 \qquad \frac{(\sigma_1)[\tau_2] \mapsto \sigma_1' \qquad \sigma_1' > \tau_1}{\forall \sigma_1 > \tau_1}$$

Fig. 4. Type instantiation relation

a monomorphic type $\mathsf{ty}(\tau_2)$, because lambda-bound variables are monomorphic. For example, the type informally written as $\lambda x.\, \lambda y.\, x$ is represented formally as $\lambda\,(\hat{\lambda}x.\, \lambda\,(\hat{\lambda}y.\,|\,x\,|_p))$ where p instantiates a monomorphic type of x to itself.

A term is formally defined as either a value $\mathsf{Val}(v)$, an application $e_1 @ e_2$, or a let term $\mathsf{let}\, v_1\, e_2$. Among them, $\mathsf{let}\, v_1\, e_2$ requires explanation on both e_2 and v_1. First, we use PHOAS to represent a let binding: e_2 is a function in the metalanguage that receives the bound value v_1. The standard (informal) notation for let terms, $\mathsf{let}\ x = v_1\ \mathsf{in}\ e_2'$, is formally represented as $\mathsf{let}\, v_1\, (\hat{\lambda}x.\, e_2')$. Since v_1 is given a polymorphic type, the type $V(\sigma_1)$ of the let-bound variable is given a polymorphic type. Consequently, we can use it polymorphically in the body of e_2. Secondly, in the standard typing rules (Fig. 3), the free type variables in the type of v_1 that does not occur free in Γ are generalized. Since we cannot represent free (type) variables in the PHOAS formalization, however, we take another approach. The definition of $\mathsf{let}\, v_1\, e_2$ in Fig. 2 can be informally written as follows:

$$\frac{\hat{\forall}\tau_1.\,(\sigma_1 > \tau_1 \to \Gamma \vdash v_1 : \tau_1) \qquad \Gamma, x : \sigma_1 \vdash e_2 : \tau_2}{\Gamma \vdash \mathsf{let}\ x = v_1\ \mathsf{in}\ e_2 : \tau_2}$$

Rather than generalizing a monomorphic type τ_1 to σ_1, we start from σ_1: for v_1 to have a type scheme σ_1, we require v_1 to have any type τ_1 that is an instantiation of σ_1. Finally, Value and Term are defined by generalizing over T and V. They are indexed by τ of type Typ.

We next describe the type instantiation relation $\sigma_1 > \tau_1$. See Fig. 4. A monomorphic type $\mathsf{ty}(\tau_1)$ is instantiated to itself. To instantiate a polymorphic type $\forall \sigma_1$, where σ_1 has a form $\hat{\lambda}\alpha.\, \sigma$, we need to substitute the topmost type variable α in σ with some (monomorphic) type τ_2. The type substitution relation $(\sigma_1)[\tau_2] \mapsto \sigma_1'$ is used for this purpose. It expresses that substituting the topmost variable α of σ_1 in the body σ of σ_1 with τ_2 yields σ_1'. The definition of the substitution relation is given in the next section.

$$(\hat{\lambda}\alpha.\,|\,\alpha\,|)[\tau] \mapsto \tau \qquad (\hat{\lambda}\alpha.\,|\,\beta\,|)[\tau] \mapsto |\,\beta\,| \qquad (\hat{\lambda}\alpha.\,\mathsf{Nat})[\tau] \mapsto \mathsf{Nat}$$

$$\frac{(\hat{\lambda}\alpha.\,\tau_1(\alpha))[\tau] \mapsto \tau_1' \qquad (\hat{\lambda}\alpha.\,\tau_2(\alpha))[\tau] \mapsto \tau_2'}{(\hat{\lambda}\alpha.\,(\tau_1(\alpha) \Rightarrow \tau_2(\alpha)))[\tau] \mapsto \tau_1' \Rightarrow \tau_2'}$$

Fig. 5. Substitution relation for types

$$\frac{(\hat{\lambda}\alpha.\,\tau_1(\alpha))[\tau] \mapsto \tau_1'}{(\hat{\lambda}\alpha.\,(\mathsf{ty}(\tau_1(\alpha))))[\tau] \mapsto \mathsf{ty}(\tau_1')} \qquad \frac{\hat{\forall}\beta.\,((\hat{\lambda}\alpha.\,((\sigma_1(\alpha))\,\beta))[\tau] \mapsto \sigma_1'\,\beta)}{(\hat{\lambda}\alpha.\,\forall(\sigma_1(\alpha)))[\tau] \mapsto \forall\sigma_1}$$

Fig. 6. Substitution relation for type schemes

2.3   Substitution Relation

Following Chlipala [6], the substitution relation for types is shown in Fig. 5. It has
the form $(\hat{\lambda}\alpha.\,\tau_1(\alpha))[\tau] \mapsto \tau_1'$, meaning that τ_1 possibly contains a type variable
α and if we substitute α in τ_1 with τ, we obtain τ_1'. If τ_1 is the type variable
$|\,\alpha\,|$ to be substituted, the result becomes τ; otherwise the result is the original
type variable $|\,\beta\,|$ unchanged. Nat has no type variable and thus no substitution
happens. For a function type, the substitution is performed recursively.

Similarly, the substitution relation for type schemes is found in Fig. 6. For
$\mathsf{ty}(\tau_1(\alpha))$, the substitution relation for types is used. For $\forall(\sigma_1(\alpha))$, first remember
that $\sigma_1(\alpha)$ is a function. It has a form $\hat{\lambda}\beta.\,((\sigma_1(\alpha))\,\beta)$, meaning that σ_1 has
possibly a type variable α (to be substituted by τ) and is generalized over β.
To substitute α in σ_1 with τ, we require that the substitution relation for $\sigma_1(\alpha)$
holds for any β. Note that the quantification over β is done in the metalanguage:
this is another instance where PHOAS is used in a non-trivial way.

Chlipala [6] shows two implementations of the substitution, one in a functional form and the other in a relational form. We take the latter approach here,
because it works uniformly for all the choices of T (and V for the substitution
relation on values and terms). We can then concentrate on the parameterized
form of types $\mathsf{ty}(T)$ only, when we prove the correctness of the CPS transformation. If we employ the functional approach, we need to instantiate T to the
type $\mathsf{ty}(T')$ (for some T') of the substituted type τ. It then forces us to consider
both $\mathsf{ty}(T)$ and Typ, resulting in complication of proofs. We tried the functional
approach, too, to formalize the CPS transformation, but so far, we have not been
able to complete the correctness proof, even if we assume well-formedness [6] of
types and terms.

The substitution relation for values is shown in Fig. 7. It has the form
$(\hat{\lambda}y.\,v_1(y))\,[v] \mapsto v_1'$, meaning that substituting y in v_1 with v yields v_1'. Because
we have let-polymorphism, the substituted value v can have a polymorphic type
σ. To account for this case, v in the substitution relation is a function in the
metalanguage that receives an instantiation relation p. If the variable y to be

$$(\hat{\lambda}y. \lfloor y \rfloor_p)[v] \mapsto v\,p \qquad (\hat{\lambda}y. \lfloor x \rfloor_p)[v] \mapsto \lfloor x \rfloor_p \qquad (\hat{\lambda}y. n)[v] \mapsto n$$

$$\frac{\hat{\forall}x. \left((\hat{\lambda}y. (e(y))\,x)[v] \mapsto e'\,x\right)}{(\hat{\lambda}y. \lambda\,(e(y)))[v] \mapsto \lambda\,e'} \qquad \frac{(\hat{\lambda}y. e_1(y))[v] \mapsto e_1' \qquad (\hat{\lambda}y. e_2(y))[v] \mapsto e_2'}{(\hat{\lambda}y. ((e_1(y)) @ (e_2(y))))[v] \mapsto e_1' @ e_2'}$$

$$\frac{\hat{\forall}p. \left((\hat{\lambda}y. (v_1(y))\,p)[v] \mapsto v_1'\,p\right) \qquad \hat{\forall}x. \left((\hat{\lambda}y. (e_2(y))\,x)[v] \mapsto e_2'\,x\right)}{(\hat{\lambda}y. \mathsf{let}\,(v_1(y))\,(e_2(y)))[v] \mapsto \mathsf{let}\,v_1'\,e_2'}$$

Fig. 7. Substitution relation for values and terms

$$\frac{(\hat{\lambda}x. e(x))[v] \mapsto e'}{(\lambda\,e)\,v \rightsquigarrow e'} \qquad \frac{e_1 \rightsquigarrow e_1'}{e_1\,e_2 \rightsquigarrow e_1'\,e_2} \qquad \frac{e_2 \rightsquigarrow e_2'}{v_1\,e_2 \rightsquigarrow v_1\,e_2'} \qquad \frac{(\hat{\lambda}x. e(x))[v] \mapsto e'}{\mathsf{let}\,v\,e \rightsquigarrow e'}$$

Fig. 8. Reduction relation for terms

substituted is found with the instantiation relation p, we replace the variable with the value v applied to p, thus correctly instantiating the polymorphic value v. Other rules are standard and follow the same pattern as the substitution relation for types and type schemes. For an abstraction, we use quantification over (monomorphic) x in the metalanguage.

The substitution relation for terms is also shown in Fig. 7. For a let term, we require that the substitution relation for the value v_1 holds for any type instantiation p. Then, the substitution relation for e_2 is required for any polymorphic x. Quantification in the metalanguage is used in both cases.

2.4   Reduction Relation

The call-by-value left-to-right reduction relation for terms is shown in Fig. 8. It consists of β-reduction, reduction under evaluation contexts, and reduction of let terms. Since v in $\mathsf{let}\,v\,e$ is restricted to a value, a let term is always a redex. Note that the substituted value v can be polymorphic in the reduction of let terms.

2.5   CPS Transformation (First Attempt)

In this section, we show our first attempt to define a CPS transformation. The CPS transformation we formalize is based on the one-pass CPS transformation presented by Danvy and Filinski [10] for the lambda calculus, which we extend with let-polymorphism. The CPS transformation $\lfloor \cdot \rfloor$ of types and type schemes is shown in Fig. 9. Since we do not have any control operators, the answer type of the CPS transformation can be arbitrary. We fix the answer type to Nat in this paper.

$$\lfloor \cdot \rfloor \;:\; \hat{\forall}T : *.\,\mathsf{typ}(T) \to \mathsf{typ}(T)$$
$$\lfloor \mathsf{Nat} \rfloor = \mathsf{Nat}$$
$$\lfloor \tau_2 \Rightarrow \tau_1 \rfloor = \lfloor \tau_2 \rfloor \Rightarrow (\lfloor \tau_1 \rfloor \Rightarrow \mathsf{Nat}) \Rightarrow \mathsf{Nat}$$

$$\lfloor \cdot \rfloor \;:\; \hat{\forall}T : *.\,\mathsf{ts}(T) \to \mathsf{ts}(T)$$
$$\lfloor \mathsf{ty}(\tau) \rfloor = \mathsf{ty}(\lfloor \tau \rfloor)$$
$$\lfloor \forall \sigma \rfloor = \forall \lfloor \sigma \rfloor$$

Fig. 9. CPS transformation for types and type schemes

$$\lfloor \cdot \rfloor_{\mathsf{V}} \;:\; \hat{\forall}T : *.\,\hat{\forall}V : \mathsf{ts}(T) \to *.\,\hat{\forall}\tau : \mathsf{typ}(T).\,\mathsf{value}(T, V \circ \lfloor \cdot \rfloor)\,\tau \to$$
$$\mathsf{value}(T, V)\,\lfloor \tau \rfloor$$
$$\lfloor n \rfloor_{\mathsf{V}} = n$$
$$\lfloor |\,x\,|_p \rfloor_{\mathsf{V}} = |\,x\,|_p$$
$$\lfloor \lambda e \rfloor_{\mathsf{V}} = \lambda\,(\hat{\lambda}x.\,\lambda\,(\hat{\lambda}k.\,\lfloor e\,x \rfloor_{\mathsf{D}}\,k))$$

$$\lfloor \cdot \rfloor_{\mathsf{S}} \;:\; \hat{\forall}T : *.\,\hat{\forall}V : \mathsf{ts}(T) \to *.\,\hat{\forall}\tau : \mathsf{typ}(T).\,\mathsf{term}(T, V \circ \lfloor \cdot \rfloor)\,\tau \to$$
$$(\mathsf{value}(T, V)\,\lfloor \tau \rfloor \to \mathsf{term}(T, V)\,\mathsf{Nat}) \to \mathsf{term}(T, V)\,\mathsf{Nat}$$
$$\lfloor v \rfloor_{\mathsf{S}} = \hat{\lambda}\kappa.\,\kappa\,\lfloor v \rfloor_{\mathsf{V}}$$
$$\lfloor e_1 @ e_2 \rfloor_{\mathsf{S}} = \hat{\lambda}\kappa.\,\lfloor e_1 \rfloor_{\mathsf{S}}\,(\hat{\lambda}m.\,\lfloor e_2 \rfloor_{\mathsf{S}}\,(\hat{\lambda}n.\,(m @ n) @ \lambda\,(\hat{\lambda}a.\,\kappa\,a)))$$
$$\lfloor \mathsf{let}\, v_1\, e_2 \rfloor_{\mathsf{S}} = \hat{\lambda}\kappa.\,\mathsf{let}\,(\hat{\lambda}p.\,\lfloor v_1\, p \rfloor_{\mathsf{V}})\,(\hat{\lambda}x.\,\lfloor e_2\, x \rfloor_{\mathsf{S}}\,\kappa) \qquad \text{-- ill typed}$$

$$\lfloor \cdot \rfloor_{\mathsf{D}} \;:\; \hat{\forall}T : *.\,\hat{\forall}V : \mathsf{ts}(T) \to *.\,\hat{\forall}\tau : \mathsf{typ}(T).\,\mathsf{term}(T, V \circ \lfloor \cdot \rfloor)\,\tau \to$$
$$\mathsf{value}(T, V)\,(\lfloor \tau \rfloor \Rightarrow \mathsf{Nat}) \to \mathsf{term}(T, V)\,\mathsf{Nat}$$
$$\lfloor v \rfloor_{\mathsf{D}} = \hat{\lambda}k.\,k @ \lfloor v \rfloor_{\mathsf{V}}$$
$$\lfloor e_1 @ e_2 \rfloor_{\mathsf{D}} = \hat{\lambda}k.\,\lfloor e_1 \rfloor_{\mathsf{S}}\,(\hat{\lambda}m.\,\lfloor e_2 \rfloor_{\mathsf{S}}\,(\hat{\lambda}n.\,(m @ n) @ k))$$
$$\lfloor \mathsf{let}\, v_1\, e_2 \rfloor_{\mathsf{D}} = \hat{\lambda}k.\,\mathsf{let}\,(\hat{\lambda}p.\,\lfloor v_1\, p \rfloor_{\mathsf{V}})\,(\hat{\lambda}x.\,\lfloor e_2\, x \rfloor_{\mathsf{D}}\,k) \qquad \text{-- ill typed}$$

Fig. 10. CPS transformation (first attempt)

The CPS transformation of values, $\lfloor \cdot \rfloor_{\mathsf{V}}$, is shown at the top of Fig. 10. Given a value of type τ, it returns a value of type $\lfloor \tau \rfloor$. A one-pass CPS transformation produces the result of a CPS transformation compactly by reducing the so-called *administrative* redexes during the transformation [10]. For this purpose, the right-hand side of the CPS transformation uses the abstraction and the application in the metalanguage. We call such constructs *static*. For example, $\lfloor \lambda e \rfloor_{\mathsf{V}}$ contains two static applications in the metalanguage. (Namely, the application of e to x and of $\lfloor e\,x \rfloor_{\mathsf{D}}$ to k.) Those static constructs are reduced during the CPS transformation and the result we obtain consists solely of values of type $\mathsf{value}(T, V)\,\lfloor \tau \rfloor$, which we call *dynamic*.

The CPS transformation of terms (also in Fig. 10) is divided into two cases depending on whether the continuation is statically known at the transformation time.[2] When it is static, $\lfloor e \rfloor_{\mathsf{S}}$ is used, where the application of κ is reduced at the

---

[2] The two cases, $\lfloor e \rfloor_{\mathsf{S}}$ and $\lfloor e \rfloor_{\mathsf{D}}$, correspond to $[\![e]\!]$ and $[\![e]\!]'$ in Danvy and Filinski [10].

transformation time. When the continuation is dynamic, $\lfloor e \rfloor_D$ is used, where the continuation k is residualized in the final result. By separating $\lfloor e \rfloor_S$ and $\lfloor e \rfloor_D$, we can remove the so-called administrative η-redex [10].

The definition of the CPS transformation in Fig. 10 is well typed if we do not have let terms. However, the cases for let terms, $\lfloor \text{let } v_1 \, e_2 \rfloor_S$ and $\lfloor \text{let } v_1 \, e_2 \rfloor_D$, do not type check. Remember that v_1 in $\text{let } v_1 \, e_2$ is a polymorphic value having the type

$$\hat{\forall}\tau_1 : \text{typ}(T). \, \sigma_1 > \tau_1 \to \text{value}(T, V) \, \tau_1.$$

Similarly, after the CPS transformation, $\hat{\lambda}p. \lfloor v_1 \, p \rfloor_V$ needs to have the type

$$\hat{\forall}\tau_1 : \text{typ}(T). \, \lfloor \sigma_1 \rfloor > \tau_1 \to \text{value}(T, V) \, \tau_1. \tag{1}$$

However, $\hat{\lambda}p. \lfloor v_1 \, p \rfloor_V$ does not have this type, because we cannot pass p of type $\lfloor \sigma_1 \rfloor > \tau_1$ to v_1 which expects an argument of type $\sigma_1 > \tau_1$. Morally, τ_1 in $\lfloor \sigma_1 \rfloor > \tau_1$ should be a CPS transform of some type τ_1' and (1) could be written as:

$$\hat{\forall}\tau_1' : \text{typ}(T). \, \lfloor \sigma_1 \rfloor > \lfloor \tau_1' \rfloor \to \text{value}(T, V) \, \lfloor \tau_1' \rfloor.$$

We could then somehow obtain a value of $\sigma_1 > \tau_1$ from p of type $\lfloor \sigma_1 \rfloor > \lfloor \tau_1' \rfloor$. However, given a general type (1), there appears to be no simple way to show that τ_1 is in the image of the CPS transformation.

In order to make precise correspondence between the types of terms before and after the CPS transformation, we will define CPS terms that keeps track of the source type information.

3 CPS Terms

In this section, we define a new term that represents the image of the CPS transformation but keeps the type information before the CPS transformation. Using this term, it becomes possible to use the same type before and after the CPS transformation, avoiding the type mismatch in the type instantiation relation. We will call this term a CPS term, and the term in Sect. 2 a DS (direct-style) term.

3.1 Continuations, Values, and Terms

By carefully observing the CPS transformation, it is possible to define the syntax of results of the CPS transformation. Based on the definition given by Danvy [8], we use the following (informal) definition:[3]

---

[3] Values and terms correspond to serious expressions and trivial expressions in Danvy's notation, respectively. Besides the introduction of let terms, our notation differs from Danvy's in that we allow a term of the form $c \, @^K \, k$ where c is not necessarily a continuation variable. We need the new form during the correctness proof.

$$\mathsf{cpscont}(T, V) \ : \ \mathsf{typ}(T) \to *$$
$$|\cdot|^{\mathsf{K}} \ : \ \hat{\forall}\tau : \mathsf{typ}(T).\ V(\mathsf{ty}(\tau \Rightarrow \mathsf{Nat})) \to \mathsf{cpscont}(T, V)\,(\tau \Rightarrow \mathsf{Nat})$$
$$\lambda^{\mathsf{K}}.\ : \ \hat{\forall}\tau : \mathsf{typ}(T).\ (V(\mathsf{ty}(\tau)) \to \mathsf{cpsterm}(T, V)\,\mathsf{Nat}) \to$$
$$\mathsf{cpscont}(T, V)\,(\tau \Rightarrow \mathsf{Nat})$$

$$\mathsf{CpsCont} \ : \ \mathsf{Typ} \to *$$
$$\mathsf{CpsCont}\,\tau = \hat{\forall}T : *.\,\hat{\forall}V : \mathsf{ts}(T) \to *.\,\mathsf{cpscont}(T, V)\,((\tau\,T) \Rightarrow \mathsf{Nat})$$

$$\mathsf{cpsvalue}(T, V) \ : \ \mathsf{typ}(T) \to *$$
$$|\cdot|^{\mathsf{C}} \ : \ \hat{\forall}\sigma : \mathsf{ts}(T).\ V(\sigma) \to \hat{\forall}\tau : \mathsf{typ}(T).\ \sigma > \tau \to \mathsf{cpsvalue}(V, T)\,\tau$$
$$n \ : \ \mathsf{cpsvalue}(T, V)\,\mathsf{Nat}$$
$$\lambda^{\mathsf{C}}.\ : \ \hat{\forall}\tau_1, \tau_2 : \mathsf{typ}(T).\ (V(\mathsf{ty}(\tau_2)) \to V(\mathsf{ty}(\tau_1 \Rightarrow \mathsf{Nat})) \to$$
$$\mathsf{cpsterm}(T, V)\,\mathsf{Nat}) \to \mathsf{cpsvalue}(T, V)\,(\tau_2 \Rightarrow \tau_1)$$

$$\mathsf{CpsValue} \ : \ \mathsf{Typ} \to *$$
$$\mathsf{CpsValue}\,\tau = \hat{\forall}T : *.\,\hat{\forall}V : \mathsf{ts}(T) \to *.\,\mathsf{cpsvalue}(T, V)\,(\tau\,T)$$

$$\mathsf{cpsterm}(T, V) \ : \ \mathsf{typ}(T) \to *$$
$$\mathsf{Val}^{\mathsf{C}}(\cdot) \ : \ \mathsf{cpsvalue}(T, V)\,\mathsf{Nat} \to \mathsf{cpsterm}(T, V)\,\mathsf{Nat}$$
$$\cdot\,@^{\mathsf{C}}\,(\cdot, \cdot) \ : \ \hat{\forall}\tau_1, \tau_2 : \mathsf{typ}(T).\ \mathsf{cpsvalue}(T, V)\,(\tau_2 \Rightarrow \tau_1) \to \mathsf{cpsvalue}(T, V)\,\tau_2 \to$$
$$\mathsf{cpscont}(T, V)\,(\tau_1 \Rightarrow \mathsf{Nat}) \to \mathsf{cpsterm}(T, V)\,\mathsf{Nat}$$
$$\cdot\,@^{\mathsf{K}}.\ : \ \hat{\forall}\tau : \mathsf{typ}(T).\ \mathsf{cpscont}(T, V)\,(\tau \Rightarrow \mathsf{Nat}) \to \mathsf{cpsvalue}(T, V)\,\tau \to$$
$$\mathsf{cpsterm}(T, V)\,\mathsf{Nat}$$
$$\mathsf{let}^{\mathsf{C}}..\ : \ \hat{\forall}\sigma : \mathsf{ts}(T).\ (\hat{\forall}\tau : \mathsf{typ}(T).\ \sigma > \tau \to \mathsf{cpsvalue}(T, V)\,\tau) \to$$
$$(V(\sigma) \to \mathsf{cpsterm}(T, V)\,\mathsf{Nat}) \to \mathsf{cpsterm}(T, V)\,\mathsf{Nat}$$

$$\mathsf{CpsTerm} \ : \ *$$
$$\mathsf{CpsTerm} = \hat{\forall}T : *.\,\hat{\forall}V : \mathsf{ts}(T) \to *.\,\mathsf{cpsterm}(T, V)\,\mathsf{Nat}$$

Fig. 11. Definition of continuations, values, and terms in CPS

$$c := k \mid \lambda^{\mathsf{K}}x.\,e \qquad\qquad \text{(continuations)}$$
$$v := x \mid n \mid \lambda^{\mathsf{C}}(x, k).\,e \qquad \text{(values)}$$
$$e := v \mid v\,@^{\mathsf{C}}\,(v, c) \mid c\,@^{\mathsf{K}}\,v \mid \mathsf{let}^{\mathsf{C}}\,v\,e \ \text{(terms)}$$

We introduce continuations as a new syntactic category. It is either a continuation variable k or a continuation $\lambda^{\mathsf{K}}x.\,e$ that receives one argument. The standard abstraction is represented as $\lambda^{\mathsf{C}}(x, k).\,e$ and receives a value and a continuation. Accordingly, we have two kinds of applications, a function application and a continuation application.

The formal definition is found in Fig. 11. In this section and the next section, we mix the formal and informal notation and write $\lambda^{\mathsf{K}}x.\,e$ and $\lambda^{\mathsf{C}}(x, k).\,e$ as abbreviations for $\lambda^{\mathsf{K}}\,(\hat{\lambda}x.\,e)$ and $\lambda^{\mathsf{C}}\,(\hat{\lambda}x.\,\hat{\lambda}k.\,e)$, respectively.

Figure 11 is a straightforward typed formalization of the above informal definition except for two points. First, the type of values is the one *before* the CPS transformation. Even though $\lambda^{\mathsf{C}}(x, k).\,e$ receives x of type τ_2 and k of type

$\tau_1 \Rightarrow$ Nat, the type of $\lambda^C(x, k). e$ is $\tau_2 \Rightarrow \tau_1$ rather than $\tau_2 \Rightarrow (\tau_1 \Rightarrow$ Nat$) \Rightarrow$ Nat. Accordingly, the type of v_1 in $v_1 @^C (v_2, k)$ is also $\tau_2 \Rightarrow \tau_1$. We attach a type before the CPS transformation to a value after the CPS transformation, thus keeping the original type.[4]

Secondly, although the definition of $\mathsf{let}^C v_1 e_2$ appears to be the same as before, the instantiation relation $\sigma > \tau$ is now with respect to the types before the CPS transformation. Namely, even if we perform the CPS transformation, we can use the type instantiation relation before the CPS transformation. With this definition, we can define the CPS transformation.

3.2 Substitution Relation

Before we show the new definition of the CPS transformation, we show the substitution relation for CPS terms. Since we have two kinds of applications, one for a function application and the other for a continuation application, we define two substitution relations. The substitution relation to be used for a function application is shown in Fig. 12. It has the form $(\hat{\lambda}(y, k). e(y, k))[v, c] \mapsto e'$, meaning that a term e possibly contains a variable y and a continuation variable k, and substituting y and k in e with v and c, respectively, yields e'. It is a straightforward adaptation of the substitution relation for DS terms. As before, v is a polymorphic value receiving an instantiation relation. Since a function in CPS is applied to its argument and a continuation at the same time, we substitute a term variable and a continuation variable at the same time.

Likewise, the substitution relation for a continuation application is shown in Fig. 13. For a continuation application, only a (term) variable is substituted, because a continuation is applied only to a value and not to a continuation. Thus, when the substituted term is a continuation variable $\lfloor k \rfloor^K$, no substitution occurs.

3.3 CPS Transformation

We now show the well-typed CPS transformation from DS terms to CPS terms in Fig. 14.

This definition is exactly the same as the one in Fig. 10 except that the output is constructed using CPS terms rather than DS terms. Because the type is shared between a DS value and its CPS counterpart, the type mismatch described in Sect. 2.5 does not occur: both v_1 in the left-hand side and $\hat{\lambda}p. \lfloor v_1 \, p \rfloor_V$ in the right-hand sides of $\lfloor \mathsf{let} \, v_1 \, e_2 \rfloor_S$ and $\lfloor \mathsf{let} \, v_1 \, e_2 \rfloor_D$ have type

$$\hat{\forall}\tau_1 : \mathsf{typ}(T). \sigma_1 > \tau_1 \to \mathsf{value}(T, V) \, \tau_1.$$

---

[4] As for continuations and terms, we keep the type after the CPS transformation. Since the answer type is always Nat, we could elide it and write the type of continuations and terms as $\neg \tau$ and $\bot$, respectively.

$$(\hat{\lambda}(y,k).\,|\,k\,|^{\mathsf{K}})[v,c] \mapsto c \qquad (\hat{\lambda}(y,k).\,|\,k'\,|^{\mathsf{K}})[v,c] \mapsto |\,k'\,|^{\mathsf{K}}$$

$$\frac{\hat{\forall}x.\,((\hat{\lambda}(y,k).\,(e(y,k))\,x)[v,c] \mapsto e'\,x)}{(\hat{\lambda}(y,k).\,\lambda^{\mathsf{K}}\,(e(y,k)))[v,c] \mapsto \lambda^{\mathsf{K}}\,e'} \qquad (\hat{\lambda}(y,k).\,|\,y\,|_p^{\mathsf{C}})[v,c] \mapsto v\,p$$

$$(\hat{\lambda}(y,k).\,|\,x\,|_p^{\mathsf{C}})[v,c] \mapsto |\,x\,|_p^{\mathsf{C}} \qquad (\hat{\lambda}(y,k).\,n)[v,c] \mapsto n$$

$$\frac{\hat{\forall}(x,z).\,((\hat{\lambda}(y,k).\,(e(y,k))\,x\,z)[v,c] \mapsto e'\,x\,z)}{(\hat{\lambda}(y,k).\,\lambda^{\mathsf{C}}\,(e(y,k)))[v,c] \mapsto \lambda^{\mathsf{C}}\,e'}$$

$$\frac{\begin{array}{c}(\hat{\lambda}(y,k).\,v_1(y,k))[v,c] \mapsto v_1' \\ (\hat{\lambda}(y,k).\,v_2(y,k))[v,c] \mapsto v_2' \qquad (\hat{\lambda}(y,k).\,k_1(y,k))[v,c] \mapsto k_1'\end{array}}{(\hat{\lambda}(y,k).\,((v_1(y,k))\,@^{\mathsf{C}}\,(v_2(y,k),k_1(y,k))))[v,c] \mapsto v_1'\,@^{\mathsf{C}}\,(v_2',k_1')}$$

$$\frac{(\hat{\lambda}(y,k).\,k_1(y,k))[v,c] \mapsto k_1' \qquad (\hat{\lambda}(y,k).\,v_2(y,k))[v,c] \mapsto v_2'}{(\hat{\lambda}(y,k).\,((k_1(y,k))\,@^{\mathsf{K}}\,(v_2(y,k))))[v,c] \mapsto k_1'\,@^{\mathsf{K}}\,v_2'}$$

$$\frac{\hat{\forall}p.\,((\hat{\lambda}(y,k).\,(v_1(y,k))\,p)[v,c] \mapsto v_1'\,p) \qquad \hat{\forall}x.\,((\hat{\lambda}(y,k).\,(e_2(y,k))\,x)[v,c] \mapsto e_2'\,x)}{(\hat{\lambda}(y,k).\,\mathsf{let}^{\mathsf{C}}\,(v_1(y,k))\,(e_2(y,k)))[v,c] \mapsto \mathsf{let}^{\mathsf{C}}\,v_1'\,e_2'}$$

Fig. 12. Substitution relation for function application

$$(\hat{\lambda}y.\,|\,k\,|^{\mathsf{K}})[v] \mapsto |\,k\,|^{\mathsf{K}} \qquad \frac{\hat{\forall}x.\,((\hat{\lambda}y.\,(e(y))\,x)[v] \mapsto e'\,x)}{(\hat{\lambda}y.\,\lambda^{\mathsf{K}}\,(e(y)))[v] \mapsto \lambda^{\mathsf{K}}\,e'} \qquad (\hat{\lambda}y.\,|\,y\,|_p^{\mathsf{C}})[v] \mapsto v\,p$$

$$(\hat{\lambda}y.\,|\,x\,|_p^{\mathsf{C}})[v] \mapsto |\,x\,|_p^{\mathsf{C}} \qquad (\hat{\lambda}y.\,n)[v] \mapsto n \qquad \frac{\hat{\forall}x,z.\,((\hat{\lambda}y.\,(e(y))\,x\,z)[v] \mapsto e'\,x\,z)}{(\hat{\lambda}y.\,\lambda^{\mathsf{C}}\,(e(y)))[v] \mapsto \lambda^{\mathsf{C}}\,e'}$$

$$\frac{(\hat{\lambda}y.\,v_1(y))[v] \mapsto v_1' \qquad (\hat{\lambda}y.\,v_2(y))[v] \mapsto v_2' \qquad (\hat{\lambda}y.\,k(y))[v] \mapsto k'}{(\hat{\lambda}y.\,((v_1(y))\,@^{\mathsf{C}}\,(v_2(y),k(y))))[v] \mapsto v_1'\,@^{\mathsf{C}}\,(v_2',k')}$$

$$\frac{(\hat{\lambda}y.\,k_1(y))[v] \mapsto k_1' \qquad (\hat{\lambda}y.\,v_2(y))[v] \mapsto v_2'}{(\hat{\lambda}y.\,((k_1(y))\,@^{\mathsf{K}}\,(v_2(y))))[v] \mapsto k_1'\,@^{\mathsf{K}}\,v_2'}$$

$$\frac{\hat{\forall}p.\,((\hat{\lambda}y.\,(v_1(y))\,p)[v] \mapsto v_1'\,p) \qquad \hat{\forall}x.\,((\hat{\lambda}y.\,(e_2(y))\,x)[v] \mapsto e_2'\,x)}{(\hat{\lambda}y.\,\mathsf{let}^{\mathsf{C}}\,(v_1(y))\,(e_2(y)))[v] \mapsto \mathsf{let}^{\mathsf{C}}\,v_1'\,e_2'}$$

Fig. 13. Substitution relation for continuation application

4   Correctness of CPS Transformation

In this section, we prove the correctness of the CPS transformation, which roughly states that if e reduces to e', then $\lfloor e \rfloor_S \kappa$ is equal to $\lfloor e' \rfloor_S \kappa$. Since we introduced CPS terms, we first define what it means for CPS terms to be equal.

$$\lfloor \cdot \rfloor_V \; : \; \hat{\forall} T : *. \hat{\forall} V : \mathsf{ts}(T) \to *. \hat{\forall} \tau : \mathsf{typ}(T). \, \mathsf{value}(T, V) \, \tau \to \mathsf{cpsvalue}(T, V) \, \tau$$
$$\lfloor n \rfloor_V = n$$
$$\lfloor \lfloor x \rfloor_p \rfloor_V = \lfloor x \rfloor_p^C$$
$$\lfloor \lambda e \rfloor_V = \lambda^C(x, k). \lfloor e \, x \rfloor_D \, k$$

$$\lfloor \cdot \rfloor_S \; : \; \hat{\forall} T : *. \hat{\forall} V : \mathsf{ts}(T) \to *. \hat{\forall} \tau : \mathsf{typ}(T). \, \mathsf{term}(T, V) \, \tau \to$$
$$(\mathsf{cpsvalue}(T, V) \, \tau \to \mathsf{cpsterm}(T, V) \, \mathsf{Nat}) \to \mathsf{cpsterm}(T, V) \, \mathsf{Nat}$$
$$\lfloor v \rfloor_S = \hat{\lambda} \kappa. \, \kappa \, \lfloor v \rfloor_V$$
$$\lfloor e_1 @ e_2 \rfloor_S = \hat{\lambda} \kappa. \lfloor e_1 \rfloor_S (\hat{\lambda} m. \lfloor e_2 \rfloor_S (\hat{\lambda} n. \, m @^C (n, (\lambda^K a. \, \kappa \, a))))$$
$$\lfloor \mathsf{let} \, v_1 \, e_2 \rfloor_S = \hat{\lambda} \kappa. \, \mathsf{let}^C (\hat{\lambda} p. \lfloor v_1 \, p \rfloor_V) (\hat{\lambda} x. \lfloor e_2 \, x \rfloor_S \kappa)$$

$$\lfloor \cdot \rfloor_D \; : \; \hat{\forall} T : *. \hat{\forall} V : \mathsf{ts}(T) \to *. \hat{\forall} \tau : \mathsf{typ}(T). \, \mathsf{term}(T, V) \, \tau \to$$
$$\mathsf{cpscont}(T, V) \, (\tau \Rightarrow \mathsf{Nat}) \to \mathsf{cpsterm}(T, V) \, \mathsf{Nat}$$
$$\lfloor v \rfloor_D = \hat{\lambda} k. \, k @^K \lfloor v \rfloor_V$$
$$\lfloor e_1 @ e_2 \rfloor_D = \hat{\lambda} k. \lfloor e_1 \rfloor_S (\hat{\lambda} m. \lfloor e_2 \rfloor_S (\hat{\lambda} n. \, m @^C (n, k)))$$
$$\lfloor \mathsf{let} \, v_1 \, e_2 \rfloor_D = \hat{\lambda} k. \, \mathsf{let}^C (\hat{\lambda} p. \lfloor v_1 \, p \rfloor_V) (\hat{\lambda} x. \lfloor e_2 \, x \rfloor_D \, k)$$

Fig. 14. CPS transformation from DS terms to CPS terms

$$\frac{(\hat{\lambda}(y, k). \, e_1(y, k))[\lfloor v \rfloor_V, k_1] \mapsto e_1'}{(\lambda^C e_1) @^C (\lfloor v \rfloor_V, k_1) \sim e_1'} \; \text{eqBeta} \qquad \frac{(\hat{\lambda} y. \, e_1(y))[\lfloor v \rfloor_V] \mapsto e_1'}{(\lambda^K e_1) @^K \lfloor v \rfloor_V \sim e_1'} \; \text{eqCont}$$

$$\frac{(\hat{\lambda} y. \, e_2(y))[\lfloor v_1 \rfloor_V] \mapsto e_2'}{\mathsf{let}^C \lfloor v_1 \rfloor_V \, e_2 \sim e_2'} \; \text{eqLet}$$

Fig. 15. Beta rules

4.1   Equality Relation for CPS Terms

The equality relations for CPS terms consist of beta rules (Fig. 15), frame rules (Fig. 16), and equivalence rules (Fig. 17).

The beta rules are induced by β-reduction, continuation applications, or let reduction. In the beta rules, we impose a restriction that the values to be substituted have always the form $\lfloor v \rfloor_V$, a CPS transform of some DS term v. The restriction is crucial: it enable us to extract the substituted DS value whenever β-equality holds for CPS terms. Without this restriction, we would need some

$$\frac{\hat{\forall}x.\,(e_1\,x \sim e_2\,x)}{\lambda^{\mathsf{K}}\,e_1 \sim \lambda^{\mathsf{K}}\,e_2}\;\text{eqFunK} \qquad \frac{\hat{\forall}x,y.\,(e_1\,x\,y \sim e_2\,x\,y)}{\lambda^{\mathsf{C}}\,e_1 \sim \lambda^{\mathsf{C}}\,e_2}\;\text{eqFunC}$$

$$\frac{v_1 \sim v_1'}{v_1\,@^{\mathsf{C}}\,(v_2,k) \sim v_1'\,@^{\mathsf{C}}\,(v_2,k)}\;\text{eqApp1} \qquad \frac{v_2 \sim v_2'}{v_1\,@^{\mathsf{C}}\,(v_2,k) \sim v_1\,@^{\mathsf{C}}\,(v_2',k)}\;\text{eqApp2}$$

$$\frac{k \sim k'}{v_1\,@^{\mathsf{C}}\,(v_2,k) \sim v_1\,@^{\mathsf{C}}\,(v_2,k')}\;\text{eqApp3} \qquad \frac{k \sim k'}{k\,@^{\mathsf{K}}\,v \sim k'\,@^{\mathsf{K}}\,v}\;\text{eqRet1}$$

$$\frac{v \sim v'}{k\,@^{\mathsf{K}}\,c \sim k\,@^{\mathsf{K}}\,v'}\;\text{eqRet2} \qquad \frac{\hat{\forall}p.\,(v_1\,p \sim v_1'\,p)}{\mathsf{let}^{\mathsf{C}}\,v_1\,e_2 \sim \mathsf{let}^{\mathsf{C}}\,v_1'\,e_2}\;\text{eqLet1}$$

$$\frac{\hat{\forall}x.\,(e_2\,x \sim e_2'\,x)}{\mathsf{let}^{\mathsf{C}}\,v_1\,e_2 \sim \mathsf{let}^{\mathsf{C}}\,v_1\,e_2'}\;\text{eqLet2}$$

Fig. 16. Frame rules

$$e \sim e \qquad \frac{e_1 \sim e_2 \quad e_2 \sim e_3}{e_1 \sim e_3} \qquad \frac{e_2 \sim e_1 \quad e_2 \sim e_3}{e_1 \sim e_3}$$

Fig. 17. Equivalence rules

kind of back translation that transforms CPS terms to DS terms (see Sect. 4.3). We prove the correctness of the CPS transformation according to this definition of equality. The validity of the proof is not compromised by this restriction, because the restricted equality entails the standard β-equality. To put it from the other side, we need only the restricted β-equality to prove the correctness of the CPS transformation.

The frame rules state that any context preserves equality, including under binders. Finally, the equivalence rules define the standard equivalence relation, i.e., reflexivity, symmetry (embedded in two kinds of transitivity), and transitivity.

4.2 Schematic Continuation

The exact statement of the theorem we prove is as follows.

Theorem 1. *Let e and e' be DS terms. If $e \rightsquigarrow e'$, then $\lfloor e \rfloor_{\mathsf{S}}\,\kappa \sim \lfloor e' \rfloor_{\mathsf{S}}\,\kappa$ for any static schematic continuation κ.*

A continuation κ is schematic, if it does not inspect the syntactic structure of its argument [10]. It is defined as follows.

Definition 1. *A static continuation κ is schematic if it satisfies $(\hat{\lambda}y.\,\kappa\,(v_1(y)))$ $[\lfloor v \rfloor_{\mathsf{V}}] \mapsto \kappa(v_1')$ for any CPS values v_1 and v_1' and a DS value v that satisfy $(\hat{\lambda}y.\,v_1(y))[\lfloor v \rfloor_{\mathsf{V}}] \mapsto v_1'$.*

In words, applying κ to $v_1(y)$ and then substituting $\lfloor v \rfloor_V$ for y is the same as applying κ to the substituted value v_1'. Notice that the substituted value has, again, the form $\lfloor v \rfloor_V$. If we imposed stronger condition where the substituted value needed to be an arbitrary CPS value for a continuation to be schematic, it would become impossible to prove the correctness of the CPS transformation.

The reason the theorem requires κ to be schematic is understood as follows. Let DS terms e and e' be (in the informal notation) as follows, where we obviously have $e \rightsquigarrow e'$.

$$e = (\lambda x. x) @ 3$$
$$e' = 3$$

Under an arbitrary continuation κ, the CPS transformation of these terms become as follows:

$$\lfloor e \rfloor_S \kappa = \lfloor (\lambda x. x) @ 3 \rfloor_S \kappa = (\lambda^C(x, k). (k @^K x)) @^C (3, (\lambda^K a. \kappa\, a))$$
$$\lfloor e' \rfloor_S \kappa = \qquad\qquad \lfloor 3 \rfloor_S \kappa = \kappa\, 3$$

These two terms appear to be equal, because applying eqBeta and eqCont to the first term would yield the second. This is not the case, however, since $\kappa\, a$ and $\kappa\, 3$ are reduced during the CPS transformation. If the continuation was κ_0 that returns 1 when its argument is a variable and returns 2 otherwise, the CPS transformation of the two terms actually goes as follows:

$$\lfloor e \rfloor_S \kappa_0 = \lfloor (\lambda x. x) @ 3 \rfloor_S \kappa_0 = (\lambda^C(x, k). (k @^K x)) @^C (3, (\lambda^K a. 1))$$
$$\lfloor e' \rfloor_S \kappa_0 = \qquad\qquad \lfloor 3 \rfloor_S \kappa_0 = 2$$

Since the first term reduces to 1, these two terms are not equal.

The theorem did not hold for κ_0, because κ_0 is not schematic: it examines the syntactic structure of the argument and does not respect the property of an abstract syntax tree where the substitution may occur. In particular, κ_0 returns 1 when applied to a variable a, but returns 2 when applied to a substituted value 3. To avoid such abnormal cases, we require that κ be schematic.

4.3   Substitution Lemmas

To prove the theorem, we need to show that the substitution relation is preserved after the CPS transformation. Because we have two kinds of substitution relations, one for function applications and the other for continuation applications, we have two kinds of substitution lemmas. We first define an equality between two continuations.

Definition 2. *We write $\kappa_1 \sim_{V,C} \kappa_2$, if for any v_1 and v_1' such that $(v_1)[\lfloor v \rfloor_V, c] \mapsto v_1'$, we have $(\hat{\lambda}(x, k). (\kappa_1\, x\, k)\, (v_1\, x\, k))[\lfloor v \rfloor_V, c] \mapsto \kappa_2\, v_1'$.*

This definition states that κ_1 (after substitution) and κ_2 behaves the same, given arguments v_1 (after substitution) and v_1' that are the same.

Using this definition, we have the following substitution lemma, proved by straightforward induction on the substitution relation.

Lemma 1. *1. If* $(v_1)[v] \mapsto v_1'$, *then* $(\lfloor v_1 \rfloor_\mathsf{V})[\lfloor v \rfloor_\mathsf{V}, c] \mapsto \lfloor v_1' \rfloor_\mathsf{V}$.
2. If $(e)[v] \mapsto e'$ *and* $\kappa_1 \sim_{\mathsf{V},\mathsf{C}} \kappa_2$, *then* $(\hat{\lambda}(x,k).\lfloor e\,x \rfloor_\mathsf{S}(\kappa_1\,x\,k))[\lfloor v \rfloor_\mathsf{V}, c] \mapsto \lfloor e' \rfloor_\mathsf{S}\,\kappa_2$.
3. If $(e)[v] \mapsto e'$ *and* $(k_1)[\lfloor v \rfloor_\mathsf{V}, c] \mapsto k_2$, *then* $(\hat{\lambda}(x,k).\lfloor e\,x \rfloor_\mathsf{D}(k_1\,x\,k))[\lfloor v \rfloor_\mathsf{V}, c] \mapsto \lfloor e' \rfloor_\mathsf{D}\,k_2$.

Notice that the conclusion of the lemma states that the substitution relation holds only for a value of the form $\lfloor v \rfloor_\mathsf{V}$. We cannot have the relation for an arbitrary CPS value. Thus, we can apply this lemma only when the goal is in this form. Otherwise, we would need a back translation to convert a CPS value into the form $\lfloor v \rfloor_\mathsf{V}$. Likewise for continuation applications.

Definition 3. *We write* $\kappa_1 \sim_\mathsf{V} \kappa_2$, *if for any* v_1 *and* v_1' *such that* $(v_1)[\lfloor v \rfloor_\mathsf{V}] \mapsto v_1'$, *we have* $(\hat{\lambda}x.(\kappa_1\,x)(v_1\,x))[\lfloor v \rfloor_\mathsf{V}] \mapsto \kappa_2\,v_1'$.

Lemma 2. *1. If* $(v_1)[v] \mapsto v_1'$, *then* $(\lfloor v_1 \rfloor_\mathsf{V})[\lfloor v \rfloor_\mathsf{V}] \mapsto \lfloor v_1' \rfloor_\mathsf{V}$.
2. If $(e)[v] \mapsto e'$ *and* $\kappa_1 \sim_\mathsf{V} \kappa_2$, *then* $(\hat{\lambda}x.\lfloor e\,x \rfloor_\mathsf{S}(\kappa_1\,x))[\lfloor v \rfloor_\mathsf{V}] \mapsto \lfloor e' \rfloor_\mathsf{S}\,\kappa_2$.
3. If $(e)[v] \mapsto e'$, *then* $(\hat{\lambda}x.\lfloor e\,x \rfloor_\mathsf{D}\,k)[\lfloor v \rfloor_\mathsf{V}] \mapsto \lfloor e' \rfloor_\mathsf{D}\,k$.

4.4   Proof of Correctness of CPS Transformation

We are now ready to prove the main theorem, reshown here.

Theorem 1. *Let* e *and* e' *be DS terms. If* $e \rightsquigarrow e'$, *then* $\lfloor e \rfloor_\mathsf{S}\,\kappa \sim \lfloor e' \rfloor_\mathsf{S}\,\kappa$ *for any static schematic continuation* κ.

The proof goes almost the same as the untyped case [10]. We explicitly note when the proof deviates from it, namely, when the reduction is not preserved and the equality is instead needed (the third subcase of the case $(\lambda\,e)\,@\,v \rightsquigarrow e'$) and when the restriction on the definition of schematic is required (the case $e_1\,@\,e_2 \rightsquigarrow e_1'\,@\,e_2$).

Proof. By induction on the derivation of $\rightsquigarrow$:

(Case $(\lambda\,e)\,@\,v \rightsquigarrow e'$ **because** $(\hat{\lambda}x.e(x))[v] \mapsto e'$**)**

$$\lfloor (\lambda\,e)\,@\,v \rfloor_\mathsf{S}\,\kappa = (\lambda^\mathsf{K}(x,k).\lfloor e\,x \rfloor_\mathsf{D}\,k)\,@^\mathsf{C}\,(\lfloor v \rfloor_\mathsf{V}, (\lambda^\mathsf{K}a.\,\kappa\,a))$$
$$\sim \lfloor e' \rfloor_\mathsf{D}\,(\lambda^\mathsf{K}a.\,\kappa\,a) \qquad \text{(eqBeta)}$$
$$\sim \lfloor e' \rfloor_\mathsf{S}\,\kappa \qquad \text{(see below)}$$

To use eqBeta, we need $(\hat{\lambda}(x,k).\lfloor e\,x \rfloor_\mathsf{D}\,k)[\lfloor v \rfloor_\mathsf{V}, (\lambda^\mathsf{K}a.\,\kappa\,a)] \mapsto \lfloor e' \rfloor_\mathsf{D}\,(\lambda^\mathsf{K}a.\,\kappa\,a)$. It is obtained from Lemma 1 (3) and the assumption $(\hat{\lambda}x.e(x))[v] \mapsto e'$. The last equality is proved by structural induction on e':

(Case $e' = v$**)**

$$\lfloor v \rfloor_\mathsf{D}\,(\lambda^\mathsf{K}a.\,\kappa\,a) = (\lambda^\mathsf{K}a.\,\kappa\,a)\,@^\mathsf{K}\,\lfloor v \rfloor_\mathsf{V}$$
$$\sim \lfloor v \rfloor_\mathsf{V}\,\kappa \qquad \text{(eqCont)}$$

To use eqCont, we need $(\hat{\lambda}a.\,\kappa\,a)[\lfloor v \rfloor_\mathsf{V}] \mapsto \lfloor v \rfloor_\mathsf{S}\,\kappa$. It is obtained from κ being schematic and a trivial substitution relation $(\hat{\lambda}a.\,a)[\lfloor v \rfloor_\mathsf{V}] \mapsto \lfloor v \rfloor_\mathsf{V}$.

(**Case** $e' = e_1 @ e_2$)

$$\lfloor e_1 @ e_2 \rfloor_D (\lambda^K a.\, \kappa\, a) = \lfloor e_1 \rfloor_S (\hat{\lambda}m.\, \lfloor e_2 \rfloor_S (\hat{\lambda}n.\, m @^C (n, (\lambda^K a.\, \kappa\, a))))$$
$$= \lfloor e_1 @ e_2 \rfloor_S \kappa$$

(**Case** $e' = \mathsf{let}\, v_1\, e_2$)

$$\lfloor \mathsf{let}\, v_1\, e_2 \rfloor_D (\lambda^K a.\, \kappa\, a) \sim \lfloor \mathsf{let}\, v_1\, e_2 \rfloor_S \kappa \qquad (\mathsf{eqLet2})$$

To use $\mathsf{eqLet2}$, we need $\hat{\forall}x.\, (\lfloor e_2\, x \rfloor_D (\lambda^K a.\, \kappa\, a) \sim \lfloor e_2\, x \rfloor_S \kappa)$. It is obtained by the induction hypothesis under arbitrary variable x. This is where reduction is not preserved. We used $\mathsf{eqLet2}$, which, in informal notation, states that:

$$\mathsf{let}\, x = v\, \mathsf{in}\, e \;\rightsquigarrow\; e[v/x] \;\sim\; e'[v/x] \;\leftsquigarrow\; \mathsf{let}\, x = v\, \mathsf{in}\, e'$$

Even if we assumed $e[v/x] \rightsquigarrow e'[v/x]$, there is no way to reduce $e'[v/x]$ to $\mathsf{let}\, x = v\, \mathsf{in}\, e'$. We thus need equality here.

(**Case** $\mathsf{let}\, v_1\, e_2 \rightsquigarrow e_2'$ **because** $(\hat{\lambda}x.\, e_2(x))[v_1] \mapsto e_2'$)

$$\lfloor \mathsf{let}\, v_1\, e_2 \rfloor_S \kappa = \mathsf{let}^C (\hat{\lambda}p.\, \lfloor v_1\, p \rfloor_V) (\hat{\lambda}x.\, \lfloor e_2\, x \rfloor_S \kappa)$$
$$\sim \lfloor e_2' \rfloor_S \kappa \qquad (\mathsf{eqLet})$$

To use eqLet, we need $(\hat{\lambda}x.\, \lfloor e_2\, x \rfloor_S \kappa)[\hat{\lambda}p.\, \lfloor v_1\, p \rfloor_V] \mapsto \lfloor e_2' \rfloor_S \kappa$. It is obtained from Lemma 2 (2), the assumption $(\hat{\lambda}x.\, e_2(x))[v_1] \mapsto e_2'$, and κ being schematic.

(**Case** $e_1 @ e_2 \rightsquigarrow e_1' @ e_2$ **because** $e_1 \rightsquigarrow e_1'$) Follows directly from the induction hypothesis on $e_1 \rightsquigarrow e_1'$ with a continuation $\kappa' = \hat{\lambda}m.\, \lfloor e_2 \rfloor_S (\hat{\lambda}n.\, m @^C (n, (\lambda^K a.\, \kappa\, a)))$. The continuation κ' being schematic is shown from Lemma 2 (2). This is where the restriction on the definition of schematic is required. Since the conclusion of Lemma 2 requires that the value to be substituted is of the form $\lfloor v \rfloor_V$, we can use the substitution relation for $\lfloor v \rfloor_V$ only. Thus, we cannot show that κ' respects the syntactic structure of its argument for an arbitrary CPS value, only for a value of the form $\lfloor v \rfloor_V$.

(**Case** $v_1 @ e_2 \rightsquigarrow v_1 @ e_2'$ **because** $e_2 \rightsquigarrow e_2'$) Follows directly from the induction hypothesis on $e_2 \rightsquigarrow e_2'$ with a continuation $\kappa' = \hat{\lambda}n.\, \lfloor v_1 \rfloor_S @^C (n, (\lambda^K a.\, \kappa\, a))$. The continuation κ' can be directly shown to be schematic. $\qquad \square$

From the theorem, we can prove the correctness of the CPS transformation for terms with arbitrary T and V by quantifying Theorem 1 over T and V.

Corollary 1. *Let E and E' be Terms such that $E\, T\, V \rightsquigarrow E'\, T\, V$ for any T and V. Then, we have $\lfloor E\, T\, V \rfloor_S \kappa \sim \lfloor E'\, T\, V \rfloor_S \kappa$ for any T and V and for any static schematic continuation κ.*

In particular, for an identity continuation id, we have the following, because an identity continuation is schematic.

Corollary 2. *Let E and E' be Terms of type Nat such that $E\, T\, V \rightsquigarrow E'\, T\, V$ for any T and V. Then, we have $\lfloor E\, T\, V \rfloor_S \mathsf{id} \sim \lfloor E'\, T\, V \rfloor_S \mathsf{id}$. for any T and V.*

5   Related Work

The most closely related work is the formalization of one-pass CPS transformations for the simply-typed lambda calculus and System F in Coq by Chlipala [6], on which the present work is based. The idea of using PHOAS and of representing substitution as a relation comes from his work. The difference is that we target a language with let-polymorphism and that we use small-step semantics as opposed to Chlipala's denotational approach. While we can define the semantics of terms easily in the denotational approach by mapping terms into the metalanguage values, instantiation of parameterized variables becomes necessary to define the mappings. Accordingly, one has to assume well-formedness of terms, meaning that different instantiations of parameterized variables have the same shape. In the small-step semantics approach, we can keep parameterized variables in an abstract form all the time. Thus, we do not have to assume the well-formedness of terms.

There are several other work on the formalization of one-pass CPS transformations but for untyped calculus, as opposed to our typeful transformation where type information is built into the CPS transformation. Minamide and Okuma [12] formalized in Isabelle/HOL the correctness of three CPS transformations for the untyped lambda calculus, one of which is the one-pass CPS transformation by Danvy and Filinski. They employ first-order abstract syntax and completely formalized α-equivalence of bound variables.

Tian [15] mechanically verified correctness of the one-pass (first-order) CPS transformation for the untyped lambda calculus using higher-order abstract syntax. He represents the CPS transformation in a relational form (rather than the standard functional form), and proved its correctness in Twelf. To represent the one-pass CPS transformation in a relational form, one needs to encode the transformation that is itself written in CPS into the relational form.

Dargaye and Leroy [11] proved in Coq the correctness of the one-pass CPS transformation for the untyped lambda calculus extended with various language constructs including n-ary functions and pattern matching. They use two kinds of de Bruijn indices, one for the ordinary variables and the other for continuation variables that are introduced during the transformation, to avoid interference between them.

6   Conclusion

In this paper, we have formalized the one-pass CPS transformation for the lambda calculus extended with let-polymorphism using PHOAS and proved its correctness in Agda. In the presence of let-polymorphism, the key to the correctness proof is to make the exact type correspondence before and after the CPS transformation. We have also pinpointed where reduction is not preserved and equality is needed.

Since the current formalization is clear enough, we regard it as a good basis for formalizations of other CPS transformations. In particular, we would like to extend the proof to include control operators, shift and reset, by Danvy and Filinski [9] and its let-polymorphic extension [2]. It would be also interesting to prove correctness of the selective CPS transformation [3,13], where many case analyses are needed and thus formalization would be of great help.

Acknowledgements. We would like to thank the reviewers for useful and constructive comments. This work was partly supported by JSPS KAKENHI under Grant No. JP18H03218.

References

1. Appel, A.W.: Compiling with Continuations. Cambridge University Press, New York (2007)
2. Asai, K., Kameyama, Y.: Polymorphic delimited continuations. In: Shao, Z. (ed.) APLAS 2007. LNCS, vol. 4807, pp. 239–254. Springer, Heidelberg (2007). https://doi.org/10.1007/978-3-540-76637-7_16
3. Asai, K., Uehara, C.: Selective CPS transformation for shift and reset. In: Proceedings of the ACM SIGPLAN Workshop on Partial Evaluation and Program Manipulation (PEPM 2018), pp. 40–52 (2018)
4. Aydemir, B.E., et al.: Mechanized metatheory for the masses: the POPLMARK challenge. In: Hurd, J., Melham, T. (eds.) TPHOLs 2005. LNCS, vol. 3603, pp. 50–65. Springer, Heidelberg (2005). https://doi.org/10.1007/11541868_4
5. de Bruijn, N.: Lambda calculus notation with nameless dummies, a tool for automatic formula manipulation, with application to the Church-Rosser theorem. In: Indagationes Mathematicae, Proceedings, vol. 75, no. 5, pp. 381–392 (1972)
6. Chlipala, A.: Parametric higher-order abstract syntax for mechanized semantics. In: Proceedings of the ACM SIGPLAN International Conference on Functional Programming (ICFP 2008), pp. 143–156, September 2008
7. Chlipala, A.: Certified Programming with Dependent Types. MIT Press, Cambridge (2013)
8. Danvy, O.: Back to Direct Style. Sci. Comput. Program. **22**, 183–195 (1994)
9. Danvy, O., Filinski, A.: Abstracting control. In: Proceedings of the ACM Conference on LISP and Functional Programming (LFP 1990), pp. 151–160 (1990)
10. Danvy, O., Filinski, A.: Representing control: a study of the CPS transformation. Math. Struct. Comput. Sci. **2**(4), 361–391 (1992)
11. Dargaye, Z., Leroy, X.: Mechanized verification of CPS transformations. In: Proceedings of the International Conference on Logic for Programming Artificial Intelligence and Reasoning (LPAR 2005), pp. 211–225 (2007)
12. Minamide, Y., Okuma, K.: Verifying CPS transformations in Isabelle/HOL. In: Proceedings of the 2003 ACM SIGPLAN Workshop on Mechanized Reasoning About Languages with Variable Binding (MERLIN 2003), pp. 1–8 (2003)
13. Nielsen, L.R.: A selective CPS transformation. Electron. Notes Theor. Comput. Sci. **45**, 311–331 (2001)
14. Pierce, B.C.: Types and Programming Languages. MIT Press, Cambridge (2002)
15. Tian, Y.H.: Mechanically verifying correctness of CPS compilation. In: Proceeding of the Twelfth Computing: The Australasian Theory Symposium (CATS 2006), vol. 51, pp. 41–51 (2006)

Model Checking Differentially Private Properties

Depeng Liu[1,2], Bow-Yaw Wang[3(✉)], and Lijun Zhang[1,2,4]

[1] State Key Laboratory of Computer Science, Institute of Software,
Chinese Academy of Sciences, Beijing, China
[2] University of Chinese Academy of Sciences, Beijing, China
[3] Institute of Information Science, Academia Sinica, Taipei, Taiwan
bywang@iis.sinica.edu.tw
[4] Institute of Intelligent Software, Guangzhou, China

Abstract. We introduce the branching time temporal logic dpCTL* for specifying differential privacy. Several differentially private mechanisms are formalized as Markov chains or Markov decision processes. Using our formal models, subtle privacy conditions are specified by dpCTL*. In order to verify privacy properties automatically, model checking problems are investigated. We give a model checking algorithm for Markov chains. Model checking dpCTL* properties on Markov decision processes however is shown to be undecidable.

1 Introduction

In the era of data analysis, personal information is constantly collected and analyzed by various parties. Privacy has become an important issue for every individual. In order to address such concerns, the research community has proposed several privacy preserving mechanisms over the years (see [18] for a slightly outdated survey). Among these mechanisms, differential privacy has attracted much attention from theoretical computer science to industry [16,24,35].

Differential privacy formalizes the tradeoff between privacy and utility in data analysis. Intuitively, a randomized data analysis mechanism is differentially private if it behaves similarly on similar input datasets [15,17]. Consider, for example, the Laplace mechanism where analysis results are perturbed by random noises with the Laplace distribution [16]. Random noises hide the differences of analysis results from similar datasets. Clearly, more noises give more privacy but less utility in released perturbed results. Under the framework of differential privacy, data analysts can balance the tradeoff rigorously in their data analysis mechanisms [16,24].

D. Liu and L. Zhang—Partially supported by the National Natural Science Foundation of China (Grants No. 61532019, 61761136011, 61472473).

B.-Y. Wang—Partially supported by the Academia Sinica Thematic Project: Socially Accountable Privacy Framework for Secondary Data Usage.

ⓒ Springer Nature Switzerland AG 2018
S. Ryu (Ed.): APLAS 2018, LNCS 11275, pp. 394–414, 2018.
https://doi.org/10.1007/978-3-030-02768-1_21

Designing differentially private mechanisms can be tedious for sophisticated data analyses. Privacy leak has also been observed in data analysis programs implementing differential privacy [26,31]. This calls for formal analysis of differential privacy on both designs and implementations. In this paper, we propose the logic dpCTL* for specifying differential privacy and investigate their model checking problems. Data analysts can automatically verify their designs and implementations with our techniques. Most interestingly, our techniques can be adopted easily by existing probabilistic model checkers. Privacy checking with existing tools is attainable with minimal efforts. More interaction between model checking [2,12] and privacy analysis hopefully will follow.

In order to illustrate applicability of our techniques, we give detailed formalizations of several data analysis mechanisms in this paper. In differential privacy, data analysis mechanisms are but randomized algorithms. We follow the standard practice in probabilistic model checking to formalize such mechanisms as Markov chains or Markov decision processes [28]. When a data analysis mechanism does not interact with its environment, it is formalized as a Markov chain. Otherwise, its interactions are formalized by non-deterministic actions in Markov decision processes. Our formalization effectively assumes that actions are controlled by adversaries. It thus considers all privacy attacks from adversaries in order to establish differential privacy as required.

Two ingredients are introduced to specify differentially private behaviors. A reflexive and symmetric user-defined binary relation over states is required to formalize similar datasets. We moreover add the path quantifier $\mathcal{D}_{\epsilon,\delta}$ for specifying similar behaviors. Informally, a state satisfies $\mathcal{D}_{\epsilon,\delta}\phi$ if its probability of having path satisfying ϕ is close to those of similar states. Consider, for instance, a data analysis mechanism computing the likelihood (*high* or *low*) of an epidemic. A state satisfying $\mathcal{D}_{\epsilon,\delta}(\mathsf{F}high) \wedge \mathcal{D}_{\epsilon,\delta}(\mathsf{F}low)$ denotes similar states have similar probabilities on every outcomes.

We moreover extend the standard probabilistic model checking algorithms to verify dpCTL* properties automatically. For Markov chains, states satisfying a subformula $\mathcal{D}_{\epsilon,\delta}\phi$ are computed by a simple variant of the model checking algorithm for Markov chains. The time complexity of our algorithm is the same as those of PCTL* for Markov chains. The logic dpCTL* obtains its expressiveness essentially for free. For Markov decision processes, checking whether a state satisfies $\mathcal{D}_{\epsilon,\delta}\phi$ is undecidable.

Related Work. An early attempt on formal verification of differential privacy is [32]. The work formalizes differential privacy in the framework of information leakage. The connection between differential privacy and information leakage is investigated in [1,20]. Type systems for differential privacy have been developed in [19,30,34]. A light-weight technique for checking differential privacy can be found in [36]. Lots of formal Coq proofs about differential privacy are reported in [4–10]. This work emphasizes on model checking differential privacy. We develop a framework to formalize and analyze differential privacy in Markov chains and Markov decision processes.

Contributions. Our main contributions are threefold.

1. We introduce the logic dpCTL* for reasoning about differential privacy. The logic is able to express subtle and generalized differentially private properties;
2. We model several differentially private mechanisms in Markov chains or Markov decision processes; and
3. We show that the model checking problem for Markov chains is standard. For Markov decision processes, we show that it is undecidable.

Organization of the Paper. Preliminaries are given in Sect. 2. In Sect. 3 we discuss how offline differentially private mechanisms are modeled as Markov chains. The logic dpCTL* and its syntax are presented in Sect. 4. The semantics over Markov chains and its model checking algorithm are given in Sect. 5. Section 6 discusses differential privacy properties using dpCTL*. More examples of online differentially private mechanisms as Markov decision processes are given in Sect. 7. The semantics over Markov decision processes and undecidability of model checking is given in Sect. 8. Finally, Sect. 9 concludes our presentation.

2 Preliminaries

Let $\mathbb{Z}$ and $\mathbb{Z}^{\geq 0}$ be the sets of integers and non-negative integers respectively. We briefly review the definitions of differential privacy, Markov chains, and Markov decision processes [28]. For differential privacy, we follow the standard definition in [16,21,22]. Our definitions of Markov chains and Markov decision processes are adopted from [2].

2.1 Differential Privacy

We denote the data universe by $\mathcal{X}$; $x \in \mathcal{X}^n$ is a *dataset* with n *rows* from the data universe. Two datasets x and x' are *neighbors* (denoted by $d(x, x') \leq 1$) if they are identical except at most one row. A *query* f is a function from $\mathcal{X}^n$ to its range $R \subseteq \mathbb{Z}$. The *sensitivity* of the query f (written $\Delta(f)$) is $\max_{d(x,x') \leq 1} |f(x) - f(x')|$. For instance, a *counting* query counts the number of rows with certain attributes (say, female). The sensitivity of a counting query is 1 since any neighbor can change the count by at most one. We only consider queries with finite ranges for simplicity. A *data analysis mechanism* (or *mechanism* for brevity) M_f for a query f is a randomized algorithm with inputs in $\mathcal{X}^n$ and outputs in $\tilde{R}$. A mechanism may not have the same output range as its query, that is, $\tilde{R} \neq R$ in general. A mechanism M_f for f is *oblivious* if $\Pr[M_f(x) = \tilde{r}] = \Pr[M_f(x') = \tilde{r}]$ for every $\tilde{r} \in \tilde{R}$ when $f(x) = f(x')$. In words, outputs of an oblivious mechanism depend on the query result $f(x)$. The order of rows, for instance, is irrelevant to oblivious mechanisms. Let x, x' be datasets and $\tilde{r} \in \tilde{R}$. The probability of the mechanism M_f outputting $\tilde{r}$ on x is (ϵ, δ)-*close* to those on x' if

$$\Pr[M_f(x) = \tilde{r}] \leq e^\epsilon \Pr[M_f(x') = \tilde{r}] + \delta.$$

A mechanism M_f is (ϵ, δ)-*differentially private* if for every $x, x' \in \mathcal{X}^n$ with $d(x, x') \leq 1$ and $\tilde{r} \in \tilde{R}$, the probability of M_f outputting $\tilde{r}$ on x is (ϵ, δ)-close to those on x'.

The non-negative parameters ϵ and δ quantify mechanism behaviors probabilistically; the smaller they are, the behaviors are more similar. Informally, a differentially private mechanism has probabilistically similar behaviors on neighbors. It will have similar output distributions when any row is replaced by another in a given dataset. Since the output distribution does not change significantly with the absence of any row in a dataset, individual privacy is thus preserved by differentially private mechanisms.

2.2 Markov Chains and Markov Decision Processes

Let AP be the set of *atomic propositions*. A *(finite) discrete-time Markov chain* $K = (S, \wp, L)$ consists of a non-empty finite set S of *states*, a *transition probability function* $\wp : S \times S \rightarrow [0, 1]$ with $\sum_{t \in S} \wp(s, t) = 1$ for every $s \in S$, and a *labeling function* $L : S \rightarrow 2^{AP}$. A *path* in K is an infinite sequence $\pi = \pi_0 \pi_1 \cdots \pi_n \cdots$ of states with $\wp(\pi_i, \pi_{i+1}) > 0$ for all $i \geq 0$. We write $\pi[j]$ for the suffix $\pi_j \pi_{j+1} \cdots$.

A *(finite) Markov decision process* (MDP)[1] $M = (S, Act, \wp, L)$ consists of a finite set of *actions* Act, a *transition probability function* $\wp : S \times Act \times S \rightarrow [0, 1]$ with $\sum_{t \in S} \wp(s, \alpha, t) = 1$ for every $s \in S$ and $\alpha \in Act$. S and L are as for Markov chains. A *path* π in M is an infinite sequence $\pi_0 \alpha_1 \pi_1 \cdots \pi_n \alpha_{n+1} \cdots$ with $\wp(\pi_i, \alpha_{i+1}, \pi_{i+1}) > 0$ for all $i \geq 0$. Similarly, we write $\pi[j]$ for the suffix $\pi_j \alpha_{j+1} \pi_{j+1} \cdots$ of π.

Let $M = (S, Act, \wp, L)$ be an MDP. A (history-dependent) *scheduler* for M is a function $\mathfrak{S} : S^+ \rightarrow Act$. A *query scheduler* for M is a function $\mathfrak{Q} : S^+ \rightarrow Act$ such that $\mathfrak{Q}(\sigma) = \mathfrak{Q}(\sigma')$ for any $\sigma, \sigma' \in S^+$ of the same length. Intuitively, decisions of a query scheduler depend only on the length of the history. A path $\pi = \pi_0 \alpha_1 \pi_1 \cdots \pi_n \alpha_{n+1} \cdots$ is an $\mathfrak{S}$-*path* if $\alpha_{i+1} = \mathfrak{S}(\pi_0 \pi_1 \cdots \pi_i)$ for all $i \geq 0$. Note that an MDP with a scheduler $\mathfrak{S}$ induces a Markov chain $M_\mathfrak{S} = (S^+, \wp_\mathfrak{S}, L')$ where $L'(\sigma s) = L(s)$, $\wp_\mathfrak{S}(\sigma s, \sigma s t) = \wp(s, \mathfrak{S}(\sigma s), t)$ for $\sigma \in S^*$ and $s, t \in S$.

3 Differentially Private Mechanisms as Markov Chains

To model differentially private mechanisms by Markov chains, we formalize inputs (such as datasets or query results) as states. Randomized computation is modeled by probabilistic transitions. Atomic propositions are used to designate intended interpretation on states (such as inputs or outputs). We demonstrate these ideas in examples.

---

[1] The MDP we consider is *reactive* in the sense that all actions are enabled in every state.

3.1 Survey Mechanism

Consider the survey question: have you been diagnosed with the disease X? In order to protect privacy, each surveyee answers the question as follows. The surveyee first flips a coin. If it is tail, she answers the question truthfully. Otherwise, she randomly answers 1 or 0 uniformly (Fig. 1a) [16].

Let us analyze the mechanism briefly. The data universe $\mathcal{X}$ is $\{+, -\}$. The mechanism M is a randomized algorithm with inputs in $\mathcal{X}$ and outputs in $\{1, 0\}$. For any $x \in \mathcal{X}$, we have $\frac{1}{4} \leq \Pr[M(x) = 1] \leq \frac{3}{4}$. Hence $\Pr[M(x) = 1] \leq \frac{3}{4} = 3 \cdot \frac{1}{4} \leq e^{\ln 3} \Pr[M(x') = 1]$ for any neighbors $x, x' \in \mathcal{X}$. Similarly, $\Pr[M(x) = 0] \leq e^{\ln 3} \Pr[M(x') = 0]$. The survey mechanism is hence $(\ln 3, 0)$-differentially private. The random noise boosts the probability of answering 1 or 0 to at least $\frac{1}{4}$ regardless of diagnoses. Inferences on individual diagnosis can be plausibly denied.

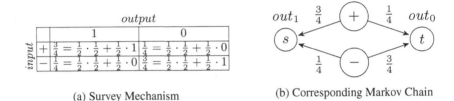

(a) Survey Mechanism   (b) Corresponding Markov Chain

Fig. 1. Survey mechanism with $\ln 3$-differential privacy

Figure 1b shows the corresponding Markov chain. In the figure, the states $+$ and $-$ denote positive or negative diagnoses respectively; the states s and t denote answers to the survey question and hence $out_1 \in L(s)$ and $out_0 \in L(t)$. States $+$ and $-$ are neighbors. Missing transitions (such as those from s and t) lead to a special state $\dagger$ with a self-loop. We omit such transitions and the state $\dagger$ for clarity.

3.2 Truncated α-Geometric Mechanism

More sophisticated differentially private mechanisms are available. Consider a query $f : \mathcal{X}^n \to \{0, 1, \ldots, m\}$. Let $\alpha \in (0, 1)$. The α-geometric mechanism outputs $f(x) + Y$ on a dataset x where Y is a random variable with the geometric distribution [21, 22] :

$$\Pr[Y = y] = \frac{1 - \alpha}{1 + \alpha} \alpha^{|y|} \text{ for } y \in \mathbb{Z}$$

The α-geometric mechanism is oblivious since it has the same output distribution on any inputs x, x' with $f(x) = f(x')$. It is $(-\Delta(f) \ln \alpha, 0)$-differentially private for any query f with sensitivity $\Delta(f)$. Observe that the privacy guarantee $(-\Delta(f) \ln \alpha, 0)$ depends on the sensitivity of the query f. To achieve $(\epsilon, 0)$-differential privacy using the α-geometric mechanism, one first decides the sensitivity of the query and then computes the parameter $\alpha = e^{-\epsilon/\Delta(f)}$.

The range of the mechanism is $\mathbb{Z}$. It may give nonsensical outputs such as negative integers for non-negative queries. The *truncated α-geometric mechanism* over $\{0, 1, \ldots, m\}$ outputs $f(x) + Z$ where Z is a random variable with the distribution:

$$\Pr[Z = z] = \begin{cases} 0 & \text{if } z < -f(x) \\ \frac{\alpha^{f(x)}}{1+\alpha} & \text{if } z = -f(x) \\ \frac{1-\alpha}{1+\alpha}\alpha^{|z|} & \text{if } -f(x) < z < m - f(x) \\ \frac{\alpha^{m-f(x)}}{1+\alpha} & \text{if } z = m - f(x) \\ 0 & \text{if } z > m - f(x) \end{cases}$$

Note the range of the truncated α-geometric mechanism is $\{0, 1, \ldots, m\}$. The truncated α-geometric mechanism is again oblivious; it is also $(-\Delta(f)\ln\alpha, 0)$-differentially private for any query f with sensitivity $\Delta(f)$. The truncated $\frac{1}{2}$-geometric mechanism over $\{0, 1, \ldots, 5\}$ is given in Fig. 2a.

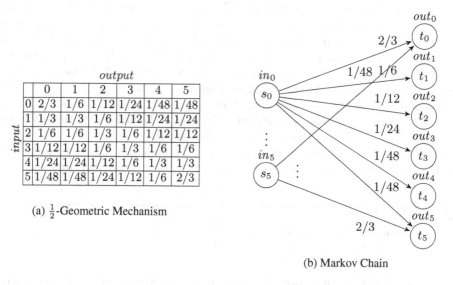

		output				
	0	1	2	3	4	5
0	2/3	1/6	1/12	1/24	1/48	1/48
1	1/3	1/3	1/6	1/12	1/24	1/24
2	1/6	1/6	1/3	1/6	1/12	1/12
3	1/12	1/12	1/6	1/3	1/6	1/6
4	1/24	1/24	1/12	1/6	1/3	1/3
5	1/48	1/48	1/24	1/12	1/6	2/3

(a) $\frac{1}{2}$-Geometric Mechanism

(b) Markov Chain

Fig. 2. A Markov chain for $\frac{1}{2}$-geometric mechanism

Similar to the survey mechanism, it is straightforward to model the truncated $\frac{1}{2}$-geometric mechanism as a Markov chain. One could naïvely take datasets as inputs in the formalization, but it is unnecessary. Recall that the truncated $\frac{1}{2}$-geometric mechanism is oblivious. The mechanism depends on query results but not datasets. It hence suffices to consider the range of query f as inputs. Let the state s_k and t_l denote the input k and output l respectively. Define $S = \{s_k, t_k : k \in \{0, 1, \ldots, m\}\}$. The probability transition $\wp(s_k, t_l)$ is the probability of the output l on the input k as defined in the mechanism. Moreover, we have $in_k \in L(s_k)$ and $out_k \in L(t_k)$ for $k \in \{0, 1, \ldots, n\}$. If $\Delta(f) = 1$, $|f(x) - f(x')| \leq 1$

for every neighbors $x, x' \in \mathcal{X}^n$. Subsequently, s_k and s_l are neighbors iff $|k-l| \leq 1$ in our model. Figure 2b gives the Markov chain for the truncated $\frac{1}{2}$-geometric mechanism over $\{0, 1, \ldots, 5\}$.

3.3 Subsampling Majority

The sensitivity of queries is required to apply the (truncated) α-geometric mechanism. Recall that the sensitivity is the maximal difference of query results on any two neighbors. Two practical problems may arise for mechanisms depending on query sensitivity. First, sensitivity of queries can be hard to compute. Second, the sensitivity over arbitrary neighbors can be too conservative for the actual dataset in use. One therefore would like to have mechanisms independent of query sensitivity.

Subsampling is a technique to design such mechanisms [16]. Concretely, let us consider $\mathcal{X} = \{R, B\}$ (for red and blue team members) and a dataset $d \in \mathcal{X}^n$. Suppose we would like to ask which team is the majority in the dataset while respecting individual privacy. This can be achieved as follows (Algorithm 1). The mechanism first samples m sub-datasets $\hat{d}_1, \hat{d}_2, \ldots, \hat{d}_m$ from d (line 3). It then computes the majority of each sub-dataset and obtains m sub-results. Let $count_R$ and $count_B$ be the number of sub-datasets with the majority R and B respectively (line 4). Since there are m sub-datasets, we have $count_R + count_B = m$. To ensure differential privacy, the mechanism makes sure the difference $|count_R - count_B|$ is significantly large after perturbation. In line 6, $Lap(p)$ denotes the continuous random variable with the probability density function $f(x) = \frac{1}{2p} e^{-|x|/p}$ of the Laplace distribution. If the perturbed difference is sufficiently large, the mechanism reports 1 if the majority of the m sub-results is R or 0 if it is B (line 7). Otherwise, no information is revealed (line 9).

Algorithm 1. Subsampling Majority

1: **function** SUBSAMPLINGMAJORITY(d, f)
Require: $d \in \{R, B\}^n$, $f : \{R, B\}^* \to \{R, B\}$
2:     $q, m \leftarrow \frac{\epsilon}{64 \ln(1/\delta)}, \frac{\log(n/\delta)}{q^2}$
3:     Subsample m data sets $\hat{d}_1, \hat{d}_2, \ldots, \hat{d}_m$ from d where each row of d is chosen with probability q
4:     $count_R, count_B \leftarrow |\{i : f(\hat{d}_i) = R\}|, |\{i : f(\hat{d}_i) = B\}|$
5:     $r \leftarrow |count_R - count_B|/(4mq) - 1$
6:     **if** $r + Lap(\frac{1}{\epsilon}) > \ln(1/\delta)/\epsilon$ **then**
7:         **if** $count_R \geq count_B$ **then return** 1 **else return** 0
8:     **else**
9:         **return** $\bot$
10: **end function**

Fix the dataset size n and privacy parameters ϵ, δ, the subsampling majority mechanism can be modeled by a Markov chain. Figure 3 gives a sketch of the Markov chain for $n = 3$. The leftmost four states represent all possible datasets. Given a dataset, m samples are taken with replacement. Outcomes of these samples are denoted by $(count_R, count_B)$. There are only $m + 1$ outcomes: $(m, 0), (m - 1, 1), \ldots, (0, m)$. Each outcome is represented by a state in Fig. 3. From each dataset, the probability distribution on all outcomes gives the transition probability. Next, observe that $|count_R - count_B|$ can have only finitely many values. The values of r (line 5) hence belong to a finite set $\{r_m, \ldots, r_M\}$ with the minimum r_m and maximum r_M. For instance, both outcomes $(m, 0)$ and $(0, m)$ transit to the state $r_M = 1/(4q) - 1$ with probability 1. For each $r \in \{r_m, \ldots, r_M\}$, the probability of having $r + Lap(\frac{1}{\epsilon}) > \ln(1/\delta)/\epsilon$ (line 6) is equal to the probability of $Lap(\frac{1}{\epsilon}) > \ln(1/\delta)/\epsilon - r$. This is equal to $\int_{\ln(1/\delta)/\epsilon - r}^{\infty} \frac{\epsilon}{2} e^{-\epsilon|x|} dx$. From each state $r \in \{r_m, \ldots, r_M\}$, it hence goes to the state $\top$ with probability $\int_{\ln(1/\delta)/\epsilon - r}^{\infty} \frac{\epsilon}{2} e^{-\epsilon|x|} dx$ and to the state $\bot$ with probability $1 - \int_{\ln(1/\delta)/\epsilon - r}^{\infty} \frac{\epsilon}{2} e^{-\epsilon|x|} dx$. Finally, the Markov chain moves from the state $\top$ to 1 if $count_R \geq count_B$; otherwise, it moves to 0. Two dataset states are neighbors if they differ at most one member. For example, rrb is a neighbor of rrr and rbb but not bbb.

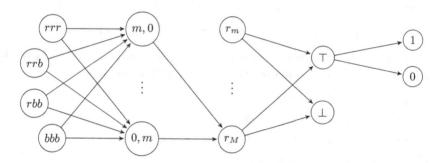

Fig. 3. Markov chain for subsampling majority

4   The Logic dpCTL*

The logic dpCTL* is designed to specify differentially private mechanisms. We introduce the differentially private path quantifier $\mathcal{D}_{\epsilon,\delta}$ and neighborhood relations for neighbors in dpCTL*. For any path formula ϕ, a state s in a Markov chain K satisfies $\mathcal{D}_{\epsilon,\delta}\phi$ if the probability of having paths satisfying ϕ from s is close to the probabilities of having paths satisfying ϕ from its neighbors.

4.1   Syntax

The syntax of dpCTL* state and path formulae is given by:

$$\Phi ::= p \mid \neg\Phi \mid \Phi \wedge \Phi \mid \mathbb{P}_J\phi \mid \mathcal{D}_{\epsilon,\delta}\phi$$
$$\phi ::= \Phi \mid \neg\phi \mid \phi \wedge \phi \mid \mathsf{X}\phi \mid \phi \,\mathsf{U}\, \phi$$

A *state* formula Φ is either an atomic proposition p, the negation of a state formula, the conjunction of two state formulae, the *probabilistic* operator $\mathbb{P}_J$ with J an interval in $[0,1]$ followed by a path formula, or the *differentially private* operator $\mathcal{D}_{\epsilon,\delta}$ with two non-negative real numbers ϵ and δ followed by a path formula. A *path* formula ϕ is simply a linear temporal logic formula, with temporal operator *next* (X) followed by a path formula, and *until* operator (U) enclosed by two path formulae. We define $F\phi \equiv true \ \mathsf{U} \ \phi$ and $G\phi \equiv \neg F(\neg\phi)$ as usual.

As in the classical setting, we consider the sublogic dpCTL by allowing only path formulae of the form $\mathsf{X}\Phi$ and $\Phi \ \mathsf{U} \ \Phi$. Moreover, one obtains PCTL [23] and PCTL* [11] from dpCTL and dpCTL* by removing the differentially private operator $\mathcal{D}_{\epsilon,\delta}$.

5   dpCTL* for Markov Chains

Given a Markov chain $K = (S, \wp, L)$, a *neighborhood relation* $N_S \subseteq S \times S$ is a reflexive and symmetric relation on S. We will write sN_St when $(s,t) \in N_S$. If sN_St, we say s and t are *neighbors* or t is a *neighbor* of s. For any Markov chain K, neighborhood relation N on S, $s \in S$, and a path formula ϕ, define

$$\mathrm{Pr}_N^K(s,\phi) = \mathrm{Pr}[\{\pi : K, N, \pi \models \phi \text{ with } \pi_0 = s\}].$$

That is, $\mathrm{Pr}_N^K(s,\phi)$ denotes the probability of paths satisfying ϕ from s on K with N. Define the satisfaction relation $K, N_S, s \models \Phi$ as follows.

$$K, N_S, s \models p \text{ if } p \in L(s)$$
$$K, N_S, s \models \neg\Phi \text{ if } K, N_S, s \not\models \Phi$$
$$K, N_S, s \models \Phi_0 \wedge \Phi_1 \text{ if } K, N_S, s \models \Phi_0 \text{ and } K, N_S, s \models \Phi_1$$
$$K, N_S, s \models \mathbb{P}_J\phi \text{ if } \mathrm{Pr}_{N_S}^K(s,\phi) \in J$$
$$K, N_S, s \models \mathcal{D}_{\epsilon,\delta}\phi \text{ if for every } t \text{ with } sN_St, \mathrm{Pr}_{N_S}^K(s,\phi) \leq e^\epsilon \mathrm{Pr}_{N_S}^K(t,\phi) + \delta \text{ and}$$
$$\mathrm{Pr}_{N_S}^K(t,\phi) \leq e^\epsilon \mathrm{Pr}_{N_S}^K(s,\phi) + \delta$$

Moreover, the relation $K, N_S, \pi \models \phi$ is defined as in the standard linear temporal logic formulae [25]. We only recall the semantics for the temporal operators X and U:

$$K, N_S, \pi \models \mathsf{X}\phi \text{ if } K, N_S, \pi[1] \models \phi$$
$$K, N_S, \pi \models \phi \ \mathsf{U} \ \psi \text{ if there is a } j \geq 0 \text{ such that } K, N_S, \pi[j] \models \psi \text{ and}$$
$$K, N_S, \pi[k] \models \phi \text{ for every } 0 \leq k < j$$

Other than the differentially private operator, the semantics of dpCTL* is standard [2]. To intuit the semantics of $\mathcal{D}_{\epsilon,\delta}\phi$, recall that $\mathrm{Pr}_N^K(s,\phi)$ is the probability of having paths satisfying ϕ from s. A state s satisfies $\mathcal{D}_{\epsilon,\delta}\phi$ if the probability of having paths satisfying ϕ from s is (ϵ,δ)-close to those from every neighbor of s. Informally, it is probabilistically similar to observe paths satisfying ϕ from s and from its neighbors.

5.1   Model Checking

We describe the model checking algorithm for dpCTL. The algorithm follows the classical algorithms for PCTL by computing the states satisfying sub state-formulae inductively [2,23]. It hence suffices to consider the inductive step where the states satisfying the subformula $\mathcal{D}_{\epsilon,\delta}(\phi)$ are to be computed.

In the classical PCTL model checking algorithm for Markov chains, states satisfying the subformula $\mathbb{P}_J\phi$ are obtained by computing $\mathrm{Pr}^K_{N_S}(s,\phi)$ for $s \in S$. These probabilities can be obtained by solving linear equations or through iterative approximations. We summarize it in the following theorem (details see [2]):

Lemma 1. *Let $K = (S,\wp,L)$ be a Markov chain, N_S a neighborhood relation on S, $s \in S$, and $B,C \subseteq S$. The probabilities $\mathrm{Pr}^K_{N_S}(s,\bigcirc B)$ and $\mathrm{Pr}^K_{N_S}(s,B\cup C)$ are computable within time polynomial in $|S|$.*

In Lemma 1, we abuse the notation slightly to admit path formulae of the form $\bigcirc B$ (next B) and $B \cup C$ (B until C) with $B,C \subseteq S$ as in [2]. They are interpreted by introducing new atomic propositions B and C for each $s \in B$ and $s \in C$ respectively.

In order to determine the set $\{s : K, N_S, s \models \mathcal{D}_{\epsilon,\delta}\phi\}$, our algorithm computes the probabilities $p(s) = \mathrm{Pr}^K_{N_S}(s,\phi)$ for every $s \in S$ (Algorithm 2). For each $s \in S$, it then compares the probabilities $p(s)$ and $p(t)$ for every neighbor t of s. If there is a neighbor t such that $p(s)$ and $p(t)$ are not (ϵ,δ)-close, the state s is removed from the result. Algorithm 2 returns all states which are (ϵ,δ)-close to their neighbors. The algorithm requires at most $O(|S|^2)$ additional steps. We hence have the following results:

Algorithm 2. SAT(K, N_S, ϕ)

```
1: procedure SAT(K, N_S, φ)
2:     match φ with                                          ▷ by Lemma 1
3:         case XΨ:
4:             B ← SAT(K, N_S, Ψ)
5:             p(s) ← Pr^K_{N_S}(s, ◯B) for every s ∈ S
6:         case Ψ U Ψ':
7:             B ← SAT(K, N_S, Ψ)
8:             C ← SAT(K, N_S, Ψ')
9:             p(s) ← Pr^K_{N_S}(s, B U C) for every s ∈ S
10:    R ← S
11:    for s ∈ S do
12:        for t with sN_St do
13:            if p(s) ≰ e^ε p(t) + δ or p(t) ≰ e^ε p(s) + δ then remove s from R
14:    return R
15: end procedure
```

Proposition 1. *Let $K = (S, \wp, L)$ be a Markov chain, N_S a neighborhood relation on S, and ϕ a dpCTL path formula. $\{s : K, N_S, s \models \mathcal{D}_{\epsilon,\delta}\phi\}$ is computable within time polynomial in $|S|$ and $|\phi|$.*

Corollary 1. *Let $K = (S, \wp, L)$ be a Markov chain, N_S a neighborhood relation on S, and Φ a dpCTL formula. $\{s : K, N_S, s \models \Phi\}$ is computable within time polynomial in $|S|$ and $|\Phi|$.*

The model checking algorithm for dpCTL* can be treated as in the classical setting [2]: all we need is to compute the probability $\mathrm{Pr}_{N_S}^K(s, \phi)$ with general path formula ϕ. For this purpose one first constructs a deterministic ω-automaton R for ϕ. Then, the probability reduces to a reachability probability in the product Markov chain obtained from K and R. There are more efficient algorithms without the product construction, see [3,13,14] for details.

6   Specifying Properties in **dpCTL***

In this section we describe how properties in the differential privacy literature can be expressed using dpCTL* formulae.

Differential Privacy. Consider the survey mechanism (Sect. 3.1). For v with uNv, we have $\mathrm{Pr}_N^K(u, \mathsf{X}out_1) \leq 3\mathrm{Pr}_N^K(v, \mathsf{X}out_1)$ for the probabilities of satisfying $\mathsf{X}out_1$ from u and v. The formula $\mathcal{D}_{\ln 3,0}(\mathsf{X}out_1)$ holds in state u and similarly for $\mathcal{D}_{\ln 3,0}(\mathsf{X}out_0)$. Recall that differential privacy requires similar output distributions on neighbors. The formula $\mathcal{D}_{\ln 3,0}(\mathsf{X}out_1) \wedge \mathcal{D}_{\ln 3,0}(\mathsf{X}out_0)$ thus specifies differential privacy for states $+$ and $-$. The survey mechanism is $(\ln 3, 0)$-differentially private.

For the $\frac{1}{2}$-geometric mechanism (Sect. 3.2), define the formula $\psi = \mathcal{D}_{\ln 2,0}(\mathsf{X}out_0) \wedge \mathcal{D}_{\ln 2,0}(\mathsf{X}out_1) \wedge \cdots \wedge \mathcal{D}_{\ln 2,0}(\mathsf{X}out_5)$. If the state s_k satisfies ψ for $k = 0, \ldots, 5$, then the $\frac{1}{2}$-geometric mechanism is $(\ln 2, 0)$-differentially private. For the subsampling majority mechanism (Sect. 3.3), consider the formula $\psi = \mathcal{D}_{\epsilon,\delta}(\mathsf{F}0) \wedge \mathcal{D}_{\epsilon,\delta}(\mathsf{F}1)$. If a state satisfies ψ, its probability of outputting is (ϵ, δ)-close to those of its neighbor for every outcomes. The subsampling majority mechanism is (ϵ, δ)-differentially private.

Compositionality. Compositionality is one of the building blocks for differential privacy. For any (ϵ_1, δ_1)-differentially private mechanism M_1 and (ϵ_2, δ_2)-differentially private mechanism M_2, their combination $(M_1(x), M_2(x))$ is $(\epsilon_1 + \epsilon_2, \delta_1 + \delta_2)$-differentially private by the compositional theorem [16, Theorem 3.16]. The degradation is rooted in the repeated releases of information. To illustrate this property, we consider the extended survey mechanism which allows two consecutive queries. In this mechanism, an input is either $+$ or $-$; but outputs are out_1out_1, out_1out_0, out_0out_1, or out_0out_0. The model is depicted in Fig. 4.

Consider the formula $\mathcal{D}_{\ln 9,0}(\mathsf{X}(out_1 \wedge \mathsf{X}out_1))$. A path satisfies $\mathsf{X}(out_1 \wedge \mathsf{X}out_1)$ if the second state satisfies out_1 and the third state satisfies out_1 as well. We verify that this formula is satisfied for states $+$ and $-$. Moreover, the bound $\epsilon =$

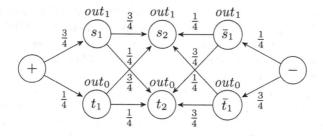

Fig. 4. Markov chain of double surveys

ln 9 is tight since the probability of satisfying $X(out_1 \wedge X out_1)$ from states $+$ and $-$ are $\frac{9}{16}$ and $\frac{1}{16}$ respectively. Finally, the formula $\wedge_{a_1,a_2} \mathcal{D}_{\ln 9,0}(X(a_1 \wedge X a_2))$ specifies differential privacy for the model, where a_1, a_2 range over atomic propositions $\{out_1, out_0\}$.

Let us consider two slightly different formulae for comparison:

- $\mathcal{D}_{\ln 3,0}(XX out_1)$. In this case we claim there is no privacy loss, even though there are two queries. The reason is that the output of the first query is not observed at all. It is easy to verify that it is indeed satisfied by $+$ and $-$.
- $\mathcal{D}_{\ln 3,0}(X(out_1 \wedge \mathcal{D}_{\ln 3,0}(X out_1)))$. This is a nested dpCTL formula, where the inner state formula $\mathcal{D}_{\ln 3,0}(X out_1)$ specifies the one-step differential privacy. Observe the inner formula is satisfied by all states. The outer formula has no privacy loss.

Tighter Privacy Bounds for Composition. An advantage of applying model checking is that we may get tighter bounds for composition. Consider the survey mechanism, and the property $\mathcal{D}_{0,.5}(X out_1)$. Obviously, it holds in states $+$ and $-$ since $\mathrm{Pr}_N^K(u, out_1) = \frac{3}{4}, \frac{1}{4}$ for $u = +, -$ respectively (Fig. 1). A careful check infers that one cannot decrease $\delta_1 = .5$ without increasing ϵ. Now consider the formula $\mathcal{D}_{\epsilon_2,\delta_2}(X(out_1 \wedge X out_1))$ in Fig. 4. Applying the compositional theorem, one has $\epsilon_2 = 2\epsilon_1 = 0$ and $\delta_2 = 2\delta_1 = 1$. However, we can check easily that one gets better privacy parameter $(0, .5)$ using the model checking algorithm because $\mathrm{Pr}_N^K(u, out_1) = \frac{9}{16}, \frac{1}{16}$ for $u = +, -$ respectively. In general, compositional theorems for differential privacy only give asymptotic upper bounds. Privacy parameters ϵ and δ must be calculated carefully and often pessimistically. Our algorithm allows data analysts to choose better parameters.

7   Differentially Private Mechanisms as Markov Decision Processes

In differential privacy, an *offline* mechanism releases outputs only once and plays no further role; an *online* (or *interactive*) mechanism allows analysts to ask queries adaptively based on previous responses. The mechanisms considered previously are offline mechanisms. Since offline mechanisms only release one query result, they are relatively easy to analyze. For online mechanisms, one has to consider all possible adaptive queries. We therefore use MDPs to model these non-deterministic behaviors. Specifically, adaptive queries are modeled by actions. Randomized computation associated with different queries is modeled by distributions associated with actions.

Consider again the survey mechanism. Suppose we would like to design an interactive mechanism which adjusts random noises on surveyors' requests. When the surveyor requests low-accuracy answers, the surveyee uses the survey mechanism in Sect. 3.1. When high-accuracy answers are requested, the surveyee answers 1 with probability $\frac{4}{5}$ and 0 with probability $\frac{1}{5}$ when she has positive diagnosis. She answers 1 with probability $\frac{1}{5}$ and 0 with probability $\frac{4}{5}$ when she is not diagnosed with the disease X. This gives an interactive mechanism corresponding to the MDP shown in Fig. 5.

In the figure, the states $+$, $-$, s, and t are interpreted as before. The actions L and H denote low- and high-accuracy queries respectively. Note that the high-accuracy survey mechanism is $(\ln 4, 0)$-differentially private. Unlike non-interactive mechanisms, the privacy guarantees vary from queries with different accuracies.

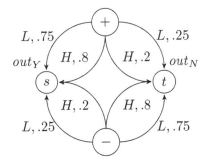

Fig. 5. Markov decision process

7.1 Above Threshold Mechanism

Below we describe an online mechanism from [16]. Given a threshold and a series of adaptive queries, we care for the queries whose results are above the threshold; queries below the threshold only disclose minimal information and hence is irrelevant. Let us assume the mechanism will halt on the first such query result for simplicity. In [16], a mechanism is designed for continuous queries by applying the Laplace mechanism. We will develop a mechanism for discrete bounded queries using the truncated geometric mechanism.

Assume that we have a threshold $t \in \{0, 1, \ldots, 5\}$ and queries $\{f_i : \Delta(f_i) = 1\}$. In order to protect privacy, our mechanism applies the truncated $\frac{1}{4}$-geometric mechanism to obtain a perturbed threshold t'. For each query f_i, the truncated $\frac{1}{2}$-geometric mechanism is applied to its result $r_i = f_i(x)$. If the perturbed result r_i' is not less than the perturbed threshold t', the mechanism halts with the output $\top$. Otherwise, it outputs $\bot$ and continues to the next query (Algorithm 3). The above threshold mechanism outputs a sequence of the form $\bot^*\top$. On similar datasets, we want to show that the above threshold mechanism outputs the same sequence with similar probabilities.

It is not hard to model the above threshold mechanism as a Markov decision process (Fig. 6). In the figure, we sketch the model where the threshold and query results are in $\{0, 1, 2\}$. The model simulates two computation in parallel: one for the dataset, the other for its neighbor. The state $t_i r_j$ represents the input

Algorithm 3. Input: private database d, queries $f_i : d \rightarrow \{0,1,\ldots,5\}$ with sensitivity 1, threshold $t \in \{0,1,\ldots,5\}$; Output: $a_1, a_2, \ldots$

1: **procedure** AboveThreshold($d, \{f_1, f_2, \ldots\}, t$)
2:     **match** t **with**   ▷ obtain t' by $\frac{1}{4}$-geometric mechanism
3:         **case** 0: $t' \leftarrow 0,1,2,3,4,5$ with probability $\frac{4}{5}, \frac{3}{20}, \frac{3}{80}, \frac{3}{320}, \frac{3}{1280}, \frac{1}{1280}$ respectively
4:         **case** 1: $t' \leftarrow 0,1,2,3,4,5$ with probability $\frac{1}{5}, \frac{3}{5}, \frac{3}{20}, \frac{3}{80}, \frac{3}{320}, \frac{1}{320}$ respectively
5:         **case** 2: $t' \leftarrow 0,1,2,3,4,5$ with probability $\frac{1}{20}, \frac{3}{20}, \frac{3}{5}, \frac{3}{20}, \frac{3}{80}, \frac{1}{80}$ respectively
6:         **case** 3: $t' \leftarrow 0,1,2,3,4,5$ with probability $\frac{1}{80}, \frac{3}{80}, \frac{3}{20}, \frac{3}{5}, \frac{3}{20}, \frac{1}{20}$ respectively
7:         **case** 4: $t' \leftarrow 0,1,2,3,4,5$ with probability $\frac{1}{320}, \frac{3}{320}, \frac{3}{80}, \frac{3}{20}, \frac{3}{5}, \frac{1}{5}$ respectively
8:         **case** 5: $t' \leftarrow 0,1,2,3,4,5$ with probability $\frac{1}{1280}, \frac{3}{1280}, \frac{3}{320}, \frac{3}{80}, \frac{3}{20}, \frac{4}{5}$ respectively
9:     **for** each query f_i **do**
10:       $r_i \leftarrow f_i(d)$
11:       **match** r_i **with**   ▷ obtain r'_i by $\frac{1}{2}$-geometric mechanism
12:         **case** 0: $r'_i \leftarrow 0,1,2,3,4,5$ with probability $\frac{2}{3}, \frac{1}{6}, \frac{1}{12}, \frac{1}{24}, \frac{1}{48}, \frac{1}{48}$ respectively
13:         **case** 1: $r'_i \leftarrow 0,1,2,3,4,5$ with probability $\frac{1}{3}, \frac{1}{3}, \frac{1}{6}, \frac{1}{12}, \frac{1}{24}, \frac{1}{24}$ respectively
14:         **case** 2: $r'_i \leftarrow 0,1,2,3,4,5$ with probability $\frac{1}{6}, \frac{1}{6}, \frac{1}{3}, \frac{1}{6}, \frac{1}{12}, \frac{1}{12}$ respectively
15:         **case** 3: $r'_i \leftarrow 0,1,2,3,4,5$ with probability $\frac{1}{12}, \frac{1}{12}, \frac{1}{6}, \frac{1}{3}, \frac{1}{6}, \frac{1}{6}$ respectively
16:         **case** 4: $r'_i \leftarrow 0,1,2,3,4,5$ with probability $\frac{1}{24}, \frac{1}{24}, \frac{1}{12}, \frac{1}{6}, \frac{1}{3}, \frac{1}{3}$ respectively
17:         **case** 5: $r'_i \leftarrow 0,1,2,3,4,5$ with probability $\frac{1}{48}, \frac{1}{48}, \frac{1}{24}, \frac{1}{12}, \frac{1}{6}, \frac{2}{3}$ respectively
18:       **if** $r'_i \geq t'$ **then halt** with $a_i = \top$ **else** $a_i = \bot$
19: **end procedure**

---

threshold i and the first query result j; the state $t'_i r'_j$ represents the perturbed threshold i and the perturbed query result j. Other states are similar. Consider the state $t_0 r_1$. After applying the truncated $\frac{1}{4}$-geometric mechanism, it goes to one of the states $t'_0 r_1, t'_1 r_1, t'_2 r_1$ accordingly. From the state $t'_1 r_1$, for instance, it moves to one of $t'_1 r'_0, t'_1 r'_1, t'_1 r'_2$ by applying the truncated $\frac{1}{2}$-geometric mechanism to the query result. If it arrives at $t'_1 r'_1$ or $t'_1 r'_2$, the perturbed query result is not less than the perturbed threshold, the model halts with the output $\top$ by entering the state with a self loop. Otherwise, it moves to one of $t'_1 r_0, t'_1 r_1$, or $t'_1 r_2$ non-deterministically (double arrows). The computation of its neighbor is similar. We just use the underlined symbols to represent threshold and query results. For instance, the state $\underline{t}'_2 \underline{r}'_1$ represents the perturbed threshold 2 and the perturbed query result 1 in the neighbor.

Now, the non-deterministic choices in the two computation cannot be independent. Recall that the sensitivity of each query is 1. If the top computation moves to the state, say, $t'_1 r_0$, it means the next query result on the dataset is 0. Subsequently, the bottom computation can only move to $\underline{t}'_j \underline{r}_0$ or $\underline{t}'_j \underline{r}_1$ depending on its perturbed threshold. This is where actions are useful. Define the actions $\{m\underline{n} : |m - n| \le 1\}$. The action $m\underline{n}$ represents that the next query result for the dataset and its neighbor are m and n respectively. For instance, the non-deterministic choice from $t'_1 r'_0$ to $t'_1 r_0$ is associated with two actions $0\underline{0}$ and $0\underline{1}$ (but not $0\underline{2}$). Similarly, the choice from $\underline{t}'_2 \underline{r}'_1$ to $\underline{t}'_2 \underline{r}_0$ is associated with the actions

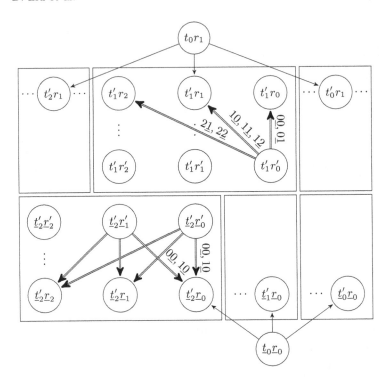

Fig. 6. Markov decision process for above threshold

$0\underline{0}$ and $1\underline{0}$ (but not $2\underline{0}$). Assume the perturbed thresholds of the top and bottom computation are i and j respectively. On the action $0\underline{0}$, the top computation moves to $t'_i r_0$ and the bottom computation moves to $\underline{t}_j \underline{r}_0$. Actions make sure the two computation of neighbors is modeled properly. Now consider the action sequence $-, -, 0\underline{1}, -, 2\underline{2}, -, 2\underline{1}$ from the states $t_0 r_1$ and $\underline{t}_0 \underline{r}_0$ ("$-$" represents the purely probabilistic action). Together with the first query results, it denotes four consecutive query results 1, 0, 2, 2 on the top computation, and 0, 1, 2, 1 on the bottom computation. Each action sequence models two sequences of query results: one on the top, the other on the bottom computation. Moreover, the difference of the corresponding query results on the two computation is at most one by the definition of the action set. Any sequence of adaptive query results is hence formalized by an action sequence in our model.

It remains to define the neighborhood relation. Recall the sensitivity is 1. Consider the neighborhood relation $\{(t_i r_m, t_i r_m), (\underline{t}_i \underline{r}_n, \underline{t}_i \underline{r}_n), (t_i r_m, \underline{t}_i \underline{r}_n), (\underline{t}_i \underline{r}_n, t_i r_m) : |m - n| \leq 1\}$. That is, two states are neighbors if they represent two inputs of the same threshold and query results with difference at most one.

8   dpCTL* for Markov Decision Processes

The logic dpCTL* can be interpreted over MDPs. Let $M = (S, Act, \wp, L)$ be an MDP and N_S a neighborhood relation on S. Define the satisfaction relation $M, N_S, s \models \Phi$ for $\mathbb{P}_J\phi$ and $\mathcal{D}_{\epsilon,\delta}\phi$ as follows (others are straightforward).

$M, N_S, s \models \mathbb{P}_J\phi$ if $\mathrm{Pr}_{N_S}^{M_\mathfrak{S}}(s, \phi) \in J$ for every scheduler $\mathfrak{S}$

$M, N_S, s \models \mathcal{D}_{\epsilon,\delta}\phi$ if for all t with sN_St and query scheduler $\mathfrak{Q}$, $\mathrm{Pr}_{N_S}^{M_\mathfrak{Q}}(s, \phi) \leq e^\epsilon \cdot$

$$\mathrm{Pr}_{N_S}^{M_\mathfrak{Q}}(t, \phi) + \delta \text{ and } \mathrm{Pr}_{N_S}^{M_\mathfrak{Q}}(t, \phi) \leq e^\epsilon \cdot \mathrm{Pr}_{N_S}^{M_\mathfrak{Q}}(s, \phi) + \delta$$

Recall that $M_\mathfrak{S}$ is but a Markov chain. The semantics of $M_\mathfrak{S}, N_S, \pi \models \phi$ and hence the probability $\mathrm{Pr}_{N_S}^{M_\mathfrak{S}}(s, \phi)$ are defined as in Markov chains. The semantics of dpCTL* on MDPs is again standard except the differentially private operator $\mathcal{D}_{\epsilon,\delta}$. For any path formula ϕ, $\mathcal{D}_{\epsilon,\delta}\phi$ specifies states whose probability of having paths satisfying ϕ are (ϵ, δ)-close to those of all its neighbors for query schedulers. That is, no query scheduler can force any of neighbors to distinguish the specified path behavior probabilistically.

Justification of Query Schedulers. We use query schedulers in the semantics for the differentially private operator. A definition with history-dependent schedulers might be

$M, N_S, s \models \mathcal{D}_{\epsilon,\delta}^{bad}\phi$ if for all t with sN_St and scheduler $\mathfrak{S}$, $\mathrm{Pr}_{N_S}^{M_\mathfrak{S}}(s, \phi) \leq e^\epsilon \cdot$

$$\mathrm{Pr}_{N_S}^{M_\mathfrak{S}}(t, \phi) + \delta \text{ and } \mathrm{Pr}_{N_S}^{M_\mathfrak{S}}(t, \phi) \leq e^\epsilon \cdot \mathrm{Pr}_{N_S}^{M_\mathfrak{S}}(s, \phi) + \delta.$$

A state satisfies $\mathcal{D}_{\epsilon,\delta}^{bad}\phi$ if no history-dependent scheduler can differentiate the probabilities of having paths satisfying ϕ from neighbors. Recall that a history-dependent scheduler chooses actions according to previous states. Such a definition would allow schedulers to take different actions from different states. Two neighbors could hence be differentiated by different action sequences. The specification might be too strong for our purposes. A query scheduler $\mathfrak{Q} : S^+ \to Act$, on the other hand, corresponds to a query sequence. A state satisfies $\mathcal{D}_{\epsilon,\delta}\phi$ if no query sequence can differentiate the probabilities of having paths satisfying ϕ from neighbors. Recall query schedulers only depend on lengths of histories. Two neighbors cannot be distinguished by the same action sequence of any length if they satisfy a differentially private subformula. Our semantics agrees with the informal interpretation of differential privacy for such systems. We therefore consider only query schedulers in our definition.

8.1   Model Checking

Given an MDP $M = (S, Act, \wp, L)$, a neighborhood relation N_S, $s \in S$, and a path formula ϕ, consider the problem of checking $M, N_S, s \models \mathcal{D}_{\epsilon,\delta}\phi$. Recall the semantics of $\mathcal{D}_{\epsilon,\delta}\phi$. Given s, t with sN_St and a path formula ϕ, we need to decide whether $\mathrm{Pr}_{N_S}^{M_\mathfrak{Q}}(s, \phi) \leq e^\epsilon\mathrm{Pr}_{N_S}^{M_\mathfrak{Q}}(t, \phi) + \delta$ for every query scheduler $\mathfrak{Q}$.

When ϕ is $\bigcirc B$ with $B \subseteq S$, only the first action in the query sequence needs to be considered. This can also be easily generalized to nested next operators: one needs only to enumerate all actions query sequences of a fixed length. The problem however is undecidable in general.

Theorem 1. *The dpCTL* model checking problem for MDPs is undecidable.*

The proof is in Appendix. We discuss some decidable special cases. Consider the formula $\phi := FB$ with $B \subseteq S$ and assume that states in B with only self-loops. For the case $\epsilon = 0$, the condition reduces to $\Pr_{N_S}^{M_\Omega}(s, FB) - \Pr_{N_S}^{M_\Omega}(t, FB) \leq \delta$. If $\delta = 0$ it is the classical language equivalence problem for probabilistic automata [29], which can be solved in polynomial time. However, if $\delta > 0$, the problem becomes an approximate version of the language equivalence problem. To the best of our knowledge, its decidability is still open except for the special case where all states are connected [33].

Despite of the negative result in Theorem 1, a sufficient condition for $M, N_S, s \models \mathcal{D}_{\epsilon,\delta}\phi$ is available. To see this, observe that for $s \in S$ and query scheduler Ω, we have

$$\min_{\mathfrak{S}} \Pr_{N_S}^{M\mathfrak{S}}(s, \phi) \leq \Pr_{N_S}^{M_\Omega}(s, \phi) \leq \max_{\mathfrak{S}} \Pr_{N_S}^{M\mathfrak{S}}(s, \phi)$$

where the minimum and maximum are taken over all schedulers $\mathfrak{S}$. Hence,

$$\Pr_{N_S}^{M_\Omega}(s, \phi) - e^\epsilon \cdot \Pr_{N_S}^{M_\Omega}(t, \phi) \leq \max_{\mathfrak{S}} \Pr_{N_S}^{M\mathfrak{S}}(s, \phi) - e^\epsilon \cdot \min_{\mathfrak{S}} \Pr_{N_S}^{M\mathfrak{S}}(t, \phi)$$

for any $s, t \in S$ and query scheduler Ω. We have the following proposition:

Proposition 2. *Let $M = (S, Act, \wp, L)$ be an MDP, N_S a neighborhood relation on S. $M, N_S, s \models \mathcal{D}_{\epsilon,\delta}\phi$ if $\max_{\mathfrak{S}} \Pr_{N_S}^{M\mathfrak{S}}(s, \phi) - e^\epsilon \cdot \min_{\mathfrak{S}} \Pr_{N_S}^{M\mathfrak{S}}(t, \phi) \leq \delta$ and $\max_{\mathfrak{S}} \Pr_{N_S}^{M\mathfrak{S}}(t, \phi) - e^\epsilon \cdot \min_{\mathfrak{S}} \Pr_{N_S}^{M\mathfrak{S}}(s, \phi) \leq \delta$ for any $s, t \in S$ with sN_St.*

For $s \in S$, recall that $\max_{\mathfrak{S}} \Pr_{N_S}^{M\mathfrak{S}}(s, \phi)$ and $\min_{\mathfrak{S}} \Pr_{N_S}^{M\mathfrak{S}}(s, \phi)$ can be efficiently computed [2]. By Proposition 2, $M, N_S, s \models \mathcal{D}_{\epsilon,\delta}\phi$ can be checked soundly and efficiently.

We model the above threshold algorithm (Algorithm 3) and apply Proposition 2 to check whether the mechanism is differentially private using the classical PCTL model checking algorithm for MDPs. Since concrete values of the parameters ϵ and δ are computed, tighter bounds for specific neighbors can be obtained. For instance, for the state t_3r_5 and its neighbor $\underline{t_3r_4}$, we verify the property $\bigwedge_{k\in\mathbb{Z}^{\geq 0}} \mathcal{D}_{0,0.17}((\mathsf{X}^k \bot)\top)$ is satisfied. Note the reachability probability goes to 0 as k goes to infinity. By repeating the computation, we verify that the property $\bigwedge_{k\in\mathbb{Z}^{\geq 0}} \mathcal{D}_{1,0.74}((\mathsf{X}^k \bot)\top)$ is satisfied for all neighbors. Subsequently, the above threshold mechanism in Algorithm 3 is $(1, 0.74)$-differentially private. Compared to the parameters for the neighbors t_3r_5 and $\underline{t_3r_4}$, the parameter δ appears to be significantly large. It means that there are two neighbors with drastically different output distributions from our mechanism. Moreover, recall that Proposition 2 is a sufficient condition. It only gives an upper bound of privacy parameters. Tighter bounds may be computed by more sophisticated sufficient conditions.

9   Conclusions

We have introduced dpCTL* to reason about properties in differential privacy, and investigated its model checking problems. For Markov chains, the model checking problem has the same complexity as for PCTL*. The general MDP model checking problem however is undecidable. We have discussed some decidable special cases and a sufficient yet efficient condition to check differentially private subformulae. An interesting future work is to identify more decidable subclasses and sufficient conditions. As an example, consider the extended dpCTL* formula $\bigwedge_{k \in \mathbb{Z}^{\geq 0}} \mathcal{D}_{\epsilon,\delta}(\mathsf{X}^k \top)$. For the case $\epsilon = \delta = 0$, it reduces to a language equivalence problem for probabilistic automata. It is interesting to characterize other cases as well. Another interesting line of further works is to consider continuous perturbation (such as Laplace distribution used in [16]). We would need Markov models with continuous state space.

A   Proof of Theorem 1

Proof. The proof follows by a reduction from the *emptiness* problem for probabilistic automata. A *probabilistic automaton* [29] is a tuple $\mathcal{A} = (S, \Sigma, M, s_0, B)$ where

- S is a finite set of states,
- Σ is the finite set of input alphabet,
- $M : S \times \Sigma \times S \to [0,1]$ such that $\sum_{t \in S} M(s, \alpha, t) = 1$ for all $s \in S$ and $\alpha \in \Sigma$,
- $s_0 \in S$ is the initial state,
- $B \subseteq S$ is a set of accepting states.

Each input alphabet α induces a stochastic matrix $M(\alpha)$ in the obvious way. Let λ denote the empty string. For $\eta \in \Sigma^*$ we define $M(\eta)$ inductively by: $M(\lambda)$ is the identity matrix, $M(x\eta') = M(x)M(\eta')$. Thus, $M(\eta)(s, s')$ denotes the probability of going from s to s' after reading η. Let v_B denote the characteristic row vector for the set B, and v_{s_0} denote the characteristic row vector for the set $\{s_0\}$. Then, the accepting probably of η by $\mathcal{A}$ is defined as $v_{s_0} \cdot M(\eta) \cdot (v_B)^c$ where $(v_B)^c$ denotes the transpose of v_B. The following *emptiness problem* is know to be undecidable [27]:

Emptiness Problem: Given a probabilistic automaton $\mathcal{A} = (S, \Sigma, M, s_0, B)$, whether there exists $\eta \in \Sigma^*$ such that $v_{s_0} \cdot M(\eta) \cdot (v_B)^c > 0$?

Now we establish the proof by reducing the emptiness problem to our dpCTL* model checking problem. Given the probabilistic automaton $\mathcal{A} = (S, \Sigma, M, s_0, B)$, assume we have a *primed* copy $\mathcal{A}' = (S', \Sigma, M', s_0', \emptyset)$.

Let $AP := \{at_B\}$. Now we construct our MDP $M = (S \uplus S', \Sigma, \wp, L)$ where $\wp(s, a, t)$ equals to $M(s, a, t)$ if $s, t \in S$ and to $M'(s, a, t)$ if $s, t \in S'$. We define the neighbor relation $N_S := \{(s_0, s_0'), (s_0', s_0)\}$ by relating states s_0, s_0'. The labelling function L is defined by $L(s) = \{at_B\}$ if $s \in B$ and $L(s) = \emptyset$ otherwise.

Now we consider the formula $\Phi = \mathcal{D}_{1,0}(Fat_B)$. For the reduction we prove $s_0 \models \mathcal{D}_{1,0}(Fat_B)$ iff for all $\eta \in \Sigma^*$ it holds $v_{s_0} \cdot M(\eta) \cdot (v_B)^c \leq 0$.

First we assume $s_0 \models \mathcal{D}_{1,0}(Fat_B)$. By dpCTL* semantics we have that for all query scheduler $\mathfrak{Q} \in \Sigma^\omega$, $\mathrm{Pr}_{N_S}^{M_\mathfrak{Q}}(s_0, Fat_B) \leq e \cdot \mathrm{Pr}_{N_S}^{M_\mathfrak{Q}}(s_0', Fat_B)$. Since the set of accepting state in the primed copy is empty, we have $\mathrm{Pr}_{N_S}^{M_\mathfrak{Q}}(s_0', Fat_B) = 0$, thus we have $\mathrm{Pr}_{N_S}^{M_\mathfrak{Q}}(s_0, Fat_B) \leq 0$. This implies $v_{s_0} \cdot M(\eta) \cdot (v_B)^c \leq 0$ for all $\eta \in \Sigma^*$.

For the other direction, assume that all $\eta \in \Sigma^*$ it holds $v_{s_0} \cdot M(\eta) \cdot (v_B)^c \leq 0$. We prove by contradiction. Assume that $s_0 \not\models \mathcal{D}_{1,0}(Fat_B)$. Since the relation $N_S = \{(s_0, s_0'), (s_0', s_0)\}$, there exists (s_0, s_0'), and a query scheduler $\mathfrak{Q} \in \Sigma^\omega$ such that

$$\mathrm{Pr}_{N_S}^{M_\mathfrak{Q}}(s_0, Fat_B) \not\leq e \cdot \mathrm{Pr}_{N_S}^{M_\mathfrak{Q}}(s_0', Fat_B)$$

which implies $\mathrm{Pr}_{N_S}^{M_\mathfrak{Q}}(s_0, Fat_B) > 0$. It is then easy to construct a finite sequence $\eta \in \Sigma^*$ with $v_{s_0} \cdot M(\eta) \cdot (v_B)^c > 0$, a contradiction.

References

1. Alvim, M.S., Andrés, M.E., Chatzikokolakis, K., Degano, P., Palamidessi, C.: On the information leakage of differentially-private mechanisms. J. Comput. Secur. **23**(4), 427–469 (2015)
2. Baier, C., Katoen, J.P.: Principles of Model Checking. The MIT Press, Cambridge (2008)
3. Baier, C., Kiefer, S., Klein, J., Klüppelholz, S., Müller, D., Worrell, J.: Markov chains and unambiguous Büchi automata. In: Chaudhuri, S., Farzan, A. (eds.) CAV 2016. LNCS, vol. 9779, pp. 23–42. Springer, Cham (2016). https://doi.org/10.1007/978-3-319-41528-4_2
4. Barthe, G., Danezis, G., Grégoire, B., Kunz, C., Zanella-Béguelin, S.: Verified computational differential privacy with applications to smart metering. In: CSF, pp. 287–301. IEEE (2013)
5. Barthe, G., et al.: Differentially private Bayesian programming. In: CCS, pp. 68–79. ACM (2016)
6. Barthe, G., Fong, N., Gaboardi, M., Grégoire, B., Hsu, J., Strub, P.Y.: Advanced probabilistic couplings for differential privacy. In: CCS, pp. 55–67. ACM (2016)
7. Barthe, G., Gaboardi, M., Arias, E.J.G., Hsu, J., Kunz, C., Strub, P.Y.: Proving differential privacy in Hoare logic. In: CSF, pp. 411–424. IEEE (2014)
8. Barthe, G., Gaboardi, M., Arias, E.J.G., Hsu, J., Roth, A., Strub, P.: Higher-order approximate relational refinement types for mechanism design and differential privacy. In: POPL, pp. 68–79. ACM (2015)
9. Barthe, G., Gaboardi, M., Gregoire, B., Hsu, J., Strub, P.Y.: Proving differential privacy via probabilistic couplings. In: LICS. IEEE (2016)
10. Barthe, G., Köpf, B., Olmedo, F., Zanella-Béguelin, S.: Probabilistic relational reasoning for differential privacy. In: POPL, pp. 97–110. ACM (2012)
11. Bianco, A., de Alfaro, L.: Model checking of probabilistic and nondeterministic systems. In: Thiagarajan, P.S. (ed.) FSTTCS 1995. LNCS, vol. 1026, pp. 499–513. Springer, Heidelberg (1995). https://doi.org/10.1007/3-540-60692-0_70
12. Clarke, E.M., Grumberg, O., Peled, D.: Model Checking. The MIT Press, Cambridge (1999)

13. Courcoubetis, C., Yannakakis, M.: The complexity of probabilistic verification. J. ACM **42**(4), 857–907 (1995)
14. Couvreur, J.-M., Saheb, N., Sutre, G.: An optimal automata approach to LTL model checking of probabilistic systems. In: Vardi, M.Y., Voronkov, A. (eds.) LPAR 2003. LNCS (LNAI), vol. 2850, pp. 361–375. Springer, Heidelberg (2003). https://doi.org/10.1007/978-3-540-39813-4_26
15. Dwork, C., McSherry, F., Nissim, K., Smith, A.: Calibrating noise to sensitivity in private data analysis. In: Halevi, S., Rabin, T. (eds.) TCC 2006. LNCS, vol. 3876, pp. 265–284. Springer, Heidelberg (2006). https://doi.org/10.1007/11681878_14
16. Dwork, C., Roth, A.: The algorithmic foundations of differential privacy. Found. Trends Theor. Comput. Sci. **9**(3–4), 211–407 (2014)
17. Dwork, C.: Differential privacy. In: Bugliesi, M., Preneel, B., Sassone, V., Wegener, I. (eds.) ICALP 2006. LNCS, vol. 4052, pp. 1–12. Springer, Heidelberg (2006). https://doi.org/10.1007/11787006_1
18. Fung, B.C.M., Wang, K., Chen, R., Yu, P.S.: Privacy-preserving data publish: a survey of recent developments. ACM Comput. Surv. **42**(4), 14:1–14:53 (2010)
19. Gaboardi, M., Haeberlen, A., Hsu, J., Narayan, A., Pierce, B.C.: Linear dependent types for differential privacy. In: POPL, pp. 357–370 (2013)
20. Gazeau, I., Miller, D., Palamidessi, C.: Preserving differential privacy under finite-precision semantics. Theor. Comput. Sci. **655**, 92–108 (2016)
21. Ghosh, A., Roughgarden, T., Sundararajan, M.: Universally utility-maximizing privacy mechanisms. In: STOC, pp. 351–360. ACM, New York (2009)
22. Ghosh, A., Roughgarden, T., Sundararajan, M.: Universally utility-maximizing privacy mechanisms. SIAM J. Comput. **41**(6), 1673–1693 (2012)
23. Hansson, H., Jonsson, B.: A logic for reasoning about time and reliability. Form. Asp. Comput. **6**(5), 512–535 (1994)
24. Ji, Z., Lipton, Z.C., Elkan, C.: Differential privacy and machine learning: a survey and review. CoRR abs/1412.7584 (2014). http://arxiv.org/abs/1412.7584
25. Manna, Z., Pnueli, A.: The Temporal Logic of Reactive and Concurrent Systems: Specification. Springer, New York (1992). https://doi.org/10.1007/978-1-4612-0931-7
26. Mironov, I.: On significance of the least significant bits for differential privacy. In: Yu, T., Danezis, G., Gligor, V.D. (eds.) ACM CCS, pp. 650–661 (2012)
27. Paz, A.: Introduction to Probabilistic Automata: Computer Science and Applied Mathematics. Academic Press, Inc., Orlando (1971)
28. Puterman, M.L.: Markov Decision Processes: Discrete Stochastic Dynamic Programming. Wiley Series in Probability and Statistics, vol. 594. Wiley, Hoboken (2005)
29. Rabin, M.: Probabilistic automata. Inf. Control. **6**(3), 230–245 (1963)
30. Reed, J., Pierce, B.C.: Distance makes the types grow stronger: a calculus for differential privacy. In: ICFP, pp. 157–168. ACM (2010)
31. Tang, J., Korolova, A., Bai, X., Wang, X., Wang, X.: Privacy loss in apple's implementation of differential privacy on MacOS 10.12. CoRR abs/1709.02753 (2017). http://arxiv.org/abs/1709.02753
32. Tschantz, M.C., Kaynar, D., Datta, A.: Formal verification of differential privacy for interactive systems (extended abstract). In: Mathematical Foundations of Programming Semantics. ENTCS, vol. 276, pp. 61–79 (2011)
33. Tzeng, W.: A polynomial-time algorithm for the equivalence of probabilistic automata. SIAM J. Comput. **21**(2), 216–227 (1992)

34. Winograd-Cort, D., Haeberlen, A., Roth, A., Pierce, B.C.: A framework for adaptive differential privacy. Proc. ACM Program. Lang. 1(ICFP), 10:1–10:29 (2017)
35. WWDC: Engineering privacy for your users (2016). https://developer.apple.com/videos/play/wwdc2016/709/
36. Zhang, D., Kifer, D.: LightDP: towards automating differential privacy proofs. In: POPL, pp. 888–901. ACM (2017)

Shallow Effect Handlers

Daniel Hillerström and Sam Lindley[(⊠)]

The University of Edinburgh, Edinburgh, UK
{Daniel.Hillerstrom,Sam.Lindley}@ed.ac.uk

Abstract. Plotkin and Pretnar's effect handlers offer a versatile abstraction for modular programming with user-defined effects. Traditional *deep handlers* are defined by folds over computation trees. In this paper we study *shallow handlers*, defined instead by case splits over computation trees. We show that deep and shallow handlers can simulate one another up to specific notions of administrative reduction. We present the first formal accounts of an abstract machine for shallow handlers and a Continuation Passing Style (CPS) translation for shallow handlers taking special care to avoid memory leaks. We provide implementations in the Links web programming language and empirically verify that neither implementation introduces unwarranted memory leaks.

Keywords: Effect handlers · Abstract machines
Continuation passing

1 Introduction

Expressive control abstractions are pervasive in mainstream programming languages, be that async/await as pioneered by C#, generators and iterators as commonly found in JavaScript and Python, or coroutines in C++20. Such abstractions may be simulated directly with higher-order functions, but at the expense of writing the entire source program in Continuation Passing Style (CPS). To retain *direct-style*, some languages build in several different control abstractions, e.g., JavaScript has both async/await and generators/iterators, but hard-wiring multiple abstractions increases the complexity of the compiler and run-time.

An alternative is to provide a single control abstraction, and derive others as libraries. Plotkin and Pretnar's effect handlers provide a modular abstraction that subsumes all of the above control abstractions. Moreover, they have a strong mathematical foundation [20,21] and have found applications across a diverse spectrum of disciplines such as concurrent programming [4], probabilistic programming [8], meta programming [24], and more [12].

With effect handlers computations are viewed as trees. Effect handlers come in two flavours *deep* and *shallow*. Deep handlers are defined by folds (specifically *catamorphisms* [18]) over computation trees, whereas shallow handlers are defined as case-splits. Catamorphisms are attractive because they are semantically well-behaved and provide appropriate structure for efficient implementations using optimisations such as fusion [23]. However, they are not always

© Springer Nature Switzerland AG 2018
S. Ryu (Ed.): APLAS 2018, LNCS 11275, pp. 415–435, 2018.
https://doi.org/10.1007/978-3-030-02768-1_22

convenient for implementing other structural recursion schemes such as mutual recursion. Most existing accounts of effect handlers use deep handlers. In this paper we develop the theory of shallow effect handlers.

As shallow handlers impose no particular structural recursion scheme, they can be more convenient. For instance, using shallow handlers it is easy to model Unix pipes as two mutually recursive functions (specifically *mutumorphisms* [7]) that alternate production and consumption of data. With shallow handlers we define a classic demand-driven Unix pipeline operator as follows

$$\text{pipe} : \langle\langle\rangle \to \alpha!\{\text{Yield} : \beta \to \langle\rangle\},\langle\rangle \to \alpha!\{\text{Await} : \beta\}\rangle \quad \to \alpha!\emptyset$$
$$\text{copipe} : \langle\beta \to \alpha!\{\text{Await} : \beta\}, \quad \langle\rangle \to \alpha!\{\text{Yield} : \beta \to \langle\rangle\}\rangle \to \alpha!\emptyset$$

$\text{pipe}\,\langle p, c\rangle = \textbf{handle}^\dagger\,c\,\langle\rangle\,\textbf{with}$	$\text{copipe}\,\langle c, p\rangle = \textbf{handle}^\dagger\,p\,\langle\rangle\,\textbf{with}$
$\quad\textbf{return}\,x \mapsto x$	$\quad\textbf{return}\,x \mapsto x$
$\quad\text{Await}\,r \quad \mapsto \text{copipe}\,\langle r, p\rangle$	$\quad\text{Yield}\,p\,r \mapsto \text{pipe}\,\langle r, \lambda\langle\rangle.c\,p\rangle$

A pipe takes two thunked computations, a producer p and a consumer c. A computation type $A!E$ is a value type A and an effect E, which enumerates the operations that the computation may perform.

The pipe function specifies how to *handle* the operations of its arguments and in doing so performs no operations of its own, thus its effect is pure $\emptyset$. Each of the thunks returns a value of type α. The producer can perform the Yield operation, which yields a value of type β and the consumer can perform the Await operation, which correspondingly awaits a value of type β. The shallow handler runs the consumer. If the consumer returns a value, then the return clause is executed and simply returns that value as is. If the consumer performs the Await operation, then the handler is supplied with a special resumption argument r, which is the continuation of the consumer computation reified as a first-class function. The copipe is now invoked with r and the producer as arguments.

The copipe function is similar. The arguments are swapped and the consumer now expects a value. The shallow handler runs the producer. If it performs the Yield operation, then pipe is invoked with the resumption of the producer along with a thunk that applies the resumption of the consumer to the yielded value.

As a simple example consider the composition of a producer that yields a stream of ones, and a consumer that awaits a single value.

$$\text{pipe}\,\langle \textbf{rec}\,ones\,\langle\rangle.\textbf{do}\,\text{Yield}\,1;\,ones\,\langle\rangle, \lambda\langle\rangle.\textbf{do}\,\text{Await}\rangle$$
$$\rightsquigarrow^+ \text{copipe}\,\langle \lambda x.x, \textbf{rec}\,ones\,\langle\rangle.\textbf{do}\,\text{Yield}\,1;\,ones\,\langle\rangle\rangle$$
$$\rightsquigarrow^+ \text{pipe}\,\langle \lambda\langle\rangle.\textbf{rec}\,ones\,\langle\rangle.\textbf{do}\,\text{Yield}\,1;\,ones\,\langle\rangle, \lambda\langle\rangle.1\rangle \rightsquigarrow^+ 1$$

(The computation $\textbf{do}\,\ell\,p$ performs operation ℓ with parameter p.)

The difference between shallow handlers and deep handlers is that in the latter the original handler is implicitly wrapped around the body of the resumption, meaning that the next effectful operation invocation is necessarily handled by the same handler. Shallow handlers allow the freedom to choose how to handle the next effectful operation; deep handlers do not. Pipes provide the quintessential example for contrasting shallow and deep handlers. To implement pipes with deep handlers, we cannot simply use term level recursion, instead we effectively have to *defunctionalise* [22] the shallow version of pipes using recursive types. Following Kammar et al. [12] we define two mutually recursive types for producers and consumers, respectively.

$$\mathsf{Producer}\,\alpha\,\beta = \langle\rangle\!\rightarrow (\mathsf{Consumer}\,\alpha\,\beta \rightarrow \alpha!\emptyset)!\emptyset$$
$$\mathsf{Consumer}\,\alpha\,\beta = \beta\!\rightarrow (\mathsf{Producer}\,\alpha\,\beta \rightarrow \alpha!\emptyset)!\emptyset$$

The underlying idea is *state-passing*: the Producer type is an alias for a suspended computation which returns a computation parameterised by a Consumer computation. Correspondingly, Consumer is an alias for a function that consumes an element of type β and returns a computation parameterised by a Producer computation. The ultimate return value has type α. Using these recursive types, we can now give types for deep pipe operators and their implementations.

$$\mathsf{pipe'} : (\langle\rangle \rightarrow \alpha!\{\mathsf{Await} : \beta\}) \qquad \rightarrow \mathsf{Producer}\,\alpha\,\beta \rightarrow \alpha!\emptyset$$
$$\mathsf{copipe'} : (\langle\rangle \rightarrow \alpha!\{\mathsf{Yield} : \beta \rightarrow \langle\rangle\}) \rightarrow \mathsf{Consumer}\,\alpha\,\beta \rightarrow \alpha!\emptyset$$

$$\begin{array}{ll}
\mathsf{pipe'}\,c = \mathbf{handle}\,c\,\langle\rangle\,\mathbf{with} & \mathsf{copipe'}\,p = \mathbf{handle}\,p\,\langle\rangle\,\mathbf{with} \\
\quad \mathbf{return}\,x \mapsto \lambda y.x & \quad \mathbf{return}\,x \mapsto \lambda y.x \\
\quad \mathsf{Await}\,r \;\; \mapsto \lambda p.p\,\langle\rangle\,r & \quad \mathsf{Yield}\,p\,r \mapsto \lambda c.c\,p\,r
\end{array}$$

$$\mathsf{runPipe}\langle p; c\rangle = \mathsf{pipe'}\,c\,(\lambda\langle\rangle.\mathsf{copipe'}\,p)$$

Application of the pipe operator is no longer direct as extra plumbing is required to connect the now decoupled handlers. The observable behaviour of runPipe is the same as the shallow pipe. Indeed, the above example yields the same result.

$$\mathsf{runPipe}\,\langle \mathbf{rec}\,\textit{ones}\,\langle\rangle.\mathbf{do}\,\mathsf{Yield}\,1;\,\textit{ones}\,\langle\rangle, \lambda\langle\rangle.\mathbf{do}\,\mathsf{Await}\rangle \rightsquigarrow^{+} 1$$

In this paper we make five main contributions, each shedding their own light on the computational differences between deep and shallow handlers:

- A proof that shallow handlers with general recursion can simulate deep handlers up to congruence and that, at the cost of performance, deep handlers can simulate shallow handlers up to administrative reductions (Sect. 3).
- The first formal account of an abstract machine for shallow handlers (Sect. 4).
- The first formal account of a CPS translation for shallow handlers (Sect. 5).
- An implementation of both the abstract machine and the CPS translation as backends for the Links web programming language [2].
- An empirical evaluation of our implementations (Sect. 6).

Section 2 introduces our core calculus of deep and shallow effect handlers. Section 7 discusses related work. Section 8 concludes.

2   Handler Calculus

In this section, we present $\lambda^{\dagger}$, a Church-style row-polymorphic call-by-value calculus for effect handlers. To support comparison within a single language we include both deep and shallow handlers. The calculus is an extension of Hillerström and Lindley's calculus of extensible deep handlers $\lambda^{\rho}_{\mathsf{eff}}$ [9] with shallow

Value types	$A, B ::= A \to C \mid \forall \alpha^K.C$	Types	$T ::= A \mid C \mid E$
	$\mid \langle R \rangle \mid [R] \mid \alpha$		$\mid F \mid R \mid P$
Computation types	$C, D ::= A!E$	Kinds	$K ::= \mathsf{Type} \mid \mathsf{Comp}$
Effect types	$E ::= \{R\}$		$\mid \mathsf{Effect} \mid \mathsf{Handler}$
Depth	$\delta ::= \mid \dagger$		$\mid \mathsf{Row}_{\mathcal{L}} \mid \mathsf{Presence}$
Handler types	$F ::= C \Rightarrow^\delta D$	Label sets	$\mathcal{L} ::= \emptyset \mid \{\ell\} \uplus \mathcal{L}$
Row types	$R ::= \ell : P; R \mid \rho \mid \cdot$	Type envs.	$\Gamma ::= \cdot \mid \Gamma, x : A$
Presence types	$P ::= \mathsf{Pre}(A) \mid \mathsf{Abs} \mid \theta$	Kind envs.	$\Delta ::= \cdot \mid \Delta, \alpha : K$

Fig. 1. Types, kinds, and environments

handlers and recursive functions. Following Hillerström and Lindley, $\lambda^\dagger$ provides a row polymorphic effect type system and is based on fine-grain call-by-value [16], which names each intermediate computation as in A-normal form [6], but unlike A-normal form is closed under β-reduction.

2.1 Types

The syntax of types, kinds, and environments is given in Fig. 1.

Value Types. Function type $A \to C$ maps values of type A to computations of type C. Polymorphic type $\forall \alpha^K.C$ is parameterised by a type variable α of kind K. Record type $\langle R \rangle$ represents records with fields constrained by row R. Dually, variant type $[R]$ represents tagged sums constrained by row R.

Computation Types and Effect Types. The computation type $A!E$ is given by a value type A and an effect type E, which specifies the operations a computation inhabiting this type may perform.

Handler Types. The handler type $C \Rightarrow^\delta D$ represent handlers that transform computations of type C into computations of type D (where δ empty denotes a deep handler and $\delta = \dagger$ a shallow handler).

Row Types. Effect, record, and variant types are given by row types. A *row type* (or just *row*) describes a collection of distinct labels, each annotated by a presence type. A presence type indicates whether a label is *present* with type A ($\mathsf{Pre}(A)$), *absent* (Abs) or *polymorphic* in its presence (θ). Row types are either *closed* or *open*. A closed row type ends in $\cdot$, whilst an open row type ends with a *row variable* ρ. The row variable in an open row type can be instantiated with additional labels. We identify rows up to reordering of labels. For instance, we consider rows $\ell_1 : P_1; \cdots; \ell_n : P_n; \cdot$ and $\ell_n : P_n; \cdots; \ell_1 : P_1; \cdot$ equivalent. Absent labels in closed rows are redundant. The unit type is the empty closed record, that is, $\langle \cdot \rangle$. Dually, the empty type is the empty, closed variant $[\cdot]$. Often we omit the $\cdot$ for closed rows.

Values
$$V, W ::= x \mid \lambda x^A.M \mid \Lambda \alpha^K.M \mid \langle\rangle \mid \langle \ell = V; W\rangle \mid (\ell\, V)^R$$
$$\mid\ \mathbf{rec}\ g^{A \to C}\ x.M$$

Computations
$$M, N ::= V\, W \mid V\, T \mid \mathbf{let}\ \langle \ell = x; y\rangle = V\ \mathbf{in}\ N$$
$$\mid\ \mathbf{case}\ V\{\ell\, x \mapsto M; y \mapsto N\} \mid \mathbf{absurd}^C\, V$$
$$\mid\ \mathbf{return}\ V \mid \mathbf{let}\ x \leftarrow M\ \mathbf{in}\ N$$
$$\mid\ (\mathbf{do}\ \ell\, V)^E \mid \mathbf{handle}^\delta\, M\ \mathbf{with}\ H$$

Handlers
$$H ::= \{\mathbf{return}\ x \mapsto M\} \mid \{\ell\, p\, r \mapsto M\} \uplus H$$

Fig. 2. Term syntax

Kinds. We have six kinds: Type, Comp, Effect, Handler, $\mathrm{Row}_{\mathcal{L}}$, Presence, which respectively classify value types, computation types, effect types, row types, presence types, and handler types. Row kinds are annotated with a set of labels $\mathcal{L}$. The kind of a complete row is $\mathrm{Row}_\emptyset$. More generally, $\mathrm{Row}_{\mathcal{L}}$ denotes a partial row that may not mention labels in $\mathcal{L}$. We write $\ell : A$ as sugar for $\ell : \mathrm{Pre}(A)$.

Type Variables. We let α, ρ and θ range over type variables. By convention we write α for value type variables or for type variables of unspecified kind, ρ for type variables of row kind, and θ for type variables of presence kind.

Type and Kind Environments. Type environments (Γ) map term variables to their types and kind environments (Δ) map type variables to their kinds.

2.2 Terms

The terms are given in Fig. 2. We let x, y, z, r, p range over term variables. By convention, we use r to denote resumption names. The syntax partitions terms into values, computations and handlers. Value terms comprise variables (x), lambda abstraction ($\lambda x^A.M$), type abstraction ($\Lambda \alpha^K.M$), the introduction forms for records and variants, and recursive functions ($\mathbf{rec}\ g^{A \to C}\ x.M$). Records are introduced using the empty record $\langle\rangle$ and record extension $\langle \ell = V; W\rangle$, whilst variants are introduced using injection $(\ell\, V)^R$, which injects a field with label ℓ and value V into a row whose type is R.

All elimination forms are computation terms. Abstraction and type abstraction are eliminated using application ($V\, W$) and type application ($V\, T$) respectively. The record eliminator ($\mathbf{let}\ \langle \ell = x; y\rangle = V\ \mathbf{in}\ N$) splits a record V into x, the value associated with ℓ, and y, the rest of the record. Non-empty variants are eliminated using the case construct ($\mathbf{case}\ V\ \{\ell\, x \mapsto M; y \mapsto N\}$), which evaluates the computation M if the tag of V matches ℓ. Otherwise it falls through to y and evaluates N. The elimination form for empty variants is ($\mathbf{absurd}^C\, V$). A trivial computation ($\mathbf{return}\ V$) returns value V. The expression ($\mathbf{let}\ x \leftarrow M\ \mathbf{in}\ N$) evaluates M and binds the result to x in N.

Operation invocation ($\mathbf{do}\ \ell\, V)^E$ performs operation ℓ with value argument V. Handling ($\mathbf{handle}^\delta\, M\ \mathbf{with}\ H$) runs a computation M using deep (δ empty) or shallow ($\delta = \dagger$) handler H. A handler definition H consists of a return clause

$\{\textbf{return } x \mapsto M\}$ and a possibly empty set of operation clauses $\{\ell \ p \ r \mapsto N_\ell\}_{\ell \in \mathcal{L}}$. The return clause defines how to handle the final return value of the handled computation, which is bound to x in M. The operation clause for ℓ binds the operation parameter to p and the resumption r in N_ℓ.

We define three projections on handlers: H^{ret} yields the singleton set containing the return clause of H and H^ℓ yields the set of either zero or one operation clauses in H that handle the operation ℓ and H^{ops} yields the set of all operation clauses in H. We write $dom(H)$ for the set of operations handled by H. Various term forms are annotated with type or kind information; we sometimes omit such annotations. We write $Id(M)$ for $\textbf{handle } M \textbf{ with } \{\textbf{return } x \mapsto \textbf{return } x\}$.

Syntactic Sugar. We make use of standard syntactic sugar for pattern matching, n-ary record extension, n-ary case elimination, and n-ary tuples.

2.3 Kinding and Typing

The kinding judgement $\Delta \vdash T : K$ states that type T has kind K in kind environment Δ. The value typing judgement $\Delta; \Gamma \vdash V : A$ states that value term V has type A under kind environment Δ and type environment Γ. The computation typing judgement $\Delta; \Gamma \vdash M : C$ states that term M has computation type C under kind environment Δ and type environment Γ. The handler typing judgement $\Delta; \Gamma \vdash H : C \Rightarrow^\delta D$ states that handler H has type $C \Rightarrow^\delta D$ under kind environment Δ and type environment Γ. In the typing judgements, we implicitly assume that Γ, A, C, and D, are well-kinded with respect to Δ. We define $FTV(\Gamma)$ to be the set of free type variables in Γ. We omit the full kinding and typing rules due to lack of space; they can be found in the extended version of the paper [10, Appendix A]. The interesting rules are those for performing and handling operations.

T-Do
$$\frac{\Delta; \Gamma \vdash V : A \qquad E = \{\ell : A \to B; R\}}{\Delta; \Gamma \vdash (\textbf{do } \ell \ V)^E : B!E}$$

T-Handle
$$\frac{\Delta; \Gamma \vdash M : C \qquad \Delta; \Gamma \vdash H : C \Rightarrow^\delta D}{\Delta; \Gamma \vdash \textbf{handle}^\delta \ M \textbf{ with } H : D}$$

T-Handler
$$\frac{\begin{array}{c} C = A!\{(\ell_i : A_i \to B_i)_i; R\} \\ D = B!\{(\ell_i : P_i)_i; R\} \\ H = \{\textbf{return } x \mapsto M\} \uplus \{\ell_i \ p \ r \mapsto N_i\}_i \\ \Delta; \Gamma, x : A \vdash M : D \\ [\Delta; \Gamma, p : A_i, r : B_i \to D \vdash N_i : D]_i \end{array}}{\Delta; \Gamma \vdash H : C \Rightarrow D}$$

T-Handler†
$$\frac{\begin{array}{c} C = A!\{(\ell_i : A_i \to B_i)_i; R\} \\ D = B!\{(\ell_i : P_i)_i; R\} \\ H = \{\textbf{return } x \mapsto M\} \uplus \{\ell_i \ p \ r \mapsto N_i\}_i \\ \Delta; \Gamma, x : A \vdash M : D \\ [\Delta; \Gamma, p : A_i, r : B_i \to C \vdash N_i : D]_i \end{array}}{\Gamma \vdash H : C \Rightarrow^\dagger D}$$

The T-Handler and T-Handler† rules are where most of the work happens. The effect rows on the computation type C and the output computation type D must share the same suffix R. This means that the effect row of D must explicitly mention each of the operations ℓ_i to say whether an ℓ_i is present with a given type signature, absent, or polymorphic in its presence. The row R describes the operations that are forwarded. It may include a row-variable, in which case an

S-APP	$(\lambda x.M)\,V \rightsquigarrow M[V/x]$
S-TYAPP	$(\Lambda\alpha.M)\,A \rightsquigarrow M[A/\alpha]$
S-SPLIT	$\textbf{let } \langle \ell = x; y \rangle = \langle \ell = V; W \rangle \textbf{ in } N \rightsquigarrow N[V/x,\,W/y]$
S-CASE$_1$	$\textbf{case } \ell\,V\{\ell\,x \mapsto M; y \mapsto N\} \rightsquigarrow M[V/x]$
S-CASE$_2$	$\textbf{case } \ell\,V\{\ell'\,x \mapsto M; y \mapsto N\} \rightsquigarrow N[\ell\,V/y],\qquad \text{if } \ell \neq \ell'$
S-REC	$(\textbf{rec } g\,x.M)\,V \rightsquigarrow M[(\textbf{rec } g\,x.M)/g,\,V/x]$
S-LET	$\textbf{let } x \leftarrow \textbf{return } V \textbf{ in } N \rightsquigarrow N[V/x]$
S-RET	$\textbf{handle}^\delta\,(\textbf{return } V)\textbf{ with } H \rightsquigarrow N[V/x],$
	$\qquad\qquad\qquad \text{where } H^{\text{ret}} = \{\textbf{return } x \mapsto N\}$
S-OP	$\textbf{handle } \mathcal{E}[\textbf{do } \ell\,V]\textbf{ with } H \rightsquigarrow$
	$\qquad N[V/p,\,\lambda y.\textbf{handle } \mathcal{E}[\textbf{return } y]\textbf{ with } H/r],$
	$\qquad\qquad \text{where } \ell \notin BL(\mathcal{E}) \text{ and } H^\ell = \{\ell\,p\,r \mapsto N\}$
S-OP†	$\textbf{handle}^\dagger\,\mathcal{E}[\textbf{do } \ell\,V]\textbf{ with } H \rightsquigarrow N[V/p,\,\lambda y.\mathcal{E}[\textbf{return } y]/r],$
	$\qquad\qquad \text{where } \ell \notin BL(\mathcal{E}) \text{ and } H^\ell = \{\ell\,p\,r \mapsto N\}$
S-LIFT	$\mathcal{E}[M] \rightsquigarrow \mathcal{E}[N],\qquad\qquad \text{if } M \rightsquigarrow N$

Evaluation contexts $\mathcal{E} ::= [\,] \mid \textbf{let } x \leftarrow \mathcal{E} \textbf{ in } N \mid \textbf{handle}^\delta\,\mathcal{E}\textbf{ with } H$

Fig. 3. Small-step operational semantics

arbitrary number of effects may be forwarded by the handler. The difference in typing deep and shallow handlers is that the resumption of the former has return type D, whereas the resumption of the latter has return type C.

2.4 Operational Semantics

Figure 3 gives a small-step operational semantics for $\lambda^\dagger$. The reduction relation $\rightsquigarrow$ is defined on computation terms. The interesting rules are the handler rules. We write $BL(\mathcal{E})$ for the set of operation labels bound by $\mathcal{E}$.

$$BL([\,]) = \emptyset \qquad BL(\textbf{let } x \leftarrow \mathcal{E} \textbf{ in } N) = BL(\mathcal{E})$$
$$BL(\textbf{handle}^\delta\,\mathcal{E}\textbf{ with } H) = BL(\mathcal{E}) \cup dom(H)$$

The S-RET rule invokes the return clause of a handler. The S-OP$^\delta$ rules handle an operation by invoking the appropriate operation clause. The constraint $\ell \notin BL(\mathcal{E})$ asserts that no handler in the evaluation context handles the operation: a handler reaches past any other inner handlers that do not handle ℓ. The difference between S-OP and S-OP† is that the former rewraps the handler about the body of the resumption. We write R^+ for transitive closure of relation R.

Definition 1. *We say that computation term N is normal with respect to effect E if N is either of the form $\textbf{return } V$ or $\mathcal{E}[\textbf{do } \ell\,W]$, where $\ell \in E$ and $\ell \notin BL(\mathcal{E})$.*

Theorem 2 (Type Soundness). *If $\vdash M : A!E$ then either $M \not\rightsquigarrow^*$ or there exists $\vdash N : A!E$ such that $M \rightsquigarrow^+ N \not\rightsquigarrow$ and N is normal with respect to E.*

3 Deep as Shallow and Shallow as Deep

In this section we show that shallow handlers and general recursion can simulate deep handlers up to congruence, and that deep handlers can simulate shallow handlers up to administrative reduction. Both translations are folklore, but we believe the precise simulation results are novel.

3.1 Deep as Shallow

The implementation of deep handlers using shallow handlers (and recursive functions) is by a rather direct local translation. Each handler is wrapped in a recursive function and each resumption has its body wrapped in a call to this recursive function. Formally, the translation $\mathcal{S}[\![-]\!]$ is defined as the homomorphic extension of the following equations to all terms.

$$\mathcal{S}[\![\mathbf{handle}\ M\ \mathbf{with}\ H]\!] = (\mathbf{rec}\ h\ f.\mathbf{handle}^\dagger\ f\ \langle\rangle\ \mathbf{with}\ \mathcal{S}[\![H]\!]h)\,(\lambda\langle\rangle.\mathcal{S}[\![M]\!])$$
$$\mathcal{S}[\![H]\!]h = \mathcal{S}[\![H^{\mathrm{ret}}]\!]h \uplus \mathcal{S}[\![H^{\mathrm{ops}}]\!]h$$
$$\mathcal{S}[\![\{\mathbf{return}\ x \mapsto N\}]\!]h = \{\mathbf{return}\ x \mapsto \mathcal{S}[\![N]\!]\}$$
$$\mathcal{S}[\![\{\ell\ p\ r \mapsto N_\ell\}_{\ell \in \mathcal{L}}]\!]h = \{\ell\ p\ r \mapsto \mathbf{let}\ r \leftarrow \mathbf{return}\ \lambda x.h\,(\lambda\langle\rangle.r\ x)\ \mathbf{in}\ \mathcal{S}[\![N_\ell]\!]\}_{\ell \in \mathcal{L}}$$

Theorem 3. *If* $\Delta; \Gamma \vdash M : C$ *then* $\Delta; \Gamma \vdash \mathcal{S}[\![M]\!] : C$.

In order to obtain a simulation result, we allow reduction in the simulated term to be performed under lambda abstractions (and indeed anywhere in a term), which is necessary because of the redefinition of the resumption to wrap the handler around its body. Nevertheless, the simulation proof makes minimal use of this power, merely using it to rename a single variable. We write R_{cong} for the compatible closure of relation R, that is the smallest relation including R and closed under term constructors for $\lambda^\dagger$.

Theorem 4 (Simulation up to Congruence). *If* $M \rightsquigarrow N$ *then* $\mathcal{S}[\![M]\!] \rightsquigarrow^+_{\mathrm{cong}} \mathcal{S}[\![N]\!]$.

Proof. By induction on $\rightsquigarrow$ using a substitution lemma. The interesting case is S-Deep-Op, which is where we apply a single β-reduction, renaming a variable, under the lambda abstraction representing the resumption.

3.2 Shallow as Deep

Implementing shallow handlers in terms of deep handlers is slightly more involved than the other way round. It amounts to the encoding of a case split by a fold and involves a translation on handler types as well as handler terms. Formally, the translation $\mathcal{D}[\![-]\!]$ is defined as the homomorphic extension of the following equations to all types, terms, and type environments.

$$\mathcal{D}[\![C \Rightarrow D]\!] = \mathcal{D}[\![C]\!] \Rightarrow \langle\langle\rangle \to \mathcal{D}[\![C]\!], \langle\rangle \to \mathcal{D}[\![D]\!]\rangle$$
$$\mathcal{D}[\![\mathbf{handle}^\dagger\ M\ \mathbf{with}\ H]\!] = \mathbf{let}\ z \leftarrow \mathbf{handle}\ \mathcal{D}[\![M]\!]\ \mathbf{with}\ \mathcal{D}[\![H]\!]\ \mathbf{in}$$
$$\mathbf{let}\ \langle f, g\rangle = z\ \mathbf{in}\ g\ \langle\rangle$$
$$\mathcal{D}[\![H]\!] = \mathcal{D}[\![H^{\mathrm{ret}}]\!] \uplus \mathcal{D}[\![H^{\mathrm{ops}}]\!]$$
$$\mathcal{D}[\![\{\mathbf{return}\ x \mapsto N\}]\!] = \{\mathbf{return}\ x \mapsto \mathbf{return}\ \langle\lambda\langle\rangle.\mathbf{return}\ x, \lambda\langle\rangle.\mathcal{D}[\![N]\!]\rangle\}$$
$$\mathcal{D}[\![\{\ell\ p\ r \mapsto N\}_{\ell \in \mathcal{L}}]\!] = \{\ell\ p\ r \mapsto$$
$$\mathbf{let}\ r = \lambda x.\mathbf{let}\ z \leftarrow r\ x\ \mathbf{in}\ \mathbf{let}\ \langle f, g\rangle = z\ \mathbf{in}\ f\ \langle\rangle\ \mathbf{in}$$
$$\mathbf{return}\ \langle\lambda\langle\rangle.\mathbf{let}\ x \leftarrow \mathbf{do}\ \ell\ p\ \mathbf{in}\ r\ x, \lambda\langle\rangle.\mathcal{D}[\![N]\!]\rangle\}_{\ell \in \mathcal{L}}$$

Each shallow handler is encoded as a deep handler that returns a pair of thunks. The first forwards all operations, acting as the identity on computations. The second interprets a single operation before reverting to forwarding.

Theorem 5. *If* $\Delta; \Gamma \vdash M : C$ *then* $\mathcal{D}[\![\Delta]\!]; \mathcal{D}[\![\Gamma]\!] \vdash \mathcal{D}[\![M]\!] : \mathcal{D}[\![C]\!]$.

As with the implementation of deep handlers as shallow handlers, the implementation is again given by a local translation. However, this time the administrative overhead is more significant. Reduction up to congruence is insufficient and we require a more semantic notion of administrative reduction.

Definition 6 (Administrative Evaluation Contexts). *An evaluation context* $\mathcal{E}$ *is administrative, admin($\mathcal{E}$), iff*

1. *For all values* V, *we have:* $\mathcal{E}[\mathbf{return}\ V] \rightsquigarrow^* \mathbf{return}\ V$
2. *For all evaluation contexts* $\mathcal{E}'$, *operations* $\ell \in BL(\mathcal{E}) \backslash BL(\mathcal{E}')$, *values* V:

$$\mathcal{E}[\mathcal{E}'[\mathbf{do}\ \ell\ V]] \rightsquigarrow^* \mathbf{let}\ x \leftarrow \mathbf{do}\ \ell\ V\ \mathbf{in}\ \mathcal{E}[\mathcal{E}'[\mathbf{return}\ x]]$$

The intuition is that an administrative evaluation context behaves like the empty evaluation context up to some amount of administrative reduction, which can only proceed once the term in the context becomes sufficiently evaluated. Values annihilate the evaluation context and handled operations are forwarded.

Definition 7 (Approximation up to Administrative Reduction). *Define* $\gtrsim$ *as the compatible closure of the following inference rules.*

$$\frac{}{M \gtrsim M} \qquad \frac{M \rightsquigarrow M' \qquad M' \gtrsim N}{M \gtrsim N} \qquad \frac{admin(\mathcal{E}) \qquad M \gtrsim N}{\mathcal{E}[M] \gtrsim N}$$

We say that M *approximates* N *up to administrative reduction if* $M \gtrsim N$.

Approximation up to administrative reduction captures the property that administrative reduction may occur anywhere within a term. The following lemma states that the forwarding component of the translation is administrative.

Lemma 8. *For all shallow handlers* H, *the following context is administrative:*

$$\mathbf{let}\ z \leftarrow \mathbf{handle}\ [\ ]\ \mathbf{with}\ \mathcal{D}[\![H]\!]\ \mathbf{in}\ \mathbf{let}\ \langle f; \_\rangle = z\ \mathbf{in}\ f\ \langle\rangle$$

Theorem 9 (Simulation up to Administrative Reduction). *If* $M' \gtrsim \mathcal{D}[\![M]\!]$ *and* $M \rightsquigarrow N$ *then there exists* N' *such that* $N' \gtrsim \mathcal{D}[\![N]\!]$ *and* $M' \rightsquigarrow^+ N'$.

Proof. By induction on $\rightsquigarrow$ using a substitution lemma and Lemma 8. The interesting case is S-$\mathrm{OP}^\dagger$, which uses Lemma 8 to approximate the body of the resumption up to administrative reduction.

4   Abstract Machine

In this section we develop an abstract machine that supports deep and shallow handlers *simultaneously*. We build upon prior work [9] in which we developed an abstract machine for deep handlers by generalising the continuation structure of a CEK machine (Control, Environment, Kontinuation) [5]. In our prior work we sketched an adaptation for shallow handlers. It turns out that this adaptation has a subtle flaw. We fix the flaw here with a full development of shallow handlers along with a proof of correctness.

The Informal Account. A machine continuation is a list of handler frames. A handler frame is a pair of a *handler closure* (handler definition) and a *pure continuation* (a sequence of let bindings). Handling an operation amounts to searching through the continuation for a matching handler. The resumption is constructed during the search by reifying each handler frame. The resumption is assembled in one of two ways depending on whether the matching handler is deep or shallow. For a deep handler, the current handler closure is included, and a deep resumption is a reified continuation. An invocation of a deep resumption amounts to concatenating it with the current machine continuation. For a shallow handler, the current handler closure must be discarded leaving behind a dangling pure continuation, and a shallow resumption is a pair of this pure continuation and the remaining reified continuation. (By contrast, the prior flawed adaptation prematurely precomposed the pure continuation with the outer handler in the current resumption.) An invocation of a shallow resumption again amounts to concatenating it with the current machine continuation, but taking care to concatenate the dangling pure continuation with that of the next frame.

Configurations	$\mathcal{C} ::= \langle M \mid \gamma \mid \kappa \circ \kappa' \rangle$	
Value environments	$\gamma ::= \emptyset \mid \gamma[x \mapsto v]$	
Values	$v, w ::= (\gamma, \lambda x^A.M) \mid (\gamma, \Lambda \alpha^K.M)$	
	$\mid \langle \rangle \mid \langle \ell = v; w \rangle \mid (\ell\, v)^R \mid \kappa^A \mid (\kappa, \sigma)^A$	

Continuations	$\kappa ::= [] \mid \theta :: \kappa$	Continuation frames	$\theta ::= (\sigma, \chi)$
		Handler closures	$\chi ::= (\gamma, H)^\delta$
Pure continuations	$\sigma ::= [] \mid \phi :: \sigma$	Pure continuation frames	$\phi ::= (\gamma, x, N)$

Fig. 4. Abstract machine syntax

The Formal Account. The abstract machine syntax is given in Fig. 4. A configuration $\mathcal{C} = \langle M \mid \gamma \mid \kappa \circ \kappa' \rangle$ of our abstract machine is a quadruple of a computation term (M), an environment (γ) mapping free variables to values, and two continuations (κ) and (κ'). The latter continuation is always the identity, except when forwarding an operation, in which case it is used to keep track of the extent to which the operation has been forwarded. We write $\langle M \mid \gamma \mid \kappa \rangle$ as syntactic sugar for $\langle M \mid \gamma \mid \kappa \circ [] \rangle$ where $[]$ is the identity continuation.

Transition function

$$M \longrightarrow \langle M \mid \emptyset \mid [([], (\emptyset, \{\mathbf{return}\ x \mapsto x\}))]\rangle$$

M-INIT

M-APPCLOSURE $\langle V\ W \mid \gamma \mid \kappa \rangle \longrightarrow \langle M \mid \gamma'[x \mapsto [\![W]\!]\gamma] \mid \kappa \rangle$,   if $[\![V]\!]\gamma = (\gamma', \lambda x^A.M)$

M-APPREC $\langle V\ W \mid \gamma \mid \kappa \rangle \longrightarrow \langle M \mid \gamma'[g \mapsto (\gamma', \mathbf{rec}\ g^{A \to C}\ x.M), x \mapsto [\![W]\!]\gamma] \mid \kappa \rangle$,   if $[\![V]\!]\gamma = (\gamma', \mathbf{rec}\ g^{A \to C}\ x.M)$

M-APPCONT $\langle V\ W \mid \gamma \mid \kappa \rangle \longrightarrow \langle \mathbf{return}\ W \mid \gamma \mid \kappa' + \kappa \rangle$,   if $[\![V]\!]\gamma = (\kappa')^A$

M-APPCONT† $\langle V\ W \mid \gamma \mid (\sigma, \chi) :: \kappa \rangle \longrightarrow \langle \mathbf{return}\ W \mid \gamma \mid \kappa' + ((\sigma' + \sigma, \chi) :: \kappa) \rangle$,   if $[\![V]\!]\gamma = (\kappa', \sigma')^A$

M-APPTYPE $\langle V\ A \mid \gamma \mid \kappa \rangle \longrightarrow \langle M[A/\alpha] \mid \gamma' \mid \kappa \rangle$,   if $[\![V]\!]\gamma = (\gamma', \Lambda\alpha^K.M)$

M-SPLIT $\langle \mathbf{let}\ \langle \ell = x; y \rangle = V\ \mathbf{in}\ N \mid \gamma \mid \kappa \rangle \longrightarrow \langle N \mid \gamma[x \mapsto v, y \mapsto w] \mid \kappa \rangle$,   if $[\![V]\!]\gamma = \langle \ell = v; w \rangle$

M-CASE $\langle \mathbf{case}\ V\ \{\ell\ x \mapsto M; y \mapsto N\} \mid \gamma \mid \kappa \rangle \longrightarrow \begin{cases} \langle M \mid \gamma[x \mapsto v] \mid \kappa \rangle, & \text{if } [\![V]\!]\gamma = \ell\ v \\ \langle N \mid \gamma[y \mapsto \ell'\ v] \mid \kappa \rangle, & \text{if } [\![V]\!]\gamma = \ell'\ v \text{ and } \ell \neq \ell' \end{cases}$

M-LET $\langle \mathbf{let}\ x \leftarrow M\ \mathbf{in}\ N \mid \gamma \mid (\sigma, \chi) :: \kappa \rangle \longrightarrow \langle M \mid \gamma \mid ((\gamma, x, N) :: \sigma, \chi) :: \kappa \rangle$

M-HANDLE $\langle \mathbf{handle}^\delta\ M\ \mathbf{with}\ H \mid \gamma \mid \kappa \rangle \longrightarrow \langle M \mid \gamma \mid ([], (\gamma, H)^\delta) :: \kappa \rangle$

M-RETCONT $\langle \mathbf{return}\ V \mid \gamma \mid (((\gamma', x, N) :: \sigma, \chi) :: \kappa \rangle \longrightarrow \langle N \mid \gamma'[x \mapsto [\![V]\!]\gamma] \mid (\sigma, \chi) :: \kappa \rangle$

M-RETHANDLER $\langle \mathbf{return}\ V \mid \gamma \mid ([], (\gamma', H)) :: \kappa \rangle \longrightarrow \langle M \mid \gamma'[x \mapsto [\![V]\!]\gamma] \mid \kappa \rangle$,   if $H^{\mathrm{ret}} = \{\mathbf{return}\ x \mapsto M\}$

M-RETTOP $\langle \mathbf{return}\ V \mid \gamma \mid [] \rangle \longrightarrow [\![V]\!]\gamma$

M-DO $\langle (\mathbf{do}\ \ell\ V)^E \mid \gamma \mid ((\sigma, (\gamma', H)) :: \kappa) \circ \kappa' \rangle \longrightarrow \langle M \mid \gamma[x \mapsto [\![V]\!]\gamma, r \mapsto (\kappa' + [(\sigma, (\gamma', H))])^B] \mid \kappa \rangle$,   if $\ell : A \to B \in E$ and $H^\ell = \{\ell\ x\ r \mapsto M\}$

M-DO† $\langle (\mathbf{do}\ \ell\ V)^E \mid \gamma \mid ((\sigma, (\gamma', H)^\dagger) :: \kappa) \circ \kappa' \rangle \longrightarrow \langle M \mid \gamma[x \mapsto [\![V]\!]\gamma, r \mapsto (\kappa', \sigma)^B] \mid \kappa \rangle$,   if $\ell : A \to B \in E$ and $H^\ell = \{\ell\ x\ r \mapsto M\}$

M-FORWARD $\langle (\mathbf{do}\ \ell\ V)^E \mid \gamma \mid ((\sigma, (\gamma', H)^\delta) :: \kappa) \circ \kappa' \rangle \longrightarrow \langle (\mathbf{do}\ \ell\ V)^E \mid \gamma \mid \kappa \circ (\kappa' + [(\sigma, (\gamma', H)^\delta)]) \rangle$,   if $H^\ell = \emptyset$

Value interpretation

$[\![x]\!]\gamma = \gamma(x)$ $[\![\lambda x^A.M]\!]\gamma = (\gamma, \lambda x^A.M)$ $[\![\Lambda\alpha^K.M]\!]\gamma = (\gamma, \Lambda\alpha^K.M)$ $[\![\mathbf{rec}\ g^{A \to C}\ x.M]\!]\gamma = (\gamma, \mathbf{rec}\ g^{A \to C}\ x.M)$

$[\![\langle\rangle]\!]\gamma = \langle\rangle$ $[\![\langle \ell = V; W \rangle]\!]\gamma = \langle \ell = [\![V]\!]\gamma; [\![W]\!]\gamma \rangle$ $[\![(\ell\ V)^R]\!]\gamma = (\ell\ [\![V]\!]\gamma)^R$

Fig. 5. Abstract machine semantics

Values consist of function closures, type function closures, records, variants, and captured continuations. A continuation κ is a stack of frames $[\theta_1, \ldots, \theta_n]$. We annotate captured continuations with input types in order to make the results of Sect. 4.1 easier to state. Each frame $\theta = (\sigma, \chi)$ represents pure continuation σ, corresponding to a sequence of let bindings, inside handler closure χ. A pure continuation is a stack of pure frames. A pure frame (γ, x, N) closes a let-binding **let** $x = [\ ]$ **in** N over environment γ. A handler closure (γ, H) closes a handler definition H over environment γ. We write $[]$ for an empty stack, $x :: s$ for the result of pushing x on top of stack s, and $s \mathbin{+\!\!+} s'$ for the concatenation of stack s on top of s'. We use pattern matching to deconstruct stacks.

The abstract machine semantics defining the transition function $\longrightarrow$ is given in Fig. 5. It depends on an interpretation function $[\![-]\!]$ for values. The machine is initialised (M-INIT) by placing a term in a configuration alongside the empty environment and identity continuation. The rules (M-APPCLOSURE), (M-APPREC), (M-APPCONT), (M-APPCONT†), (M-APPTYPE), (M-SPLIT), and (M-CASE) enact the elimination of values. The rules (M-LET) and (M-HANDLE) extend the current continuation with let bindings and handlers respectively. The rule (M-RETCONT) binds a returned value if there is a pure continuation in the current continuation frame; (M-RETHANDLER) invokes the return clause of a handler if the pure continuation is empty; and (M-RETTOP) returns a final value if the continuation is empty. The rule (M-DO) applies the current handler to an operation if the label matches one of the operation clauses. The captured continuation is assigned the forwarding continuation with the current frame appended to the end of it. The rule (M-DO†) is much like (M-DO), except it constructs a shallow resumption, discarding the current handler but keeping the current pure continuation. The rule (M-FORWARD) appends the current continuation frame onto the end of the forwarding continuation.

4.1 Correctness

The (M-INIT) rule provides a canonical way to map a computation term onto a configuration. Figure 6 defines an inverse mapping $(\!|-|\!)$ from configurations to computation terms via a collection of mutually recursive functions defined on configurations, continuations, computation terms, handler definitions, value terms, and values. We write $dom(\gamma)$ for the domain of γ and $\gamma \backslash \{x_1, \ldots, x_n\}$ for the restriction of environment γ to $dom(\gamma) \backslash \{x_1, \ldots, x_n\}$.

The $(\!|-|\!)$ function enables us to classify the abstract machine reduction rules according to how they relate to the operational semantics. The rules (M-INIT) and (M-RETTOP) are concerned only with initial input and final output, neither a feature of the operational semantics. The rules (M-APPCONT$^\delta$), (M-LET), (M-HANDLE), and (M-FORWARD) are administrative in that $(\!|-|\!)$ is invariant under them. This leaves β-rules (M-APPCLOSURE), (M-APPREC), (M-APPTYPE), (M-SPLIT), (M-CASE), (M-RETCONT), (M-RETHANDLER), (M-DO†), and (M-DO†), each of which corresponds directly to performing a reduction in the operational semantics. We write $\longrightarrow_a$ for administrative steps, $\longrightarrow_\beta$ for β-steps, and $\Longrightarrow$ for a sequence of steps of the form $\longrightarrow_a^* \longrightarrow_\beta$.

Configurations

$$(\!|\langle M \mid \gamma \mid \kappa \circ \kappa'\rangle|\!) = (\!|\kappa' \mathbin{+\!\!+} \kappa|\!)((\!|M|\!)\gamma) = (\!|\kappa'|\!)((\!|\kappa|\!)(\!|M|\!)\gamma)$$

Pure continuations

$$(\!|[]|\!)M = M \qquad (\!|((\gamma, x, N) :: \sigma)|\!)M = (\!|\sigma|\!)(\mathbf{let}\ x \leftarrow M\ \mathbf{in}\ (\!|N|\!)(\gamma\backslash\{x\}))$$

Continuations

$$(\!|[]|\!)M = M \qquad (\!|(\sigma, \chi) :: \kappa|\!)M = (\!|\kappa|\!)((\!|\chi|\!)((\!|\sigma|\!)(M)))$$

Handler closures

$$(\!|(\gamma, H)|\!)^\delta M = \mathbf{handle}^\delta\ M\ \mathbf{with}\ (\!|H|\!)\gamma$$

Computation terms

$$(\!|V\ W|\!)\gamma = (\!|V|\!)\gamma\,(\!|W|\!)\gamma$$
$$(\!|V\ A|\!)\gamma = (\!|V|\!)\gamma\,A$$
$$(\!|\mathbf{let}\ \langle \ell = x; y\rangle = V\ \mathbf{in}\ N|\!)\gamma = \mathbf{let}\ \langle \ell = x; y\rangle = (\!|V|\!)\gamma\ \mathbf{in}\ (\!|N|\!)(\gamma\backslash\{x, y\})$$
$$(\!|\mathbf{case}\ V\ \{\ell\ x \mapsto M; y \mapsto N\}|\!)\gamma = \mathbf{case}\ (\!|V|\!)\gamma\ \{\ell\ x \mapsto (\!|M|\!)(\gamma\backslash\{x\}); y \mapsto (\!|N|\!)(\gamma\backslash\{y\})\}$$
$$(\!|\mathbf{return}\ V|\!)\gamma = \mathbf{return}\ (\!|V|\!)\gamma$$
$$(\!|\mathbf{let}\ x \leftarrow M\ \mathbf{in}\ N|\!)\gamma = \mathbf{let}\ x \leftarrow (\!|M|\!)\gamma\ \mathbf{in}\ (\!|N|\!)(\gamma\backslash\{x\})$$
$$(\!|\mathbf{do}\ \ell\ V|\!)\gamma = \mathbf{do}\ \ell\ (\!|V|\!)\gamma$$
$$(\!|\mathbf{handle}^\delta\ M\ \mathbf{with}\ H|\!)\gamma = \mathbf{handle}^\delta\ (\!|M|\!)\gamma\ \mathbf{with}\ (\!|H|\!)\gamma$$

Handler definitions

$$(\!|\{\mathbf{return}\ x \mapsto M\}|\!)\gamma = \{\mathbf{return}\ x \mapsto (\!|M|\!)(\gamma\backslash\{x\})\}$$
$$(\!|\{\ell\ x\ k \mapsto M\} \uplus H|\!)\gamma = \{\ell\ x\ k \mapsto (\!|M|\!)(\gamma\backslash\{x, k\}\} \uplus (\!|H|\!)\gamma$$

Value terms and values

$$(\!|x|\!)\gamma = (\!|v|\!), \quad \text{if}\ \gamma(x) = v \qquad\qquad (\!|\kappa^A|\!) = \lambda x^A.(\!|\kappa|\!)(\mathbf{return}\ x)$$
$$(\!|x|\!)\gamma = x, \quad \text{if}\ x \notin dom(\gamma) \qquad (\!|(\kappa, \sigma)^A|\!) = \lambda x^A.(\!|\sigma|\!)((\!|\kappa|\!)(\mathbf{return}\ x))$$
$$(\!|\lambda x^A.M|\!)\gamma = \lambda x^A.(\!|M|\!)(\gamma\backslash\{x\}) \qquad (\!|(\gamma, \lambda x^A.M)|\!) = \lambda x^A.(\!|M|\!)(\gamma\backslash\{x\})$$
$$(\!|\Lambda \alpha^K.M|\!)\gamma = \Lambda \alpha^K.(\!|M|\!)\gamma \qquad\qquad (\!|(\gamma, \Lambda \alpha^K.M)|\!) = \Lambda \alpha^K.(\!|M|\!)\gamma$$
$$(\!|\langle\rangle|\!)\gamma = \langle\rangle \qquad\qquad\qquad\qquad (\!|\langle\rangle|\!) = \langle\rangle$$
$$(\!|\langle\ell = V; W\rangle|\!)\gamma = \langle\ell = (\!|V|\!)\gamma; (\!|W|\!)\gamma\rangle \qquad (\!|\langle\ell = v; w\rangle|\!) = \langle\ell = (\!|v|\!); (\!|w|\!)\rangle$$
$$(\!|(\ell\ V)^R|\!)\gamma = (\ell\ (\!|V|\!)\gamma)^R \qquad\qquad (\!|(\ell\ v)^R|\!) = (\ell\ (\!|v|\!))^R$$
$$(\!|\mathbf{rec}\ g^{A \to C}\ x.M|\!)\gamma = \mathbf{rec}\ g^{A \to C}\ x.(\!|M|\!)(\gamma\backslash\{g, x\}) = (\!|(\gamma, \mathbf{rec}\ g^{A \to C}\ x.M)|\!)$$

Fig. 6. Mapping from abstract machine configurations to terms

Each reduction in the operational semantics is simulated by a sequence of administrative steps followed by a single β-step in the abstract machine. The *Id* handler (Sect. 2.2) implements the top-level identity continuation.

Theorem 10 (Simulation). *If $M \rightsquigarrow N$, then for any C such that $(\!|C|\!) = Id(M)$ there exists C' such that $C \Longrightarrow C'$ and $(\!|C'|\!) = Id(N)$.*

Proof. By induction on the derivation of $M \rightsquigarrow N$.

Corollary 11. *If $\vdash M : A!E$ and $M \rightsquigarrow^+ N \not\rightsquigarrow$, then $M \longrightarrow^+ C$ with $(\!|C|\!) = N$.*

5 Higher-Order CPS Translation

In this section we formalise a CPS translation for deep and shallow handlers. We adapt the higher-order translation of Hillerström et al. [11]. They formalise a translation for deep handlers and then briefly outline an extension for shallow handlers. Alas, there is a bug in their extension. Their deep handler translation takes advantage of the rewrapping of the body of a resumption with the current handler to combine the current return clause with the current pure continuation. Their shallow handler translation attempts to do the same, but the combination is now unsound as the return clause must be discarded by the resumption. We fix the bug by explicitly separating out the return continuation. Moreover, our translation is carefully designed to avoid memory leaks. The key insight is that to support the typical tail-recursive pattern of shallow handlers without generating useless identity continuations it is essential that we detect and eliminate them. We do so by representing pure continuations as lists of pure frames whereby the identity continuation is just an empty list, much like the abstract machine of Sect. 4.

Following Hillerström et al. [11], we present a higher-order uncurried CPS translation into an untyped lambda calculus. In the style of Danvy and Nielsen [3], we adopt a two-level lambda calculus notation to distinguish between *static* lambda abstraction and application in the meta language and *dynamic* lambda abstraction and application in the target language: overline denotes a static syntax constructor; underline denotes a dynamic syntax constructor. To facilitate this notation we write application as an infix "at" symbol (@). We assume the meta language is pure and hence respects the usual β and η equivalences.

5.1 Target Calculus

The target calculus is given in Fig. 7. As in $\lambda^\dagger$ there is a syntactic distinction between values (V) and computations (M). Values (V) comprise: lambda abstractions ($\underline{\lambda} x\, k.M$) and recursive functions ($\mathbf{rec}\ g\, x\, k.M$), each of which take an additional continuation parameter; first-class labels (ℓ); pairs $\langle V, W \rangle$; and two special convenience constructors for building deep ($\mathbf{res}\ V$) and shallow ($\mathbf{res}^\dagger\ V$) resumptions, which we will explain shortly. Computations (M) comprise: values (V); applications ($U\ \underline{@}\ V\ \underline{@}\ W$); pair elimination ($\mathbf{let}\ \langle x, y \rangle = V\ \mathbf{In}\ N$); label elimination ($\mathbf{case}\ V\ \{\ell \mapsto M; x \mapsto N\}$); and a special convenience constructor for continuation application ($\mathbf{app}\ V\ W$).

Lambda abstraction, pairs, application, and pair elimination are underlined to distinguish them from equivalent constructs in the meta language. We define syntactic sugar for variant values, record values, list values, let binding, variant eliminators, and record eliminators. We assume standard n-ary generalisations and use pattern matching syntax for deconstructing variants, records, and lists.

The reductions for functions, pairs, and first-class labels are standard. To explain the reduction rules for continuations, we first explain the encoding of continuations. Much like the abstract machine, a continuation (k) is given by a

Syntax

Values $V, W ::= x \mid \lambda x\, k.M \mid \mathbf{rec}\, g\, x\, k.M \mid \ell \mid \langle V, W \rangle \mid \mathbf{res}^{\delta}$

Computations $M, N ::= V \mid U @ V @ W \mid \mathbf{let}\ \langle x, y \rangle = V\ \mathbf{in}\ N$
$\mid\ \mathbf{case}\ V\ \{\ell \mapsto M; x \mapsto N\} \mid \mathbf{app}\ V\ W$

Syntactic sugar

$$\mathbf{let}\ x = V\ \mathbf{in}\ N \equiv N[V/x] \qquad \langle\rangle \equiv \ell_{\langle\rangle} \qquad [] \equiv \ell_{[]}$$
$$\ell\ V \equiv \langle \ell, V \rangle \qquad \langle \ell = V; W \rangle \equiv \ell\ \langle V, W \rangle \qquad V :: W \equiv \ell_{::}\ \langle V, W \rangle$$

$$\mathbf{case}\ V\ \{\ell\, x \mapsto M; y \mapsto N\} \equiv \qquad \mathbf{let}\ \langle \ell = x; y \rangle = V\ \mathbf{in}\ N \equiv$$
$$\mathbf{let}\ y = V\ \mathbf{in}\ \mathbf{let}\ \langle z, x \rangle = y\ \mathbf{in} \qquad \mathbf{let}\ \langle z, z' \rangle = V\ \mathbf{in}\ \mathbf{let}\ \langle x, y \rangle = z'\ \mathbf{in}$$
$$\mathbf{case}\ z\ \{\ell \mapsto M; z \mapsto N\} \qquad \mathbf{case}\ z\ \{\ell \mapsto N; z \mapsto \ell_{\perp}\}$$

Reductions

U-APP $(\lambda x\, k.M) @ V @ W \rightsquigarrow M[V/x, W/k]$

U-REC $(\mathbf{rec}\, g\, x\, k.M) @ V @ W \rightsquigarrow M[\mathbf{rec}\, g\, x\, k.M/g, V/x, W/k]$

U-SPLIT $\mathbf{let}\ \langle x, y \rangle = \langle V, W \rangle\ \mathbf{in}\ N \rightsquigarrow N[V/x, W/y]$

U-CASE$_1$ $\mathbf{case}\ \ell\ \{\ell \mapsto M; x \mapsto N\} \rightsquigarrow M$

U-CASE$_2$ $\mathbf{case}\ \ell\ \{\ell' \mapsto M; x \mapsto N\} \rightsquigarrow N[\ell/x], \qquad\qquad \text{if } \ell \neq \ell'$

U-KAPPNIL $\mathbf{app}\ (\langle [], \langle v, e \rangle \rangle :: k)\ V \rightsquigarrow v @ V @ k$

U-KAPPCONS $\mathbf{app}\ (\langle f :: s, h \rangle :: k)\ V \rightsquigarrow f @ V @ (\langle s, h \rangle :: k)$

U-RES $\mathbf{res}\ (q_n :: \cdots :: q_1 :: []) \rightsquigarrow \lambda x\, k.\mathbf{app}\ (q_1 :: \cdots :: q_n :: k)\ x$

U-RES† $\mathbf{res}^{\dagger}\ (\langle f_1 :: \cdots :: f_m, h \rangle :: q_n :: \cdots :: q_1 :: []) \rightsquigarrow$
$\lambda x\, k.\mathbf{let}\ (\langle s', h' \rangle :: k') = k\ \mathbf{in}$
$\mathbf{app}\ (q_1 :: \cdots :: q_n :: \langle f_1 :: \cdots :: f_m :: s', h' \rangle :: k')\ x$

Fig. 7. Untyped target calculus

list of continuation frames. A continuation frame ($\langle s, h \rangle$) consists of a pair of a pure continuation (s) and a handler (h). A pure continuation is a list of pure continuation frames (f). A handler is a pair of a return continuation (v) and an effect continuation (e) which dispatches on the operations provided by a handler. There are two continuation reduction rules, both of which inspect the first frame of the continuation. If the pure continuation of this frame is empty then the return clause is invoked (U-KAPPNIL). If the pure continuation of this frame is non-empty then the first pure continuation frame is invoked (U-KAPPCONS). A crucial difference between our representation of continuations and that of Hillerström et al. [11] is that they use a flat list of frames whereas we use a nested structure in which each pure continuation is a list of pure frames.

To explain the reduction rules for continuations, we first explain the encoding of resumptions. Reified resumptions are constructed frame-by-frame as reversed continuations—they grow a frame at a time as operations are forwarded through the handler stack. Hillerström et al. [11] adopt such an intensional representation in order to obtain a relatively tight simulation result. We take further advantage of this representation to discard the handler when constructing a shallow handler's resumption. The resumption reduction rules turn reified resumptions into actual resumptions. The deep rule (U-RES) simply appends the reified resumption onto the continuation. The shallow rule (U-RES†) appends the tail of the reified resumption onto the continuation after discarding the topmost handler from the resumption and appending the topmost pure continuation from the resumption onto the topmost pure continuation of the continuation.

The continuation application and resumption constructs along with their reduction rules are macro-expressible in terms of the standard constructs. We choose to build them in order to keep the presentation relatively concise.

Values

$$[\![x]\!] = x \qquad\qquad [\![\Lambda\alpha.M]\!] = \underline{\lambda}z\,k.[\![M]\!]\,\overline{@}\,k \qquad [\![\langle \ell = V; W \rangle]\!] = \langle \ell = [\![V]\!]; [\![W]\!] \rangle$$
$$[\![\lambda x.M]\!] = \underline{\lambda}x\,k.[\![M]\!]\,\overline{@}\,k \qquad\qquad [\![\langle\rangle]\!] = \langle\rangle \qquad\qquad\qquad [\![\ell\,V]\!] = \ell\,[\![V]\!]$$
$$[\![\mathbf{rec}\,g\,x.M]\!] = \mathbf{rec}\,g\,x\,k.[\![M]\!]\,\overline{@}\,k$$

Computations

$$[\![V\,W]\!] = \overline{\lambda}\kappa.[\![V]\!]\,\underline{@}\,[\![W]\!]\,\underline{@}\,{\downarrow}\kappa$$
$$[\![V\,T]\!] = \overline{\lambda}\kappa.[\![V]\!]\,\underline{@}\,\langle\rangle\,\underline{@}\,{\downarrow}\kappa$$
$$[\![\mathbf{let}\,\langle\ell = x; y\rangle = V\,\mathbf{in}\,N]\!] = \overline{\lambda}\kappa.\mathbf{let}\,\langle\ell = x; y\rangle = [\![V]\!]\,\mathbf{in}\,[\![N]\!]\,\overline{@}\,\kappa$$
$$[\![\mathbf{case}\,V\,\{\ell\,x \mapsto M; y \mapsto N\}]\!] = \overline{\lambda}\kappa.\mathbf{case}\,[\![V]\!]\,\{\ell\,x \mapsto [\![M]\!]\,\overline{@}\,\kappa; y \mapsto [\![N]\!]\,\overline{@}\,\kappa\}$$
$$[\![\mathbf{absurd}\,V]\!] = \overline{\lambda}\kappa.\mathbf{absurd}\,[\![V]\!]$$
$$[\![\mathbf{return}\,V]\!] = \overline{\lambda}\kappa.\mathbf{app}\,{\downarrow}\kappa\,[\![V]\!]$$
$$[\![\mathbf{let}\,x \leftarrow M\,\mathbf{in}\,N]\!] = \overline{\lambda}\langle s,\chi\rangle\,\overline{::}\,\kappa.[\![M]\!]\,\overline{@}\,(\langle(\underline{\lambda}x\,k.[\![N]\!]\,\overline{@}\,k)\,\underline{::}\,s,\chi\rangle\,\overline{::}\,\kappa)$$
$$[\![\mathbf{do}\,\ell\,V]\!] = \overline{\lambda}\langle s,\langle v,e\rangle\rangle\,\overline{::}\,\kappa.e\,\underline{@}\,(\ell\,\langle[\![V]\!],\langle s,\langle v,e\rangle\rangle\,\underline{::}\,[]\rangle)\,\underline{@}\,{\downarrow}\kappa$$
$$[\![\mathbf{handle}^\delta\,M\,\mathbf{with}\,H]\!] = \overline{\lambda}\kappa.[\![M]\!]\,\overline{@}\,\langle[],[\![H]\!]^\delta\rangle\,\overline{::}\,\kappa$$
$$[\![H]\!]^\delta = \overline{\langle}[\![H^{\mathbf{ret}}]\!],[\![H^{\mathbf{ops}}]\!]^\delta\overline{\rangle}$$
$$[\![\{\mathbf{return}\,x \mapsto N\}]\!] = \underline{\lambda}x\,k.[\![N]\!]\,\overline{@}\,k$$
$$[\![\{(\ell\,p\,r \mapsto N_\ell)_{\ell \in \mathcal{L}}\}]\!]^\delta = \underline{\lambda}x\,k.\mathbf{let}\,\langle z,\langle p,rk\rangle\rangle = x\,\mathbf{in}$$
$$\mathbf{case}\,z\,\{(\ell \mapsto \mathbf{let}\,r = \mathbf{res}^\delta\,rk\,\mathbf{in}\,[\![N_\ell]\!]\,\overline{@}\,k)_{\ell \in \mathcal{L}}$$
$$y \mapsto M_{\mathrm{forward}}((y,p,rk),k)\}$$
$$M_{\mathrm{forward}}((y,p,rk),k) = \mathbf{let}\,\langle s',\langle v',e'\rangle\rangle\,\underline{::}\,k' = k\,\mathbf{in}$$
$$e'\,\underline{@}\,(y\,\underline{\langle}p,\langle s',\langle v',e'\rangle\rangle\,\underline{::}\,rk\underline{\rangle})\,\underline{@}\,k'$$

Top-level program

$$\top[\![M]\!] = [\![M]\!]\,\overline{@}\,(\langle[],\langle\underline{\lambda}x\,k.x,\underline{\lambda}z\,k.\mathbf{absurd}\,z\rangle\rangle\,\overline{::}\,[])$$

Fig. 8. Higher-order uncurried CPS translation of $\lambda^\dagger$

5.2   Static Terms

Redexes marked as $\overline{\text{static}}$ are reduced as part of the translation (at compile time), whereas those marked as $\underline{\text{dynamic}}$ are reduced at runtime.

We make use of static lambda abstractions, pairs, and lists. We let κ range over static continuations and χ range over static handlers. We let $\mathcal{V},\mathcal{W}$ range over meta language values, $\mathcal{M}$ range over meta language expressions, and $\mathcal{P},\mathcal{Q}$ over meta language patterns. We use list and record pattern matching in the meta language.

$$(\overline{\lambda\langle P, Q\rangle}.\mathcal{M}) \overline{@} \langle V, W\rangle = (\overline{\lambda P.\overline{\lambda} Q}.\mathcal{M}) \overline{@} V \overline{@} W = (\overline{\lambda(P \bar{::} Q)}.\mathcal{M}) \overline{@} (V \bar{::} W)$$
$$(\overline{\lambda\langle P, Q\rangle}.\mathcal{M}) \overline{@} V = \mathbf{let} \; \langle f, s\rangle = V \; \mathbf{in} \; (\overline{\lambda P.\overline{\lambda} Q}.\mathcal{M}) \overline{@} f \overline{@} s = (\overline{\lambda(P \bar{::} Q)}.\mathcal{M}) \overline{@} V$$

A meta language value V can be reified as a target language value $\downarrow V$.

$$\downarrow V = V \quad \downarrow(V \bar{::} W) = \downarrow V :: \downarrow W \quad \downarrow\langle V, W\rangle = \langle\downarrow V, \downarrow W\rangle$$

5.3   The Translation

The CPS translation is given in Fig. 8. Its behaviour on constructs for introducing and eliminating values is standard. Where necessary static continuations in the meta language are reified as dynamic continuations in the target language. The translation of **return** V applies the continuation to $[\![V]\!]$. The translation of **let** $x \leftarrow M$ **in** N adds a frame to the pure continuation on the topmost frame of the continuation. The translation of **do** $\ell\ V$ dispatches the operation to the effect continuation at the head of the continuation. The resumption is initialised with the topmost frame of the continuation. The translations of deep and shallow handling each add a new frame to the continuation. The translation of the operation clauses of a handler dispatches on the operation. If a match is found then the reified resumption is turned into a function and made available in the body of the operation clause. If there is no match, then the operation is forwarded by unwinding the continuation, transferring the topmost frame to the head of the reified resumption before invoking the next effect continuation. The only difference between the translations of a deep handler and a shallow handler is that the reified resumption of the latter is specially marked in order to ensure that the handler is disposed of in the body of a matching operation clause.

Example. The following example illustrates how the higher-order CPS translation avoids generating administrative redexes by performing static reductions.

$$\begin{aligned}
\mathsf{T}[\![\mathbf{handle} \; (\mathbf{do} \; \mathsf{Await} \; \langle\rangle) \; \mathbf{with} \; H]\!] &= [\![\mathbf{handle} \; (\mathbf{do} \; \mathsf{Await} \; \langle\rangle) \; \mathbf{with} \; H]\!] \; \overline{@} \; \mathcal{K}_\mathsf{T} \\
&= [\![\mathbf{do} \; \mathsf{Await} \; \langle\rangle]\!] \; \overline{@} \; \langle[], [\![H]\!]\rangle \bar{::} \mathcal{K}_\mathsf{T} \\
&= [\![\mathbf{do} \; \mathsf{Await} \; \langle\rangle]\!] \; \overline{@} \; \langle[], \langle[\![H^{\mathrm{ret}}]\!], [\![H^{\mathrm{ops}}]\!]\rangle\rangle \bar{::} \mathcal{K}_\mathsf{T} \\
&= [\![H^{\mathrm{ops}}]\!] \; @ \; \mathsf{Await} \; \langle\langle\rangle, \langle[], [\![H]\!]\rangle :: []\rangle \; @ \; \downarrow\mathcal{K}_\mathsf{T}
\end{aligned}$$

where $\mathcal{K}_\mathsf{T} = (\langle[], \langle\lambda x \, k.x, \lambda z \, k.\mathbf{absurd} \; z\rangle\rangle \bar{::} [])$. The resulting term passes Await directly to the dispatcher that implements the operation clauses of H.

5.4   Correctness

The translation naturally lifts to evaluation contexts.

$$\begin{aligned}
[\![[\;]]\!] &= \overline{\lambda}\kappa.\kappa \\
[\![\mathbf{let} \; x \leftarrow \mathcal{E} \; \mathbf{in} \; N]\!] &= \overline{\lambda}\langle s, \chi\rangle \bar{::} \kappa.[\![\mathcal{E}]\!] \; \overline{@} \; (\langle(\lambda x \, k.[\![N]\!] \; \overline{@} \; k) :: s, \chi\rangle \bar{::} \kappa) \\
[\![\mathbf{handle}^\delta \; \mathcal{E} \; \mathbf{with} \; H]\!] &= \overline{\lambda}\kappa.[\![\mathcal{E}]\!] \; \overline{@} \; (\langle[], [\![H]\!]^\delta\rangle \bar{::} \kappa)
\end{aligned}$$

Lemma 12 (Decomposition). $[\![\mathcal{E}[M]]\!] \,\overline{@}\, (\mathcal{V} :: \mathcal{W}) = [\![M]\!] \,\overline{@}\, ([\![\mathcal{E}]\!] \,\overline{@}\, (\mathcal{V} :: \mathcal{W}))$

Though it eliminates static administrative redexes, the translation still yields administrative redexes that cannot be eliminated statically, as they only appear at run-time, which arise from deconstructing a reified stack of continuations. We write $\leadsto_a$ for the compatible closure of U-SPLIT, U-CASE$_1$ and U-CASE$_2$.

The following lemma is central to our simulation theorem. It characterises the sense in which the translation respects the handling of operations.

Lemma 13 (Handling). *If* $\ell \notin BL(\mathcal{E})$ *and* $H^\ell = \{\ell\, p\, r \mapsto N_\ell\}$ *then:*

1. $[\![\mathbf{do}\ \ell\ V]\!] \,\overline{@}\, ([\![\mathcal{E}]\!] \,\overline{@}\, (\langle\overline{[]}, [\![H]\!]\rangle :: \mathcal{W})) \leadsto^+\leadsto_a^*$
   $\quad ([\![N_\ell]\!] \,\overline{@}\, \mathcal{W})[[\![V]\!]/p, \underline{\lambda} y\, k.[\![\mathbf{return}\ y]\!] \,\overline{@}\, ([\![\mathcal{E}]\!] \,\overline{@}\, (\langle\overline{[]}, [\![H]\!]\rangle :: k))/r]$

2. $[\![\mathbf{do}\ \ell\ V]\!] \,\overline{@}\, ([\![\mathcal{E}]\!] \,\overline{@}\, (\langle\overline{[]}, [\![H]\!]^\dagger\rangle :: \mathcal{W})) \leadsto^+\leadsto_a^*$
   $\quad ([\![N_\ell]\!] \,\overline{@}\, \mathcal{W})[[\![V]\!]/p, \underline{\lambda} y\, k.\mathbf{let}\ (\langle s, \langle v, e\rangle\rangle :: k) = k\ \mathbf{in}$
   $\quad\quad\quad\quad [\![\mathbf{return}\ y]\!] \,\overline{\overline{@}}\, ([\![\mathcal{E}]\!] \,\overline{@}\, (\langle s, \overline{\langle v, e\rangle}\rangle :: k))/r]$

We now give a simulation result in the style of Plotkin [19]. The theorem shows that the only extra behaviour exhibited by a translated term is the necessary bureaucracy of dynamically deconstructing the continuation stack.

Theorem 14 (Simulation). *If* $M \leadsto N$ *then for all static values* $\mathcal{V}$ *and* $\mathcal{W}$, *we have* $[\![M]\!] \,\overline{@}\, (\mathcal{V} :: \mathcal{W}) \leadsto^+\leadsto_a^* [\![N]\!] \,\overline{@}\, (\mathcal{V} :: \mathcal{W})$.

Proof. By induction on the reduction relation ($\leadsto$) using Lemma 13.

As a corollary, we obtain that the translation simulates full reduction to a value.

Corollary 15. $M \leadsto^* V$ *iff* $\top[\![M]\!] \leadsto^*\leadsto_a^* \top[\![V]\!]$.

6 Empirical Evaluation

We conducted a basic empirical evaluation using an experimental branch of the Links web programming language [2] extended with support for shallow handlers and JavaScript backends based on the CEK machine (Sect. 4) and CPS translation (Sect. 5). We omit the full details due to lack of space; they can be found in the extended version of the paper [10, Appendix B]. Here we give a brief high-level summary. Our benchmarks are adapted from Kammar et al. [12], comprising: pipes, a count down loop, and n-Queens. Broadly, our results align with those of Kammar et al. Specifically, the shallow implementation of pipes outperforms the deep implementation. The shallow-as-deep translation fails to complete most benchmarks as it runs out of memory. The memory usage pattern exhibited by deep, shallow, and shallow-as-deep implementations are all stable.

Deep handlers perform slightly better than shallow handlers except on the pipes benchmark (CEK and CPS) and the countdown benchmark on the CEK machine. The former is hardly surprising given the inherent indirection in the deep implementation of pipes, which causes unnecessary closure allocations to happen when sending values from one end of the pipe to the other. We conjecture that the relatively poor performance of deep handlers on the CEK version of the countdown benchmark is also due to unnecessary closure allocation in the interpretation of state. Kammar et al. avoid this problem by adopting *parameterised handlers*, which thread a parameter through each handler.

7 Related Work

Shallow Handlers. Most existing accounts of effect handlers use deep handlers. Notable exceptions include Haskell libraries based on free monads [12–14], and the Frank programming language [17]. Kiselyov and Ishii [13] optimise their implementation by allowing efficient implementations of catenable lists to be used to support manipulation of continuations. We conjecture that both our abstract machine and our CPS translation could benefit from a similar representation.

Abstract Machines for Handlers. Lindley et al. [17] implement Frank using an abstract machine similar to the one described in this paper. Their abstract machine is not formalised and differs in several ways. In particular, continuations are represented by a single flattened stack, rather than a nested stack like ours, and Frank supports multihandlers, which handle several computations at once. Biernacki et al. [1] present an abstract machine for deep effect handlers similar to that of Hillerström and Lindley [9] but factored slightly differently.

CPS for Handlers. Leijen [15] implements a selective CPS translation for deep handlers, but does not go all the way to plain lambda calculus, relying on a special built in handling construct.

8 Conclusion and Future Work

We have presented the first comprehensive formal analysis of shallow effect handlers. We introduced the handler calculus $\lambda^\dagger$ as a uniform calculus of deep and shallow handlers. We specified formal translations back and forth between deep and shallow handlers within $\lambda^\dagger$, an abstract machine for $\lambda^\dagger$, and a higher-order CPS translation for $\lambda^\dagger$. In each case we proved a precise simulation result, drawing variously on different notions of administrative reduction. We have implemented the abstract machine and CPS translation as backends for Links and evaluated the performance of deep and shallow handlers and their encodings, measuring both execution time and memory consumption. Though deep and shallow handlers can always encode one another, the results suggest that the shallow-as-deep encoding is not viable in practice due to administrative overhead, whereas the deep-as-shallow encoding may be viable. In future we intend to perform a more comprehensive performance evaluation for a wider range of effect handler implementations.

Another outstanding question is to what extent shallow handlers are really needed at all. We have shown that we can encode them generically using deep handlers, but the resulting cruft hinders performance in practice. Extensions to deep handlers not explored in this paper, such as *parameterised handlers* [12,21] or a deep version of the *multihandlers* of Lindley et al. [17], offer the potential for expressing certain shallow handlers without the cruft. Parameterised handlers thread a parameter through each handler, avoiding unnecessary closure allocation. Deep multihandlers directly capture mutumorphisms over computations, allowing a direct implementation of pipes. In future we plan to study the precise relationship between shallow handlers, parameterised handlers, deep multihandlers, and perhaps handlers based on other structural recursion schemes.

Acknowledgements. We would like to thank John Longley for insightful discussions about the inter-encodings of deep and shallow handlers. Daniel Hillerström was supported by EPSRC grant EP/L01503X/1 (EPSRC Centre for Doctoral Training in Pervasive Parallelism). Sam Lindley was supported by EPSRC grant EP/K034413/1 (From Data Types to Session Types—A Basis for Concurrency and Distribution).

References

1. Biernacki, D., Piróg, M., Polesiuk, P., Sieczkowski, F.: Handle with care: relational interpretation of algebraic effects and handlers. PACMPL **2**(POPL), 8:1–8:30 (2018)
2. Cooper, E., Lindley, S., Wadler, P., Yallop, J.: Links: web programming without tiers. In: de Boer, F.S., Bonsangue, M.M., Graf, S., de Roever, W.-P. (eds.) FMCO 2006. LNCS, vol. 4709, pp. 266–296. Springer, Heidelberg (2007). https://doi.org/10.1007/978-3-540-74792-5_12
3. Danvy, O., Nielsen, L.R.: A first-order one-pass CPS transformation. Theor. Comput. Sci. **308**(1–3), 239–257 (2003)
4. Dolan, S., White, L., Sivaramakrishnan, K., Yallop, J., Madhavapeddy, A.: Effective concurrency through algebraic effects. In: OCaml Workshop (2015)
5. Felleisen, M., Friedman, D.P.: Control operators, the SECD-machine, and the λ-calculus. In: Formal Description of Programming Concepts **III**, pp. 193–217 (1987)
6. Flanagan, C., Sabry, A., Duba, B.F., Felleisen, M.: The essence of compiling with continuations. In: PLDI, pp. 237–247. ACM (1993)
7. Fokkinga, M.M.: Tupling and mutumorphisms. Squiggolist **1**(4), 81–82 (1990)
8. Goodman, N.: Uber AI Labs open sources Pyro, a deep probabilistic programming language, November 2017. https://eng.uber.com/pyro/
9. Hillerström, D., Lindley, S.: Liberating effects with rows and handlers. In: TyDe@ICFP, pp. 15–27. ACM (2016)
10. Hillerström, D., Lindley, S.: Shallow effect handlers (extended version) (2018). http://homepages.inf.ed.ac.uk/slindley/papers/shallow-extended.pdf
11. Hillerström, D., Lindley, S., Atkey, R., Sivaramakrishnan, K.C.: Continuation passing style for effect handlers. In: FSCD. LIPIcs, vol. 84, pp. 18:1–18:19 (2017)
12. Kammar, O., Lindley, S., Oury, N.: Handlers in action. In: ICFP, pp. 145–158. ACM (2013)
13. Kiselyov, O., Ishii, H.: Freer monads, more extensible effects. In: Haskell, pp. 94–105. ACM (2015)

14. Kiselyov, O., Sabry, A., Swords, C.: Extensible effects: an alternative to monad transformers. In: Haskell, pp. 59–70. ACM (2013)
15. Leijen, D.: Type directed compilation of row-typed algebraic effects. In: POPL, pp. 486–499. ACM (2017)
16. Levy, P.B., Power, J., Thielecke, H.: Modelling environments in call-by-value programming languages. Inf. Comput. **185**(2), 182–210 (2003)
17. Lindley, S., McBride, C., McLaughlin, C.: Do be do be do. In: POPL, pp. 500–514. ACM (2017)
18. Meijer, E., Fokkinga, M., Paterson, R.: Functional programming with bananas, lenses, envelopes and barbed wire. In: Hughes, J. (ed.) FPCA 1991. LNCS, vol. 523, pp. 124–144. Springer, Heidelberg (1991). https://doi.org/10.1007/3540543961_7
19. Plotkin, G.D.: Call-by-name, call-by-value and the λ-calculus. Theor. Comput. Sci. **1**(2), 125–159 (1975)
20. Plotkin, G., Power, J.: Adequacy for algebraic effects. In: Honsell, F., Miculan, M. (eds.) FoSSaCS 2001. LNCS, vol. 2030, pp. 1–24. Springer, Heidelberg (2001). https://doi.org/10.1007/3-540-45315-6_1
21. Plotkin, G.D., Pretnar, M.: Handling algebraic effects. Log. Methods Comput. Sci. **9**(4), 1–36 (2013)
22. Reynolds, J.C.: Definitional interpreters for higher-order programming languages. High.-Order Symb. Comput. **11**(4), 363–397 (1998)
23. Wu, N., Schrijvers, T.: Fusion for free. In: Hinze, R., Voigtländer, J. (eds.) MPC 2015. LNCS, vol. 9129, pp. 302–322. Springer, Cham (2015). https://doi.org/10.1007/978-3-319-19797-5_15
24. Yallop, J.: Staged generic programming. PACMPL **1**(ICFP), 29:1–29:29 (2017)

Author Index

Printed in the United States
By Bookmasters